Collins

Primary illustrated

Spanish
Dictionary

HarperCollins Publishers
Westerhill Road
Bishopbriggs
Glasgow
G64 2QT
Great Britain

www.collinsdictionary.com
www.collins.co.uk

First Edition 2015
Previously published as Collins First Time
Spanish Dictionary 2003, 2008, 2012

10 9 8 7 6 5 4 3 2 1

© HarperCollins Publishers 2015

ISBN   978-0-00-811196-0

Collins® is a registered trademark of
HarperCollins Publishers Limited

A catalogue record for this book is available
from the British Library

Art direction by Mark Thomson
Designed by Wolfgang Homola
Typeset by Davidson Pre-Press, Glasgow

Printed in Italy by Grafica Veneta Spa

Acknowledgements
We would like to thank those authors and
publishers who kindly gave permission for
copyright material to be used in the Collins
Corpus. We would also like to thank Times
Newspapers Ltd for providing valuable data.

PUBLISHING DIRECTOR
Rob Scriven

MANAGING EDITOR
Gaëlle Amiot-Cadey

PROJECT MANAGEMENT
Alex Hepworth
Susanne Reichert

CONTRIBUTORS
Morven Dooner
Cordelia Lilly
Julie Muleba
José María Ruiz Vaca
Malihé Forghani-Nowbari
José Antonio Gálvez Castiella

ILLUSTRATIONS
Q2A Media

ILLUSTRATED SUPPLEMENT
Marcella Grassi
© Boroli Editore 2008

Contents

The **Collins Primary Illustrated Spanish Dictionary** is a new bilingual dictionary aimed at primary school children who are starting to learn Spanish.

Access to a dictionary which is pitched at an appropriate level is a vital part of the language-learning process. The content of this dictionary has been carefully selected to reflect current trends in primary education and help children with acquiring basic language-learning skills.

The key aims of the **Collins Primary Illustrated Spanish Dictionary** are:
- to develop both language skills in Spanish and language learning skills in general
- to cover the four key areas of language attainment: listening, speaking, reading and writing
- to reinforce key aspects of the language by the use of notes and feature boxes throughout the entries
- to extend cultural awareness by providing information about Spain, especially where traditions differ from those in Britain

The **Collins Primary Illustrated Spanish Dictionary** supports language learning in a number of specific ways:
- it develops children's knowledge of how language works by encouraging them to understand, analyse and use simple aspects of grammar
- it develops children's individual learning skills by using a wide range of notes that explain things in a simple but interesting way
- it enables children to make comparisons between Spanish and English by encouraging them to explore the similarities and differences between the two languages and cultures
- it introduces young learners to all the basic elements of a bilingual dictionary and provides detailed instructions on how to get the most out of using the dictionary

The **Collins Primary Illustrated Spanish Dictionary** is presented in an easy-to-use format which is intended to appeal to children of primary school age. It provides lots of simple, relevant examples and tips on how to remember words, and how to avoid some of the pitfalls of translation. It also features key phrases, illustrations and information about life in Spain, making it an invaluable and exciting new resource.

Step one:
Pick the right side

Remember there are two halves to the dictionary. If you want to know what a Spanish word means, look in the first half of the dictionary.

If you want to translate an English word into Spanish, look in the second half, which is English-Spanish. It comes after the supplement in the middle of the dictionary.

1 Which of these words would you look up on the Spanish-English side of the dictionary?
ver brother horse teléfono

2 Look at page 51 of the dictionary. Is this the Spanish side or the English side? How can you tell?

3 Look at page 150 of the dictionary. What is shown at the top of the page, down the side?

4 Is **invite** the first or the last word on page 437?

Remember that you do not read across the whole page in a dictionary – you have to read down the columns.

5 Which word comes immediately after **aburrido** on page 3?

Step two:
Find the right word

A B C D E F G H I J K L M N O P Q R S T U V W X Y Z

Words are in alphabetical order in the dictionary – like names in the phone book, and in a school register. The alphabet is shown down the edge of each page of the dictionary. You can sort words into alphabetical order by looking at the first letter of each word.

6 Can you put these names in alphabetical order?
María, Isabel, Juan, Jorge, David, Arturo, Carmen
When two words start with the same letter, look at their second letters.

7 In alphabetical order which comes first – **Juan** or **Jorge**?

8 This is the order of the days of the week on a calendar:
Monday, Tuesday, Wednesday, Thursday, Friday, Saturday, Sunday
Which day comes first in a dictionary? Which comes last?

9 **Thursday** comes before **Tuesday** in a dictionary. Why?

10 Put the seven days of the week into alphabetical order.
If the first letters are the same, and the second letters are the same, look at the third letters.

11 **June, July, August**: which comes last in the dictionary?

Step three:
Pick the right translation
The translations are easy to spot in this dictionary because they are blue on the English-Spanish side and red on the Spanish-English side.

Spanish words can be masculine or feminine, and singular or plural. In the dictionary you will come across the abbreviations *masc* and *fem*, which tell you the gender of a Spanish word. PL tells you the word is plural. The dictionary also shows you the Spanish word for 'the' (this can be **el**, **la**, **los** or **las**). In the Language plus supplement, NOUN is abbreviated to N and ADJECTIVE is abbreviated to ADJ.

When you look up 'doll' you can see that the word for 'doll' in Spanish is **muñeca**. You can tell that the Spanish word for 'doll' is feminine because it is given with **la** and the dictionary says that it is '*fem*' (feminine).

So 'the doll' is **la muñeca** and 'a doll' would be **una muñeca**.

Sometimes there is more than one translation, and each one has a number. If there is more than one translation, don't just pick the first one! Check to see which is the right one.

12 Which is the Spanish word for **a ball** that you kick – **la pelota** or **el balón**? Look for the clue.

ball NOUN
  1 la **pelota** *fem (for tennis, golf, cricket)*
    Hit the ball!
    ¡Dale a la pelota!
  2 el **balón** *masc* (PL los **balones**) *(for football, rugby)*
    Pass the ball!
    ¡Pasa el balón!

Step four:
Parts of Speech
Sometimes, to pick the right translation, you need to know the part of speech of a word, for example whether a word is a noun, an adjective, an adverb or a verb.

NOUNS
Nouns are naming words for things or people. You often use the words 'a' or 'the' with a noun – eg a **girl**, a **boy**, the **school**, the **windows**.

Nouns can be singular, eg an **accident**, the **playground**, my **dad**, **football** – or plural, eg **sweets**, the **children**, my **friends**.

13 How many nouns are there in this sentence? What are they?
The car has got a flat tyre and a big dent in the door.

ADJECTIVES
An **adjective** is a describing word which tells you what things are like: **flat** shoes are shoes that don't have high heels. A **flat** tyre is a tyre with no air in it.

14 How many adjectives are there in this sentence? What are they?
She's got brown hair and blue eyes.

Some words have a **noun** meaning and an **adjective** meaning. In the dictionary there is a box to tell you about this. The different meanings usually have different translations in Spanish.

patient

patient *can be a noun or an adjective.*

A NOUN
el/la **paciente** *masc/fem*
B ADJECTIVE
paciente *masc & fem*
The teacher is very patient.
El maestro es muy paciente.
Be patient, Joshua.
Ten paciencia, Joshua.

ADVERBS
An **adverb** is a word which describes a verb or an adjective:
She writes **neatly**. The film was **very** good.

15 How many adverbs are in this sentence? What are they?
The children sat quietly and played happily.

VERBS
Verbs are sometimes called 'doing words'. They often go with words like 'I' and 'you', and with names, eg I **play** football, what **do** you **want**?, Hugo **likes** mashed potato.

Verbs tell you about the present, eg I'm **listening** – the past, eg I **scored** a goal – and the future, eg I'm **going to get** an ice cream.

16 How many verbs are there in this sentence? What are they?
School starts at 9.00 and finishes at 3.30.

Some words have a **noun** meaning and a **verb** meaning. In the dictionary there is a box to tell you about this. The different meanings have different translations in Spanish.

rain

> **rain** *can be a noun or a verb.*

A NOUN
la **lluvia** *fem*
in the rain
bajo la lluvia
B VERB
to rain
llover
It's going to rain.
Va a llover.
It rains a lot here.
Llueve mucho aquí.

> **It's raining.**
> Está lloviendo.

17 What is the Spanish word for 'rain'?

18 Why is 'It's going to rain.' in part **B**?

19 How do you say 'It's raining.' in Spanish?

20 Is 'llover' a noun or a verb?

Learn useful phrases
In the dictionary you'll see phrases that are especially important in orange boxes. Try to learn these when you come across them, and you'll soon know lots of useful things to say in Spanish.

> **What time is it?**
> Qué hora es?
> **It's lunch time.**
> Es la hora de comer.
> **How many times?**
> ¿Cuántas veces?
> **Have a good time, Amanda!**
> ¡Que lo pases bien, Amanda!

Find out about life in Spain
There are also boxes which tell you about Spanish customs, and about differences between life in Spain and Britain.

> **Did you know?**
> **churros** *are a kind of fritter that people often eat on the streets in a paper bag or order in a café typically with a cup of thick, hot chocolate:* **chocolate con churros**.

Even more words
At school you will learn to talk about subjects such as the time and the weather, your family, your pets, and your clothes. The most important words for talking about these subjects are shown in the dictionary itself, and even more words are given in **Language Plus**, the middle part of the dictionary. Have a look!

Answer key

1 ver and teléfono
2 It is the Spanish side. It has Spanish words on it and Spanish–English written at the side near the top.
3 Spanish-English
4 The last word
5 aburrirse
6 Arturo, Carmen, David, Isabel, Jorge, Juan, María
7 Jorge – because 'o' comes before 'u'
8 Friday; Wednesday
9 Because the second letter of Thursday is 'h', which comes before 'u', the second letter of Tuesday.
10 Friday, Monday, Saturday, Sunday, Thursday, Tuesday, Wednesday
11 June
12 el balón – The clue is (for football, rugby).
13 four – car, tyre, dent, door
14 two – brown and blue
15 two – quietly and happily
16 two – starts and finishes
17 la lluvia
18 It is an example of the verb and so is in the verb section of the entry.
19 Está lloviendo.
20 a verb

Spanish - English

A a

a PREPOSITION

> **Language tip**
>
> *When **a** is followed by a masculine noun, **a** and the article **el** turn into **al**.*

1 **to** *(with places)*
Fueron a Madrid.
They went to Madrid.

2 *(with movement)*
Me caí al río.
I fell into the river.
Se subieron al tejado.
They climbed onto the roof.
Marta llegó tarde a la estación.
Marta arrived at the station late.

3 *(with distances)*
Está a quince kilómetros de aquí.
It's fifteen kilometres from here.

4 **at** *(with time, ages, speed)*
a las diez
at ten o'clock
a medianoche
at midnight

a los veinticuatro años
at the age of twenty-four
Íbamos a más de noventa kilómetros por hora.
We were going at over ninety kilometres an hour.

5 *(with dates)*
Estamos a nueve de julio.
It's the ninth of July.

6 *(with prices)*
Los huevos están a un euro con cincuenta la docena.
Eggs are one euro fifty a dozen.

7 *(before an infinitive or a direct object)*
Voy a verla.
I'm going to see her.
Vine a decírtelo.
I came to tell you.
Me obligaban a comer.
They forced me to eat.
Nos cruzamos al salir.
We bumped into each other as we were going out.
Se lo di a Ana.
I gave it to Ana.
Le enseñé a Pablo el libro que me dejaste.
I showed Pablo the book you lent me.
Se lo compré a él.
I bought it from him.
Vi a Juan.
I saw Juan.
Llamé al médico.
I called the doctor.

abajo ADVERB

1 **below**
Los platos y las tazas están abajo.
The plates and cups are below.
La montaña no parece tan alta desde abajo.
The mountain doesn't seem so high from below.
Mete las cervezas abajo del todo.
Put the beers right at the bottom.
El estante de abajo.
The bottom shelf.

Spanish

English

a
b
c
d
e
f
g
h
i
j
k
l
m
n
ñ
o
p
q
r
s
t
u
v
w
x
y
z

2 downstairs
Abajo están la cocina y el salón.
The kitchen and lounge are downstairs.
Hay una fiesta en el piso de abajo.
There's a party in the flat downstairs.

la **abeja** NOUN
bee

el **abeto** NOUN
fir tree

abierto

abierto can be an adjective or a verb.

A (FEM **abierta**) ADJECTIVE
1 open
¿Están abiertas las tiendas?
Are the shops open?
2 on
No dejes el gas abierto.
Don't leave the gas on.
B VERB ▷ *see* **abrir**
He abierto la puerta.
I've opened the door.

abrazar VERB
to hug
Al verme me abrazó.
He hugged me when he saw me.
¡Abrázame fuerte!
Give me a big hug!
■ **abrazarse**
to hug
Se abrazaron y se besaron.
They hugged and kissed.

el **abrazo** NOUN
hug
¡Dame un abrazo!
Give me a hug!

un abrazo
love

Did you know…?
Did you know that Spanish speakers sometimes end e-mails, postcards, and letters to friends with **un abrazo**?

abrigar VERB
Esta chaqueta abriga mucho.
This jacket's really warm.
■ **abrigarse**
to wrap up well

el **abrigo** NOUN
coat
un abrigo de pieles
a fur coat
ropa de abrigo
warm clothing

abril MASC NOUN
April

Language tip
Months are not spelled with a capital letter in Spanish.

Nació el veinte de abril.
He was born on the twentieth of April.

en abril
in April

abrir VERB
1 to open
Las tiendas abren a las diez.
The shops open at ten o'clock.
Abre la ventana.
Open the window.
¡Abre, soy yo!
Open the door, it's me!
2 to turn on
Abre el gas.
Turn the gas on.

■ **abrirse**
to open
De repente se abrió la puerta.
Suddenly the door opened.

abrocharse VERB
to do up
Abróchate la camisa.
Do your shirt up.
Abróchense los cinturones.
Please fasten your seatbelts.

la **abuela** NOUN
grandmother
mi abuela
my grandmother
¿Dónde está la abuela?
Where's Gran?

el **abuelo** NOUN
grandfather
mi abuelo
my grandfather
¿Dónde está el abuelo?
Where's Granddad?
mis abuelos
my grandparents

aburrido (FEM **aburrida**)
ADJECTIVE
1 **bored**
Estaba aburrida y me marché.
I was bored so I left.
2 **boring**
No seas aburrida y vente al cine.
Don't be boring and come to the cinema.
una película muy aburrida
a very boring film

aburrirse VERB
to get bored
Me aburro viendo la tele.
I get bored watching television.

acabar VERB
to finish
Ayer acabé de pintar la valla.
Yesterday I finished painting the fence.
Acabo de ver a tu padre.
I've just seen your father.
■ **acabarse**
to run out
La impresora te avisa cuando se acaba el papel.
The printer tells you when the paper runs out.

acaso ADVERB
por si acaso
just in case

el **accidente** NOUN
accident
los accidentes de carretera
road accidents
Han tenido un accidente.
They've had a car accident.

la **acción** (PL las **acciones**) NOUN
action
una película llena de acción
an action-packed film

el **aceite** NOUN
oil
el aceite de oliva
olive oil

la **aceituna** NOUN
olive
aceitunas rellenas
stuffed olives

el **acento** NOUN
accent
'Té' lleva acento cuando significa 'tea'.
'Té' has an accent when it means 'tea'.
Tiene un acento cerrado del sur.
He has a strong southern accent.

aceptar VERB
to accept
Acepté su invitación.
I accepted his invitation.
Acepté ayudarles.
I agreed to help them.

la **acera** NOUN
pavement

acerca ADVERB
acerca de
about
un documental acerca de la fauna africana
a documentary about African wildlife

acercar VERB
1 **to pass**
¿Me acercas la sal?
Could you pass me the salt?
2 **to bring over**
Acerca la silla.
Bring your chair over here.
¿Acerco más la cama a la ventana?
Shall I put the bed nearer the window?
Nos acercaron al aeropuerto.
They gave us a lift to the airport.

■ **acercarse**
1 **to come closer**
Acércate, que te vea.
Come closer so that I can see you.
2 **to go over**
Me acerqué a la ventana.
I went over to the window.
Acércate a la tienda y trae una botella de agua.
Go over to the shop and get a bottle of water.

acertar VERB
1 **to get … right**
He acertado todas las respuestas.
I got all the answers right.
No acerté.
I got it wrong.
2 **to guess**
Si aciertas cuántos caramelos hay, te los regalo todos.
If you guess how many sweets there are, I'll give you all of them.

el **acierto**

acierto can be a noun or a verb.

A NOUN
right answer
Tuve más aciertos que fallos en el examen.
I got more right answers than wrong ones in the exam.
B VERB ▷ see **acertar**
No acierto a entenderlo.
I can't understand it at all.

aclarar VERB
to clear up
Necesito que me aclares unas dudas.
I need you to clear up some doubts for me.
Con tantos números no me aclaro.
There are so many numbers that I can't make head nor tail of it.

acompañar VERB
acompañar a alguien
to come with somebody/to go with somebody

Language tip
acompañar a alguien *has two meanings. Look at the examples.*

Si quieres te acompaño.
I'll come with you if you like.
Me pidió que la acompañara a la estación.
She asked me to go to the station with her.

aconsejar VERB
to advise
Te aconsejo que lo hagas.
I'd advise you to do it.

acordarse VERB
to remember
Ahora mismo no me acuerdo.
Right now I can't remember.

acordarse de
to remember
¿Te acuerdas de mí?
Do you remember me?
Acuérdate de cerrar la puerta con llave.
Remember to lock the door.

acostado (FEM **acostada**)
ADJECTIVE
estar acostado
to be in bed

acostarse VERB
1 **to lie down**
2 **to go to bed**

acostumbrarse VERB
acostumbrarse a
to get used to
No me acostumbro a la vida en la ciudad.
I can't get used to city life.
Ya me he acostumbrado a trabajar de noche.
I've got used to working at night now.

el **acto** NOUN
ceremony

en el acto
instantly

el **actor** NOUN
actor

la **actriz** (PL las **actrices**) NOUN
actress

la **actuación** (PL las **actuaciones**) NOUN
performance
Fue una actuación muy buena.
It was a very good performance.

actual (FEM **actual**) ADJECTIVE
present
la situación actual del país
the country's present situation
uno de los mejores pintores del arte actual
one of the greatest painters of today

Language tip
Be careful! **actual** *does not mean the same as* **actual***.*

actualmente ADVERB
1 **nowadays**
Actualmente apenas se utilizan las máquinas de escribir.
Typewriters are hardly used nowadays.
2 **currently**
Es geólogo, pero actualmente está en el paro.
He's a geologist but he's currently out of work.

Language tip
Be careful! **actualmente** *does not mean the same as* **actually***.*

actuar VERB
1 **to act**
Es difícil actuar con naturalidad delante de las cámaras.
It's hard to act naturally in front of the cameras.
No comprendo tu forma de actuar.
I can't understand your behaviour.
No actuó en esa película.
He wasn't in that film.
2 **to perform**
Hoy actúan en el Café del Jazz.
Today they'll be performing at the Café del Jazz.

el **acuario** NOUN
1 **aquarium**
2 **fish tank**

el **acuerdo**

acuerdo *can be a noun or part of the verb* **acordar***.*

A NOUN
agreement

> **llegar a un acuerdo**
> to reach an agreement
> **¡De acuerdo!**
> All right!

B VERB ▷ see **acordar**
Ahora no me acuerdo.
I can't remember it now.

acusar VERB
to accuse
Su novia lo acusaba de mentiroso.
His girlfriend accused him of being a liar.

adelantado (FEM adelantada)
ADJECTIVE
1 **advanced**
Suecia es un país muy adelantado.
Sweden is a very advanced country.
los niños más adelantados de la clase
the children who are doing best in the class
2 **fast**
Este reloj va adelantado.
This watch is fast.

adelantar VERB
1 **to bring ... forward**
Tuvimos que adelantar la boda.
We had to bring the wedding forward.
2 **to overtake**
Adelanta a ese camión cuando puedas.
Overtake that lorry when you can.
3 **to put ... forward**
El domingo hay que adelantar los relojes una hora.
On Sunday we'll have to put the clocks forward an hour.

adelantarse VERB
to go on ahead

Me adelanté para coger asiento.
I went on ahead to get a seat.

adelante

> adelante *can be an adverb or an exclamation.*

A ADVERB
Se inclinó hacia adelante.
He leant forward.
más adelante
further on/later

> **Language tip**
> **más adelante** *has two meanings. Look at the examples.*

El pueblo está más adelante.
The village is further on.
Más adelante hablaremos de los resultados.
We'll discuss the results later.
B EXCLAMATION
1 **come on!**
2 **come in!**

adelgazar VERB
to lose weight
¡Cómo has adelgazado!
You've really lost weight!
He adelgazado cinco kilos.
I've lost five kilos.

además ADVERB
1 **as well**
Es profesor y además carpintero.
He's a teacher and a carpenter as well.
2 **what's more**
El baño es demasiado pequeño y, además, no tiene ventana.
The bathroom's too small and, what's more, it hasn't got a window.
3 **besides**
Además, no tienes nada que perder.
Besides, you've got nothing to lose.

adentro ADVERB
inside
> Empezó a llover y se
> metieron adentro.
> It began to rain so they went
> inside.

adhesivo (FEM **adhesiva**)
ADJECTIVE
sticky
> cinta adhesiva
> sticky tape

adiós EXCLAMATION
goodbye!

> decir adiós a alguien
> to say goodbye to somebody

adivinar VERB
to guess
> Adivina quién viene.
> Guess who's coming.
> adivinar el pensamiento a
> alguien
> to read somebody's mind

el **adjetivo** NOUN
adjective

admirar VERB
to admire
> Todos la admiran.
> Everyone admires her.
> Me admira lo poco que
> gastas en ropa.
> I'm amazed at how little you
> spend on clothes.

admitir VERB
1 **to admit**
> Admite que estabas
> equivocado.
> Admit you were wrong.
2 **to accept**
> La máquina no admite
> monedas de dos euros.
> The machine doesn't accept
> two-euro coins.
> Espero que me admitan a la
> universidad.
> I hope I'll get a place at
> university.

el/la **adolescente** NOUN
teenager

adónde ADVERB
where
> ¿Adónde ibas?
> Where were you going?

adornar VERB
to decorate

el **adulto**
la **adulta** NOUN
adult

el **adverbio** NOUN
adverb

advertir VERB
to warn
> Ya te advertí que sería difícil.
> I warned you it would be difficult.
> Te advierto que no va a ser
> nada fácil.
> I must warn you that it won't be
> at all easy.

aéreo (FEM **aérea**) ADJECTIVE
air
> un ataque aéreo
> an air raid

el **aeropuerto** NOUN
airport

afectar VERB
to affect
> Esto a ti no te afecta.
> This doesn't affect you.

afeitar VERB
to shave
■ **afeitarse**
to shave
> Voy a afeitarme.
> I'm going to shave.
> Se afeitó la barba.
> He shaved off his beard.

Spanish **English**

a
b
c
d
e
f
g
h
i
j
k
l
m
n
ñ
o
p
q
r
s
t
u
v
w
x
y
z

la **afición** (PL las **aficiones**)
NOUN
hobby
> **Su afición es la filatelia.**
> His hobby is stamp collecting.
> **Tengo mucha afición por el ciclismo.**
> I'm very keen on cycling.

aficionado
aficionada

> **aficionado** *can be a noun or an adjective.*

A MASC/FEM NOUN
1 **enthusiast**
> **un libro para los aficionados al ciclismo**
> a book for cycling enthusiasts
2 **amateur**
> **un partido para aficionados**
> a game for amateurs

B ADJECTIVE
1 **keen**
> **Es muy aficionada a la pintura.**
> She's very keen on painting.

2 **amateur**
> **un equipo de fútbol aficionado**
> an amateur football team

aficionarse VERB
> **aficionarse a algo**
> to take up something/to become interested in something

> **Language tip**
> **aficionarse a algo** *has two meanings. Look at the examples.*

> **Raúl se aficionó al tenis.**
> Raúl took up tennis.
> **Me he aficionado al teatro.**
> I've become interested in theatre.

afirmar VERB
> **afirmar que ...**
> to say that ...
> **Afirmaba que no la conocía.**
> He said that he didn't know her.

aflojar VERB
to loosen
- **aflojarse**
  to come loose
> **Se ha aflojado un tornillo.**
> A screw has come loose.

afónico (FEM **afónica**) ADJECTIVE
> **Estoy afónico.**
> I've lost my voice.

afortunado (FEM **afortunada**)
ADJECTIVE
lucky
> **Es un tipo afortunado.**
> He's a lucky guy.

afuera ADVERB
outside
> **Vámonos afuera.**
> Let's go outside.

las **afueras** NOUN
outskirts
> **en las afueras de Barcelona**
> on the outskirts of Barcelona

agacharse VERB
to crouch down

agarrar VERB
1 **to grab**
> **Agarró a su hermano por el hombro.**
> He grabbed his brother by the shoulder.
2 **to hold**
> **Agarra bien la sartén.**
> Hold the frying pan firmly.
- **agarrarse**
  to hold on
> **Agárrate a la barandilla.**
> Hold on to the rail.

la **agenda** NOUN
1 **diary**
2 **address book**

Language tip

Be careful! **agenda** *does not mean the same as* **agenda**.

agitar VERB
to shake
Agítese antes de usar.
Shake before use.

agosto MASC NOUN
August

Language tip

Months are not spelled with a capital letter in Spanish.

en agosto
in August
el ocho de agosto
the eighth of August
Nació el ocho de agosto.
He was born on the eighth of August.

agotado (FEM **agotada**)
ADJECTIVE
1 **exhausted**
Estoy agotado.
I'm exhausted.
2 **sold out**
Ese modelo en concreto está agotado.
That particular model is sold out.

agotar VERB
1 **to use up**
Agotamos todas nuestras reservas.
We used up all our supplies.
2 **to tire out**
Me agota tanto ejercicio.
All this exercise is tiring me out.
■ **agotarse**
to run out
Se está agotando la leña.
The firewood's running out.
Se agotaron todas las entradas.
The tickets all sold out.

agradable (FEM **agradable**)
ADJECTIVE
nice

agradecer VERB
agradecer algo a alguien
to thank somebody for something
Te agradezco tu interés.
Thank you for your interest.

la agresión (PL las **agresiones**)
NOUN
attack

el agricultor
la agricultora NOUN
farmer

la agricultura NOUN
farming

el agua FEM NOUN
water
agua corriente
running water
agua potable
drinking water

aguantar VERB
1 **to stand**
No aguanto la ópera.
I can't stand opera.
Su vecina no la aguanta.
Her neighbour can't stand her.
Últimamente estás que no hay quien te aguante.
You've been unbearable lately.
2 **to take**
La estantería no va a aguantar el peso.
The shelf won't take the weight.
3 **to hold**
Aguántame el martillo un momento.
Can you hold the hammer for me for a moment?
Aguanta la respiración.
Hold your breath.
No pude aguantar la risa.
I couldn't help laughing.

**Si no puede venir, que se
aguante.**
If he can't come, he'll just have
to lump it.

agudo (FEM **aguda**) ADJECTIVE
1 **sharp**
2 **high-pitched**
3 **witty**

la **aguja** NOUN
1 **needle**
2 **hand**

el **agujero** NOUN
hole
hacer un agujero
to make a hole

ahí ADVERB
there
¡Ahí están!
There they are!
Lo tienes ahí mismo.
You've got it right there.

> **Language tip**
> **por ahí** *has several meanings. It
> can be translated as* **over there**,
> **somewhere**, *and* **thereabouts**.
> *Look at the examples.*

Tú busca por ahí.
You look over there.
**¿Has visto las tijeras? —
Andarán por ahí.**
Have you seen the scissors?
— They must be somewhere
around.
doscientos o por ahí
two hundred or thereabouts

ahogarse VERB
to drown
Se ahogó en el río.
He drowned in the river.

ahora ADVERB
now
¿Dónde vamos ahora?
Where are we going now?
Ahora mismo está de viaje.
He's away on a trip right now.

Ahora te lo digo.
I'll tell you in a moment.
Por ahora no cambies nada.
Don't change anything for the
moment.
Ahora mismo voy.
I'm just coming.

> **ahora mismo**
> right now
> **de ahora en adelante**
> from now on
> **por ahora**
> for now

ahorrar VERB
to save

el **aire** NOUN
1 **air**
**Necesitamos aire para
respirar.**
We need air to breathe.
aire acondicionado
air conditioning
2 **wind**
El aire le voló la gorra.
The wind blew his cap off.

al aire libre
outdoors/outdoor

> **Language tip**
> **al aire libre** *has two meanings.
> Look at the examples.*

Comimos al aire libre.
We had lunch outdoors.
una fiesta al aire libre
an outdoor party

el **ajo** NOUN
garlic

al PREPOSITION *(= a + el)* ▷*see* **a**
Fui al cine.
I went to the cinema.

el **ala** FEM NOUN
wing

alargar VERB
1 **to make ... longer**
Hay que alargar un poco las mangas.
We'll need to make the sleeves a bit longer.
2 **to extend**
Decidieron alargar las vacaciones.
They decided to extend their holidays.
■ **alargarse**
to get longer
Ya van alargándose los días.
The days are getting longer.

la **alarma** NOUN
alarm
Saltó la alarma.
The alarm went off.
dar la voz de alarma
to raise the alarm
alarma de incendios
fire alarm

el **alboroto** NOUN
racket
¡Vaya alboroto!
What a racket!

alcanzar VERB
1 **to catch up with**
La alcancé cuando salía por la puerta.
I caught up with her just as she was going out of the door.
2 **to reach**
alcanzar la cima de la montaña
to reach the top of the mountain
3 **to pass**
¿Me alcanzas las tijeras?
Could you pass me the scissors?

alegrar VERB
to cheer up
Intenté alegrarlos con unos chistes.
I tried to cheer them up with a few jokes.

Me alegra que hayas venido.
I'm glad you've come.
■ **alegrarse**
to be glad
¿Te gusta? Me alegro.
You like it? I'm glad.
Me alegro de su éxito.
I'm glad about his success.
alegrarse por alguien
to be happy for somebody
Me alegro por ti.
I'm happy for you.

alegre (FEM **alegre**) ADJECTIVE
cheerful

la **alegría** NOUN
Sentí una gran alegría.
I was really happy.

¡Qué alegría!
How lovely!

alejarse VERB
to move away
Aléjate un poco del fuego.
Move a bit further away from the fire.

la **alergia** NOUN
allergy
¿Tienes alguna alergia?
Have you got any allergies?
alergia al polen
hay fever

las **aletas** PL NOUN
flippers

la **alfombra** NOUN
1 **rug**
2 **carpet**

algo

algo *can be a pronoun or an adverb.*

Spanish

English

a
b
c
d
e
f
g
h
i
j
k
l
m
n
ñ
o
p
q
r
s
t
u
v
w
x
y
z

A PRONOUN

1 something

Algo se está quemando.
Something is burning.
¿Quieres algo de comer?
Would you like something to eat?
¿Te pasa algo?
Is something the matter?
Aún queda algo de zumo.
There's still some juice left.

2 anything

¿Algo más?
Anything else?

B ADVERB

rather

La falda te está algo corta.
The skirt's rather short on you.

el **algodón** (PL los **algodones**)
NOUN

cotton

Me puse algodones en los oídos.
I put cotton wool in my ears.
el algodón de azúcar
candyfloss

alguien PRONOUN

1 somebody

Alguien llama a la puerta.
There's somebody knocking at the door.
¿Necesitas que te ayude alguien?
Do you need somebody to help you?

2 anybody

¿Conoces a alguien aquí?
Do you know anybody here?

algún ADJECTIVE (FEM **alguna**, MASC PL **algunos**)

1 some

Algún día iré.
I'll go there some day.

2 any

¿Compraste algún cuadro?
Did you buy any pictures?
¿Quieres alguna cosa más?
Was there anything else?

algún que otro ...
the odd ...

alguno PRONOUN (FEM **alguna**)

1 somebody

Siempre hay alguno que se queja.
There's always somebody who complains.
Algunos piensan que no ocurrió así.
Some people think that's not what happened.

2 some

Solo conozco a algunos de los vecinos.
I only know some of the neighbours.
Tiene que estar en alguna de estas cajas.
It must be in one of these boxes.

3 any

Necesito una aspirina. ¿Te queda alguna?
I need an aspirin. Have you got any left?
Si alguno quiere irse que se vaya.
If any of them want to leave, fine.
¿Lo sabe alguno de vosotros?
Do any of you know?

el **alimento** NOUN
food

alimentos congelados
frozen food

allá ADVERB
over there

Tu libro está allá.
Your book is over there.
Échate un poco más allá.
Move over that way a bit.

allí ADVERB
there

Allí está.
There it is.
Allí viene tu hermana.
Here comes your sister.

el **alma** FEM NOUN
soul
> **Lo siento en el alma.**
> I'm really sorry.

la **almohada** NOUN
pillow

almorzar VERB
to have lunch
> **No he almorzado todavía.**
> I haven't had lunch yet.
> **¿Qué has almorzado?**
> What did you have for lunch?

el **almuerzo** NOUN
lunch

alrededor ADVERB
> **alrededor de**
> around/about

Language tip
alrededor de *has two meanings.*
Look at the examples.

> **El satélite gira alrededor de
> la Tierra.**
> The satellite goes around the
> Earth.
> **Deben de ser alrededor de
> las dos.**
> It must be about two o'clock.

los **alrededores**
PL NOUN
> **Ocurrió en los alrededores
> de Madrid.**
> It happened near Madrid.
> **Hay muchas tiendas en los
> alrededores del museo.**
> There are a lot of shops in the
> area around the museum.

alto (FEM **alta**)

alto *can be an adjective, a pronoun
or an exclamation.*

A ADJECTIVE
1 tall
> **Es un chico muy alto.**
> He's a very tall boy.

> **un edificio
> muy alto**
> a very tall
> building

2 high
> **El Everest es
> la montaña más
> alta del mundo.**
> Everest is the
> highest mountain
> in the world.
> **Sacó notas altas en todos
> los exámenes.**
> He got high marks in all his exams.

3 loud
> **La música está demasiado
> alta.**
> The music's too loud.

B ADVERB
high
> **subir muy alto**
> to go up very high
> **Pepe habla muy alto.**
> Pepe has got a very loud voice.
> **¡Más alto, por favor!**
> Speak up, please!
> **Pon el volumen más alto.**
> Turn the volume up.

C EXCLAMATION
stop!

la **altura** NOUN
height
> **Volamos a una altura de
> quince mil pies.**
> We're flying at a height of fifteen
> thousand feet.
> **La pared tiene dos metros de
> altura.**
> The wall's two metres high.

el **alumno**
la **alumna** NOUN
pupil

amable (FEM **amable**) ADJECTIVE
kind

amanecer

amanecer *can be a verb or a noun.*

A VERB
to get light
Amanece a las siete.
It gets light at seven.
B MASC NOUN
dawn

al amanecer
at dawn

amar VERB
to love

amargo (FEM **amarga**) ADJECTIVE
bitter

amarillo (FEM **amarilla**)
ADJECTIVE, MASC NOUN
yellow

el **ambiente** NOUN
atmosphere
Se respira un ambiente tenso.
There's a tense atmosphere.
el medio ambiente
the environment

amenace VERB ▷ see **amenazar**
No voy a hacerlo aunque me amenace.
I'm not going to do it even if he threatens me.

la **amenaza** NOUN
threat

amenazar VERB
to threaten
Le amenazó con decírselo al profesor.
He threatened to tell the teacher.

el **amigo**
la **amiga** NOUN
friend

hacerse amigos
to become friends

el **amor**
NOUN
love

ancho (FEM **ancha**)
ADJECTIVE
1 **wide**
una calle ancha
a wide street
2 **loose**
Le gusta llevar ropa ancha.
He likes to wear loose clothing.
Me está ancho el vestido.
The dress is too big for me.

anda EXCLAMATION
1 **well I never!**
¡Anda, un billete de cincuenta euros!
Well I never, a fifty-euro note!
2 **come on**
¡Anda, ponte el abrigo y vámonos!
Come on, put your coat on and let's go!

¡Anda ya!
You're not serious!

andar VERB
1 **to walk**
Anduvimos varios kilómetros.
We walked several kilometres.
Iremos andando a la estación.
We'll walk to the station.
2 **to be**
Últimamente ando muy liado.
I've been very busy lately.
No sé por dónde anda.
I don't know where he is.
¿Qué tal andas?
How are you?
andar mal de dinero
to be short of money

anduve VERB
▷ see **andar**
Anduve dos horas.
I walked for two hours.

el **ángel** NOUN
angel

el **ángulo** NOUN
angle
en ángulo recto
at right angles

el **anillo** NOUN
ring
un anillo de boda
a wedding ring

animado (FEM **animada**)
ADJECTIVE
1 **cheerful**
Últimamente parece que
está más animada.
She has seemed more cheerful
lately.
2 **lively**
Fue una fiesta muy
animada.
It was a very lively party.
dibujos animados
cartoons

el **animal** NOUN
animal
los animales domésticos
pets

animar VERB
1 **to cheer up**
Lo ha pasado muy mal y
necesita que la animen.
She has had a rough time and
needs cheering up.
2 **to cheer on**
Estuvimos animando al
equipo.
We were cheering the team on.

animar a alguien a que haga
algo
to encourage somebody to do
something
**Nos animaron a que
fuésemos a la fiesta.**
They encouraged us to go to the
party.
■ **animarse**
to cheer up
¡Vamos, anímate hombre!
Come on, cheer up mate!
animarse a hacer algo
to make up one's mind to do
something

ánimo EXCLAMATION
cheer up!
¡Ánimo, chaval, que no es el
fin del mundo!
Cheer up mate, it's not the end
of the world!

anoche ADVERB
last night
antes de anoche
the night before last

anochecer VERB
to get dark
En invierno anochece muy
temprano.
It gets dark very early in winter.

anteayer ADVERB
the day before yesterday

la **antena** NOUN
aerial
una antena parabólica
a satellite dish

anterior (FEM **anterior**)
ADJECTIVE
before
La semana anterior llovió
mucho.
It rained a lot the week before.
Su examen fue anterior al
nuestro.
Their exam was before ours.

antes ADVERB
 1 **before**
 Esta película ya la he visto antes.
 I've seen this film before.
 antes de la cena
 before dinner
 antes de que te vayas
 before you go
 Él estaba aquí antes que yo.
 He was here before me.
 Antes no había tantos juguetes.
 People didn't use to have so many toys.
 2 **first**
 Nosotros llegamos antes.
 We arrived first.

lo antes posible
as soon as possible

antiguo (FEM **antigua**) ADJECTIVE
 old
 Este reloj es muy antiguo.
 This clock is very old.

antipático (FEM **antipática**)
 ADJECTIVE
 unfriendly

anual (FEM **anual**) ADJECTIVE
 annual

anunciar VERB
 to announce
 anunciar una decisión
 to announce a decision

el **anuncio** NOUN
 1 **advertisement**
 Pusieron un anuncio en el periódico.
 They put an advertisement in the paper.
 2 **announcement**
 Tengo que hacer un anuncio importante.
 I have an important announcement to make.

añadir VERB
 to add

el **año** NOUN
 year
 Estuve allí el año pasado.
 I was there last year.
 ¿Cuántos años tiene?
 How old is he?
 Tiene siete años.
 He's seven.

¡Feliz Año Nuevo!
Happy New Year!
el año que viene
next year
el año pasado
last year
los años ochenta
the eighties

apagar VERB
 to switch off
 Apaga la tele.
 Switch the TV off.

aparecer VERB
 1 **to appear**
 De repente apareció la policía.
 The police suddenly appeared.
 2 **to turn up**
 ¿Han aparecido ya las tijeras?
 Have the scissors turned up yet?

el **apartamento** NOUN
 flat

apartar VERB
 to move out of the way
 Aparta todas las sillas.
 Move all the chairs out of the way.
 ¡Aparta!
 Stand back!

■ **apartarse**
to stand back
Apártense de la puerta.
Stand back from the door.

el **apellido** NOUN
surname

apenas ADVERB, CONJUNCTION
1 hardly
No tenemos apenas nada de comer.
We've got hardly anything to eat.
Apenas podía levantarse.
He could hardly stand up.
2 hardly ever
Apenas voy al cine.
I hardly ever go to the cinema.
3 barely
Hace apenas diez minutos que hablé con ella.
I spoke to her barely ten minutes ago.
Terminé en apenas dos horas..
It only took me two hours to finish.

el **aperitivo** NOUN
aperitif

apestar VERB
to stink
Te apestan los pies.
Your feet stink.
apestar a
to stink of

apetecer VERB
¿Te apetece una tortilla?
Do you fancy an omelette?
No, gracias, ahora no me apetece.
No, thanks, I don't feel like it just now.

el **apetito** NOUN
appetite
Eso se va a quitar el apetito.
You won't have any appetite left.
No tengo apetito.
I'm not hungry.

aplastar VERB
to squash
Me senté encima del regalo y lo aplasté.
I sat on the present and squashed it.

aplaudir VERB
to clap
Todos aplaudían.
Everyone clapped.

el **aplauso** NOUN
applause
Los aplausos duraron varios minutos.
The applause lasted for several minutes.

aplazar VERB
to postpone

apostar VERB
to bet
apostar por algo
to bet on something
¿Qué te apuestas a que ... ?
How much do you bet that...?

apoyar VERB
1 to lean
Apoya el espejo contra la pared.
Lean the mirror against the wall.
2 to rest
Apoya la espalda en este cojín.
Rest your back against this cushion.
3 to support
Todos mis compañeros me apoyan.
All my colleagues support me.
■ **apoyarse**
to lean
No te apoyes en la mesa.
Don't lean on the table.

aprender VERB
to learn
Ya me he aprendido los verbos irregulares.

I've already learnt the irregular verbs.
aprender a hacer algo
to learn to do something
Estoy aprendiendo a tocar la guitarra.
I'm learning to play the guitar.

> **aprender algo de memoria**
> to learn something off by heart

apretado (FEM **apretada**)
ADJECTIVE
1 **tight**
Estos pantalones me están muy apretados.
These trousers are very tight on me.
2 **cramped**
Íbamos muy apretados en el autobús.
We were very cramped on the bus.

apretar VERB
1 **to tighten**
Aprieta bien los tornillos.
Tighten up the screws.
2 **to press**
Aprieta este botón.
Press this button.
Me aprietan los zapatos.
My shoes are too tight.

aprobar VERB
to pass
aprobar un examen
to pass an exam
aprobar por los pelos
to scrape through

aprovechar VERB
1 **to make good use of**
No aprovecha el tiempo.
He doesn't make good use of his time.
2 **to use**
Aprovecharé los ratos libres para estudiar.
I'll use my spare time to study.
aprovecharse de
to take advantage of

Me aproveché de la situación.
I took advantage of the situation.
Todos se aprovechan del pobre chico.
Everyone takes advantage of the poor boy.

> **¡Que aproveche!**
> Enjoy your meal!

apruebo VERB ▷see **aprobar**
Si no apruebo, mis padres se enfadarán.
If I fail, my parents will be angry.

apuesto VERB ▷see **apostar**
Te apuesto a que no le va a gustar.
I bet you she won't like it.

apuntar VERB
1 **to write down**
Apúntalo o se te olvidará.
Write it down or you'll forget.
Apunta mis datos.
Can you take a note of my details?
2 **to point**
Me apuntó con el dedo.
He pointed at me.
■ **apuntarse**
to put one's name down
Nos hemos apuntado para el viaje a Marruecos.
We've put our names down for the trip to Morocco.
apuntarse a un curso
to enrol on a course

> **¡Yo me apunto!**
> Count me in!

los **apuntes** NOUN
notes

> **tomar apuntes**
> to take notes

aquel (FEM **aquella**) ADJECTIVE
that
Me gusta más aquella mesa.
I prefer that table.

aquél (FEM **aquélla**) PRONOUN
that one
>**Aquél no es el mío.**
>That one isn't mine.
>**Dame aquélla de allí.**
>Give me that one over there.

aquello PRONOUN
>**aquello que hay allí**
>that thing over there

aquí ADVERB
1 **here**
>**Aquí está el informe que me pediste.**
>Here's the report you asked me for.
2 **now**
>**de aquí en adelante**
>from now on
>**por aquí**
>around here/this way

Language tip

por aquí *has two meanings. Look at the examples.*

>**Lo tenía por aquí en alguna parte.**
>I had it around here somewhere.
>**Pasa por aquí, por favor.**
>Please come this way.

la **araña**
NOUN
spider

>**¡Hay una araña en la bañera!**
>There's a spider in the bath!

arañar VERB
to scratch
>**El gato me arañó.**
>The cat scratched me.

el **árbitro**
la **árbitra** NOUN
referee

el **árbol** NOUN
tree

>**un árbol frutal**
>a fruit tree
>**el árbol de Navidad**
>the Christmas tree

el **arco** NOUN
1 **bow**
2 **arch**
>**el arco iris**
>the rainbow

arder VERB
to burn
>**Ese tronco no va a arder.**
>That log won't burn.
>**¡La sopa está ardiendo!**
>The soup's boiling hot!

la **ardilla** NOUN
squirrel

el **área** FEM NOUN
area

la **arena** NOUN
sand
>**arenas movedizas**
>quicksand

armar VERB
1 **to assemble**
>**El juguete viene desmontado y luego tú lo armas.**
>The toy comes in pieces and you assemble it.
2 **to make**
>**Los vecinos de arriba arman mucho jaleo.**
>Our upstairs neighbours make a lot of noise.
>**armarse un lío**
>to get in a muddle
>**Me voy a armar un lío con tantos números.**
>I'm going to get into a muddle with all these numbers.

el **armario** NOUN
1 **cupboard**
un armario de cocina
a kitchen cupboard
2 **wardrobe**

arrancar VERB
1 **to pull up**
Estaba arrancando malas hierbas.
I was pulling up weeds.
2 **to pull out**
Le arranqué una espina del dedo.
I pulled a thorn out of his finger.

arrastrar VERB
to drag
Arrastraba una maleta enorme.
He was dragging an enormous suitcase.
■ **arrastrarse**
to crawl
Llegaron hasta la valla arrastrándose.
They crawled up to the fence.

arreglar VERB
to fix
¿Sabrás arreglarme el grifo?
Could you fix the tap for me?

arreglarse VERB
1 **to get ready**
Se arregló para salir.
She got ready to go out.
2 **to work out**
Ya verás como todo se arregla.
It'll all work out, you'll see.

el **arreglo** NOUN
repair
El tostador sólo necesita un pequeño arreglo.
The toaster only needs a minor repair.
Esta tele no tiene arreglo.
This TV is unrepairable.
Este problema no tiene arreglo.
There's no solution to this problem.

arriba ADVERB
1 **above**
Los platos y las tazas están arriba.
The plates and mugs are above.
Visto desde arriba parece más pequeño.
Seen from above it looks smaller.
Pon esos libros arriba del todo.
Put those books on top.
2 **upstairs**
Arriba están los dormitorios.
The bedrooms are upstairs.
los vecinos de arriba
our upstairs neighbours

más arriba
further up

arriesgado (FEM **arriesgada**)
ADJECTIVE
risky

la **arroba** NOUN
at
Mi e-mail es loveday arroba collins punto E-S (loveday@ collins.es).
My email address is loveday at collins dot E-S (loveday@ collins.es).

arrojar VERB
to throw
Arrojaban piedras y palos.
They were throwing sticks and stones.

el **arroyo** NOUN
stream

el **arroz** NOUN
rice
arroz blanco
white rice
arroz con leche
rice pudding

Spanish
English

la **arruga** NOUN
1 **wrinkle**
2 **crease**

el **arte** (PL las **artes**) NOUN
art
el arte abstracto
abstract art

el **artículo** NOUN
article
el artículo determinado
the definite article
el artículo indeterminado
the indefinite article

artificial (FEM **artificial**)
ADJECTIVE
artificial

el/la **artista**
NOUN
1 **artist**
2 **un artista**
an actor
una artista
an actress

asar VERB
to roast
asar algo a la parrilla
to grill something

Me aso de calor.
I'm boiling.

el **ascensor**
NOUN
lift

el **asco** NOUN
El ajo me da asco.
I think garlic's revolting.
La casa está hecha un asco.
The house is filthy.

¡Qué asco!
How revolting!

el **aseo** NOUN
el aseo personal
personal hygiene
los aseos
the toilets

así ADVERB
1 **like this**
Se hace así.
You do it like this.
2 **like that**
Es así: como lo hace Jorge.
It's like that: the way Jorge is
doing it.
**¿Ves aquel abrigo? Quiero
algo así.**
Do you see that coat? I'd like
something like that.
un tomate así de grande
a tomato this big

el **asiento** NOUN
seat
el asiento delantero
the front seat
el asiento trasero
the back seat

la **asignatura** NOUN
subject
**Tiene dos asignaturas
pendientes.**
He's got two subjects to retake.

asomar VERB
**No asomes la cabeza por la
ventanilla.**
Don't lean out of the window.
Asómate a la ventana.
Look out of the window.

asombrar VERB
to amaze
Me asombra que no lo sepas.
I'm amazed you don't know.
■ **asombrarse**
to be amazed
**Se asombró de lo tarde que
era.**
He was amazed at how late it
was.

a
b
c
d
e
f
g
h
i
j
k
l
m
n
ñ
o
p
q
r
s
t
u
v
w
x
y
z

el **aspecto** NOUN
appearance
> **A ver si cuidas más tu aspecto.**
> You need to take a bit more care with your appearance.

la **aspiradora** NOUN
vacuum cleaner

asqueroso (FEM **asquerosa**)
ADJECTIVE
1 **disgusting**
2 **filthy**
> **Esta cocina está asquerosa.**
> This kitchen is filthy.

el **asunto** NOUN
matter
> **Es un asunto muy delicado.**
> It's a very delicate matter.
> **No me gusta que se metan en mis asuntos.**
> I don't like anyone meddling in my affairs.
> **¡Eso no es asunto tuyo!**
> That's none of your business!

asustar VERB
1 **to frighten**
> **No me asustan los fantasmas.**
> I'm not frightened of ghosts.

2 **to startle**
> **¡Huy! Me has asustado.**
> Goodness! You startled me.
- **asustarse**
  to get frightened
  > **Se asusta por nada.**
  > He gets frightened over nothing.

atacar VERB
to attack

el **atajo** NOUN
short cut
> **Cogeremos un atajo.**
> We'll take a short cut.

el **ataque** NOUN
attack
> **un ataque contra alguien**
> an attack on somebody
> **Le dio un ataque de risa.**
> He burst out laughing.

atar VERB
to tie
> **Ata al perro a la farola.**
> Tie the dog to the lamppost.
> **Átate los cordones.**
> Tie your shoelaces up.

atardecer

> atardecer *can be a verb or a noun.*

A VERB
to get dark
> **Está atardeciendo.**
> It's getting dark.
B MASC NOUN
dusk

> **al atardecer**
> at dusk

el **atasco** NOUN
traffic jam

atención

> atención *can be a noun or an exclamation.*

A FEM NOUN
> **Hay que poner más atención.**
> You should pay more attention.
> **Escucha con atención.**
> Listen carefully.
> **El director del colegio le llamó la atención.**
> The headmaster gave him a talking-to.
> **Estás llamando la atención con esa ropa.**
> You're attracting attention to yourself in those clothes.

B EXCLAMATION
¡Atención, por favor!
May I have your attention please?
'¡Atención!'
'Danger!'

el **atentado** NOUN
attack
   un atentado terrorista
   a terrorist attack

atento (FEM **atenta**) ADJECTIVE
thoughtful
   Es un chico muy atento.
   He's a very thoughtful boy.
   Estaban atentos a las explicaciones del profesor.
   They were paying attention to the teacher's explanations.

el **aterrizaje** NOUN
landing
   un aterrizaje forzoso
   an emergency landing

aterrizar VERB
to land

atiendo VERB ▷ see **atender**
   Ahora mismo la atiendo.
   I will be with you right away.

la **atracción** (PL las **atracciones**) NOUN
attraction
   una atracción turística
   a tourist attraction
   sentir atracción por algo
   to be attracted to something
   Sentía atracción por él.
   I was attracted to him.

atractivo (FEM **atractiva**) ADJECTIVE
attractive
   un hombre muy atractivo
   a very attractive man

atrapar VERB
to catch
   Mi gato atrapa pájaros.
   My cat catches birds.

atrás ADVERB
1 **Los niños viajan siempre atrás.**
   The children always travel in the back.
   la parte de atrás
   the back
   el asiento de atrás
   the back seat
2 **Mirar hacia atrás.**
   To look back.
   Está más atrás.
   It's further back.
   ir para atrás
   to go backwards
3 **El coche de atrás va a adelantarnos.**
   The car behind is going to overtake us.
   Yo me quedé atrás porque iba muy cansado.
   I stayed behind because I was very tired.

atrasado (FEM **atrasada**)
ADJECTIVE
1 **backward**
   Es un país muy atrasado.
   It's a very backward country.
2 **behind**
   Va bastante atrasado en la escuela.
   He's rather behind at school.
   Tengo mucho trabajo atrasado.
   I'm very behind with my work.
3 **El reloj está atrasado.**
   The clock's slow.

atravesar VERB
to cross
   Atravesamos el río.
   We crossed the river.

atreverse VERB
to dare
   No me atreví a decírselo.
   I didn't dare tell him.
   No me atrevo.
   I daren't.

a b c d e f g h i j k l m n ñ o p q r s t u v w x y z

Spanish **English**

a b c d e f g h i j k l m n ñ o p q r s t u v w x y z

atropellar VERB
to run over
> **Un coche atropelló al perro.**
> The dog was run over by a car.

el **aula** FEM NOUN
classroom

el **aumento** NOUN
increase
> **Ha habido un aumento de los precios.**
> There's been an increase in prices.

aun ADVERB
even
> **Aun sentado me duele la pierna.**
> Even when I'm sitting down, my leg hurts.

aun así
even so

aún ADVERB
1 **still**
> **Aún me queda un poco para terminar.**
> I've still got a little bit left to finish.
> **¿Aún te duele?**
> Is it still hurting?
2 **yet**
> **Aún no ha llegado mi madre.**
> My mum hasn't arrived yet.
> **Y aún no me has devuelto el libro.**
> You still haven't given me the book back.
3 **even**
> **La película es aún más aburrida de lo que creía.**
> The film's even more boring than I thought it would be.

aunque CONJUNCTION
1 **although**
> **Me gusta el francés, aunque prefiero el alemán.**
> I like French, although I prefer German.
> **Estoy pensando en ir, aunque no sé cuándo.**
> I'm thinking of going, though I don't know when.
> **Seguí andando, aunque me dolía mucho la pierna.**
> I went on walking, even though my leg was hurting a lot.
> **No te lo daré, aunque protestes.**
> You can complain all you like but you're not getting it.
2 **even if**
> **Pienso irme, aunque tenga que salir por la ventana.**
> I shall leave, even if I have to climb out of the window.

ausente (FEM **ausente**)
ADJECTIVE
absent

auténtico (FEM **auténtica**)
ADJECTIVE
1 **real**
> **Es un auténtico campeón.**
> He's a real champion.
2 **genuine**
> **El cuadro era auténtico.**
> The painting was genuine.

el **autobús** (PL los **autobuses**)
NOUN
bus

en autobús
by bus

automático (FEM **automática**)
ADJECTIVE
automatic

la **autopista** NOUN
motorway
> **autopista de peaje**
> toll motorway

el **autor**
la **autora** NOUN
author

la **autoridad** NOUN
authority

autorizar VERB
to authorize
No le han autorizado la entrada al país.
His entry into the country hasn't been authorized.

auxilio EXCLAMATION
help!

avanzar VERB
to make progress
Isabel avanzó mucho el pasado trimestre.
Isabel made a lot of progress last term.

el **ave** FEM NOUN
bird
un ave de rapiña
a bird of prey

la **aventura** NOUN
adventure
Te contaré nuestras aventuras en la playa.
I'll tell you about our adventures at the beach.

avergonzar VERB
to embarrass
Me avergonzaste delante de todos.
You embarrassed me in front of everyone.
Me avergüenzan estas situaciones.
I find this sort of situation embarrassing.
avergonzarse de algo
to be ashamed of something
No hay de qué avergonzarse.
There's nothing to be ashamed of.

la **avería** NOUN
El coche tiene una avería.
The car has broken down.

averiarse VERB
to break down

el **avión** (PL los **aviones**) NOUN
plane

ir en avión
to fly

avisar VERB
1 **to warn**
Ya nos avisaron de que haría mucho frío.
They warned us that it would be very cold.
2 **to let ... know**
Avísanos si hay alguna novedad.
Let us know if there's any news.

el **aviso** NOUN
notice
Había un aviso en la puerta.
There was a notice on the door.

la **avispa** NOUN
wasp

ay EXCLAMATION
1 **ow!**
¡Ay! ¡Me has pisado!
Ow! You've trodden on my toe!
2 **oh no!**
¡Ay! ¡Creo que nos han engañado!
Oh no! I think they've cheated us!

ayer ADVERB
yesterday
ayer por la mañana
yesterday morning
ayer por la tarde
yesterday afternoon/yesterday evening

Language tip

ayer por la tarde *has two meanings. It can be translated as* **yesterday afternoon** *and* **yesterday evening**.

Spanish English

ayer por la noche
last night

antes de ayer
the day before yesterday

la **ayuda** NOUN
help
> **Gracias por tu ayuda.**
> Thanks for your help.

el/la **ayudante** NOUN
assistant

ayudar VERB
to help
> **¿Me ayudas con los ejercicios?**
> Could you help me with these exercises?
> **Me está ayudando a hacer los deberes.**
> He's helping me do my homework.

el **ayuntamiento** NOUN
1 **town hall**
2 **city hall**

la **azafata** NOUN
air-hostess

el **azúcar** NOUN
sugar

azul ADJECTIVE, MASC NOUN
blue
> **una puerta azul**
> a blue door
> **azul celeste**
> sky blue
> **azul marino**
> navy blue
> **Yo iba de azul.**
> I was wearing blue.

B b

el **bache** NOUN
1 **pothole**
2 **bump**

el **Bachillerato** NOUN

Did you know…?
The **Bachillerato** *is a two-year secondary school course leading to university.*

la **bacteria** NOUN
bacterium

la **bahía** NOUN
bay

bailar VERB
to dance
 sacar a bailar a alguien
 to ask somebody to dance

el **bailarín**
 la **bailarina** NOUN (MASC PL
los **bailarines**)
 dancer

el **baile** NOUN
dance
 Me han invitado a un baile.
 I have been invited to a dance.

bajar VERB
1 **to go down**
 Bajó la escalera muy despacio.
 He went down the stairs very slowly.

2 **to come down**
 Baja y ayúdame.
 Come down and help me.
3 **to take down**
 ¿Has bajado la basura?
 Have you taken the rubbish down?
4 **to bring down**
 ¿Me bajas el abrigo?
 Could you bring my coat down?
5 **to fall**
 Han bajado los precios.
 Prices have fallen.
6 **to turn down**
 Baja la radio.
 Turn the radio down.
7 **to download**
 ▪ **bajarse de**
 to get off/to get out of/ to get down from

Language tip
bajarse de *has three meanings. Look at the examples.*

 Se bajó del autobús antes que yo.
 He got off the bus before me.
 ¡Bájate del coche!
 Get out of the car!
 ¡Bájate del árbol!
 Get down from the tree!

bajo (FEM **baja**)

bajo *can be an adjective, a preposition or an adverb.*

A ADJECTIVE
1 **low**
 una silla muy baja
 a very low chair
 la temporada baja
 the low season
 Hablaban en voz baja.
 They were speaking quietly.

2 short
Mi hermano es muy bajo.
My brother is very short.

3 ground
Viven en la planta baja.
They live on the ground floor.

B PREPOSITION
under
Juan llevaba un libro bajo el brazo.
Juan was carrying a book under his arm.

C ADVERB

1 low
El avión volaba muy bajo.
The plane was flying very low.

2 quietly
¡Habla bajo!
Speak quietly!

la **bala** NOUN
bullet

el **balcón** (PL los **balcones**) NOUN
balcony

la **baldosa** NOUN
tile

la **ballena** NOUN
whale

el **ballet** (PL los **ballets**) NOUN
ballet

el **balón**
(PL los **balones**)
NOUN
ball
balón de fútbol
football

el **baloncesto** NOUN
basketball
jugar al baloncesto
to play basketball

el **balonvolea** NOUN
volleyball
jugar al balonvolea
to play volleyball

el **banco** NOUN
1 bench
2 bank

la **banda** NOUN
1 band
Toca la trompeta en una banda.
He plays the trumpet with a band.

2 gang
La policía ha cogido a toda la banda.
The police have caught the whole gang.
la banda ancha
broadband
la banda sonora
the soundtrack

la **bandeja** NOUN
tray

la **bandera** NOUN
flag

la **banqueta** NOUN
stool

el **banquillo** NOUN
bench
El entrenador está en el banquillo.
The trainer is sitting on the bench.

el **bañador** NOUN
1 swimming trunks
2 swimming costume

bañarse VERB
1 to have a bath

Me gusta más bañarme que ducharme.
I prefer having a bath to having a shower.
2 to go for a swim
Estuve en la playa pero no me bañé.
I went to the beach but I didn't go for a swim.

la **bañera** NOUN
bath

el **baño** NOUN
1 bathroom
La casa tiene dos baños.
The house has two bathrooms.
darse un baño
to have a bath/to go for a swim

Language tip
darse un baño *has two meanings. It can be translated by* **to have a bath** *or* **to go for a swim**.

2 toilet
¿Puedo usar el baño, por favor?
Can I use the toilet, please?

el **bar** NOUN
bar

la **baraja** NOUN
pack of cards

barato (FEM **barata**)

barato *can be an adjective or an adverb.*

A ADJECTIVE
cheap
Esta marca es más barata que aquélla.
This brand is cheaper than that one.
B ADVERB
cheaply
Aquí se come muy barato.
You can eat really cheaply here.

la **barba** NOUN
beard

dejarse barba
to grow a beard

la **barbaridad** NOUN
1 atrocity
Hicieron barbaridades en la guerra.
They committed atrocities during the war.
2 Pablo come una barbaridad.
Pablo eats an awful lot.

la **barbilla** NOUN
chin

la **barca** NOUN
boat

el **barco** NOUN
1 ship
2 boat
un barco de vela
a sailing boat

la **barra** NOUN
bar
una barra metálica
a metal bar
Me tomé un café en la barra.
I had a coffee at the bar.
una barra de pan
a French stick
una barra de labios
a lipstick

barrer VERB
to sweep

la **barrera** NOUN
barrier

la **barriga** NOUN
belly
Estás echando barriga.
You're getting a bit of a belly.
Me duele la barriga.
I've got a stomachache.

el barrio NOUN
area
> **Ese chico no es del barrio.**
> That's boy's not from this area.

el barro NOUN
mud
> **Me llené los zapatos de barro.**
> My shoes got covered in mud.

el barullo NOUN
racket
> **armar barullo**
> to make a racket

la báscula NOUN
scales

la base NOUN
base
> **la base de la columna**
> the base of the column

básico (FEM **básica**) ADJECTIVE
basic

bastante (FEM **bastante**)

> **bastante** can be an adjective or an adverb.

A ADJECTIVE
1 enough
> **No tengo bastante dinero.**
> I haven't got enough money.
> **¿Hay bastante?**
> Is there enough?
2 quite a lot of
> **Vino bastante gente.**
> Quite a lot of people came.
> **Se tarda bastante tiempo en llegar.**
> It takes quite a while to get there.
B ADVERB
quite
> **Son bastante ricos.**
> They are quite rich.

bastar VERB
to be enough
> **Con esto basta.**
> That's enough.

> **¡Basta ya de tonterías!**
> That's enough of your nonsense!

> **¡Basta!**
> That's enough!

la basura NOUN
1 rubbish
> **Eso es basura.**
> That's rubbish.
> **tirar algo a la basura**
> to put something in the bin
2 litter

el basurero NOUN
dustman

la bata NOUN
overall

la batalla NOUN
battle

batería

> **batería** can be a feminine or masculine noun.

A FEM NOUN
1 battery
> **Se ha agotado la batería.**
> The battery is flat.
2 drums
> **¿Tocas la batería?**
> Do you play the drums?
B MASC/FEM NOUN
drummer

el batido NOUN
1 milkshake
> **un batido de fresa**
> a strawberry milkshake
2 smoothie

batir VERB
1 to break
2 to beat

el baúl NOUN
1 chest
2 trunk

el bautizo NOUN
christening

beber VERB
to drink
>**Hay que beber mucha agua en verano.**
>You need to drink a lot of water in the summer.

la **bebida** NOUN
drink
>**bebidas alcohólicas**
>alcoholic drinks

la **beca** NOUN
1 **grant**
2 **scholarship**

el **beicon** NOUN
bacon

la **belleza** NOUN
beauty

bello (FEM **bella**) ADJECTIVE
beautiful

bendecir VERB
to bless

la **bendición** (PL las **bendiciones**) NOUN
blessing

las **bermudas** NOUN
Bermuda shorts
>**Le compré unas bermudas.**
>I bought him a pair of Bermuda shorts.

besar VERB
to kiss
>**Ana y Pepe se besaron.**
>Ana and Pepe kissed each other.

el **beso** NOUN
kiss
>**Dame un beso.**
>Give me a kiss.

besos
love

la **bestia** NOUN
beast

la **Biblia** NOUN
Bible

la **biblioteca** NOUN
library

el **bicho** NOUN
insect
>**Me ha picado un bicho.**
>I've been bitten by an insect.
>**David es un bicho raro.**
>David's weird.

la **bici** NOUN
bike

la **bicicleta** NOUN
bicycle
>**una bicicleta de montaña**
>a mountain bike

bien

bien *can be an adverb or a noun.*

A ADVERB
1 **well**
>**Habla bien el español.**
>He speaks Spanish well.
2 **good**
>**Huele bien.**
>It smells good.
>**Lo pasamos muy bien.**
>We had a very good time.
>**Ese libro está muy bien.**
>That's a very good book.
>**Has contestado bien.**
>You gave the right answer.

Hiciste bien en decírselo.
You were right to tell him.
¡Está bien! Lo haré.
OK! I'll do it.
3 very
un café bien caliente
a very hot coffee

¡Qué bien!
Excellent!

B MASC NOUN
good
Lo digo por tu bien.
I'm telling you for your own good.
los bienes
possessions
todos los bienes de la familia
all the family's possessions

la **bienvenida** NOUN
dar la bienvenida a alguien
to welcome somebody
una fiesta de bienvenida
a welcome party

bienvenido (FEM **bienvenida**)

bienvenido can be an adjective or an exclamation.

A ADJECTIVE
welcome
Siempre serás bienvenido aquí.
You will always be welcome here.
B EXCLAMATION
welcome!

el **bigote** NOUN
moustache

el **bikini** NOUN
bikini

bilingüe (FEM **bilingüe**)
ADJECTIVE
bilingual

el **billar** NOUN
billiards
el billar americano
pool

el **billete** NOUN
1 ticket
un billete de metro
an underground ticket
un billete de ida y vuelta
a return ticket
2 note
un billete de veinte euros
a twenty-euro note

el **billón** (PL los **billones**) NOUN
un billón
a million million

Language tip
Be careful! **billón** does not mean **billion**.

biodegradable
(FEM **biodegradable**) ADJECTIVE
biodegradable

la **biografía** NOUN
biography

la **biología** NOUN
biology

biológico (FEM **biológica**)
ADJECTIVE
1 organic
2 biological

el **biquini** NOUN
bikini

la **bisabuela** NOUN
great-grandmother

el **bisabuelo** NOUN
great-grandfather
mis bisabuelos
my great-grandparents

el **bistec** (PL los **bistecs**) NOUN
steak

bizco (FEM **bizca**) ADJECTIVE
cross-eyed

el **bizcocho** NOUN
sponge cake

blanco

blanco can be an adjective or a noun.

A (FEM **blanca**) ADJECTIVE
white
un vestido blanco
a white dress

B MASC NOUN
white
Me gusta el blanco.
I like white.
Me quedé en blanco.
My mind went blank.

blando (FEM **blanda**) ADJECTIVE
soft
Este colchón es muy blando.
This mattress is very soft.

el **bloc** (PL los **blocs**) NOUN
writing pad
un bloc de dibujo
a drawing pad

el **blog** NOUN
blog

el **bloque** NOUN
block
un bloque de pisos
a block of flats

bloquear VERB
to block
La nieve bloqueó las carreteras.
The snow blocked the roads.

la **blusa** NOUN
blouse

la **bobada** NOUN
Este programa es una bobada.
This programme is stupid.

decir bobadas
to talk nonsense

bobo (FEM **boba**) ADJECTIVE
silly

la **boca** NOUN
mouth
No debes hablar con la boca llena.
You shouldn't talk with your mouth full.
No abrió la boca en toda la tarde.
He didn't open his mouth all afternoon.
Me quedé con la boca abierta.
I was speechless.

boca abajo
face down
boca arriba
face up

el **bocadillo** NOUN
sandwich
un bocadillo de queso
a cheese sandwich

Did you know...?
In Spain, a **bocadillo** *is usually made with a baguette.*

el **bocado** NOUN
bite
Dame un bocado de tu bocadillo.
Let me have a bite of your sandwich.
No he probado bocado desde ayer.
I haven't had a bite to eat since yesterday.

el **bocata** NOUN
sandwich
Ya me he comido el bocata.
I've already had my sandwich.
un bocata de queso
a cheese sandwich

Did you know...?
In Spain, a **bocata** *is usually made with a baguette.*

Spanish | English

a
b
c
d
e
f
g
h
i
j
k
l
m
n
ñ
o
p
q
r
s
t
u
v
w
x
y
z

la **boda** NOUN
wedding

la **bofetada** NOUN
slap
> **Le dio una bofetada.**
> She slapped him.

la **bola** NOUN
1 **ball**
> **una bola de nieve**
> a snowball
2 **scoop**

el **boli** NOUN
pen

el **bolígrafo** NOUN
pen

el **bollo** NOUN
bun
> **Me he comido un bollo para desayunar.**
> I had a bun for breakfast.

los **bolos** NOUN
tenpin bowling

la **bolsa** NOUN
bag
> **una bolsa de plástico**
> a plastic bag

el **bolsillo** NOUN
pocket
> **Sacó las llaves del bolsillo.**
> He took the keys out of his pocket.
> **un libro de bolsillo**
> a paperback

el **bolso** NOUN
bag

la **bomba** NOUN
bomb

el **bombero** NOUN
fireman

la **bombilla** NOUN
lightbulb

el **bombón** (PL los **bombones**)
NOUN
chocolate

la **bombona** NOUN
gas cylinder

bonito (FEM **bonita**) ADJECTIVE
pretty
> **una casa muy bonita**
> a very pretty house

el **borde** NOUN
edge
> **al borde de la mesa**
> at the edge of the table

borracho (FEM **borracha**)
ADJECTIVE
drunk
> **Estás borracho.**
> You're drunk.

el **borrador** NOUN
1 **duster**
> **Usó un trapo como borrador.**
> He used a rag as a duster.
2 **rough draft**
> **Escribe primero un borrador.**
> First write a rough draft.

borrar VERB
1 **to rub out**
> **Borra toda la palabra.**
> Rub out the whole word.
2 **to clean**
> **Borra la pizarra.**
> Clean the blackboard.
> **borrarse de**
> to take one's name off/to leave

Language tip

borrarse de *has two meanings. Look at the examples.*

> **Voy a borrarme de la lista.**
> I'm going to take my name off the list.
> **Se borró del club.**
> He left the club.

el **bosque** NOUN
1 **wood**
2 **forest**

34

bostezar VERB
to yawn

la **bota** NOUN
boot

botar VERB
to bounce
Esta pelota no bota.
This ball doesn't bounce.

el **bote** NOUN
1 **boat**
un bote salvavidas
a lifeboat
2 **jar**

pegar un bote
to jump

la **botella** NOUN
bottle

el **botón** (PL los **botones**) NOUN
button
He perdido un botón de la camisa.
I've lost a button off my shirt.
pulsar un botón
to press a button

boxear VERB
to box

el **boxeo** NOUN
boxing

las **bragas** NOUN
knickers
unas bragas
a pair of knickers

la **bragueta** NOUN
fly

bravo EXCLAMATION
well done!

la **braza** NOUN
breaststroke

nadar a braza
to do the breaststroke

el **brazo** NOUN
arm
Me duele el brazo.
My arm hurts.
Estaba sentada con los brazos cruzados.
She was sitting with her arms folded.

breve (FEM **breve**) ADJECTIVE
short
un relato breve
a short story

brillante

brillante *can be an adjective or a noun.*

A (FEM **brillante**) ADJECTIVE
shiny
Tenía el pelo brillante.
Her hair was shiny.
B MASC NOUN
diamond

brillar VERB
1 **to shine**
Hoy brilla el sol.
The sun is shining today.
2 **to sparkle**

el **brillo** NOUN
1 **shine**
2 **sparkle**

británico
británica

británico *can be an adjective or a noun.*

A ADJECTIVE
British
B MASC/FEM NOUN
British person
los británicos
the British

la **brocha** NOUN
paintbrush

el **broche** NOUN
1 **clasp**
2 **brooch**

la **broma** NOUN
joke
> **Le gastamos una broma al profesor.**
> We played a joke on the teacher.
> **decir algo en broma**
> to say something as a joke
> **una broma pesada**
> a practical joke

bromear VERB
to joke

el/la **bromista** NOUN
joker

la **bronca** NOUN
1 **row**
> **Tuvieron una bronca muy gorda.**
> They had a huge row.
2 **fuss**

> **echar una bronca a alguien**
> to tell somebody off

el **bronce** NOUN
bronze

el **bronceado** NOUN
suntan

el **bronceador** NOUN
suntan lotion

la **bruja**
NOUN
witch

el **brujo** NOUN
wizard

la **brújula** NOUN
compass

bruto (FEM **bruta**) ADJECTIVE
rough
> **¡No seas bruto!**
> Don't be so rough!

bucear VERB
to dive

buen ADJECTIVE ▷ see **bueno**

> **Language tip**
> When **bueno** goes in front of a masculine singular noun it is shortened to **buen**.

> **Es un buen hombre.**
> He's a good man.

bueno (FEM **buena**) ADJECTIVE
good
> **Es un buen libro.**
> It's a good book.
> **Hace buen tiempo.**
> The weather's good.
> **Es buena persona.**
> He's a good person.
> **un buen trozo**
> a good slice
> **ser bueno para**
> to be good for
> **Está muy bueno este bizcocho.**
> This sponge cake is lovely.
> **¡Buenos días!**
> Good morning!
> **¡Buenas tardes!**
> Good afternoon!/Good evening!
> **¡Buenas noches!**
> Good evening!/Good night!

> **Language tip**
> Did you know that the Spanish use **¡buenas tardes!** in the afternoon and early evening and **¡buenas noches!** when it starts to get dark as well as when they say good night?

> **¡Bueno!**
> OK!

la **bufanda** NOUN
scarf

el **búho** NOUN
owl

el **bulto** NOUN
lump
> **Tengo un bulto en la frente.**
> I have a lump on my forehead.

la **burbuja** NOUN
  bubble
    un refresco sin burbujas
    a still drink
    un refresco con burbujas
    a fizzy drink

la **burla** NOUN
    Siempre hacen burla de mí.
    They are always making fun of
    me.

burlarse VERB
    Siempre se burlan de mí.
    They are always making fun of
    me.

la **burrada** NOUN
    **Siempre andan haciendo
    burradas.**
    They're always messing around.

burro

> **burro** *can be a noun or an
> adjective.*

A MASC NOUN
1 **donkey**
2 **idiot**
    Eres un burro.
    You're an idiot.
B (FEM **burra**) ADJECTIVE
1 **thick**
2 **rough**

el **buscador** NOUN
  search engine

buscar VERB
1 **to look for**
    Estoy buscando las gafas.
    I'm looking for my glasses.
2 **to pick up**
    **Mi madre siempre me viene
    a buscar al colegio en coche.**
    My mother always picks me up
    from school in the car.
3 **to look up**
    **Busca la palabra en el
    diccionario.**
    Look the word up in the
    dictionary.
    Él se lo ha buscado.
    He was asking for it.

la **búsqueda** NOUN
  search

la **butaca** NOUN
  armchair

el **buzo** NOUN
  diver

el **buzón** (PL los **buzones**) NOUN
1 **letterbox**

> ### *Did you know...?*
> *Spanish* **letterboxes** *tend to be
> American-Style boxes in which the
> postman leaves mail rather than the
> hole in the door that is common in
> the UK.*

2 **postbox**
    echar una carta al buzón
    to post a letter
    buzón de voz
    voice mail

C c

el caballo NOUN
horse
> **¿Te gusta montar a caballo?**
> Do you like horseriding?

el cabello NOUN
hair

caber VERB
to fit
> **No cabe en mi armario.**
> It won't fit in my cupboard.
> **No cabe nadie más.**
> There's no room for anyone else.

la cabeza NOUN
head
> **Se rascó la cabeza.**
> He scratched his head.

la cabina NOUN
phone box

el cable NOUN
cable

la cabra NOUN
goat

cabrá VERB ▷ *see* **caber**
> **No sé si cabrá.**
> I don't know whether it will fit.

el cachorro
la cachorra
NOUN
1 puppy

2 cub

cada (FEM **cada**) ADJECTIVE
1 each
> **Cada libro es de un color distinto.**

Each book is a different colour.
cada uno
each one

2 every
> **cada año**
> every year
> **cada vez que la veo**
> every time I see her
> **Viene cada vez más gente.**
> More and more people are coming.
> **Viene cada vez menos.**
> He comes less and less often.
> **Cada vez hace más frío.**
> It's getting colder and colder.

la cadena NOUN
1 chain
> **una cadena de oro**
> a gold chain
2 channel
> **Por la cadena tres ponen una película.**
> There's a film on channel three.

> **tirar de la cadena**
> to flush the toilet

caer VERB
to fall
> **¡Cuidado que vas a caer!**
> Careful or you'll fall!
> **Su hermano me cae muy bien.**
> I really like his brother.
> **Eva me cae muy mal.**
> I can't stand Eva.

■ **caerse**
to fall
> **Tropecé y me caí.**
> I tripped and fell.
> **Se me cayeron las monedas.**
> I dropped the coins.

el café (PL los **cafés**) NOUN
1 coffee

Spanish English

un café con leche
a white coffee
2 café

caigo VERB ▷see **caer**
¡Ahora caigo!
Now I remember!

la **caja** NOUN
1 box
una caja de zapatos
a shoe box
2 checkout

el **cajón** (PL los **cajones**) NOUN
drawer

el **calcetín** (PL los **calcetines**)
NOUN
sock

la **calculadora** NOUN
calculator

la **calefacción** NOUN
heating
calefacción central
central heating

el **calendario** NOUN
calendar

el **calentamiento** NOUN
el calentamiento global
global warming
ejercicios de calentamiento
warm-up exercises

calentar VERB
1 to heat up
**¿Quieres que te caliente la
leche?**
Do you want me to heat up the
milk for you?

2 to warm up

calentarse VERB
1 to heat up
**Espera a que se caliente el
agua.**
Wait for the water to heat up.
2 to warm up
**Deja que se caliente el
motor.**
Let the engine warm up.

caliente (FEM **caliente**)
ADJECTIVE
hot
Esta sopa está muy caliente.
This soup is very hot.

la **calificación** (PL las
calificaciones) NOUN
mark
**Obtuvo buenas
calificaciones.**
He got good marks.
boletín de calificaciones
school report

callado (FEM **callada**) ADJECTIVE
quiet
una persona muy callada
a very quiet person

callar VERB
to be quiet
**Calla, que no me dejas
concentrarme.**
Be quiet, I can't concentrate.
■ **callarse**
to keep quiet/to stop talking

Language tip

callarse *has two meanings. Look at
the examples.*

Prefirió callarse.
He preferred to keep quiet.
**Al entrar el profesor, todos se
callaron.**
When the teacher came in,
everyone stopped talking.

la **calle** NOUN
street

a b **c** d e f g h i j k l m n ñ o p q r s t u v w x y z

Viven en la calle Peñalver, 13.
They live at number 13, Peñalver Street.
Hoy no he salido a la calle.
I haven't been out today.

calmar VERB
to calm down
Intenté calmarla un poco.
I tried to calm her down a little.
¡Cálmate!
Calm down!

el **calor** NOUN
heat
No se puede trabajar con este calor.
It's impossible to work in this heat.

Hace calor.
It's hot.
Tengo calor.
I'm hot.

los **calzoncillos** NOUN
underpants
unos calzoncillos
a pair of underpants

la **cama** NOUN
bed
Está en la cama.
He's in bed.

hacer la cama
to make the bed
irse a la cama
to go to bed

la **cámara** NOUN
camera
una cámara digital
a digital camera

la **camarera** NOUN
waitress

el **camarero** NOUN
waiter

cambiar VERB
1 **to change**
No has cambiado nada.
You haven't changed a bit.
He cambiado de idea.
I've changed my mind.
Voy a cambiarme.
I'm going to get changed.
2 **to swap**
Me gusta el tuyo, te lo cambio.
I like yours, let's swap.

cambiar de idea
to change one's mind

el **cambio** NOUN
change
un cambio brusco de temperatura
a sudden change in temperature
¿Tiene cambio de veinte euros?
Have you got change of twenty euros?

caminar VERB
to walk

el **camino** NOUN
1 **path**
2 **way**
¿Sabes el camino a su casa?
Do you know the way to his house?
La farmacia me pilla de camino.
The chemist's is on my way.

el **camión** (PL los **camiones**) NOUN
lorry

la **camisa** NOUN
shirt

la **camiseta** NOUN
1 **T-shirt**
2 **vest**
3 **shirt**

el **campamento** NOUN
camp

un campamento de verano
a summer camp

la **campana** NOUN
bell

el **campeón**
la **campeona** NOUN
champion

el **camping** (PL los **campings**)
NOUN
1 **camping**
Fuimos de camping este verano.
We went camping this summer.
2 **campsite**
Estamos en un camping.
We're at a campsite.

el **campo** NOUN
1 **country**
Prefiero vivir en el campo.
I prefer living in the country.
2 **pitch**
un campo de fútbol
a football pitch

el **canal** NOUN
1 **channel**
Por el canal dos ponen una película.
They're showing a film on channel two.
2 **channel**
el Canal de la Mancha
the English Channel

la **canción** (PL las **canciones**)
NOUN
song

el **cangrejo** NOUN
crab

cansado (FEM **cansada**)
ADJECTIVE
tired
Estoy muy cansado.
I'm very tired.

Estoy cansado de hacer lo mismo todos los días.
I'm tired of doing the same thing every day.

cansarse VERB
to get tired
Está muy débil y enseguida se cansa.
He is very weak and gets tired quickly.
Me cansé de esperarlo y me marché.
I got tired of waiting for him and I left.

el/la **cantante** NOUN
singer

cantar VERB
to sing

la **cantidad** NOUN
1 **quantity**
La calidad es más importante que la cantidad.
Quality is more important than quantity.
¡Qué cantidad de gente!
What a lot of people!
2 **amount**
una cierta cantidad de dinero
a certain amount of money

la **capa** NOUN
layer
> **la capa de ozono**
> the ozone layer

el **capitán**
la **capitana** NOUN
captain

el **capítulo** NOUN
chapter

la **capucha** NOUN
hood

la **cara** NOUN
1 face
> **Tiene la cara alargada.**
> He has a long face.
> **Tienes mala cara.**
> You don't look well.
> **No pongas esa cara.**
> Don't look like that.
2 cheek
> **¡Qué cara!**
> What a cheek!
3 side
> **un folio escrito por las dos caras**
> a sheet written on both sides

¿Cara o cruz?
Heads or tails?

el **caramelo** NOUN
sweet

la **carga** NOUN
refill

cargar VERB
1 to load
> **Cargaron el coche de maletas.**
> They loaded the car with suitcases.
2 to charge

la **caries** (PL las **caries**) NOUN
1 tooth decay
2 cavity

cariñoso (FEM **cariñosa**)
ADJECTIVE
affectionate
> **Es muy cariñosa con los niños.**
> She is very affectionate towards the children.

la **carne** NOUN
meat
> **No como carne.**
> I don't eat meat.

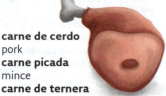

> carne de cerdo
> pork
> **carne picada**
> mince
> **carne de ternera**
> veal
> **carne de vaca**
> beef

el **carnet** (PL los **carnets**) NOUN
card
> **el carnet de identidad**
> identity card
> **un carnet de conducir**
> a driving licence

caro (FEM **cara**) ADJECTIVE, ADVERB
expensive
> **Aquí todo lo venden tan caro.**
> Everything is so expensive here.

la **carpeta** NOUN
folder

la **carrera** NOUN
race
> **una carrera de caballos**
> a horse race

la **carretera** NOUN
road

el **carrito** NOUN
trolley

el **carro** NOUN
1 cart
2 trolley

la **carta** NOUN
  1 letter
    Le he escrito una carta a Juan.
    I've written Juan a letter.
  2 card
    jugar a las cartas
    to play cards

el **cartel** NOUN
  1 poster
  2 sign

la **cartera** NOUN
  1 satchel
  2 wallet

el **cartero** NOUN
  postman

el **cartón** (PL los **cartones**) NOUN
  cardboard
    una caja de cartón
    a cardboard box

el **cartucho** NOUN
  cartridge

la **cartulina** NOUN
  card

la **casa** NOUN
  1 house
  2 home
    Estábamos en casa.
    We were at home.
    Nos vamos a casa.
    We're going home.
    Estábamos en casa de Juan.
    We were at Juan's.

casado (FEM **casada**) ADJECTIVE
  married
    una mujer casada
    a married woman
    Está casado con una francesa.
    He's married to a French woman.

casarse VERB
  to get married

    Quieren casarse.
    They want to get married.

la **cascada** NOUN
  waterfall

la **cáscara** NOUN
  1 shell
  2 skin

casi ADVERB
  almost
    Casi me ahogo.
    I almost drowned.
    Son casi las cinco.
    It's nearly five o'clock.
    Casi no comí.
    I hardly ate.

la **casilla** NOUN
  box

el **caso** NOUN
  case
    En casos así es mejor callarse.
    In such cases it's better to keep quiet.
    El caso es que no me queda dinero.
    The thing is, I haven't got any money left.
    No le hagas caso.
    Don't take any notice of him.

la **caspa** NOUN
  dandruff

la **castaña** NOUN
  chestnut

castaño (FEM **castaña**) ADJECTIVE
  brown
    Mi hermana tiene el pelo castaño.
    My sister has brown hair.

castigar VERB
  to punish
    Mi padre me castigó por contestarle.
    My father punished me for answering him back.

a b c d e f g h i j k l m n ñ o p q r s t u v w x y z

el **castigo** NOUN
punishment
> **Tuve que escribirlo diez**
> **veces, como castigo.**
> I had to write it out ten times, as
> punishment.

el **castillo** NOUN
castle
> **un castillo de arena**
> a sandcastle

la **casualidad** NOUN
coincidence
> **¡Qué casualidad!**
> What a coincidence!
> **Nos encontramos por**
> **casualidad.**
> We met by chance.

el **catarro** NOUN
cold
> **Vas a pillar un catarro.**
> You're going to catch a cold.

la **catástrofe** NOUN
catastrophe

catorce (FEM **catorce**) ADJECTIVE,
PRONOUN
fourteen

> **el catorce de enero**
> the fourteenth of January
> **Nació el catorce de enero.**
> He was born on the fourteenth of
> January.

la **causa** NOUN
cause
> **No se sabe la causa del**
> **accidente.**
> The cause of the accident is
> unknown.

> **a causa de**
> because of

causar VERB
to cause
> **La lluvia causó muchos daños.**
> The rain caused a lot of damage.

cayendo VERB
> ▷ see **caer**
> **Está cayendo**
> **nieve.**
> It's snowing.

la **cazadora** NOUN
jacket

la **cebolla** NOUN
onion

la **ceja** NOUN
eyebrow

celebrar VERB
to celebrate

el **celo** NOUN
Sellotape®

los **celos** NOUN
jealousy
> **Lo hizo por celos.**
> He did it out of jealousy.
> **Tiene celos de su mejor**
> **amiga.**
> She's jealous of her best friend.

celoso (FEM **celosa**) ADJECTIVE
jealous
> **Está celoso de su hermano.**
> He's jealous of his brother.

el **cemento** NOUN
cement

la **cena** NOUN
dinner
> **La cena es a las ocho.**
> Dinner is at eight o'clock.

cenar VERB
to have dinner
> **No he cenado.**
> I haven't had dinner.
> **¿Qué quieres cenar?**
> What do you want for dinner?

Did you know…?
*In Spain, people generally eat later
than in the UK. Lunch is usually
around two and people tend to have
dinner around nine or ten.*

Spanish | English

a b c d e f g h i j k l m n ñ o p q r s t u v w x y z

el **cenicero** NOUN
ashtray

la **ceniza** NOUN
ash

centígrado (FEM **centígrada**)
ADJECTIVE
centigrade
veinte grados centígrados
twenty degrees centigrade

el **centímetro** NOUN
centimetre

el **céntimo** NOUN
cent

central (FEM **central**) ADJECTIVE
central

el **centro** NOUN
centre
un centro comercial
a shopping centre
Fui al centro a hacer unas compras.
I went into town to do some shopping.

cepillar VERB
to brush
Se está cepillando los dientes.
He's brushing his teeth.

el **cepillo** NOUN
brush
un cepillo de dientes
a toothbrush

la **cera** NOUN
wax

cerca ADVERB
near
El colegio está muy cerca.
The school is very near.

cerca de la iglesia
near the church
cerca de dos horas
nearly two hours
Quería verlo de cerca.
I wanted to see it close up.

el **cerdo** NOUN
1 **pig**
2 **pork**
No comemos cerdo.
We don't eat pork.

el **cereal** NOUN
cereal
Los niños desayunan cereales.
The children have cereal for breakfast.

el **cerebro** NOUN
brain

la **cerilla** NOUN
match
una caja de cerillas
a box of matches

el **cero** NOUN
zero
Estamos a cinco grados bajo cero.
It's five degrees below zero.
cero coma tres
zero point three
Van dos a cero.
The score is two-nil.
Tuve que empezar desde cero.
I had to start from scratch.

cerrado (FEM **cerrada**) ADJECTIVE
closed
Las tiendas están cerradas.
The shops are closed.

la **cerradura** NOUN
lock

cerrar VERB
1 **to close**
No cierran al mediodía.
They don't close at lunchtime.

Cerró el libro.
He closed the book.
Cerré la puerta con llave.
I locked the door.
Se me cierran los ojos.
I can't keep my eyes open.
No puedo cerrar la maleta.
I can't shut this suitcase.
2 to turn off
Cierra el grifo.
Turn off the tap.

la **cerveza** NOUN
beer

el **césped** NOUN
grass
'no pisar el césped'
'keep off the grass'

el **chaleco** NOUN
waistcoat
un chaleco salvavidas
a life-jacket

el **chalet** (PL los **chalets**) NOUN
1 house
2 cottage

el **champú** (PL los **champús**)
NOUN
shampoo

el **chándal** (PL los **chándals**)
NOUN
tracksuit

la **chaqueta** NOUN
1 cardigan
2 jacket

charlar VERB
to chat

el **chat** NOUN
chatroom

la **chatarra** NOUN
scrap metal

la **chica** NOUN
1 girl
2 girlfriend
Fui al cine con mi chica.
I went to the cinema with my
girlfriend.

el **chichón** (PL los **chichones**)
NOUN
bump
**Me ha salido un chichón en
la frente.**
I've got a bump on my forehead.

el **chicle** NOUN
chewing gum

el **chico** NOUN
1 boy
**Fueron todos
los chicos
de la clase.**
All the boys
in the class
went.

2 boyfriend
Iré con mi chico.
I'll go with my boyfriend.

chillar VERB
to scream

la **chimenea** NOUN
1 chimney
2 fireplace

la **chincheta** NOUN
drawing pin

el **chiste** NOUN
joke
El maestro nos contó un chiste.
The teacher told us a joke.

chocar VERB
chocar contra
**to hit/to bump into/to crash
into**

Spanish English

Language tip
chocar contra *has various meanings. Look at the examples.*

El coche chocó contra un árbol.
The car hit a tree.
Choqué contra una farola.
I bumped into a lamppost.
Chocó contra un muro.
He crashed into a wall.

el **chocolate** NOUN
chocolate

el **chorizo** NOUN
chorizo

Did you know...?
Chorizo *is a kind of spicy sausage.*

el **chubasquero** NOUN
cagoule

chulo (FEM **chula**) ADJECTIVE
1 cocky
2 cool
¡Qué mochila más chula!
What a cool rucksack!

chupar VERB
to suck
Se chupaba el dedo.
He was sucking his thumb.

los **churros** PL NOUN
long sweet fritters

Did you know...?
churros *are a kind of fritter that people often eat on the streets in a paper bag or order in a café typically with a cup of thick, hot chocolate:* **chocolate con churros**.

el **cíber** NOUN
Internet café

el **cibercafé** NOUN
Internet café

el/la **ciclista** NOUN
cyclist

ciego
ciega

ciego *can be an adjective or a noun.*

A ADJECTIVE
blind
Mi abuelo es ciego.
My grandfather is blind.

quedarse ciego
to go blind

B MASC/FEM NOUN
un ciego
a blind man
una ciega
a blind woman
los ciegos
the blind

el **cielo** NOUN
sky
No había ni una nube en el cielo.
There wasn't a single cloud in the sky.

cien (FEM **cien**) ADJECTIVE,
PRONOUN
a hundred
Había unos cien invitados en la boda.
There were about a hundred guests at the wedding.

cien mil
a hundred thousand
cien por cien
a hundred percent

la **ciencia** NOUN
science
Me gustan mucho las ciencias.
I really enjoy science.

Spanish English

a b **c** d e f g h i j k l m n ñ o p q r s t u v w x y z

ciento (FEM **ciento**) ADJECTIVE, PRONOUN
a hundred
ciento cuarenta y dos libras
a hundred and forty two pounds
Recibimos cientos de cartas.
We received hundreds of letters.
el diez por ciento de la población
ten percent of the population

cierro VERB ▷see **cerrar**
Cuando cierro al puerta hace un ruido extraño.
When I close the door it makes a funny noise.

cierto (FEM **cierta**) ADJECTIVE
true
No, eso no es cierto.
No, that's not true.

por cierto
by the way

el **ciervo** NOUN
deer

la **cifra** NOUN
figure
un número de cuatro cifras
a four-figure number

el **cigarrillo** NOUN
cigarette

cinco (FEM **cinco**) ADJECTIVE, PRONOUN
five
Tiene cinco años.
He's five.

el cinco de enero
the fifth of January
Nació el cinco de enero.
He was born on the fifth of January.
Son las cinco.
It's five o'clock.

cincuenta (FEM **cincuenta**) ADJECTIVE, PRONOUN
fifty
Tiene cincuenta años.
He's fifty.

el **cine** NOUN
cinema
Mañana voy al cine.
I'm going to the cinema tomorrow.

la **cintura** NOUN
waist
¿Cuánto mides de cintura?
What's your waist size?

el **cinturón** (PL los **cinturones**) NOUN
belt
el cinturón de seguridad
the safety belt

el **circo** NOUN
circus

el **círculo** NOUN
circle
Dibuja un círculo.
Draw a circle.

el **cisne** NOUN
swan

la **cita** NOUN
1 **date**
No llegues tarde a la cita.
Don't be late for your date.
2 **appointment**
Tengo cita con el médico.
I've got a doctor's appointment.

la **ciudad** NOUN
1 **city**
2 **town**

la **clara** NOUN
white

claro (FEM **clara**)

claro *can be an adjective or an adverb.*

A ADJECTIVE
1 **clear**

Lo quiero mañana. ¿Está claro?
I want it tomorrow. Is that clear?
Está claro que esconden algo.
It's obvious that they are hiding
something.

2 light
una camisa azul claro
a light blue shirt

B ADVERB
clearly
Lo oí muy claro.
I heard it very clearly.
¡Claro!
Of course!
¿Te oyó? —
¡Claro que me oyó!
Did he hear you? —
Of course he heard me!

la **clase** NOUN
1 class
A las diez tengo clase de física.
I have a physics class at ten.
Mi hermana da clases de
inglés.
My sister teaches English.
Hoy no hay clase.
There's no school today.
clases particulares
private lessons

2 classroom
3 kind
Había juguetes de todas
clases.
There were all kinds of toys.

clásico (FEM **clásica**) ADJECTIVE
classical
Me gusta la música clásica.
I like classical music.

clasificar VERB
to classify
■ **clasificarse**
to qualify
Esperan clasificarse para la
final.
They hope to qualify for the final.
Se clasificaron en tercer lugar.
They came third.

la **clave** NOUN
code
un mensaje en clave
a coded message

el **clic** NOUN
click
hacer clic en algo
to click on something

el **clima** NOUN
climate
Es un país de clima tropical.
It's a country with a tropical
climate.

la **clínica** NOUN
hospital

el **clip** (PL los **clips**) NOUN
paper clip

cobarde (FEM **cobarde**)
ADJECTIVE
cowardly
¡No seas cobarde!
Don't be such a coward!

el **coche** NOUN
car
Fuimos a Sevilla en coche.
We went to Sevilla by car.
un coche de carreras
a racing car
los coches de choque
the bumper cars
un coche de bomberos
a fire engine

la **cocina** NOUN
1 kitchen
Comemos en la cocina.
We eat in the kitchen.

2 cooker
una cocina de gas
a gas cooker
la cocina vasca
Basque cuisine
un libro de cocina
a cookery book

cocinar VERB
to cook

No sabe cocinar.
He can't cook.
Cocinas muy bien.
You're a very good cook.

el **codo** NOUN
 elbow

coger VERB
 1 **to take**
 Coge el que más te guste.
 Take the one you like best.
 2 **to catch**
 ¡Coge la pelota!
 Catch the ball!
 La cogieron robando.
 They caught her stealing.
 He cogido un resfriado.
 I've caught a cold.
 Voy a coger el autobús.
 I'm going to get the bus.

el **cohete** NOUN
 rocket

el **cojín** (PL los **cojines**) NOUN
 cushion

cojo

 cojo *can be an adjective or a verb.*

 A (FEM **coja**) ADJECTIVE
 Es algo cojo.
 He has a bit of a limp.
 B VERB ▷ *see* **coger**
 ¡Si te cojo!
 If I catch you!

la **cola** NOUN
 1 **tail**
 2 **queue**
 Había mucha cola para el baño.
 There was a long queue for the toilets.
 3 **glue**

 hacer cola
 to queue

colarse VERB
 to push in
 No te cueles.
 Don't push in.

Nos colamos en el cine.
We sneaked into the cinema without paying.

el/la **colega** NOUN
 1 **mate**
 2 **colleague**

el **colegio** NOUN
 school

 ¿Todavía vas al colegio?
 Are you still at school?
 un colegio público
 a state school

colgar VERB
 1 **to hang**
 Colguemos el cuadro en esta pared.
 Let's hang the picture on this wall.
 ¡No dejes la chaqueta en la silla, cuélgala!
 Don't leave your jacket on the chair, hang it up!
 2 **to hang up**
 ¡No cuelgues!
 Don't hang up!
 Me colgó el teléfono.
 He hung up on me.

el **collar** NOUN
 1 **necklace**
 2 **collar**

el **colmo** NOUN
 ¡Esto ya es el colmo!
 This really is the last straw!

colocar VERB
 to put
 Colocamos la mesa en medio del comedor.
 We put the table in the middle of the dining room.

¡Colocaos en fila!
Get into a line!

la **colonia** NOUN
perfume
¿Qué colonia llevas?
What perfume are you wearing?

una colonia de verano
a summer camp

el **color** NOUN
colour
¿De qué color son?
What colour are they?
un vestido de color azul
a blue dress

la **columna** NOUN
column

el **columpio** NOUN
swing

la **coma** NOUN
comma
Separa las palabras con una coma.
Separate the words with a comma.
cero coma ocho
zero point eight

Did you know…?
In Spanish you use a comma instead of a point in decimal numbers.

la **comba** NOUN
skipping rope

saltar a la comba
to skip

el **comedor** NOUN
1 **dining room**
2 **refectory**

comenzar VERB
to begin
Comenzó a llover.
It began to rain.

comer VERB
1 **to eat**
¿Quieres comer algo?
Do you want something to eat?

Le estaba dando de comer a su hijo.
She was feeding her son.

2 **to have lunch**
Comimos en el hotel.
We had lunch in the hotel.
Hemos comido paella.
We had paella for lunch.
¿Qué hay para comer?
What's for lunch?

Did you know…?
In Spain, people generally eat later than in the UK. Lunch is usually around two and people tend to have dinner around nine or ten.

cometa

cometa can be a masculine or a feminine noun.

A MASC NOUN
comet
B FEM NOUN
kite

el **cómic** NOUN
comic

la **comida** NOUN
1 **food**
La comida del hotel es muy buena.
The food in the hotel is very good.

2 **lunch**
La comida es a la una y media.
Lunch is at half past one.

Did you know…?
In Spain, people generally eat later than in the UK. Lunch is usually around two and people tend to have dinner around nine or ten.

3 meal
Es la comida más importante del día.
It's the most important meal of the day.

comienzo VERB ▷see
comenzar
Yo comienzo y después tú me sigues.
I go first and then you follow me.

como ADVERB, CONJUNCTION
1 like
Tienen un perro como el nuestro.
They've got a dog like ours.
blanco como la nieve
as white as snow
Es tan alto como tú.
He is as tall as you.
2 as
Como ella no llegaba, me fui.
As she didn't arrive, I left.
Lo usé como cuchara.
I used it as a spoon.
3 if
Como lo vuelvas a hacer se lo digo a tu madre.
If you do it again, I'll tell your mother.
4 about
Vinieron como unas diez personas.
About ten people came.
como si
as if
Siguió leyendo, como si no hubiera oído nada.
He kept on reading, as if he had heard nothing.

cómo ADVERB
how
¿Cómo se dice en inglés?
How do you say it in English?
¿Cómo están tus padres?
How are your parents?
¿Cómo es de grande?
How big is it?
¿Cómo es el clima?
What's the weather like?
Perdón, ¿cómo has dicho?
Sorry, what did you say?
¡Cómo! ¿Mañana?
What? Tomorrow?

cómodo (FEM **cómoda**)
ADJECTIVE
comfortable
un sillón cómodo
a comfortable chair

el **compañero**
la **compañera** NOUN
1 classmate

2 workmate
3 partner

la **compañía** NOUN
company
Ana vino a hacerme compañía.
Ana came to keep me company.

comparar VERB
to compare
Siempre me comparan con mi hermana.
I'm always being compared to my sister.

compartir VERB
to share

el **compás** (PL los **compases**)
NOUN
compass

la **competición** (PL las **competiciones**) NOUN
competition

el **complejo** NOUN
complex
Tiene complejo porque está gordo.
He's got a complex about being fat.
un complejo deportivo
a sports complex

completo (FEM **completa**)
ADJECTIVE
full
> **Los hoteles estaban completos.**
> The hotels were full.
> **Me olvidé por completo.**
> I completely forgot.

complicado (FEM **complicada**)
ADJECTIVE
complicated

la **compra** NOUN
shopping

> **ir de compras**
> to go shopping

comprar VERB
to buy
> **Quiero comprarme unos zapatos.**
> I want to buy a pair of shoes.

comprender VERB
to understand
> **¡No lo comprendo!**
> I don't understand it!

común (FEM **común**) ADJECTIVE
common
> **un apellido muy común**
> a very common surname
> **No tenemos nada en común.**
> We have nothing in common.
> **Hicimos el trabajo en común.**
> We did the work between us.

la **comunidad** NOUN
community

con PREPOSITION
with
> **Vivo con mis padres.**
> I live with my parents.
> **¿Con quién vas a ir?**
> Who are you going with?
> **Lo he escrito con bolígrafo.**
> I wrote it in pen.
> **Voy a hablar con Luis.**
> I'll talk to Luis.
> **con tal de que no llegues tarde**
> as long as you don't arrive late

la **concha** NOUN
shell

el **concurso** NOUN
competition

la **condición** (PL las **condiciones**) NOUN
condition
> **a condición de que apruebes**
> on condition that you pass
> **El piso está en muy malas condiciones.**
> The flat is in a very bad state.
> **No está en condiciones de viajar.**
> He's not fit to travel.

conducir VERB
to drive
> **Mi madre no sabe conducir.**
> My mum can't drive.

el **conductor**
la **conductora** NOUN
driver

conduzco VERB ▷ see **conducir**
> **Siempre tomo mucho cuidado cuando conduzco.**
> I'm always very careful when I'm driving.

el **conejo**
NOUN
rabbit

la **conferencia** NOUN
lecture

confesar VERB
to admit
> **Confesó que había sido él.**
> He admitted that it had been him.

la **confianza** NOUN
trust
> **Tengo confianza en ti.**
> I trust you.

No tiene confianza en sí mismo.
He has no self-confidence.

confiar VERB
to trust
> **No confío en ella.**
> I don't trust her.

confieso VERB ▷ see **confesar**
> **Confieso que estaba equivocado.**
> I admit I was wrong.

conformarse VERB
> **conformarse con**
> to make do with
> **Tendrás que conformarte con uno más barato.**
> You'll have to make do with a cheaper one.

confundir VERB
1 **to mistake**
> **La gente me confunde con mi hermana.**
> People mistake me for my sister.
2 **to confuse**
> **Su explicación me confundió todavía más.**
> His explanation confused me even more.
> **Confundí las fechas.**
> I got the dates mixed up.

congelado (FEM **congelada**)
ADJECTIVE
frozen

el **congelador** NOUN
freezer

congelar VERB
to freeze
> **Me estoy congelando.**
> I'm freezing.

el **conjunto** NOUN
group

un conjunto de música pop
a pop group

conmigo PRONOUN
with me
> **¿Por qué no vienes conmigo?**
> Why don't you come with me?
> **Rosa quiere hablar conmigo.**
> Rosa wants to talk to me.
> **No estoy satisfecho conmigo mismo.**
> I'm not proud of myself.

conocer VERB
1 **to know**
> **Conozco a todos sus hermanos.**
> I know all his brothers.
> **Nos conocemos desde el colegio.**
> We know each other from school.
2 **to meet**
> **La conocí en una fiesta.**
> I met her at a party.

conocido (FEM **conocida**)
ADJECTIVE
well-known
> **un actor muy conocido**
> a well-known actor

el **conocimiento** NOUN
consciousness
> **perder el conocimiento**
> to lose consciousness

conozco VERB ▷ see **conocer**
> **No la conozco.**
> I don't know her.

conseguir VERB
to get
> **Él me consiguió la entrada.**
> He got me the ticket.

el **consejo** NOUN
advice
> **¿Quieres que te dé un consejo?**
> Would you like me to give you some advice?

consigo

consigo can be a pronoun or part of the verb **conseguir**.

Spanish English

a b c d e f g h i j k l m n ñ o p q r s t u v w x y z

A PRONOUN
1 with him
Se llevó a Marta consigo.
He took Marta with him.
2 with her
3 with you
B VERB ▷ see **conseguir**
No consigo olvidarme de lo que pasó.
I can't forget what happened.

constipado

> **constipado** *can be and adjective or a noun.*

A (FEM **constipada**) ADJECTIVE
estar constipado
to have a cold
B MASC NOUN
cold
coger un constipado
to catch a cold

Language tip

Be careful! **constipado** *does not mean the same as* **constipated**.

construir VERB
to build

la **consulta** NOUN
surgery
horas de consulta
surgery hours

consultar VERB
to consult
Deberías consultar a un médico.
You should consult a doctor.
Tengo que consultarlo con mi familia.
I need to discuss it with my family.

contagioso (FEM **contagiosa**)
ADJECTIVE
infectious

la **contaminación** NOUN
pollution
la contaminación del aire
air pollution

contar VERB
1 to count
Sabe contar hasta diez.
He can count to ten.
2 to tell
Les conté un cuento a los niños.
I told the children a story.
Cuéntame lo que pasó.
Tell me what happened.
Cuento contigo.
I'm counting on you.

el **contenido** NOUN
contents
el contenido de la maleta
the contents of the suitcase

contento (FEM **contenta**)
ADJECTIVE
happy
Estaba contento porque era su cumpleaños.
He was happy because it was his birthday.
Estoy contento con la bici nueva.
I'm pleased with my new bike.

contestar VERB
to answer
Contesté a todas las preguntas.
I answered all the questions.
Me escribieron y tengo que contestarles.
They wrote to me and I have to reply to them.

contigo PRONOUN
with you
Quiero ir contigo.
I want to go with you.
Necesito hablar contigo.
I need to talk to you.

el **continente** NOUN
continent

a b **c** d e f g h i j k l m n ñ o p q r s t u v w x y z

contra PREPOSITION
against
Eran dos contra uno.
They were two against one.
El domingo jugamos contra el Málaga.
We play against Málaga on Sunday.

contrario (FEM **contraria**)
ADJECTIVE
1 **opposing**
2 **opposite**
Los dos coches iban en dirección contraria.
The two cars were travelling in opposite directions.
Ella opina lo contrario.
She thinks the opposite.
Al contrario, me gusta mucho.
On the contrary, I like it a lot.
De lo contrario, tendré que castigarte.
Otherwise, I will have to punish you.

la contraseña NOUN
password

el control NOUN
control
Nunca pierde el control.
He never loses control.

la conversación (PL las **conversaciones**) NOUN
conversation
Necesito clases de conversación.
I need conversation classes.

convertir VERB
to turn
Convirtieron la casa en colegio.
They turned the house into a school.
■ **convertirse en**
to become/to turn into

Language tip
convertirse en *has two meanings. Look at the examples.*

Se convirtió en un hombre rico.
He became a rich man.
Se convirtió en una pesadilla.
It turned into a nightmare.

la copa
NOUN
glass

la copia NOUN
copy
hacer una copia
to make a copy

copiar VERB
to copy
copiar y pegar
to copy and paste

el corazón (PL los **corazones**)
NOUN
heart

el cordón (PL los **cordones**)
NOUN
shoelace

la corona NOUN
crown

la correa NOUN
1 **lead**
2 **strap**

correcto (FEM **correcta**)
ADJECTIVE
correct
Las respuestas eran correctas.
The answers were correct.

el corredor
la corredora NOUN
runner

corregir VERB
1 **to correct**
Corrígeme si me equivoco.
Correct me if I'm wrong.
2 **to mark**
El profesor corrigió los exámenes.
The teacher marked the exams.

el **correo** NOUN
post
Me lo mandó por correo.
He sent it to me by post.
Correos
the post office
correo electrónico
email

correr VERB
1 **to run**
Tuve que correr para coger el autobús.
I had to run to catch the bus.
2 **to hurry**
Corre que llegamos tarde.
Hurry or we'll be late.
3 **to go fast**
No corras tanto, que hay hielo en la carretera.
Don't go so fast, the road's icy.
4 **to move**
Córrete un poco hacia la izquierda.
Move a bit to the left.

la **corriente** NOUN
1 **current**
2 **draught**

corrijo VERB ▷*see* **corregir**
Ahora mismo lo corrijo.
I'll correct it right away.

cortado (FEM **cortada**) ADJECTIVE
1 **sour**
2 **chapped**
3 **closed**

cortar VERB
to cut
Corta la manzana por la mitad.

Cut the apple in half.
Me corté el dedo.
I cut my finger.
Te vas a cortar.
You're going to cut yourself.
Estas tijeras no cortan.
These scissors are blunt.
Fui a cortarme el pelo.
I went to get my hair cut.

el **corte** NOUN
cut
Tenía un corte en la frente.
He had a cut on his forehead.
un corte de pelo
a haircut

Me da corte pedírselo.
I'm embarrassed to ask him.

la **corteza** NOUN
crust

la **cortina** NOUN
curtain

corto (FEM **corta**) ADJECTIVE
short
Susana tiene el pelo corto.
Susana has short hair.

la **cosa** NOUN
thing
¿Qué es esa cosa redonda?
What's that round thing?
Cogí mis cosas y me fui.
I picked up my things and left.
¿Me puedes decir una cosa?
Can you tell me something?
¡Qué cosa más rara!
How strange!

cualquier cosa
anything

coser VERB
to sew

las **cosquillas** NOUN
hacer cosquillas a alguien
to tickle somebody
Tiene muchas cosquillas.
He's very ticklish.

la **costa** NOUN
coast
Pasamos el verano en la costa.
We spent the summer on the coast.

costar VERB
to cost
Cuesta mucho dinero.
It costs a lot of money.
Me costó diez euros.
It cost me ten euros.
Las matemáticas le cuestan mucho.
He finds maths very difficult.

¿Cuánto cuesta?
How much is it?

la **costilla** NOUN
rib

la **costumbre** NOUN
1 **habit**
Tiene la mala costumbre de mentir.
He has the bad habit of lying.
2 **custom**
una costumbre británica
a British custom
Se le olvidó, como de costumbre.
He forgot, as usual.

cotillear VERB
to gossip

crecer VERB
to grow
Me crece mucho el pelo.
My hair grows very fast.
¡Cómo has crecido!
Haven't you grown!

creer VERB
1 **to believe**
Nadie me cree.
Nobody believes me.
¿Crees en los fantasmas?
Do you believe in ghosts?
2 **to think**
No creo que pueda ir.
I don't think I'll be able to go.

Creo que sí.
I think so.
Creo que no.
I don't think so.

la **crema** NOUN
cream
Me pongo crema en las manos.
I put cream on my hands.
la crema solar
suncream

la **cremallera** NOUN
zip
Súbete la cremallera.
Do your zip up.

el **cristal** NOUN
1 **glass**
una botella de cristal
a glass bottle
En el suelo había cristales rotos.
There was some broken glass on the floor.
2 **window pane**
Los niños rompieron el cristal.
The children broke the window pane.
limpiar los cristales
to clean the windows

el **cromo** NOUN
picture card

la **croqueta** NOUN
croquette
croquetas de pollo
chicken croquettes

el **cruce** NOUN
crossroads

En el cruce hay un semáforo.
There are traffic lights at the crossroads.
un cruce de peatones
a pedestrian crossing

crudo (FEM **cruda**) ADJECTIVE
raw
las zanahorias crudas
raw carrots

crujiente (FEM **crujiente**) ADJECTIVE
crunchy

la **cruz** (PL las **cruces**) NOUN
cross

cruzar VERB
1 **to cross**
2 **to fold**
Nos cruzamos en la calle.
We passed each other in the street.

el **cuaderno** NOUN
notebook
un cuaderno de ejercicios
an exercise book

la **cuadra** NOUN
stable

cuadrado (FEM **cuadrada**)
ADJECTIVE, MASC NOUN
square
dos metros cuadrados
two square metres

el **cuadro** NOUN
painting

cual PRONOUN (PL **cuales**)
1 **who**
el primo del cual te estuve hablando
the cousin who I was telling you about
2 **which**
la ventana desde la cual nos observaban
the window from which they were watching us

cuál PRONOUN (PL **cuáles**)
1 **what**
No sé cuál es la solución.
I don't know what the solution is.
2 **which one**
¿Cuál te gusta más?
Which one do you like best?
¿Cuáles quieres?
Which ones do you want?

cualquier ADJECTIVE ▷ see
cualquiera

cualquiera (FEM **cualquiera**)

cualquiera *can be an adjective or a pronoun.*

A ADJECTIVE
any
Puedes usar un bolígrafo cualquiera.
You can use any pen.
No es un empleo cualquiera.
It's not just any job.

cualquier cosa
anything
en cualquier sitio
anywhere

B PRONOUN
1 **anyone**
Cualquiera puede hacer eso.
Anyone can do that.
cualquiera que le conozca
anyone who knows him
2 **any one**
Me da igual, cualquiera.
It doesn't matter, any one.
en cualquiera de las habitaciones
in any one of the rooms
cualquiera que elijas
whichever one you choose
3 **either**
¿Cuál de los dos prefieres? — Cualquiera.
Which of the two do you prefer? — Either.

cuando CONJUNCTION
when
> **Lo haré cuando tenga tiempo.**
> I'll do it when I have time.
> **Puedes venir cuando quieras.**
> You can come whenever you like.

cuándo ADVERB
when
> **¿Cuándo te va mejor?**
> When suits you?
> **No sabe cuándo ocurrió.**
> He doesn't know when it happened.

cuanto (FEM **cuanta**) ADJECTIVE, PRONOUN
> **Termínalo cuanto antes.**
> Finish it as soon as possible.
> **Cuanto más lo pienso menos lo entiendo.**
> The more I think about it, the less I understand it.
> **Cuantas menos personas haya mejor.**
> The fewer people the better.
> **En cuanto oí su voz me eché a llorar.**
> As soon as I heard his voice I began to cry.
> **Había sólo unos cuantos invitados.**
> There were only a few guests.

> **en cuanto a**
> as for

cuánto (FEM **cuánta**) ADJECTIVE, PRONOUN
1 **how much**
> **¿Cuánto dinero tienes?**
> How much money do you have?
> **Me dijo cuánto costaba.**
> He told me how much it was.
2 **how many**
> **¿Cuántas sillas?**
> How many chairs?
> **No sé cuántos necesito.**
> I don't know how many I need.

> **¿A cuántos estamos?**
> What's the date?
> **¡Cuánta gente!**
> What a lot of people!
> **¿Cuánto hay de aquí a Bilbao?**
> How far is it from here to Bilbao?
> **¿Cuánto tiempo llevas estudiando inglés?**
> How long have you been studying English?

cuarenta (FEM **cuarenta**) ADJECTIVE, PRONOUN
forty
> **Tiene cuarenta años.**
> He's forty.

cuarto

> **cuarto** can be an adjective, pronoun or noun.

A (FEM **cuarta**) ADJECTIVE, PRONOUN
fourth
> **Vivo en el cuarto piso.**
> I live on the fourth floor.
B MASC NOUN
1 **room**
> **Los niños jugaban en su cuarto.**
> The children were playing in their room.
> **el cuarto de estar**
> the living room
> **el cuarto de baño**
> the bathroom
2 **quarter**
> **un cuarto de hora**
> a quarter of an hour

> **Son las once y cuarto.**
> It's a quarter past eleven.
> **A las diez menos cuarto.**
> At a quarter to ten.

cuatro (FEM **cuatro**) ADJECTIVE, PRONOUN
four

> **Son las cuatro.**
> It's four o'clock.
> **el cuatro de julio**

the fourth of July
Nació el cuatro de julio.
He was born on the fourth of July.

cuatrocientos
(FEM **cuatrocientas**) ADJECTIVE,
PRONOUN
four hundred

cubierto

> **cubierto** *can be an adjective or part of the verb* **cubrir**.

A (FEM **cubierta**) ADJECTIVE
covered
Estaba todo cubierto de nieve.
Everything was covered in snow.
B VERB ▷see **cubrir**
Ha cubierto el piano con una lona.
He's covered the piano with a tarpaulin.

los **cubiertos** NOUN
cutlery

el **cubito de hielo** NOUN
ice-cube

el **cubo** NOUN
bucket
el cubo y la pala
the bucket and spade
el cubo de la basura
the dustbin

cubrir VERB
to cover
Tenemos que cubrir los cuadernos.
We have to cover our exercise books.
El agua casi me cubría.
I was almost out of my depth.

la **cuchara** NOUN
spoon

la **cucharada** NOUN
spoonful
una cucharada de jarabe
a spoonful of syrup

la **cucharilla** NOUN
teaspoon

cuchichear VERB
to whisper

el **cuchillo** NOUN
knife

el **cucurucho** NOUN
cone

cuelgo VERB ▷see **colgar**
¿Dónde cuelgo el abrigo?
Where can I hang the coat?

el **cuello** NOUN
neck

la **cuenta** NOUN
1 bill
El camarero nos trajo la cuenta.
The waiter brought us the bill.
2 account
una cuenta de correo
an email account
darse cuenta
to realize/to notice

> *Language tip*
>
> **darse cuenta** *has two meanings. Look at the examples.*

Perdona, no me di cuenta de que eras vegetariano.
Sorry, I didn't realize you were a vegetarian.
¿Te has dado cuenta de que han cortado el árbol?
Did you notice they've cut down that tree?

cuento

> **cuento** *can be an adjective or part of the verb* **contar**.

A MASC NOUN
story

a b c d e f g h i j k l m n ñ o p q r s t u v w x y z

Spanish | English

a b **c** d e f g h i j k l m n ñ o p q r s t u v w x y z

La abuela nos contaba cuentos.
Grandma used to tell us stories.
un cuento de hadas
a fairy-tale
B VERB ▷ see **contar**
Si quieres te cuento lo que pasó.
If you want, I'll tell you what happened.

la **cuerda** NOUN
1 rope
Le ataron las manos con una cuerda.
They tied his hands together with a rope.
2 string
Necesito una cuerda para atar este paquete.
I need some string to tie up this parcel.

el **cuero** NOUN
leather
una chaqueta de cuero
a leather jacket

el **cuerpo** NOUN
body
el cuerpo humano
the human body
el cuerpo de bomberos
the fire-brigade

cuesta

cuesta *can be an adjective or part of the verb* **costar**.

A FEM NOUN
slope
una cuesta muy empinada
a very steep slope

ir cuesta abajo
to go downhill
ir cuesta arriba
to go uphill

B VERB ▷ see **costar**
¿Cuánto cuesta esa bicicleta?
How much does that bicycle cost?

la **cueva** NOUN
cave

el **cuidado** NOUN
care
Conducía con cuidado.
He was driving carefully.

¡Cuidado!
Careful!

cuidar VERB
to look after
Ella cuida de los niños.
She looks after the children.
▪ **cuidarse**
to look after oneself
Tienes que cuidarte.
You need to look after yourself.

¡Cuídate!
Take care!

la **culpa** NOUN
fault
La culpa es mía.
It's my fault.
Siempre me echan la culpa a mí.
They're always blaming me.

culpable

culpable *can be an adjective or a noun*.

A (FEM **culpable**) ADJECTIVE
guilty
Yo no soy culpable.
I'm not guilty.
B MASC/FEM NOUN
culprit
Ella es la culpable de todo.
She is to blame for everything.

la **cultura** NOUN
culture

la **cumbre** NOUN
summit

el **cumpleaños** (PL los **cumpleaños**) NOUN
birthday

¡Feliz cumpleaños!
Happy birthday!

cumplir VERB
1 **to carry out**
2 **to keep**
   Mañana cumplo dieciséis años.
   I'll be sixteen tomorrow.

la **cuna** NOUN
cradle

la **cuñada** NOUN
sister-in-law

el **cuñado** NOUN
brother-in-law

cupo VERB ▷ see **caber**
   No cupo por la puerta.
   It wouldn't go through the door.

el **cura** NOUN
priest

curar VERB
1 **to cure**
   un remedio para curar una pulmonía
   a treatment to cure pneumonia
   Espero que te cures pronto.
   I hope that you get better soon.
2 **to heal**
   Ya se le ha curado la herida.
   His wound has already healed.

cursi (FEM **cursi**) ADJECTIVE
1 **affected**
2 **twee**

el **cursillo** NOUN
course
   un cursillo de informática
   a computer course
   hacer un cursillo de natación
   to have swimming lessons

el **curso** NOUN
1 **year**
   un chico de mi curso
   a boy in my year
   Hago segundo curso.
   I'm in Year two.
2 **course**
   Hice un curso de alemán.
   I did a German course.

la **curva** NOUN
bend
   Hay algunas curvas muy cerradas.
   There are some very sharp bends.

a
b
c
d
e
f
g
h
i
j
k
l
m
n
ñ
o
p
q
r
s
t
u
v
w
x
y
z

D d

la **dama** NOUN
> **lady**
>> **damas y caballeros**
>> ladies and gentlemen
>> **las damas**
>> draughts
>> **jugar a las damas**
>> to play draughts

el **daño** NOUN
> **damage**
>> **El daño producido no es muy grave.**
>> The damage isn't very serious.
>> **¡Me estás haciendo daño!**
>> You're hurting me!

hacerse daño
to hurt oneself

dar VERB
> **to give**
>> **Se lo di a Teresa.**
>> I gave it to Teresa.
>> **Se me dan bien las ciencias.**
>> I'm good at science.

de PREPOSITION

Language tip
de + **el** = **del**.

1 **of**
>> **un paquete de caramelos**
>> a packet of sweets
>> **un vaso de agua**
>> a glass of water
>> **las clases de inglés**
>> English lessons
>> **un anillo de oro**
>> a gold ring
>> **la casa de Isabel**
>> Isabel's house

2 **from**
>> **Soy de Madrid.**
>> I'm from Madrid.

>> **una carta de mi tía**
>> a letter from my aunt
>> **Son del año pasado.**
>> They're from last year.

3 **than**
>> **Es más difícil de lo que creía.**
>> It's more difficult than I thought.

dé VERB ▷*see* **dar**
>> **Quiero que me dé el móvil.**
>> I want him to give me the mobile phone.

debajo ADVERB
> **underneath**
>> **Levanta la maceta, la llave está debajo.**
>> Lift up the flowerpot, the key's underneath.
>> **debajo de**
>> under
>> **debajo de la mesa**
>> under the table

deber

deber can be a noun or a verb.

A MASC NOUN
> **duty**
>> **Sólo cumplí con mi deber.**
>> I simply did my duty.
>> **los deberes**
>> homework

B VERB
1 **must**
>> **Debo intentarlo.**
>> I must try it.
>> **No debes preocuparte.**
>> You mustn't worry.
>> **No deberías haberla dejado sola.**

You shouldn't have left her alone.
deber de
must
Debe de ser canadiense.
He must be Canadian.

2 to owe
¿Cuánto le debo?
How much do I owe you?

débil (FEM **débil**) ADJECTIVE
weak

decidir VERB
to decide
Tú decides.
You decide.
Me decidí a aprender inglés.
I decided to learn English.
¡Decídete!
Make up
your mind!

décimo (FEM **décima**) ADJECTIVE,
PRONOUN
tenth
Vivo en el décimo.
I live on the tenth floor.

decir VERB
1 to say
¿Qué dijo?
What did he say?
¿Cómo se dice 'casa' en inglés?
How do you say 'casa' in English?
No sé lo que quiere decir.
I don't know what it means.

2 to tell
Nunca me dice la verdad.
He never tells me the truth.
Me dijo que esperara fuera.
He told me to wait outside.

es decir
that's to say
¡No me digas!
Really?

el **dedo** NOUN
1 finger
2 toe
el dedo gordo
the thumb/the big toe

dejar VERB
1 to leave
He dejado las llaves en la mesa.
I've left the keys on the table.
No me dejes sola.
Don't leave me on my own.

2 to let
Mis padres no me dejan salir de noche.
My parents won't let me go out at night.
dejar caer
to drop
Dejó caer la bandeja.
She dropped the tray.

3 to lend
Le dejé mi libro de matemáticas.
I lent him my maths book.
dejar de
to stop
He dejado de morderme las uñas.
I've stopped biting my nails.

del PREPOSITION ▷ *see* **de**
Vengo del colegio.
I'm coming from school.

delante ADVERB
in front
Siéntate delante.
You sit in front.
la parte de delante
the front

de delante
front
la rueda de delante
the front wheel
Se inclinó hacia delante.
He leaned forward.
delante de
in front of/opposite

Language tip

delante de *has two meanings.*
Look at the examples.

No digas nada delante de Anna.
Don't say anything in front of Anna.
Mi casa está delante de la escuela.
My house is opposite the school.

delgado (FEM delgada)
ADJECTIVE
thin
Estás muy delgado.
You're too thin.

demás

demás *can be an adjective or a pronoun.*

A (FEM **demás**) ADJECTIVE
other
los demás niños
the other children
B PRONOUN
los demás
the others
lo demás
the rest
Yo limpio las ventanas y lo demás lo limpias tú.
I'll clean the windows and you clean the rest.

demasiado

demasiado *can be an adjective or an adverb.*

A (FEM **demasiada**) ADJECTIVE
too much

demasiado tiempo
too much time
demasiados libros
too many books

B ADVERB
too much
Hablas demasiado.
You talk too much.
Es demasiado pesado para levantarlo.
It's too heavy to lift.
Caminas demasiado deprisa.
You walk too quickly.

el **dentífrico** NOUN
toothpaste

el/la **dentista** NOUN
dentist
Mi madre es dentista.
My mum is a dentist.

dentro ADVERB
inside
¿Qué hay dentro?
What's inside?
dentro de
in
Métalo dentro del sobre.
Put it in the envelope.
dentro de tres meses
in three months
por dentro
inside
Mira bien por dentro.
Have a good look inside.
Está aquí dentro.
It's in here.

dentro de poco
soon

depender VERB
depender de
to depend on
El precio depende de la calidad.
The price depends on the quality.

Depende.
It depends.

el **deporte** NOUN
sport
No hago mucho deporte.
I don't do much sport.

deportista

deportista *can be an adjective or a noun.*

A (FEM **deportista**)
ADJECTIVE
sporty

Alicia es poco deportista.
Alicia is not very sporty.
B MASC NOUN
sportsman
C FEM NOUN
sportswoman

deprisa ADVERB
quickly
Acabaron muy deprisa.
They finished very quickly.
Lo hacen todo deprisa y corriendo.
They do everything in a rush.

¡Deprisa!
Hurry up!

la **derecha** NOUN
1 right hand
Escribo con la derecha.
I write with my right hand.

2 right
doblar a la derecha
to turn right
a la derecha
on the right
Coge la segunda calle a la derecha.
Take the second turning on the right.

derecho

derecho *can be an adjective, an adverb or a noun.*

A (FEM **derecha**) ADJECTIVE
1 right
Escribo con la mano derecha.
I write with my right hand.
2 straight
¡Ponte derecho!
Stand up straight!
B ADVERB
straight
Siga derecho.
Carry straight on.
C MASC NOUN
right
los derechos humanos
human rights

¡No hay derecho!
It's not fair!

desagradable
(FEM **desagradable**) ADJECTIVE
unpleasant
un olor muy desagradable
a very unpleasant smell
Fuiste muy desagradable con tu prima.
You were really nasty to your cousin.

desaparecer VERB
to disappear
La mancha ha desaparecido.
The stain has disappeared.

el **desastre** NOUN
disaster
La función fue un desastre.
The show was a disaster.

Spanish | **English**

a b c **d** e f g h i j k l m n ñ o p q r s t u v w x y z

Soy un desastre para la gimnasia.
I'm hopeless at gymnastics.

desayunar VERB
1 to have breakfast
Nunca desayuno.
I never have breakfast.

2 to have ... for breakfast
Desayuné café con leche y un bollo.
I had coffee and a roll for breakfast.

el **desayuno** NOUN
breakfast

descalzarse VERB
to take one's shoes off
Descálzate.
Take your shoes off.

descalzo (FEM descalza)
ADJECTIVE
barefoot
Paseaban descalzos por la playa.
They walked barefoot along the beach.
No entres en la cocina descalzo.
Don't come into the kitchen in bare feet.

descansar VERB
to rest
Tienes que descansar.
You must rest.

el **descanso** NOUN
1 rest
He caminado mucho, necesito un descanso.
I've done a lot of walking, I need a rest.

2 break
Cada dos horas me tomo un descanso.
I have a break every two hours.

descarado (FEM descarada)
ADJECTIVE
cheeky
¡No seas descarado!
Don't be cheeky!

descargar VERB
to download
■ **descargarse**
to go flat

desconectar VERB
to unplug

el **descubrimiento** NOUN
discovery

desde PREPOSITION
1 from
Desde Burgos hasta mi casa hay treinta kilómetros.
It's thirty kilometres from Burgos to my house.
2 since
La conozco desde niño.
I've known her since I was a child.
¿Desde cuándo vives aquí?
How long have you been living here?

desde entonces
since then
desde luego
of course

desear VERB
to wish

Te deseo mucha suerte.
I wish you lots of luck.

desenchufar VERB
to unplug

el **deseo** NOUN
wish

el **desfile** NOUN
parade

la **desgracia** NOUN
tragedy
Su muerte fue una auténtica desgracia.
His death was an absolute tragedy.
por desgracia
unfortunately
Por desgracia he vuelto a suspender.
Unfortunately I've failed again.

deshacer VERB
to untie

el **desierto** NOUN
desert

desnatado (FEM **desnatada**)
ADJECTIVE
skimmed

desnudarse VERB
to get undressed

desnudo (FEM **desnuda**)
ADJECTIVE
naked

desobedecer VERB
to disobey

desobediente
(FEM **desobediente**) ADJECTIVE
disobedient

el **desodorante** NOUN
deodorant

desordenado
(FEM **desordenada**) ADJECTIVE
untidy
Tengo la habitación muy desordenada.
My room's really untidy.

despacio ADVERB
slowly
Conduce despacio.
Drive slowly.

¡Despacio!
Take it easy!

despedir VERB
to say goodbye to
Se despidieron en la estación.
They said goodbye at the station.

el **despertador**
NOUN
alarm clock

despertar VERB
to wake up
No me despiertes hasta las once.
Don't wake me up until eleven o'clock.

despierto (FEM **despierta**)
ADJECTIVE
awake
A las siete ya estaba despierto.
He was already awake by seven o'clock.

después ADVERB
1 **later**
Ellos llegaron después.
They arrived later.

un año después
a year later

2 next
¿Qué viene después?
What comes next?
después de
after
Tu nombre está después del mío.
Your name comes after mine.
Después de comer fuimos de paseo.
After lunch we went for a walk.

el **destornillador** NOUN
screwdriver

destrozar VERB
to wreck
Tu perro ha destrozado la silla.
Your dog has wrecked the chair.

destruir VERB
to destroy
Los huracanes destruyen edificios enteros.
Hurricanes can destroy whole buildings.

la **desventaja** NOUN
disadvantage

el **detalle** NOUN
detail
No recuerdo todos los detalles.
I don't remember all the details.

detener VERB
1 to stop
¡Detenlos!
Stop them!
2 to arrest
Han detenido a los ladrones.
They've arrested the thieves.

■ **detenerse**
to stop
Nos detuvimos en el semáforo.
We stopped at the lights.

el **detergente** NOUN
detergent

detrás ADVERB
behind
El resto de los niños vienen detrás.
The rest of the children are coming on behind.
detrás de
behind
Se escondió detrás de un árbol.
He hid behind a tree.

devolver VERB
1 to give back
¿Me puedes devolver el libro que te presté?
Could you give me back the book I lent you?
2 to take back
Devolví la falda porque me iba pequeña.
I took the skirt back as it was too small for me.
3 to throw up

di VERB
1 ▷ see **decir**
Di, ¿qué te parece?
Tell me, what do you think?
2 ▷ see **dar**
Se lo di a ella.
I gave it to her.

el **día** NOUN
day
Pasaré dos días en la playa.
I'll spend a couple of days at the beach.
Es de día.
It's daylight.
¿Qué día es hoy?
What day is it today?/What's the date today?

Language tip
¿qué día es hoy? *has two meanings. It can be translated as* **what day is it today?** *and* **what's the date today?**

un día de fiesta
a public holiday
el día de los enamorados
Saint Valentine's Day
el día de los Santos Inocentes
the Feast of the Holy Innocents

Did you know...?
In Spanish-speaking countries the day people play practical jokes on each other is 28 December, **día de los Santos Inocentes**.

al día siguiente
the following day
¡Buenos días!
Good morning!
todos los días
every day

el **diablo** NOUN
devil

diagonal ADJECTIVE, FEM NOUN
diagonal
en diagonal
diagonally

el **diamante** NOUN
diamond

el **diámetro** NOUN
diameter

diario

diario *can be an adjective or a noun.*

A (FEM **diaria**) ADJECTIVE
daily
la rutina diaria
the daily routine
la ropa de diario
everyday clothes
a diario
every day
Va al gimnasio a diario.
He goes to the gym every day.

B MASC NOUN
diary

la **diarrea** NOUN
diarrhoea

dibujar VERB
to draw

No sé dibujar.
I can't draw.

el **dibujo** NOUN
drawing
Me hizo un dibujo.
She did me a drawing.
los dibujos animados
cartoons

el **diccionario** NOUN
dictionary

dicho VERB ▷ see **decir**
Ya te he dicho que no lo quiero.
I've already told you that I don't want it.

diciembre MASC NOUN
December

Language tip
Months are not written with a capital letter in Spanish.

en diciembre
in December
Nació el seis de diciembre.
He was born on the sixth of December.

diciendo VERB ▷ see **decir**
Como iba diciendo ...
As I was saying ...

diecinueve (FEM **diecinueve**)
ADJECTIVE, PRONOUN
nineteen
> Tengo diecinueve años.
> I'm nineteen.

el diecinueve de julio
the nineteenth of July
Nació el diecinueve de julio.
He was born on the nineteenth of July.

dieciocho (FEM **dieciocho**)
ADJECTIVE, PRONOUN
eighteen
> Tengo dieciocho años.
> I'm eighteen.

el dieciocho de abril
the eighteenth of April
Nació el dieciocho de abril.
He was born on the eighteenth of April.

dieciséis (FEM **dieciséis**)
ADJECTIVE, PRONOUN
sixteen
> Tengo dieciséis años.
> I'm sixteen.

el dieciséis de febrero
the sixteenth of February
Nació el dieciséis de febrero.
He was born on the sixteenth of February.

diecisiete (FEM **diecisiete**)
ADJECTIVE, PRONOUN
seventeen
> Tengo diecisiete años.
> I'm seventeen.

el diecisiete de enero
the seventeenth of January
Nació el diecisiete de enero.
He was born on the seventeenth of January.

el **diente** NOUN
tooth
> Me lavo los dientes tres
> veces al día.

I clean my teeth three times a day.
un diente de leche
a milk tooth
un diente de ajo
a clove of garlic

la **dieta** NOUN
diet
> una dieta vegetariana
> a vegetarian diet

estar a dieta
to be on a diet

diez (FEM **diez**) ADJECTIVE,
PRONOUN
ten
> Tengo diez años.
> I'm ten.

Son las diez.
It's ten o'clock.
el diez de agosto
the tenth of August
Nació el diez de agosto.
He was born on the tenth of August.

la **diferencia** NOUN
difference
> ¿Qué diferencia hay entre los
> dos?
> What's the difference between
> the two?

diferenciar VERB
> ¿En qué se diferencian?
> What's the difference between
> them?
> Sólo se diferencian en el
> tamaño.
> The only difference between
> them is their size.

diferente (FEM **diferente**)
ADJECTIVE
different

difícil (FEM **difícil**) ADJECTIVE
difficult
> Es un problema difícil de
> entender.

It's a difficult problem to understand.

la **digestión** NOUN
digestion

> **hacer la digestión**
> to digest

digital (FEM **digital**) ADJECTIVE
digital
una cámara digital
a digital camera

una huella digital
a fingerprint

digo VERB ▷ see **decir**
Porque lo digo yo.
Because I say so.

dije VERB ▷ see **decir**
¡Yo no dije eso!
I didn't say that!

el **dinero** NOUN
money
No tengo más dinero.
I haven't got any more money.
dinero suelto
loose change

dio VERB ▷ see **dar**
Me dio un libro.
He gave me a book.

Dios MASC NOUN
God

el **dios** (PL los **dioses**) NOUN
god

dirá VERB ▷ see **decir**
¿Qué dirá mi madre cuando se entere?
¿What will my mother say when she finds out?

la **dirección** (PL las **direcciones**) NOUN

1 **direction**
Íbamos en dirección equivocada.
We were going in the wrong direction.
una calle de dirección única
a one-way street

2 **address**
Apúntame tu dirección aquí.
Can you write your address down here for me?
dirección de correo electrónico
e-mail address

directo (FEM **directa**) ADJECTIVE
direct
Hay un tren directo a Valencia.
There's a direct train to Valencia.
una pregunta directa
a direct question

el **director**
la **directora** NOUN
1 **headteacher**
2 **manager**
3 **director**

el **disco** NOUN
record
un disco compacto
a compact disc
el disco duro
the hard disk

la **discusión** (PL las **discusiones**) NOUN
argument
Tuve una discusión con mi madre.
I had an argument with my mother.

discutir VERB
to argue
Siempre discuten por dinero.
They're always arguing about money.
Discutió con su madre.
He had an argument with his mother.

el **disfraz** (PL los **disfraces**)
NOUN
costume
> **un disfraz de vaquero**
> a cowboy costume
> **una fiesta de disfraces**
> a fancy-dress party

disfrazarse VERB
> **disfrazarse de**
> to dress up as
> **Mi amiga se disfrazó de hada.**
> My friend dressed up as a fairy.

disfrutar VERB
to enjoy oneself
> **Disfruté mucho en la fiesta.**
> I really enjoyed myself
> at the party.

> **Disfruto leyendo.**
> I enjoy reading.

disgustado (FEM **disgustada**)
ADJECTIVE
upset

> ***Language tip***
> *Be careful!* **disgustado** *does not*
> *mean* **disgusted**.

disimular VERB
to hide
> **Intentó disimular su enfado.**
> He tried to hide his annoyance.
> **No disimules, sé que has sido
> tú.**
> Don't bother pretending, I know
> it was you.

el **disparate** NOUN
silly thing
> **He hecho muchos disparates
> en mi vida.**
> I've done a lot of silly things in
> my life.

> **No digas disparates.**
> Don't talk rubbish.

el **disparo** NOUN
shot

la **distancia** NOUN
distance
> **la distancia entre dos coches**
> the distance between two cars
> **¿Qué distancia hay entre
> Madrid y Barcelona?**
> How far is Madrid from
> Barcelona?
> **¿A qué distancia está la
> estación?**
> How far's the station?
> **a veinte kilómetros de
> distancia**
> twenty kilometres away

distinguir VERB
to distinguish
> **Resulta difícil distinguir el
> macho de la hembra.**
> It's difficult to distinguish the
> male from the female.
> **No distingue entre el rojo
> y el verde.**
> He can't tell the difference
> between red and green.
> **Se parecen tanto que no los
> distingo.**
> They're so alike that I can't tell
> them apart.

distinto (FEM **distinta**)
ADJECTIVE
different
> **Carlos es distinto a los
> demás.**
> Carlos is different to everyone
> else.

distintos
several
distintas clases de coches
several types of car

la **distracción** (PL las **distracciones**) NOUN
pastime
Cocinar es mi distracción favorita.
My favourite pastime is cooking.

distraer VERB
1 **to keep ... entertained**
Les pondré un vídeo para distraerlos.
I'll put a video on to keep them entertained.
Me distrae mucho escuchar música.
I really enjoy listening to music.

2 **to distract**
No me distraigas, que tengo trabajo.
Don't distract me. I've got work to do.

distraído (FEM **distraída**)
ADJECTIVE
absent-minded
Mi padre es muy distraído.
My father is very absent-minded.
Perdona, estaba distraído.
Sorry, I wasn't paying attention.

la **diversión** (PL las **diversiones**)
NOUN
entertainment

Language tip
Be careful! **diversión** does not mean **diversion**.

divertido (FEM **divertida**)
ADJECTIVE
funny
Fue muy divertido.
It was great fun.

divertir VERB
to entertain
Nos divirtió con sus cuentos.
He entertained us with his stories.
■ **divertirse**
to have a good time

dividir VERB
to divide
El libro está dividido en dos partes.
The book is divided into two parts.
Divide cuatro entre dos.
Divide four by two.
■ **dividirse**
to divide/to share

Language tip
dividirse has two meanings. Look at the examples.

Nos dividimos el trabajo entre los tres.
We divided the work between the three of us.
Se dividieron el dinero de la lotería.
They shared the lottery money.

divierto VERB ▷ see **divertir**
Me divierto mucho con ellos.
I have a good time when I'm with them.

la **división** (PL las **divisiones**)
NOUN
division
en primera división
in the first division
Ya sabe hacer divisiones.
He already knows how to do division.

a
b
c
d
e
f
g
h
i
j
k
l
m
n
ñ
o
p
q
r
s
t
u
v
w
x
y
z

Spanish English

el **DNI** ABBREVIATION
(= **Documento Nacional de Identidad**)
ID card

el **doble** NOUN
twice as much
> **Comes el doble que yo.**
> You eat twice as much as I do.
> **Trabaja el doble que tú.**
> He works twice as hard as you do.

doce (FEM **doce**) ADJECTIVE, PRONOUN
twelve
> **Tengo doce años.**
> I'm twelve.

> **Son las doce.**
> It's twelve o'clock.
> **el doce de diciembre**
> the twelfth of December
> **Nació el doce de diciembre.**
> He was born on the twelfth of December.

la **docena** NOUN
dozen

el **doctor**
la **doctora** NOUN
doctor
> **Cuando crezca me gustaría ser doctor.**
> I want to be a doctor when I grow up.

el **documental** NOUN
documentary

el **documento** NOUN
document
> **un documento oficial**
> an official document
> **el documento nacional de identidad**
> the identity card

doler VERB
to hurt
> **Me duele el brazo.**
> My arm hurts.

> **Me duele la cabeza.**
> I've got a headache.
> **Me duele la garganta.**
> I've got a sore throat.

el **dolor** NOUN
pain
> **Gritó de dolor.**
> He cried out in pain.

> **Tengo dolor de cabeza.**
> I've got a headache.
> **Tengo dolor de garganta.**
> I've got a sore throat.
> **Tengo dolor de estómago.**
> I've got a stomachache.

doméstico (FEM **doméstica**) ADJECTIVE
domestic
> **para uso doméstico**
> for domestic use
> **las tareas domésticas**
> the housework
> **un animal doméstico**
> a pet

el **domingo** NOUN
Sunday

Language tip
The days of the week are not spelled with a capital letter in Spanish.

> **La vi el domingo.**
> I saw her on Sunday.

> **todos los domingos**
> every Sunday
> **el domingo pasado**
> last Sunday
> **el domingo que viene**
> next Sunday

Spanish English

a b c **d** e f g h i j k l m n ñ o p q r s t u v w x y z

don MASC NOUN
don Juan Gómez
Mr Juan Gómez

donde ADVERB
where
La nota está donde la dejaste.
The note's where you left it.

dónde ADVERB
where
¿Dónde vas?
Where are you going?
Le pregunté dónde estaba la catedral.
I asked him where the cathedral was.
¿Sabes dónde está?
Do you know where he is?
¿De dónde eres?
Where are you from?
¿Por dónde se va al cine?
How do you get to the cinema?

doña FEM NOUN
doña Marta García
Mrs Marta García

dorado (FEM **dorada**)
ADJECTIVE
golden

dormir VERB
to sleep
Antonio durmió diez horas.
Antonio slept for ten hours.
dormir la siesta
to have a nap
estar medio dormido
to be half asleep
■ **dormirse**
to fall asleep
Me dormí en el tren.
I fell asleep on the train.
Se me ha dormido el brazo.
My arm has gone to sleep.

el **dormitorio** NOUN
bedroom

dos (FEM **dos**) ADJECTIVE, PRONOUN
1 **two**
Tenemos dos gatos.
We have two cats.
2 **both**
Al final vinieron los dos.
In the end they both came.
Los hemos invitado a los dos.
We've invited both of them.

Tiene dos años.
He's two.
Son las dos.
It's two o'clock.
el dos de enero
the second of January
Nació el dos de enero.
He was born on the second of January.

doscientos (FEM **doscientas**)
ADJECTIVE, PRONOUN
two hundred
doscientos cincuenta
two hundred and fifty

doy VERB ▷ see **dar**
Si quieres, te doy uno.
If you want, I'll give you one.

el **drogadicto**
la **drogadicta** NOUN
drug addict

la **ducha** NOUN
shower

darse una ducha
to have a shower

ducharse VERB
to have a shower

la **duda** NOUN
doubt

Spanish

English

a
b
c
d
e
f
g
h
i
j
k
l
m
n
ñ
o
p
q
r
s
t
u
v
w
x
y
z

Tengo mis dudas.
I have my doubts.
Tengo una duda.
I have a query.
¿Alguna duda?
Any questions?

dudar VERB
  to doubt
Lo dudo.
I doubt it.
Dudo que sea cierto.
I doubt if it's true.
Dudó si comprarlo o no.
He wasn't sure whether to buy it or not.

el **dueño**
  la **dueña** NOUN
  owner

duermo VERB ▷ see **dormir**
Duermo ocho horas todos los días.
I sleep eight hours every day.

dulce

dulce *can be an adjective or a noun.*

A (FEM **dulce**) ADJECTIVE
  sweet
B MASC NOUN
  sweet

durante ADVERB
  during
Tuvo que trabajar durante las vacaciones.
He had to work during the holidays.
durante toda la noche
all night long
Habló durante una hora.
He spoke for an hour.

durar VERB
  to last
La película dura dos horas.
The film lasts two hours.

durmiendo VERB ▷ see **dormir**
Me estoy durmiendo.
I'm falling asleep.

duro

duro *can be an adjective or an adverb.*

A (FEM **dura**) ADJECTIVE
1 **hard**
Los diamantes son muy duros.
Diamonds are very hard.
2 **tough**
Esta carne está dura.
This meat's tough.
B ADVERB
  hard
trabajar duro
to work hard

E e

e CONJUNCTION

> **Language tip**
>
> **e** *is used instead of* **y** *in front of words beginning with 'i' and 'hi', but not 'hie'.*

and
> **Pablo e Inés.**
> Pablo and Inés.

echar VERB
1 **to throw**
> **Échame las llaves.**
> Throw me the keys.
2 **to throw out**
> **Me echó de su casa.**
> He threw me out of the house.
3 **to expel**
> **Lo han echado del colegio.**
> He's been expelled from school.
> **Echo de menos a mi familia.**
> I miss my family.

ecológico (FEM **ecológica**)
ADJECTIVE
ecological
> **un desastre ecológico**
> an ecological disaster
> **un producto ecológico**
> an environmentally friendly product

ecologista
ecologista

> **ecologista** *can be an adjective or a noun.*

A ADJECTIVE
environmental
> **un grupo ecologista**
> an environmental group
B MASC/FEM NOUN
environmentalist

la **edad** NOUN
age

> **Tenemos la misma edad.**
> We're the same age.

> **¿Qué edad tiene?**
> How old is he?

el **edificio** NOUN
building

la **educación** NOUN
1 **education**
> **educación física**
> PE
2 **upbringing**
> **Rosa recibió una educación muy estricta.**
> Rosa had a very strict upbringing.
> **Señalar es de mala educación.**
> It's rude to point.
> **Es una falta de educación hablar con la boca llena.**
> It's bad manners to speak with your mouth full.

educado (FEM **educada**)
ADJECTIVE
polite
> **Es un chico bien educado.**
> He's a polite boy.

egoísta (FEM **egoista**)
ADJECTIVE
selfish

el **ejemplo** NOUN
example
> **¿Puedes ponerme un ejemplo?**
> Can you give me an example?

> **por ejemplo**
> for example

el **ejercicio** NOUN
exercise

a b c d **e** f g h i j k l m n ñ o p q r s t u v w x y z

La maestra nos puso varios ejercicios.
The teacher gave us several exercises to do.

> **hacer ejercicio**
> to do exercise

el (FEM SING **la**, MASC PL **los**, FEM PL **las**) ARTICLE
the
Perdí el autobús.
I missed the bus.
Yo fui el que lo encontró.
I was the one who found it.
Ayer me lavé la cabeza.
I washed my hair yesterday.
Me puse el abrigo.
I put my coat on.
Tiene unos zapatos bonitos, pero prefiero los míos.
Her shoes are nice but I prefer mine.
No me gusta el pescado.
I don't like fish.

él PRONOUN
1 he
Me lo dijo él.
He told me.
2 him
Se lo di a él.
I gave it to him.
Su mujer es más alta que él.
His wife is taller than him.
él mismo
himself
No lo sabe ni él mismo.
He doesn't even know himself.
de él
his
El coche es de él.
The car's his.

la **electricidad** NOUN
electricity

eléctrico (FEM **eléctrica**)
ADJECTIVE
electric
una guitarra eléctrica
an electric guitar

el **elefante** NOUN
elephant

elegir VERB
to choose
No sabía qué color elegir.
I didn't know what colour to choose.

elijo VERB ▷ see **elegir**
Yo elijo el blanco.
I choose the white one.

ella PRONOUN
1 she
Ella no estaba en casa.
She was not at home.
2 her
El regalo es para ella.
The present's for her.
Él estaba más nervioso que ella.
He was more nervous than her.
ella misma
herself
Me lo dijo ella misma.
She told me herself.
de ella
hers
Este abrigo es de ella.
This coat's hers.

e-mail NOUN
1 email
2 email address

embarazada ADJECTIVE
pregnant
Estaba embarazada de cuatro meses.
She was four months pregnant.

Spanish English

a b c d e f g h i j k l m n ñ o p q r s t u v w x y z

Language tip
Be careful! **embarazada** *does not mean the same as* **embarrassed**.

embarazoso
(FEM **embarazosa**) ADJECTIVE
embarrassing

la **emergencia** NOUN
emergency
> **la salida de emergencia**
> the emergency exit

emocionante
(FEM **emocionante**) ADJECTIVE
exciting
> **El partido fue muy emocionante.**
> The match was very exciting.

el **empaste** NOUN
filling

empatar VERB
to draw
> **Empatamos a uno.**
> We drew one-all.

el **empate** NOUN
draw
> **un empate a cero**
> a goalless draw

empezar VERB
to start
> **Las vacaciones empiezan el día uno.**
> The holidays start on the first.
> **Ha empezado a nevar.**
> It's started snowing.
> **volver a empezar**
> to start again

el **empleo** NOUN
job
> **Ha encontrado empleo en un restaurante.**
> He has found a job in a restaurant.
> **estar sin empleo**
> to be unemployed

empollar VERB
to swot
> **Me pasé la noche empollando.**
> I spent the whole night swotting.

el **empollón**
la **empollona** (MASC PL los empollones) NOUN
swot

la **empresa** NOUN
firm
> **Mi padre trabaja en una empresa de informática.**
> My dad works for a computer firm.

empujar VERB
to push
> **Empuja la puerta.**
> Push the door.

en PREPOSITION
1 in
> **en el armario**
> in the wardrobe
> **Viven en Granada.**
> They live in Granada.
> **Nació en invierno.**
> He was born in winter.
> **Lo hice en dos días.**
> I did it in two days.
> **Está en el hospital.**
> She's in hospital.
2 into
> **Entré en la cocina.**
> I went into the kitchen.
3 on
> **Las llaves están en la mesa.**
> The keys are on the table.
> **La librería está en la calle Pelayo.**

a
b
c
d
e
f
g
h
i
j
k
l
m
n
ñ
o
p
q
r
s
t
u
v
w
x
y
z

The bookshop is on Pelayo street.
La oficina está en el quinto piso.
The office is on the fifth floor.
4 **at**
Yo estaba en casa.
I was at home.
Te veo en el cine.
See you at the cinema.
5 **by**
Vinimos en avión.
We came by plane.

enamorado (FEM **enamorada**)
ADJECTIVE
estar enamorado de alguien
to be in love with somebody

enamorarse VERB
to fall in love
Se ha enamorado de Yolanda.
He's fallen in love with Yolanda.

encantado (FEM **encantada**)
ADJECTIVE
Está encantada con su abrigo nuevo.
She loves her new coat.

¡Encantado de conocerle!
Pleased to meet you!

encantar VERB
to love
Me encantan los animales.
I love animals.

Les encanta esquiar.
They love skiing.

encargar VERB
to order
Encargamos dos pizzas.
We ordered two pizzas.

encender VERB
1 **to light**
2 **to switch on**

encendido (FEM **encendida**)
ADJECTIVE
on
La tele estaba encendida.
The telly was on.

el **enchufado**
la **enchufada** NOUN
Amelia es la enchufada del profesor.
Amelia's the teacher's pet.

enchufar VERB
to plug in
Enchufa la tele.
Plug the TV in.

el **enchufe** NOUN
1 **plug**
2 **socket**

enciendo VERB ▷ *see* **encender**
¿Cómo enciendo la calefacción?
How do I switch the heating on?

encima ADVERB
on
Pon la taza aquí encima.
Put the cup on here.
encima de
on/on top of

Language tip

encima de *has two meanings. Look at the examples.*

Ponlo encima de la mesa.
Put it on the table.
Mi maleta está encima del armario.
My case is on top of the wardrobe.

encontrar VERB
to find

No encuentro las llaves.
I can't find the keys.

encontrarse VERB
1 to feel

Ahora se encuentra mejor.
Now she's feeling better.

2 to meet

Nos encontramos en el cine.
We met at the cinema.
Me encontré con Manolo en la calle.
I bumped into Manolo in the street.

el **enemigo** (FEM la **enemiga**)
ADJECTIVE, NOUN
enemy

la **energía** NOUN
energy

enero MASC NOUN
January

Language tip

Months are not written with a capital letter in Spanish.

en enero
in January
Nació el seis de enero.
He was born on the sixth of January.

enfadado (FEM **enfadada**)
ADJECTIVE
angry

Mi padre estaba muy enfadado conmigo.
My father was very angry with me.

enfadarse VERB
to be angry

Papá se va a enfadar mucho contigo.
Dad will be very angry with you.

la **enfermedad** NOUN
illness

Adelgazó mucho durante su enfermedad.
He lost a lot of weight during his illness.

el **enfermero**
la **enfermera** NOUN
nurse

Mi madre es enfermera.
My mother's a nurse.

enfermo
enferma

enfermo *can be an adjective or a noun.*

A ADJECTIVE
ill

He estado enferma toda la semana.
I've been ill all week.

B MASC/FEM NOUN
patient

un enfermo del Dr. Rojas
one of Dr Rojas' patients
Los enfermos deben tomar precauciones especiales.
Sick people need to take special precautions.

enfrente ADVERB
opposite

Luisa estaba sentada enfrente.
Luisa was sitting opposite.
La panadería está enfrente.
The baker's is across the street.
de enfrente
opposite
la casa de enfrente
the house opposite

enfriarse VERB
1 to get cold

La sopa se ha enfriado.
The soup has got cold.

2 to cool down
Deja que la sopa se enfríe un poco.
Let the soup cool down a bit.

3 to catch cold
Ponte el abrigo que te vas a enfriar.
Put your coat on or you'll catch cold.

engordar VERB

1 to put on weight
No quiero engordar.
I don't want to put on weight.
He engordado dos kilos.
I've put on two kilos.

2 to be fattening
Los caramelos engordan mucho.
Sweets are very fattening

la **enhorabuena** NOUN
¡Enhorabuena!
Congratulations!

enorme (FEM **enorme**) ADJECTIVE
enormous
Tienen una casa enorme.
They have an enormous house.

la **ensalada** NOUN
salad

enseguida ADVERB
straight away
La ambulancia llegó enseguida.
The ambulance arrived straight away.

la **enseñanza** NOUN
1 teaching
2 education
la enseñanza primaria
primary education

enseñar VERB

1 to teach
Ricardo enseña inglés en un colegio.
Ricardo teaches English in a school.
Mi padre me enseñó a nadar.
My father taught me to swim.

2 to show
Ana me enseñó todos sus videojuegos.
Ana showed me all her video games.

ensuciar VERB
to get ... dirty

Vas a ensuciar el sofá.
You'll get the sofa dirty.
No quiero ensuciarme.
I don't want to get dirty.
Me he ensuciado las manos.
I've got my hands dirty.

entender VERB
to understand
No entiendo el francés.
I don't understand French.
¿Lo entiendes?
Do you understand?

enterarse VERB

1 to find out
Me enteré por Manolo.
I found out from Manolo.
Se enteraron del accidente por la tele.
They heard about the accident on the TV.

2 to notice

Me sacaron una muela y ni me enteré.
They took out a tooth and I didn't notice a thing.

entero (FEM **entera**) ADJECTIVE
whole

Se comió el paquete entero de galletas.
He ate the whole packet of biscuits.

Se pasó la noche entera estudiando.
He spent the whole night studying.

entiendo VERB ▷ see **entender**
No lo entiendo.
I can't understand it.

el **entierro** NOUN
funeral

entonces ADVERB
then

Me recogió y entonces fuimos al cine.
He picked me up and then we went to the cinema.

la **entrada** NOUN
1 **entrance**
Nos vemos en la entrada.
I'll see you at the entrance.
2 **ticket**
Tengo entradas para el teatro.
I've got tickets for the theatre.
'prohibida la entrada'
'no entry'

entrar VERB
1 **to go in**
Abrí la puerta y entré.
I opened the door and went in.
2 **to come in**
¿Se puede? — Sí, entra.
May I? — Yes, come in.
Le entraron ganas de reír.
She wanted to laugh.
De repente le entró sueño.
He suddenly felt sleepy.

Me ha entrado hambre al verte comer.
Watching you eat has made me hungry.

entre PREPOSITION
1 **between**
Lo terminamos entre los dos.
Between the two of us we finished it.
Vendrá entre las diez y las once.
He'll be coming between ten and eleven.
2 **among**
Las mujeres hablaban entre sí.
The women were talking among themselves.
Le compraremos un regalo entre todos.
We'll buy her a present between all of us.

entregar VERB
to hand in
Marta entregó el examen.
Marta handed her exam paper in.

el **entrenamiento** NOUN
training

entrenarse VERB
to train

entretenerse VERB
to amuse oneself
Se entretienen viendo los dibujos animados.
They amuse themselves watching cartoons.
No os entretengáis jugando.
Don't hang about playing.

la **entrevista** NOUN
interview

entrevistar VERB
to interview

entusiasmado
(FEM **entusiasmada**) ADJECTIVE

excited
Estaba entusiasmado con su fiesta de cumpleaños.
He was excited about his birthday party.

entusiasmarse VERB
to get excited
Se entusiasmó con la idea de hacer una fiesta.
He got very excited about the idea of having a party.

enviar VERB
to send
Envíame las fotos.
Send me the photos.

la **envidia** NOUN
envy
¡Qué envidia!
I'm so jealous!
Le tiene envidia a Ana.
He's jealous of Ana.

envidiar VERB
to envy
¡No te envidio!
I don't envy you!

envolver VERB
to wrap up
¿Quiere que se lo envuelva?
Would you like me to wrap it up for you?

envuelto VERB ▷ *see* envolver
Estaba envuelto con papel de embalar.
It was wrapped in brown paper.

el **equipaje** NOUN
luggage
equipaje de mano
hand luggage

el **equipo**
NOUN
team
un equipo de baloncesto
a basketball team

equivocado (FEM equivocada)
ADJECTIVE
wrong
Estás equivocada.
You're wrong.
Elena me dio el número equivocado.
Elena gave me the wrong number.

equivocarse VERB

1 **to make a mistake**
Perdona. Me equivoqué.
Sorry. I made a mistake.

2 **to be wrong**
Si crees que voy a dejarte ir, te equivocas.
If you think I'm going to let you go, you're wrong.
Perdone, me he equivocado de número.
Sorry, wrong number.

era VERB ▷ *see* ser
Era yo.
It was me.

eres VERB ▷ *see* ser
Eres muy amable.
You're very kind.

el **erizo** NOUN
hedgehog

el **error** NOUN
mistake
Fue un error contárselo a Lola.
Telling Lola about it was a mistake.

Cometí muchos errores en el examen.
I made a lot of mistakes in the exam.

es VERB ▷*see* **ser**
Es un árbol.
It's a tree.

esa ADJECTIVE ▷*see* **ese**
Dame esa raqueta.
Give me that racket.

ésa PRONOUN ▷*see* **ése**
Ésa es mía.
That one is mine.

la **escalera** NOUN
stairs
bajar las escaleras
to go down the stairs
una escalera mecánica
an escalator

el **escándalo** NOUN
scandal
La pelea produjo un gran escándalo.
The fight caused a huge scandal.

escaparse VERB
to escape
El ladrón se escapó de la cárcel.
The thief escaped from prison.

la **escayola** NOUN
plaster
Mañana me quitan la escayola.
I'm getting my plaster taken off tomorrow.

la **escoba** NOUN
broom

escocés
escocesa (MASC PL **escoceses**)

escocés *can be an adjective or a noun.*

A ADJECTIVE
Scottish
B MASC/FEM NOUN
un escocés
a Scotsman
una escocesa
a Scotswoman
los escoceses
Scottish people

Escocia FEM NOUN
Scotland

escoger VERB
to choose
Yo escogí el azul.
I chose the blue one.

escolar (FEM **escolar**) ADJECTIVE
school
el uniforme escolar
the school uniform

esconder VERB
to hide
Lo escondí en el cajón.
I hid it in the box.
Me escondí debajo de la cama.
I hid under the bed.

escondidas FEM PL NOUN
a escondidas
in secret
Se ven a escondidas.
They meet in secret.

el **escondite** NOUN
jugar al escondite
to play hide-and-seek

la **escopeta** NOUN
shotgun

Spanish **English**

a b c d e f g h i j k l m n ñ o p q r s t u v w x y z

escribir VERB
to write
> **Les escribí una carta.**
> I wrote them a letter.
> **Escribe pronto.**
> Write soon.
> **Nos escribimos de vez en cuando.**
> We write to each other from time to time.
> **¿Cómo se escribe tu nombre?**
> How do you spell your name?

escrito (FEM **escrita**) ADJECTIVE
written
> **un examen escrito**
> a written exam

el **escritor**
la **escritora** NOUN
writer
> **Pablo es escritor.**
> Pablo's a writer.

escuchar VERB
to listen
> **Juan escuchaba con atención.**
> Juan was listening attentively.
> **Me gusta escuchar música.**
> I like listening to music.

la **escuela** NOUN
school
> **Hoy no tengo que ir a la escuela.**
> I don't have to go to school today.
> **la escuela primaria**
> primary school

escupir VERB
to spit

ese (FEM **esa**, MASC PL **esos**)
ADJECTIVE
that
> **Dame ese libro.**
> Give me that book.
> **Trae esas sillas aquí.**
> Bring those chairs over here.

ése (FEM **ésa**, MASC PL **ésos**)
PRONOUN

that one
> **Ése es mío.**
> That one is mine.
> **Ésos de ahí son mejores.**
> Those ones over there are better.
> **¿Cuánto valen ésos?**
> How much are those?

Language tip
*Traditionally, the pronouns **ése**, **ésa**, **ésos**, and **ésas** were written with an accent to distinguish them from the unaccented adjective forms. Nowadays, you don't have to give the accents unless the sentence would be confusing otherwise.*

esforzarse VERB
to make an effort
> **Tienes que esforzarte si quieres ganar.**
> You have to make an effort if you want to win.

el **esfuerzo** NOUN
effort
> **Tuve que hacer un esfuerzo para aprobar el examen.**
> I had to make an effort to pass the exam.

el **esguince** NOUN
sprain
> **Me hice un esguince en el tobillo.**
> I sprained my ankle.

la **ESO** ABBREVIATION
(= **Enseñanza Secundaria obligatoria**)

Did you know…?
ESO is the compulsory secondary education course done by 12 to 16 year-olds.

eso PRONOUN
that
> **Eso es mentira.**
> That's a lie.
> **Por eso te lo dije.**
> That's why I told you.
> **¡Y eso que estaba lloviendo!**

And it was raining and everything!

¡Eso es!
That's it!

esos ADJECTIVE ▷see **ese**
Dame esos lápices.
Give me those pencils.

ésos PRONOUN ▷see **ése**
Ésos son míos.
Those ones are mine.

el **espacio** NOUN
1 **room**
El piano ocupa mucho espacio.
The piano takes up a lot of room.
2 **space**
Deja más espacio entre las líneas.
Leave more space between the lines.

la **espada**
NOUN
sword

Language tip
Be careful! **espada** does not mean **spade**.

la **espalda** NOUN
back
Estaba tumbada de espaldas.
She was lying on her back.

España FEM NOUN
Spain

español

español can be an adjective or a noun.

A (FEM **española**) ADJECTIVE
Spanish
B MASC/FEM NOUN
español/española
Spaniard
los españoles
the Spanish
C MASC NOUN
Spanish
¿Hablas español?
Do you speak Spanish?

especial (FEM **especial**)
ADJECTIVE
special
Fue un día muy especial.
It was a very special day.

especialmente ADVERB
1 **especially**
Me gusta mucho el pan, especialmente el integral.
I love bread, especially wholemeal bread.
2 **specially**
un vestido diseñado especialmente para ella
a dress designed specially for her

la **especie** NOUN
species

el **espectador**
la **espectadora** NOUN
spectator
los espectadores
the audience

el **espejo**
NOUN
mirror

Me miré en el espejo.
I looked at myself in the mirror.

esperar VERB
1 **to wait**
Espera en la puerta, ahora mismo voy.
Wait at the door. I'm just coming.
2 **to wait for**
No me esperéis.
Don't wait for me.
Me hizo esperar una hora.
He kept me waiting for an hour.

Fuimos a esperarla a la estación.
We went to the station to meet her.

3 to expect
Llegaron antes de lo que yo esperaba.
They arrived sooner than I expected.

4 to hope
Espero que no sea nada grave.
I hope it isn't anything serious.
¿Vendrás a la fiesta? — Espero que sí.
Are you coming to the party? — I hope so.
¿Crees que Carmen se enfadará? — Espero que no.
Do you think Carmen will be angry? — I hope not.

la **espina** NOUN
  1 thorn
  2 bone

la **esponja** NOUN
  sponge

la **esposa** NOUN
  1 wife

  2 las esposas
  handcuffs

el **esposo** NOUN
  husband

la **espuma** NOUN
  foam

el **esqueleto** NOUN
  skeleton
    el **esquiador**
    la **esquiadora** NOUN
  skier

esquiar VERB
  to ski
    ¿Sabes esquiar?
    Can you ski?

la **esquina** NOUN
  corner

esta (FEM **esta**) ADJECTIVE ▷ see **este**
  Esta pelota es mía.
  This ball is mine.

ésta PRONOUN ▷ see **éste**
  Mi casa es ésta.
  My house is this one.

está VERB ▷ see **estar**
  Está frío.
  It's cold.

la **estación** (PL las **estaciones**) NOUN
  1 station
    la estación de autobuses
    the bus station
    la estación de ferrocarril
    the railway station
  2 season
    las cuatro estaciones del año
    the four seasons of the year

estacionar VERB
  to park

el **estadio** NOUN
  stadium

los **Estados Unidos** NOUN
  the United States
    en Estados Unidos
    in the United States

estadounidense ADJECTIVE, MASC/FEM NOUN
  American

estallar VERB
  to explode

el **estanco** NOUN
  tobacconist's

Did you know...?

In Spain, an **estanco** is recognizable by the brown and yellow 'T' sign that hangs over the door. As well as tobacco, they sell stamps and coupons for the football pools.

Spanish English

el **estanque** NOUN
pond

la **estantería** NOUN
1 **shelves**
2 **bookshelves**

estar VERB
1 **to be**
Madrid está en el centro de España.
Madrid is in the centre of Spain.
Papá está en la cocina.
Dad's in the kitchen.
¿Dónde estabas?
Where were you?
¿Está Mónica?
Is Mónica there?
¿Cómo estás?
How are you?
Estoy muy cansada.
I'm very tired.
Estamos de vacaciones.
We're on holiday.
Estamos a treinta de enero.
It's the thirtieth of January.
Estábamos a 30°C.
The temperature was 30°C.
Estamos esperando a Manolo.
We're waiting for Manolo.
María estaba sentada en la arena.
María was sitting on the sand.
2 **to look**
Ese vestido te está muy bien.
That dress looks very good on you.

la **estatua** NOUN
statue

este

> *este can be an adjective or a noun.*

A (FEM **esta**, MASC PL **estos**)
ADJECTIVE
this
este libro
this book

estas revistas
these magazines
B MASC NOUN, ADJECTIVE
east
el este del país
the east of the country

> ### Language tip
> When it means 'east', the adjective **este** *never changes its ending, no matter what it describes.*

en la costa este
on the east coast

éste (FEM **ésta**, MASC PL **éstos**)
PRONOUN
this one
Me gusta más éste.
I prefer this one.
Éstos son muy caros.
These ones are very expensive.
¿Cuánto valen éstos?
How much are these?

> ### Language tip
> *Traditionally, the pronouns* **éste**, **ésta**, **éstos** *and* **éstas** *were written with an accent to distinguish them from the unaccented adjective forms. Nowadays, you don't have to give the accents unless the sentence would be confusing otherwise.*

esté VERB ▷ *see* **estar**
Espero que no esté muy lejos.
I hope it won't be too far.

estimado (FEM **estimada**)
ADJECTIVE
Estimado Sr. Pérez:
Dear Mr Pérez,

> ### Language tip
> *Did you notice that there's a colon (:) at the end of the opening line of a letter in Spanish, not a comma?*

estirar VERB
to stretch
No quiero estirar el jersey.
I don't want to stretch my jumper.

a b c d e f g h i j k l m n ñ o p q r s t u v w x y z

esto PRONOUN
this
> **¿Para qué es esto?**
> What's this for?

el **estómago** NOUN
stomach
> **Me dolía el estómago.**
> I had a stomachache.

estorbar VERB
to be in the way
> **Las maletas estorban aquí.**
> The cases are in the way here.

estornudar VERB
to sneeze

estos PL ADJECTIVE ▷ see **este**
Estos libros son bastante baratos.
These books are quite cheap.

éstos PL PRONOUN ▷ see **éste**
Éstos son míos.
These ones are mine.

estoy VERB ▷ see **estar**
Estoy cansado.
I'm tired.

estrecho (FEM **estrecha**)
ADJECTIVE
1 **narrow**
2 **tight**
> **La falda me queda muy estrecha.**
> The skirt is very tight on me.

la **estrella** NOUN
star
> **una estrella de cine**
> a film star
> **una estrella de mar**
> a starfish

estreñido (FEM **estreñida**)
ADJECTIVE
constipated

estropeado (FEM **estropeada**)
ADJECTIVE
1 **broken**
2 **broken down**

estropear VERB
1 **to break**
2 **to ruin**
> **La lluvia nos estropeó las vacaciones.**
> The rain ruined our holidays.
■ **estropearse**
to break
> **Se nos ha estropeado la tele.**
> The TV's broken.

el **estuche** NOUN
case

el/la **estudiante** NOUN
student

estudiar VERB

1 **to study**
> **Quiere estudiar medicina.**
> She wants to study medicine.
2 **to learn**
> **Tengo que estudiar cuatro lecciones para el examen.**
> I have to learn four lessons for the exam.

el **estudio** NOUN
> **Ha dejado los estudios.**
> He's given up his studies.

la **estufa** NOUN
heater
> **una estufa eléctrica**
> an electric heater

estupendo (FEM **estupenda**)
ADJECTIVE
great
> **Pasamos unas Navidades estupendas.**
> We had a great Christmas.

¡Estupendo!
Great!

la **estupidez** (PL las **estupideces**) NOUN
No dice más que estupideces.
He just talks rubbish.
Lo que hizo fue una estupidez.
What he did was stupid.

estúpido
estúpida

> **estúpido** *can be an adjective or a noun.*

A ADJECTIVE
stupid
B MASC/FEM NOUN
idiot
Ese tío es un estúpido.
That guy's an idiot.

estuve VERB ▷ *see* **estar**
Estuve una semana de vacaciones.
I was on holiday for a week.

la **etiqueta** NOUN
label

el **euro** NOUN
euro

Europa FEM NOUN
Europe

el **europeo**
(FEM la **europea**) ADJECTIVE, NOUN
European

evitar VERB
1 to avoid
Quiero evitar ese riesgo.
I want to avoid that risk.
Intento evitar a Carmen.
I'm trying to avoid Carmen.
No pude evitarlo.
I couldn't help it.
2 to save
Esto nos evitará muchos problemas.
This will save us a lot of problems.

exacto (FEM **exacta**) ADJECTIVE
exact
el precio exacto
the exact price

exagerado (FEM **exagerada**)
ADJECTIVE
exaggerated
una descripción exagerada
an exaggerated description
¡No seas exagerado, el pez no era tan grande!
Don't exaggerate! The fish wasn't that big.
El precio me parece exagerado.
The price seems far too high.

el **examen** (PL los **exámenes**)
NOUN
exam

examinar VERB
to examine
El médico la examinó.
The doctor examined her.
Mañana me examino de inglés.
Tomorrow I've got an English exam.

excelente (FEM **excelente**)
ADJECTIVE
excellent

excepto PREPOSITION
except for
todos, excepto Juan
everyone, except for Juan

excluyendo VERB ▷ see **excluir**
Excluyendo a mis padres, somos tres.
Not counting my parents, there are three of us.

la **excursión** (PL las **excursiones**) NOUN
trip
Mañana vamos de excursión con el colegio.
Tomorrow we're going on a school trip.

la **excusa** NOUN
excuse

existir VERB
to exist
¿Existen los fantasmas?
Do ghosts exist?

el **éxito** NOUN
success
Esa novela será un gran éxito.
That novel will be a great success.
Su película tuvo mucho éxito.
His film was very successful.
Acabaron con éxito el proyecto.
They completed the project successfully.

Language tip
Be careful! **éxito** does not mean the same as **exit**.

la **experiencia** NOUN
experience

el **experimento** NOUN
experiment

el **experto**
la **experta** NOUN
expert
Es un experto en informática.
He's a computer expert.

la **explicación** (PL las **explicaciones**) NOUN
explanation

explicar VERB
to explain
¿Quieres que te explique cómo hacerlo?
Do you want me to explain to you how to do it?

la **explosión** (PL las **explosiones**) NOUN
explosion

la **exposición** (PL las **exposiciones**) NOUN
exhibition
montar una exposición
to put on an exhibition

expresar VERB
to express
No sabe expresarse.
He doesn't know how to express himself.

la **expresión** (PL las **expresiones**) NOUN
expression

extender VERB
to spread
Extendí la toalla sobre la arena.
I spread the towel out on the sand.
El fuego se extendió rápidamente.
The fire spread quickly.

exterior (FEM **exterior**)
ADJECTIVE
outside

extinto (FEM **extinta**) ADJECTIVE
extinct

extra (FEM **extra**) ADJECTIVE
extra
>**una manta extra**
>an extra blanket

extraescolar
>(FEM **extraescolara**) ADJECTIVE
>**actividades extraescolares**
>extracurricular activities

extranjero
extranjera

>**extranjero** *can be an adjective or a noun.*

A ADJECTIVE
>**foreign**
B MASC/FEM NOUN
>**foreigner**

>**viajar al extranjero**
>to travel abroad

extrañar VERB
to miss
>**Extraña mucho a sus padres.**
>He misses his parents a lot.
>**Me extraña que no haya llegado.**
>I'm surprised he hasn't arrived.
>**¡Ya me extrañaba a mí!**
>I thought it was strange!

extraño (FEM **extraña**) ADJECTIVE
strange
>**¡Qué extraño!**
>How strange!

extraordinario
>(FEM **extraordinaria**) ADJECTIVE
>**extraordinary**

el **extremo** NOUN
end
>**Cogí la cuerda por un extremo.**
>I took hold of one end of the rope.
>**pasar de un extremo a otro**
>to go from one extreme to the other

F f

la **fábrica** NOUN
factory

> **Language tip**
> Be careful! *fábrica* does not mean
> the same as **fabric**.

fácil (FEM **fácil**) ADJECTIVE
easy
> **un ejercicio fácil**
> an easy exercise

la **falda** NOUN
skirt

el **fallo** NOUN
1 **fault**
2 **mistake**
> **¡Qué fallo!**
> What a stupid mistake!

falso (FEM **falsa**) ADJECTIVE
1 **false**
2 **forged**

la **falta** NOUN
1 **lack**
> **la falta de dinero**
> lack of money
2 **mistake**
> **una falta de ortografía**
> a spelling mistake

> **Me hace falta un ordenador.**
> I need a computer.
> **No hace falta que vengáis.**
> You don't need to come.

faltar VERB
1 **to be missing**
> **Me falta un bolígrafo.**
> One of my pens is missing.
> **No podemos irnos. Falta
> Manolo.**
> We can't go. Manolo isn't here
> yet.
> **A la sopa le falta sal.**
> There isn't enough salt in the soup.

> **faltar al colegio**
> to miss school
> **You mustn't miss school.**
> No debes faltar al colegio.
2 **Falta media hora para comer.**
> There's half an hour to go before
> lunch.
> **¿Te falta mucho?**
> Will you be long?

la **fama** NOUN
1 **fame**
2 **reputation**
> **tener fama de**
> to have a reputation for
> **Tiene fama de mandona.**
> She has a reputation for being
> bossy.

la **familia** NOUN
family

familiar (FEM **familiar**)
ADJECTIVE
1 **family**
> **la vida familiar**
> family life
2 **familiar**
> **Su cara me es familiar.**
> His face is familiar.

famoso (FEM **famosa**) ADJECTIVE
famous

el **fantasma** NOUN
ghost

la **farmacia** NOUN
chemist's
> **Lo compré en la farmacia.**
> I bought it at the chemist's.

> **Did you know...?**
> Spanish chemists are identifiable
> by a red or green cross outside the
> shop. If you want to buy cosmetics
> or toiletries, go to a **perfumería**.

el **faro** NOUN
1 **headlight**
2 **lighthouse**

fastidiar
VERB
to annoy
Lo que más me fastidia es tener que decírselo.
What annoys me most is having to tell him.

fatal

> **fatal** *can be an adjective or an adverb.*

A (FEM **fatal**) ADJECTIVE
awful
Me siento fatal.
I feel awful.
B ADVERB
Lo pasé fatal.
I had an awful time.
Lo hice fatal.
I made a mess of it.

el **favor** NOUN
favour
¿Puedes hacerme un favor?
Can you do me a favour?

por favor
please

favorito (FEM **favorita**)
ADJECTIVE
favourite
¿Cuál es tu color favorito?
What's your favourite colour?

febrero MASC NOUN
February

> *Language tip*
> *Months are not spelled with a capital letter in Spanish.*

Nació el veintiocho de febrero.
She was born on the twenty-eighth of February.

en febrero
in February

Nació el quince de febrero.
He was born on the fifteenth of February.

la **fecha** NOUN
date
¿En qué fecha estamos?
What's the date today?
su fecha de nacimiento
his date of birth

la **felicidad** NOUN
happiness
¡Felicidades!
Happy birthday!/
Congratulations!

> *Language tip*
> **¡Felicidades!** *has two meanings.*

felicitar VERB
to congratulate
La felicité por sus notas.
I congratulated her on her exam results.
Felicítale por su cumpleaños.
Wish her a happy birthday.

feliz (FEM **feliz**, PL **felices**)
ADJECTIVE
happy

Se la ve muy feliz.
She looks very happy.

¡Feliz cumpleaños!
Happy birthday!
¡Feliz Año Nuevo!
Happy New Year!
¡Felices Navidades!
Happy Christmas!

femenino (FEM **femenina**)
ADJECTIVE
1 **feminine**
2 **female**
el sexo femenino
the female sex

feo (FEM **fea**) ADJECTIVE
ugly

festivo (FEM **festiva**) ADJECTIVE
un día festivo
a holiday

fiar VERB
fiarse de alguien
to trust somebody
No me fío de él.
I don't trust him.

la **ficha** NOUN
counter

los **fideos** NOUN
noodles

la **fiebre** NOUN
temperature
Tiene fiebre.
She has a temperature.
fiebre de heno
hay fever

la **fiesta** NOUN
1 **party**
Voy a dar una fiesta para celebrarlo.
I'm going to have a party to celebrate.
El pueblo está en fiestas.
There's a fiesta on in the town.
una fiesta de cumpleaños
a birthday party

2 **holiday**
El lunes es fiesta.
Monday is a holiday.

la **fila** NOUN
1 **row**

Nos sentamos en la segunda fila.
We sit in the second row.
2 **line**
Los niños se pusieron en fila.
The children got into line.

el **filete** NOUN
1 **steak**
un filete con patatas fritas
steak and chips
2 **fillet**
un filete de merluza
a hake fillet

el **fin** NOUN
end
a fines de abril
at the end of April
En fin, ¿qué le vamos a hacer?
Oh well, what can we do about it?
por fin
at last
¡Por fin hemos llegado!
We've got here at last!
el fin de año
New Year's Eve
el fin de semana
the weekend

final

final *can be an adjective or a noun.*

A (FEM **final**) ADJECTIVE
final
el resultado final
the final result
B MASC NOUN
end
Al final de la calle hay un colegio.
At the end of the street there's a school.
a finales de mayo
at the end of May
al final
in the end
Al final tuve que darle la razón.

In the end I had to admit that he was right.
un final feliz
a happy ending

C FEM NOUN
final
la final de la copa
the cup final

fingir VERB
to pretend
Fingió no haberme oído.
He pretended not to have heard me.
Finge dormir.
He's pretending to be asleep.

fino (FEM **fina**) ADJECTIVE
1 **thin**
2 **fine**

la firma NOUN
signature

firmar VERB
to sign

firme (FEM **firme**) ADJECTIVE
steady
Mantén la escalera firme.
Can you hold the ladder steady?

la flauta NOUN
1 **recorder**
2 **flute**

la flecha NOUN
arrow

el flequillo NOUN
fringe

flojo (FEM **floja**) ADJECTIVE
1 **loose**
2 **weak**
Todavía tengo las piernas muy flojas.
My legs are still very weak.
Está flojo en matemáticas.
He's weak at maths.

la flor NOUN
flower

el flotador NOUN
rubber ring

el folio NOUN
1 **sheet of paper**
2 **page**

el folleto NOUN
1 **brochure**
2 **leaflet**

el fondo NOUN
1 **bottom**
en el fondo del mar
at the bottom of the sea
2 **end**
Mi habitación está al fondo del pasillo.
My room's at the end of the corridor.

el fontanero
la fontanera NOUN
plumber

la forma NOUN
way
Me miraba de una forma extraña.
She was looking at me in a strange way.
de todas formas
anyway
De todas formas, debes ir a verlo.
You should go to see him anyway.

formal (FEM **formal**) ADJECTIVE
responsible
un chico muy formal
a very responsible boy

forrar VERB
to cover

la **foto** NOUN
photo
> **Les hice una foto a los niños.**
> I took a photo of the children.

la **fotocopia** NOUN
photocopy

fotocopiar VERB
to photocopy

la **fotografía** NOUN
photograph
> **una fotografía de mis padres**
> a photograph of my parents

la **frambuesa** NOUN
raspberry

la **frase** NOUN
sentence

la **frecuencia** NOUN
frequency
> **Nos vemos con frecuencia.**
> We often see each other.

frecuente (FEM **frecuente**)
ADJECTIVE
common
> **un error bastante frecuente**
> a fairly common mistake

el **fregadero** NOUN
sink

fregar VERB
to wash
> **Tengo que fregar la cazuela.**
> I've got to wash the pan.
> **Yo estaba en la cocina fregando.**
> I was in the kitchen washing the dishes.
> **Deberías fregar el suelo.**
> You should mop the floor.

freír VERB
to fry

el **freno** NOUN
brake
> **el freno de mano**
> the handbrake

la **frente** NOUN
forehead
> **Tiene una cicatriz en la frente.**
> He has a scar on his forehead.

el **frente** NOUN
front
> **frente a**
> opposite
> **Frente al hotel hay un banco.**
> There's a bank opposite the hotel.

la **fresa** NOUN
strawberry

fresco

> **fresco** *can be an adjective or a noun.*

A (FEM **fresca**) ADJECTIVE
1 cool
2 fresh
B MASC NOUN
fresh air
> **Salimos fuera a tomar el fresco.**
> We went outside to get some fresh air.
> **Hace fresco.**
> It's chilly./It's cool.

> **Language tip**
> **hace fresco** *has two meanings. Look at the examples.*

> **No quiero salir porque hace fresco.**
> I don't want to go out because it's a bit chilly.
> **En esta casa hace fresco en verano.**
> This house is cool in summer.

Hace más fresco dentro.
It's cooler inside.

friego VERB ▷*see* **fregar**
Yo friego y tu seca.
I'll wash and you dry.

frío

> **frío** *can be an adjective, noun or part of the verb* **freír**.

A (FEM **fría**) ADJECTIVE
cold
Tengo las manos frías.
My hands are cold.

B MASC NOUN
cold
Hace frío.
It's cold.

Tengo mucho frío.
I'm very cold.

C VERB ▷*see* **freír**
¿Te frío un huevo?
Shall I fry you an egg?

frito

> **frito** *can be an adjective or part of the verb* **freír**.

A (FEM **frita**) ADJECTIVE
fried
huevos fritos
fried eggs

B VERB ▷*see* **freír**
He frito un huevo.
I've fried an egg.

la **frontera** NOUN
border

Nos pararon en la frontera.
We were stopped at the border.

la **fruta** NOUN
fruit
La fruta está muy cara.
Fruit is very expensive.

fue VERB ▷*see* **ir, ser**
Fue a la escuela en Barcelona.
He went to school in Barcelona.
Fue él.
It was him.

el **fuego** NOUN
fire

Enciende el fuego.
Light the fire.
Puse la cazuela al fuego.
I put the pot on to heat.
¿Tiene fuego, por favor?
Have you got a light, please?
fuegos artificiales
fireworks

la **fuente** NOUN
fountain

fuera

> **fuera** *can be an adverb or a verb.*

A ADVERB
outside
Los niños estaban jugando fuera.
The children were playing outside.
Por fuera es blanco.
It's white on the outside.
¡Estamos aquí fuera!
We are out here!
Hoy vamos a cenar fuera.
We're going out for dinner tonight.

B VERB ▷*see* **ir, ser**
Quería que fuera con ella.
She wanted me to go with her.

Si fuera yo, no se lo diría.
If I were you, I wouldn't tell him.

fuerte

> **fuerte** *can be an adjective or an adverb.*

A (FEM **fuerte**) ADJECTIVE
1 **strong**
2 **loud**
3 **hard**
B ADVERB
loudly
Siempre habla fuerte.
He always talks loudly.
Agárrate fuerte.
Hold on tight.
No le des tan fuerte.
Don't hit it so hard.

la **fuerza** NOUN
strength
No le quedaban fuerzas.
He had no strength left.
No te lo comas a la fuerza.
Don't force yourself to eat it.
la fuerza de la gravedad
the force of gravity
la fuerza de voluntad
willpower

fuerzo VERB ▷*see* **forzar**
Solo se abrirá si la fuerzo.
It will only open if I force it.

fui VERB ▷*see* **ir, ser**
Ayer fui al cine.
I went to the cinema yesterday.
Fui yo.
It was me.

el **fumador**
la **fumadora** NOUN
smoker

fumar VERB
to smoke
Mi padre quiere dejar de fumar.
My dad wants to give up smoking.

funcionar VERB
to work
El ascensor no funciona.
The lift isn't working.
Funciona con pilas.
It runs on batteries.

el **funeral** NOUN
funeral

la **furgoneta** NOUN
van

furioso (FEM **furiosa**) ADJECTIVE
furious

el **fútbol** NOUN
football
jugar al fútbol
to play football

el **futbolín** (PL los **futbolines**) NOUN
table football

el/la **futbolista** NOUN
footballer
Quiere ser futbolista.
He wants to be a footballer.

G g

las **gafas** NOUN
  1 **glasses**
    Lleva gafas.
    He wears glasses.
    Había unas gafas encima de la mesa.
    There was a pair of glasses on the table.
    gafas de sol
    sunglasses
  2 **goggles**

Gales MASC NOUN
  Wales
    el País de Gales
    Wales

la **galleta** NOUN
  biscuit
    una galleta salada
    a cracker

gallina FEM NOUN
  hen

el **gallo** NOUN
  cock

el **gamberro**
  la **gamberra** NOUN
  hooligan

la **gana** NOUN
    Hazlo como te dé la gana.
    Do it however you like.
    Lo hizo de mala gana.
    She did it reluctantly.
    Tengo ganas de que llegue el sábado.
    I'm looking forward to Saturday.

  ¡No me da la gana!
  I don't want to!

el **ganador**
  la **ganadora** NOUN
  winner

ganar VERB
  1 **to win**
    Lo importante no es ganar.
    Winning isn't the most important thing.
    Con eso no ganas nada.
    You won't achieve anything by doing that.
  2 **ganar a**
    to beat
    Ganamos al Olimpic tres a cero.
    We beat Olimpic three-nil.
  3 **to earn**
    Gana un buen sueldo.
    He earns a good wage.

el **garaje** NOUN
  garage

la **garganta** NOUN
  throat
    Me duele la garganta.
    I've got a sore throat.

el **gas** (PL los **gases**) NOUN
  gas
    ¿Te huele a gas?
    Can you smell gas?
    agua mineral sin gas
    still mineral water
    agua mineral con gas
    sparkling mineral water

la **gaseosa** NOUN

Did you know...?
Gaseosa *is a sweet fizzy drink a bit like lemonade or soda.*

Spanish | English

a
b
c
d
e
f
g
h i j
k
l
m
ñ
o
p
q
r
s
t
u
v
w
x
y
z

la **gasolina** NOUN
petrol

la **gasolinera** NOUN
petrol station

gastado (FEM **gastada**)
ADJECTIVE
worn

gastar VERB
1 to spend
2 to use
Gastamos mucha electricidad.
We use a lot of electricity.
Se han gastado las pilas.
The batteries have run out.
Le gastamos una broma a Juan.
We played a joke on Juan.

la **gata** NOUN
cat
andar a gatas
to crawl
El niño todavía anda a gatas.
The baby is still crawling.

el **gato** NOUN
cat

la **gaviota** NOUN
seagull

el **gemelo**
la **gemela** NOUN
identical twin

los **gemelos**
NOUN
binoculars

general (FEM **general**) ADJECTIVE
general
por lo general
generally

genial (FEM **genial**) ADJECTIVE
brilliant

el **genio** NOUN
1 temper
¡Menudo genio tiene tu padre!
Your father has got such a temper!
Tiene mal genio.
He has a bad temper
2 genius
¡Eres un genio!
You're a genius!

la **gente** NOUN
people
Había poca gente en la sala.
There weren't many people in the room.

la **geografía** NOUN
geography

el **gesto** NOUN
Hizo un gesto de alivio.
He looked relieved.
Me hizo un gesto para que me sentara.
He signalled for me to sit down.

la **gimnasia** NOUN
gymnastics
Mi madre hace gimnasia todas las mañanas.
My mother does some exercise every morning.

el **gimnasio** NOUN
gym

girar VERB
  to turn
    Giré la cabeza para ver quién era.
    I turned my head to see who it was.

global (FEM **global**) ADJECTIVE
  global

el **globo** NOUN
  balloon

el **gobierno** NOUN
  government

el **gol** NOUN
  goal
    Metió un gol.
    He scored a goal.

la **golosina** NOUN
  sweet

goloso (FEM **golosa**) ADJECTIVE
    Soy muy golosa.
    I've got a very sweet tooth.

el **golpe** NOUN
  knock
    Oímos un golpe en la puerta.
    We heard a knock at the door.
    Me he dado un golpe en el codo.
    I banged my elbow.
    Se dio un golpe contra la pared.
    He hit the wall.
    de golpe
    suddenly
    De golpe decidió marcharse.
    He suddenly decided to leave.

golpear VERB
  1 **to hit**
    Me golpeó en la cara con su raqueta.
    He hit me in the face with his racquet.
  2 **to bang**
    El maestro golpeó el pupitre con la mano.

The teacher banged the desk with his hand.

la **goma** NOUN
  1 **rubber**
    ¿Me prestas la goma?
    Can you lend me your rubber?
  2 **elastic band**
    Necesito una goma para el pelo.
    I need an elastic band for my hair.

gordo (FEM **gorda**) ADJECTIVE
  fat
    Estoy muy gordo.
    I'm very fat.

la **gorra** NOUN
  cap
    de gorra
    for free
    Entramos de gorra.
    We got in for free.

el **gorro** NOUN
  hat

    Llevaba un gorro de lana.
    He wore a woolly hat.
    un gorro de baño
    a swimming cap

la **gota** NOUN
  drop
    Solo bebí una gota de zumo.
    I only had a drop of juice.
    Están cayendo cuatro gotas.
    It's spitting.

grabar VERB
  1 **to record**
    Lo grabaron en directo.
    It was recorded live.
  2 **to tape**
    Quiero grabar esta película.
    I want to tape this film.

a b c d e f **g** h i j k l m n ñ o p q r s t u v w x y z

a
b
c
d
e
f
g
h i j
k
l
m n ñ
o p
q
r
s
t
u v
w
x y
z

3 to engrave

la **gracia** NOUN

Sus chistes tienen mucha gracia.
His jokes are very funny.
Yo no le veo la gracia.
I don't see what's so funny.
Me hizo mucha gracia.
It was so funny.
No me hace gracia tener que salir con este tiempo.
I'm not too pleased about having to go out in this weather.

gracias a
thanks to
¡Gracias!
Thank you!
¡Muchas gracias!
Thanks very much!
dar las gracias a alguien
to thank somebody

gracioso (FEM **graciosa**)
ADJECTIVE
funny

¡Qué gracioso!
How funny!

el **grado** NOUN
degree

Estaban a diez grados bajo cero.
It was ten degrees below zero.

la **gramática** NOUN
grammar

el **gramo** NOUN
gram

gran ADJECTIVE ▷ see **grande**
un gran artista
a great artist
un gran número de gente
a large number of people

Gran Bretaña FEM NOUN
Great Britain

grande (FEM **grande**) ADJECTIVE

Language tip
grande becomes **gran** before a
singular noun.

1 big
¿Cómo es de grande?
How big is it?
La camisa me está grande.
The shirt is too big for me.
unos grandes almacenes
a department store
2 large
un gran número de visitantes
a large number of visitors

el **granizo** NOUN
hail

la **granja**
NOUN
farm

el **grano** NOUN
1 spot
Me ha salido un grano en la frente.
I've got a spot on my forehead.
2 grain

gratis

gratis can be an adjective or an adverb.

A (FEM, PL **gratis**) ADJECTIVE
free
La entrada es gratis.
Entry is free.
B ADVERB
for free
Te lo arreglan gratis.
They'll fix it for free.

grave (FEM **grave**) ADJECTIVE
serious
Tenemos un problema grave.
We've got a serious problem.

el **grifo** NOUN
tap
Abre el grifo.
Turn on the tap.

Cierra el grifo.
Turn off the tap.

la **gripe** NOUN
flu

Tengo la gripe
I've got flu.

gris ADJECTIVE, MASC NOUN
grey

gritar VERB
1 **to shout**
Niños, no gritéis tanto.
Children, stop shouting so much.
2 **to scream**
El enfermo no podía dejar de gritar.
The patient couldn't stop screaming.

el **grito** NOUN
1 **shout**
¡No des esos gritos!
Stop shouting like that!
2 **scream**
Oímos un grito en la calle.
We heard a scream outside.

grosero (FEM **grosera**) ADJECTIVE
rude

la **grúa** NOUN
crane

el **grupo** NOUN
1 **group**
Los alumnos trabajan en grupo.
The students work in groups.
2 **band**
un grupo de rock
a rock band

el **guante** NOUN
glove
unos guantes
a pair of gloves

guapo (FEM **guapa**) ADJECTIVE
1 **handsome**
2 **pretty**

guardar VERB
1 **to put away**
Los niños guardaron los juguetes.
The children put away their toys.
2 **to keep**
No sabe guardar un secreto.
He can't keep a secret.
3 **to save**
Debes guardar el fichero.
You must save the file.

la **guardería** NOUN
nursery

el/la **guardia** NOUN
police officer

el **guarro**
la **guarra** NOUN
¡Eres un guarro!
You're disgusting!

guay (FEM **guay**) ADJECTIVE
cool
¡Qué moto más guay!
What a cool bike!

la **guerra** NOUN
war

guía
A MASC/FEM NOUN
guide
B FEM NOUN
guidebook
Compré una guía turística de Londres.
I bought a tourist guidebook to London.

guiñar VERB
to wink
Me guiñó el ojo.
He winked at me.

a b c d e f **g** h i j k l m n ñ o p q r s t u v w x y z

la **guitarra** NOUN
guitar

el **gusano** NOUN
worm

gustar VERB
Me gustan las uvas.
I like grapes.

¿Te gusta viajar?
Do you like travelling?
Me gusta su hermana.
I fancy his sister.
Le gusta más llevar pantalones.
She prefers to wear trousers.

H h

ha VERB ▷ see **haber**
Me ha comprado un libro.
He has bought me a book.

haber VERB
to have

> *Language tip*
> **haber** *is used to make the past tense of verbs.*

He comido.
I've eaten.
¿Habéis comido?
Have you eaten?
Había comido.
I'd eaten.
Se ha sentado.
She's sat down.
hay
there is/there are

> *Language tip*
> **hay** *has two meanings:* **there is** *and* **there are.** *Look at the examples.*

Hay una iglesia en la esquina.
There's a church on the corner.
Hay treinta alumnos en mi clase.
There are thirty pupils in my class.
¿Hay entradas?
Are there any tickets?
hay que
you must
Hay que ser respetuoso.
You must be respectful.

la **habitación** (PL las
habitaciones) NOUN
1 bedroom
**Ésta es la
habitación de
mi hermana.**
This is my
sister's bedroom.

2 room
una habitación doble
a double room
una habitación individual
a single room

el/la **habitante** NOUN
inhabitant
los habitantes de la zona
people living in the area

hablar VERB
1 to speak
¿Hablas español?
Do you speak Spanish?
2 to talk
**Estuvimos hablando toda
la tarde.**
We were talking all afternoon.
¿Has hablado con el profesor?
Have you spoken to the teacher?
Solo hablan de fútbol.
They only talk about football.
¡Ni hablar!
No way!

habré VERB ▷ see **haber**
**¿Dónde habré puesto las
llaves?**
Where did I put my keys?

hacer VERB
1 to make
Tengo que hacer la cama.
I've got to make the bed.
Estáis haciendo mucho ruido.
You're making a lot of noise.
2 to do
¿Qué haces?
What are you doing?
Tengo que hacer los deberes.
I have to do my homework.
Hace mucho deporte.
She does a lot of sport.
hacer clic en algo
to click on something

3 to be
Hace calor.
It's hot.
hace
ago/for

> **Language tip**
> When talking about time, **hace** can mean **ago** or **for**. Look at the examples.

Terminé hace una hora.
I finished an hour ago.
Hace un mes que voy.
I've been going for a month.
¿Hace mucho que esperas?
Have you been waiting long?

■ **hacerse**
to become
Quiere hacerse famoso.
He wants to become famous.

hacia PREPOSITION
towards
Venía hacia mí.
He was coming towards me.
hacia adelante
forwards
hacia atrás
backwards
hacia dentro
inside
hacia fuera
outside
hacia abajo
down
hacia arriba
up

hago VERB ▷see **hacer**
Y ahora, ¿qué hago?
And now, what do I do?

el **hambre** NOUN
hunger
tener hambre
to be hungry
No tengo mucha hambre.
I'm not very hungry.

la **hamburguesa**
NOUN
hamburger

haré VERB ▷see **hacer**
Lo haré mañana.
I'll do it tomorrow.

hartar VERB
hartarse de algo
to get fed up with something
Me harté de estudiar.
I got fed up with studying.

harto (FEM **harta**) ADJECTIVE
fed up
Estoy harto de repetirlo.
I'm fed up with repeating it.
¡Me tienes harto!
I'm fed up with you!

hasta

> **hasta** can be a preposition, conjunction or adverb.

A PREPOSITION, CONJUNCTION
till
Está abierto hasta las cuatro.
It's open till four o'clock.
¿Hasta cuándo?
How long?
¿Hasta cuándo te quedas? —
Hasta la semana que viene.
How long are you staying? —
Till next week.
hasta que
until
Espera aquí hasta que te
llamen.
Wait here until you're called.

¡Hasta luego!
See you!
¡Hasta mañana!
See you tomorrow!
¡Hasta el sábado!
See you on Saturday!

B ADVERB
even

Estudia hasta cuando está
de vacaciones.
He even studies when he's
on holiday.

hay VERB ▷ see **haber**
Hay tres casas.
There are three houses.

haz VERB ▷ see **hacer**
Haz lo que quieras.
Do whatever you like.

he VERB ▷ see **haber**
No he estado nunca en Londres.
I've never been to London.

hecho

> **hecho** *can be an adjective or part
> of the verb* **hacer**.

A (FEM **hecha**) ADJECTIVE
made
¿De qué está hecho?
What's it made of?
hecho a mano
handmade
¡Bien hecho!
Well done!
B VERB ▷ see **hacer**
Ya lo he hecho.
I've done it already.

helado

> **helado** *can be a noun or an adjective.*

A MASC NOUN
ice cream
**un helado de
chocolate**
a chocolate ice
cream

B (FEM **helada**) ADJECTIVE
1 frozen
El lago está helado.
The lake's frozen over.
2 freezing
¡Estoy helado!
I'm freezing!

el **helicóptero** NOUN
helicopter

hemos VERB ▷ see **haber**
Ya hemos llegado.
We've arrived.

la **herida** NOUN
wound

herido (FEM **herida**) ADJECTIVE
1 wounded
2 injured

herir VERB
to wound
Lo hirieron en el pecho.
He was wounded in the chest.

la **hermana** NOUN
sister

la **hermanastra** NOUN
stepsister

el **hermanastro** NOUN
stepbrother
mis hermanastros
my stepbrothers/my
stepbrothers and sisters

> *Language tip*
>
> **mis hermanastros** *has two
> meanings. It can be translated as*
> **my stepbrothers** *or* **my
> stepbrothers and sisters**.

el **hermano** NOUN
brother
mis hermanos
my brothers/my brothers and sisters

> *Language tip*
>
> **mis hermanos** *has two meanings.
> It can be translated as* **my
> brothers** *or* **my brothers and
> sisters**.

el **héroe** NOUN
hero

la **herramienta** NOUN
tool

hervir VERB
to boil
El agua está hirviendo.
The water's boiling.

a
b
c
d
e
f
g
h
i
j
k
l
m
n
ñ
o
p
q
r
s
t
u
v
w
x
y
z

hice VERB ▷*see* **hacer**
Lo hice yo solo.
I did it on my own.

el **hielo** NOUN
ice

la **hierba** NOUN
grass

el **hierro** NOUN
iron

la **higiene** NOUN
hygiene

higiénico (FEM **higiénica**)
ADJECTIVE
hygienic
poco higiénico
unhygienic

la **hija** NOUN
daughter
Soy hija única.
I'm an only child.

la **hijastra** NOUN
stepdaughter

el **hijastro** NOUN
stepson
mis hijastros
my stepsons/my stepchildren

Language tip
mis hijastros *has two meanings.*
It can be translated as **my**
stepsons *or* **my stepchildren**.

el **hijo** NOUN
son
su hijo mayor
his oldest son
Soy hijo único.
I'm an only child.
mis hijos
my sons/
my children

Language tip
mis hijos *has two meanings. It can*
be translated as **my sons** *or* **my**
children.

hinchado (FEM **hinchada**)
ADJECTIVE
swollen

el **hipo** NOUN
hiccups
Tengo hipo.
I've got hiccups.

hirviendo VERB ▷*see* **hervir**
La leche está hirviendo.
The milk is boiling.

la **historia** NOUN
history
mi profesor de historia
my history teacher

hizo VERB ▷*see* **hacer**
Lo hizo mi hermana.
My sister did it.

el **hobby** NOUN
hobby
Lo hago por hobby.
I do it as a hobby.

el **hogar** NOUN
home

la **hoja** NOUN
1 leaf
2 sheet
una hoja de papel
a sheet of paper
3 page
las hojas de un libro
the pages of a book

hola EXCLAMATION
hello!

holgazán (FEM **holgazana**, MASC
PL **holgazanes**) ADJECTIVE
lazy

el **hombre** NOUN
man
un hombre de negocios
a businessman

el **hombro** NOUN
shoulder

hondo (FEM **honda**) ADJECTIVE
deep
> **la parte honda de la piscina**
> the deep end of the pool

la **hora** NOUN

1 hour
> **El viaje dura una hora.**
> The journey lasts an hour.

2 time
> **¿A qué hora te levantas?**
> What time do you get up?
> **¿Tienes hora?**
> Have you got the time?
> **la hora de cenar**
> dinner time
> **a última hora**
> at the last minute

¿Qué hora es?
What's the time?

el **horario** NOUN
timetable

horizontal (FEM **horizontal**)
ADJECTIVE
horizontal

el **horizonte** NOUN
horizon

la **hormiga** NOUN
ant

el **horno** NOUN
oven
> **pollo al horno**
> roast chicken

el **horóscopo** NOUN
horoscope

la **horquilla** NOUN
hairgrip

horrible (FEM **horrible**)
ADJECTIVE
awful
> **Ha hecho un tiempo horrible.**
> The weather has been awful.

el **hospital** NOUN
hospital
> **La llevaron al hospital.**
> She was taken to hospital.

el **hotel** NOUN
hotel

hoy ADVERB
today
> **¿Qué día es hoy?**
> What's the date today?
> **de hoy en adelante**
> from now on
> **hoy por la mañana**
> this morning

la **hucha** NOUN
moneybox

hueco

hueco *can be an adjective or a noun.*

A (FEM **hueca**) ADJECTIVE
hollow

B MASC NOUN
space
> **Deja un hueco para la respuesta.**
> Leave a space for the answer.

la **huella** NOUN
footprint
> **las huellas del ladrón**
> the thief's footprints
> **huella digital**
> fingerprint

Spanish **English**

a
b
c
d
e
f
g
h
i
j
k
l
m
n
ñ
o
p
q
r
s
t
u
v
w
x
y
z

huelo VERB ▷ see **oler**
Lo huelo desde aquí.
I can smell it from here.

el **hueso** NOUN
1 **bone**
2 **stone**

el **huevo** NOUN
egg
un huevo duro
a hard-boiled egg
un huevo frito
a fried egg
huevos revueltos
scrambled eggs
un huevo pasado por agua
a soft-boiled egg

humano (FEM **humana**)
ADJECTIVE
human
el cuerpo humano
the human body
los seres humanos
human beings

húmedo (FEM **húmeda**)
ADJECTIVE
1 **damp**

Mi camiseta está húmeda todavía.
My t-shirt is still damp.
2 **humid**

el **humo** NOUN
smoke
Salía humo de la chimenea.
Smoke was coming out of the chimney.

el **humor** NOUN
mood
No está de humor para bromas.
He's not in the mood for jokes.
estar de buen humor
to be in a good mood
estar de mal humor
to be in a bad mood

hundirse VERB
to sink
El barco se hundió durante la tormenta.
The boat sank during the storm.

huyendo VERB ▷ see **huir**
Estaban huyendo de un perro.
They were running away from a dog.

I i

iba VERB ▷*see* **ir**
Iba por la calle.
He was walking down the street.

la **ida** NOUN
single
¿Cuánto cuesta la ida?
How much does a single cost?
El viaje de ida duró dos horas.
The journey there took two hours.
un billete de ida y vuelta
a return ticket

la **idea** NOUN
idea
¡Qué buena idea!
What a good idea!
Ya me voy haciendo a la idea.
I'm beginning to get used to the idea.
cambiar de idea
to change one's mind
He cambiado de idea.
I've changed my mind.

No tengo ni idea.
I have no idea.

ideal (FEM **ideal**) ADJECTIVE
ideal
Es el lugar ideal para las vacaciones.
It's the ideal place for a holiday.

idéntico (FEM **idéntica**)
ADJECTIVE
identical
Tiene una falda idéntica a la mía.
She has an identical skirt to mine.
Es idéntica a su padre.
She's the spitting image of her father.

el **idioma** NOUN
language
Habla tres idiomas.
He speaks three languages.

idiota

idiota *can be an adjective or a noun.*

A (FEM **idiota**) ADJECTIVE
stupid
¡No seas tan idiota!
Don't be so stupid!
B MASC/FEM NOUN
idiot

la **iglesia** NOUN
church
Voy a la iglesia todos los domingos.
I go to church every Sunday.
la Iglesia católica
the Catholic Church

ignorante (FEM **ignorante**)
ADJECTIVE
ignorant

igual

igual *can be an adjective or an adverb.*

A (FEM **igual**) ADJECTIVE
1 equal
Se repartieron el dinero en partes iguales.
They divided the money into equal shares.

a b c d e f g h i j k l m n ñ o p q r s t u v w x y z

X es igual a Y.
X is equal to Y.

2 the same
Todas las casas son iguales.
All the houses are the same.
Es igual a su madre.
She looks just like her mother./
She's just like
her mother.

Language tip
ser igual a *has two meanings. It can be translated as* **to look just like** *and* **to be just like**.

Tengo una falda igual que la tuya.
I've got a skirt just like yours.

Me da igual.
I don't mind.

B ADVERB
1 the same
Se visten igual.
They dress the same.
2 maybe
Igual no lo saben todavía.
Maybe they don't know yet.
3 anyway
No hizo nada pero la castigaron igual.
She didn't do anything but they punished her anyway.

igualmente ADVERB
the same to you
¡Feliz Navidad! —
Gracias, igualmente.
Happy Christmas! —
Thanks, the same to you.

ilegal (FEM **ilegal**) ADJECTIVE
illegal

la **ilusión** (PL las **ilusiones**)
NOUN

dream
Mi mayor ilusión es llegar a ser médico.
My dream is to become a doctor.
Le hace mucha ilusión que vengas.
He's really looking forward to you coming.
Tu regalo me hizo mucha ilusión.
I was really pleased with your present.

la **imagen** (PL las **imágenes**)
NOUN
image
Han decidido cambiar de imagen.
They've decided to change their image.
Es la viva imagen de su madre.
She's the spitting image of her mother.

la **imaginación** (PL las **imaginaciones**) NOUN
imagination
Tiene mucha imaginación.
He has a vivid imagination.
Ni se me pasó por la imaginación.
It never even occurred to me.

imaginarse VERB
to imagine
Me imagino que seguirá en Madrid.
I imagine that he's still in Madrid.
¿Se enfadó mucho? — ¡imagínate!
Was he very angry? —
What do you think!

imbécil (FEM **imbécil**)
ADJECTIVE
stupid
¡No seas imbécil!
Don't be stupid!

imitar VERB
1 **to copy**
Imita todo lo que hace su hermano.
He copies everything his brother does.
2 **to do an impression of**
Imita muy bien a la directora.
She does a very good impression of the headmistress.

impar

> **impar** *can be an adjective or a noun.*

A (FEM **impar**) ADJECTIVE
odd
un número impar
an odd number
B MASC NOUN
odd number

el **imperdible** NOUN
safety pin

la **importancia** NOUN
importance
tener importancia
to be important
La educación tiene mucha importancia.
Education is very important.

importante (FEM **importante**)
ADJECTIVE
important
lo importante
the important thing
Lo importante es que vengas.
The important thing is that you come.

importar VERB
to matter
¿Y eso qué importa?
And what does that matter?
no importa
it doesn't matter/never mind

> *Language tip*
> **no importa** *has two meanings. Look at the examples.*

No importa lo que piensen los demás.
It doesn't matter what other people think.
No importa, podemos hacerlo mañana.
Never mind, we can do it tomorrow.
No me importa levantarme temprano.
I don't mind getting up early.
¿Le importa que abra la ventana?
Do you mind if I open the window?

imposible (FEM **imposible**)
ADJECTIVE
impossible
Es imposible predecir quién ganará.
It's impossible to predict who will win.
Es imposible que lo sepan.
They can't possibly know.

imprescindible
(FEM **imprescindible**) ADJECTIVE
essential

la **impresión** (PL las
impresiones) NOUN
impression
Le causó muy buena impresión a mis padres.
He made a very good impression on my parents.
Tengo la impresión de que no va a venir.
I have a feeling that he won't come.

impresionante
(FEM **impresionante**) ADJECTIVE
1 **impressive**
una colección de sellos impresionante
an impressive stamp collection
2 **amazing**
una cantidad impresionante de videojuegos

a b c d e f g h i j k l m n ñ o p q r s t u v w x y z

Spanish

English

a
b
c
d
e
f
g
h
i
j
k
l
m
n
ñ
o
p
q
r
s
t
u
v
w
x
y
z

an amazing number of videogames

imprimir VERB
to print

inaceptable
(FEM **inaceptable**) ADJECTIVE
unacceptable

incapaz (FEM **incapaz**,
PL **incapaces**) ADJECTIVE
incapable
Es incapaz de estarse callado.
He is incapable of keeping quiet.
Hoy soy incapaz de concentrarme.
I can't concentrate today.

el **incendio** NOUN
fire
Se declaró un incendio en el hotel.
A fire broke out in the hotel.

el **incidente** NOUN
incident

inclinarse VERB
to lean
inclinarse hacia delante
to lean forward
inclinarse hacia atrás
to lean back

incluido (FEM **incluida**)
ADJECTIVE
included
El servicio no está incluido en el precio.
Service is not included.

incluir VERB
to include
El precio incluye las comidas.
The price includes meals.

incluso ADVERB
even
He tenido que estudiar incluso los domingos.
I've even had to study on Sundays.

incluyendo VERB ▷see **incluir**
Somos cinco, incluyendo a mi abuela.
It's five of us, including my grandmother.

incómodo (FEM **incómoda**)
ADJECTIVE
uncomfortable
Este asiento es muy incómodo.
This seat is very uncomfortable.

inconsciente
(FEM **inconsciente**) ADJECTIVE
unconscious
Quedó inconsciente con el golpe.
The force of the blow left him unconscious.

inconveniente

inconveniente *can be an adjective or a noun.*

A (FEM **inconveniente**) ADJECTIVE
inconvenient
a una hora inconveniente
at an inconvenient time
B MASC NOUN
problem
Ha surgido un inconveniente.
A problem has come up.

incorrecto (FEM **incorrecta**)
ADJECTIVE
incorrect
una respuesta incorrecta
an incorrect answer

increíble (FEM **increíble**)
ADJECTIVE
incredible

indicar VERB
to indicate
El termómetro indicaba treinta grados.
The thermometer indicated thirty degrees.

el **índice** NOUN
1 **index**
un índice alfabético
an alphabetical index
el índice de materias
the table of contents
2 **index finger**

la **indirecta** NOUN
hint

individual (FEM **individual**)
ADJECTIVE
1 **individual**
Los venden en paquetes individuales.
They're sold in individual packets.
2 **single**
Quisiera una habitación individual.
I'd like a single room.

la **industria** NOUN
industry

inesperado (FEM **inesperada**)
ADJECTIVE
unexpected
una visita inesperada
an unexpected visit

infantil (FEM **infantil**) ADJECTIVE

1 **children's**
un programa infantil
a children's programme
2 **childish**
¡No seas tan infantil!
Don't be so childish!

el **infarto** NOUN
heart attack
Le dio un infarto.
He had a heart attack.

la **infección** (PL las **infecciones**)
NOUN
infection
tener una infección
to have an infection
Tiene una infección de oídos.
He has got an ear infection.

el **infierno** NOUN
hell

el **infinitivo** NOUN
infinitive

inflar VERB
1 **to blow up**
2 **to inflate**

la **información** (PL las **informaciones**) NOUN
information
Quisiera información sobre cursos de inglés.
I'd like some information on English courses.
una información muy importante
a very important piece of information

informal (FEM **informal**)
ADJECTIVE
1 **informal**
un ambiente muy informal
a very informal atmosphere
Prefiero la ropa informal.
I prefer casual clothes.
2 **unreliable**
Es una persona muy informal.
He's a very unreliable person.

Spanish **English**

a b c d e f g h i j k l m n ñ o p q r s t u v w x y z

informar VERB
to inform
Nos informaron de que venía con retraso.
They informed us that it was going to be late.
¿Me podría informar sobre los cursos de inglés?
Could you give me some information about English courses?

la **informática** NOUN
1 **computing**
los avances de la informática
advances in computing
Quiere estudiar informática.
He wants to study computer science.

2 **computer expert**

informático

informático *can be an adjective or a noun.*

A (FEM **informática**) ADJECTIVE
computer
un programa informático
a computer program
B MASC NOUN
computer expert

el **informe** NOUN
report
Presentó un informe detallado sobre lo ocurrido.
He gave a detailed report about what had happened.

Inglaterra FEM NOUN
England

inglés

inglés *can be an adjective or a noun.*

A (FEM **inglesa**, MASC PL **ingleses**)
ADJECTIVE
English
la comida inglesa
English food
B MASC/FEM NOUN
un inglés
an Englishman
una inglesa
an Englishwoman
los ingleses
English people
C MASC NOUN
English
Estudio inglés.
I'm studying English.

el **ingrediente** NOUN
ingredient

ingresar VERB
ingresar en el hospital
to go into hospital
ingresar en un club
to join a club

el **inhalador** NOUN
inhaler

la **inicial** NOUN
initial

injusto (FEM **injusta**) ADJECTIVE
unfair

inmediato (FEM **inmediata**)
ADJECTIVE
immediate

de inmediato
immediately

el/la **inmigrante** NOUN
immigrant

inocente (FEM **inocente**)
ADJECTIVE
innocent
Soy inocente.
I'm innocent.

inolvidable (FEM **inolvidable**)
ADJECTIVE
unforgettable

inquietante (FEM **inquietante**)
ADJECTIVE
worrying

inquieto (FEM **inquieta**)
ADJECTIVE
worried
> **Estaba inquieta porque su hijo no había llegado a casa.**
> She was worried because her son hadn't come home.

insatisfecho
(FEM **insatisfecha**) ADJECTIVE
dissatisfied

inscribirse VERB
to enrol
> **Se inscribió en un curso de idiomas.**
> He enrolled on a language course.

inscrito VERB ▷see **inscribirse**
> **Estoy inscrito en un curso de informática.**
> I've enrolled on a computing course.

el **insecto** NOUN
insect

inseguro (FEM **insegura**)
ADJECTIVE
1 **insecure**
2 **unsafe**

insistir VERB
to insist
> **Insistió en hablar conmigo.**
> He insisted on talking to me.

insolente (FEM **insolente**)
ADJECTIVE
insolent

insoportable
(FEM **insoportable**) ADJECTIVE
unbearable

el **inspector**

la **inspectora** NOUN
inspector

el **instante** NOUN
moment
> **A cada instante suena el teléfono.**
> The phone rings all the time.

el **instinto** NOUN
instinct

el **instituto** NOUN
institute
> **un instituto de enseñanza secundaria**
> a secondary school
> **un instituto de bachillerato**
> a secondary school

Did you know...?

In Spain the **institutos de bachillerato** *are state secondary schools for 12- to 18-year-olds.*

las **instrucciones** NOUN
instructions

el **instructor**
la **instructora** NOUN
instructor
> **un instructor de esquí**
> a ski instructor
> **un instructor de autoescuela**
> a driving instructor

el **instrumento** NOUN
instrument

insuficiente

insuficiente *can be an adjective or a noun.*

A (FEM **insuficiente**) ADJECTIVE
insufficient
> **una cantidad insuficiente de dinero**
> an insufficient amount of money

B MASC NOUN
> **Sacó un insuficiente en francés.**
> He got an F in French.

Spanish

English

a
b
c
d
e
f
g
h
i
j
k
l
m
n
ñ
o
p
q
r
s
t
u
v
w
x
y
z

insultar VERB
to insult

el **insulto** NOUN
insult

la **inteligencia** NOUN
intelligence

inteligente (FEM **inteligente**)
ADJECTIVE
intelligent

la **intención** (PL las
intenciones) NOUN
intention
> **No tengo la más mínima
intención de hacerlo.**
> I haven't got the slightest
> intention of doing it.
> **tener intención de hacer algo**
> to intend to do something
> **Tenía intención de descansar
un rato.**
> He intended to rest for a while.

intensivo (FEM **intensiva**)
ADJECTIVE
intensive
> **un curso intensivo de inglés**
> an intensive English course

intenso (FEM **intensa**) ADJECTIVE
intense

intentar VERB
to try
> **¿Por qué no lo intentas
otra vez?**
> Why don't you try again?
> **intentar hacer algo**
> to try to do something
> **Voy a intentar llamarle esta
noche.**
> I'm going to try to call him
> tonight.

el **intento** NOUN
attempt
> **Aprobó al primer intento.**
> He passed at the first attempt.

el **intercambio** NOUN
exchange

el **interés** (PL los **intereses**)
NOUN
interest
> **Tienes que poner más interés
en tus estudios.**
> You must take more of an
> interest in your studies.

interesante (FEM **interesante**)
ADJECTIVE
interesting

interesar VERB
to interest
> **Eso es algo que siempre me
ha interesado.**
> That's something that has
> always interested me.
> **Me interesa mucho la física.**
> I'm very interested in physics.

interior

> interior *can be an adjective or a
noun.*

A (FEM **interior**) ADJECTIVE
inside
B MASC NOUN
inside
> **el interior del túnel**
> the inside of the tunnel

el **intermedio** NOUN
interval

el **intermitente** NOUN
indicator

internacional
(FEM **internacional**) ADJECTIVE
international

el/la **internauta** NOUN
internet user

el/la **Internet** NOUN
the internet
> **en Internet**
> on the internet

interno
interna

> *interno can be an adjective or a noun.*

A ADJECTIVE
> **estar interno en un colegio**
> to be at boarding school

B MASC/FEM NOUN
boarder

interpretar VERB
to play
> **Interpreta el papel de Victoria.**
> She plays the part of Victoria.

el/la **intérprete** NOUN
interpreter
> **Quiere ser intérprete.**
> She wants to be an interpreter.

interrogar VERB
to question
> **Fue interrogado por la policía.**
> He was questioned by the police.

interrumpir VERB
to interrupt

la **interrupción** (PL las interrupciones) NOUN
interruption

el **interruptor** NOUN
switch

intervenir VERB
1 to take part
> **No intervino en el debate.**
> He did not take part in the debate.
2 to intervene
> **La policía intervino para separarlos.**
> The police intervened to separate them.

intimidar VERB
to intimidate

íntimo (FEM **íntima**) ADJECTIVE
intimate
> **mis secretos íntimos**
> my intimate secrets
> **Es un amigo íntimo.**
> He's a close friend.

la **introducción** (PL las introducciones) NOUN
introduction

introducir VERB
1 to introduce
2 to insert
> **Introdujo la moneda en la ranura.**
> He inserted the coin in the slot.

la **inundación** (PL las inundaciones) NOUN
flood

inundar VERB
to flood
> **El río inundó el pueblo.**
> The river flooded the village.
■ **inundarse**
to be flooded
> **Se nos inundó el baño.**
> Our bathroom was flooded.

inútil (FEM **inútil**)

> *inútil can be an adjective or a noun.*

A ADJECTIVE
useless
> **La oficina está llena de trastos inútiles.**
> The office is full of useless rubbish.
> **Es inútil tratar de hacerle entender.**
> It's useless trying to make him understand.

B MASC/FEM NOUN
> **¡Es un inútil!**
> He's useless!

a
b
c
d
e
f
g
h
i
j
k
l
m
n
ñ
o
p
q
r
s
t
u
v
w
x
y
z

a b c d e f g h i j k l m n ñ o p q r s t u v w x y z

invadir VERB
   to invade

inventar VERB
   1 to invent
      Inventaron un nuevo sistema.
      They invented a new system.
   2 to make up
      Inventó toda la historia.
      He made up the whole story.

el **invento** NOUN
   invention

el **inventor**
la **inventora** NOUN
   inventor

el **invernadero** NOUN
   greenhouse
      el efecto invernadero
      the greenhouse effect

invernar VERB
   to hibernate

invertir VERB
   to invest
      Hemos invertido muchas horas en el proyecto.
      We've invested a lot of time in the project.

el **invierno** NOUN
   winter

en invierno
in winter

invisible (FEM **invisible**)
   ADJECTIVE
   invisible

la **invitación** (PL las **invitaciones**) NOUN
   invitation

el **invitado**
la **invitada** NOUN
   guest
      Es el invitado de honor.
      He's the guest of honour.

invitar VERB
   to invite
      Me invitó a una fiesta.
      He invited me to a party.
      Me gustaría invitarla a cenar.
      I'd like to invite her to dinner.
      Te invito a una Coca-Cola.
      I'll buy you a Coke.
      Esta vez invito yo.
      This time it's on me.

la **inyección** (PL las **inyecciones**) NOUN
   injection
      poner una inyección a alguien
      to give someone an injection

el **iPod**® NOUN
   iPod®

ir VERB
   1 to go
      ¿A qué colegio vas?
      What school do you go to?
      Anoche fuimos al cine.
      We went to the cinema last night.
      ir a por
      to go and get
      Voy a por el paraguas.
      I'll go and get the umbrella.
      Voy a hacerlo mañana.
      I'm going to do it tomorrow.
      vamos
      let's go

Vamos a casa.
Let's go home.
¡Vamos!
Come on!
¡Vamos! ¡Di algo!
Come on! Say something!
2 **to come**
¡Ahora voy!
I'm just coming!
¿Puedo ir contigo?
Can I come with you?
3 **to be**
Va muy bien vestido.
He's very well dressed.
Iba con su madre.
He was with his mother.
Va a ser difícil.
It's going to be difficult.

ir a pie
to walk
ir en avión
to fly
ir de vacaciones
to go on holiday
¡Qué va!
No way!

■ **irse** VERB
to leave
Acaba de irse.
He has just left.
Vete a hacer los deberes.
Go and do your homework.
¡Vámonos!
Let's go!
¡Vete!
Go away!

Irlanda FEM NOUN
Ireland

irlandés
irlandesa
(MASC PL **irlandeses**)

irlandés can be an adjective or
a noun.

A ADJECTIVE
Irish
un café irlandés
an Irish coffee

B MASC/FEM NOUN
un irlandés
an Irishman
una irlandesa
an Irishwoman
los irlandeses
Irish people

irónico (FEM **irónica**) ADJECTIVE
ironic

irresistible (FEM **irresistible**)
ADJECTIVE
irresistible

irresponsable
(FEM **irresponsable**) ADJECTIVE
irresponsible

irritar VERB
to irritate

la **isla** NOUN
island
una isla desierta
a desert island

el **Islam** NOUN
Islam

la **izquierda** NOUN
1 **left hand**
Escribo con la izquierda.
I write with my left hand.
2 **left**
doblar a la izquierda
to turn left
a la izquierda
on the left
**la segunda calle a la
izquierda**
the second turning on the left
a la izquierda del edificio
to the left of the building

izquierdo (FEM **izquierda**)
ADJECTIVE
left
Levanta la mano izquierda.
Raise your left hand.
Escribo con la mano izquierda.
I write with my left hand.

a
b
c
d
e
f
g
h
i
j
k
l
m
n
ñ
o
p
q
r
s
t
u
v
w
x
y
z

Language tip
*In Spanish you usually use an article
like* **el**, **la** *or* **los**, **las** *with parts of
the body.*

el lado izquierdo
the left side
a mano izquierda
on the left-hand side

a b c d e f g h i j k l m n ñ o p q r s t u v w x y z

J j

el **jabón** (PL los **jabones**) NOUN
soap

jamás ADVERB
never
> **Jamás he visto nada parecido.**
> I've never seen anything like it.

el **jamón** (PL los **jamones**) NOUN
ham
> **un bocadillo de jamón**
> a ham sandwich
> **jamón serrano**
> cured ham
> **jamón de York**
> cooked ham

el **jarabe** NOUN
syrup
> **un jarabe para la tos**
> a cough syrup

el **jardín** (PL los **jardines**) NOUN
garden
> **Tienen una piscina en el jardín.**
> They have a swimming pool in the garden.
> **jardín de infancia**
> nursery school

la **jarra** NOUN
jug
> **una jarra de agua**
> a jug of water

el **jarrón** (PL los **jarrones**) NOUN
vase

el **jefe**
la **jefa** NOUN
boss
> **Carlos es el jefe.**
> Carlos is the boss.

el **jersey**
(PL los **jerséis**)
NOUN
jumper

Jesús
EXCLAMATION
Bless you!

joven (FEM **joven**, PL **jóvenes**)

> *joven can be an adjective or a noun.*

A ADJECTIVE
young
> **una chica joven**
> a young girl

B MASC/FEM NOUN
> **un joven**
> a young man
> **una joven**
> a young woman
> **los jóvenes**
> young people

la **joya** NOUN
jewel
> **Me han robado las joyas.**
> My jewellery has been stolen.

jubilado
jubilada

> *jubilado can be an adjective or a noun.*

A ADJECTIVE
retired
> **estar jubilado**
> to be retired

B MASC/FEM NOUN
pensioner

jubilarse VERB
  to retire

la **judía** NOUN
  1 Jew
  2 bean
    judía verde
    green bean

el **judío** NOUN
  Jew

el **judo** NOUN
  judo

juego

> **juego** *can be a noun or part of the verb* **jugar**.

A MASC NOUN
  game
    un juego de ordenador
    a computer game
    juegos de cartas
    card games
    un juego de café
    a coffee set
    No hace juego con la falda.
    It doesn't go with the skirt.
B VERB ▷*see* **jugar**
    Juego al tenis todos los días.
    I play tennis every day.

la **juerga** NOUN
    irse de juerga
    to go out on the town

el **jueves** (PL los **jueves**) NOUN
  Thursday

> **Language tip**
> *Days of the week are not spelled with a capital letter in Spanish.*

    La vi el jueves.
    I saw her on Thursday.

> **el jueves que viene**
> next Thursday
> **el jueves pasado**
> last Thursday
> **todos los jueves**
> every Thursday

el **jugador**
  la **jugadora** NOUN
  player

jugar VERB
  to play
    Los domingos jugamos al fútbol.
    We play football on Sundays.
    jugar una partida de dominó
    to have a game of dominoes

el **juguete** NOUN
  toy
    un avión de juguete
    a toy plane

julio MASC NOUN
  July

> **Language tip**
> *Months are not spelled with a capital letter in Spanish.*

> **en julio**
> in July
> **Nació el cuatro de julio.**
> He was born on the fourth of July.

junio MASC NOUN
  June

> **Language tip**
> *Months are not written with a capital letter in Spanish.*

> **en junio**
> in June
> **Nació el veinte de junio.**
> He was born on the twentieth of June.

juntar VERB
  to put together
    Vamos a juntar los pupitres.
    Let's put the desks together.
  ■ **juntarse**
    to move closer together/to get together

> **Language tip**
> **juntarse** *has two meanings. Look at the examples.*

Si os juntáis más, cabremos todos.
If you move closer together, we'll all fit in.
Nos juntamos para ver el partido.
We got together to watch the match.

junto (FEM **junta**)

junto *can be an adjective or an adverb.*

A ADJECTIVE
together

Cuando estamos juntos lo pasamos muy bien.
We have a good time when we're together.
todo junto
all together
Ponlo todo junto en una bolsa.
Put it all together in one bag.
Los muebles están muy juntos.
The furniture is too close together.

B ADVERB
junto a
by
Hay una mesa junto a la ventana.
There's a table by the window.
Mi apellido se escribe todo junto.
My surname is all one word.

jurar VERB
to swear

la **justicia** NOUN
justice

justo (FEM **justa**)

justo *can be an adjective or an adverb.*

A ADJECTIVE
1 **fair**
No es justo.
It's not fair.
2 **tight**
Me están muy justos estos pantalones.
These trousers are tight on me.
3 **just enough**
Tengo el dinero justo para un bocadillo.
I have just enough money for a sandwich.
en el momento justo
at the right time
B ADVERB
just
Está justo al doblar la esquina.
It's just round the corner.
Me dio un golpe justo en la nariz.
He hit me right on the nose.

juvenil (FEM **juvenil**) ADJECTIVE
young
la moda juvenil
young people's fashion
el equipo juvenil
the youth team

la **juventud** NOUN
youth
Fue soldado en su juventud.
He was a soldier in his youth.

a b c d e f g h i **j** k l m n ñ o p q r s t u v w x y z

K k

el kárate NOUN
karate

el kilo NOUN
kilo
> **un kilo de tomates**
> a kilo of tomatoes

el kilogramo NOUN
kilogramme

el kilómetro NOUN
kilometre
> **Está a tres kilómetros de aquí.**
> It's three kilometres from here.
> **a noventa kilómetros por hora**
> at ninety kilometres an hour

el kiosco NOUN
news stand

> **Did you know…?**
>
> In Spain you'll come across **kioscos**, newsstands on the street which sell newspapers, magazines and other items.

L l

la

la can be an article or a pronoun.

A ARTICLE
the
la pared
the wall
la del sombrero rojo
the girl in the red hat
Yo fui la que te desperté.
I was the one who woke you up.
Ayer me lavé la cabeza.
I washed my hair yesterday.
Abróchate la camisa.
Do your shirt up.
No me gusta la fruta.
I don't like fruit.

Vendrá la semana que viene.
He'll come next week.
Me he encontrado a la Sra. Sendra.
I bumped into Mrs Sendra.
B PRONOUN
1 her
La quiero.
I love her.
La han despedido.
She has been sacked.
2 you
La acompaño hasta la puerta.
I'll see you out.
3 it
No la toques.
Don't touch it.

el **labio** NOUN
lip

el **lado** NOUN
side
a los dos lados de la carretera
on both sides of the road
Hay gente por todos lados.
There are people everywhere.
Tiene que estar en otro lado.
It must be somewhere else.
Mi casa está aquí al lado.
My house is right nearby.
al lado de
beside
la silla que está al lado del armario
the chair beside the wardrobe
Felipe se sentó a mi lado.
Felipe sat beside me.

ladrar VERB
to bark
El perro les ladró.
The dog barked at them.

el **ladrillo** NOUN
brick

el **ladrón**
la **ladrona** NOUN
1 thief
Un ladrón me quitó el bolso.
A thief took my bag.
2 burglar
Los ladrones entraron en la casa.
The burglars broke into the house.
3 robber
Tres ladrones atracaron el banco.
Three robbers raided the bank.

el **lago** NOUN
lake

la **lágrima** NOUN
tear

lamentar VERB
>**Lamento lo ocurrido.**
>I am sorry about what happened.
- **lamentarse**
  to complain
  >**De nada vale lamentarse.**
  >There's no use complaining.

la **lámpara** NOUN
lamp

la **lancha** NOUN
motorboat
>**una lancha de salvamento**
>a lifeboat

lanzar VERB
to throw
>**Lanzó una piedra al río.**
>He threw a stone into the river.
- **lanzarse**
  to dive
  >**Los niños se lanzaron a la piscina.**
  >The children dived into the swimming pool.

el **lápiz** (PL los **lápices**) NOUN
pencil
>**Escríbelo a lápiz.**
>Write it in pencil.

>**los lápices de colores**
>crayons

largo

largo can be an adjective or a noun.

A (FEM **larga**) ADJECTIVE
long
>**Esta cuerda es demasiado larga.**
>This piece of string is too long.

B MASC NOUN
length
>**Nadé cuatro largos de la piscina.**
>I swam four lengths of the pool.
>**¿Cuánto mide de largo?**
>How long is it?
>**Tiene nueve metros de largo.**
>It's nine metres long.
>**a lo largo del río**
>along the river
>**a lo largo de la semana**
>throughout the week
>**Pasó de largo sin saludar.**
>He passed by without saying hello.

Language tip
Be careful! **largo** *does not mean the same as* **large**.

las

las can be an article or a pronoun.

A ARTICLE
the
>**las paredes**
>the walls
>**las del estante de arriba**
>the ones on the top shelf
>**Me duelen las piernas.**
>My legs hurt.
>**Poneos las bufandas.**
>Put on your scarves.
>**No me gustan las arañas.**
>I don't like spiders.
>**Vino a las seis de la tarde.**
>He came at six in the evening.
B PRONOUN
1 them
>**Las vi por la calle.**
>I saw them in the street.
>**Las han despedido.**
>They've been sacked.
2 you
>**Las acompañaré hasta la puerta, señoras.**
>I'll see you out, ladies.

la **lata** NOUN
1 tin

2 can
  Deja de dar la lata.
  Stop being a pain.

el **latido** NOUN
  beat

el **lavabo** NOUN
  1 sink
  Llené el lavabo de agua.
  I filled the sink with water.
  2 toilet

  Voy al lavabo.
  I'm going to the toilet.

la **lavadora** NOUN
  washing machine

lavar VERB
  to wash
  Lava estos vasos.
  Wash these glasses.
  lavar la ropa
  to do the washing
  ▪ **lavarse**
  to wash
  Me lavo todos los días.
  I wash every day.
  Ayer me lavé la cabeza.
  I washed my hair yesterday.
  Lávate los dientes.
  Brush your teeth.

el **lazo** NOUN
  1 bow
  2 ribbon

le PRONOUN
  1 him
  Le mandé una carta.
  I sent him a letter.
  Le miré con atención.
  I watched him carefully.

Le abrí la puerta.
I opened the door for him.
Le huelen los pies.
His feet smell.
  2 her
  Le mandé una carta.
  I sent her a letter.
  No le hablé de ti.
  I didn't speak to her about you.
  Le busqué el libro.
  I looked for the book for her.
  3 you
  Le presento a la Sra. Gutiérrez.
  Let me introduce you to Mrs Gutiérrez.
  Le he arreglado el ordenador.
  I've fixed the computer for you.

la **lección** (PL las **lecciones**)
NOUN
  lesson

la **leche** NOUN
  milk
  la leche desnatada
  skimmed milk

leer VERB
  to read

lejos ADVERB
  far
  ¿Está lejos?
  Is it far?
  No está lejos de aquí.
  It's not far from here.
  De lejos parecía un avión.
  From a distance it looked like a plane.

la **lengua** NOUN
  tongue
  Me he mordido la lengua.
  I've bitten my tongue.
  mi lengua materna
  my mother tongue

el **lenguaje** NOUN
  language

a b c d e f g h i j k l m n ñ o p q r s t u v w x y z

la **lente** NOUN
lense
> **las lentes de contacto**
> contact lenses

la **lentilla** NOUN
contact lens

lento

> *lento can be an adjective or an adverb.*

> **A** (FEM **lenta**) ADJECTIVE
> **slow**
> > **un proceso lento**
> > a slow progress
> **B** ADVERB
> **slowly**
> > **Vas un poco lento.**
> > You're going a bit slowly.

el **león** (PL los **leones**) NOUN
lion

la **leona** NOUN
lioness

les PRONOUN
> **1** **them**
> > **Les mandé una carta.**
> > I sent them a letter.
> > **Les miré con atención.**
> > I watched them carefully.
> > **Les abrí la puerta.**
> > I opened the door for them.
> > **Les eché de comer a los gatos.**
> > I gave the cats something to eat.
> **2** **you**
> > **Les presento a la Sra. Gutiérrez.**
> > Let me introduce you to Mrs Gutiérrez.

> **Les he arreglado el ordenador.**
> I've fixed the computer for you.

la **lesión** (PL las **lesiones**) NOUN
injury

la **letra** NOUN
> **1** **letter**
> > **la letra 'a'**
> > the letter 'a'
> **2** **handwriting**
> > **Tengo muy mala letra.**
> > My handwriting's very poor.

el **letrero** NOUN
sign

levantar VERB
to lift
> > **Levanta la tapa.**
> > Lift the lid.
> > **Levantad la mano si tenéis alguna duda.**
> > Raise your hand if you are unclear.
> ■ **levantarse**
> **to get up**
> > **Hoy me he levantado temprano.**
> > I got up early this morning.
> > **Me levanté y seguí caminando.**
> > I got up and carried on walking.

la **ley** (PL las **leyes**) NOUN
law
> > **la ley de la gravedad**
> > the law of gravity

leyendo VERB ▷ *see* **leer**
> **Estaba leyendo el periódico.**
> I was reading the newspaper.

liar VERB
to confuse
> > **Me liaron con tantas explicaciones.**
> > They confused me with all their explanations.
> > **A mí no me líes en esto.**
> > Don't get me mixed up in this.

■ **liarse**
to get muddled up
Me estoy liando, empezaré otra vez.
I'm getting muddled up, I'll start again.

la **libra** NOUN
pound
libra esterlina
pound sterling

librarse VERB
librarse de
to get out of/to get rid of

Language tip
librarse de *has two meanings. Look at the examples.*

¡No te librarás de fregar los platos!
You're not going to get out of doing the washing-up!
Logré librarme de mi hermana.
I managed to get rid of my sister.

libre (FEM **libre**) ADJECTIVE
free
¿Está libre este asiento?
Is this seat free?
El martes estoy libre.
I'm free on Tuesday.

la **librería** NOUN
bookshop

Language tip
Be careful! **librería** *does not mean* **library**.

la **libreta** NOUN
notebook

el **libro** NOUN
book
un libro de texto
a text book

ligero (FEM **ligera**) ADJECTIVE
1 **light**
Me gusta llevar ropa ligera.
I like to wear light clothing.

Comimos algo ligero.
We ate something light.
2 **slight**
Tengo un ligero dolor de cabeza.
I have a slight headache.
Andaba a paso ligero.
He walked quickly.

el **límite** NOUN
limit
el límite de velocidad
the speed limit
fecha límite
deadline

el **limón** (PL los **limones**) NOUN
lemon

limpiar VERB
1 **to clean**
El sábado voy a limpiar mi habitación.
I'm going to clean my room on Saturday.
2 **to wipe**
¿Has limpiado la mesa?
Have you wiped the table?
Límpiate la nariz.
Wipe your nose.

la **limpieza** NOUN
cleaning
Mi madre hace la limpieza los sábados.
My mum does the cleaning on Saturdays.

limpio (FEM **limpia**) ADJECTIVE
clean
El baño está muy limpio.
The bathroom's very clean.
Voy a pasar esto a limpio.

I'm going to write this out in neat.

la línea NOUN
line
> **Dibujó una línea recta.**
> He drew a straight line.
> **una línea aérea**
> an airline
> **estar en línea**
> to be online

el lío NOUN
muddle
> **hacerse un lío**
> to get muddled up
> **Se hizo un lío con tantos nombres.**
> He got muddled up with all the names.

el líquido NOUN
liquid

liso (FEM **lisa**) ADJECTIVE
1 **smooth**
2 **straight**

la lista NOUN
list
> **la lista de espera**
> the waiting list
> **pasar lista**
> to call the register

listo (FEM **lista**) ADJECTIVE
1 **clever**
> **Es una chica muy lista.**
> She's a very clever girl.
2 **ready**
> **¿Estás listo?**
> Are you ready?

la litera NOUN
bunk bed

la literatura NOUN
literature

el litro NOUN
litre

la llama NOUN
flame

la llamada NOUN
call
> **hacer una llamada telefónica**
> to make a phone call

llamar VERB
1 **to call**
> **Me llamaron mentiroso.**
> They called me a liar.
> **llamar a la policía**
> to call the police
> **llamar por teléfono a alguien**
> to phone somebody
> **Te llamaré por teléfono mañana.**
> I will phone you tomorrow.
2 **to ring**
3 **to knock**
> **llamar a la puerta**
> to knock at the door

> **¿Cómo te llamas?**
> What's your name?
> **Me llamo Adela.**
> My name's Adela.

llano (FEM **llana**) ADJECTIVE
flat

la llave NOUN
key

> **las llaves del coche**
> the car keys

el llavero NOUN
keyring

la llegada NOUN
1 **arrival**
2 **finish**

llegar VERB
1 **to arrive**

a b c d e f g h i j k l m n ñ o p q r s t u v w x y z

El avión llega a las dos.
The plane arrives at two o'clock.
Acabamos de llegar.
We've just arrived.
Llegamos tarde.
We were late.

2 **llegar a**
to get to
Llegamos a Granada a las cinco.
We got to Granada at five o'clock.
¿A qué hora llegaste a casa?
What time did you get home?

3 **to reach**
No llego al estante de arriba.
I can't reach the top shelf.
El agua me llegaba hasta las rodillas.
The water came up to my knees.

llenar VERB
to fill
Llena la jarra de agua.
Fill the jug with water.

lleno (FEM **llena**) ADJECTIVE
full
Todos los hoteles están llenos.
All the hotels are full.
El restaurante estaba lleno de gente.
The restaurant was full of people.

llevar VERB
1 **to take**
¿Llevas los vasos a la cocina?
Can you take the glasses to the kitchen?
No llevará mucho tiempo.
It won't take long.

2 **to wear**
María llevaba un abrigo muy bonito.
María was wearing a nice coat.

3 **to give a lift**
Sofía nos llevó a casa.
Sofía gave us a lift home.

4 **to carry**
Yo te llevo la maleta.
I'll carry your case.
¿Cuánto tiempo llevas aquí?
How long have you been here?
Llevo horas esperando aquí.
I've been waiting here for hours.
Mi hermana mayor me lleva ocho años.
My elder sister is eight years older than me.
llevarse algo
to take something
Llévatelo.
Take it with you.
¿Le gusta? — Sí, me lo llevo.
Do you like it? — Yes, I'll take it.
Me llevo bien con mi hermano.
I get on well with my brother.
Nos llevamos muy mal.
We don't get on at all.

llorar VERB
to cry

llover VERB
to rain

llueve VERB ▷ see **llover**
Llueve mucho.
It's raining hard.

la **lluvia** NOUN
rain

bajo la lluvia
in the rain

lluvioso (FEM **lluviosa**)
ADJECTIVE
rainy

Spanish
English

a
b
c
d
e
f
g
h
i
j
k
l
m
n
ñ
o
p
q
r
s
t
u
v
w
x
y
z

lo

> **lo** *can be an article or a pronoun.*

A ARTICLE

Lo peor fue que no pudimos entrar.
The worst thing was we couldn't get in.

Pon en mi habitación lo de Pedro.
Put Pedro's things in my room.

Lo mío son las matemáticas.
Maths is my thing.

Olvida lo de ayer.
Forget what happened yesterday.

¡No sabes lo aburrido que es!
You don't know how boring he is!

lo que
what/whatever

Language tip

lo que *has two meanings. Look at the examples.*

Lo que más me gusta es nadar.
What I like most is swimming.

Ponte lo que quieras.
Wear whatever you like.

más de lo que
more than

Cuesta más de lo que crees.
It costs more than you think.

B PRONOUN

1 him

No lo conozco.
I don't know him.

Lo han despedido.
He's been sacked.

2 you

Yo a usted lo conozco.
I know you.

3 it

No lo veo.
I can't see it.

Voy a pensarlo.
I'll think about it.

No lo sabía.
I didn't know.

No parece lista pero lo es.
She doesn't seem clever but she is.

local (FEM local) ADJECTIVE
local

un producto local
a local product

loco
loca

> **loco** *can be an adjective or a noun.*

A ADJECTIVE
mad

volver loco a alguien
to drive somebody mad

Me estás volviendo loco.
You're driving me mad.

volverse loco
to go mad

¿Estás loco?
Are you mad?

Está loco con su moto nueva.
He's mad about his new motorbike.

Me vuelve loco el marisco.
I'm mad about seafood.

B MASC/FEM NOUN

un loco
a madman

una loca
a madwoman

la locura NOUN
madness

Es una locura ir solo.
It's madness to go on your own.

lógico (FEM lógica) ADJECTIVE
natural

Es lógico que no quiera venir.
It's only natural he doesn't want to come.

lograr VERB
to manage

Logré escaparme de ellos.
I managed to get away from them.

la **longitud** NOUN
length
>Tiene tres metros de longitud.
>It's three metres long.

los

>**los** can be an article or a pronoun.

A ARTICLE
the
los barcos
the boats
los de las bufandas rojas
the people in the red scarves
Se lavaron los pies en el río.
They washed their feet in the river.
Abrochaos los abrigos.
Button up your coats.
Me gustan sus cuadros, pero prefiero los de Ana.
I like his paintings, but I prefer Ana's.
No me gustan los melocotones.
I don't like peaches.
Solo vienen los lunes.
They only come on Mondays.

B PRONOUN
1 them
Los vi por la calle.
I saw them in the street.
Los han despedido.
They've been sacked.

2 you
Los acompaño hasta la puerta, señores.
I'll see you to the door, gentlemen.

la **lotería** NOUN
lottery
>Le tocó la lotería.
>He won the lottery.

la **lucha** NOUN
fight
lucha libre
wrestling

luchar VERB
to fight

luego ADVERB
1 then
Primero se puso de pie y luego habló.
First he stood up and then he spoke.

2 later
Mi hermana viene luego.
My sister's coming later.
desde luego
of course
¡Desde luego que me gusta!
Of course I like it!

¡Hasta luego!
See you!

el **lugar** NOUN
place
>Este lugar es muy bonito.
>This is a lovely place.
Llegó en último lugar.
He came last.

el **lujo** NOUN
luxury
un apartamento de lujo
a luxury apartment

la **luna** NOUN
moon
la luna de miel
honeymoon

el **lunar** NOUN
mole

el **lunes** (PL los **lunes**) NOUN
Monday

Language tip
The days of the week are not spelled with a capital letter in Spanish.

>La vi el lunes.
>I saw her on Monday.

todos los lunes
every Monday
el lunes pasado
last Monday
el lunes que viene
next Monday

139

Spanish English

a
b
c
d
e
f
g
h
i
j
k
l
m
n
ñ
o
p
q
r
s
t
u
v
w
x
y
z

la **lupa** NOUN
magnifying glass

la **luz** (PL las **luces**) NOUN
light

Enciende la luz, por favor.
Put on the light please.

M m

los **macarrones** NOUN
macaroni
>**Me gustan los macarrones.**
>I like macaroni.

la **maceta** NOUN
flowerpot

macho ADJECTIVE, MASC NOUN
male
>**una rata macho**
>a male rat

la **madera** NOUN
wood
>**Está hecho de madera.**
>It's made of wood.
>**un juguete de madera**
>a wooden toy

la **madre** NOUN
mother

la **madrugada** NOUN
early morning
>**a las cuatro de la madrugada**
>at four o'clock in the morning

madrugar VERB
to get up early

maduro (FEM **madura**)
ADJECTIVE
1 ripe
2 mature

el **maestro**
la **maestra** NOUN
teacher
>**Mi tía es maestra.**
>My aunt's a teacher.

la **magia** NOUN
magic

mágico
(FEM **mágica**)
ADJECTIVE
magic
>**una varita mágica**
>a magic wand

majo (FEM **maja**) ADJECTIVE
1 nice
2 pretty

mal

> **mal** *can be an adverb, a noun or an adjective.*

A ADVERB
1 badly
>**Toca la guitarra muy mal.**
>He plays the guitar very badly.
>**Esta habitación huele mal.**
>This room smells bad.
>**Lo pasé muy mal.**
>I had a terrible time.
>**Me entendió mal.**
>He misunderstood me.
2 wrong
>**Han escrito mal mi apellido.**
>They've spelt my surname wrong.
>**Está mal mentir.**
>It's wrong to tell lies.

B MASC NOUN
evil

C ADJECTIVE ▷see **malo**

maleducado
(FEM **maleducada**) ADJECTIVE
bad-mannered

la **maleta** NOUN
suitcase

> **hacer la maleta**
> to pack

el **maletero** NOUN
boot

malo
mala

> **malo** *can be a noun or an adjective.*

A MASC/FEM NOUN
el malo de la película
the villain in the film
B ADJECTIVE

Language tip
*Use **mal** before a masculine noun.*

1 bad
un mal día
a bad day
Este programa es muy malo.
This is a very bad programme.
Soy muy mala para las
matemáticas.
I'm very bad at maths.
Lo malo es que ...
The trouble is that ...

2 naughty
¿Por qué eres tan malo?
Why are you so naughty?

3 ill
Mi hija está mala.
My daughter's ill.
Se puso malo después de
comer.
He started to feel ill after lunch.

la **mamá** (PL las **mamás**) NOUN
mum
¡Hola, mamá!
Hi Mum!

la **mancha** NOUN
stain

manchar VERB
to stain
El agua no mancha.
Water doesn't stain.
■ **mancharse**
to get dirty
No te manches la camisa.
Don't get your shirt dirty.

Me he manchado el vestido
de tinta.
I've got ink stains on my dress.

Language tip
In Spanish, the person is the direct subject of the action.

mandar VERB
1 to tell
¿Qué te mandaron hacer?
What did they tell you to do?
Nos mandó callar.
He told us to be quiet.
Aquí mando yo.
I'm the boss here.

2 to send
Se lo mandaremos
por correo.
We'll send
it to you
by post.

Me mandaron a hacer un
recado.
They sent me on an errand.

el **mando** NOUN
el mando a distancia
the remote control
los mandos
the controls

manejar VERB
to operate

la **manera** NOUN
way
Lo hice a mi manera.
I did it my way.
No hay manera de
convencerla.
There's nothing one can do
to convince her.

la **manga** NOUN
sleeve
Súbete las mangas.
Roll your sleeves up.

de manga corta
short-sleeved
de manga larga
long-sleeved

la **manía** NOUN
Tiene la manía de repetir todo lo que digo.
He has an irritating habit of repeating everything I say.
El profesor me tiene manía.
The teacher has it in for me.

la **mano** NOUN
hand
Dame la mano.
Give me your hand.
tener algo a mano
to have something to hand
Ahora no tengo ese libro a mano.
I don't have that book to hand right now.
hecho a mano
handmade
de segunda mano
secondhand

echar una mano
to lend a hand

la **manta** NOUN
blanket

el **mantel** NOUN
tablecloth

mantener VERB
to keep
Les mantendremos informados.
We'll keep you informed.
mantener la calma
to keep calm
mantenerse en forma
to keep fit
mantenerse en pie
to remain standing

la **mantequilla** NOUN
butter

mantuve VERB ▷ see **mantener**

Mantuve la calma.
I stayed calm.

la **manzana**
NOUN
apple

mañana

mañana *can be a noun or an adverb.*

A FEM NOUN
morning
Llegó a las nueve de la mañana.
He arrived at nine o'clock in the morning.
Por la mañana voy al gimnasio.
In the mornings I go to the gym.
a media mañana
mid-morning
B ADVERB
tomorrow

¡Hasta mañana!
See you tomorrow!
pasado mañana
the day after tomorrow
mañana por la mañana
tomorrow morning
mañana por la noche
tomorrow night

el **mapa** NOUN
map
El pueblo no está en el mapa.
The village isn't on the map.

el **maquillaje** NOUN
make-up

maquillarse VERB
to put one's make-up on
Está maquillándose.
She's putting her make-up on.

la **máquina** NOUN
machine
una máquina de coser
a sewing machine

Spanish English

a b c d e f g h i j k l **m** n ñ o p q r s t u v w x y z

una máquina de afeitar
an electric razor
una máquina fotográfica
a camera

la **maquinilla** NOUN
razor
una maquinilla eléctrica
an electric razor

el **mar** NOUN
sea
por mar
by sea

> **Language tip**
> Note that in some set phrases, **mar** is feminine.

Lo hizo la mar de bien.
He did it really well.

la **maravilla** NOUN
¡Qué maravilla de casa!
What a wonderful house!
ser una maravilla
to be wonderful
Se llevan de maravilla.
They get on wonderfully well together.

maravilloso (FEM **maravillosa**)
ADJECTIVE
marvellous

la **marca** NOUN
1 **mark**
Había marcas de neumático en la arena.
There were tyre marks in the sand.
2 **make**
¿De qué marca es tu tele?
What make's your TV?

3 **brand**
una conocida marca de chocolate
a well-known brand of chocolate
la ropa de marca
designer clothes

el **marcador** NOUN
1 **scoreboard**
2 **bookmark**

marcar VERB
1 **to dial**
2 **to score**

marcharse VERB
to leave

la **marea** NOUN
tide
una marea negra
an oil slick

mareado (FEM **mareada**)
ADJECTIVE
Estoy mareado.
I feel dizzy./I feel sick.

> **Language tip**
> **estoy mareado** has two meanings. It can be translated as **I feel dizzy** and **I feel sick**.

marear VERB
to make ... feel sick
Ese olor me marea.
That smell makes me feel sick.

marearse VERB
1 **to get dizzy**
Te marearás si das tantas vueltas.
You'll get dizzy going round and round like that.
¡No me marees!
Stop going on!
2 **to get sick**
¿Te mareas cuando vas en barco?
Do you get seasick when you travel by boat?
Siempre me mareo en coche.
I always get carsick.

el **mareo** NOUN
1 sea sickness
2 car sickness

la **margarina** NOUN
margarine

el **margen** (PL los **márgenes**)
NOUN
margin
Escribe las notas al margen.
Write your notes in the
margin.

el **marido** NOUN
husband

la **mariposa** NOUN
butterfly

el **martes** (PL los **martes**) NOUN
Tuesday

Language tip
The days of the week are not spelled with a capital letter in Spanish.

La vi el martes.
I saw her on Tuesday.

todos los martes
every Tuesday
el martes pasado
last Tuesday
el martes que viene
next Tuesday
Martes de Carnaval
Shrove Tuesday

Did you know…?
During the week before Lent, all over Spain and Latin America there are fiestas and fancy-dress parades, with the main celebrations taking place on **Martes de Carnaval** *(literally Carnival Tuesday).*

marzo MASC NOUN
March

Language tip
Months are not spelled with a capital letter in Spanish.

en marzo
in March
Nació el diecisiete de marzo.
He was born on the seventeenth of March.

más ADJECTIVE, ADVERB
more
Ahora salgo más.
I go out more these days.
Últimamente nos vemos más.
We've been seeing more of each other lately.
¿Quieres más?
Would you like some more?
No tengo más dinero.
I haven't got any more money.
deprisa – más deprisa
quickly – more quickly
barato – más barato
cheap – cheaper
lejos – más lejos
far – further
grande – más grande
big – bigger
temprano – más temprano
early – earlier
caro – más caro
expensive – more expensive
Es más grande que el tuyo.
It's bigger than yours.
Corre más rápido que yo.
He runs faster than I do.
más de mil libros
more than a thousand books
más de lo que yo creía
more than I thought
el niño más joven
the youngest child
el coche más grande
the biggest car
el punto más lejano
the furthest point
el más inteligente de todos
the most intelligent of all of them
Paco es el que come más.
Paco's the one who eats the most.

a
b
c
d
e
f
g
h
i
j
k
l
m
n
ñ
o
p
q
r
s
t
u
v
w
x
y
z

Fue el que más trabajó.
He was the one who worked the hardest.
¿Qué más?
What else?
¡Qué perro más sucio!
What a filthy dog!
Tenemos uno de más.
We have one too many.
Por más que estudio no apruebo.
However hard I study I don't pass.
Dos más dos son cuatro.
Two plus two is four.

masculino (FEM **masculina**) ADJECTIVE

1 **male**
el sexo masculino
the male sex
2 **men's**
la ropa masculina
men's clothing
3 **masculine**

masticar VERB
to chew

matar VERB
to kill
Mi padre me va a matar.
My dad will kill me.

las **matemáticas** NOUN
mathematics

la **materia** NOUN
subject

Es un experto en la materia.
He's an expert on the subject.

material ADJECTIVE, MASC NOUN
material

matricularse VERB
to enrol

máximo

máximo *can be a noun or an adjective.*

A MASC NOUN
maximum
un máximo de cincuenta euros
a maximum of fifty euros
como máximo
at the most/at the latest

Language tip

como máximo *has two meanings. Look at the examples.*

Te costará cinco libras como máximo.
It'll cost you five pounds at the most.
Llegaré a las diez como máximo.
I'll be there by ten o'clock at the latest.
B (FEM **máxima**) ADJECTIVE
maximum
la velocidad máxima
the maximum speed

mayo MASC NOUN
May

Language tip

Months are not spelled with a capital letter in Spanish.

en mayo
in May
Nació el veintiocho de mayo.
He was born on the twenty-eighth of May.

la **mayonesa** NOUN
mayonnaise

Spanish English

a b c d e f g h i j k l m ñ o p q r s t u v w x y z

mayor (FEM **mayor**)

> **mayor** *can be an adjective, pronoun or noun.*

A ADJECTIVE, PRONOUN
older
Paco es mayor que Nacho.
Paco is older than Nacho.
Es tres años mayor que yo.
He is three years older than me.
el hermano mayor
the older brother/the oldest brother

> **Language tip**
> **el hermano mayor** *has two meanings. It can be translated as* **the older brother** *and* **the oldest brother**.

Soy el mayor.
I'm the older./I'm the oldest.

> **Language tip**
> **Soy el mayor** *has two meanings. It can be translated as* **I'm the older (of the two)** *and* **I'm the oldest**.

Sus hijos ya son mayores.
Their children are grown-up now.
la gente mayor
the elderly
B MASC/FEM NOUN
un mayor de edad
an adult
los mayores
grown-ups

la **mayúscula** NOUN
capital letter
Empieza cada frase con mayúscula.
Start each sentence with a capital letter.
Escríbelo con mayúsculas.
Write it in capitals.
una M mayúscula
a capital M

me PRONOUN
1 me
Me quiere.
He loves me.

Me regaló una pulsera.
He gave me a bracelet.
Me lo dio.
He gave it to me.
¿Me echas esta carta?
Will you post this letter for me?
2 myself
No me hice daño.
I didn't hurt myself.
me dije a mí mismo
I said to myself
Me duelen los pies.
My feet hurt.
Me puse el abrigo.
I put my coat on.

la **medalla** NOUN
medal

la **media** NOUN
average
la media de edad
the average age
medias
stockings/tights

> **Language tip**
> **medias** *has two meanings. It can be translated either as* **stockings** *or* **tights**.

mediados PL NOUN
a mediados de
around the middle of

la **medianoche** NOUN
midnight
a medianoche
at midnight

el **medicamento** NOUN
medicine

la **medicina** NOUN
medicine

Spanish
English

a
b
c
d
e
f
g
h
i
j
k
l
m
n
ñ
o
p
q
r
s
t
u
v
w
x
y
z

Mi hermano estudia medicina en la universidad.
My brother's studying medicine at university.
¿Te has tomado ya la medicina?
Have you taken your medicine yet?

el **médico**
la **médica** NOUN
doctor
Quiere ser médica.
She wants to be a doctor.
el médico de cabecera
the family doctor

la **medida** NOUN
measure
medidas de seguridad
security measures
a medida que …
as …
Saludaba a los invitados a medida que iban llegando.
He greeted the guests as they arrived.

medio

medio *can be an adjective, an adverb or a noun.*

A (FEM **media**) ADJECTIVE
1 **half**
medio litro
half a litre
Nos queda media botella de leche.
We've got half a bottle of milk left.
media hora
half an hour
una hora y media
an hour and a half
Son las ocho y media.
It's half past eight.
2 **average**
la temperatura media
the average temperature
B ADVERB
half

Estaba medio dormido.
He was half asleep.
C MASC NOUN
1 **middle**
Está en el medio.
It's in the middle.
2 **means**
un medio de transporte
a means of transport
los medios de comunicación
the media
el medio ambiente
the environment

el **mediodía** NOUN
al mediodía
at midday/at lunchtime

> *Language tip*
>
> **al mediodía** *has two meanings. It can be translated as* **at midday** *and* **at lunchtime**.

medir VERB
to measure
¿Has medido la ventana?
Have you measured the window?
¿Cuánto mides? — Mido un metro cincuenta.
How tall are you? — I'm one metre fifty.
¿Cuánto mide esta habitación? — Mide tres metros por cuatro.
How big is this room? — It measures three metres by four.

la **mejilla** NOUN
cheek

mejor (FEM **mejor**)

mejor *can be an adjective or an adverb.*

A ADJECTIVE
1 **better**
Éste es mejor que el otro.
This one is better than the other one.
Es el mejor de los dos.
He's the better of the two.

2 best
mi mejor amiga
my best friend

el mejor de la clase
the best in the class
Es el mejor de todos.
He's the best of the lot.

B ADVERB
1 better
La conozco mejor que tú.
I know her better than you do.
2 best
¿Quién lo hace mejor?
Who does it best?
Mejor nos vamos.
We had better go.

a lo mejor
probably

mejorar VERB
to improve
El tiempo está mejorando.
The weather's improving.
Han mejorado el servicio.
They have improved the service.

¡Que te mejores!
Get well soon!

la **melena** NOUN
long hair
Lleva una melena rubia.
She has long blond hair.

el **mellizo** (FEM la **melliza**)
ADJECTIVE, NOUN
twin
Son mellizos.
They're twins.

el **melocotón** (PL los
melocotones) NOUN
peach

el **melón** (PL los **melones**) NOUN
melon

la **memoria** NOUN
memory
tener mala memoria
to have a bad memory
aprender algo de memoria
to learn something by heart

menor (FEM **menor**)

*menor can be an adjective, a
pronoun or a noun.*

A ADJECTIVE, PRONOUN
1 younger
Es tres años menor que yo.
He's three years younger than
me.
Juanito es menor que Pepe.
Juanito is younger than Pepe.
el hermano menor
the younger brother/the
youngest brother

Language tip

el hermano menor *has two
meanings. It can be translated as*
the younger brother *and* **the
youngest brother**.

Yo soy el menor.
I'm the younger./I'm the
youngest.

Language tip

yo soy el menor *has two
meanings. It can be translated as*
I'm the younger *and* **I'm the
youngest**.

2 smaller
una talla menor
a smaller size
**No tiene la menor
importancia.**
It's not in the least important.
B MASC/FEM NOUN
un menor de edad
a minor
los menores
the under-18s

a b c d e f g h i j k l **m** n ñ o p q r s t u v w x y z

menos

> **menos** *can be an adjective, an adverb or a preposition.*

A ADJECTIVE, ADVERB

1 **less**

Ahora salgo menos.
I go out less these days.

Últimamente nos vemos menos.
We've been seeing less of each other recently.

menos caro
less expensive

menos harina
less flour

menos gatos
fewer cats

menos gente
fewer people

menos ... que
less ... than

Me gusta menos que el otro.
I like it less than the other one.

Trabaja menos que yo.
He doesn't work as hard as I do.

Es menos nerviosa que antes.
She's less nervous than she was.

menos de cincuenta cajas
fewer than fifty boxes

2 **least**

el chico menos desobediente de la clase
the least disobedient boy in the class

Fue el que menos trabajó.
He was the one who worked the least hard.

el examen con menos errores
the exam paper with the fewest mistakes

No quiero verle y menos visitarle.
I don't want to see him, let alone visit him.

¡Menos mal!
Thank goodness!

B PREPOSITION

except

todos menos él
everyone except him

Cinco menos dos son tres.
Five minus two is three.

a menos que
unless

el **mensaje** NOUN
message

un mensaje de texto
a text message

mentir VERB
to lie

No me mientas.
Don't lie to me.

la **mentira** NOUN
lie

No digas mentiras.
Don't tell lies.

Parece mentira que aún no te haya pagado.
It's incredible that he still hasn't paid you.

una pistola de mentira
a toy pistol

el **mentiroso**
la **mentirosa** NOUN
liar

el **menú** (PL los **menús**) NOUN
menu

el menú del día
the set menu

menudo (FEM **menuda**)
ADJECTIVE

¡Menudo lío!
What a mess!

a menudo
often

el **meñique** NOUN
little finger

el **mercado** NOUN
market

150

merecer VERB
to deserve
> **Mereces que te castiguen.**
> You deserve to be punished.

merece la pena
it's worthwhile

merendar VERB
to have tea

la **merienda** NOUN
tea

el **mes** (PL los **meses**) NOUN
month

el mes que viene
next month

la **mesa** NOUN
table

poner la mesa
to lay the table

el **metal** NOUN
metal

meter VERB
to put
> **¿Dónde has metido las llaves?**
> Where have you put the keys?
> **meterse en**
> to go into
> **Se metió en la cueva.**
> He went into the cave.
> **No te metas donde no te llaman.**
> Don't poke your nose in where it doesn't belong.
> **meterse con alguien**
> to pick on somebody
> **No te metas con tu hermano.**
> Don't pick on your brother.

el **metro** NOUN
  1 underground
> **coger el metro**
> to take the underground
  2 metre
> **Mide tres metros de largo.**
> It's three metres long.

la **mezcla** NOUN
mixture

mezclar VERB
to mix
> **Hay que mezclar el azúcar y la harina.**
> You have to mix the sugar and the flour.

mi (FEM **mi**, PL **mis**) ADJECTIVE
my
> **mis hermanas**
> my sisters

mí PRONOUN
me
> **para mí**
> for me
> **Para mí que ...**
> I think that ...
> **Por mí no hay problema.**
> There's no problem as far as I'm concerned.

el **micrófono** NOUN
microphone

el **microondas** (PL los **microondas**) NOUN
microwave
> **un horno microondas**
> a microwave oven

el **microscopio** NOUN
microscope

midiendo VERB ▷ see **medir**
> **Estaba midiendo la habitación.**
> I was measuring the room.

el **miedo** NOUN
fear
> **el miedo a la oscuridad**
> fear of the dark

tener miedo
to be afraid
Le tenía miedo a su padre.
He was afraid of his father.
Tengo miedo a caerme.
I'm afraid of falling over.
dar miedo a
to scare
Me daba miedo hacerlo.
I was scared of doing it.

la **miel** NOUN
honey

el/la **miembro** NOUN
member

mientras ADVERB, CONJUNCTION
while
Lava tú mientras yo seco.
You wash while I dry.
Seguiré jugando al fútbol mientras pueda.
I'll carry on playing football for as long as I can.

mientras tanto
meanwhile

el **miércoles** (PL los **miércoles**)
NOUN
Wednesday

Language tip
The days of the week are not spelled with a capital letter in Spanish.

La vi el miércoles.
I saw her on Wednesday.

todos los miércoles
every Wednesday
el miércoles pasado
last Wednesday
el miércoles que viene
next Wednesday

mil (FEM **mil**) ADJECTIVE, PRONOUN
thousand
miles de personas
thousands of people
dos mil euros
two thousand euros

el **milagro** NOUN
miracle
No nos hemos matado de milagro.
It was a miracle we weren't killed.

el **milímetro** NOUN
millimetre

el **millón** (PL los **millones**) NOUN
million
millones de personas
millions of people
mil millones
a billion

el **millonario**
la **millonaria** NOUN
millionaire

mimado (FEM **mimada**)
ADJECTIVE
spoiled

mineral ADJECTIVE, MASC NOUN
mineral

mínimo

mínimo *can be a noun or an adjective.*

A MASC NOUN
minimum
un mínimo de diez euros
a minimum of ten euros
lo mínimo que puede hacer
the least he can do
Como mínimo podrías haber llamado.
You could at least have called.

B (FEM **mínima**) ADJECTIVE
minimum
la puntuación mínima
the minimum score
No tienes ni la más mínima idea.
You haven't the faintest idea.

la **minoría** NOUN
minority
las minorías étnicas
ethnic minorities

la **minúscula** NOUN
small letter

la **minusválida** NOUN
disabled woman

el **minusválido** NOUN
disabled man
los minusválidos
the disabled

el **minuto** NOUN
minute
Espera un minuto.
Wait a minute.

mío (FEM **mía**) ADJECTIVE,
PRONOUN
mine
Estos caballos son míos.
Those horses are mine.
¿De quién es esta bufanda? — Es mía.
Whose scarf is this? — It's mine.
El mío está en el armario.
Mine's in the cupboard.
Éste es el mío.
This one's mine.
un amigo mío
a friend of mine

la **mirada** NOUN
look
con una mirada de odio
with a look of hatred
echar una mirada a algo
to have a look at something
¿Le has echado una mirada a mi informe?

Have you had a look at my report?

mirar VERB
to look
¡Mira! Un ratón.
Look! A mouse.
Mira a ver si está ahí.
Look and see if he is there.
mirar algo
to look at something
Mira esta foto.
Look at this photo.
mirar por la ventana
to look out of the window

mirar algo fijamente
to stare at something
¡Mira que es tonto!
What an idiot!
mirarse al espejo
to look at oneself in the mirror
Se miraron asombrados.
They looked at each other in amazement.

la **misa** NOUN
mass

mismo

mismo *can be an adjective, an adverb or a pronoun.*

A (FEM **misma**) ADJECTIVE
same
Nos gustan los mismos libros.
We like the same books.
Vivo en su misma calle.
I live in the same street as him.
yo mismo
myself

a b c d e f g h i j k l **m** n ñ o p q r s t u v w x y z

Lo hice yo mismo.
I did it myself.
B ADVERB
Hoy mismo le escribiré.
I'll write to him today.
Nos podemos encontrar aquí mismo.
We can meet right here.
C PRONOUN
lo mismo
the same
Yo tomaré lo mismo.
I'll have the same.
Da lo mismo.
It doesn't matter.
No ha llamado pero lo mismo viene.
He hasn't phoned but he may well come.

el **misterio** NOUN
mystery

la **mitad** NOUN
half
Se comió la mitad del pastel.
He ate half the cake.
más de la mitad de los alumnos
more than half the pupils
La mitad son chicas.
Half of them are girls.
a mitad de precio
half-price
a mitad de camino
halfway there
Corta el pan por la mitad.
Cut the loaf in half.

mixto (FEM **mixta**) ADJECTIVE
mixed
una escuela mixta
a mixed school

la **mochila** NOUN
rucksack

el **moco** NOUN
Límpiate los mocos.
Wipe your nose.

tener mocos
to have a runny nose

la **moda** NOUN
fashion
estar de moda
to be in fashion
pasado de moda
old-fashioned

los **modales** NOUN
manners
buenos modales
good manners

el/la **modelo** ADJECTIVE, NOUN
model
una niña modelo
a model child
Quiero ser modelo.
I want to be a model.

moderno (FEM **moderna**)
ADJECTIVE
modern

modesto (FEM **modesta**)
ADJECTIVE
modest

el **modo** NOUN
way
Le gusta hacerlo todo a su modo.
She likes to do everything her own way.
de modo que
so/so that

Language tip
de modo que *has two meanings.*
Look at the examples.

No has hecho los deberes, de modo que no puedes salir.
You haven't done your homework so you can't go out.
Mueve la tele de modo que todos la podamos ver.
Move the TV so that we can all see it.
'modo de empleo'
'instructions for use'
de todos modos
anyway

mojado (FEM **mojada**) ADJECTIVE
wet

mojar VERB
to get ... wet
¡No mojes la alfombra!
Don't get the carpet wet!
Me he mojado las mangas.
I got my sleeves wet.
Moja el pan en la salsa.
Dip the bread in the sauce.
■ **mojarse**
to get wet

molestar VERB
1 **to bother**
¿Te molesta la radio?
Is the radio bothering you?
Siento molestarle.
I'm sorry to bother you.
2 **to disturb**
No me molestes, que estoy trabajando.
Don't disturb me, I'm working.
■ **molestarse**
to get upset
Se molestó por algo que dije.
She got upset because of something I said.

el **momento** NOUN
moment
Espera un momento.
Wait a moment.

en este momento
at the moment
Tenemos mucho trabajo en este momento.
We've got a lot of work at the moment.

de un momento a otro
any moment now
Llegarán de un momento a otro.
They'll be here any moment now.
Llegó el momento de irnos.
The time came for us to go.

la **moneda** NOUN
coin
una moneda de dos euros
a two-euro coin

el **monedero** NOUN
purse

mono

mono *can be an adjective or a noun.*

A (FEM **mona**) ADJECTIVE
pretty
¡Qué piso tan mono!
What a pretty flat!
¡Qué niña tan mona!
What a sweet little girl!
B MASC NOUN
monkey

el **monopatín** (PL los monopatines) NOUN
skateboard

el **monstruo** NOUN
monster

la **montaña** NOUN
mountain
Fuimos de vacaciones a la montaña.
We went to the mountains on holiday.

Spanish

English

a
b
c
d
e
f
g
h
i
j
k
l
m
n
ñ
o
p
q
r
s
t
u
v
w
x
y
z

la **montaña rusa**
the roller coaster

montar VERB
to assemble
■ **montarse**
to get on
Se montó en el autobús.
He got on the bus.

montar en bici
to ride a bike

el **montón** (PL los **montones**)
NOUN
pile
Puso el montón de libros sobre la mesa.
He put the pile of books on the table.
un montón de ...
loads of ...
un montón de gente
loads of people
un montón de dinero
loads of money

la **moral** NOUN
morale
levantar la moral a alguien
to cheer somebody up

morder VERB
to bite
morderse las uñas
to bite one's nails
No te muerdas las uñas.
Don't bite your nails.

el **mordisco** NOUN
bite
Dame un mordisco de tu bocadillo.
Let me have a bite of your sandwich.
dar un mordisco
to bite
Me dio un mordisco.
He bit me.

moreno (FEM **morena**) ADJECTIVE
dark
Es moreno.

Language tip
Es moreno *has two meanings. It can be translated as* **he has dark hair** *and* **he is dark-skinned**.

ponerse moreno
to get brown

morir VERB
to die
¿Cuándo murió?
When did he die?
¡Me muero de hambre!
I'm starving!
Me muero de vergüenza.
I'm so embarrassed.
Me muero de ganas de ir a nadar.
I'm dying to go for a swim.

la **mosca** NOUN
fly

el **mosquito**
NOUN
mosquito

el **mostrador**
NOUN
counter

mostrar VERB
to show
Nos mostró el camino.
He showed us the way.

el **mote** NOUN
nickname

el **motivo** NOUN
reason
Dejó el trabajo por motivos personales.
He left the job for personal reasons.

la **moto** NOUN
motorbike

el **motor** NOUN
engine

el/la **motorista** NOUN
motorcyclist

mover VERB
   to move
      **Mueve un poco las cajas para
      que podamos pasar.**
      Move the boxes a bit so that we
      can get past.
   ■ **moverse**
    to move
     ¡No te muevas!
     Don't move!

el **móvil** NOUN
   mobile
      un móvil con cámara
      a camera phone

el **movimiento** NOUN
   movement

el **MP3** NOUN
   MP3
      un reproductor de MP3
      an MP3 player

la **muchacha** NOUN
   girl

el **muchacho** NOUN
   boy

mucho (FEM **mucha**)

> **mucho** *can be an adjective, a
> pronoun or an adverb.*

A ADJECTIVE
1 **a lot of**
    Había mucha gente.
    There were a lot of people.
    Tiene muchas plantas.
    He has got a lot of plants.
2 **much**
    No tenemos mucho tiempo.
    We haven't got much time.
    ¿Conoces a mucha gente?
    Do you know many people?
    **Muchas personas creen
    que ...**
    Many people think that ...
    no hace mucho tiempo
    not long ago
    Hace mucho calor.
    It's very hot.

Tengo mucho frío.
I'm very cold.
**Tengo mucha
hambre.**
I'm very
hungry.

Tengo mucha sed.
I'm very thirsty.

B PRONOUN
1 **a lot**
    Tengo mucho que hacer.
    I've got a lot to do.
    ¿Cuántos había? — Muchos.
    How many were there? — A lot.
2 **much**
    No tengo mucho que hacer.
    I haven't got much to do.
    **¿Hay manzanas? —
    Sí, pero no muchas.**
    Are there any apples? —
    Yes, but not many.
    ¿Vinieron muchos?
    Did many people come?
    Muchos dicen que ...
    Many people say that ...

C ADVERB
1 **very much**
    Te quiero mucho.
    I love you very much.
    **No me gusta mucho la
    carne.**
    I don't like meat very much.
    Me gusta mucho el jazz.
    I really like jazz.
2 **a lot**
    Come mucho.
    He eats a lot.
    mucho más
    a lot more
    mucho antes
    long before
    No tardes mucho.
    Don't be long.

mudarse VERB
   to move

Spanish | English

a b c d e f g h i j k l **m** n ñ o p q r s t u v w x y z

Spanish **English**

a
b
c
d
e
f
g
h
i
j
k
l
m
n
ñ
o
p
q
r
s
t
u
v
w
x
y
z

mudarse de casa
to move house

el **mueble** NOUN
un mueble
a piece of furniture
seis muebles
six pieces of furniture
los muebles
furniture

la **muela**
NOUN
tooth

una muela del juicio
a wisdom tooth

el **muelle** NOUN
1 **spring**
2 **quay**

muerdo VERB ▷see **morder**
Me duele cuando muerdo.
It hurts when I bite.

la **muerte** NOUN
death
Nos dio un susto de muerte.
He nearly frightened us to death.

muerto
muerta

> **muerto** can be an adjective or a
> noun.

A ADJECTIVE
dead
Está muerto de cansancio.
He's dead tired.
B MASC/FEM NOUN
un muerto
a dead man
una muerta
a dead woman
los muertos
the dead

Hubo tres muertos.
Three people were killed.

la **muestra** NOUN
sign
dar muestras de
to show signs of

muestro VERB ▷see **mostrar**
Ahora te muestro cómo se hace.
I'll show you now how it's done.

muevo VERB ▷see **mover**
Yo no me muevo de aquí.
I'm not moving from here.

la **mujer** NOUN
1 **woman**
Vino a verte una mujer.
A woman came to see you.
2 **wife**
la mujer del médico
the doctor's wife

la **multa** NOUN
fine
una multa de cincuenta euros
a fifty-euro fine

multiplicar VERB
to multiply
**Hay que multiplicarlo por
cinco.**
You have to multiply it by five.
la tabla de multiplicar
the times tables

mundial

> **mundial** can be an adjective or a
> noun.

A (FEM **mundial**) ADJECTIVE
1 **world**
un récord mundial
a world record
2 **worldwide**
B MASC NOUN
world championship

el **mundo** NOUN
world
todo el mundo
everybody

Spanish
English

Se lo ha dicho a todo el mundo.
He has told everybody.
No lo cambiaría por nada del mundo.
I wouldn't change it for anything in the world.

la **muñeca** NOUN
1 **wrist**
2 **doll**

el **muñeco** NOUN
doll
   un muñeco de peluche
   a soft toy
   un muñeco de nieve
   a snowman

el **museo** NOUN
museum
   un museo de arte
   an art gallery

la **música** NOUN
music

   la música pop
   pop music

muy ADVERB
very
   muy bonito
   very pretty

a
b
c
d
e
f
g
h
i
j
k
l
m
n
ñ
o
p
q
r
s
t
u
v
w
x
y
z

N n

nacer VERB
to be born
> **Nació en 1964.**
> He was born in 1964.

nacional (FEM **nacional**)
ADJECTIVE
national
> **vuelos nacionales**
> domestic flights

nada

> **nada** *can be a pronoun or an adverb.*

A PRONOUN
1 nothing
> **¿Qué has comprado? —
> Nada.**
> What have you bought? —
> Nothing.
> **No hace nada.**
> He does nothing.
2 anything
> **No quiero nada.**
> I don't want anything.
> **No dijo nada más.**
> He didn't say anything else.
> **Encendió la tele nada más
> llegar.**
> He turned on the TV as soon as
> he came in.
> **No sabe nada de español.**
> He knows no Spanish at all.

> **¡Gracias! — De nada.**
> Thanks! — You're welcome!

B ADVERB
at all
> **Esto no me gusta nada.**
> I don't like this at all.

el nadador
la nadadora NOUN
swimmer

nadar VERB
to swim

nadie PRONOUN
1 nobody
> **Nadie habló.**
> Nobody spoke.
> **No había nadie.**
> There was nobody there.
2 anybody
> **No quiere ver a nadie.**
> He doesn't want to see anybody.

naranja

> **naranja** *can be an adjective or a noun.*

A ADJECTIVE
orange

> *Language tip*
> The colour **naranja** never changes
> its ending no matter what it
> describes.

> **un anorak naranja**
> an orange anorak
B FEM NOUN
orange (*fruit*)

C MASC NOUN
orange (*colour*)

la nariz (PL **las narices**) NOUN
nose

la nata NOUN
cream

la natación NOUN
swimming

natural (FEM **natural**) ADJECTIVE
natural

la **naturaleza** NOUN
nature

las **náuseas** NOUN
tener náuseas
to feel sick

la **navaja** NOUN
penknife

la **nave** NOUN
ship
una nave espacial
a spaceship

navegar VERB
to sail

navegar por Internet
to surf the Net

la **Navidad**
NOUN
Christmas

¡Feliz Navidad!
Happy Christmas!

necesario (FEM **necesaria**)
ADJECTIVE
necessary
No es necesario.
It isn't necessary.
Ya tengo el dinero necesario para el billete.
I've now got the money I need for the ticket.
No es necesario que vengas.
You don't have to come.

la **necesidad** NOUN
need
No hay necesidad de hacerlo.
There is no need to do it.

necesitar VERB
to need
Necesito cien euros.
I need a hundred euros.
Necesito sacar un notable en el examen.
I need to get a good mark in the exam.
Necesito que me ayudes.
I need you to help me.
'Se necesita camarero'
'Waiter wanted'

negar VERB
1 **to deny**
No lo puedes negar.
You can't deny it.
Negó con la cabeza.
He shook his head.
2 **to refuse**
Se negó a hacer las compras.
He refused to do the shopping.

negativo (FEM **negativa**)
ADJECTIVE
negative

negro

negro *can be an adjective or a noun.*

A (FEM **negra**) ADJECTIVE
black
B MASC/FEM NOUN
un negro
a black man
una negra
a black woman
los negros
black people
C MASC NOUN
black *(colour)*

el **nervio** NOUN
nerve
Me pone de los nervios.
She gets on my nerves.

nervioso (FEM **nerviosa**)
ADJECTIVE
nervous

a
b
c
d
e
f
g
h
i
j
k
l
m
n
ñ
o
p
q
r
s
t
u
v
w
x
y
z

Spanish
English

a
b
c
d
e
f
g
h
i
j
k
l
m
n
ñ
o
p
q
r
s
t
u
v
w
x
y
z

Me pongo muy nervioso en los exámenes.
I get very nervous during exams.
¡Me pone nervioso!
He gets on my nerves!

nevar VERB
to snow

la **nevera** NOUN
refrigerator

ni CONJUNCTION
neither
Ella no fue, ni yo tampoco.
She didn't go and neither did I.
ni ... ni
neither ... nor
No vinieron ni Carlos ni Sofía.
Neither Carlos nor Sofía came.
No me gustan ni el bacalao ni el hígado.
I don't like either cod or liver.
No compré ni uno ni otro.
I didn't buy either of them.
Ni siquiera me saludó.
He didn't even say hello.

el **nido** NOUN
nest

la **niebla** NOUN
fog
Hay niebla.
It's foggy.

niego VERB ▷ see **negar**
No niego que esté enfadado.

I'm not denying I'm angry.

la **nieta** NOUN
granddaughter

el **nieto** NOUN
grandson
mis nietos
my grandsons/my grandchildren

Language tip
mis nietos *has two meanings. It can be translated as* **my grandsons** *or* **my grandchildren**.

nieva VERB ▷ see **nevar**
Nieva.
It's snowing.

la **nieve** NOUN
snow

ningún PRONOUN ▷ see **ninguno**
No tengo ningún caramelo.
I don't have any sweets.

ninguno (FEM **ninguna**)
ADJECTIVE, PRONOUN
1 no
No hay ninguna prisa.
There's no hurry.
2 any
No vimos a ningún amigo en las vacaciones.
We didn't see any friends in the holidays.
3 none
¿Cuál eliges? — Ninguno.
Which one do you want? — None of them.
No me queda ninguno.
I have none left.
Ninguno de nosotros va a ir a la fiesta.
None of us is going to the party.
No lo encuentro por ningún sitio.
I can't find it anywhere.
ninguno de los dos
neither of them/either of them

> **Language tip**
> **ninguno de los dos** *has two meanings. Look at the examples.*

> **A ninguna de las dos les gusta el café.**
> Neither of them likes coffee.
> **No me gusta ninguno de los dos.**
> I don't like either of them.

la **niña** NOUN
girl

el **niño** NOUN
boy
los niños
the boys/the children

> **Language tip**
> **los niños** *has two meanings. It can be translated as* **the boys** *or* **the children**.

el **nivel** NOUN
1 **level**
el nivel del agua
the water level
2 **standard**
el nivel de vida
the standard of living

no ADVERB
no
¿Quieres venir? — No.
Do you want to come? — No.
¿Te gusta? — No mucho.
Do you like it? — Not really.
No me gusta.
I don't like it.
María no habla inglés.
María doesn't speak English.
No puedo venir esta noche.
I can't come tonight.
No tengo tiempo.
I haven't got time.
No debes preocuparte.
You mustn't worry.
No hace frío.
It isn't cold.
No conozco a nadie.
I don't know anyone.

Esto es tuyo, ¿no?
This is yours, isn't it?
Fueron al cine, ¿no?
They went to the cinema, didn't they?
¿Puedo salir esta noche? — ¡Que no!
Can I go out tonight? — I said no!
los no fumadores
non-smokers

la **noche** NOUN
night

Pasó la noche sin dormir.
He had a sleepless night.
¡Buenas noches!
Good evening!/Good night!

> **Language tip**
> **¡buenas noches!** *has two meanings. It can be translated as* **good evening!** *and* **good night!**

Era de noche cuando llegamos a casa.
It was night time when we got home.

> **el sábado por la noche**
> on Saturday night
> **esta noche**
> tonight
> **por la noche**
> at night

la **Nochebuena** NOUN
Christmas Eve

la **Nochevieja** NOUN
New Year's Eve

nombrar VERB
to mention
Me nombró en su discurso.
He mentioned me in his speech.

el **nombre** NOUN
1 **name**
nombre de pila
first name
nombre y apellidos
full name
2 **noun**

noreste MASC NOUN, ADJECTIVE
northeast

> *Language tip*
> *The adjective **noreste** never changes its ending, no matter what it describes.*

la **noria** NOUN
big wheel

la **norma** NOUN
rule

normal (FEM **normal**) ADJECTIVE
normal
una persona normal
a normal person
Es normal que quiera divertirse.
It's natural that he should want to enjoy himself.

noroeste MASC NOUN, ADJECTIVE
northwest

> *Language tip*
> *The adjective **noroeste** never changes its ending, no matter what it describes.*

norte MASC NOUN, ADJECTIVE
north
el norte del país
the north of the country

> *Language tip*
> *The adjective **norte** never changes its ending, no matter what it describes.*

en la costa norte
on the north coast

el **norteamericano** (FEM la **norteamericana**) ADJECTIVE, NOUN
American

nos PRONOUN
1 **us**
Nos vinieron a ver.
They came to see us.
Nos dio un consejo.
He gave us some advice.
Nos lo dio.
He gave it to us.
Nos tienen que arreglar el ordenador.
They have to fix the computer for us.
2 **ourselves**
Tenemos que defendernos.
We must defend ourselves.
Nos levantamos a las ocho.
We got up at eight o'clock.
Nos dolían los pies.
Our feet were hurting.
Nos pusimos los abrigos.
We put our coats on.
3 **each other**
No nos hablamos desde hace tiempo.
We haven't spoken to each other for a long time.

la **nota** NOUN
1 **mark**
Saca muy malas notas.
He gets very bad marks.
2 **note**
Tomó muchas notas en la conferencia.
He took a lot of notes during the lecture.

notar VERB
1 **to notice**
Notó que le seguían.
He noticed they were following him.
2 **to feel**

Con este abrigo no noto el
frío.
I don't feel the cold with this
coat on.
**Se nota que has estudiado
mucho este trimestre.**
You can tell that you've studied
a lot this term.

la **noticia** NOUN
news
**Tengo una buena noticia que
darte.**
I've got some good news for
you.
**Fue una noticia excelente
para la escuela.**.
It was an excellent piece of news
for the school.
Vi las noticias de las nueve.
I watched the nine o'clock news.

> *Language tip*
> *Be careful! noticia does not mean
> the same as notice.*

el **novato**
la **novata** NOUN
beginner

novecientos
(FEM **novecientas**) ADJECTIVE,
PRONOUN
nine hundred

la **novedad** NOUN
**Las últimas novedades en
moda infantil.**
The latest in children's fashions.

la **novela** NOUN
novel

noveno (FEM **novena**) ADJECTIVE,
PRONOUN
ninth

Vivo en el noveno.
I live on the ninth floor.

noventa (FEM **noventa**)
ADJECTIVE, PRONOUN
ninety
el noventa aniversario
the ninetieth anniversary

la **novia** NOUN
girlfriend

noviembre MASC NOUN
November

> *Language tip*
> *Months are not spelled with a
> capital letter in Spanish.*

en noviembre
in November
Nació el treinta de noviembre.
He was born on the thirtieth of
November.

los **novillos** NOUN
hacer novillos
to play truant

el **novio** NOUN
boyfriend
los novios
the bride and groom

la **nube** NOUN
cloud

nublado (FEM **nublada**)
ADJECTIVE
cloudy

nublarse VERB
to cloud over

a b c d e f g h i j k l m **n** ñ o p q r s t u v w x y z

la **nuca** NOUN
nape

nuclear ADJECTIVE
nuclear
    una central nuclear
    a nuclear power station

el **nudo** NOUN
knot

nuestro (FEM **nuestra**)
ADJECTIVE, PRONOUN
1 **our**
    nuestro perro
    our dog
    nuestras bicicletas
    our bicycles
2 **ours**
    **¿De quién es esto? —
    Es nuestro.**
    Whose is this? — It's ours.
    La nuestra es blanca.
    Ours is white.
    un amigo nuestro
    a friend of ours

nueve (FEM **nueve**) ADJECTIVE,
PRONOUN
nine
    Son las nueve.
    It's nine o'clock.

> **el nueve de marzo**
> the ninth of March
> **Nació el nueve de marzo.**
> He was born on the ninth of
> March.

nuevo (FEM **nueva**) ADJECTIVE
new
    **Necesito un ordenador
    nuevo.**
    I need a new computer.

**Tuve que leer el libro de
nuevo.**
I had to read the book again.

la **nuez** (PL las **nueces**) NOUN
walnut

el **número** NOUN
1 **number**
    Calle Aribau, sin número.
    Aribau street, no number.
    número de teléfono
    telephone number
2 **size** (of shoe)

nunca ADVERB
1 **never**
    No viene nunca.
    He never comes.
    No la veré nunca más.
    I'll never see her again.
2 **ever**
    **Ninguno de nosotros había
    esquiado nunca.**
    Neither of us had ever skied
    before.
    Casi nunca me escribe.
    He hardly ever writes to me.

> ### Language tip
> *The Spanish alphabet has an extra
> letter in it:* **ñ**. *Not many words begin
> with it but you will see it in lots of
> common words e.g.* **niño**, **cariño**.

Ñ ñ

ñoño
ñoña

ñoño can be an adjective or a noun.

A ADJECTIVE
wet

Me parece algo ñoña.
I think she's a bit wet.
B MASC/FEM NOUN
drip
Tu hermano es un ñoño.
Your brother's a drip.

O o

a b c d e f g h i j k l m n ñ **o** p q r s t u v w x y z

o CONJUNCTION
or
> **¿Quieres té o café?**
> Would you like tea or coffee?
> **¿Vas a ayudarme o no?**
> Are you going to help me or not?
> **o … o …**
> either … or …
> **O ha salido o no coge el teléfono.**
> Either he's out or he's not answering the phone.

obedecer VERB
> **to obey**

obediente (FEM **obediente**) ADJECTIVE
> **obedient**

el **objeto** NOUN
> **object**
> **un objeto metálico**
> a metal object

obligar VERB
> **to force**
> **Nadie te obliga a ir a clases de karate.**
> Nobody's forcing you to do karate.

obligatorio (FEM **obligatoria**) ADJECTIVE
> **compulsory**

la **obra** NOUN
> **1 work**
> **una obra de arte**
> a work of art

> **una obra de teatro**
> a play
> **2 building site**
> **'obras'**
> 'roadworks'

observar VERB
> **to observe**

el **obstáculo** NOUN
> **obstacle**

obtener VERB
> **to obtain**

obvio (FEM **obvia**) ADJECTIVE
> **obvious**

la **ocasión** (PL las **ocasiones**) NOUN
> **opportunity**
> **Ésta es la ocasión que esperábamos.**
> This is the opportunity we've been waiting for.

el **océano** NOUN
> **ocean**

> **el océano Atlántico**
> the Atlantic Ocean

ochenta (FEM **ochenta**) ADJECTIVE, PRONOUN
> **eighty**
> **Tiene ochenta años.**
> He's eighty.
> **el ochenta aniversario**
> the eightieth anniversary

ocho (FEM **ocho**) ADJECTIVE, PRONOUN
eight
> **Son las ocho.**
> It's eight o'clock.

> **el ocho de agosto**
> the eighth of August
> **Nació el ocho de agosto.**
> He was born on the eighth of August.

ochocientos
(FEM **ochocientas**) ADJECTIVE, PRONOUN
eight hundred

octavo (FEM **octava**) ADJECTIVE, PRONOUN
eighth
> **Vivo en el octavo.**
> I live on the eighth floor.

octubre MASC NOUN
October

> *Language tip*
> *Months are not spelled with a capital letter in Spanish.*

> **en octubre**
> in October
> **Nació el tres de octubre.**
> He was born on the third of October.

ocupado (FEM **ocupada**)
ADJECTIVE
1 **busy**
> **Estoy muy ocupado.**
> I'm very busy.
2 **engaged**
> **La línea está ocupada.**
> The line's engaged.
> **'ocupado'**
> 'engaged'
> **¿Está ocupado este asiento?**
> Is this seat taken?

ocupar VERB
to take up

> **Ocupa casi todo mi tiempo.**
> It takes up almost all my time.
> **Los espectadores ocuparon sus asientos.**
> The spectators took their seats.
> **ocuparse de algo**
> to look after something
> **Juan se ocupa de las ventas.**
> Juan looks after sales.

ocurrir VERB
to happen
> **¿Qué ocurrió?**
> What happened?
> **¿Qué te ocurre?**
> What's the matter?
> **Se nos ocurrió una idea brillante.**
> We had a brilliant idea.

odiar VERB
to hate
> **Odio tener que levantarme pronto.**
> I hate having to get up early.

oeste MASC NOUN, ADJECTIVE
west
> **el oeste del país**
> the west of the country

> *Language tip*
> *The adjective **oeste** never changes its ending, no matter what it describes.*

> **en la costa oeste**
> on the west coast

Spanish English

a
b
c
d
e
f
g
h
i
j
k
l
m
n
ñ
o
p
q
r
s
t
u
v
w
x
y
z

la **oferta** NOUN
offer

> **estar de oferta**
> to be on special offer

la **oficina** NOUN
office
> **la oficina de turismo**
> the tourist office
> **la oficina de correos**
> the post office
> **la oficina de objetos perdidos**
> the lost property office

ofrecer VERB
to offer
> **Nos ofrecieron un refresco.**
> They offered us something to drink.
> **Me ofrecí para ayudar.**
> I offered to help.

el **oído** NOUN
1 **ear**
2 **hearing**

oír VERB
1 **to hear**
> **He oído un ruido.**
> I heard a noise.
> **¿Me oyes bien desde ahí?**
> Can you hear me all right from there?
2 **to listen to**
> **Óyeme bien.**
> Listen to me.
> **oír la radio**
> to listen to the radio
> **¡Oye!**
> Hey!
> **¡Oiga, por favor!**
> Excuse me!

ojalá EXCLAMATION
I hope
> **¡Ojalá Toni venga hoy!**
> I hope Toni comes today!

el **ojo** NOUN
eye
> **Tengo algo en el ojo.**
> I've got something in my eye.

> **¡Ojo! Es muy mentiroso.**
> Watch out! He's a real liar.

la **ola** NOUN
wave

oler VERB
to smell
> **Huele a tabaco.**
> It smells of cigarette smoke.
> **Esta salsa huele muy bien.**
> This sauce smells very good.

> **¡Qué mal huelen estos zapatos!**
> These shoes smell awful!

el **olfato** NOUN
sense of smell

la **oliva** NOUN
olive
> **el aceite de oliva**
> olive oil

la **olla** NOUN
pot
> **una olla a presión**
> a pressure cooker

el **olor** NOUN
smell
> **un olor a tabaco**
> a smell of cigarette smoke
> **¡Qué mal olor!**
> What a horrible smell!

olvidar VERB
1 **to forget**
> **No olvides comprar el pan.**
> Don't forget to buy the bread.

Se me olvidó por completo.
I completely forgot.
2 to leave
Olvidé las llaves en la mesa.
I left the keys on the table.

once (FEM **once**) ADJECTIVE,
PRONOUN
eleven

Tengo once años.
I'm eleven.
Son las once.
It's eleven o'clock.
el once de agosto
the eleventh of August
Nació el once de agosto.
He was born on the eleventh
of August.

la **onda** NOUN
wave

la **operación** (PL **operaciones**)
NOUN
operation
una operación de estómago
a stomach operation

operar VERB
Lo tienen que operar.
He has to have an operation.
■ **operarse**
to have an operation
Me tengo que operar de la
rodilla.
I have to have a knee operation.

opinar VERB
to think
¿Y tú qué opinas del nuevo
gimnasio?
So what do you think about the
new gym?

la **opinión** (PL las **opiniones**)
NOUN
opinion

la **oportunidad** NOUN
chance
No tuvo la oportunidad de
hacerlo.
He didn't have a chance to do it.

opuesto (FEM **opuesta**)
ADJECTIVE
opposite

oral (FEM **oral**) ADJECTIVE
oral
un examen oral
an oral exam

orden

orden *can be a masculine or a*
feminine noun.

A MASC NOUN
order

en orden alfabético
in alphabetical order

B (PL las **órdenes**) FEM NOUN
order

el **ordenador**
NOUN
computer

un ordenador portátil
a laptop

ordenar VERB
1 to tidy
¿Por qué no ordenas tu
habitación?
Why don't you tidy your room?
2 to order
El policía nos ordenó que
saliéramos del edificio.
The policeman ordered us to
leave the building.

ordinario (FEM **ordinaria**)
ADJECTIVE
ordinary
los acontecimientos
ordinarios
ordinary events

la **oreja** NOUN
ear

a b c d e f g h i j k l m n ñ o p q r s t u v w x y z

organizar VERB
to organize
> Te tienes que organizar
> mejor.
> You need to organize yourself
> better.

orgulloso (FEM **orgullosa**)
ADJECTIVE
proud

el **origen** (PL los **orígenes**) NOUN
origin

original (FEM **original**) ADJECTIVE
original

la **orilla** NOUN
1 **shore**
> un paseo a la orilla del mar
> a walk along the seashore
2 **bank**
> a orillas de
> on the shores of/on the banks of

> *Language tip*
> *a orillas de has two meanings.*
> *It can be translated as* **on the**
> **shores of** *and* **on the banks of**.

el **oro** NOUN
gold
> un collar de oro
> a gold necklace

la **orquesta** NOUN
orchestra
> una orquesta de jazz
> a jazz band

la **ortografía** NOUN
spelling

os PRONOUN
1 **you**
> No os
> oigo.
> I can't
> hear
> you.

> Os he comprado un libro a
> cada uno.
> I've bought each of you a book.
> Os lo doy.
> I'll give it to you.
> ¿Os han arreglado ya el
> ordenador?
> Have they fixed your computer
> yet?
2 **yourselves**
> ¿Os habéis hecho daño?
> Did you hurt yourselves?
> Os tenéis que levantar antes
> de las ocho.
> You have to get up before eight.
> Lavaos las manos.
> Wash your hands.
3 **each other**
> Quiero que os pidáis perdón.
> I want you to say sorry to each
> other.

oscurecer VERB
to get dark

la **oscuridad** NOUN
dark
> Estaban hablando en la
> oscuridad.
> They were talking in the dark.

oscuro (FEM **oscura**) ADJECTIVE
dark
> una habitación muy oscura
> a very dark room
> azul oscuro
> dark blue

> **a oscuras**
> in the dark

el **oso**
la **osa** NOUN
bear
> un oso de
> peluche
> a teddy bear

el **otoño** NOUN
autumn

en otoño
in autumn

otro (FEM **otra**)

otro *can be an adjective or a pronoun.*

A ADJECTIVE
1 another
otro coche
another car
¿Me das otra manzana, por favor?
Can I have another apple, please?
¿Hay alguna otra manera de hacerlo?
Is there any other way of doing it?

otra vez
again

2 other
Tengo otros planes.
I have other plans.

B PRONOUN
1 another one
**¿Has perdido el lápiz? —
No importa, tengo otro.**
Have you lost your pencil? —
It doesn't matter, I've got another one.
el otro/la otra
the other one
No quiero éste, quiero el otro.
I don't want this one, I want the other one.

2 other
Tengo otros planes.
I have other plans.

la **oveja** NOUN
sheep

el **oxígeno** NOUN
oxygen

oyendo VERB ▷ *see* **oír**
¿Estás oyendo lo que te dice?
Are you listening to what she's saying?

Spanish English

a
b
c
d
e
f
g
h
i
j
k
l
m
n
ñ
o
p
q
r
s
t
u
v
w
x
y
z

P p

la **paciencia** NOUN
patience

paciente ADJECTIVE, MASC/FEM
NOUN
patient

pacífico (FEM **pacífica**)
ADJECTIVE
peaceful

el **padre** NOUN
father
> mis padres
> my parents

el **padrino** NOUN
godfather
> mis padrinos
> my godparents

> **Did you know…?**
> *At a wedding, the **padrino** is the person who escorts the bride down the aisle and gives her away, usually her father.*

la **paga** NOUN
pocket money
> **Me dan la paga los domingos.**
> I get my pocket money on Sundays.

pagar VERB
to pay for
> **Tengo que pagar las entradas.**
> I have to pay for the tickets.
> **¿Dónde pago?**
> Where do I pay?

la **página** NOUN
page
> **Está en la página diez.**
> It's on page ten.
> **una página web**
> a Web page

el **país** (PL los **países**) NOUN
country
> **el País Vasco**
> the Basque Country

el **paisaje** NOUN
landscape
> **el paisaje de Castilla**
> the Castilian landscape

la **paja** NOUN
straw
> **un sombrero de paja**
> a straw hat

el **pájaro** NOUN
bird

la **pajita** NOUN
straw

la **pala** NOUN
1 **spade**
2 **shovel**

la **palabra** NOUN
word

pálido (FEM **pálida**) ADJECTIVE
pale
> **Se puso pálida.**
> She turned pale.

la **palma** NOUN
palm

el **palo** NOUN
stick
> **Le pegó con un palo.**
> He hit him with a stick.
> **una cuchara de palo**
> a wooden spoon

la **paloma** NOUN
pigeon

las **palomitas** NOUN
> **las palomitas de maíz**
> popcorn

Spanish English

el **pan** NOUN
  1 bread
    pan integral
    wholemeal bread
    pan de molde
    sliced bread
    una barra de pan
    a loaf of bread
  2 loaf
    Compré dos panes.
    I bought two loaves.

la **panadería** NOUN
  bakery

la **pandilla** NOUN
  gang

el **pánico** NOUN
  panic

    en un momento de pánico
    in a moment of panic
    Me entró pánico.
    I panicked.
    Les tengo pánico a las arañas.
    I'm terrified of spiders.

la **pantalla** NOUN
  screen
    una pantalla plana
    a flat screen

los **pantalones** NOUN
  trousers
    unos pantalones
    a pair of trousers
    pantalones cortos
    shorts
    pantalones vaqueros
    jeans

el **pañal** NOUN
  nappy

el **paño** NOUN
  cloth
    un paño de cocina
    a dishcloth

el **pañuelo** NOUN
  handkerchief

el **papa** NOUN
  pope
    el Papa
    the Pope

el **papá** (PL los **papás**) NOUN
  dad
    mis papás
    my mum and dad

    Papá Noel
    Father Christmas

el **papel** NOUN
  1 paper
    una bolsa de papel
    a paper bag
    papel de aluminio
    foil
    papel higiénico
    toilet paper
  2 piece of paper
    Lo escribí en un papel.
    I wrote it on a piece of paper.

la **papelera** NOUN
  1 wastepaper bin
  2 litter bin

el **paquete** NOUN
  1 packet
  2 parcel
    Me mandaron un paquete por correo.
    I got a parcel in the post.

par

---

par *can be a noun or an adjective.*

a b c d e f g h i j k l m n ñ o **p** q r s t u v w x y z

175

A MASC NOUN
1 **couple**
un par de horas al día
a couple of hours a day
2 **pair**
un par de calcetines
a pair of socks
Abrió la ventana de par en par.
He opened the window wide.
B (FEM **par**) ADJECTIVE
un número par
an even number

para PREPOSITION
for
Es para ti.
It's for you.
Tengo muchos deberes para mañana.
I have a lot of homework to do for tomorrow.
¿Para qué lo quieres?
What do you want it for?
¿Para qué sirve?
What's it for?
Estoy ahorrando para comprarme una moto.
I'm saving up to buy a motorbike.
para que te acuerdes de mí
so that you remember me

la **parada** NOUN
stop
una parada de autobús
a bus stop
una parada de taxis
a taxi rank

parado (FEM **parada**) ADJECTIVE
out of work
Hace seis meses que está parada.
She's been out of work for six months.
No te quedes ahí parado.
Don't just stand there.

el **paraguas** (PL los **paraguas**)
NOUN
umbrella

parar VERB
to stop
Paramos a poner gasolina.
We stopped to get some petrol.
No paró de llover en toda la noche.
It didn't stop raining all night.
■ **pararse**
to stop
El reloj se ha parado.
The clock has stopped.

el **parasol** NOUN
umbrella

parecer VERB
1 **to seem**
Parece muy simpática.
She seems very nice.
2 **to look**
Esos zapatos no parecen muy cómodos.
Those shoes don't look very comfortable.
Parece una modelo.
She looks like a model.
Parece que va a llover.
It looks as if it's going to rain.
3 **to think**
¿Qué te pareció la película?
What did you think of the film?

Me parece que sí.
I think so.
Me parece que no.
I don't think so.

■ **parecerse**
to look alike
María y Ana se parecen mucho.
María and Ana look very much alike.

parecerse a
to look like
Te pareces mucho a tu madre.
You look very like your mother.

parecido (FEM **parecida**)
ADJECTIVE
similar
Tu blusa es parecida a la mía.
Your blouse is similar to mine.

la **pared** NOUN
wall

la **pareja** NOUN
1 **couple**
Había varias parejas bailando.
There were several couples dancing.
2 **pair**
En este juego hay que formar parejas.
For this game you have to get into pairs.

el **paréntesis** (PL los paréntesis) NOUN
bracket

entre paréntesis
in brackets

el/la **pariente** NOUN
relative
Es pariente mío.
He's a relative of mine.

Language tip
Be careful! **pariente** *does not mean the same as* **parent**.

el **parking** (PL los **parkings**)
NOUN
car park

Language tip
Be careful! **parking** *does not mean the same as* **parking**.

el **parque**
NOUN
park

un parque de atracciones
an amusement park
un parque zoológico
a zoo

el **párrafo** NOUN
paragraph

la **parrilla** NOUN
grill
carne a la parrilla
grilled meat

la **parte** NOUN
part
¿De qué parte de Inglaterra eres?
What part of England are you from?
la mayor parte de los españoles
most Spanish people
la parte delantera
the front
la parte de atrás
the back
la parte de arriba
the top
la parte de abajo
the bottom
alguna parte
somewhere
Tengo que haberlo dejado en alguna parte.
I must have left it somewhere.
por todas partes
everywhere
¡Hay gatos por todas partes!
There are cats everywhere!

Spanish English

a b c d e f g h i j k l m n ñ o **p** q r s t u v w x y z

177

Spanish English

a b c d e f g h i j k l m n ñ o **p** q r s t u v w x y z

¿De parte de quién?
Who's calling please?

participar VERB
to take part
Voy a participar en un concurso.
I'm going to take part in a competition.

el **participio** NOUN
participle

particular (FEM **particular**)
ADJECTIVE
private
clases particulares
private classes

la **partida** NOUN
game

echar una partida de cartas
to have a game of cards

el **partido** NOUN
1 **match**
2 **party**

partir VERB
1 **to cut**
2 **to crack**
3 **to break off**

a partir de ahora
from now on

■ **partirse**
to break
El remo se partió en dos.
The oar broke in two.

la **pasada** NOUN
¡Ese coche es una pasada!
This car is amazing!

pasado

pasado can be an adjective or a noun.

A (FEM **pasada**) ADJECTIVE
1 **last**
el verano pasado
last summer
2 **after**
Pasado el semáforo, verás un cine.
After the traffic lights you'll see a cinema.

pasado mañana
the day after tomorrow

B NOUN
past
en el pasado
in the past

el **pasajero**
la **pasajera** NOUN
passenger

el **pasaporte** NOUN
passport

pasar VERB
1 **to pass**
¿Me pasas la sal, por favor?
Can you pass me the salt, please?
Cuando termines pásasela a Isabel.
When you've finished pass it on to Isabel.
Un momento, te paso con Pedro.
Just a moment, I'll put you on to Pedro.
2 **to go past**
Pasaron varios coches.
Several cars went past.
Pasaron cinco años.
Five years went by.
3 **to spend**
Voy a pasar unos días con ella.
I'm going to spend a few days with her.
Me pasé el fin de semana estudiando.
I spent the weekend studying.
4 **to happen**
Por suerte no le pasó nada.
Luckily nothing happened to him.

¿Qué pasa?
What's the matter?
¿Qué le pasa a Juan?
What's the matter with Juan?
Hemos pasado mucho frío.
We were very cold.

¡Pase, por favor!
Please come in.
pasarlo bien
to have a good time

el **pasatiempo** NOUN
hobby

la **Pascua** NOUN
Easter

¡Felices Pascuas!
Happy Christmas!

pasear VERB
to walk
ir a pasear
to go for a walk

el **paseo** NOUN
walk
Salimos a dar un paseo.
We went out for a walk.
un paseo en barco
a boat trip
un paseo en bicicleta
a bike ride

dar un paseo
to go for a walk

el **pasillo** NOUN
1 **corridor**
2 **aisle**

pasmado (FEM **pasmada**)
ADJECTIVE
amazed

Cuando me enteré, me quedé pasmado.
I was amazed when I found out.

el **paso** NOUN
1 **step**
Dio un paso hacia atrás.
He took a step backwards.
He oído pasos.
I heard footsteps.
2 **way**
Han cerrado el paso.
They've blocked the way.
El banco me pilla de paso.
The bank is on my way.
un paso de peatones
a pedestrian crossing
un paso de cebra
a zebra crossing

la **pasta**
NOUN
pasta

pasta de dientes
toothpaste

el **pastel** NOUN
cake

la **pastelería** NOUN
cake shop

la **pastilla** NOUN
pill
pastillas para la tos
cough sweets

la **pata** NOUN
leg
saltar a la pata coja
to hop

la **patada** NOUN
Me dio una patada.
He kicked me.

la **patata** NOUN
potato
un filete con patatas fritas
steak and chips
una bolsa de patatas fritas
a bag of crisps

a b c d e f g h i j k l m n ñ o **p** q r s t u v w x y z

179

Spanish English

a b c d e f g h i j k l m n ñ o **p** q r s t u v w x y z

el **patín** (PL los **patines**) NOUN
1 **roller skate**
   los patines en línea
   Rollerblades
2 **skate**

el **patinaje** NOUN
1 **roller skating**
2 **ice skating**

patinar VERB
1 **to roller-skate**
2 **to skate**

el **patinete** NOUN
   scooter

el **patio** NOUN
   playground
      el patio de recreo
      the playground

el **pato** NOUN
   duck

el **payaso**
   la **payasa** NOUN
   clown
      Deja de hacer el payaso.
      Stop clowning around.

la **paz** (PL las **paces**) NOUN
   peace

   ¡Déjame en paz!
   Leave me alone!

el **PC** ABBREVIATION
   PC

el **peatón** (PL los **peatones**)
   NOUN
   pedestrian

la **peca** NOUN
   freckle

el **pecho** NOUN
   chest

pedalear VERB
   to pedal

el **pedazo** NOUN
   piece
      un pedazo de pan

a piece of bread
   hacer pedazos
   to smash

pedir VERB
   to ask for
      Le pedí dinero a mi padre.
      I asked my father for some money.
      **He pedido hora para el
      médico.**
      I've asked for a doctor's
      appointment.
      ¿Te puedo pedir un favor?
      Can I ask you a favour?
      pedir disculpas a alguien
      to apologize to somebody
      Le pedí disculpas.
      I apologized to him.
      **Tuve que pedir dinero
      prestado.**
      I had to borrow some money.

el **pegamento** NOUN
   glue

pegar VERB
1 **to hit**
      Andrés me ha pegado.
      Andrés hit me.
      La pelota pegó en el árbol.
      The ball hit the tree.
2 **to stick**
      Lo puedes pegar con celo.
      You can stick it on with sellotape.
      **Tengo que pegar las fotos en
      el álbum.**
      I have to stick the photos in the
      album.
3 **to give**
      Le pegó una bofetada.
      She gave him a slap.
      ¡Qué susto me has pegado!
      What a fright you gave me!
      Pegó un grito.
      He shouted.

la **pegatina** NOUN
   sticker

peinar VERB
      peinar a alguien
      to comb somebody's hair

Péinate antes de salir.
Comb your hair before you go out.

el **peine** NOUN
comb

p.ej. ABBREVIATION
(= **por ejemplo**)
e.g.

pelar VERB
to peel
Se me está pelando la espalda.
My back is peeling.

la **pelea** NOUN
1 **fight**
Hubo una pelea en la discoteca.
There was a fight at the disco.
2 **argument**
Tuvo una pelea con su novio.
She had an argument with her boyfriend.

pelear VERB
1 **to fight**
¡Deja de pelear con tu hermano!
Stop fighting with your brother!
2 **to argue**
Pelean por cualquier tontería.
They argue over the slightest thing.

la **película** NOUN
film
A las ocho ponen una película.
There's a film on at eight.

el **peligro** NOUN
danger

peligroso (FEM **peligrosa**)
ADJECTIVE
dangerous

pelirrojo (FEM **pelirroja**)
ADJECTIVE
Es pelirrojo.
He has red hair.

pellizcar
VERB
to pinch

Me pellizcó el brazo.
He pinched my arm.

el **pellizco** NOUN
pinch
un pellizco de sal
a pinch of salt

el **pelo** NOUN
hair
Tiene el pelo rizado.
He has curly hair.
No perdí el avión por un pelo.
I only just caught the plane.
Se me pusieron los pelos de punta.
It made my hair stand on end.
Me estás tomando el pelo.
You're pulling my leg.

la **pelota** NOUN
ball
jugar a la pelota
to play ball

peludo (FEM **peluda**) ADJECTIVE
hairy

la **peluquería** NOUN
hairdresser's

el **peluquero**
la **peluquera** NOUN
hairdresser

la **pena** NOUN
shame
> **Es una pena que no puedas venir.**
> It's a shame you can't come.
> **Me dio tanta pena el pobre animal.**
> I felt so sorry for the poor animal.
> **Me da pena tener que marcharme.**
> I'm so sad to have to go away.

> **Vale la pena.**
> It's worth it.
> **¡Qué pena!**
> What a shame!

el **penalty** (PL los **penaltys**) NOUN
penalty

el **pendiente** NOUN
earring

la **pendiente** NOUN
slope

pensar VERB
to think
> **Piénsalo bien antes de contestar.**
> Think carefully before you answer.
> **¿Piensas que vale la pena?**
> Do you think it's worth it?
> **¿Qué piensas de Manolo?**
> What do you think of Manolo?
> **Tengo que pensarlo.**
> I'll have to think about it.

la **pensión** (PL las **pensiones**) NOUN
pension
> **pensión completa**
> full board
> **media pensión**
> half board

penúltimo
penúltima
A ADJECTIVE
> **la penúltima estación**
> the last station but one

B MASC/FEM NOUN
> **Soy el penúltimo.**
> I'm second to last.

peor (FEM **peor**) ADJECTIVE, ADVERB
1 **worse**
> **Su situación es peor que la nuestra.**
> Their situation is worse than ours.
> **Hoy me siento peor.**
> I feel worse today.
2 **worst**
> **el peor día de mi vida**
> the worst day of my life
> **Sacó la peor nota de toda la clase.**
> He got the worst mark in the whole class.

el **pepino** NOUN
cucumber
> **Me importa un pepino lo que piense.**
> I couldn't care less what he thinks.

la **pepita** NOUN
pip

pequeño (FEM **pequeña**)
ADJECTIVE
small
> **un niño pequeño**
> a small child
> **Estos zapatos me quedan pequeños.**
> These shoes are too small for me.
> **¿Cuál prefieres? — El pequeño.**
> Which would you prefer? — The small one.
> **mi hermana pequeña**
> my younger sister

la **pera** NOUN
pear

el **perdedor**
la **perdedora** NOUN
loser
> **Eres mal perdedor.**
> You're a bad loser.

perder VERB

1 to lose

He perdido el monedero.
I've lost my purse.

Está intentando perder peso.
He's trying to lose weight.
perder el conocimiento
to lose consciousness
Perdimos dos a cero.
We lost two nil.

2 to miss

Date prisa o perderás el tren.
Hurry up or you'll miss the train.
No quiero perder esta oportunidad.
I don't want to miss this opportunity.
Tenía miedo de perderme.
I was afraid of getting lost.

la **pérdida** NOUN
loss

Fue una pérdida de tiempo.
It was a waste of time.

perdido (FEM **perdida**) ADJECTIVE
lost

el **perdón** NOUN
Le pedí perdón.
I apologized to him.
¡Perdón!
Sorry!/Excuse me!

> **Language tip**
>
> **¡perdón!** has two meanings. It can be translated as **sorry!** and **excuse me!**

perdonar VERB
to forgive

¿Me perdonas?
Will you forgive me?
¡Perdona! ¿Tienes hora?
Excuse me, do you have the time?
¡Perdona! ¿Te he hecho daño?
I'm so sorry! Did I hurt you?

la **pereza** NOUN
laziness
¡Qué pereza tengo!
I feel so lazy!
Me da pereza levantarme.
I can't be bothered to get up.

perezoso (FEM **perezosa**)
ADJECTIVE
lazy

perfecto (FEM **perfecta**)
ADJECTIVE
perfect

el **periódico** NOUN
newspaper

el **periodo** NOUN
period
un periodo de tres meses
a three-month period

el **permiso** NOUN
permission
Tengo que pedirles permiso a mis padres.
I have to ask my parents' permission.

permitir VERB
to allow
No nos permiten llevar zapatillas de deporte.
We're not allowed to wear trainers.
No me lo puedo permitir.
I can't afford it.

pero CONJUNCTION
but
> Me gustaría, pero no puedo.
> I'd like to, but I can't.

el **perro**
la **perra** NOUN
dog

> un perro callejero
> a stray dog
> Es una perra muy buena.
> She's a very good dog.
> ¿Es perra o perro?
> Is it a bitch or a dog?
> un perro pastor
> a sheepdog

perseguir VERB
to chase
> Mi perro persigue a los gatos.
> My dog chases cats.
> Me persigue la policía.
> The police are after me.

persiguiendo VERB ▷see
perseguir
> Me venían persiguiendo por la calle.
> They were chasing me down the street.

la **persona** NOUN
person
> Es una persona encantadora.
> He's a really nice person.
> personas
> people
> Había unas diez personas en la sala.
> There were about ten people in the hall.

el **personaje** NOUN
character
> los personajes de la novela
> the characters in the novel

personal (FEM **personal**)
ADJECTIVE
personal

pertenecer VERB
> pertenecer a
> to belong to
> Este reloj perteneció a su abuelo.
> This watch belonged to his grandfather.
> Esto me pertenece a mí.
> This belongs to me.

la **pesa** NOUN
weight

la **pesadilla** NOUN
nightmare

pesado
pesada

> **pesado** *can be an adjective or a noun.*

A ADJECTIVE
heavy
> ¡No seas pesado!
> Don't be a pain!
B MASC/FEM NOUN
> Mi primo es un pesado.
> My cousin is a pain.
> Mi hermana es una pesada.
> My sister is a pain.

pesar VERB
1 **to weigh**
> El paquete pesaba dos kilos.
> The parcel weighed two kilos.
> ¿Cuánto pesas?
> How much do you weigh?
> Tengo que pesarme.
> I must weigh myself.
2 **to be heavy**
> Esta maleta pesa mucho.
> This suitcase is very heavy.

a b c d e f g h i j k l m n ñ o **p** q r s t u v w x y z

¡No pesa nada!
It isn't heavy at all!
a pesar del mal tiempo
in spite of the bad weather
a pesar de que la quiero
even though I love her

la **pesca** NOUN
fishing

la **pescadería** NOUN
fishmonger's

el **pescado**
NOUN
fish

Quiero comprar pescado.
I want to buy some fish.

el **pescador** NOUN
fisherman
Mi tío es pescador.
My uncle is a fisherman.

pescar VERB
1 **to fish**
Los domingos íbamos a pescar.
On Sundays we used to go fishing.
2 **to catch**
Pescamos varias truchas.
We caught several trout.

el **peso** NOUN
weight
ganar peso
to put on weight
Ha perdido mucho peso.
He's lost a lot of weight.

la **pestaña** NOUN
eyelash

la **peste** NOUN
stink
¡Qué peste hay aquí!
There's a real stink in here!

el **pestillo** NOUN
1 **bolt**
2 **latch**

el **petardo** NOUN
banger

la **petición** (PL las **peticiones**)
NOUN
request

el **petróleo** NOUN
oil

el **pez** (PL los **peces**) NOUN
fish
Cogimos tres peces.
We caught three fish.
un pez de colores
a goldfish

el **piano** NOUN
piano

la **picadura** NOUN
1 **bite**
2 **sting**

picante (FEM **picante**) ADJECTIVE
hot

picar VERB
1 **to bite**
Me ha picado algo.
I've been bitten by something.
2 **to sting**
3 **to chop up**
Luego picas un poquito de jamón.
Then you chop up a bit of ham.
La salsa pica bastante.
The sauce is quite hot.
Saqué algunas cosas para picar.
I put out some nibbles.

Me pica la espalda.
I've got an itchy back.

el **pico** NOUN
Eran las tres y pico.
It was just after three.
doscientos y pico euros
just over two hundred euros

pidiendo VERB ▷*see* **pedir**
Siempre anda pidiendo algo.
She's always asking for something.

el **pie** NOUN
foot
Fuimos a pie.
We went on foot.
Estaba de pie junto a mi cama.
She was standing next to my bed.

ponerse de pie
to stand up

la **piedra** NOUN
stone
Nos tiraban piedras.
They were throwing stones at us.

la **piel** NOUN
1 **skin**
Tengo la piel grasa.
I have greasy skin.
2 **peel**
3 **fur**
un abrigo de pieles
a fur coat
4 **leather**
un bolso de piel
a leather bag

pienso VERB ▷*see* **pensar**
Pienso que sí.
I think so.

pierdo VERB ▷*see* **perder**
Siempre pierdo.
I always lose.

la **pierna** NOUN
leg

la **pieza** NOUN
piece
una pieza del rompecabezas
a piece of the jigsaw puzzle

el **pijama** NOUN
pyjamas
un pijama
a pair of pyjamas

la **pila** NOUN
1 **battery**
Funciona con pilas.
It goes on batteries.
2 **pile**
una pila de revistas
a pile of magazines

pillar VERB
to catch
Pillaron al ladrón.
They caught the thief.
Lo pillé haciendo trampa.
I caught him cheating.

pillo (FEM **pilla**) ADJECTIVE
1 **crafty**
2 **naughty**

el/la **piloto** NOUN
pilot

la **pimienta** NOUN
pepper
pimienta negra
black pepper

el **pimiento** NOUN
pepper

el **pincel** NOUN
paintbrush

el/la **pinchadiscos** (PL los/las **pinchadiscos**) NOUN
disc jockey

pinchar VERB
1 **to prick**
Me pinché con un alfiler.
I pricked myself on a pin.
Me pincharon en el brazo.
They gave me an injection in the arm.

2 to burst
El clavo pinchó la pelota.
The nail burst the ball.
Se me pinchó una rueda.
I had a puncture.

el **pinchazo** NOUN
puncture
Tuvimos un pinchazo en la autopista.
We got a puncture on the motorway.

el **ping-pong** NOUN
table tennis
jugar al ping-pong
to play table tennis

el **pino** NOUN
pine tree

> **hacer el pino**
> to do a headstand

la **pinta** NOUN
tener buena pinta
to look good
La paella tiene muy buena pinta.
The paella looks delicious.
Con esas gafas tienes pinta de maestra.
You look like a teacher with those glasses on.

el **pintalabios** NOUN (PL los pintalabios)
lipstick

pintar VERB
1 to paint
Quiero pintar la habitación de azul.
I want to paint the room blue.
2 to colour in
Dibujó un árbol y lo pintó.
He drew a tree and coloured it in.
Me estoy pintando las uñas.
I'm painting my nails.

el **pintor**
la **pintora** NOUN
painter

Soy pintor.
I'm a painter.

la **pintura** NOUN
1 paint
Tengo que comprar más pintura.
I've got to buy some more paint.
2 painting
varias pinturas al óleo
several oil paintings

la **pinza** NOUN
1 clothes peg
2 hairgrip

la **piña** NOUN
pineapple

la **pipa** NOUN
1 pipe
Fuma en pipa.
He smokes a pipe.
2 seed
comer pipas
to eat sunflower seeds

> *Did you know...?*
> **pipas** *are a common snack which both children and adults enjoy.*

el/la **pirata**
NOUN
pirate

un pirata informático
a hacker
un DVD pirata
a pirate DVD

la **pisada** NOUN
1 footprint
2 footstep

pisar VERB
1 to walk on
¿Se puede pisar el suelo de la cocina?
Can I walk on the kitchen floor?

2 to tread on
Perdona, te he pisado.
Sorry, I trod on your toe.

la **piscina** NOUN
swimming pool

el **piso** NOUN
1 flat
Vivimos en un piso céntrico.
We live in a flat in the town
centre.
2 floor
**Su oficina está en el
segundo piso.**
His office is on the second
floor.

la **pista** NOUN
1 clue
¿Te doy una pista?
Shall I give you a clue?
2 court
la pista de aterrizaje
the runway
la pista de esquí
the ski slope
la pista de patinaje
the ice rink

la **pistola** NOUN
pistol

pitar VERB
to blow one's whistle
El policía nos pitó.
The policeman blew his whistle
at us.

el **pito** NOUN
whistle

la **pizarra** NOUN
board
una pizarra interactiva
an interactive whiteboard

la **pizca** NOUN
pinch
una pizca de sal
a pinch of salt

el **plan** NOUN
plan

**¿Qué planes tienes para este
verano?**
What are your plans for the
summer?
Lo dije en plan de broma.
I said it as a joke.

la **plancha** NOUN
iron
pescado a la plancha
grilled fish

planchar VERB
1 to iron
**Tengo que planchar esta
camisa.**
I've got to iron this shirt.
2 to do the ironing
¿Quieres que planche?
Do you want me to do the
ironing?

el **planeta** NOUN
planet

el **plano** NOUN
street plan
en primer plano
in close-up

la **planta** NOUN
1 plant
Tengo que regar las plantas.
I have to water the plants.
2 floor
El edificio tiene tres plantas.
The building has three floors.
la planta baja
the ground floor

plantar VERB
to plant

el **plástico** NOUN
plastic
cubiertos de plástico
plastic cutlery

la **plata** NOUN
silver

el **plátano** NOUN
banana

el **plato** NOUN
1 **plate**
¿Me pasas un plato?
Could you pass me a plate?
2 **dish**
un plato típico de Galicia
a typical Galician dish
el plato del día
the dish of the day
3 **course**
¿Qué hay de segundo plato?
What's for the main course?

la **playa** NOUN
1 **beach**

Los niños jugaban en la playa.
The children were playing on
the beach.
2 **seaside**
Prefiero la playa a la montaña.
I prefer the seaside to the
mountains.

la **plaza** NOUN
square
la plaza del pueblo
the town square
la plaza mayor
the main square
una plaza de toros
a bullring

el **plazo** NOUN
period

en un plazo de diez días
within a period of ten days
El viernes se cumple el plazo.
Friday is the deadline.

pleno (FEM **plena**) ADJECTIVE
en pleno verano
in the middle of summer
a plena luz del día
in broad daylight

el **pliegue** NOUN
fold

el **plomo** NOUN
1 **lead**
gasolina sin plomo
unleaded petrol
2 **fuse**
Se han fundido los plomos.
The fuses have blown.

la **pluma** NOUN
1 **feather**
2 **pen**
una pluma estilográfica
a fountain pen

plural ADJECTIVE, MASC NOUN
plural

la **población** (PL las
poblaciones) NOUN
1 **population**
2 **town**

pobre (FEM **pobre**) ADJECTIVE
poor
Somos pobres.
We're poor.
los pobres
the poor

la **pobreza** NOUN
poverty

poco (FEM **poca**)

poco *can be an adjective, adverb
or pronoun.*

A ADJECTIVE
not much
Hay poca leche.
There isn't much milk.

189

a b c d e f g h i j k l m n ñ o **p** q r s t u v w x y z

Tenemos muy poco tiempo.
We haven't got much time.
pocos
not many
Tiene pocos amigos.
He hasn't got many friends.
B ADVERB
Sus libros son poco conocidos aquí.
His books are not very well known here.
por poco
nearly
Por poco me caigo.
I nearly fell.
C PRONOUN
unos pocos
a few
Me llevé unos pocos.
I took a few with me.
un poco
a bit
¿Tienes frío? — Un poco.
Are you cold? — A bit.
¿Me das un poco?
Can I have a bit?
Tomé un poco de zumo.
I had a bit of juice.

dentro de poco
soon
hace poco
not long ago

poder VERB
1 can
Yo puedo ayudarte.
I can help you.
¿Puedo usar tu teléfono?
Can I use your phone?
Aquí no se puede jugar.
You can't play here.
¡Me lo podías haber dicho!
You could have told me!
¡No puede ser!
That's impossible!
2 to be able to
Creo que mañana no voy a poder ir.
I don't think I'll be able to come tomorrow.

Puede que llegue mañana.
He may arrive tomorrow.

poderoso (FEM **poderosa**)
ADJECTIVE
powerful

podrido (FEM **podrida**) ADJECTIVE
rotten

la **poesía** NOUN
1 poetry
Me gusta la poesía.
I like poetry.
2 poem
una poesía de Machado
a poem by Machado

el/la **poeta** NOUN
poet

policía

policía can be a masculine or a feminine noun.

A MASC NOUN
policeman
Es policía.
He's a policeman.
B FEM NOUN
1 police
Llamamos a la policía.
We called the police.
2 policewoman
Soy policía.
I'm a policewoman.

el **polideportivo** NOUN
sports centre

la **política** NOUN
1 politics
Hablaban de política.
They were talking about politics.

Language tip
When talking about people's jobs in Spanish, you do not use an article.

2 politician
político

político can be an adjective or a noun.

A (FEM **política**) ADJECTIVE
political

B NOUN
politician
Soy político.
I'm a politician.

el **pollo** NOUN
chicken
pollo asado
roast chicken

el **polo** NOUN
1 ice lolly
2 polo shirt

el **polvo** NOUN
dust
quitar el polvo
to do the dusting
quitar el polvo a algo
to dust something
polvos de talco
talcum powder
Estoy hecho polvo.
I'm shattered.

pondrá VERB ▷see **poner**
Ya lo pondrá en su sitio cuando acabe.
He'll put it back when he's finished.

poner VERB
1 to put
¿Dónde pongo mis cosas?
Where shall I put my things?
Se puso a mi lado en clase.
He sat down beside me in class.
2 to put on
Me puse el abrigo.
I put my coat on.
¿Pongo música?
Shall I put some music on?
Pon el radiador.
Put the heater on.
No sé que ponerme.
I don't know what to wear.
¿Ponen alguna película esta noche?
Is there a film on tonight?
3 to set
La maestra nos puso un examen.
Our teacher set us an exam.

Puse el despertador para las siete.
I set the alarm for seven o'clock.
poner la mesa
to lay the table
¿Me pone con el Sr. García, por favor?
Could you put me through to Mr García, please?
¿Qué te pongo?
What can I get you?
Cuando se lo dije se puso muy triste.
He was very sad when I told him.
ponerse a hacer algo
to start doing something
Se puso a llorar.
He started crying.

pongo VERB ▷see **poner**
¿Lo pongo aquí?
Shall I put it here?

por PREPOSITION
1 for
Lo hice por mis padres.
I did it for my parents.
Lo vendió por cien euros.
He sold it for a hundred euros.
Me castigaron por mentir.
I was punished for lying.
2 through
Pasamos por Valencia.
We went through Valencia.
3 by
Fueron apresados por la policía.
They were captured by the police.
Me agarró por el brazo.
He grabbed me by the arm.

191

Spanish English

a b c d e f g h i j k l m n ñ o p q r s t u v w x y z

4 along
Paseábamos por la playa.
We were walking along the beach.

5 per
cien kilómetros por hora
a hundred kilometres per hour
diez euros por persona
ten euros per person

por la mañana
in the morning
por la noche
at night
¿Por qué?
Why?

la **porción** (PL las **porciones**)
NOUN
portion

porque CONJUNCTION
because
No fuimos porque llovía.
We didn't go because it was raining.

la **porquería** NOUN
Este CD es una porquería.
This CD's rubbish.

la **portada** NOUN
1 front page
2 cover

el **portal** NOUN
1 hallway
Los buzones están en el portal.
The letterboxes are in the hallway.
el portal de Belén
the nativity scene
2 portal

portarse VERB
to behave
Se está portando muy mal.
He's behaving very badly.

¡Pórtate bien!
Behave yourself!

portátil (FEM **portátil**) ADJECTIVE
portable

el **portazo** NOUN
Dio un portazo.
He slammed the door.

la **portería** NOUN
goal
El balón entró en la portería.
The ball went into the goal.

el **portero**
la **portera** NOUN
1 caretaker
2 goalkeeper
un portero automático
an entryphone

poseer VERB
to possess

la **posibilidad** NOUN
1 possibility
Es una posibilidad.
It's a possibility.
2 chance
Tendrás la posibilidad de viajar.
You'll have the chance to travel.
Tiene muchas posibilidades de ganar.
He has a good chance of winning.

posible (FEM **posible**) ADJECTIVE
possible
>**Es posible.**
>It's possible.
>**Haremos todo lo posible.**
>We'll do everything we can.
>**Es posible que ganen.**
>They might win.

la **posición** (PL las **posiciones**)
NOUN
position
>**una posición estratégica**
>a strategic position
>**Está en primera posición.**
>He's in first place.

positivo (FEM **positiva**)
ADJECTIVE
positive
>**El test dio positivo.**
>The test was positive.

la **postal** NOUN
postcard

el **poste** NOUN
post

el **póster** (PL los **pósters**) NOUN
poster

el **postre** NOUN
dessert
>**De postre tomé un helado.**
>I had ice cream for dessert.
>**¿Qué hay de postre?**
>What's for dessert?

potable (FEM **potable**) ADJECTIVE
>**agua potable**
>drinking water

potente (FEM **potente**)
ADJECTIVE
powerful

el **pozo** NOUN
well

la **práctica** NOUN
practice
>**No tengo mucha práctica.**
>I haven't had much practice.

practicar VERB
to practise
>**Tengo que practicar un poco más.**
>I need to practise a bit more.
>**No practico ningún deporte.**
>I don't do any sports.

práctico (FEM **práctica**)
ADJECTIVE
practical

el **precio** NOUN
price
>**Han subido los precios.**
>Prices have gone up.

precioso (FEM **preciosa**)
ADJECTIVE
beautiful
>**¡Es precioso!**
>It's beautiful!

preciso (FEM **precisa**) ADJECTIVE
1 **precise**
>**en ese preciso momento**
>at that precise moment
2 **accurate**
>**un reloj muy preciso**
>a very accurate watch
>**No es preciso que vengas.**
>There's no need for you to come.

preferido (FEM **preferida**)
ADJECTIVE
favourite

preferir VERB
to prefer
>**Prefiero un buen libro a una película.**
>I prefer a good book to a film.
>**Prefiero ir mañana.**
>I'd rather go tomorrow.

prefiero VERB ▷ see **preferir**
>**Prefiero el verde.**
>I prefer the green one.

la **pregunta** NOUN
question
>**hacer una pregunta**
>to ask a question

preguntar VERB
to ask
> **Siempre me preguntas lo mismo.**
> You're always asking me the same question.
> **Me preguntó por ti.**
> He asked after you.
> **Me pregunto si estará enterado.**
> I wonder if he's heard yet.

el **premio** NOUN
prize
> **llevarse un premio**
> to get a prize

preocupado
(FEM **preocupada**) ADJECTIVE
worried
> **Estoy preocupado por el examen.**
> I'm worried about the exam.

preocupar VERB
to worry
> **No te preocupes.**
> Don't worry.
> **preocuparse por algo**
> to worry about something
> **Se preocupa por sus gatitos.**
> She worries about her kittens.
> **Si llego un poco tarde se preocupa.**
> If I arrive a bit late he gets worried.

preparar VERB
1 **to prepare**
> **No he preparado el discurso.**
> I haven't prepared my talk.
2 **to prepare for**
> **¿Te has preparado el examen?**
> Have you prepared for the exam?
3 **to cook**
> **Mi madre estaba preparando la cena.**
> My mother was cooking dinner.
> **Me estaba preparando para salir.**
> I was getting ready to go out.

el **presentador**
la **presentadora** NOUN
presenter

presentar VERB
1 **to introduce**

> **Me presentó a sus padres.**
> He introduced me to his parents.
2 **to hand in**
> **Mañana tengo que presentar un trabajo.**
> I have to hand in an essay tomorrow.

presentarse VERB
1 **to turn up**
> **Se presentó en mi casa sin avisar.**
> He turned up at my house without warning.
2 **to introduce oneself**
> **Me voy a presentar.**
> Let me introduce myself.
> **presentarse a un examen**
> to sit an exam

el **presente** ADJECTIVE, NOUN
present
> **Juan no estaba presente en la reunión.**
> Juan was not present at the meeting.
> **el presente**
> the present
> **los presentes**
> those present

> **¡Presente!**
> Here!

el **presidente**
la **presidenta** NOUN
president

el **preso**
la **presa** NOUN
prisoner

prestado (FEM **prestada**)
ADJECTIVE
La cinta no es mía, es prestada.
It's not my tape, somebody lent it to me.
Le pedí prestada la bicicleta.
I asked if I could borrow his bicycle.
Me dejó el coche prestado.
He lent me his car.

prestar VERB
to lend
Un amigo me prestó el diccionario.
A friend lent me the dictionary.
¿Me prestas el boli?
Can I borrow your pen?
Tienes que prestar atención.
You must pay attention.

presumido (FEM **presumida**)
ADJECTIVE
vain

presumir VERB
to show off
Lleva ropa cara para presumir.
He wears expensive clothes just to show off.

pretender VERB
1 **to intend**
Pretendo sacar al menos un notable.
I intend to get at least a B.
2 **to expect**
¡No pretenderás que te pague la comida!
You're not expecting me to pay for your meal, are you?
¿Qué pretendes decir con eso?
What do you mean by that?

> *Language tip*
> Be careful! **pretender** *does not mean the same as* **to pretend**.

prevenir VERB
to prevent

prevenir un accidente
to prevent an accident

previsto (FEM **prevista**)
ADJECTIVE
Tengo previsto volver mañana.
I plan to return tomorrow.
El avión tiene prevista su llegada a las dos.
The plane is due in at two o'clock.
Como estaba previsto, ganó él.
As expected, he won.

la **primavera** NOUN
spring
en primavera
in spring

primero (FEM **primera**)
ADJECTIVE, PRONOUN
first

> *Language tip*
> **primero** *becomes* **primer** *before a masculine singular noun.*

el primer día
the first day
la primera planta
the first floor
Primero vamos a comer.
Let's eat first.
en primera fila
in the front row
En primer lugar, veamos los datos.
Firstly, let's look at the facts.
Vivo en el primero.
I live on the first floor.
Fui la primera en llegar.
I was the first to arrive.
Juan es el primero de la clase.
Juan is top of the class.
El examen será a primeros de mayo.
The exam will be at the beginning of May.

el **primo**
la **prima** NOUN
cousin

la **princesa** NOUN
princess

principal (FEM **principal**)
ADJECTIVE
main
> **el personaje principal**
> the main character
> **Lo principal es que estás mejor.**
> The main thing is that you're better.

principalmente ADVERB
mainly

el **príncipe** NOUN
prince

el/la **principiante** NOUN
beginner

el **principio** NOUN
beginning
> **El principio me gustó.**
> I liked the beginning.
> **Al principio parecía fácil.**
> It seemed easy at first.

la **prisa** NOUN
rush
> **Con las prisas me olvidé el paraguas.**
> In the rush I forgot my umbrella.

> **¡Date prisa!**
> Hurry up!
> **Tengo prisa.**
> I'm in a hurry.

la **prisión** (PL las **prisiones**) NOUN
prison

el **prisionero**
la **prisionera** NOUN
prisoner

los **prismáticos** NOUN
binoculars

privado (FEM **privada**) ADJECTIVE
private
> **un colegio privado**
> a private school

probable (FEM **probable**)
ADJECTIVE
likely
> **Es muy probable.**
> It's very likely.
> **Es probable que llegue tarde.**
> He'll probably arrive late.

probablemente ADVERB
probably

el **probador** NOUN
changing room

probar VERB
1 **to prove**
> **La policía no pudo probarlo.**
> The police could not prove it.
2 **to taste**
> **Probé la sopa para ver si le faltaba sal.**
> I tasted the soup to see if it needed more salt.
3 **to try**
> **Prueba estas patatas a ver si te gustan.**
> Try these potatoes and see if you like them.
> **Me probé un vestido.**
> I tried on a dress.

el **problema** NOUN
problem

la **procesión** (PL las **procesiones**) NOUN
procession

el **proceso** NOUN
process

procurar VERB
to try

Procura terminarlo mañana.
Try to finish it tomorrow.

la **producción** (PL las
producciones) NOUN
production

producir VERB
to produce
No producimos lo suficiente.
We are not producing enough.
**¿Cómo se produjo el
accidente?**
How did the accident happen?

el **producto** NOUN
product
productos de limpieza
cleaning products
productos lácteos
dairy products

la **profesión** (PL las
profesiones) NOUN
profession

profesional ADJECTIVE, MASC/
FEM NOUN
professional

el **profesor**
la **profesora** NOUN
teacher
**Amelia es profesora de
inglés.**
Amelia is an English teacher.
mi profesor particular
my private tutor

Language tip
Be careful! **profesor** does not mean
the same as **professor**.

la **profundidad** NOUN
depth
la profundidad de la piscina
the depth of the pool
**Tiene dos metros de
profundidad.**
It's two metres deep.

profundo (FEM **profunda**)
ADJECTIVE
deep

una piscina poco profunda
a shallow pool

el **programa** NOUN
1 **programme**
un programa de televisión
a television programme
un programa-concurso
a quiz show
2 **program**
un programa informático
a computer program

el **progreso** NOUN
progress
**Carmen ha hecho muchos
progresos este trimestre.**
Carmen has made great progress
this term.

prohibir VERB
to ban
**Le prohibieron la entrada
en el edificio.**
He was banned from entering
the building.
**terminantemente
prohibido**
strictly forbidden

el **promedio** NOUN
average

la **promesa** NOUN
promise

prometer VERB
to promise
Prometió llevarnos al cine.
He promised to take us to the
cinema.

la **promoción**
(PL **promociones**) NOUN
promotion
Está en promoción.
It's on offer.

el **pronombre** NOUN
pronoun

el **pronóstico** NOUN
el pronóstico del tiempo
the weather forecast

197

pronto ADVERB
1 **soon**
   Los invitados llegarán pronto.
   The guests will be here soon.
2 **early**
   ¿Por qué has llegado tan pronto?
   Why are you so early?
   Hoy me he levantado muy pronto.
   I got up very early this morning.

De pronto, empezó a nevar.
All of a sudden it began to snow.

¡Hasta pronto!
See you soon!

pronunciar VERB
  to pronounce
   ¿Cómo se pronuncia esta palabra?
   How do you pronounce this word?

la **propina** NOUN
  tip
   ¿Vamos a dejar propina?
   Shall we leave a tip?

propio (FEM **propia**) ADJECTIVE
1 **own**
   Tengo mi propia habitación.
   I have my own room.
2 **himself**
   Lo anunció el propio ministro.
   It was announced by the minister himself.
   un nombre propio
   a proper noun

proponer VERB
  to suggest

Nos propuso pagar la cena a medias.
He suggested that we should go halves on the cost of the meal.
Se ha propuesto adelgazar.
He's decided to lose some weight.

el **propósito** NOUN
  purpose
   ¿Cuál es el propósito de su visita?
   What is the purpose of your visit?
   A propósito, ya tengo los billetes.
   By the way, I've got the tickets.
   Lo hizo a propósito.
   He did it deliberately.

propuesto VERB ▷see **proponer**
  He propuesto ayudarles.
  I've suggested helping them.

el/la **protagonista** NOUN
  main character
   El protagonista no muere en la película.
   The main character doesn't die in the film.
   El protagonista es Tom Cruise.
   Tom Cruise plays the lead.

proteger VERB
  to protect
   El muro le protegió de las balas.
   The wall protected him from the bullets.
   Nos protegimos de la lluvia en la cabaña.
   We sheltered from the rain in the hut.

protestar VERB
1 **to protest**
   Protestaron contra la subida de la gasolina.
   They protested against the rise in petrol prices.

2 to complain
Cómete la verdura y no protestes.
Eat your vegetables and don't complain.

el **provecho** NOUN
¡Buen provecho!
Enjoy your meal!
Sacó mucho provecho del curso.
He got a lot out of the course.

provocar VERB
1 to provoke
No quería pegarle pero me provocó.
I didn't mean to hit him but he provoked me.
2 to cause
La lluvia ha provocado graves inundaciones.
The rain caused serious flooding.
El incendio fue provocado.
The fire was started deliberately.

próximo (FEM **próxima**)
ADJECTIVE
next
Lo haremos la próxima semana.
We'll do it next week.
la próxima calle a la izquierda
the next street on the left

la próxima vez
next time

el **proyecto** NOUN
project

prueba

prueba can be a noun or part of the verb **probar**.

A FEM NOUN
1 test
El médico me hizo más pruebas.
The doctor did some more tests.

2 proof
Eso es la prueba de que lo hizo él.
This is the proof that he did it.
B VERB ▷ see **probar**
Prueba esto.
Try this.

pruebo VERB ▷ see **probar**
A ver que pruebo yo.
Let me try.

la **publicidad** NOUN
advertising
una campaña de publicidad
an advertising campaign

público

público can be an adjective or a noun.

A (FEM **pública**) ADJECTIVE
public
B MASC NOUN
1 public
cerrado al público
closed to the public
2 spectators

pude VERB ▷ see **poder**
No pude hacerlo.
I couldn't do it.

el **pueblo** NOUN
1 village

2 town

puedo VERB ▷ see **poder**
Yo puedo ayudarte.
I can help you.

el **puente** NOUN
bridge

hacer puente
to make a long weekend of it

Did you know...?
When a public holiday falls on a Tuesday or Thursday people often take off Monday or Friday as well to give themselves a long weekend.

la **puerta** NOUN
door
Llaman a la puerta.
There's somebody at the door.
Susana me acompañó a la puerta.
Susana saw me out.

el **puerto** NOUN
port
un puerto pesquero
a fishing port
un puerto de montaña
a mountain pass

pues CONJUNCTION
1 **then**
Tengo sueño. — ¡Pues vete a la cama!
I'm tired. — Then go to bed!
2 **well**
Pues, como te iba contando ...
Well, as I was saying ...
¡Pues no lo sabía!
Well I didn't know!

¡Pues claro!
Yes, of course!

puesto

puesto *can be a noun or part of the verb* **poner**.

A MASC NOUN
place
Acabé en primer puesto.
I finished in first place.
un puesto de trabajo
a job
B VERB ▷*see* **poner**
Han puesto un cartel en la ventana.

They've put a sign in the window.

el **pulgar** NOUN
thumb

el **pulmón** (PL los **pulmones**) NOUN
lung

pulsar VERB
to press

la **pulsera** NOUN
bracelet
un reloj de pulsera
a wrist watch

el **pulso** NOUN
pulse
El doctor le tomó el pulso.
The doctor took his pulse.
Tengo muy mal pulso.
My hand is very unsteady.
Echamos un pulso y le gané.
We had an arm-wrestling match and I won.

la **punta** NOUN
1 **tip**
2 **point**
Sácale punta al lápiz.
Sharpen your pencil.
la hora punta
the rush hour

la **puntería** NOUN
tener buena puntería
to be a good shot

la **puntilla** NOUN
andar de puntillas
to tiptoe
ponerse de puntillas
to stand on tiptoe

el **punto** NOUN
1 **point**
Perdieron por tres puntos.
They lost by three points.
Ése es un punto importante.
That's an important point.

2 dot

Mi e-mail es loveday arroba collins punto E-S (loveday@ collins.es).
My email address is loveday at collins dot E-S (loveday@collins. es).

3 full stop

punto y seguido
full stop, new sentence
punto y aparte
full stop, new paragraph
punto y coma
semi-colon
dos puntos
colon
puntos suspensivos
dot, dot, dot
Estábamos a punto de salir cuando llamaste.
We were about to go out when you phoned.
Estuve a punto de perder el tren.
I very nearly missed the train.

a la una en punto
at one o'clock sharp

la **puntuación** (PL las **puntuaciones**) NOUN

1 punctuation

los signos de puntuación
punctuation marks

2 score

Recibió una puntuación alta.
He got a high score.

el **puñado** NOUN
handful

un puñado de arena
a handful of sand

el **puñetazo** NOUN
punch

un puñetazo en la cara
a punch in the face
Le pegó un puñetazo.
He punched him.

el **puño** NOUN
fist

el **puré** (PL los **purés**) NOUN

puré de verduras
vegetable soup
puré de patatas
mashed potato

puro (FEM **pura**) ADJECTIVE
pure

pura lana
pure wool
Es la pura verdad.
That's the absolute truth.

puse VERB ▷ see **poner**
Yo lo puse allí.
I put it there.

Spanish English

a
b
c
d
e
f
g
h
i
j
k
l
m
n
ñ
o
p
q
r
s
t
u
v
w
x
y
z

Q q

el **quad** NOUN
quad bike

que

> **que** *can be a conjunction or a pronoun.*

A CONJUNCTION

1 **than**
Es más alto que tú.
He's taller than you.

2 **that**
José sabe que estás aquí.
José knows that you're here.
Dijo que vendría.
He said he'd come.
Dile que me llame.
Ask her to call me.
¡Que te mejores!
Get well soon!

B PRONOUN

1 **which**
la película que ganó el premio
the film which won the award
el juego que te compraste ayer
the game you bought yesterday

2 **who**
el hombre que vino ayer
the man who came yesterday
la chica que conocí
the girl I met

qué ADJECTIVE, ADVERB, PRONOUN

1 **what**
¿Qué haces?
What are you doing?
¿Qué hora es?
What's the time?

2 **which**
¿Qué película quieres ver?
Which film do you want to see?
¿Qué tal?
How are things?

No lo he hecho. ¿Y qué?
I haven't done it. So what?
¡Qué asco!
How revolting!

quedar VERB

1 **to be left**
Quedan dos manzanas.
There are two apples left.
Me quedan diez euros.
I've got ten euros left.

2 **to be**
Eso queda muy lejos de aquí.
That's a long way from here.

3 **to suit**
No te queda bien ese vestido.
That dress doesn't suit you.

4 **to arrange to meet**
Hemos quedado en el cine.
We've arranged to meet at the cinema.

▪ **quedarse**
to stay
Ve tú, yo me quedo.
You go, I'll stay.
quedarse con algo
to keep something
Quédese con el cambio.
Keep the change.

la **queja** NOUN
complaint

quejarse VERB
to complain
quejarse de algo
to complain about something
Se quejan de la comida.
They complain about the food.

quejarse de que ...
to complain that ...
Pablo se queja de que nadie lo escucha.
Pablo complains that nobody listens to him.

quemado (FEM **quemada**)
ADJECTIVE
burnt
El arroz estaba quemado.
The rice was burnt.
quemado por el sol
sunburnt

quemar VERB
to burn
He quemado la camisa con la plancha.
I burned my shirt with the iron.
Esta sopa quema.
This soup's boiling hot.
■ **quemarse**
to burn oneself
Me quemé con una cerilla.
I burned myself with a match.

quepa VERB ▷ see **caber**
No creo que quepa ahí.
I don't think it will fit in there.

querer VERB
1 **to want**
No quiero jugar.
I don't want to play.
¿Quieres un bocadillo?
Would you like a sandwich?
2 **to love**
Te quiero.
I love you.
3 **to mean**
No quería hacerte daño.
I didn't mean to hurt you.
Lo hice sin querer.
It was an accident.
querer decir
to mean
¿Qué quieres decir?
What do you mean?

querido (FEM **querida**) ADJECTIVE
dear

Querido Sr. Lobos
Dear Mr Lobos

querré VERB ▷ see **querer**
Jamás querré ir allí.
I'll never want to go there.

el **queso** NOUN
cheese

un bocadillo de queso
a cheese sandwich

quien PRONOUN
who
Fue Juan quien nos lo dijo.
It was Juan who told us.
Vi al chico con quien sales.
I saw the boy you're going out with.

quién PRONOUN
who
¿Quién es ésa?
Who's that?
¿A quién viste?
Who did you see?
¿De quién es ... ?
Whose is...?
¿De quién es este libro?
Whose is this book?
¿Quién es?
Who's there?/Who's calling?

> *Language tip*
> **¿Quién es?** *has two meanings. It can be translated as* **Who's there?** *when there's somebody at the door and* **Who's calling?** *when you answer the phone.*

quiero VERB ▷ see **querer**
Quiero un bocadillo.
I want a sandwich.

quieto (FEM **quieta**) ADJECTIVE
still
¡Estáte quieto!
Keep still!

la **química** NOUN

1 chemistry
clase de química
chemistry class
2 chemist
Es química.
She's a chemist.

el **químico** NOUN
chemist
Es químico.
He's a chemist.

quince (FEM **quince**) ADJECTIVE, PRONOUN
fifteen
quince euros
fifteen euros
Mi hermano tiene quince años.
My brother's fifteen.

el quince de enero
the fifteenth of January
Nació el quince de enero.
He was born on the fifteenth of January.

quinientos (FEM **quinientas**) ADJECTIVE, PRONOUN
five hundred

quinto (FEM **quinta**) ADJECTIVE, PRONOUN
fifth
Vivo en el quinto.
I live on the fifth floor.

el **quiosco** NOUN
un quiosco de periódicos
a news stand

Did you know…?
*In Spain, people traditionally buy their newspapers, lottery tickets, etc from the **quioscos** that are dotted around a town.*

quise VERB ▷ *see* **querer**
No quise ir al cine con él.
I didn't want to go to the cinema with him.

quisquilloso
(FEM **quisquillosa**) ADJECTIVE
fussy
No soy quisquillosa con la comida.
I'm not fussy about what I eat.

quitar VERB
to take away
Su hermana le quitó la pelota.
His sister took the ball away from him.
Me han quitado la cartera.
I've had my wallet stolen.
▪ **quitarse**
to take off
Juan se quitó la chaqueta.
Juan took his jacket off.
¡Quítate de en medio!
Get out of the way!

quizás ADVERB
perhaps

R r

la **rabia** NOUN
Me da mucha rabia.
It's really annoying.

la **rabieta** NOUN
tantrum
agarrarse una rabieta
to throw a tantrum

el **rabo** NOUN
tail
Ese perro tiene un rabo muy corto.
That dog has a very short tail.

la **racha** NOUN
una racha de buen tiempo
a spell of good weather
pasar una mala racha
to go through a bad patch

el **racimo** NOUN
bunch
un racimo de uvas
a bunch of grapes

la **ración** (PL las **raciones**) NOUN
portion
una ración de patatas fritas
a portion of chips

la **radio** NOUN
radio
El abuelo escucha la radio.
Granddad listens to the radio.
Lo oí por la radio.
I heard it on the radio.
la radio digital
digital radio

el **radio** NOUN
radius
en un radio de cincuenta kilómetros
within a fifty-kilometre radius

la **radiografía** NOUN
X-ray
Tengo que hacerme una radiografía.
I've got to have an X-ray.

la **raíz** (PL las **raíces**) NOUN
root
a raíz de
as a result of

rallar VERB
to grate
Primero rallas el queso.
First you grate the cheese.

la **rama** NOUN
branch

el **ramo** NOUN
bunch
un ramo de rosas
a bunch of roses

rápidamente ADVERB
quickly

rápido

rápido *can be an adjective or an adverb.*

A (FEM **rápida**) ADJECTIVE
fast
un coche muy rápido
a very fast car
Fue una visita muy rápida.
It was a very quick visit.
B ADVERB
fast
Conduces demasiado rápido.
You drive too fast.

Lo hice tan rápido como pude.
I did it as quickly as I could.
¡Rápido!
Hurry up!

la **raqueta** NOUN
1 **racket**

2 **bat**

raro (FEM **rara**) ADJECTIVE
strange
Es una cosa muy rara.
It's a very strange thing.
¡Qué raro!
How strange!
Sabe un poco raro.
It tastes a bit funny.
Es raro que haga tan buen tiempo.
It's unusual to have such good weather.

rascar VERB
to scratch
¿Me rascas la espalda?
Could you scratch my back for me?
■ **rascarse**
to scratch
No deja de rascarse.
He can't stop scratching.

el **rastro** NOUN
trail
seguir el rastro de alguien
to follow somebody's trail

la **rata** NOUN
rat

el **rato** NOUN
while
después de un rato
after a while
hace un rato
a little while ago

al poco rato
shortly after
Pasamos un buen rato.
We had a good time.
Pasamos un mal rato.
We had a dreadful time.
en mis ratos libres
in my free time
Tengo para rato con los deberes.
My homework's going to take me quite a while.

el **ratón** (PL los **ratones**) NOUN
mouse

dos ratones blancos
two white mice

la **raya** NOUN
1 **line**
trazar una raya
to draw a line
pasarse de la raya
to overstep the mark
un jersey a rayas
a striped jumper
2 **parting**
Me hago la raya en medio.
I have a middle parting.

rayar VERB
to scratch

el **rayo** NOUN
lightning

Cayó un rayo en la iglesia.
The church was struck by lightning.
los rayos del sol
the sun's rays

la **raza** NOUN
  race
  la raza humana
  the human race
  ¿De qué raza es tu perro?
  What breed's your dog?

la **razón** (PL las **razones**) NOUN
  reason
  la razón de su visita
  the reason for his visit
  Pedro tiene razón.
  Pedro's right.
  no tener razón
  to be wrong

la **reacción** (PL las **reacciones**)
  NOUN
  reaction

reaccionar VERB
  to react

real (FEM **real**) ADJECTIVE
  real
  en la vida real
  in real life
  la familia real
  the royal family

la **realidad** NOUN
  reality
  en realidad
  actually
  Parece mayor, pero en realidad es menor que yo.
  He looks older but actually he's younger than I am.
  Mi sueño se hizo realidad.
  My dream came true.

realista (FEM **realista**)
  ADJECTIVE
  realistic

el **reality** (PL los **realitys**) NOUN
  reality show

realmente ADVERB
  really
  un problema realmente difícil
  a really difficult problem

la **rebaja** NOUN
  discount
  Me hizo una rebaja.
  He gave me a discount.
  las rebajas
  the sales
  Las tiendas están de rebajas.
  The sales are on.

rebajar VERB
  to reduce
  Han rebajado los abrigos.
  Coats have been reduced.

la **rebanada** NOUN
  slice

  una rebanada de pan
  a slice of bread

rebelde (FEM **rebelde**) ADJECTIVE
  rebellious

rebotar VERB
  to bounce
  La pelota rebotó en el poste.
  The ball bounced off the post.

el **recado** NOUN
  errand
  Ha ido a hacer unos recados.
  She's gone to do some errands.

el **recambio** NOUN
  refill

la **receta** NOUN
  1 recipe
  Me dió la receta de los raviolis.

a
b
c
d
e
f
g
h i j
k
l
m
ñ
ñ
o p q
r
s
t
u v
w
x y
z

He gave me the recipe for the ravioli.
2 prescription

> *Language tip*
> Be careful! **receta** does not mean the same as **receipt**.

recetar VERB
to prescribe

rechazar VERB
to reject
Rechazaron mi sugerencia.
They rejected my suggestion.

recibir VERB
to receive
No he recibido tu carta.
I haven't received your letter.
Recibí muchos regalos.
I got a lot of presents.

el **recibo** NOUN
receipt
No te lo devuelven sin recibo.
They won't give you a refund without a receipt.

reciclar VERB
to recycle

recién ADVERB
just
El comedor está recién pintado.
The dining room has just been painted.

un recién nacido
a newborn baby

reciente (FEM **reciente**)
ADJECTIVE
recent

recientemente ADVERB
recently

el **recipiente** NOUN
container

la **reclamación** (PL las **reclamaciones**) NOUN
complaint
hacer una reclamación
to make a complaint

reclamar VERB
to complain
Fuimos a reclamar al director.
We went and complained to the manager.

recoger VERB
to pick up
Me agaché para recoger la cuchara.
I bent down to pick up the spoon.
Me recogen en la estación.
They pick me up at the station.
Recógelo todo antes de marcharte.
Clear up everything before you leave.
recoger la mesa
to clear the table

recomendar VERB
to recommend
¿Qué nos recomienda?
What do you recommend?

la **recompensa** NOUN
reward

reconocer VERB
to recognize
> **No lo reconocí con ese traje.**
> I didn't recognize him in that suit.

el **récord** (PL los **récords**) NOUN
record
> **el récord mundial de salto de altura**
> the world record in the high jump
> **batir el récord**
> to break the record

recordar VERB
to remember
> **No recuerdo dónde lo puse.**
> I can't remember where I put it.
> **Me recuerda a su padre.**
> He reminds me of his father.

Language tip
*Be careful! **recordar** does not mean the same as **to record**.*

recorrer VERB
to travel around
> **Recorrimos toda Francia.**
> We travelled all around France.

recortar VERB
to cut out
> **Lo recorté de una revista.**
> I cut it out from a magazine.

el **recreo** NOUN
break
> **Tenemos veinte minutos de recreo.**
> We have a twenty-minute break.
> **Salimos al recreo a las once.**
> We have a break at eleven o'clock.
> **a la hora del recreo**
> at playtime

rectangular (FEM **rectangular**) ADJECTIVE
rectangular

el **rectángulo** NOUN
rectangle

recto (FEM **recta**) ADJECTIVE, ADVERB
straight
> **una línea recta**
> a straight line
> **Siga todo recto.**
> Go straight on.

el **recuadro** NOUN
box

recuerdo

recuerdo *can be a noun or part of the verb* **recordar**.

A MASC NOUN
1 **memory**
> **Me trae buenos recuerdos.**
> It brings back happy memories.
2 **souvenir**
> **una tienda de recuerdos**
> a souvenir shop
> **Dale recuerdos de mi parte.**
> Give him my regards.
B VERB ▷ *see* **recordar**
> **No recuerdo su nombre.**
> I can't remember his name.

recuperar VERB
to get back
> **Nunca recuperó la maleta.**
> She never got her suitcase back.
> **recuperar fuerzas**
> to get one's strength back
> **Se está recuperando de la operación.**
> He's recovering from the operation.

la **red** NOUN
1 **net**
> **La pelota dio contra la red.**
> The ball went into the net.
2 **la Red**
> **the Net**

redondo (FEM **redonda**) ADJECTIVE
round
> **una mesa redonda**
> a round table

Todo salió redondo.
Everything worked out perfectly.

reducir VERB
to reduce
Reduzca la velocidad.
Reduce speed.

referirse VERB
referirse a
to refer to
¿Te refieres a mí?
Are you referring to me?
¿A qué te refieres con eso?
What exactly do you mean by that?

reflejar VERB
to reflect

el **refresco** NOUN
soft drink

el **refugio** NOUN
refuge
un refugio de montaña
a mountain refuge

la **regadera** NOUN
watering can

regalar VERB
to give
¿Y si le regalamos un libro?
What about giving him a book?
Me lo regalaron para mi cumpleaños.
I got it for my birthday.

el **regalo** NOUN
present
un regalo de Navidad
a Christmas present
hacer un regalo a alguien
to give somebody a present
papel de regalo
wrapping paper
de regalo
free
Te dan un CD de regalo.
They give you a free CD.

regañar VERB
to tell off

Me regañó por llegar tarde.
He told me off for being late.

regar VERB
to water

el **régimen** (PL los **regímenes**)
NOUN
diet
estar a régimen
to be on a diet
ponerse a régimen
to go on a diet

la **región** (PL las **regiones**) NOUN
region

la **regla** NOUN
1 ruler

Trazó la línea con una regla.
He drew the line with a ruler.
2 rule
saltarse las reglas
to break the rules

regresar VERB
to go back
Regresó a casa por el paraguas.
He went back home for his umbrella.
Regresamos tarde.
We got back late.

el **regreso** NOUN
return
el viaje de regreso
the return journey
de regreso
on the way back
De regreso paramos en Ávila.
On the way back we stopped in Ávila.

regular

regular can be an adjective or an adverb.

A (FEM **regular**) ADJECTIVE
regular
un verbo regular
a regular verb

B ADVERB
El examen me fue regular.
My exam didn't go brilliantly.
Me encuentro regular.
I'm not too bad.

la **reina** NOUN
queen

el **Reino Unido** NOUN
the United Kingdom

reír VERB
to laugh

No te rías.
Don't laugh.
echarse a reír
to burst out laughing
Siempre nos reímos con él.
We always have a good laugh
with him.
reírse de
to laugh at
¿De qué te ríes?
What are you laughing at?

la **relación** (PL las **relaciones**)
NOUN
1 link
la relación entre los dos casos
the link between the two cases
2 relationship
una relación de amistad
a friendly relationship
con relación a
in relation to

relajar VERB
to relax

¡Relájate!
Relax!
**La música clásica la relaja
mucho.**
She finds classical music really
relaxing.

el **relámpago** NOUN
flash of lightning
Vimos un relámpago.
We saw a flash of lightning.
**No me gustan los
relámpagos.**
I don't like lightning.

relativo (FEM **relativa**) ADJECTIVE
relative
un pronombre relativo
a relative pronoun
Eso es muy relativo.
That's all relative.

religión (PL **religiones**) NOUN
religion

rellenar VERB
to fill in
**Tienes que rellenar un
impreso.**
You have to fill in a form.

relleno (FEM **rellena**) ADJECTIVE
stuffed
aceitunas rellenas
stuffed olives

el **reloj** NOUN
1 clock
**El reloj de la cocina va
atrasado.**
The kitchen clock's slow.
un reloj despertador
an alarm clock

contra reloj
against the clock
2 watch
Se me ha parado el reloj.
My watch has stopped.
un reloj sumergible
a waterproof watch

remar VERB
to row

el **remedio** NOUN
remedy
un remedio contra la tos
a cough remedy
No tuve otro remedio.
I had no other choice.

el **remolque** NOUN
trailer

remover VERB
to stir
Remueve la leche con una cuchara.
Stir the milk with a spoon.

rendirse VERB
1 to give up
No sé la respuesta; me rindo.
I don't know the answer; I give up.
2 to surrender
El enemigo se rindió.
The enemy surrendered.

el **renglón** (PL los **renglones**)
NOUN
line

reñir VERB
1 to tell somebody off
Mis padres me riñeron.
My parents told me off.
2 to quarrel
Mi hermana y yo siempre estamos riñendo.
My sister and I are always quarrelling.

repartir VERB
1 to hand out
El profesor repartió los

exámenes.
The teacher handed out the exam papers.
2 to share out
Nos repartimos el dinero.
We shared out the money between us.

repasar VERB
1 to check
Repasa la ortografía.
Check the spelling.
2 to revise
repasar para un examen
to revise for an exam

el **repaso** NOUN
revision
Tengo que darle un repaso a los apuntes.
I have to revise my notes.

repente ADVERB
de repente
suddenly

repetir VERB
1 to repeat
¿Podría repetirlo, por favor?
Could you repeat that, please?
2 to have seconds
Todavía tengo hambre. Voy a repetir.
I'm still hungry. I'm going to have seconds.

repitiendo VERB ▷see **repetir**
Repitiendo las tablas se aprenden.
Repeating your tables helps you learn them.

representar VERB
1 to represent
Van a representar a España.
They will be representing Spain.
2 to put on
Vamos a representar una obra de teatro.
We're going to put on a play.

reproducirse VERB
to reproduce

el **reproductor** NOUN
player
> **un reproductor de CD**
> a CD player
> **un reproductor de MP3**
> an MP3 player

el **reptil** NOUN
reptile

repugnante (FEM **repugnante**)
ADJECTIVE
revolting

la **reputación** (PL las
reputaciones) NOUN
reputation
> **tener buena reputación**
> to have a good reputation

resbalar VERB
to be slippery
> **Este suelo resbala.**
> This floor's slippery.
- **resbalarse**
  to slip
  > **Me resbalé y me caí.**
  > I slipped and fell down.

rescatar VERB
to rescue

el/la **reserva** NOUN
reserve

reservar VERB
to reserve

resfriado

> resfriado *can be an adjective or a
> noun.*

A (FEM **resfriada**) ADJECTIVE
estar resfriado
to have a cold
Estaba muy resfriado.
I had a bad cold.
B MASC NOUN
cold

agarrarse un resfriado
to catch a cold

resfriarse VERB
to catch a cold

la **residencia** NOUN
residence
> **la residencia del primer
> ministro**
> the prime minister's residence

resistir VERB
1 to resist
> **No pude resistir la tentación.**
> I couldn't resist the temptation.
2 to stand
> **No puedo resistir este frío.**
> I can't stand this cold.

resolver VERB
to solve

respetar VERB
to respect
> **Hay que respetar a los
> ancianos.**
> We should respect old people.

el **respeto** NOUN
respect
> **tener respeto a alguien**
> to respect somebody
> **No le faltes al respeto.**
> Don't be disrespectful to him.

la **respiración** NOUN
> **quedarse sin respiración**
> to be out of breath
> **la respiración boca a boca**
> the kiss of life
> **Le hicieron la respiración
> boca a boca.**
> They gave him the kiss of life.

a b c d e f g h i j k l m n ñ o p q r s t u v w x y z

respirar VERB
to breathe

responder VERB
1 **to answer**
Tienes que responder sí o no.
You have to answer yes or no.
2 **to reply**
No han respondido a mi carta.
They haven't replied to my letter.

la **responsabilidad** NOUN
responsibility

responsable

> **responsable** *can be an adjective or a noun.*

A (FEM **responsable**) ADJECTIVE
responsible
No parece muy responsable.
She doesn't seem very responsible.
Todos somos responsables de nuestros actos.
We are all responsible for our actions.
hacerse responsable de algo
to take responsibility for something
B MASC/FEM NOUN
Tú eres la responsable de lo ocurrido.
You're responsible for what happened.
Juan es el responsable de la cocina.
Juan is in charge of the kitchen.

la **respuesta** NOUN
answer

la **resta** NOUN
subtraction

restar VERB
to subtract
Está aprendiendo a restar.
He's learning to subtract.
Tienes que restar tres de ocho.
You have to take three away from eight.

el **restaurante** NOUN
restaurant

el **resto** NOUN
rest
Yo haré el resto.
I'll do the rest.
Juan se comió los restos.
Juan ate the leftovers.

resuelto VERB ▷ *see* **resolver**
El problema ha quedado resuelto.
The problem has been solved.

resuelvo VERB ▷ *see* **resolver**
Yo te resuelvo el problema.
I'll solve the problem for you.

el **resultado** NOUN
result
el resultado de los exámenes
the exam results

resultar VERB
to turn out
Al final resultó que él tenía razón.
In the end it turned out that he was right.

el **resumen** (PL los **resúmenes**)
NOUN
summary
un resumen de las noticias
a news summary
hacer un resumen de algo
to summarize something
en resumen
in short

retirarse VERB
to retire
Mi abuelo se retira el año que viene.
My granddad will be retiring next year.

retorcer VERB
to twist
Me retorció el brazo.
He twisted my arm.

retrasado (FEM **retrasada**)
ADJECTIVE
1 **slow**
Este reloj va retrasado.
This clock is slow.
2 **delayed**
Todos los vuelos iban retrasados.
All flights were delayed.

retrasar VERB
to postpone
Retrasaron el viaje.
They postponed the trip.
■ **retrasarse**
to be late
El tren de las nueve se retrasó.
The nine o'clock train was late.

el **retraso** NOUN
Date prisa que vamos con retraso.
Hurry up, we're running late.
El autobús lleva una hora de retraso.
The bus is an hour late.

retuerzo VERB ▷see **retorcer**
Suéltame o te retuerzo el brazo.
Let go of me or I'll twist your arm.

reunir VERB
to gather together
Reviento de ganas de decírselo.
She gathered the children together in her office.

Estamos reuniendo dinero para el viaje.
We're raising money for the trip.

reunirse VERB
1 **to get together**
En Navidad nos reunimos toda la familia.
The whole family gets together at Christmas.
2 **to meet**
Los profesores se reúnen una vez a la semana.
The teachers meet once a week.

revelar VERB
to develop
Luis revela sus propias fotos.
Luis develops his own photos.

reventar VERB
to burst
No revientes los globos.
Don't burst the balloons.

el **revés** NOUN
al revés
the wrong way round
Lo tienes puesto al revés.
You've got it on the wrong way round.
El dibujo está al revés.
The picture's upside down.

reviento VERB ▷see **reventar**
Reviento de ganas de decírselo.
I'm bursting to tell him.

revisar VERB
to check

Spanish | **English**

Revisa que esté bien la cuenta.
Check the sum is right.

la **revista** NOUN
magazine
una revista de modas
a fashion magazine

revuelto

revuelto can be an adjective or part of the verb **revolver**.

A (FEM **revuelta**) ADJECTIVE
in a mess
Todo estaba revuelto.
Everything was in a mess.
Tengo el estómago revuelto.
I've got an upset stomach.

B VERB ▷ *see* **revolver**
Eso me ha revuelto el estómago.
That's turned my stomach.

el **rey** (PL los **reyes**)
NOUN
king

Los reyes visitaron China.
The King and Queen visited China.
los Reyes Magos
the Three Wise Men

Did you know…?
As part of the Christmas festivities, the Spanish celebrate **el día de Reyes** (Epiphany) on the 6th of January, when the Three Wise Men bring presents for children.

rezar VERB
to pray
rezar por algo
to pray for something

rico
rica

rico can be an adjective or a noun.

A ADJECTIVE
rich
Son muy ricos.
They're very rich.
¡Esto está muy rico!
This is delicious!

B MASC/FEM NOUN
un rico
a rich man
una rica
a rich woman
los ricos
the rich

ridículo (FEM **ridícula**)
ADJECTIVE
ridiculous
¿A que suena ridículo?
Doesn't it sound ridiculous?
hacer el ridículo
to make a fool of oneself
poner a alguien en ridículo
to make a fool of somebody

riendo VERB ▷ *see* **reír**
Se estaba riendo de mí.
He was laughing at me.

el **riesgo** NOUN
risk
correr riesgos
to take risks
No quiero correr ese riesgo.
I don't want to take that risk.

la **rifa** NOUN
raffle

el **rincón** (PL los **rincones**) NOUN
corner
Pon la silla en ese rincón.
Put the chair in that corner.

riñendo VERB ▷ *see* **reñir**
La profesora le estaba riñendo.
The teacher was telling him off.

río

río can be a noun or part of the verb **reír**.

A MASC NOUN
river

el río Támesis
the River Thames
B VERB ▷ *see* **reír**
No me río.
I'm not laughing.

la **risa** NOUN
laugh
una risa contagiosa
an infectious laugh
Me da risa.
It makes me laugh.
Daba risa cómo lo explicaba.
It was so funny the way he told it.
¡Qué risa!
What a laugh!

el **ritmo** NOUN
rhythm

el/la **rival** ADJECTIVE, NOUN
rival

rizado (FEM **rizada**) ADJECTIVE
curly
Tiene el pelo rizado.
He has curly hair.

rizar VERB
to curl
Se riza el pelo.
She curls her hair.

robar VERB
to steal
Le robaba dinero a su amigo.
He was stealing money from his friend.
¡Nos han robado!
We've been robbed!

el **robo** NOUN
theft
un robo de banco
a bank robbery

la **roca** NOUN
rock

la **rodaja** NOUN
slice
cortar algo en rodajas
to cut something into slices

rodar VERB
to roll
La pelota rodó por la calle.
The ball rolled down the street.
rodar una película
to shoot a film

rodear VERB
to surround
El bosque rodea el palacio.
The forest surrounds the palace.
rodeado de
surrounded by

la **rodilla** NOUN
knee
ponerse de rodillas
to kneel down

rojo (FEM **roja**) ADJECTIVE, MASC
NOUN
red
Va vestida de rojo.
She's wearing red.
ponerse rojo de vergüenza
to go red with embarrassment

el **rollo** NOUN
roll
un rollo de papel higiénico
a roll of toilet paper
¡Qué rollo de película!
What a boring film!
Nos soltó el rollo de siempre.
He gave us the same old lecture.

el **romántico** (FEM la
romántica) ADJECTIVE, NOUN
romantic

el **rompecabezas**
(PL los **rompecabezas**)
NOUN
jigsaw

a
b
c
d
e
f
g
h
i
j
k
l
m
ñ
o
p
q
r
s
t
u
v
w
x
y
z

romper VERB
1 **to break**
Me rompí el brazo.
I broke my arm.
2 **to tear up**
Rompió la carta en pedazos.
He tore the letter up.
Se me han roto los pantalones.
I've torn my trousers.

roncar VERB
to snore

la **ropa** NOUN
clothes
Voy a cambiarme de ropa.
I'm going to change my clothes.
la ropa interior
underwear
ropa de deporte
sportswear

rosa

> *rosa can be an adjective or a noun.*

A ADJECTIVE
pink

> **Language tip**
> *The colour **rosa** never changes its ending no matter what it describes.*

Llevaba unos calcetines rosa.
She was wearing pink socks.
B FEM NOUN
rose
una rosa amarilla
a yellow rose
C MASC NOUN
pink
Va vestida de rosa.
She's wearing pink.

el **roscón**
(PL los **roscones**)
NOUN
cake

> **Did you know...?**
> *In Spain it's traditional to eat **el roscón de Reyes** on 6th January. Hidden in this fruit-studded ring-shaped cake is a little figure or other surprise that is meant to bring good luck to the person that finds it.*

roto

> *roto can be an adjective or part of the verb **romper**.*

A (FEM **rota**) ADJECTIVE
broken
un vaso roto
a broken glass
Llevas la camisa rota.
Your shirt is torn.
B VERB ▷ *see* **romper**
Se ha roto.
It's broken.

el **rotulador** NOUN
felt-tip pen

rubio (FEM **rubia**) ADJECTIVE
fair
Luis tiene el pelo rubio.
Luis has got fair hair.
Es rubia con los ojos azules.
She has got fair hair and blue eyes.
Quiero teñirme el pelo de rubio.
I want to dye my hair blond.

la **rueda** NOUN
wheel
la rueda delantera
the front wheel
Se nos pinchó la rueda.
We got a puncture.

ruego VERB ▷ *see* **rogar**
Te lo ruego.
I'm begging you.

el **ruido** NOUN
 noise

> **Hacen mucho ruido.**
> They make a lot of noise.

ruidoso (FEM **ruidosa**) ADJECTIVE
 noisy

la **ruina** NOUN
 las ruinas
 the ruins

El castillo está en ruinas.
The castle is in ruins.

la **ruta** NOUN
 route

la **rutina** NOUN
 routine

> **la rutina diaria**
> the daily routine

a
b
c
d
e
f
g
h
i
j
k
l
m
n
ñ
o
p
q
r
s
t
u
v
w
x
y
z

S s

el sábado NOUN
Saturday

Jugamos los sábados.
We play on Saturdays.

todos los sábados
every Saturday
el sábado pasado
last Saturday
el sábado que viene
next Saturday

la sábana NOUN
sheet

saber VERB
1 **to know**
No lo sé.
I don't know.
Sabe mucho de ordenadores.
He knows a lot about computers.
No sabe nadar.
She can't swim.
¿Sabes inglés?
Can you speak English?

Se sabe la lista de memoria.
He knows the list off by heart.
2 **to taste**
Sabe a pescado.
It tastes of fish.

el sabor NOUN
1 **taste**
Tiene un sabor muy raro.
It's got a very strange taste.
2 **flavour**
¿De qué sabor lo quieres?
What flavour do you want?

sabré VERB ▷*see* **saber**
Pronto lo sabré.
I'll soon know.

sabroso (FEM **sabrosa**) ADJECTIVE
tasty

el sacapuntas (PL los **sacapuntas**) NOUN
pencil sharpener

sacar VERB
1 **to take out**
Se sacó las llaves del bolsillo.
He took the keys out of his pocket.
sacar la basura
to take the rubbish out
sacar al perro a pasear
to take the dog out for a walk
2 **to get**
Hoy sacaremos las entradas.
We'll get the tickets today.
sacar buenas notas
to get good marks
Le sacamos una foto a Jaime.
We took a photo of Jaime.
sacarse las botas
to take off one's boots

el saco NOUN
sack
un saco de patatas
a sack of potatoes
un saco de dormir
a sleeping bag

sacudir VERB
to shake
Hay que sacudir la alfombra.
The carpet needs shaking.

la **sal** NOUN
salt

la **sala** NOUN
room
sala de estar
living room
sala de espera
waiting room
sala de profesores
staffroom

salado (FEM **salada**) ADJECTIVE
salty

la **salchicha** NOUN
sausage

el **salchichón** (PL los **salchichones**) NOUN
spiced salami sausage

saldré VERB ▷ see **salir**
Saldré después de almorzar.
I'm going out after lunch.

salgo VERB ▷ see **salir**
Siempre salgo los sábados por la tarde.
I always go out on Saturday afternoons.

la **salida** NOUN
exit
salida de emergencia
emergency exit

salir VERB
1 **to come out**
Salió a jugar con nosotros.
She came out to play with us.
Sal del coche.
Get out of the car.
2 **to go out**
Ha salido a la tienda.
He's gone out to the shop.
Mi hermana está saliendo con Juan.
Mi sister's going out with Juan.
3 **to leave**
El autocar sale a las ocho.
The coach leaves at eight.

Sale a quince euros por persona.
It works out at fifteen euros each.
Todo salió bien.
Everything worked out well.

el **salón** (PL los **salones**) NOUN
living room

salpicar VERB
to splash

la **salsa** NOUN
sauce
salsa de tomate
tomato sauce

saltar VERB
to jump
saltar por la ventana
to jump out of the window
Te has saltado una página.
You've skipped a page.

el **salto** NOUN
jump
salto de altura
high jump
salto de longitud
long jump
dar un salto
to jump

salud

salud can be a noun or an exclamation.

a b c d e f g h i j k l m n ñ o p q r s t u v w x y z

Spanish
English

a
b
c
d
e
f
g
h
i
j
k
l
m
n
ñ
o
p
q
r
s
t
u
v
w
x
y
z

A FEM NOUN
health
B EXCLAMATION
bless you!

saludable (FEM **saludable**)
ADJECTIVE
healthy

saludar VERB
to say hello
Entramos a saludarla.
We went in to say hello to her.

el **saludo** NOUN
greeting

saludos
best wishes

salvaje (FEM **salvaje**) ADJECTIVE
wild

salvar VERB
to save
Me has salvado la vida.
You saved my life.
He salvado el archivo.
I've saved the file.

la **sandalia** NOUN
sandal
unas sandalias
a pair of sandals

la **sandía** NOUN
watermelon

el **sándwich** (PL los **sándwiches**) NOUN
sandwich

un sándwich de queso
a cheese sandwich

la **sangre** NOUN
blood

sano (FEM **sana**) ADJECTIVE
healthy

una dieta sana
a healthy diet

santo
santa

santo *can be a noun or an adjective.*

A MASC/FEM NOUN
saint
Santa Clara
Saint Clara
Mañana es mi santo.
Tomorrow is my saint's day.

Did you know...?
Besides birthdays, some people in Spain also celebrate the feast day of the saint they are named after.

B ADJECTIVE
holy
un lugar santo
a holy place

el **sapo** NOUN
toad

la **sartén** (PL las **sartenes**) NOUN
frying pan

satisfecho (FEM **satisfecha**)
ADJECTIVE
satisfied

se PRONOUN

Language tip
When **se** *is an indirect object and appears in a sentence with another pronoun, it means* **him, her, them,** *or* **you,** *when it refers to* **él, ella, ellos, ellas,** *and* **usted** *or* **ustedes.**

Pedro necesitaba la calculadora y se la dejé.
Pedro needed the calculator and I lent it to him.

Rosa no lo sabe. No se lo digas.
Rosa doesn't know. Don't tell her.

Language tip

*When the object is repeated, **se** isn't translated.*

No se lo digas a Susana.
Don't tell Susana.
¿Se lo has preguntado a tus padres?
Have you asked your parents?

Language tip

*When **se** is reflexive, it means **himself, herself, itself, themselves, yourself,** or **yourselves** when it refers to **él, ella, ellos, ellas,** and **usted** or **ustedes**.*

Se ha cortado con un cristal.
He cut himself on a piece of broken glass.
¿Se ha hecho usted daño?
Have you hurt yourself?

Language tip

*When it refers to parts of the body or clothes you wear, **se** isn't translated.*

Pablo se lavó los dientes.
Pablo brushed his teeth.
Me puse los guantes.
I put my gloves on.

Language tip

*When **se** is reciprocal, it is translated by **each other**.*

Se dieron un beso.
They gave each other a kiss.

Language tip

*When **se** is impersonal it is usually translated by **it** or **you**.*

Eso pasa cuando se come tan deprisa.
That's what happens when you eat so fast.

sé VERB ▷ *see* **saber**
No sé.
I don't know.

sea VERB ▷ *see* **ser**
siempre que sea razonable
as long as it's reasonable

el **secador** NOUN
hair dryer

secar VERB
to dry
Voy a secarme el pelo.
I'm going to dry my hair.

■ **secarse**
to dry oneself

Sécate con la toalla.
Dry yourself with the towel.

la **sección** NOUN
1 **section**
Lo leí en la sección de deportes.
I read it in the sports section.
2 **department**
la sección de zapatos
the shoes department

seco (FEM **seca**) ADJECTIVE
dry
La pintura ya está seca.
The paint's dry already.
flores secas
dried flowers

el **secretario**
la **secretaria** NOUN
secretary
Es secretaria.
She's a secretary.

secreto

secreto *can be a noun or an adjective.*

A MASC NOUN
secret
Te voy a contar un secreto.
I'm going to tell you a secret.

a b c d e f g h i j k l m n ñ o p q r s t u v w x y z

a
b
c
d
e
f
g
h
i
j
k
l
m
n
ñ
o
p
q
r
s
t
u
v
w
x
y
z

en secreto
in secret
B (FEM **secreta**) ADJECTIVE
secret
un agente secreto
a secret agent

la **sed** NOUN
thirst
apagar la sed
to quench one's thirst
Tengo sed.
I'm thirsty.

la **seda** NOUN
silk
una camisa de seda
a silk shirt

seguido (FEM **seguida**)
ADJECTIVE
in a row
tres días seguidos
three days in a row
en seguida
straight away
Vino en seguida.
He came straight away.
todo seguido
straight on
Vaya todo seguido hasta la plaza.
Go straight on until the square.

seguir VERB
1 **to carry on**
¡Sigue, no pares!
Carry on, don't stop!
Siguió hablando.
She carried on talking.
Sigue lloviendo.
It's still raining.
2 **to follow**
Tú ve primero que yo te sigo.
You go first and I'll follow you.

seguir adelante
to go ahead
Siguieron adelante con su plan.
They went ahead with their plan.

según PREPOSITION
1 **according to**
Según el testigo, el coche no paró.
According to the witness, the car didn't stop.
2 **depending on**
Iremos o no, según esté el tiempo.
We might go, depending on the weather.

segundo

segundo *can be an adjective, pronoun or noun.*

A (FEM **segunda**) ADJECTIVE, PRONOUN
second
el segundo plato
the second course
la segunda planta
the second floor
Vive en el segundo.
He lives on the second floor.
B MASC NOUN
second
Es un segundo nada más.
It'll only take a second.

seguramente ADVERB
probably
Seguramente llegarán mañana.
They'll probably arrive tomorrow.

seguro (FEM **segura**) ADJECTIVE
1 **safe**
Aquí estaremos seguros.
We'll be safe here.
2 **sure**
¿Estás seguro?
Are you sure?
seguro que
it's bound to

Seguro que llueve.
It's bound to rain.

seis (FEM **seis**) ADJECTIVE, PRONOUN
six
Tiene seis años.
She's six.

Son las seis.
It's six o'clock.
el seis de enero
the sixth of January

seiscientos (FEM **seiscientas**) ADJECTIVE, PRONOUN
six hundred

la **selección** (PL las **selecciones**) NOUN
1 **selection**
una selección de juguetes
a selection of toys
2 **team**
la selección nacional
the national team

el **sello** NOUN
stamp
Colecciono sellos.
I collect stamps.

la **selva** NOUN
jungle

el **semáforo** NOUN
traffic lights
El semáforo está en rojo.
The lights are red.

la **semana** NOUN
week
dentro de una semana
in a week's time
una vez a la semana
once a week

la **semilla** NOUN
seed

sencillo (FEM **sencilla**) ADJECTIVE
simple
Es muy sencillo.
It's really simple.

sensible (FEM **sensible**) ADJECTIVE
sensitive
Es un chico muy sensible.
He's a very sensitive boy.

> ***Language tip***
> *Be careful!* **sensible** *does not mean the same as* **sensible***.*

sentar VERB
1 **to suit**
Ese vestido te sienta muy bien.
That dress really suits you.
2 **to agree with**
El arroz no me sentó bien.
The rice didn't agree with me.
Le sentó mal lo que dije.
He didn't like what I said.
▪ **sentarse**
to sit down
Me senté en el banco.
I sat down on the bench.

el **sentido** NOUN
sense
Eso no tiene sentido.
That doesn't make sense.
sentido común
common sense
Eso es de sentido común.
That's common sense.
sentido del humor
sense of humour
No tiene sentido del humor.
He doesn't have a sense of humour.

el **sentimiento** NOUN
feeling

sentir VERB
1 **to feel**
Sentí un dolor en la pierna.
I felt a pain in my leg.
2 **to be sorry**
Lo siento mucho.
I'm very sorry.

a b c d e f g h i j k l m n ñ o p q r s t u v w x y z

a b c d e f g h i j k l m n ñ o p q r s t u v w x y z

Siento llegar tarde.
I'm sorry I'm late.
■ **sentirse**
to feel
No me siento bien.
I don't feel well.

la **seña** NOUN
sign
Nos comunicamos por señas.
We communicate by signs.

la **señal** NOUN
1 **sign**
Eso es mala señal.
That's a bad sign.
una señal de tráfico
a road sign
2 **signal**
Yo daré la señal.
I'll give the signal.

señalar VERB
to mark
Señálalo con un bolígrafo rojo.
Mark it with a red pen.
señalar con el dedo
to point

el **señor** NOUN
1 **man**
¿Quién es ese señor?
Who's that man?
¿Qué le pongo, señor?
What would you like, sir?

> **Language tip**
> **Señor** *is a handy way of attracting somebody's attention. Look at the example.*

¡Señor! ¡Se le ha caído el billete!
Excuse me! You've dropped your ticket!
2 **Mr**
el señor Delgado
Mr Delgado
Muy señor mío: ...
Dear Sir, ...

la **señora** NOUN
1 **lady**
Deja pasar a esta señora.
Let the lady past.
¿Qué le pongo, señora?
What would you like, madam?

> **Language tip**
> **Señora** *is a handy way of attracting somebody's attention. Look at the example.*

¡Señora! ¡Se ha dejado las gafas!
Excuse me! You've forgotten your glasses!
2 **Mrs**
la señora Delgado
Mrs Delgado
3 **wife**
Vino con su señora.
He came with his wife.

la **señorita** NOUN
1 **young lady**
Hay una señorita esperando.
There's a young lady waiting.
2 **Miss**
la señorita Delgado
Miss Delgado

sepa VERB ▷ *see* **saber**
Que yo sepa no.
Not as far as I know.

separado (FEM **separada**)
ADJECTIVE
separate
Ponlos en dos montones separados.
Put them in two separate piles.
Sus padres están separados.
His parents are separated.

separar VERB
to separate

septiembre NOUN
September

> **Language tip**
> *Months are not spelled with a capital letter in Spanish.*

en septiembre
in September
Nació el once de septiembre.
He was born on the eleventh of September.

séptimo (FEM **séptima**)
ADJECTIVE, PRONOUN
seventh
Vivo en el séptimo.
I live on the seventh floor.

ser

ser can be a verb or a noun.

A VERB
to be
Juan es muy alto.
Juan is very tall.
Es médico.
He's a doctor.
Era de noche.
It was night.
Soy Lucía.
It's Lucía.
Son las seis y media.
It's half past six.
Éramos cinco en el coche.
There were five of us in the car.
Es de Joaquín.
It's Joaquín's.
¿De dónde eres?
Where are you from?
Soy de Barcelona
I'm from Barcelona
Es de plástico.
It's made of plastic.
a no ser que ...
unless ...
a no ser que vayamos mañana
unless we go tomorrow
B MASC NOUN
being
Son seres humanos.
They're human beings.

serio (FEM **seria**) ADJECTIVE
serious
No te pongas tan serio.
Don't look so serious.
No hablaba en serio.
I didn't mean it.

en serio
seriously

la **serpiente** NOUN
snake

el **servicio** NOUN
1 **service**
2 **toilet**
Está en el servicio.
He's in the toilet.
el servicio de caballeros
the gents'
el servicio de señoras
the ladies'

la **servilleta** NOUN
napkin

servir VERB
to be useful for
Estas cajas sirven para muchas cosas.
These boxes are useful for a lot of things.
¿Para qué sirve esto?
What's this for?
no servir para nada
to be useless
Este mapa no sirve para nada.
This map is useless.

Spanish English

a b c d e f g h i j k l m n ñ o p q r s t u v w x y z

sesenta (FEM **sesenta**)
ADJECTIVE, PRONOUN
sixty
> **Tiene sesenta años.**
> He's sixty.

la **seta** NOUN
mushroom

setecientos
(FEM **setecientas**) ADJECTIVE,
PRONOUN
seven hundred

setenta (FEM **setenta**)
ADJECTIVE, PRONOUN
seventy
> **Tiene setenta años.**
> He's seventy.

sexto (FEM **sexta**) ADJECTIVE,
PRONOUN
sixth
> **Vivo en el sexto.**
> I live on the sixth floor.

si CONJUNCTION
1 **if**
> **Si quieres te dejo mi bici.**
> I'll lend you my bike if you like.
> **¿Y si llueve?**
> And what if it rains?
2 **whether**
> **No sé si ir o no.**
> I don't know whether to go or not.
> **si no**
> otherwise/if not

> *Language tip*
> **si no** *has two meanings. Look at the examples.*

> **Ponte crema. Si no, te quemarás.**
> Put some cream on, otherwise you'll get sunburned.
> **Avísame si no puedes venir.**
> Let me know if you can't come.

sí

> **sí** *can be an adverb or a pronoun.*

A ADVERB
yes
> **¿Quieres un helado? — Sí, gracias.**
> Do you want an ice-cream? — Yes, please.
> **¿Te gusta? — Sí.**
> Do you like it? — Yes, I do.
> **Creo que sí.**
> I think so.
> **Él no quiere pero yo sí.**
> He doesn't want to but I do.
B PRONOUN
> **Solo piensa en sí misma.**
> She only thinks about herself.
> **Hablaban entre sí.**
> They were talking among themselves.
> **Es mejor aprender las cosas por sí mismo.**
> It's better to learn things by yourself.

siempre ADVERB
always
> **Siempre llega tarde.**
> She always arrives late.

para siempre
forever

siendo VERB ▷*see* **ser**
> **Sigue siendo feliz.**
> She's still happy.

siento VERB ▷*see* **sentir**
> **Siento pena por ellos.**
> I feel sorry for them.

Lo siento.
I'm sorry.

la **siesta** NOUN
nap

> **echarse la siesta**
> to have a nap

A mi abuela le gusta echarse la siesta.
My grandma likes to have an afternoon nap.

siete (FEM **siete**) ADJECTIVE, PRONOUN
seven
> **Tiene siete años.**
> She's seven.

> **Son las siete.**
> It's seven o'clock.
> **el siete de marzo**
> the seventh of March
> **Nació el siete de marzo.**
> He was born on the seventh of March.

el **siglo** NOUN
century
> **el siglo veintiuno**
> the twenty-first century

el **significado** NOUN
meaning

significar VERB
to mean
> **¿Qué significa 'wild'?**
> What does 'wild' mean?
> **No sé lo que significa.**
> I don't know what it means.

el **signo** NOUN
sign
> **Eso es signo de buena salud.**
> That's a sign of good health.
> **¿De qué signo eres?**
> What star sign are you?
> **signo de admiración**
> exclamation mark
> **signo de interrogación**
> question mark

Did you know...?
Don't forget that in Spanish you also need an upside-down exclamation mark or question mark at the beginning of your phrase or question.

siguiendo VERB ▷*see* **seguir**
> **Nos están siguiendo.**
> We're being followed.

siguiente (FEM **siguiente**)
ADJECTIVE
next
> **Al día siguiente visitamos Toledo.**
> The next day we visited Toledo.
> **¡Que pase el siguiente, por favor!**
> Next please!

silbar VERB
to whistle

el **silencio** NOUN
silence
> **guardar silencio**
> to keep quiet
> **En la biblioteca hay que guardar silencio.**
> You need to keep quiet in the library.

¡Silencio!
Quiet!

la **silla** NOUN
chair
> **silla de paseo**
> pushchair
> **silla de ruedas**
> wheelchair

el **sillón** (PL los **sillones**) NOUN
armchair

el **símbolo** NOUN
symbol

simpático (FEM **simpática**)
ADJECTIVE
nice
> **Luisa es muy simpática.**
> Luisa is very nice.
> **Me cae simpático.**
> I think he's really nice.

Language tip
Be careful! **simpático** *does not mean* **sympathetic**.

a
b
c
d
e
f
g
h
i
j
k
l
m
n
ñ
o
p
q
r
s
t
u
v
w
x
y
z

simple (FEM **simple**) ADJECTIVE
simple

simplemente ADVERB
simply

sin PREPOSITION
without
Salió sin abrigo.
She went out without a coat.
sin hacer ruido
without making a noise

singular ADJECTIVE, MASC NOUN
singular
en singular
in the singular

sino CONJUNCTION
but
No son ingleses sino galeses.
They're not English, but Welsh.

sintiendo VERB ▷ see **sentir**
¿Te sigues sintiendo mal?
Do you still feel ill?

siquiera ADVERB
ni siquiera
not even
Ni siquiera se despidió.
She didn't even say goodbye.

sirviendo VERB ▷ see **servir**
**Estas clases no me están
sirviendo para nada.**
I'm not finding these classes at all
useful.

el **sitio** NOUN
1 place
Es un sitio tranquilo.
It's a quiet place.
¿Me puedo cambiar de sitio?
Can I change places?

en cualquier sitio
anywhere
en algún sitio
somewhere

2 room
Hay sitio de sobra.
There's room to spare.

Hacedme sitio.
Can you make some room for me?
un sitio web
a website

la **situación** (PL las **situaciones**)
NOUN
situation

el **SMS** NOUN
text message
enviar un SMS
to send a text
**enviarle un SMS
a alguien**
to text somebody

sobra FEM NOUN
Tenemos comida de sobra.
We've got more than enough
food.

sobrar VERB
to be left over
Ha sobrado mucha comida.
There's plenty of food left over.
Con diez euros sobrará.
Ten euros will be more than
enough.

sobre

sobre *can be a preposition or a
noun.*

A PREPOSITION
1 on
Deja el dinero sobre la mesa.
Leave the money on the table.
2 about
información sobre hoteles
information about hotels

sobre las seis
at about six o'clock
sobre todo
above all
Me gustan los deportes, sobre
todo la natación.
I like sport, especially swimming.

B MASC NOUN
envelope

el **sobresaliente** NOUN
distinction
> He sacado sobresaliente en matemáticas.
> I got top marks in maths.

sobrevivir VERB
to survive

la **sobrina** NOUN
niece

el **sobrino** NOUN
nephew
> mis sobrinos
> my nephews/my nieces and nephews

> **Language tip**
> **mis sobrinos** *has two meanings. It can be translated as* **my nephews** *or* **my nephews and nieces**.

la **sociedad** NOUN
society

el **socio**
la **socia** NOUN
1 partner
2 member

el/la **socorrista** NOUN
lifeguard

el **socorro** NOUN
help
> pedir socorro
> to ask for help
> La mujer pedía socorro.
> The woman was asking for help.

> **¡Socorro!**
> Help!

el **sofá** (PL los **sofás**) NOUN
sofa

> un sofá-cama
> a sofa bed

sois VERB ▷ *see* **ser**
> ¿Sois hermanas?
> Are you sisters?

el **sol** NOUN
sun
> estar al sol
> to be in the sun
> Hace sol.
> It's sunny.
> tomar el sol
> to sunbathe

solamente ADVERB
only

el **soldado** NOUN
soldier

soler VERB

> **Language tip**
> *In the present, English normally uses the adverb* **usually** *to translate* **soler**.

> Suele salir a las ocho.
> He usually leaves at eight.

> **Language tip**
> *In the past, English normally uses the structure* **used to** *to translate* **soler**.

> Solíamos ir a la playa.
> We used to go to the beach.

solo

> **solo** *can be an adjective or an adverb.*

A (FEM **sola**) ADJECTIVE
1 alone
> Me quedé solo.
> I was left alone.
> ¿Estás solo?
> Are you on your own?
> Lo hice yo solo.
> I did it on my own.
> Había un solo problema.
> There was just one problem.

a
b
c
d
e
f
g
h
i
j
k
l
m
n
ñ
o
p
q
r
s
t
u
v
w
x
y
z

2 lonely
A veces me siento solo.
Sometimes I feel lonely.

B ADVERB
only
Solo cuesta diez libras.
It only costs ten pounds.
no solo ... sino ...
not only ... but ...
No solo es bonito, sino barato.
It's not only nice, but cheap.

Language tip
You may sometimes see **sólo** *written with an accent when it is an adverb.*

soltar VERB
to let go of
No sueltes la cuerda.
Don't let go of the rope.
¡Suéltame!
Let go of me!

soltero (FEM **soltera**) ADJECTIVE
single
Es soltero.
He's single.

la **solución** (PL las **soluciones**) NOUN
solution

solucionar VERB
to solve

la **sombra** NOUN
1 shade
Prefiero quedarme a la sombra.
I prefer to stay in the shade.
2 shadow
Solo vi una sombra.
I only saw a shadow.
sombra de ojos
eye shadow

el **sombrero** NOUN
hat

la **sombrilla** NOUN
sunshade

sonar VERB
1 to sound
Sonaba un poco triste.
She sounded a bit sad.
Se escribe tal y como suena.
It's written as it sounds.
2 to ring
Sonó el timbre.
The bell rang.
sonarse la nariz
to blow one's nose

el **sonido** NOUN
sound

sonreír VERB
to smile
Me sonrió.
She smiled at me.

la **sonrisa** NOUN
smile

soñar VERB
to dream
Ayer soñé con él.
I dreamed about him yesterday.

la **sopa** NOUN
soup

soplar VERB
to blow
¡Sopla con fuerza!
Blow hard!
Soplaba un viento fuerte.
A strong wind was blowing.

soportar VERB
to stand
No la soporto.
I can't stand her.

Language tip
Be careful! **soportar** *does not mean* **to support**.

sordo (FEM **sorda**) ADJECTIVE
deaf

sorprender VERB
to surprise

No me sorprende.
It doesn't surprise me.
Me sorprendí al verlos.
I was surprised to see them.

la **sorpresa** NOUN
surprise
¡Qué sorpresa!
What a surprise!
Me pilló de sorpresa.
It took me by surprise.

el **sorteo** NOUN
draw

soso (FEM **sosa**) ADJECTIVE
1 **dull**
Es un poco soso.
He's a bit dull.
2 **bland**
estar soso
to need more salt
Estas patatas fritas están sosas.
These chips need more salt.

sospechar VERB
to suspect
Sospechan de Luisa.
They suspect Luisa.

sospechoso (FEM **sospechosa**) ADJECTIVE
suspicious

sostener VERB
1 **to support**
Está sostenido por dos columnas.
It is supported by two columns.
2 **to hold**
Sostenían la caja entre los dos.
They held the box between the two of them.

soy VERB ▷see **ser**
Soy española.
I'm Spanish.

Sr. ABBREVIATION
Mr

Sra. ABBREVIATION
Mrs

Sres. ABBREVIATION
Messrs

Srta. ABBREVIATION
Miss

su ADJECTIVE
1 **his**
su mochila
his backpack
Antonio y sus padres
Antonio and his parents
2 **her**
su falda
her skirt
Marta y sus amigas
Marta and her friends
3 **its**
un oso y su cachorro
a bear and its cub
4 **their**
mis padres y sus amigos
my parents and their friends
5 **your**
No olviden sus paraguas.
Don't forget your umbrellas.

suave (FEM **suave**) ADJECTIVE
1 **gentle**
2 **soft**

subir VERB
1 **to go up**
Subimos las escaleras.
We went up the stairs.
La gasolina ha subido.
Petrol's gone up.
2 **to come up**
Sube, que te voy a enseñar una cosa.
Come up, I've got something to show you.
3 **to take up**
Ayúdame a subir las maletas.
Help me take the cases up.
4 **to turn up**
Sube la tele, que no se oye.
Turn the TV up. I can't hear it.

Language tip
subirse a *has several meanings. Look at the examples.*

subirse al coche
to get into the car
subirse al tren
to get on the train
subirse a la bici
to get onto the bike

subirse a un árbol
to climb a tree

subrayar VERB
to underline

el **suceso** NOUN
incident
    El suceso ocurrió sobre las tres de la tarde.
    The incident happened at around three in the afternoon.

> *Language tip*
> Be careful! **suceso** *does not mean* **success**.

sucio (FEM **sucia**) ADJECTIVE
dirty
    Tienes las manos sucias.
    You've got dirty hands.

sudamericano
sudamericana ADJECTIVE,
MASC/FEM NOUN
South American

sudar VERB
to sweat

sudeste MASC NOUN, ADJECTIVE
southeast

> *Language tip*
> The adjective **sudeste** *never changes its ending, no matter what it describes.*

sudoeste MASC NOUN, ADJECTIVE
southwest

> *Language tip*
> The adjective **sudoeste** *never changes its ending, no matter what it describes.*

el **sudor** NOUN
sweat

la **suegra** NOUN
mother-in-law

el **suegro** NOUN
father-in-law

los **suegros** PL NOUN
in-laws

el **sueldo** NOUN
salary

suelo

> **suelo** *can be a noun or part of the verb* **soler**.

A MASC NOUN
1 **floor**
    un suelo de madera
    a wooden floor
2 **ground**
    El suelo está mojado.
    The ground is wet.
    Me caí al suelo.
    I fell over.
B VERB ▷*see* **soler**
    Suelo ir al cine los domingos.
    I usually go to the cinema on Sundays.

suelto

> **suelto** *can be an adjectivo, a noun or part of the verb* **soltar**.

A (FEM **suelta**) ADJECTIVE
loose
    Tiene varias hojas sueltas.
    Some of the pages are loose.
    Lleva el pelo suelto.
    She wears her hair loose.
B MASC NOUN
change
    No llevo suelto.
    I don't have any change on me.
C VERB ▷*see* **soltar**
    Si lo suelto, se cae.
    If I let go, it will fall.

Spanish **English**

sueno VERB ▷*see* **sonar**
Sueno rara cuando hablo inglés.
I sound strange when I speak English.

sueño

sueño *can be a noun or part of the verb* **soñar**.

A MASC NOUN
dream
Anoche tuve un mal sueño.
I had a bad dream last night.

Tengo sueño.
I'm sleepy.

B VERB ▷*see* **soñar**
Siempre sueño.
I always dream.

la **suerte** NOUN
luck
No tiene mucha suerte.
She doesn't have much luck.
Tuvo suerte.
She was lucky.
por suerte
luckily

¡Buena suerte!
Good luck!
¡Qué suerte!
How lucky!

suficiente (FEM **suficiente**)
ADJECTIVE
enough
No tenía dinero suficiente.
I didn't have enough money.

sufrir VERB
to suffer
Sufre de artritis.
He suffers from arthritis.

la **sugerencia** NOUN
suggestion
hacer una sugerencia
to make a suggestion

sugerir VERB
to suggest

Sugirió que fuéramos al cine.
She suggested going to the cinema.

sugiero VERB ▷*see* **sugerir**
Sugiero que lo dejemos para mañana.
I suggest we leave it until tomorrow.

sujetar VERB
to hold
Sujeta la escalera.
Hold the ladder.
Sujeta al perro, que no se escape.
Hold on to the dog so it doesn't get away.

la **suma** NOUN
sum
hacer una suma
to do a sum

sumar VERB
to add up

supe VERB ▷*see* **saber**
Siempre lo supe.
I always knew it.

el **supermercado** NOUN
supermarket

el/la **superviviente** NOUN
survivor

suponer VERB
to suppose
Supongo que vendrá.
I suppose she'll come.

Supongo que sí.
I suppose so.
Supongo que no.
I suppose not.

a b c d e f g h i j k l m n ñ o p q r **s** t u v w x y z

235

a b c d e f g h i j k l m n ñ o p q r s t u v w x y z

supuesto VERB ▷ *see* **suponer**

por supuesto
of course

supuse VERB ▷ *see* **suponer**
Ya supuse que no vendría.
I thought he wouldn't come.

sur MASC NOUN, ADJECTIVE
south
el sur del país
the south of the country

Language tip
The adjective **sur** never changes its ending, no matter what it describes.

sureste MASC NOUN, ADJECTIVE
southeast

Language tip
The adjective **sureste** never changes its ending, no matter what it describes.

el **surf** NOUN
surfing

surf a vela
windsurfing
practicar el surf
to surf

surgir VERB
to come up
Ha surgido un problema.
A problem has come up.

suroeste MASC NOUN, ADJECTIVE
southwest

Language tip
The adjective **suroeste** never changes its ending, no matter what it describes.

la **suscripción** (PL las **suscripciones**) NOUN
subscription

suspender VERB
1 **to fail**
He suspendido Matemáticas.
I've failed maths.
2 **to call off**
Suspendieron el partido.
They called off the match.

suspirar VERB
to sigh

el **sustantivo** NOUN
noun

el **susto** NOUN
fright
dar un susto a alguien
to give somebody a fright
Me has dado un susto.
You gave me a fright.

T t

el tabaco NOUN
1 **tobacco**
2 **cigarettes**

la tabla NOUN
plank
 El agujero estaba cubierto con tablas.
 The hole was covered with planks.
 la tabla de multiplicar
 the multiplication table
 una tabla de cocina
 a chopping board
 la tabla de surf
 the surfboard

el tablero NOUN
board
 el tablero de ajedrez
 the chessboard

la tableta NOUN
1 **bar**
2 **tablet**

tachar VERB
to cross out
 No lo taches, bórralo.
 Don't cross it out, rub it out.

el taco NOUN
1 **stud**
2 **cube**
3 **swearword**
 soltar tacos
 to swear

el tacón (PL los **tacones**) NOUN
heel
 zapatos de tacón
 high-heeled shoes

tal (FEM **tal**) ADJECTIVE, PRONOUN
such
 En tales casos es mejor consultar con un médico.
 In such cases it's better to see

a doctor.
 Lo dejé tal como estaba.
 I left it just as it was.
 con tal de que
 as long as
 con tal de que regreséis antes de las once
 as long as you get back before eleven
 ¿Qué tal has dormido?
 How did you sleep?

 ¿Qué tal?
 How are things?
 tal vez
 perhaps

la talla NOUN
size
 ¿Tienen esta camisa en la talla cuatro?
 Do you have this shirt in a size four?

el taller NOUN
garage
 Tenemos el coche en el taller.
 Our car is in the garage.

el tamaño NOUN
size
 ¿Qué tamaño tiene?
 What size is it?

también ADVERB
also
 Canta flamenco y también baila.
 He sings flamenco and also dances.
 Tengo hambre. — Yo también.
 I'm hungry. — So am I.
 Yo estoy de acuerdo. — Nosotros también.
 I agree. — So do we.

el **tambor**
NOUN
drum

tampoco ADVERB
1 **either**
Yo tampoco lo compré.
I didn't buy it either.
2 **neither**
Yo no la vi. — Yo tampoco.
I didn't see her. — Neither did I.
**Nunca he estado en París.
— Yo tampoco.**
I've never been to Paris. —
Neither have I.

tan ADVERB
so
**No creí que fueras a venir tan
pronto.**
I didn't think you'd come so soon.
¡No es tan difícil!
It's not so difficult!
¡Qué hombre tan amable!
What a kind man!
tan ... como ...
as ... as ...
**No es tan guapa como su
madre.**
She's not as pretty as her
mother.
Vine tan pronto como pude.
I came as soon as I could.
tan ... que ...
so ... that ...
**Habla tan deprisa que no la
entiendo.**
She talks so fast I can't
understand her.

tanto

tanto *can be an adjective, adverb,
pronoun or noun.*

A (FEM **tanta**) ADJECTIVE, PRONOUN
so much

Ahora no bebo tanta leche.
I don't drink so much milk now.
**¡Tengo tantos ejercicios que
hacer hoy!**
I have so many exercises to do
today!
**Vinieron tantos que no
cabían en la sala.**
So many people came that they
couldn't fit into the room.
B ADVERB
1 **so much**
**Se preocupa tanto que no
puede dormir.**
He worries so much that he
can't sleep.
¡No corras tanto!
Don't run so fast!
tanto tú como yo
both you and I
2 **so often**
Ahora no la veo tanto.
I don't see her so often these days.
C MASC NOUN
goal
**Juárez marcó el segundo
tanto.**
Juárez scored the second goal.
un tanto por ciento
a percentage
**Había cuarenta y tantos
invitados.**
There were forty-odd guests.

la **tapa** NOUN
1 **lid**
2 **top**
3 **cover**
4 **tapa**
**Pedimos unas tapas en
el bar.**
We ordered some tapas in
the bar.

tapar VERB
to cover
La tapé con una manta.
I covered her with a blanket.
Tapa la olla.
Put the lid on the pan.

Tápate bien que hace frío.
Wrap up well as it's cold.

el tapón (PL **los tapones**) NOUN
1 **plug**
2 **top**

la taquilla NOUN
1 **box office**
2 **ticket office**

tardar VERB
to be late
Te espero a las ocho. No tardes.
I expect you at eight. Don't be late.
Tardaron una semana en contestar.
They took a week to reply.
En avión se tarda dos horas.
The plane takes two hours.

tarde

tarde *can be a noun or an adverb.*

A FEM NOUN
1 **afternoon**
a las tres de la tarde
at three in the afternoon
¡Buenas tardes!
Good afternoon!
por la tarde
in the afternoon
hoy por la tarde
this afternoon
2 **evening**
a las ocho de la tarde
at eight in the evening
¡Buenas tardes!
Good evening!
por la tarde
in the evening
hoy por la tarde
this evening
B ADVERB
late
Se está haciendo tarde.
It's getting late.
más tarde
later

Llegaré a las nueve como muy tarde.
I'll arrive at nine at the latest.

tarde o temprano
sooner or later

la tarea NOUN
task
Una de sus tareas es repartir la correspondencia.
One of his tasks is to hand out the mail.
las tareas domésticas
housework

la tarjeta NOUN
card
Me mandó una tarjeta de Navidad.
He sent me a Christmas card.
una tarjeta de crédito
a credit card
una tarjeta telefónica
a phonecard
una tarjeta de embarque
a boarding card

el tarro NOUN
jar

la tarta NOUN
1 **cake**
una tarta de cumpleaños
a birthday cake

2 **tart**

el tatuaje NOUN
tattoo

el taxi NOUN
taxi
Cogimos un taxi.
We got a taxi.

el/la taxista NOUN
taxi driver

a b c d e f g h i j k l m n ñ o p q r s t u v w x y z

la taza NOUN
  1 cup
  Mis padres tomaron una taza de café.
  My parents had a cup of coffee.
  2 cupful
  una taza de arroz
  a cupful of rice
  3 bowl

el tazón (PL los **tazones**) NOUN
  bowl

te PRONOUN
  1 you
  Te quiero.
  I love you.
  Te voy a dar un consejo.
  I'm going to give you some advice.
  Me gustaría comprártelo.
  I'd like to buy it for you.
  2 yourself
  ¿Te has hecho daño?
  Have you hurt yourself?
  ¿Te duelen los pies?
  Do your feet hurt?
  Te tienes que poner el abrigo.
  You should put your coat on.

el té (PL los **tés**) NOUN
  tea
  Me hice un té.
  I made myself a cup of tea.

Did you know...?
People don't tend to drink as much tea in Spain as in England and tea with lemon or herbal teas are more common than the tea we are used to in Britain.

el teatro NOUN
  theatre
  Por la noche fuimos al teatro.
  At night we went to the theatre.
  una obra de teatro
  a play

el tebeo NOUN
  comic

el techo NOUN
  ceiling

El techo está pintado de blanco.
The ceiling is painted white.

la tecla NOUN
  key
  pulsar una tecla
  to press a key

el teclado NOUN
  keyboard

teclear VERB
  to type

la técnica NOUN
  1 technique
  2 technology
  3 technician
  Mi hermana es técnica de laboratorio.
  My sister is a laboratory technician.

técnico

técnico can be a noun or an adjective.

A MASC NOUN
  1 technician
  Es técnico de laboratorio.
  He is a laboratory technician.
  2 repairman
  El técnico me arregló la lavadora.
  The repairman fixed my washing machine.
B (FEM **técnica**) ADJECTIVE
  technical

la tecnología NOUN
  technology
  tecnología punta
  state-of-the-art technology

el tejado NOUN
  roof

la **tela** NOUN
 fabric

la **telaraña** NOUN
 cobweb

la **tele** NOUN
 TV
   Estábamos viendo la tele.
   We were watching TV.

el **telediario** NOUN
 news
   el telediario de las nueve
   the nine o'clock news

el **teléfono** NOUN
 telephone
   No tengo teléfono.
   I don't have a telephone.
   Está hablando por teléfono.
   He's on the phone.
   un teléfono móvil
   a mobile phone

la **telenovela** NOUN
 soap opera

el **telesilla** NOUN
 chairlift

la **televisión** (PL las
 televisiones) NOUN
 television

   **Dieron la noticia por la
   televisión.**
   They gave the news on the
   television.
   **¿Qué ponen en la televisión
   esta noche?**
   What's on the television
   tonight?

   la televisión por cable
   cable television
   la televisión digital
   digital TV

el **televisor** NOUN
 television set

el **tema** NOUN
 1 topic
   **El tema de la redacción era
   'Las vacaciones'.**
   The topic of the essay was
   'The holidays'.
 2 subject
   **Luego hablaremos de ese
   tema.**
   We'll talk about that subject
   later.

temblar VERB
 to tremble
   Me temblaban las manos.
   My hands were trembling.
   temblar de miedo
   to tremble with fear
   temblar de frío
   to shiver

temer VERB
 1 to be afraid
   No temas.
   Don't be afraid.
 2 to be afraid of
   Le teme al profesor.
   He's afraid of the teacher.

el **temor** NOUN
 fear
   por temor a equivocarme
   for fear of making a mistake

la **temperatura** NOUN
 temperature
   **El médico le tomó la
   temperatura.**
   The doctor took his
   temperature.

la **temporada** NOUN
 season
   la temporada alta
   the high season

la **temporada baja**
the low season

el **temporal** NOUN
storm

temprano ADVERB
early
por la mañana temprano
early in the morning

ten VERB ▷see **tener**
Ten el mío si quieres.
Have mine if you like.

tender VERB
to hang out
Marta estaba tendiendo la ropa.
Marta was hanging out the
washing.
tenderse en el sofá
to lie down on the sofa

tendrá VERB ▷see **tener**
Tendrá que hacerlo.
She'll have to do it.

el **tenedor** NOUN
fork

tener VERB
to have
Tengo dos hermanas.
I have two sisters.
¿Tienes dinero?
Do you have any money?
Tiene el pelo rubio.
He has blond hair.
Mi tía va a tener un niño.
My aunt's going to have a baby.
¿Cuántos años tienes?
How old are you?
Tiene cinco metros de largo.
It's five metres long.
Ten cuidado.
Be careful.
tener que hacer algo
to have to do something

Tengo que llamar a mi padre.
I have to call my father.

tenga VERB ▷see **tener**
No creo que tenga tiempo.
I don't think I'll have time.

el **tenis** NOUN
tennis
¿Juegas al tenis?
Do you play tennis?
tenis de mesa
table tennis

el/la **tenista** NOUN
tennis player

la **tentación** (PL las
tentaciones) NOUN
temptation

el **tentempié** (PL los
tentempiés) NOUN
snack

teñir VERB
to dye
Se ha teñido el pelo.
He's dyed his hair.

la **teoría** NOUN
theory
En teoría es fácil.
In theory it's easy.

tercero (FEM **tercera**) ADJECTIVE,
PRONOUN
third
la tercera vez
the third time
la tercera planta
the third floor
Llegué el tercero.
I arrived third.
**una tercera parte de la
población**
a third of the population
Vivo en el tercero.
I live on the third floor.

> *Language tip*
>
> **tercero** *becomes* **tercer** *before a
> masculine singular noun.*

el **tercio** NOUN
third

terco (FEM **terca**) ADJECTIVE
obstinate

terminar VERB
1 **to finish**
He terminado el libro.
I've finished the book.
cuando terminó de hablar
when he finished talking
2 **to end**
¿A qué hora termina la clase?
At what time does the class end?
Terminaron peleándose.
They ended up fighting.
Se nos ha terminado la leche.
We've run out of milk.
He terminado con Andrés.
I've broken up with Andrés.

la **ternera** NOUN
veal

la **terraza** NOUN
1 **balcony**
2 **roof terrace**

el **terremoto** NOUN
earthquake

el **terreno** NOUN
1 **land**
una granja con mucho terreno
a farm with a lot of land
2 **un terreno**
a plot of land
Mis padres han comprado un terreno.
My parents have bought a plot of land.
3 **field**
terrenos plantados de naranjos
fields planted with orange trees
el terreno de juego
the pitch

terrestre (FEM **terrestre**)
ADJECTIVE
land
los animales terrestres
land animals

terrible (FEM **terrible**) ADJECTIVE
terrible
Fue una experiencia terrible.
It was a terrible experience.

el **texto** NOUN
text
un libro de texto
a textbook

ti PRONOUN
you
una llamada para ti
a call for you
Solo piensas en ti mismo.
You only think of yourself.

la **tía** NOUN
1 **aunt**
mi tía
my aunt
2 **girl**
Es una tía majísima.
She's a really nice girl.

tiemblo VERB ▷ *see* **temblar**
Tiemblo de miedo.
I'm shaking with fear.
Tiemblo de frío.
I'm shivering.

el **tiempo** NOUN
1 **time**
No tengo tiempo.
I don't have time.
¿Qué haces en tu tiempo libre?
What do you do in your spare time?
Me llevó bastante tiempo.
It took me quite a long time.
¿Cuánto tiempo hace que vives aquí?
How long have you been living here?
Hace mucho tiempo que no la veo.

Spanish English

a b c d e f g h i j k l m n ñ o p q r s **t** u v w x y z

I haven't seen her for a long time.
al mismo tiempo
at the same time
a tiempo
in time
Llegamos a tiempo de ver la película.
We got there in time to see the film.

2 weather
¿Qué tiempo hace ahí?
What's the weather like there?
Hizo buen tiempo.
The weather was fine.
Hace mal tiempo.
The weather's bad.

3 half
Metieron el gol durante el segundo tiempo.
They scored the goal during the second half.

perder el tiempo
to waste time

la **tienda** NOUN
shop
una tienda de comestibles
a grocer's
una tienda de discos
a record shop
una tienda de campaña
a tent

ir de tiendas
to go shopping

tiendo VERB ▷ see **tender**
En el verano tiendo la ropa fuera.
I hang out the washing outside in the summer.

tiene VERB ▷ see **tener**
Tiene dos hermanas.
She has two sisters.

la **tierra** NOUN
land
la Tierra
the Earth

tieso (FEM **tiesa**) ADJECTIVE
1 stiff
quedarse tieso de frío
to be frozen stiff
2 straight
Ponte tiesa.
Stand up straight.

el **tigre** NOUN
tiger

las **tijeras** NOUN
scissors
Es más fácil cortarlo con las tijeras.
It's easier to cut it with scissors.
¿Tienes unas tijeras?
Do you have a pair of scissors?

el **timbre** NOUN
bell
Ya ha sonado el timbre.
The bell has already gone.

llamar al timbre
to ring the bell

tímido (FEM **tímida**) ADJECTIVE
shy

el **timo** NOUN
1 con
2 rip off
¡Vaya timo!
What a rip-off!

la **tinta** NOUN
ink

el **tinto** NOUN
red wine

tiñendo VERB ▷ see **teñir**
Mamá se está tiñendo el pelo.
Mum is dyeing her hair.

el **tío** NOUN
1 **uncle**
mis tíos
my uncle and aunt
2 **guy**
Es un tío muy simpático.
He's a really nice guy.
Oye, tío, me alegro de verte.
Hey, man, nice to see you.

el **tiovivo** NOUN
merry-go-round

típico (FEM **típica**) ADJECTIVE
typical
Eso es muy típico de ella.
That's very typical of her.

el **tipo** NOUN
1 **kind**
No me gusta este tipo de fiestas.
I don't like this kind of party.
todo tipo de ...
all sorts of ...
2 **figure**
Marisa tiene un tipo muy bonito.
Marisa has a lovely figure.

la **tira** NOUN
strip
una tira de papel
a strip of paper
una tira cómica
a comic strip
Hace la tira de tiempo que no la veo.
I haven't seen her for ages.

tirado (FEM **tirada**) ADJECTIVE
1 **dirt-cheap**
2 **dead easy**

tirar VERB
1 **to throw**
Tírame la pelota.
Throw me the ball.
Se tiró al suelo.
He threw himself to the ground.
2 **to throw away**
No tires la comida.
Don't throw away the food.

tirar algo a la basura
to throw something out
3 **to knock down**
Queremos tirar esta pared.
We want to knock this wall down.
tirar de la cadena
to pull the chain
tirarse al agua
to plunge into the water

tirarse de cabeza
to dive in head first
Se tiró toda la mañana estudiando.
He spent the whole morning studying.

la **tirita** NOUN
plaster

el **tiro** NOUN
shot
Oímos un tiro.
We heard a shot.
un tiro libre
a free kick

titular VERB
to call
La novela se titula 'Marcianos'.
The novel is called 'Marcianos'.

el **título** NOUN
title
Necesito un título para el poema.
I need a title for the poem.

la **tiza** NOUN
chalk
una tiza
a piece of chalk

la **toalla** NOUN
towel
una toalla de baño
a bath towel

Spanish **English**

a
b
c
d
e
f
g
h
i
j
k
l
m
n
ñ
o
p
q
r
s
t
u
v
w
x
y
z

el **tobillo** NOUN
ankle
> **Me he torcido el tobillo.**
> I've twisted my ankle.

el **tobogán** (PL los **toboganes**) NOUN
slide

tocar VERB
1 **to touch**
> **Si lo tocas te quemarás.**
> If you touch it you'll burn yourself.
2 **to play**
> **Toca el violín.**
> He plays the violin.
3 **Te toca fregar los platos.**
> It's your turn to do the dishes.
> **Le tocó la lotería.**
> He won the lottery.

todavía ADVERB
1 **still**
> **¿Todavía estás en la cama?**
> Are you still in bed?
> **¡Y todavía se queja!**
> And he still complains!
2 **yet**
> **Todavía no han llegado.**
> They haven't arrived yet.
> **¿Todavía no has comido?**
> Haven't you eaten yet?
> **Todavía no.**
> Not yet.

todo (FEM **toda**) ADJECTIVE, PRONOUN
1 **all**
> **todos los niños**
> all the children
> **Todos son caros.**
> They're all expensive.
> **toda la noche**
> all night
> **todos vosotros**
> all of you
2 **every**
> **todos los días**
> every day
3 **the whole**
> **Me he aprendido toda la canción.**
> I've learnt the whole song.
4 **everything**
> **Lo sabemos todo.**
> We know everything.
5 **everybody**
> **Todos estaban de acuerdo.**
> Everybody agreed.
> **Todo el mundo lo sabe.**
> Everybody knows.

tomar VERB
1 **to take**
> **En clase tomamos apuntes.**
> We take notes in class.
2 **to have**
> **¿Qué quieres tomar?**
> What are you going to have?
> **De postre tomé un helado.**
> I had an ice cream for dessert.
> **Toma, esto es tuyo.**
> Here, this is yours.
> **tomar el pelo a alguien**
> to pull somebody's leg
> **¡Me estás tomando el pelo!**
> You're pulling my leg!

> **tomar el sol**
> to sunbathe

el **tomate** NOUN
tomato

el **tono** NOUN
1 **tone**
> **Lo dijo en tono cariñoso.**
> He said it in an affectionate tone.
> **un tono de llamada**
> a ringtone
2 **shade**
> **un tono un poco más oscuro**
> a slightly darker shade

la **tontería** NOUN
silly thing
Se pelearon por una tontería.
They fell out over a silly thing.
tonterías
nonsense
¡Eso son tonterías!
That's nonsense!
¡No digas tonterías!
Don't talk nonsense!

tonto
tonta

tonto *can be an adjective or a noun.*

A ADJECTIVE
silly
¡Qué error más tonto!
What a silly mistake!
B MASC/FEM NOUN
fool

hacer el tonto
to mess around

el **tope** NOUN
El autobús iba a tope.
The bus was packed.

el **toque** NOUN
dar los últimos toques a algo
to put the finishing touches to
something

torcer VERB
1 **to twist**
¡Me estás torciendo el brazo!
You're twisting my arm!
Se torció el tobillo.
He sprained his ankle.
2 **to turn**
torcer a la derecha
to turn right
torcer la esquina
to turn the corner

la **tormenta** NOUN
storm

Hubo tormenta.
There was a storm.
un día de tormenta
a stormy day

el **torneo** NOUN
tournament

el **tornillo** NOUN
screw

el **toro** NOUN
bull
los toros
bullfighting

torpe (FEM **torpe**) ADJECTIVE
1 **clumsy**
2 **dim**

la **torre** NOUN
tower
la torre de control
the control tower

la **torta** NOUN
small flat cake

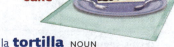

la **tortilla** NOUN
omelette
una tortilla de patatas
a Spanish omelette

la **tos** (PL las **toses**) NOUN
cough
Tengo mucha tos.
I have a bad cough.

toser VERB
to cough

la **tostada** NOUN
piece of toast
¿Quieres una tostada?
Do you want a piece of toast?
tostadas
toast
Tomé café con tostadas.
I had coffee and toast.

tostar VERB
to toast

Spanish English

a b c d e f g h i j k l m n ñ o p q r s **t** u v w x y z

total

total *can be an adjective, noun or adverb.*

A (FEM **total**) ADJECTIVE
total

B MASC NOUN
El total son cuarenta y cinco euros con cincuenta.
The total is forty-five euros fifty.
En total éramos catorce.
There were fourteen of us altogether.

C ADVERB
Total, que perdimos.
So, anyway, we lost.

totalmente ADVERB
totally
Mario es totalmente distinto a Carlos.
Mario is totally different from Carlos.
Estoy totalmente de acuerdo.
I completely agree.
¿Estás seguro? — Totalmente.
Are you sure? — Absolutely.

tóxico (FEM tóxica) ADJECTIVE
toxic

el **trabajador**
la **trabajadora** NOUN
worker

trabajar VERB
to work
No trabajes tanto.
Don't work so hard.
¿En qué trabajas?
What's your job?
Trabajo de camarero.
I work as a waiter.

el **trabajo** NOUN
1 work
Tengo mucho trabajo.
I have a lot of work.

2 job
Mi hermano no encuentra trabajo.
My brother can't find a job.

la **tradición** (PL las **tradiciones**)
NOUN
tradition

tradicional (FEM tradicional)
ADJECTIVE
traditional

la **traducción** (PL las **traducciones**) NOUN
translation
Una traducción del español al inglés.
A translation from Spanish into English.

traducir VERB
to translate
traducir del inglés al español
to translate from English into Spanish

traer VERB
to bring
He traído el paraguas por si acaso.
I've brought the umbrella just in case.

el **tráfico** NOUN
traffic
un accidente de tráfico
a road accident

tragar VERB
1 to swallow
Traga esta pastilla.
Swallow this tablet.
2 to stand
No la trago.
I can't stand her.

la **tragedia** NOUN
tragedy

el **traidor**
la **traidora** NOUN
traitor

traigo VERB
▷ see **traer**
¿Te traigo un vaso de leche?
Shall I bring you a glass of milk?

el **traje** NOUN
suit
Pedro llevaba un traje gris.
Pedro was wearing a grey suit.
un traje de baño
a pair of swimming trunks/a swimsuit

Language tip
un traje de baño *can mean either* a pair of swimming trunks *or* a swimsuit.

la **trampa** NOUN
trap
caer en la trampa
to fall into the trap

hacer trampa
to cheat

el **tramposo**
la **tramposa** NOUN
cheat

tranquilamente ADVERB
calmly
Háblale tranquilamente.
Speak to him calmly.

la **tranquilidad** NOUN
peace and quiet
Necesito un poco de tranquilidad.
I need a little peace and quiet.

tranquilizar VERB
to calm down
¡Tranquilízate!
Calm down!

tranquilo (FEM **tranquila**)
ADJECTIVE

1 calm
El día del examen estaba bastante tranquilo.
On the day of the exam I was quite calm.
2 peaceful

transgénico
(FEM **transgénica**) ADJECTIVE
genetically modified

la **transmisión** (PL las **transmisiones**) NOUN
broadcast
una transmisión en directo
a live broadcast

transmitir VERB
to transmit

transparente
(FEM **transparente**) ADJECTIVE
transparent

el **transporte** NOUN
transport
el transporte público
public transport

el **trapo** NOUN
cloth
Lo limpié con un trapo.
I wiped it with a cloth.
un trapo de cocina
a dishcloth
Pásale un trapo al espejo.
Give the mirror a wipe.
el trapo del polvo
the duster

tras PREPOSITION
after
Salimos corriendo tras ella.
We ran out after her.
semana tras semana
week after week

el **trasero** NOUN
bum

el **trasto** NOUN
piece of junk
El desván está lleno de trastos.
The loft is full of junk.

trastornado
(FEM **trastornada**) ADJECTIVE
disturbed

tratar VERB
to treat
> **Su padrastro los trata muy bien.**
> Their stepfather treats them really well.

> **¿De qué se trata?**
> What's it about?

el **trato** NOUN
deal
> **hacer un trato**
> to make a deal

> **¡Trato hecho!**
> It's a deal!

través PREPOSITION
> **a través de**
> across/through

Language tip
a través de *has two meanings. Look at the examples.*

> **Nadó a través del río.**
> He swam across the river.
> **Se enteraron a través de un amigo.**
> They found out through a friend.

travieso (FEM **traviesa**) ADJECTIVE
naughty

el **trayecto** NOUN
1 journey
2 way
> **¿Qué trayecto hace ese autobús?**
> What way does that bus go?

el **trébol** NOUN
clover

trece (FEM **trece**) ADJECTIVE, PRONOUN
thirteen
> **Tengo trece años.**
> I'm thirteen.

> **el trece de enero**
> the thirteenth of January
> **Nació el trece de enero.**
> He was born on the thirteenth of January.

treinta (FEM **treinta**) ADJECTIVE, PRONOUN
thirty
> **Tiene treinta años.**
> He's thirty.
> **el treinta de enero**
> the thirtieth of January
> **Nació el treinta de enero.**
> He was born on the thirtieth of January.

tremendo (FEM **tremenda**) ADJECTIVE
1 terrible
> **Tenía un tremendo dolor de cabeza.**
> I had a terrible headache.
> **Hacía un frío tremendo.**
> It was terribly cold.
2 tremendous
> **La película tuvo un éxito tremendo.**
> The film was a tremendous success.

el **tren** NOUN
train
> **viajar en tren**
> to travel by train

la **trenza** NOUN
plait
> **Le hice una trenza.**
> I put her hair up in a plait.

tres (FEM **tres**) ADJECTIVE, PRONOUN
three

Son las tres.
It's three o'clock.
el tres de febrero
the third of February
Nació el tres de febrero.
He was born on the third of February.

trescientos (FEM **trescientas**)
ADJECTIVE, PRONOUN
three hundred

el **triángulo** NOUN
triangle

el **trimestre** NOUN
term

el **trineo** NOUN
1 **sledge**
2 **sleigh**

el **trío** NOUN
trio

la **tripa** NOUN
gut

el **triple** NOUN
Esta habitación es el triple de grande.
This room is three times as big.
Gastan el triple que nosotros.
They spend three times as much as we do.

la **tripulación** (PL las **tripulaciones**) NOUN
crew

triste (FEM **triste**)
ADJECTIVE
sad

Me puse muy triste cuando me enteré.
I was very sad when I heard.

la **tristeza** NOUN
sadness

triunfar VERB
to triumph

el **triunfo** NOUN
triumph

el **trofeo** NOUN
trophy

la **trompeta** NOUN
trumpet

tronar VERB
to thunder
Ha estado tronando toda la noche.
It has been thundering all night.

troncharse VERB
Yo me tronchaba de risa.
I was killing myself laughing.

el **tronco** NOUN
1 **trunk**
2 **log**

el **trono** NOUN
throne

tropezar VERB
to trip
Tropecé y me caí.
I tripped and fell.
tropezar contra un árbol
to bump into a tree

el **tropezón** (PL los **tropezones**) NOUN
trip

tropical (FEM **tropical**)
ADJECTIVE
tropical

tropiece VERB ▷*see* **tropezar**
Mira que no tropiece con la puerta.
Make sure it doesn't bang into the door.

a
b
c
d
e
f
g
h
i
j
k
l
m
n
ñ
o
p
q
r
s
t
u
v
w
x
y
z

el **trozo** NOUN
piece
> **un trozo de madera**
> a piece of wood
> **Dame un trocito solo.**
> Just give me a small piece.

la **trucha** NOUN
trout

el **truco** NOUN
trick
> **Ya le he cogido el truco.**
> I've got the hang of it already.

truena VERB ▷ see **tronar**
> **Truena.**
> It's thundering.

el **trueno** NOUN
> **Oímos un trueno.**
> We heard a clap of thunder.
> **Me despertaron los truenos.**
> The thunder woke me up.

tu ADJECTIVE
your
> **tu bicicleta**
> your bicycle
> **tus familiares**
> your relations

tú PRONOUN
you
> **Cuando tú quieras.**
> Whenever you like.

la **tubería** NOUN
pipe
> **Ha reventado una tubería.**
> A pipe has burst.

el **tubo** NOUN
1 **pipe**
2 **tube**
> **un tubo de crema para las manos**
> a tube of hand cream

tuerzo VERB ▷ see **torcer**
> **Si no me sueltas, te tuerzo el brazo.**
> Let go or I'll twist your arm.

la **tumba** NOUN
grave

tumbar VERB
to knock down
> **El perro me tumbó.**
> The dog knocked me down.
- **tumbarse**
to lie down
> **Me tumbé en el sofá.**
> I lay down on the sofa.

el **túnel** NOUN
tunnel

el **turismo** NOUN
tourism
> **El turismo es importante para nuestra economía.**
> Tourism is important for our economy.
> **turismo rural**
> tourism in rural areas

el/la **turista**
NOUN
tourist

turístico (FEM **turística**)
ADJECTIVE
tourist

turnarse VERB
to take it in turns
> **Nos turnamos para fregar los platos.**
> We take it in turns to do the washing-up.

el **turno** NOUN
turn
> **cuando me tocó el turno**
> when it was my turn

el **turrón** (PL los **turrones**)
NOUN
nougat

tutear VERB

  Se tutean con el profesor.
They address their teacher in
familiar terms.

el **tutor**
  la **tutora** NOUN
  tutor

tuve VERB ▷*see* **tener**
  Tuve fiebre.
  I had a temperature.

tuyo (FEM **tuya**) ADJECTIVE,
PRONOUN
  yours
    ¿Es tuyo este abrigo?
    Is this coat yours?
    La tuya está en el armario.
    Yours is in the cupboard.
    mis amigos y los tuyos
    my friends and yours
    un amigo tuyo
    a friend of yours

a b c d e f g h i j k l m n ñ o p q r **t** u v w x y z

U u

u CONJUNCTION
or

> **Language tip**
> **u** *is used instead of* **o** *before words starting with* **o-** *or* **ho-**.

¿Minutos u horas?
Minutes or hours?

Ud. ABBREVIATION = **usted**

Uds. ABBREVIATION = **ustedes**

la **UE** ABBREVIATION
= **Unión Europea**
EU

uf EXCLAMATION
1 **phew!**
2 **ugh!**

últimamente ADVERB
recently

último
última

> **último** *can be an adjective or a noun.*

A ADJECTIVE
1 **last**
 la última vez que hablé con ella
 the last time I spoke to her
2 **top**
 No llego al último estante.
 I can't reach the top shelf.
3 **back**
 Nos sentamos en la última fila.
 We sat in the back row.
 la última moda
 the latest fashion
 llegar en último lugar
 to come last

a última hora
at the last minute

B MASC/FEM NOUN
the last one
 a últimos de mes
 towards the end of the month
 por último
 lastly

un
una ARTICLE
1 **a**
 una silla
 a chair

2 **an**
 un paraguas
 an umbrella
3 **some**
 Fui con unos amigos.
 I went with some friends.
 Había unas veinte personas.
 There were about twenty people.
 Me he comprado unos zapatos de tacón.
 I have bought a pair of high-heels.

undécimo (FEM **undécima**)
ADJECTIVE, PRONOUN
eleventh
 Vivo en el undécimo piso.
 I live on the eleventh floor.

único
única

> **único** *can be an adjective or a noun.*

A ADJECTIVE
 only
 el único día que tengo libre
 the only day I have free

Soy hija única.
I'm an only child.
Lo único que no me gusta ...
The only thing I don't like ...
B MASC/FEM NOUN
el único/la única
the only one
el único que me queda
the only one I've got left

la **unidad** NOUN
unit
una unidad de peso
a unit of weight

unido (FEM **unida**) ADJECTIVE
close
una familia muy unida
a very close family

el **uniforme** NOUN
uniform
Llevaba el uniforme del colegio.
He was wearing his school
uniform.

la **unión** (PL las **uniones**) NOUN
union
la Unión Europea
the European Union

unir VERB
1 to link
**Este pasaje une los dos
edificios.**
This passage links the two
buildings.
2 to join
**Unió los dos extremos con
una cuerda.**
He joined the two ends with
some string.
unirse a algo
to join something
Andrés se unió a la expedición.
Andrés joined the expedition.

la **universidad** NOUN
university
**Mi hermana va a la
universidad.**
My sister's at university.

el **universo** NOUN
universe

uno (FEM **una**) ADJECTIVE,
PRONOUN
one
Vivo en el número uno.
I live at number one.
Uno de ellos era mío.
One of them was mine.
Entraron uno a uno.
They came in one by one.
unas diez personas
about ten people

el uno de abril
the first of April
Es la una.
It's one o'clock.

untar VERB
untar algo con algo
to spread something on
something
**Primero hay que untar el pan
con mantequilla.**
First you have to spread the
butter on the bread.
**Te has untado las manos de
chocolate.**
You've got chocolate all over
your hands.

la **uña** NOUN
nail

la **urbanización** (PL las
urbanizaciones) NOUN
housing estate

la **urgencia** NOUN
emergency
los servicios de urgencia
the emergency services
urgencias
accident and emergency
department

urgente (FEM **urgente**)
ADJECTIVE
urgent

Spanish English

a b c d e f g h i j k l m n ñ o p q r s t **u** v w x y z

usado (FEM **usada**) ADJECTIVE
1 **secondhand**
   una tienda de ropa usada
   a secondhand clothes shop
2 **worn**
   Estas zapatillas están ya muy usadas.
   These slippers are very worn now.

usar VERB
1 **to use**
   ¿Usaste el grande o el pequeño?
   Did you use the small one or the big one?
2 **to wear**
   Esta falda está sin usar.
   This skirt has never been worn.
   ¿Qué número de zapato usas?
   What size shoe do you take?

el **uso** NOUN
   use
   instrucciones de uso
   instructions for use

usted PRONOUN
   you
   Quisiera hablar con usted en privado.
   I'd like to speak to you in private.

útil (FEM **útil**) ADJECTIVE
   useful

utilizar VERB
   to use

la **uva** NOUN
   grape

Did you know…?

in Spain, people celebrate the start of the New Year by eating twelve grapes, one with each of the twelve chimes, representing a month's luck for each grape that is eaten.

V v

va VERB ▷*see* **ir**
Va a la escuela del barrio.
He goes to the local school.

la **vaca** NOUN
1 **cow**
2 **beef**
No como carne de vaca.
I don't eat beef.

las **vacaciones** NOUN
holidays
las vacaciones de Navidad
the Christmas holidays
La secretaria está de vacaciones.
The secretary is on holiday.
En agosto me voy de vacaciones.
I'm going on holiday in August.

vaciar VERB
to empty
Ayúdame a vaciar este cajón.
Help me empty this drawer.

vacío (FEM **vacía**) ADJECTIVE
empty

el **vagabundo**
la **vagabunda** NOUN
tramp

vago (FEM **vaga**) ADJECTIVE
lazy

el **vagón** (PL los **vagones**) NOUN
carriage

la **vainilla** NOUN
vanilla

un helado de vainilla
a vanilla ice cream

el **vale** NOUN
voucher
un vale de regalo
a gift voucher

valer VERB
1 **to cost**
¿Cuánto vale?
How much does it cost?
2 **to be worth**
El terreno vale más que la casa.
The land is worth more than the house.
vale la pena
it's worth it
no vale la pena
it's not worth it
No vale la pena gastar tanto dinero.
It's not worth spending that much money.
Este cuchillo no vale para nada.
This knife is useless.
¿Vamos a tomar algo? — ¡Vale!
Shall we go for a drink? — OK!

¡Eso no vale!
That's not fair!
¿Vale?
OK?

válido (FEM **válida**) ADJECTIVE
valid

valiente (FEM **valiente**)
ADJECTIVE
brave

la **valla** NOUN
fence

257

a b c d e f g h i j k l m n ñ o p q r s t u **v** w x y z

el **valle** NOUN
valley

el **valor** NOUN
1 value
valor sentimental
sentimental value
objetos de valor
valuables
2 courage
armarse de valor
to pluck up courage

el **vapor** NOUN
steam
al vapor
steamed

el **vaquero** NOUN
cowboy
una película de vaqueros
a western
vaqueros
jeans
Llevaba unos vaqueros negros.
He was wearing black jeans.

variado (FEM **variada**) ADJECTIVE
varied
Tenemos un programa muy variado.
Our timetable is really varied.

variar VERB
to vary
Los precios varían según las tallas.
Prices vary according to size.
Decidí ir en tren, para variar.
I decided to go by train for a change.

la **variedad** NOUN
variety

varios (FEM **varias**) ADJECTIVE, PRONOUN
several
Estuve enfermo varios días.
I was ill for several days.
Le hicimos un regalo entre varios.

Several of us clubbed together to get him a present.

varón (PL **varones**)

> **varón** *can be an adjective or a noun.*

A ADJECTIVE
male
B MASC NOUN
Tiene dos hembras y un varón.
She has two girls and a boy.
Sexo: varón.
Sex: male.

vasco

> **vasco** *can be an adjective or a noun.*

A (FEM **vasca**) ADJECTIVE
Basque
el País Vasco
the Basque Country
B MASC/FEM NOUN
vasco/vasca
Basque
C MASC NOUN
Basque
Hablamos vasco.
We speak Basque.

el **vaso** NOUN
glass
Bebí un vaso de leche.
I drank a glass of milk.
un vaso de plástico
a plastic cup

vaya VERB ▷ *see* **ir**
¿Quieres que vaya contigo?
Do you want me to go with you?

Vd. ABBREVIATION = **usted**

Vds. ABBREVIATION = **ustedes**

ve VERB ▷ *see* **ir**, **ver**
Ve con él.
Go with him.
Mi perro no ve bien.
My dog can't see very well.

el **vecindario** NOUN
neighbourhood

el **vecino**
la **vecina** NOUN
neighbour
los vecinos de al lado
the next door neighbours

vegetal ADJECTIVE, MASC NOUN
vegetable
aceite vegetal
vegetable oil

el **vehículo** NOUN
vehicle

veinte (FEM **veinte**) ADJECTIVE,
PRONOUN
twenty

Tiene veinte años.
He's twenty.
el veinte de enero
the twentieth of January
Nació el veinte de enero.
He was born on the twentieth of
January.
el siglo veinte
the twentieth century

la **vejez** NOUN
old age

la **vela** NOUN
1 **candle**

Encendimos una vela.
We lit a candle.
2 **sail**

la **velocidad** NOUN
speed

**Pasó una moto a toda
velocidad.**
A motorbike went past at full
speed.
¿A qué velocidad ibas?
How fast were you going?

veloz (FEM **veloz**, PL **veloces**)
ADJECTIVE
swift

ven VERB ▷ see **ir, ver**
Ven conmigo.
Come with me.
Sus padres no ven el problema.
Her parents can't see the problem.

la **vena** NOUN
vein

vencer VERB
1 **to defeat**
2 **to overcome**

la **venda** NOUN
bandage
**Me pusieron una venda en
el brazo.**
They bandaged my arm.

vendar VERB
to bandage
Me vendaron el codo.
They bandaged my elbow.
vendar los ojos a alguien
to blindfold somebody

vender VERB
to sell
He vendido la bici.
I've sold my bike.

'se vende'
'for sale'

vendré VERB ▷ see **venir**
Mañana vendré de nuevo.
I'll come again tomorrow.

el **veneno** NOUN
poison

venenoso (FEM **venenosa**)
ADJECTIVE
poisonous

a
b
c
d
e
f
g
h
i
j
k
l
m
n
ñ
o
p
q
r
s
t
u
v
w
x
y
z

vengo VERB ▷ see **venir**
> **No vengo aquí mucho.**
> I don't come here much.

venir VERB
1 to come
> **Vino en taxi.**
> He came by taxi.
> **Vinieron a verme al hospital.**
> They came to see me in hospital.
> **¡Ven aquí!**
> Come here!
2 to be
> **La noticia venía en el periódico.**
> The news was in the paper.
> **¿Te viene bien el sábado?**
> Is Saturday all right for you?

> **el año que viene**
> next year
> **¡Venga, vámonos!**
> Come on, let's go!
> **¡Venga ya!**
> Come off it!

la **ventaja** NOUN
advantage
> **Tiene la ventaja de que está cerca de casa.**
> It has the advantage of being close to home.

la **ventana** NOUN
window

la **ventanilla** NOUN
window

> **Baja la ventanilla.**
> Open the window.

ver VERB
1 to see
> **Te vi en el parque.**
> I saw you in the park.
> **¡Cuánto tiempo sin verte!**
> I haven't seen you for ages!
> **No he visto esa película.**
> I haven't seen that film.
> **¿Ves? Ya te lo dije.**
> See? I told you so.
> **Eso no tiene nada que ver.**
> That has nothing to do with it.
> **¡No la puede ver!**
> He can't stand her!
> **Se ve que no tiene idea de informática.**
> It's clear he's got no idea about computers.
2 to watch
> **¿Te apetece ver la tele?**
> Do you feel like watching TV?

> **A ver ...**
> Let's see ...

el **verano** NOUN
summer
> **En verano hace mucho calor.**
> It's very hot in summer.
> **las vacaciones de verano**
> the summer holidays

> **en verano**
> in summer

el **verbo** NOUN
verb

la **verdad** NOUN
truth
> **Les dije la verdad.**
> I told them the truth.
> **La verdad es que no tengo ganas.**
> I don't really feel like it.
> **De verdad que yo no dije eso.**
> I didn't say that, honestly.
> **Es bonito, ¿verdad?**
> It's pretty, isn't it?
> **No te gusta, ¿verdad?**
> You don't like it, do you?

verdadero (FEM **verdadera**)
ADJECTIVE
real
> **Su apellido verdadero es Rodríguez.**
> His real surname is Rodríguez.

verde

> **verde** *can be an adjective or a noun.*

A (FEM **verde**) ADJECTIVE
green
> **Tiene los ojos verdes.**
> She has green eyes.
> **Estos plátanos están todavía verdes.**
> These bananas are still green.
B MASC NOUN
green

la **verdura** NOUN
vegetables
> **Comemos mucha verdura.**
> We eat a lot of vegetables.

vergonzoso (FEM **vergonzosa**)
ADJECTIVE
1 **shy**
> **Es muy vergonzosa.**
> She is very shy.
2 **disgraceful**
> **Es vergonzoso cómo los trataron.**
> It's disgraceful the way they were treated.

la **vergüenza** NOUN
1 **embarrassment**
> **Casi me muero de vergüenza.**
> I almost died of embarrassment.

> **¡Qué vergüenza!**
> How embarrassing!
> **Le da vergüenza pedirle ayuda.**
> He's embarrassed to ask her for help.
2 **shame**
> **No tienen vergüenza.**
> They have no shame.
> **¡Es una vergüenza!**
> It's disgraceful!

la **versión** (PL las **versiones**) NOUN
version

vertical (FEM **vertical**) ADJECTIVE
vertical
> **Ponlo vertical.**
> Put it upright.

vestido

> **vestido** *can be a noun or an adjective.*

A NOUN
dress
B (FEM **vestida**) ADJECTIVE
> **Iba vestida de negro.**
> She was dressed in black.
> **Yo iba vestido de payaso.**
> I was dressed as a clown.

vestir VERB
to wear
> **Vestía pantalones vaqueros y una camiseta.**
> He was wearing jeans and a T-shirt.
■ **vestirse**
to get dressed
> **Se está vistiendo.**
> He's getting dressed.
> **Se vistió de princesa.**
> She dressed up as a princess.

el **veterinario**
la **veterinaria** NOUN
vet

la **vez** (PL las **veces**) NOUN
time
> **¿Cuántas veces al año?**
> How many times a year?
> **¿La has visto alguna vez?**
> Have you ever seen her?
> **una vez**
> once
> **La veo una vez a la semana.**
> I see her once a week.
> **dos veces**
> twice

> **a veces**
> sometimes
> **algunas veces**
> sometimes
> **de vez en cuando**
> from time to time
> **en vez de**
> instead of
> **otra vez**
> again
> **tal vez**
> maybe

vi VERB ▷ see **ver**
> **Lo vi ayer.**
> I saw him yesterday.

viajar VERB
to travel
> **viajar en autocar**
> to travel by coach

el **viaje** NOUN
1 **trip**
> **¡Buen viaje!**
> Have a good trip!
2 **journey**
> **Es un viaje muy largo.**
> It's a very long journey.

> **estar de viaje**
> to be away

el **viajero**
la **viajera** NOUN
passenger

la **vida** NOUN
life

> **He vivido aquí toda mi vida.**
> I've lived here all my life.

el **vídeo** NOUN
video

la **videocámara** NOUN
video camera

el **videojuego** NOUN
video game

el **vidrio** NOUN
glass
> **botellas de vidrio**
> glass bottles
> **Me corté el dedo con un vidrio.**
> I cut my finger on a piece of glass.

viejo
vieja

> viejo *can be an adjective or a noun.*

A ADJECTIVE
old
> **un viejo amigo mío**
> an old friend of mine
> **Estos zapatos ya están muy viejos.**
> These shoes are very old now.

B MASC/FEM NOUN
> **un viejo**
> an old man
> **una vieja**
> an old woman
> **los viejos**
> old people

viene VERB ▷ see **venir**
> **¿Viene o no?**
> Is she coming or not?

el **viento** NOUN
wind

el **vientre** NOUN
stomach

el **viernes** (PL los **viernes**) NOUN
Friday

> **Language tip**
> *Days are not spelled with a capital letter in Spanish.*

La vi el viernes.
I saw her on Friday.
Viernes Santo
Good Friday

> **todos los viernes**
> every Friday
> **el viernes pasado**
> last Friday
> **el viernes que viene**
> next Friday

vigilar VERB
1 **to guard**
 Un policía vigilaba al preso.
 A policeman was guarding the prisoner.
2 **to watch**
 Nos vigilan.
 They're watching us.

el **vinagre** NOUN
vinegar

vine VERB ▷*see* **venir**
Vine sola.
I came on my own.

viniendo VERB ▷*see* **venir**
¿Nos veías viniendo por la montaña?
Could you see us coming down the mountain?

el **vino** NOUN
wine
 vino blanco
 white wine
 vino tinto
 red wine

la **violencia** NOUN
violence

violento (FEM **violenta**)
ADJECTIVE
violent

La película contiene algunas escenas violentas.
The film contains some violent scenes.

el **violín** (PL los **violines**) NOUN
violin

el/la **violinista** NOUN
violinist

el **virus** (PL los **virus**) NOUN
virus

visible (FEM **visible**) ADJECTIVE
visible

la **visión** (PL las **visiones**) NOUN
vision
 la visión nocturna
 night vision

la **visita** NOUN
1 **visit**
 hacer una visita a alguien
 to visit somebody
 Hice una visita a mi abuela.
 I visited my grandmother.

2 **visitor**
 Tienes visita.
 You've got visitors.
 horario de visita
 visiting hours

visitar VERB
to visit
 Miles de personas han visitado ya la exposición.
 Thousands of people have already visited the exhibition.

la **víspera** NOUN
the day before
 la víspera del partido
 the day before the match

la **vista** NOUN
1 **sight**

a b c d e f g h i j k l m n ñ o p q r s t u **v** w x y z

conocer a alguien de vista
to know somebody by sight
La conozco de vista.
I know her by sight.

2 view
una habitación con vistas al mar
a room with a sea view

> **¡Hasta la vista!**
> See you!

el **vistazo** NOUN
echar un vistazo a algo
to have a look at something
Échale un vistazo a esta revista.
Have a look at this magazine.

vistiendo VERB ▷see **vestir**
Se está vistiendo.
She's getting dressed.

visto (FEM **vista**)

> **visto** can be an adjective or part of the verb **ver**.

A ADJECTIVE
Está visto que ...
It's clear that ...

> **por lo visto**
> apparently

B VERB ▷see **ver**
¿Has visto a Elena?
Have you seen Elena?

viuda

> **viuda** can be an adjective or a noun.

A ADJECTIVE
Es viuda.
She's a widow.
B FEM NOUN
widow

viudo

> **viudo** can be an adjective or a noun.

A ADJECTIVE
Es viudo.

He's a widower.
B MASC NOUN
widower

vivir VERB
1 to live
¿Dónde vives?
Where do you live?
2 to be alive
¿Todavía vive?
Is he still alive?

> **¡Viva!**
> Hurray!

vivo (FEM **viva**) ADJECTIVE
1 alive
Estaba vivo.
He was alive.
en vivo
live
una retransmisión en vivo
a live broadcast
2 bright

el **vocabulario** NOUN
vocabulary

la **vocal** NOUN
vowel

el **volante** NOUN
steering wheel

volar VERB
to fly
El helicóptero volaba muy bajo.
The helicopter was flying very low.
Se me pasó la semana volando.
The week just flew by.
Tuvimos que ir volando al hospital.
We had to rush to the hospital.

el **voleibol** NOUN
volleyball

la **voltereta** NOUN
somersault
dar una voltereta
to do a somersault

el **volumen** (PL los **volúmenes**)
NOUN
volume
> **bajar el volumen**
> to turn the volume down
> **subir el volumen**
> to turn the volume up

la **voluntad** NOUN
1 **will**
> **Lo hizo contra mi voluntad.**
> He did it against my will.
2 **willpower**
> **Le cuesta, pero tiene mucha voluntad.**
> It's difficult for him, but he has a lot of willpower.

voluntario
voluntaria

> **voluntario** can be an adjective or a noun.

A ADJECTIVE
voluntary
B MASC/FEM NOUN
volunteer

volver VERB
1 **to come back**
2 **to go back**
3 **to turn**
> **Me volvió la espalda.**
> He turned away from me.
> **Me volví para ver quién era.**
> I turned round to see who it was.
4 **to become**
> **Se ha vuelto muy cariñoso.**
> He's become very affectionate.
> **volver a hacer algo**
> to do something again
> **Volví a abrir la puerta.**
> I opened the door again.

vomitar VERB
to be sick
> **Ha vomitado dos veces.**
> He's been sick twice.
> **Vomitó todo lo que había comido.**
> He threw up everything he'd eaten.

votar VERB
to vote
> **Voté por Alcántara.**
> I voted for Alcántara.

voy VERB ▷ see **ir**
> **Voy al parque.**
> I'm going to the park.

la **voz** (PL las **voces**) NOUN
voice
> **No tengo buena voz.**
> I don't have a very good voice.

vuelo

> **vuelo** can be a noun or part of the verb **volar**.

A MASC NOUN
flight
B VERB ▷ see **volar**
> **Esta vez vuelo en primera clase.**
> I'm flying first class this time.

la **vuelta** NOUN
1 **return**
> **un billete de ida y vuelta**
> a return ticket
2 **lap**
> **Di tres vueltas a la pista.**
> I did three laps of the track.
3 **change**
> **Quédese con la vuelta.**
> Keep the change.
> **Vive a la vuelta de la esquina.**
> He lives round the corner.
> **dar una vuelta**
> to go for a walk/to go for a drive

Language tip
dar una vuelta *has two meanings. It can be translated as* **to go for a walk** *and* **to go for a drive**.

vuelto VERB ▷ *see* **volver**
Ya ha vuelto del viaje.
He's back from his trip already.

vuelvo VERB ▷ *see* **volver**
Mañana vuelvo.
I'll be back tomorrow.

vuestro (FEM **vuestra**)

vuestro *can be an adjective or a pronoun.*

A ADJECTIVE
your
vuestra casa
your house
vuestros amigos
your friends
un amigo vuestro
a friend of yours

B PRONOUN
yours
¿Son vuestros?
Are they yours?
¿Es ésta la vuestra?
Is this one yours?
**¿Y los bocadillos? —
Los vuestros están aquí.**
Where are the sandwiches? —
Yours are over here.

W w

el **walkman®**
(PL los **walkmans**) NOUN
Walkman®

el **wáter** NOUN
loo

Language tip
Be careful! **wáter** *does not mean*
water.

la **web** NOUN
1 **website**
2 **(World Wide) Web**

la **webcam** NOUN
webcam

el **windsurf** NOUN
windsurfing

WWW ABBREVIATION
(= **World Wide Web**)
WWW

X x

el **xilófono** NOUN
xylophone

a
b
c
d
e
f
g
h
i
j
k
l
m
n
ñ
o
p
q
r
s
t
u
v
w
x
y
z

Y y

y CONJUNCTION
  and
    Andrés y su novia.
    Andrés and his girlfriend.
    Yo quiero una ensalada.
    ¿Y tú?
    I'd like a salad. What about you?
    Son las tres y cinco.
    It's five minutes past three.

ya ADVERB
  already
    Ya se han ido.
    They've already left.
    ¿Ya has terminado?
    Have you finished already?
    ya no
    not … any more
    Ya no salimos juntos.
    We aren't going out together
    any more.

> **ya que**
> since
> **Ya lo sé.**
> I know.
> **¡Ya voy!**
> I'm coming!

el **yate** NOUN
  yacht

la **yema** NOUN
  1 **yolk**
  2 **fingertip**

yendo VERB ▷ see **ir**
  **Llevo todo el día yendo y
  viniendo.**
  I've spent all day coming and going.

el **yeso** NOUN
  plaster

yo PRONOUN
  1 **I**
    Carlos y yo no fuimos.
    Carlos and I didn't go.
  2 **me**
    **¿Quién ha visto la película?
    — Ana y yo.**
    Who's seen the film? —
    Ana and me.
    Es más alta que yo.
    She's taller than me.
    Soy yo, María.
    It's me, María.
    yo mismo
    myself
    Lo hice yo misma.
    I did it myself.

> **¡Yo también!**
> Me too!
> **yo que tú**
> if I were you

el **yoga** NOUN
  yoga

el **yogur** NOUN
  yoghurt

Z z

zamparse VERB
to wolf down
> **Se zampó todas las galletas.**
> He wolfed down all the biscuits.

la **zanahoria** NOUN
carrot

la **zancadilla** NOUN
> **Me puso la zancadilla.**
> He tripped me up.

la **zanja** NOUN
ditch

la **zapatería** NOUN
shoe shop

la **zapatilla** NOUN
slipper

> **Tráeme las zapatillas.**
> Bring me my slippers.
> **zapatillas de ballet**
> ballet shoes
> **zapatillas de deporte**
> trainers

el **zapato** NOUN
shoe
> **zapatos cómodos**
> comfortable shoes

zapatos de tacón
high-heeled shoes

el **zapping** NOUN
channel hopping
> **hacer zapping**
> to channel-hop

la **zona** NOUN
area
> **Viven en una zona muy tranquila.**
> They live in a very quiet area.
> **una zona peatonal**
> a pedestrian precinct
> **una zona verde**
> a green space

el **zoo** NOUN
zoo

el **zoológico** NOUN
zoo

el **zorro** NOUN
fox

zumbar VERB
to buzz
> **Me zumban los oídos.**
> My ears are buzzing.

el **zumo** NOUN
juice
> **zumo de naranja**
> orange juice

zurdo (FEM **zurda**) ADJECTIVE
1 **left-handed**
2 **left-footed**

zurrar VERB
to thrash

Language plus

Language plus

• Pets - Los animales domésticos

budgie N el **periquito**

canary N el **canario**

cat N el **gato**

dog N el **perro**

goldfish N el **pez de colores**
(PL los **peces de colores**)

guinea pig N el **conejillo de Indias**

hamster N el **hámster**
(PL los **hámsters**)

kitten N el **gatito**

mouse N el **ratón**
(PL los **ratones**)

parrot N el **loro**

poodle N el **caniche**

puppy N el **cachorro**

rabbit N el **conejo**

tortoise N la **tortuga**

• Farm animals - Los animales de la granja

bull N el **toro**

calf N el **ternero**

chick N el **polluelo**

chicken N el **pollo**

cock N el **gallo**

cow N la **vaca**

donkey N el **burro**

goat N la **cabra**

goose N la **oca**

hen N la **gallina**

horse N el **caballo**

lamb N el **cordero**

mare N la **yegua**

peacock N el **pavo real**

pheasant N el **faisán**
(PL los **faisanes**)

pig N el **cerdo**

pony N el **poney** (PL los **poneys**)

ram N el **carnero**

sheep N la **oveja**

sheepdog N el **perro pastor**

turkey N el **pavo**

• Wild animals - Los animales salvajes

ant N la **hormiga**

ape N el **simio**

bat N el **murciélago**

bear N el **oso**

bee N la **abeja**

beetle N el **escarabajo**

bird N el **pájaro**

butterfly N la **mariposa**

camel N el **camello** *(two humps)*

camel N el **dromedario**
(one hump)

cheetah N el **guepardo**
crab N el **cangrejo**
crocodile N el **cocodrilo**
cub N el **cachorro**
deer N el **ciervo**
dolphin N el **delfín**
  (PL los **delfines**)
duck N el **pato**
elephant N el **elefante**
fish N el **pez** (PL los **peces**)
fly N la **mosca**
fox N el **zorro**
frog N la **rana**
giraffe N la **jirafa**
gorilla N el **gorila**
hare N la **liebre**
hedgehog N el **erizo**
hippo N el **hipopótamo**
insect N el **insecto**
jellyfish N la **medusa**
kangaroo N el **canguro**

koala N el **koala**
ladybird N la **mariquita**
leopard N el **leopardo**

lion N el **león** (PL los **leones**)
lioness N la **leona**
lizard N el **lagarto**
mammoth N el **mamut**
mole N el **topo**
monkey N el **mono**
mosquito N el **mosquito**
moth N la **polilla**
octopus N el **pulpo**
ostrich N el **avestruz**
  (PL los **avestruces**)
owl N el **búho**
panther N la **pantera**
penguin N el **pingüino**

pigeon N la **paloma**
polar bear N el **oso polar**
rat N la **rata**
raven N el **cuervo**
reindeer N el **reno**
reptile N el **reptil**
rhino N el **rinoceronte**
robin N el **petirrojo**
seagull N la **gaviota**
seal N la **foca**

shark N el **tiburón**
(PL los **tiburones**)

slug N la **babosa**

snail N el **caracol**

snake N la **serpiente**

sparrow N el **gorrión**
(PL los **gorriones**)

spider N la **araña**

squirrel N la **ardilla**

swallow N la **golondrina**

swan N el **cisne**

tadpole N el **renacuajo**

tiger N el **tigre**

toad N el **sapo**

turtle N la **tortuga de mar**

wasp N la **avispa**

whale N la **ballena**

wolf N el **lobo**

worm N el **gusano**

zebra N la **cebra**

ankle N el **tobillo**

arm N el **brazo**

back N la **espalda**

beard N la **barba**

blood N la **sangre**

body N el **cuerpo**

brain N el **cerebro**

cheek N la **mejilla**

chest N el **pecho**

chin N la **barbilla**

ear N la **oreja**

elbow N el **codo**

eye N el **ojo**

eyebrow N la **ceja**

eyelash N la **pestaña**

eyelid N el **párpado**

face N la **cara**

finger N el **dedo (de la mano)**

fist N el **puño**

foot N el **pie**

forehead N la **frente**

freckles N las **pecas**

fringe N el **flequillo**

hair N el **pelo**

hand N la **mano**

head N la **cabeza**

heart N el **corazón**
(PL los **corazones**)

heel N el **talón**
(PL los **talones**)

hip N la **cadera**

jaw N la **mandíbula**

kidney N el **riñón**
(PL los **riñones**)

knee N la **rodilla**

leg N la **pierna**

lip N el **labio**

liver N el **hígado**

lung N el **pulmón**
(PL los **pulmones**)

moustache N el **bigote**

mouth N la **boca**

muscle N el **músculo**

nail N la **uña**

neck N el **cuello**

nerve N el **nervio**

nose N la **nariz** (PL las **narices**)

organ N el **órgano**

palm N la **palma**

rib N la **costilla**

shoulder N el **hombro**

skeleton N el **esqueleto**

skin N la **piel**

skull N el **cráneo**

spine N la **columna vertebral**

stomach N el **estómago**

thigh N el **muslo**

throat N la **garganta**

thumb N el **pulgar**

toe N el **dedo (del pie)**

tongue N la **lengua**
tonsils N PL las **amígdalas**
tooth N el **diente**

tummy N la **barriga**
waist N la **cintura**
wrist N la **muñeca**

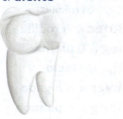

anorak N el **anorak**

apron N el **delantal**

ballet shoes N PL las **zapatillas de ballet**

baseball cap N la **gorra de béisbol**

belt N el **cinturón** (PL los **cinturones**)

beret N la **boina**

bikini N el **bikini**

blouse N la **blusa**

boots N PL las **botas**

bow tie N la **pajarita**

boxer shorts N el **boxer**

bra N el **sujetador**

cagoule N el **chubasquero**

cap N la **gorra**

cardigan N la **rebeca**

clothes N la **ropa**

coat N el **abrigo**

dress N el **vestido**

dressing gown N la **bata**

dungarees N el **peto**

fleece N el **forro polar**

flippers N PL las **aletas**

football boots N PL las **botas de fútbol**

football shirt N la **camiseta de fútbol**

glasses N PL las **gafas**

glove N el **guante**

goggles N PL las **gafas de piscina**

hat N el **sombrero**

helmet N el **casco**

hood N la **capucha**

hoodie N el **jersey con capucha**

jacket N la **chaqueta**

jeans N PL los **vaqueros**

jumper N el **jersey**

kilt N la **falda escocesa**

knickers N PL las **bragas**

leather jacket N la **chaqueta de cuero**

leggings N PL las **mallas**

miniskirt N PL la **minifalda**

nightdress N el **camisón** (PL los **camisones**)

overall N la **bata**

polo shirt N el **polo**

polo-necked sweater N el **jersey de cuello alto**

pyjamas N el **pijama**

raincoat N el **impermeable**

sandals N PL las **sandalias**

scarf N la **bufanda**

shirt N la **camisa**

shoes N PL los **zapatos**

shorts N PL los **pantalones cortos**

ski boots N PL las **botas de esquí**

skirt N la **falda**

slippers N PL las **zapatillas**

sock N el **calcetín** (PL los calcetines)

suit N el **traje**

sunglasses NPL las **gafas de sol**

sweatshirt N la **sudadera**

swimming costume N el **bañador**

tie N la **corbata**

tights N las **medias**

top N el **top**

tracksuit N el **chándal** (PL los **chándals**)

trainers N PL las **zapatillas de deporte**

trousers N PL los **pantalones**

trunks N el **bañador**

T-shirt N la **camiseta**

underpants N PL los **calzoncillos**

underwear N la **ropa interior**

uniform N el **uniforme**

vest N la **camiseta**

waistcoat N el **chaleco**

wellingtons N PL las **botas de agua**

wetsuit N el **traje de neopreno**

beige ADJ **beige**
(FEM, PL **beige**)

black ADJ **negro** (FEM **negra**)

blonde ADJ **rubio**
(FEM **rubia**)

blue ADJ **azul** (FEM **azul**)

brown ADJ **marrón**
(FEM **marrón**)

cream ADJ **crema**
(FEM, PL **crema**)

green ADJ **verde** (FEM **verde**)

grey ADJ **gris** (FEM **gris**)

maroon ADJ **burdeos**
(FEM, PL **burdeos**)

navy blue ADJ **azul
marino** (FEM, PL **azul marino**)

orange ADJ **naranja**
(FEM, PL **naranja**)

pink ADJ **rosa** (FEM, PL **rosa**)

purple ADJ **morado**
(FEM **morada**)

red ADJ **rojo** (FEM **roja**)

turquoise ADJ **turquesa**
(FEM, PL **turquesa**)

white ADJ **blanco**
(FEM **blanca**)

yellow ADJ **amarillo**
(FEM **amarilla**)

aunt N la **tía**
baby N el **bebé**
brother N el **hermano**
brother-in-law N el **cuñado**
child N la **niña**
child N el **niño**
cousin N la **prima**
cousin N el **primo**
dad N el **papá**
daughter N la **hija**
daughter-in-law N
  la **nuera**
family N la **familia**
father N el **padre**
father-in-law N el **suegro**
fiancé N el **prometido**
fiancée N la **prometida**
grandchildren N PL
  los **nietos**
granddad N el **abuelo**
granddaughter N la **nieta**
grandparents N PL
  los **abuelos**
grandson N el **nieto**
granny N la **abuela**
half-brother N
  el **hermanastro**
half-sister N
  la **hermanastra**

husband N el **marido**
in-laws N PL los **suegros**
mother N la **madre**
mother-in-law N la **suegra**
mum N la **mamá**

nephew N el **sobrino**
niece N la **sobrina**
parents N los **padres**
sister N la **hermana**
sister-in-law N la **cuñada**
son N el **hijo**
son-in-law N el **yerno**
stepdaughter N la **hijastra**
stepfather N el **padastro**
stepmother N la **madrastra**
stepson N el **hijastro**
uncle N el **tío**
wife N la **mujer**

• Days of the week – Los días de la semana

Monday el **lunes**
Tuesday el **martes**
Wednesday el **miércoles**
Thursday el **jueves**
Friday el **viernes**
Saturday el **sábado**
Sunday el **domingo**

• Months of the year – Los meses del año

January **enero**
February **febrero**
March **marzo**
April **abril**
May **mayo**
June **junio**
July **julio**
August **agosto**
September **septiembre**
October **octubre**
November **noviembre**
December **diciembre**

• Special days – Fiestas señaladas

New Year's Day N el **Día de Año Nuevo**
Mother's Day N el **Día de la Madre**
Father's Day N el **Día del Padre**
Valentine's Day N el **Día de San Valentín**
Christmas N la **Navidad**
Christmas Eve N la **Nochebuena**
New Year's Eve N la **Nochevieja**
Easter N la **Semana Santa**

It's chilly. Hace fresco.

It's cloudy. Está nublado.

It's cold. Hace frío.

It's foggy. Hay niebla.

It's freezing. Hace mucho frío.

It's frosty. Hay escarcha.

It's hot. Hace calor.

It's icy. Hay hielo.

It's misty. Hay niebla.

It's nice. Hace buen tiempo.

It's overcast. El cielo está nublado.

It's raining. Llueve.

It's snowing. Nieva.

It's stormy. Hay tormenta.

It's sunny. Hace sol.

It's windy. Hace viento.

● **Seasons – Las estaciones del año**

spring N la **primavera**

summer N el **verano**

autumn N el **otoño**

winter N el **invierno**

Africa N África

Albania N Albania

Algeria N Argelia

America N América

Asia N Asia

Australia N Australia

Austria N Austria

Belgium N Bélgica

Brazil N Brasil

Brussels N Bruselas

Bulgaria N Bulgaria

Canada N Canadá

China N China

Cornwall N Cornualles

Corsica N Córcega

Croatia N Croacia

Cyprus N Chipre

Denmark N Dinamarca

Dublin N Dublín

Edinburgh N Edimburgo

Egypt N Egipto

Eire N la República de Irlanda

England N Inglaterra

Estonia N Estonia

Ethiopia N Etiopia

Europe N Europa

Far East N Extremo Oriente

Finland N Finlandia

Francia N France

Germany N Alemania

Great Britain N Gran Bretaña

Greece N Grecia

Holland N Holanda

Hungary N Hungría

Iceland N Islandia

India N India

Iran N Irán

Iraq N Irak

Ireland N Irlanda

Israel N Israel

Italy N Italia

Japan N Japón

Jordan N Jordania

Korea N Corea

Latin America N América Latina

Latvia N Letonia

Lebanon N Líbano

Libya N Libia

Lithuania N Lituania

London N Londres

Luxembourg N Luxemburgo

Majorca N Mallorca

Malaysia N Malasia

Malta N Malta

Mexico N México

Middle East N Oriente Medio

Milan N Milán

Monaco N Mónaco

Morocco N Marruecos

Naples N Nápoles

New Zealand N Nueva Zelanda

North America N
América del Norte

Northern Ireland N
Irlanda del Norte

Norway N Noruega

Orkneys N Órcadas

Pakistan N Paquistán

Palestine N Palestina

Paris N París

Poland N Polonia

Portugal N Portugal

Romania N Rumania

Rome N Roma

Russia N Rusia

Sardinia N Cerdeña

Saudi Arabia N Arabia
Saudí

Scandinavia N los países
escandinavos

Scotland N Escocia

Shetland Islands N PL
las Islas Shetland

Sicily N Sicilia

Slovakia N Eslovaquia

Slovenia N Eslovenia

South Africa N Sudáfrica

South America N
Sudamérica

Spain N España

Sweden N Suecia

Switzerland N Suiza

the Alps N PL los Alpes

the Atlantic N el Atántico

the British Isles las Islas
Británicas

the Caribbean N
el Caribe

the Czech Republic N
la República Checa

the English Channel N
el Canal de la Mancha

the Mediterranean N
el Mediterráneo

the Netherlands N PL
los Países Bajos

the North Pole N el Polo
Norte

the North Sea N el Mar
del Norte

the South Pole N el Polo
Sur

the Thames N el Támesis

the United Kingdom N
el Reino Unido

the United States N PL
los Estados Unidos

the US N los EE. UU.

the West Indies N PL
las Antillas

Tunisia N Túnez

Turkey N Turquía

Vietnam N Vietnam

Wales N Gales

• Savoury – Alimentos salados

bacon N la **panceta**

baked potato N la **patata asada**

beans N PL las **alubias**

beef N la **carne de vaca**

beefburguer N la **hamburguesa**

biscuit N la **galleta**

bread N el **pan**

butter N la **mantequilla**

cereal N los **cereales**

cheese N el **queso**

chicken N el **pollo**

chips N las **patatas fritas**

chop N la **chuleta**

cod N el **bacalao**

corn on the cob N la **mazorca de maíz**

cracker N la **galleta salada**

cream N la **nata**

cream cheese N el **queso para untar**

crisps N las **patatas fritas**

egg N el **huevo**

fish N el **pescado**

fried egg N el **huevo frito**

garlic N el **ajo**

gravy N el **jugo de carne**

ham N el **jamón**

hard-boiled egg N el **huevo cocido**

herbs N PL las **hierbas aromáticas**

hot dog N el **perrito caliente**

ketchup N el **ketchup**

kidney N el **riñón** (PL los **riñones**)

lamb N el **cordero**

lamb chop N la **chuleta de cordero**

lentil N la **lenteja**

liver N el **hígado**

loaf of bread N el **pan**

lobster N la **langosta**

macaroni N los **macarrones**

mackerel N la **caballa**

margarine N la **margarina**

mashed potatoes N el **puré de patatas**

mayonnaise N la **mayonesa**

meat N la **carne**

mince N la **carne picada**

muesli N el **muesli**

mushroom N el **champiñón** (PL los **champiñones**) (*button mushrooms*)

mushroom N la **seta** (*open-cup*)

mussel N el **mejillón** (PL los **mejillones**)

mustard N la **mostaza**

noodles N PL los **fideos**

oats N la **avena**

oil N el **aceite**

olive N la **aceituna**

olive oil N el **aceite de oliva**

omelette N la **tortilla**

oyster N la **ostra**

parsley N el **perejil**

pasta N la **pasta**

pâté N el **paté**

pepper N la **pimienta**

pizza N la **pizza**

sauce N la **salsa**

sausage N la **salchicha**

scampi N las **gambas rebozadas**

scrambled eggs N PL los **huevos revueltos**

seafood N el **marisco**

shellfish N el **marisco**

shrimps N PL los **camarones**

soft-boiled egg N el **huevo pasado por agua**

soup N la **sopa**

pork N la **carne de cerdo**

potato N la **patata**

prawn N la **gamba**

rice N el **arroz**

roast potatoes N las **patatas asadas**

roll N el **bollo**

rye N el **centeno**

rye bread N el **pan de centeno**

salad N la **ensalada**

salad dressing N el **aliño**

salami N el **salami**

salmon N el **salmón**

salt N la **sal**

sandwich N el **bocadillo**

sardine N la **sardina**

soy sauce N la **salsa de soja**

steak N el **bistec**

stew N el **estofado**

sweetcorn N el **maíz**

thyme N el **tomillo**

toast N las **tostadas**

toasted sandwich N el **sándwich caliente**

trout N la **trucha**

tuna N el **atún**

turkey N el **pavo**

veal N la **ternera**

vinegar N el **vinagre**

wheat N el **trigo**

wholemeal bread N el **pan integral**

- **Sweet – Alimentos dulces**

apple tart N la **tarta de manzana**

biscuit N la **galleta**

cake N el **pastel** *(small)*

cake N la **tarta** *(big)*

candyfloss N el **algodón de azúcar**

caramel N el **caramelo líquido**

caramel N el **flan**

chewing gum N el **chicle**

chocolate N el **chocolate**

chocolate mousse N la **mousse de chocolate**

cone N el **cucurucho**

cream N la **nata**

cream cake N la **tarta de nata**

custard N las **natillas**

dessert N el **postre**

fruit salad N la **macedonia**

honey N la **miel**

ice cream N el **helado**

ice lolly N el **polo**

jam N la **mermelada**

jelly N la **gelatina**

lollipop N el **pirulí**

marmalade N la **mermelada de naranja**

marzipan N el **mazapán**

meringue N el **merengue**

mint N el **caramelo de menta**

mousse N la **mousse**

pancake N la **tortita**

popcorn N las **palomitas**

rice pudding N el **arroz con leche**

sponge cake N el **bizcocho**

sugar N el **azúcar**

sweet N el **caramelo**

vanilla N la **vainilla**

whipped cream N la **nata montada**

yoghurt N el **yogur**

apple N la **manzana**

apricot N el **albaricoque**

aubergine N la **berenjena**

avocado N el **aguacate**

banana N el **plátano**

beetroot N la **remolacha**

blackberry N la **mora**

blackcurrant N la **grosella negra**

broccoli N el **brécol**

Brussels sprouts N PL las **coles de Bruselas**

cabbage N la **col**

carrot N la **zanahoria**

cauliflower N la **coliflor**

celery N el **apio**

cherry N la **cereza**

chestnut N la **castaña**

clementine N la **clementina**

coconut N el **coco**

courgette N el **calabacín** (PL los **calabacines**)

cress N el **berro**

cucumber N el **pepino**

French beans N PL las **judías verdes**

fruit N la **fruta**

fruit salad N la **macedonia**

gooseberry N la **grosella espinosa**

grapefruit N el **pomelo**

grapes N PL las **uvas**

hazelnut N la **avellana**

leek N el **puerro**

lemon N el **limón** (PL los **limones**)

lettuce N la **lechuga**

lime N la **lima**

mango N el **mango**

melón N el **melón** (PL los **melones**)

onion N la **cebolla**

orange N la **naranja**

pea N el **guisante**

peach N el **melocotón** (PL los **melocotones**)

peanut N el **cacahuete**

pear N la **pera**

pepper N el **pimiento**

pineapple N la **piña**

plum N la **ciruela**

pumpkin N la **calabaza**

radish N el **rábano**

raisin N la **pasa**

raspberry N la **frambuesa**

redcurrant N la **grosella roja**

spinach N las **espinacas**

strawberry N la **fresa**

sultana N la **pasa sultana**

tangerine N la **mandarina**

tomato N el **tomate**

turnip N el **nabo**

vegetables N PL las **verduras**

walnut N la **nuez**

watermelon N la **sandía**

apple juice N el **zumo de manzana**

beer N la **cerveza**

black coffee N el **café solo**

champagne N el **champán**

cocoa N el **cacao**

coffee N el **café**

Coke® N la **Coca-Cola®**

decaffeinated coffee N el **café descafeinado**

fruit juice N el **zumo de fruta**

hot chocolate N el **chocolate caliente**

juice N el **zumo**

latte N el **café con leche**

lemonade N la **gaseosa**

milk N la **leche**

milkshake N el **batido**

mineral water N el **agua mineral**

orange juice N el **zumo de naranja**

peach juice N el **zumo de melocotón**

pineapple juice N el **zumo de piña**

tea N el **té**

water N el **agua**

wine N el **vino**

armchair N el **sillón**
(PL los **sillones**)

bath tub N la **bañera**

bed N la **cama**

bench N el **banco**

bookcase N la **librería**

bookshelf N la **estantería**

bunk beds N PL las **camas literas**

chair N la **silla**

chest of drawers N
la **cómoda**

coffee table N la **mesa de centro**

cooker N la **cocina**

couch N el **sofá**

cupboard N el **armario**

curtain N la **cortina**

cushion N el **cojín**
(PL los **cojines**)

deckchair N la **tumbona**

dishwasher N
el **lavavajillas**
(PL los **lavavajillas**)

double bed N la **cama de matrimonio**

easy chair N la **butaca**

freezer N el **congelador**

fridge N la **nevera**

microwave N el **microondas**
(PL los **microondas**)

oven N el **horno**

refrigerator N el **frigorífico**

rug N la **alfombra**

sink N el **fregadero**

sink N el **lavabo**

table N la **mesa**

television N la **televisión**

tumble dryer N
la **secadora**

washing machine N
la **lavadora**

All the jobs in the following list can be done by both men and women. For reasons of space, only the masculine forms have been given for nouns that end in **-o** in the masculine and **-a** in the feminine, so don't forget to change el to la and the **-o** ending to **-a** when referring to a woman.

Where the article is shown as el/la, it means that the same noun works for both males and females, eg el/la **juez** N **judge**. Where two translations are given, the one that starts with el is the masculine form while the one that starts with la is the feminine form.

accountant N el/la **contable**

actor N el **actor**

actress N la **actriz**

air hostess N la **azafata de vuelo**

archaeologist N el **arqueólogo**

architect N el **arquitecto**

artist N el/la **artista**

athlete N el/la **atleta**

au pair N el/la **au pair**

baker N el **panadero**

barber N el **barbero**

boxer N el **boxeador**, la **boxeadora**

builder N el **albañil**

bus driver N el **conductor de autobús**, la **conductora de autobús**

butcher N el **carnicero**

captain N el **capitán**, la **capitana**

caretaker N el **guardián**, la **guardiana**

chef N el **cocinero**

chemist N el **químico**

child minder N el/la **canguro**

conductor N el **director de orquesta**, la **directora de orquesta**

dancer N el **bailarín** (PL los **bailarines**), la **bailarina**

dentist N el/la **dentista**

detective N el/la **detective**

director N el **director**, la **directora**

disc jockey N el/la **disc jockey**

doctor N el **médico**

drummer N el/la **batería**

dustman N el **basurero**

electrician N el/la **electricista**

engineer N el **ingeniero**

farmer N el **agricultor**, la **agricultora**

film star N el/la **artista de cine**

fireman N el **bombero**

fisherman N el **pescador**

flight attendant N el/la **auxiliar de vuelo**

florist N el/la **florista**

football player N el **jugador de fútbol**, la **jugadora de fútbol**

footballer N el/la **futbolista**

gardener N el **jardinero**

goalkeeper N el **portero**

hairdresser N el **peluquero**

head teacher N el **director de colegio**, la **directora de colegio**

housewife N **ama de casa** *(fem)*

iman N el **imán**

instructor N el **instructor**, la **instructora**

interior designer N el **diseñador de interiores**, la **diseñadora de interiores**

interpreter N el/la **intérprete**

interviewer N el **entrevistador**, la **entrevistadora**

inventor N el **inventor**, la **inventora**

jeweller N el **joyero**

jockey N el/la **jockey**

joiner N el **carpintero**

journalist N el/la **periodista**

judge N el/la **juez**

labourer N el **obrero**

lawyer N el **abogado**

lecturer N el **profesor universitario**, la **profesora universitaria**

librarian N el **bibliotecario**

lorry driver N el **camionero**

magician N el **mago**

mayor N el **alcalde**, la **alcaldesa**

mechanic N el **mecánico**

midwife N la **comadrona**

miner N el **minero**

minister N el **ministro**

model N el/la **modelo**

monk N el **monje**

MP N el **diputado**

musician N el **músico**

nanny N la **niñera**

nun N la **monja**

nurse N la **enfermera**, el **enfermero**

operator N el **teleoperador**, la **teleoperadora**

optician N el **óptico**

painter N el **pintor**, la **pintora**

paperboy N el **repartidor de periódicos**

· ·

papergirl N la **repartidora de periódicos**

pharmacist N el **farmacéutico**

physicist N el **físico**

physiotherapist N el/la **fisioterapeuta**

pianist N el/la **pianista**

pilot N el/la **piloto**

plumber N el **fontanero**

policeman N el **policía**

policewoman N la **policía**

pop singer N el/la **cantante pop**

postman N el **cartero**

priest N el **sacerdote**

prison officer N el/la **guardia de prisiones**

professor N el **catedrático**

programmer N el **programador**, la **programadora**

psychiatrist N el/la **psiquiatra**

psychoanalyst N el/la **psicoanalista**

psychologist N el **psicólogo**

rabbi N el **rabino**

receptionist N el/la **recepcionista**

rep N el/la **representante**

reporter N el **reportero**

sailor N el **marinero**

salesman N el **comercial**

scientist N el **científico**

secretary N el **secretario**

shepherd N el **pastor**, la **pastora**

shop assistant N el **dependiente**, la **dependienta**

shopkeeper N el/la **comerciante**

social worker N el/la **asistente social**

soldier N el/la **soldado**

solicitor N el **notario**

supply teacher N el **maestro suplente**, la **maestra suplente** *(primary)*

supply teacher N el **profesor suplente**, la **profesora suplente** *(secondary)*

surgeon N el **cirujano**

surveyor N el **tasador**, la **tasadora**

taxi driver N el/la **taxista**

teacher N el **maestro** *(primary school)*

teacher N el **profesor**, la **profesora** *(secondary school)*

technician N el **técnico**

translator N el **traductor**, la **traductora**

vet N el **veterinario**

vicar N el **cura**

waiter N el **camarero**

waitress N la **camarera**

writer N el **escritor**, la **escritora**

atlas N el **atlas**

bell N la **campana**

Biro® N el **bolígrafo**

blackboard N la **pizarra**

book N el **libro**

break time N el **recreo**

calculator N la **calculadora**

canteen N el **comedor**

cassette player N
  el **casete**

chair N la **silla**

chalk N la **tiza**

chart N el **gráfico**

class N la **clase**

classroom N el **aula** *(fem)*

clock N el **reloj**

computer N el **ordenador**

corridor N el **pasillo**

curriculum N el **programa**

deputy head N
  el **subdirector**,
  la **subdirectora**

desk N la **mesa**

diagram N el **esquema**

dictionary N el **diccionario**

door N la **puerta**

drawing N el **dibujo**

drawing pin N
  la **chincheta**

essay N la **redacción**
  (PL las **redacciones**)

exam N el **examen**
  (PL los **exámenes**)

exercise N el **ejercicio**

exercise book N
  el **cuaderno**

felt-tip pen N el **rotulador**

folder N la **carpeta**

general knowledge N
  la **cultura general**

grammar N la **gramática**

gym N el **gimnasio**

gym kit N la **ropa de
  gimnasia**

head teacher N el **director**,
  la **directora**

homework N los **deberes**

ink N la **tinta**

jotter N el **bloc de notas**

language laboratory N
  el **laboratorio de idiomas**

lesson N la **lección** (PL las
  lecciones)

library N la **biblioteca**

mouse N el **ratón** (PL los
  ratones)

mousemat N la **alfombrilla
  del ratón**

page N la **página**

pen N la **pluma**

pencil N el **lápiz** (PL los **lápices**)

pencil case N el **lapicero**

pencil sharpener N
el **sacapuntas** (PL los **sacapuntas**)

photocopier N
la **fotocopiadora**

photocopy N la **fotocopia**

playground N el **patio de recreo**

printer N la **impresora**

pupil N el **alumno**

registration N la **inscripción**

rubber N la **goma**

ruler N la **regla**

school N el **colegio**

schoolbag N la **cartera**

schoolboy N el **colegial**

secondary school N
el **instituto de secundaria**

teacher N el **maestro**

test N la **prueba**

textbook N el **libro de texto**

whiteboard N la **pizarra blanca**

window N la **ventana**

● **School subjects – Las asignaturas**

art N el **dibujo**

English N el **inglés**

French N el **francés**

geography N la **geografía**

gym N la **gimnasia**

history N la **historia**

ICT N la **informática**

literacy N la **lengua**

maths N las **matemáticas**

music N la **música**

numeracy N las **matemáticas**

PE N la **educación física**

RE N la **religión**

science N las **ciencias**

attic N el **ático**

basement N el **sótano**

bedroom N el **dormitorio**

canteen N el **comedor**

changing room N
el **vestuario**

classroom N el **aula**

cloakroom N
el **guardarropa**

garage N el **garaje**

hall N la **entrada**

kitchen N la **cocina**

library N la **biblioteca**

living room N la **sala de estar**

lounge N el **salón**
(PL los **salones**)

office N la **oficina**

staircase N la **escalera**

study N el **despacho**

toilet N el **baño**

1	uno	**14**	catorce	**70**	setenta
2	dos	**15**	quince	**80**	ochenta
3	tres	**16**	dieciséis	**90**	noventa
4	cuatro	**17**	diecisiete	**100**	cien
5	cinco	**18**	dieciocho	**101**	ciento uno
6	seis	**19**	diecinueve	**200**	doscientos
7	siete	**20**	veinte	**250**	doscientos
8	ocho	**21**	veintiuno		cincuenta
9	nueve	**22**	veintidós		
10	diez	**30**	treinta	**1,000**	mil
11	once	**40**	cuarenta	**2,000**	dos mil
12	doce	**50**	cincuenta	**1,000,000**	un millón
13	trece	**60**	sesenta		

What time is it?
¿Qué hora es?

It's ...
Es .../Son ...

one o'clock
la una

ten past one
la una y diez

quarter past one
la una y cuarto

half past one
la una y media

twenty to two
las dos menos veinte

quarter to two
las dos menos cuarto

What time...?

¿A qué hora ... ?

at midnight
a medianoche

at midday
a mediodía

at one o'clock
(in the afternoon)
a la una (de la tarde)

at eight o'clock
(at night)
a las ocho
(de la noche)

**at quarter past
eleven**
(in the morning)
a las once y cuarto
(de la mañana)

at quarter to nine
(at night)
a las nueve menos cuarto
(de la noche)

The tables that follow show how the main Spanish verbs work in the present tense.

In Spanish the ending of the verb changes according to the person. This means that the form of the verb used for **yo** is different from the form used for **nosotros**, **ellos** etc.

The first three verbs given (**hablar**, **comer** and **vivir**) can be used as models for any other regular -**ar**, -**er** or -**ir** verb.

At the end of each table, there are some useful phrases which require other tenses. The examples throughout the dictionary use a variety of basic tenses that children and teachers alike will find useful.

1 hablar (to speak)

(yo)	hablo	(nosotros/as)	hablamos
(tú)	hablas	(vosotros/as)	habláis
(él/ella/usted)	habla	(ellos/ellas/ustedes)	hablan

Hoy he hablado con mi hermana. I've spoken to my sister today.
No hables tan alto. Don't talk so loud.
No se hablan. They don't talk to each other.

2 comer (to eat)

(yo)	como	(nosotros/as)	comemos
(tú)	comes	(vosotros/as)	coméis
(él/ella/usted)	come	(ellos/ellas/ustedes)	comen

No come carne. He doesn't eat meat.
No comas tan deprisa. Don't eat so fast.
Se lo ha comido todo. He's eaten it all.

3 vivir (to live)

(yo)	vivo	(nosotros/as)	vivimos
(tú)	vives	(vosotros/as)	vivís
(él/ella/usted)	vive	(ellos/ellas/ustedes)	viven

¿Dónde vives? Where do you live?
Viven en Valencia. They live in Valencia.
Vivimos en Inglaterra dos años. We lived in England for two years.

4 **estar** (to be)

(yo)	estoy	(nosotros/as)	estamos
(tú)	estás	(vosotros/as)	estáis
(él/ella/usted)	está	(ellos/ellas/ustedes)	están

Estoy cansado. I'm tired.
Estuvimos en casa de mi tía. We went to my aunt's.
¿A qué hora estarás en casa? What time will you be home?

5 **ser** (to be)

(yo)	soy	(nosotros/as)	somos
(tú)	eres	(vosotros/as)	sois
(él/ella/usted)	es	(ellos/ellas/ustedes)	son

Soy español. I'm Spanish.
¿Fuiste tú el que llamó? Was it you who phoned?
Era de noche. It was dark.

6 **ir** (to go)

(yo)	voy	(nosotros/as)	vamos
(tú)	vas	(vosotros/as)	vais
(él/ella/usted)	va	(ellos/ellas/ustedes)	van

Voy al colegio del barrio. I go to the local school.
Vamos al parque. Let's go to the park.
Ayer fuimos al cine. We went to the cinema yesterday.

7 **tener** (to have)

(yo)	tengo	(nosotros/as)	tenemos
(tú)	tienes	(vosotros/as)	tenéis
(él/ella/usted)	tiene	(ellos/ellas/ustedes)	tienen

Tengo dos hermanos. I have two brothers.
¿Cuántos años tienes? How old are you?
Tengo que hacer los deberes. I have to do my homework.

8 **haber** (to have [auxiliary])

(yo)	he	(nosotros/as)	hemos
(tú)	has	(vosotros/as)	habéis
(él/ella/usted)	ha	(ellos/ellas/ustedes)	han

¿Has visto eso? Did you see that?
Ya hemos ido a ver esa película. We've already been to see that film.
Ya te lo había dicho. I'd already told you.

9 **decir** (to say)

(yo)	digo	(nosotros/as)	decimos
(tú)	dices	(vosotros/as)	decís
(él/ella/usted)	dice	(ellos/ellas/ustedes)	dicen

Pero ¿qué dices? What are you saying?
Me lo dijo ayer. He told me yesterday.
¿Te ha dicho lo del profesor? Has he told you about the teacher?

10 **dar** (to give)

(yo)	doy	(nosotros/as)	damos
(tú)	das	(vosotros/as)	dais
(él/ella/usted)	da	(ellos/ellas/ustedes)	dan

Me da miedo la oscuridad. I'm scared of the dark.
Nos dieron un par de entradas gratis. They gave us a couple of free tickets.
Te daré el número de mi móvil. I'll give you my mobile phone number.

la estación

mi villa

el hospital

HOSPITAL

el río

la oficina de correos

el puente

el museo

la farmacia

la plaza

la iglesia

el banco

el mercado

el cine

ODEON

la calle

el patio de recreo

la acera

la escuela

el supermercado

el semáforo

ESCUELA

303

Mi habitación

el armario

la cortina

el ordenador

el libro

la mesa

el juguete

la silla

el cajón

el juego de ordenador

la librería

el despertador

los cómics

la cama

las zapatillas

el edredón

el pijama

la almohada

la guitarra

mi fiesta de cumpleaños

la vela

el globo

la tarta

el algodon de azúcar

la pajita

el tenedor

el vaso

la servilleta

el plato

la cuchara

el zumo

las patatas fritas

la limonada

la cámara

el regalo

los caramelos

en el parque

el tiovivo

la cometa

el tobogán

el columpio

el césped

el monopatín

el balón

la flor

los patines en línea

REFRESCOS

el helado

el estanque

el banco

el cisne

la bici

el pato

307

En la playa

el sol

la gaviota

la ola

las aletas

el pez

la roca

la nadadora

el mar

el socorrista

el flotador

el parasol

la arena

el bañador

la estrella de mar

las gafas de sol

el cangrejo

la crema solar

el castillo de arena

el cubo y la pala

la concha

En el bosque

el búho
la ardilla
el árbol
la hoja
el zorro
el abeto
el ciervo
el conejo
el trébol
la seta
el arroyo
la castaña
la frambuesa
la hormiga
el erizo

English - Spanish

A a

a ARTICLE
un *masc*
una *fem*

> **Language tip**
> Use **un** for masculine nouns and **una** for feminine nouns.

a book
un libro
a girl
una chica

> **Language tip**
> **a** isn't always translated by **un** and **una**.

He's a mechanic.
Es mecánico.
It costs ten pence a packet.
Cuesta diez peniques el paquete.
a hundred pounds
cien libras

able ADJECTIVE
to be able to
poder
Will you be able to come?
¿Podrás venir?
I won't be able to help you.
No podré ayudarte.

about ADVERB, PREPOSITION
1 **alrededor de** *(approximately)*
about fifty euros
alrededor de cincuenta euros
at about eleven o'clock
alrededor de las once
2 **sobre** *(concerning)*
a programme about lions
un programa sobre los leones
How about a game of cards?
¿Por qué no jugamos a las cartas?
I'm hungry, how about you?
Yo tengo hambre, ¿y tú?
We're about to go out.
Estamos a punto de salir.

above PREPOSITION

> **Language tip**
> When something is located above something, use **encima de**. When there is movement involved, use **por encima de**.

1 **encima de**
There's a picture above the fireplace.
Hay un cuadro encima de la chimenea.
2 **por encima de**
Throw the ball above your head.
Lanza el balón por encima de la cabeza.

> **Language tip**
> In Spanish you usually use an article like **el**, **la** or **los**, **las** with parts of the body.

3 **más de** *(more than)*
above thirty degrees
más de treinta grados

abroad ADVERB
1 **en el extranjero** *(in a foreign country)*
They live abroad.
Viven en el extranjero.
2 **al extranjero** *(to a foreign country)*
We're going abroad this year.
Vamos al extranjero este año.

absent ADJECTIVE
Who's absent today?
¿Quién falta hoy?
Tom's absent.
Falta Tom.

absurd ADJECTIVE
absurdo *masc*
absurda *fem*

That's absurd!
¡Eso es absurdo!

academy NOUN
la **academia** *fem*

accent NOUN
el **acento** *masc*
He's got a good accent.
Tiene buen acento.

accident NOUN
el **accidente** *masc*
It was an accident.
Fue un accidente.
a car accident
un accidente de coche
by accident
por casualidad/sin querer

> **Language tip**
> **by accident** *has two translations.*
> *Look at the examples.*

They discovered it by accident.
Lo descubrieron por casualidad.
The player touched the ball by accident.
El jugador tocó el balón sin querer.

ace NOUN
el **as** *masc* **the ace of hearts**
el as de corazones

to **ache** VERB
My leg's aching.
Me duele la pierna.

> **Language tip**
> *In Spanish you usually use an article*
> *like* **el**, **la** *or* **los**, **las** *with parts of*
> *the body.*

across PREPOSITION
al otro lado de
It's across the road.
Está al otro lado de la calle.
You mustn't run across the road.
No debes cruzar la calle corriendo.

to **act** VERB
actuar
He's acting in a play.
Actúa en una obra de teatro.

activity NOUN
la **actividad** *fem*
outdoor activities
actividades al aire libre

actor NOUN
el **actor** *masc*
la **actriz** *fem* (PL las **actrices**)
He's an actor.
Es actor.

> **Language tip**
> *When you say what someone's job is*
> *in Spanish, you do not use an article.*

actress NOUN
la **actriz** *fem* (PL las **actrices**)

actually ADVERB
en realidad
Actually, it's good fun.
En realidad, es bastante divertido.

> **Language tip**
> *Be careful! The translation of*
> **actually** *is not* **actualmente**.

AD ABBREVIATION
(= **Anno Domini**)
d.C. (= *después de Cristo*)
in 800 AD
en el 800 d.C.

to **add** VERB
añadir
Add some sugar.
Añade un poco de azúcar.

to **add up** VERB
sumar
You have to add the figures up.
Hay que sumar las cantidades.

address NOUN
la **dirección** *fem* (PL las **direcciones**)
What's your address, Emma?
¿Cuál es tu dirección, Emma?

adjective NOUN
　el **adjetivo** *masc*

admission NOUN
　la **entrada** *fem*
　　'admission free'
　　'entrada libre'

adopted ADJECTIVE
　I'm adopted.
　Soy adoptado.

adult NOUN
　el **adulto** *masc*
　la **adulta** *fem*
　　two adults and one child
　　dos adultos y un menor

advantage NOUN
　la **ventaja** *fem*
　　It's an advantage to be able to speak English.
　　Es una ventaja saber hablar inglés.

adventure NOUN
　la **aventura** *fem*
　　Harry has lots of adventures.
　　A Harry le suceden muchas aventuras.

adverb NOUN
　el **adverbio** *masc*

advert NOUN
　el **anuncio** *masc*
　　They put an advert in the newspaper.
　　Pusieron un anuncio en el periódico.

advice NOUN
　los **consejos** *masc pl*
　　Can you give me some advice?
　　¿Puedes darme algunos consejos?
　　That's good advice.
　　Es un buen consejo.
　　a piece of advice
　　un consejo

> **Language tip**
> *Be careful! The translation of* **advice** *is not* **aviso**.

aerobics NOUN
　el **aerobic** *masc*

aeroplane NOUN
　el **avión** *masc* (PL los **aviones**)

　　on an aeroplane
　　en un avión

affectionate ADJECTIVE
　cariñoso *masc*
　cariñosa *fem*
　　My cat is very affectionate.
　　Mi gato es muy cariñoso.

to **afford** VERB
　permitirse
　　I can't afford a new pair of jeans.
　　No puedo permitirme comprar unos vaqueros nuevos.

> **Language tip**
> *There isn't really a verb in Spanish that translates* **afford**. *You need to use a phrase with* **permitirse**.

afraid ADJECTIVE
　　to be afraid
　　tener miedo
　　I'm afraid.
　　Tengo miedo.
　　I'm afraid of spiders.
　　Me dan miedo las arañas.
　　Are you afraid of the dark?
　　¿Te da miedo la oscuridad?

after PREPOSITION
　después de
　　after break
　　después del recreo
　　after lunch
　　después de comer

afternoon NOUN
　la **tarde** *fem*
　　In the morning or in the afternoon?

¿Por la mañana o por la tarde?
at three o'clock in the afternoon
a las tres de la tarde
I'm playing football on Saturday afternoon.
Voy a jugar al fútbol el sábado por la tarde.

this afternoon
esta tarde
in the afternoon
por la tarde
Good afternoon!
¡Buenas tardes!

afters PL NOUN
el **postre** *masc*
What do you want for afters?
¿Qué quieres de postre?

again ADVERB
otra vez
I'd like to hear it again.
Quiero escucharlo otra vez.
Try again!
¡Inténtalo otra vez!

Language tip
You can also use **volver a** *followed by the main verb to translate* **again**.

Try again!
¡Vuelve a intentarlo!

against PREPOSITION
contra
You mustn't lean your chair against the wall.
No debes apoyar la silla contra la pared.

age NOUN
la **edad** *fem*
Write your name and age.
Escribe tu nombre y tu edad.
at the age of thirteen
a la edad de trece años

I am the same age as you.
Tengo la misma edad que tú.

Language tip
Note that in Spanish you use the verb **tener** to talk about somebody's age.

ago ADVERB
I bought it six months ago.
Lo compré hace seis meses.

a week ago
hace una semana
a long time ago
hace mucho tiempo

to **agree** VERB
estar de acuerdo
I agree.
Estoy de acuerdo.
I agree with Carol.
Estoy de acuerdo con Carol.

ahead ADVERB
Look straight ahead!
¡Mira hacia adelante!
The red team is five points ahead.
El equipo rojo lleva cinco puntos de ventaja.
There were a lot of people ahead of us in the queue.
Había mucha gente delante de nosotros en la cola.

air NOUN
el **aire** *masc*
Throw the ball into the air.
Lanza el balón al aire.
I prefer to travel by air.
Prefiero viajar en avión.

air-conditioned ADJECTIVE
climatizado *masc*
climatizada *fem*

airmail NOUN
by airmail
por avión

airport NOUN
el **aeropuerto** *masc*

alarm clock NOUN
el **despertador** masc

album NOUN
el **álbum** masc

alcohol NOUN
el **alcohol** masc
I don't drink alcohol.
No bebo alcohol.

A levels PL NOUN
el **bachillerato** masc
My brother is doing his A levels.
Mi hermano está haciendo el bachillerato.

Did you know…?
In Spain, the **bachillerato** is the equivalent of **A levels**.

alive ADJECTIVE
vivo masc
viva fem
They're still alive.
Todavía siguen vivos.

all ADJECTIVE, PRONOUN
todo masc
toda fem
all the time
todo el tiempo
all night
toda la noche
all my friends
todos mis amigos
all the girls
todas las chicas
The score is five all.
El marcador está empatado a cinco.

Is that all?
¿Eso es todo?

allergic ADJECTIVE
alérgico masc
alérgica fem
I'm allergic to cats.
Soy alérgica a los gatos.

allergy NOUN
la **alergia** fem
Have you got any allergies?
¿Tienes alguna alergia?

allowed ADJECTIVE
permitido masc
permitida fem
It's not allowed.
No está permitido.
We're not allowed to use calculators in the exam.
No se nos permite usar calculadora en el examen.

all right ADVERB, ADJECTIVE
1 **bien** (not bad)
Are you all right?
¿Estás bien?
Is that all right?
¿Está bien así?
Do you like school? — It's all right.
¿Te gusta ir al colegio? — Regular.
2 **de acuerdo** (when agreeing)
I'd like a coffee. — All right.
Quiero un café. — De acuerdo.

almost ADVERB
casi
Are you ready? — Almost.
¿Estás lista? — Casi.

alone ADJECTIVE
1 **solo** masc
sola fem
to be alone
estar solo
He was alone in the house.
Estaba solo en la casa.
She lives alone.
Vive sola.
2 **tranquilo** masc
tranquila fem (in peace)
Paul, leave Graham alone!
¡Paul, deja tranquilo a Graham!
Leave him alone!
¡Déjalo tranquilo!
Leave me alone!
¡Déjame tranquilo!

Leave my things alone!
¡No toques mis cosas!

along PREPOSITION
por
a walk along the beach
un paseo por la playa

aloud ADVERB
en voz alta
Read the words aloud, children.
Leed las palabras en voz alta, niños.
Read the words aloud, Richard.
Lee las palabras en voz alta, Richard.

alphabet NOUN
el **alfabeto** masc

alphabetical order NOUN
in alphabetical order
por orden alfabético

already ADVERB
ya
I've already done it.
Ya lo he hecho.
Have you finished already?
¿Ya has terminado?

also ADVERB
también
I also play the flute.
También toco la flauta.

alternate ADJECTIVE
on alternate days
cada dos días

alternative NOUN
la **alternativa** fem
You have no alternative.
No tienes alternativa.

altogether ADVERB
en total
That's twenty pounds altogether.
Son veinte libras en total.

always ADVERB
siempre
The bus is always late.
El autobús siempre llega tarde.

am VERB ▷see **be**

a.m. ABBREVIATION
de la mañana
at four a.m.
a las cuatro de la mañana

amazing ADJECTIVE
1 **increíble** masc & fem (surprising)
That's amazing!
¡Eso es increíble!
2 **excelente** masc & fem (excellent)
Vivian's an amazing cook.
Vivian es una cocinera excelente.

ambulance NOUN
la **ambulancia** fem

America NOUN
los **Estados Unidos** masc pl
We're going to America.
Vamos a Estados Unidos.

American

American can be an adjective or a noun.

A ADJECTIVE
americano masc
americana fem
American food
la cocina americana

He's American.
Es americano.
She's American.
Es americana.

B NOUN
el **americano** masc
la **americana** fem
the Americans
los americanos

Language tip
americano is not spelled with a capital letter in Spanish.

English **Spanish**

amount NOUN
  la **cantidad** *fem*
    a huge amount of rice
    una enorme cantidad de arroz
    a large amount of money
    una gran suma de dinero

amusement arcade NOUN
  el **salón recreativo** *masc* (PL
  los **salones recreativos**)

an ARTICLE
  un *masc*
  una *fem*

> *Language tip*
> Use **un** for masculine nouns and
> **una** for feminine nouns.

    an animal
    un animal
    an apple
    una manzana

> *Language tip*
> Sometimes the article **an** isn't
> translated.

    He's an actor.
    Es actor.
    ten kilometres an hour
    diez kilómetros por hora

and CONJUNCTION
  y
    my brother and me
    mi hermano y yo
    Two and two are four.
    Dos y dos son cuatro.

> *Language tip*
> Use **e** instead of **y** before words
> beginning with **i-** or **hi-** but not
> **hie-**.

    Miguel and Ignacio
    Miguel e Ignacio

> *Language tip*
> Don't translate **and** in numbers.

    two hundred and fifty
    doscientos cincuenta

angel NOUN
  el **ángel** *masc*

> *Language tip*
> Even though **ángel** is a masculine
> word, you can use it to refer to a
> woman or girl.

    You're an angel!
    ¡Eres un ángel!

angry ADJECTIVE
  enfadado *masc*
  enfadada *fem*
    He's very angry.
    Está muy enfadado.
    to get angry
    enfadarse
    **Mum gets angry if
    I'm late.**
    Mi madre se enfada
    si llego tarde.

animal NOUN
  el **animal** *masc*

anniversary NOUN
  el **aniversario** *masc*
    **my parents' wedding
    anniversary**
    el aniversario de bodas de mis
    padres

> **Happy anniversary!**
> ¡Feliz aniversario!

> *Language tip*
> Have you noticed the upside-down
> exclamation mark at the start of
> Spanish exclamations?

announcement NOUN
  el **anuncio** *masc*
    an important announcement
    un anuncio importante

anorak NOUN
  el **anorak** *masc*
    my new anorak
    mi anorak nuevo

another ADJECTIVE, PRONOUN
  otro *masc*
  otra *fem*

a b c d e f g h i j k l m n o p q r s t u v w x y z

319

English **Spanish**

a b c d e f g h i j k l m n o p q r s t u v w x y z

Would you like another sandwich?
¿Quieres otro sándwich?
There are plenty of apples. Would you like another one?
Hay muchas manzanas. ¿Quieres otra?

answer

answer *can be a verb or a noun.*

A VERB
to answer
contestar
Isabel, you have to answer yes or no.
Isabel, tienes que contestar sí o no.
Think before you answer.
Piensa antes de contestar.
to answer a question
contestar a una pregunta
Who can answer the question?
¿Quién puede contestar a la pregunta?
B NOUN
la **respuesta** *fem*
the right answer
la respuesta correcta

anthem NOUN
the national anthem
el himno nacional

any

any *can be an adjective or a pronoun.*

A ADJECTIVE

Language tip
You usually don't translate **any** *in questions.*

Do you want any bread?
¿Quieres pan?
Have you got any brothers or sisters?
¿Tienes hermanos?

Language tip
However, you can use **algún** *with a masculine singular noun and* **alguna** *with a feminine singular noun when the emphasis is on each individual person or thing.*

Do you have any hobbies?
¿Tienes algún pasatiempo?

Language tip
Similarly, you usually don't translate **any** *in negative sentences.*

I don't want any bread.
No quiero pan.
There aren't any oranges.
No hay naranjas.

Language tip
However, you can use **ningún** *with a masculine singular noun and* **ninguna** *with a feminine singular noun when* **not ... any** *is equivalent to* **not a single**.

I haven't got any CDs left.
No me queda ningún CD.
I can't see any flowers.
No veo ninguna flor.

Have you got any money?
¿Tienes dinero?
Have you got any pets?
¿Tienes alguna mascota?
There isn't any milk.
No hay leche.

B PRONOUN
1 **alguno** *masc*
alguna *fem (in questions)*
I need a stamp. Have you got any left?
Necesito un sello. ¿Te queda alguno?

Language tip
Only use **alguno/alguna** *when you mean one or two of something. Otherwise, don't translate* **any**.

I fancy some soup. Have we got any?
Me apetece sopa. ¿Tenemos?

I need some oil. Is there any?
Necesito aceite. ¿Hay?
2 **ninguno** *masc*
ninguna *fem (in negatives)*
I don't like any of them.
No me gusta ninguno.
A stamp? Sorry, I haven't got any.
¿Un sello? Lo siento, no tengo ninguno.

> **Language tip**
> *Only use* **ninguno/ninguna** *when* **not any** *means* **not a single one.** *Otherwise, don't translate* **any.**

I prefer apple juice, but we haven't got any.
Prefiero zumo de manzana, pero no tenemos.
I don't want any more.
No quiero más.

anybody PRONOUN
1 **alguien** *(in questions)*
Does anybody want a sweet?
¿Alguien quiere un caramelo?
2 **nadie** *(in negatives)*
I didn't see anybody.
No vi a nadie.

anyone PRONOUN
1 **alguien** *(in questions)*
Does anyone want to try?
¿Alguien quiere probar?
2 **nadie** *(in negatives)*
I can't see anyone.
No veo a nadie.

> **Language tip**
> *Don't forget the personal* **a** *in example sentences like this one.*

anything PRONOUN
1 **algo** *(in questions)*
Do you want anything to eat?
¿Quieres comer algo?
2 **nada** *(in negatives)*
I don't want anything.
No quiero nada.

anywhere PRONOUN
1 **en algún sitio** *(in questions)*

Have you seen my pen anywhere?
¿Has visto mi bolígrafo en algún sitio?
Are you going anywhere?
¿Vas a algún sitio?
2 **en ningún sitio** *(in negatives)*
I can't find it anywhere.
No lo encuentro en ningún sitio.
I'm not going anywhere.
No voy a ningún sitio.

apart ADVERB
Stand with your feet apart.
Ponte de pie con los pies separados.

> **Language tip**
> *In Spanish you usually use an article like* **el**, **la**, *or* **los**, **las** *with parts of the body.*

apart from
aparte de
Apart from that, everything's fine.
Aparte de eso, todo va bien.

apartment NOUN
el **piso** *masc*

apostrophe NOUN
el **apóstrofo** *masc*
Don't forget the apostrophe!
¡Que no se te olvide el apóstrofo!

app NOUN
la **aplicación** *fem*
for phone

apple NOUN
la **manzana** *fem*
a big red apple
una manzana grande y roja

apple juice NOUN
el **zumo de manzana** *masc*

apple pie NOUN
el **pastel de manzana** *masc*

English
Spanish

a
b
c
d
e
f
g
h
i
j
k
l
m
n
o
p
q
r
s
t
u
v
w
x
y
z

appointment NOUN
la **cita** *fem*
I've got a dental appointment.
Tengo cita con el dentista.

April NOUN
abril *masc*
My birthday's in April.
Mi cumpleaños es en abril.
It's the fifth of April today.
Hoy es cinco de abril.

in April
en abril
on the ninth of April
el nueve de abril

Language tip
Months are not spelled with a capital letter in Spanish.

April Fool NOUN
April Fool!
¡Inocente!

April Fools' Day NOUN
el **día de los Santos Inocentes** *masc*

Did you know...?
In Spanish-speaking countries people play practical jokes on each other on 28 December, and this day is called **el día de los Santos Inocentes**.

apron NOUN
el **delantal** *masc*
a white apron
un delantal blanco

are VERB ▷*see* **be**

area NOUN
la **zona** *fem*
a mountainous area of Spain
una zona montañosa de España

to **argue** VERB
discutir
Stop arguing!
¡Dejad de discutir!

arm NOUN
el **brazo** *masc*
I've hurt my arm.
Me he hecho daño en el brazo.

Language tip
In Spanish you usually use an article like **el**, **la** *or* **los**, **las** *with parts of the body.*

armchair NOUN
el **sillón** *masc* (PL los **sillones**)

army NOUN
el **ejército** *masc*
He's in the army.
Está en el ejército.

around PREPOSITION
1 **alrededor de**
The pupils are sitting around the teacher.
Los alumnos están sentados alrededor del profesor.
I go to bed around ten o'clock.
Me voy a la cama alrededor de las diez.
2 *(near)*
around here
por aquí
Is there a chemist's around here?
¿Hay una farmacia por aquí?

to **arrive** VERB
llegar

What time does the train arrive?
¿A qué hora llega el tren?

arrow NOUN
la **flecha** *fem*
Follow the arrows.
Siga las flechas.

art NOUN
1 el **dibujo** *masc* (at school)

Art is my favourite subject.
El dibujo es mi asignatura
preferida.
2 el **arte** *masc (artwork)*
modern art
el arte moderno

art gallery NOUN
el **museo** *masc*
The art gallery is closed.
El museo está cerrado.

artist NOUN
el/la **artista**
masc/fem

as CONJUNCTION,
PREPOSITION
1 **como** *(since)*
**Alice, as it's
your birthday you can
choose.**
Alice, como es tu cumpleaños,
puedes elegir.
2 **de** *(in the role of)*
**He works as a waiter in the
holidays.**
Trabaja de camarero en las
vacaciones.
as ... as
tan ... como
Edward's as tall as Stephen.
Edward es tan alto como
Stephen.
**Write to me as soon as
possible.**
Escríbeme lo antes posible.

ashamed ADJECTIVE
avergonzado *masc*
avergonzada *fem*

He's ashamed.
Está avergonzado.
**You should be ashamed
of yourself!**
¡Debería darte vergüenza!

ashtray NOUN
el **cenicero** *masc*

to **ask** VERB
1 **preguntar** *(make inquiry)*
Ask his name.
Pregúntale el nombre.
Ask your friend.
Pregúntale a tu amigo.

> **Language tip**
> *Don't forget the personal **a** in
> example sentences like this one.*

**Who wants to ask a
question?**
¿Quién quiere hacer una
pregunta?
Ask the question.
Haz la pregunta.
2 **pedir** *(request)*
If you need help, ask!
Si necesitas ayuda, ¡pídela!
3 **invitar** *(invite)*
**Are you going to ask
Matthew to the party?**
¿Vas a invitar a Matthew a
la fiesta?

> **Language tip**
> *Don't forget the personal **a** in
> examples like this one.*

to **ask for** VERB
pedir
**Ask for some chips and
a drink.**
Pide patatas fritas y una
bebida.

asleep ADJECTIVE
dormido *masc*
dormida *fem*
to be asleep
estar dormido
Are you asleep?
¿Estás dormido?

assembly NOUN
la **reunión de los profesores y alumnos** *fem*

Did you know…?
There is not normally **assembly** *in Spanish schools.*

assistant NOUN
1 el **dependiente** *masc*
la **dependienta** *fem (shop assistant)*
Ask the assistant.
Pregúntale a la dependienta.
2 el/la **ayudante** *masc/fem (helper)*
my assistant
mi ayudante

asthma NOUN
el **asma** *fem*
I've got asthma.
Tengo asma.

Language tip
Even though it's a feminine noun, remember that you use **el** with **asma**.

astronomy NOUN
la **astronomía** *fem*

at PREPOSITION
1 **en** *(with place, festival)*
at the café
en el café
at Christmas
en Navidad
2 **a** *(with time, speed)*
at four o'clock
a las cuatro
at fifty kilometres an hour
a cincuenta kilómetros por hora
What time did you arrive at the station?
¿A qué hora llegaste a la estación?

Language tip
a combines with **el** to form **al**.

What time did you arrive at the airport?
¿A qué hora llegaste al aeropuerto?
3 la **arroba** *fem (at sign)*
My email address is loveday at collins dot co dot U-K (loveday@collins.co.uk).
Mi e-mail es loveday arroba collins punto co punto U-K (loveday@collins.co.uk).

at night
por la noche
What are you doing at the weekend?
¿Qué vas a hacer el fin de semana?
at school
en el colegio
at home
en casa
two at a time
dos a la vez

ate VERB ▷ see **eat**

athlete NOUN
el/la **atleta** *masc/fem*

Atlantic NOUN
el **Atlántico** *masc*

atlas NOUN
el **atlas** *masc* (PL los **atlas**)

attention NOUN
la **atención** *fem*
Pay attention, everyone!
¡Prestad atención todos!
Pay attention, Mark!
¡Presta atención, Mark!

attic NOUN
el **desván** *masc* (PL los **desvanes**)

attractive ADJECTIVE
atractivo *masc*
atractiva *fem*
She's very attractive.
Es muy atractiva.

August NOUN
agosto *masc*

> **My birthday's in August.**
> Mi cumpleaños es en agosto.
> **It's the tenth of August today.**
> Hoy es diez de agosto.

> **in August**
> en agosto
> **on the fifth of August**
> el cinco de agosto

> *Language tip*
> *Months are not spelled with a capital letter in Spanish.*

aunt NOUN
la **tía** *fem*

> **my aunt**
> mi tía
> **my aunt and uncle**
> mis tíos

au pair NOUN
el/la **au pair** *masc/fem* (PL los/las **au pair**)

> **She's working as an au pair in London.**
> Está de au pair en Londres.

Australia NOUN
Australia *fem*

Australian

> **Australian** *can be an adjective or a noun.*

A ADJECTIVE
australiano *masc*
australiana *fem*

> **He's Australian.**
> Es australiano.
> **She's Australian.**
> Es australiana.

B NOUN
el **australiano** *masc*
la **australiana** *fem*

> *Language tip*
> **australiano** *is not spelled with a capital letter in Spanish.*

author NOUN
1 el **autor** *masc*
la **autora** *fem (of particular book)*

> **the author of the book**
> el autor del libro

2 el **escritor** *masc*
la **escritora** *fem (as a job)*

> **a famous author**
> un escritor famoso

autumn NOUN
el **otoño** *masc*

> **in autumn**
> en otoño

avenue NOUN
la **avenida** *fem*

average

> **average** *can be a noun or an adjective.*

A NOUN
la **media** *fem*

> **on average**
> de media
> **above average**
> por encima de la media

B ADJECTIVE
medio *masc*
media *fem*

> **the average age**
> la edad media
> **I'm average height.**
> Soy de estatura media.

English Spanish

a
b
c
d
e
f
g
h
i
j
k
l
m
n
o
p
q
r
s
t
u
v
w
x
y
z

away ADVERB
fuera
  He's away on a business trip.
  Está fuera en viaje de negocios.
  He'll be away for a week.
  Estará fuera una semana.

awful ADJECTIVE
  horroroso *masc*
  horrorosa *fem*

The food's awful.
La comida está horrorosa.
That's awful!
¡Eso es horroroso!
I feel awful.
Me siento fatal.

B b

baby NOUN
el **bebé** *masc*

The baby's asleep.
El bebé está durmiendo.
She's going to have a baby.
Va a tener un niño.
Don't be a baby!
¡No seas crío!

to **babysit** VERB
hacer de canguro
I babysit at the weekends.
Hago de canguro los fines de semana.

babysitter NOUN
el/la **canguro** *masc/fem*

back

A NOUN
1 la **espalda** *fem (of person)*
My back hurts.
Me duele la espalda.

Lie on your back!
¡Túmbate de espaldas!
2 el **fondo** *masc (of room)*
at the back
al fondo
Tony and I sit at the back.
Tony y yo nos sentamos al fondo.

at the back of the house
en la parte de atrás de la casa
3 el **final** *masc (of book)*
The verb tables are at the back of the book.
Las conjugaciones verbales están al final del libro.
B ADJECTIVE
trasero *masc*
trasera *fem*
the back seat
el asiento trasero
He came in the back door.
Entró por la puerta de atrás.

backache NOUN
I've got backache.
Me duele la espalda.

background NOUN
el **fondo** *masc*
a house in the background
una casa en el fondo

backstroke NOUN
la **espalda** *fem*
I can do the backstroke.
Sé nadar a espalda.

backwards ADVERB
hacia atrás
Take a step backwards!
¡Da un paso hacia atrás!

English Spanish

a **b** c d e f g h i j k l m n o p q r s t u v w x y z

bacon NOUN
el **beicon** *masc*
  bacon and eggs
  huevos con beicon

bad ADJECTIVE
1 **malo** *masc*
  mala *fem (awful)*
  a bad film
  una mala película
  Smoking is bad for you.
  Fumar es malo para la salud.

> *Language tip*
> Shorten **malo** to **mal** before a masculine singular noun.

  bad weather
  mal tiempo

> *Language tip*
> **mal** is also used in some phrases.

  That's not bad.
  No está mal.
  I'm bad at drawing.
  Se me da mal el dibujo.
2 **grave** *masc & fem (serious)*
  a bad accident
  un accidente grave
3 **travieso** *masc*
  traviesa *fem (naughty)*
  You bad boy!
  ¡Eres un chico travieso!

Bad luck!
¡Mala suerte!

badge NOUN
la **chapa** *fem*

badly ADVERB
mal
  He behaved badly.
  Se portó mal.

badminton NOUN
el **bádminton** *masc*
  I play badminton.
  Juego al bádminton.

> *Language tip*
> In Spanish, you need to add **al** or **a la** before the name of the sport or game.

bag NOUN
1 la **bolsa** *fem*
  a plastic bag
  una bolsa de plástico
2 el **bolso** *masc (handbag)*

bagpipes PL NOUN
la **gaita** *fem*
  Jimmy plays the bagpipes.
  Jimmy toca la gaita.

baked beans
PL NOUN
las **alubias con tomate** *fem pl*
  I like baked beans.
  Me gustan las alubias con tomate.

baked potato NOUN
la **patata asada** *fem*

baker's NOUN
la **panadería** *fem*

bakery NOUN
la **panadería** *fem*

balcony NOUN
el **balcón** *masc* (PL los **balcones**)

bald ADJECTIVE
calvo *masc*
calva *fem*
  My grandfather is bald.
  Mi abuelo es calvo.

ball NOUN
1 la **pelota** *fem (for tennis, golf, cricket)*
  Hit the ball!
  ¡Dale a la pelota!
2 el **balón** *masc*
  (PL los **balones**)
  (for football, rugby)
  Pass the ball!
  ¡Pasa el balón!

ballet NOUN
el **ballet** *masc*
  I do ballet.
  Hago ballet.

ballet dancer NOUN
　el **bailarín** *masc* (PL los
　　bailarines)
　la **bailarina** *fem*

ballet shoes PL NOUN
　las **zapatillas de ballet** *fem pl*

balloon NOUN
　el **globo** *masc*
　　a red balloon
　　un globo rojo

banana NOUN
　el **plátano** *masc*

band NOUN
　1 el **grupo de rock** *masc* (rock
　　band)
　2 la **banda de música** *fem*
　　(brass band)

bandage NOUN
　la **venda** *fem*
　　**He's got a bandage round his
　　arm.**
　　Lleva una venda en el brazo.

> **Language tip**
>
> *In Spanish you usually use an article
> like* **el**, **la** *or* **los**, **las** *with parts of
> the body.*

bang

> **bang** *can be a noun or a verb.*

A NOUN
　el **golpe** *masc*
　I heard a bang.
　Oí un golpe.
　**I got a nasty bang on my
　head.**
　Me di un golpe fuerte en la
　cabeza.
　The door shut with a bang.
　La puerta se cerró de un portazo.

B VERB
　to bang
　golpear
　**Mind you don't bang your
　head!**
　¡Cuidado no te vayas a golpear la
　cabeza!
　Don't bang the door!
　¡No des un portazo!

banger NOUN
　1 la **salchicha** *fem* (sausage)
　　bangers and mash
　　salchichas con puré de patatas
　2 el **petardo** *masc* (firework)
　　Peter is scared of bangers.
　　A Peter le asustan los petardos.

bank NOUN
　1 el **banco** *masc* (for money)
　　She works in a bank.
　　Trabaja en un banco.
　2 la **orilla** *fem* (of river, lake)
　　the banks of the Thames
　　las orillas del Támesis

bank holiday NOUN
　el **día festivo** *masc*
　　It's a bank holiday today.
　　Hoy es día festivo.

bar NOUN
　1 (piece)
　　a bar of chocolate
　　una tableta de chocolate
　　a bar of soap
　　una pastilla de jabón

　2 el **bar** *masc* (place)
　　She works in a bar.
　　Trabaja en un bar.

barbecue NOUN
　la **barbacoa** *fem*

barber's NOUN
　la **barbería** *fem*
　　at the barber's
　　en la barbería

English Spanish

a **b** c d e f g h i j k l m n o p q r s t u v w x y z

bare ADJECTIVE
desnudo *masc*
desnuda *fem*
She had bare arms.
Tenía los brazos desnudos.
Don't run about in bare feet.
No andes por ahí descalzo.

bargain NOUN
la **ganga** *fem*
It's a bargain!
¡Es una ganga!

to **bark** VERB
ladrar
My dog barks a lot.
Mi perro ladra mucho.

baseball NOUN
el **béisbol** *masc*
I play baseball.
Juego al béisbol.

> ### *Language tip*
> *In Spanish, you need to add* **al** *or* **a la** *before the name of the sport or game.*

baseball cap NOUN
la **gorra de béisbol** *fem*

basement NOUN
el **sótano** *masc*

basin NOUN
el **lavabo** *masc (washbasin)*

basket NOUN
la **cesta** *fem*

basketball NOUN
el **baloncesto** *masc*
Do you play basketball?
¿Juegas al baloncesto?

> ### *Language tip*
> *In Spanish, you need to add* **al** *or* **a la** *before the name of the sport or game.*

bat NOUN
1 el **bate** *masc (for cricket, rounders)*
2 la **raqueta** *fem (for table tennis)*
3 el **murciélago** *masc (animal)*

bath NOUN
1 el **baño** *masc (wash)*
a hot bath
un baño caliente
to have a bath
bañarse
I have a bath every night.
Me baño todas las noches.

2 la **bañera** *fem (tub)*
There's a spider in the bath!
¡Hay una araña en la bañera!

> ### *Language tip*
> *Don't confuse* **la bañera** *(the bathtub) with* **el baño** *(the wash you have in it).*

bathroom NOUN
el **cuarto de baño** *masc*

battery NOUN
1 la **pila** *fem (for torch, toy)*
I need a battery.
Necesito una pila.
2 la **batería** *fem (for car)*
The battery's flat.
La batería está descargada.

battle NOUN
la **batalla** *fem*

BC ABBREVIATION (= **before Christ**)
a.C. (= *antes de Cristo*)
in 200 BC
en el 200 a.C.

to **be** VERB

> ### *Language tip*
> *In Spanish there are two main verbs* **ser** *and* **estar** *for* **to be**.

1 **ser**

> ### *Language tip*
> *Use* **ser** *to talk about size, shape, colour, and characteristics which are generally permanent.*

I'm quite tall.
Soy bastante alto.
She's blonde.
Es rubia.
It's green.
Es verde.
It isn't very big.
No es muy grande.
It's round.
Es redondo.
They're wooden.
Son de madera.
It's easy.
Es fácil.

Language tip
*Use **ser** to talk about where someone's from.*

I'm English.
Soy inglesa.
I'm from Manchester.
Soy de Manchester.

Language tip
*Use **ser** with a following noun (naming word) to say what someone or something is.*

He's a teacher.
Es profesor.
It's a table.
Es una mesa.
It's the 28th of October today.
Hoy es 28 de octubre.

It's me.
Soy yo.

2 estar

Language tip
*Use **estar** to talk about where people, places, and objects are.*

I'm at home.
Estoy en casa.
Lima is in Peru.
Lima está en Perú.
Where are the keys?
¿Dónde están las llaves?

Language tip
*Use **estar** with adjectives (describing words) to talk about passing or temporary states.*

I'm tired.
Estoy cansado.
Are you ready?
¿Estás listo?
The coffee's cold.
El café está frío.
He's ill today.
Hoy está enfermo.

Language tip
*Use **estar** when talking about what someone is doing now.*

I'm writing a letter.
Estoy escribiendo una carta.
What are you doing?
¿Qué estás haciendo?

3 tener

Language tip
*Use **tener** when saying you're 'hot', 'cold', 'hungry', 'thirsty', or 'sleepy'.*

I'm hot.
Tengo calor.
I'm cold.
Tengo frío.
I'm hungry.
Tengo hambre.
I'm thirsty.
Tengo sed.
I'm sleepy.
Tengo sueño.

Language tip
*Use **tener** when talking about somebody's age.*

I'm eleven.
Tengo once años.
My brother is thirteen.
Mi hermano tiene trece años.

4 hacer

Language tip
*Use **hacer** when talking about the weather.*

It's cold.
Hace frío.
It's hot.
Hace calor.
It's a nice day.
Hace buen día.

beach NOUN
la **playa** *fem*

beans
PL NOUN
1 las **alubias con tomate** *fem
pl (baked beans)*
Would you like some beans?
¿Quieres unas alubias con
tomate?
2 las **judías verdes** *fem pl
(green beans)*

beard NOUN
la **barba** *fem*
Our teacher's got a beard.
Nuestro profesor tiene barba.

to **beat** VERB
ganar a *(in game)*
We're going to beat you!
¡Os vamos a ganar!

beautiful ADJECTIVE
1 **precioso** *masc*
preciosa *fem (thing, place)*
Your garden is beautiful.
Tu jardín es precioso.
2 **guapo** *masc*
guapa *fem (person)*
Emma is very beautiful.
Emma es muy guapa.

because CONJUNCTION
porque
**We can't play outside
because it's too cold.**
No podemos jugar fuera porque
hace mucho frío.

**Why don't you eat meat? —
Because I don't like it.**
¿Por qué no comes carne? —
Porque no me gusta.
**I can't sleep because of the
noise.**
No puedo dormir por el ruido.
because of the weather
debido al mal tiempo
because of you
por ti

to **become** VERB
hacerse
He became a footballer.
· Se hizo futbolista.

bed NOUN
la **cama** *fem*
in bed
en la cama
to go to bed
acostarse
I go to bed at ten o'clock.
Me acuesto a las diez.
What time do you go to bed?
¿A qué hora te acuestas?

bed and breakfast NOUN
la **pensión** *fem* (PL las **pensiones**)

bedroom NOUN
la **habitación** *fem* (PL las
habitaciones)
my bedroom
mi habitación

bedtime NOUN
**Ten o'clock is my usual
bedtime.**
Casi siempre me acuesto a las
diez.

Bedtime!
¡A la cama!

bee NOUN
la **abeja** *fem*

beef NOUN
la **ternera** *fem*
Would you like beef or chicken?
¿Quieres ternera o pollo?
roast beef
el rosbif

beefburger NOUN
la **hamburguesa** *fem*

been VERB ▷ *see* **be**

beer NOUN
la **cerveza** *fem*
a can of beer
una lata de cerveza

before

before *can be a preposition, conjunction or adverb.*

A PREPOSITION
antes de
before three o'clock
antes de las tres
B CONJUNCTION
Think before you answer, Rose!
¡Piensa antes de contestar, Rose!
C ADVERB
antes
Why didn't you say so before?
¿Por qué no lo has dicho antes?
I've never been to Scotland before.
Nunca había estado en Escocia.

to **begin** VERB
empezar
It begins with 'b'.
Empieza por 'b'.
It's beginning to get cold.
Está empezando a hacer frío.

beginner NOUN
el/la **principiante** *masc/fem*
I'm a beginner.
Soy principiante.

beginning NOUN
el **principio** *masc*
at the beginning
al principio

begun VERB ▷ *see* **begin**

to **behave** VERB
portarse
He behaves badly.
Se porta mal.
She's behaving like an idiot.
Se está portando como una idiota.
Behave!
¡Pórtate bien!

behind PREPOSITION
detrás de
It's behind the television.
Está detrás del televisor.
one behind the other
uno detrás del otro

beige

beige *can be an adjective or a noun.*

A ADJECTIVE
beige *masc & fem*
It's beige.
Es beige.
a beige skirt
una falda beige

Language tip
Colour adjectives come after the noun in Spanish.

B NOUN
el **beige** *masc*

to **believe** VERB
creer
I don't believe you.
No te creo.

bell NOUN
1 la **campana** *fem* (at school, in church)

The bell rang.
Sonó la campana.

2 el **timbre** *masc (at door, on reception)*
Ring the bell.
Llama al timbre.

3 el **cascabel** *masc (small bell)*
My cat has a bell on its collar.
Mi gato lleva un cascabel en el collar.

to **belong** VERB
to belong to somebody
pertenecer a alguien
That belongs to me.
Eso me pertenece a mí.
Does this belong to you?
¿Es tuyo esto?
Who does it belong to?
¿De quién es?
The ball belongs to Tony.
El balón es de Tony.

below PREPOSITION
bajo
below ground
bajo tierra
ten degrees below freezing
diez grados bajo cero

belt NOUN
el **cinturón** *masc* (PL los **cinturones**)

bench NOUN
el **banco** *masc*

bend

bend can be a noun or a verb.

A NOUN
la **curva** *fem*
a dangerous bend
una curva peligrosa
B VERB
to bend
doblar

Bend your legs!
¡Dobla las piernas!

Language tip

*In Spanish you usually use an article like **el**, **la** or **los**, **las** with parts of the body.*

---

beneath PREPOSITION
debajo de
beneath the table
debajo de la mesa

bent VERB ▷*see* **bend**

beside PREPOSITION
al lado de
beside the television
al lado del televisor
Sit beside me.
Siéntate a mi lado.

best

best can be an adjective, noun or adverb.

A ADJECTIVE
mejor *masc & fem*
Francis is my best friend.
Francis es mi mejor amigo.
Mary and Olga are my best friends.
Mary y Olga son mis mejores amigas.
the best team in the world
el mejor equipo del mundo
B NOUN
el/la **mejor** *masc/fem*
He's the best in the class.
Es el mejor de la clase.
C ADVERB
mejor
Emily sings best.
Emily es la que canta mejor.

English **Spanish**

Best wishes!
¡Saludos cordiales!

Language tip
Have you noticed the upside-down exclamation mark at the start of Spanish exclamations?

best man NOUN
el **padrino de boda** *masc*

better

better *can be an adjective or an adverb.*

A ADJECTIVE
mejor *masc & fem*
The ice cream is better than the cake.
El helado está mejor que el pastel.
That's better!
¡Eso está mejor!
B ADVERB
mejor
I can sing better than you.
Yo canto mejor que tú.

Get better soon!
¡Que te mejores pronto!

Language tip
Have you noticed the upside-down exclamation mark at the start of Spanish exclamations?

between PREPOSITION
entre
Think of a number between one and twelve.
Piensa en un número entre uno y doce.

Bible NOUN
la **Biblia** *fem*

bicycle
NOUN
la **bicicleta**
fem
by bicycle
en bicicleta

big ADJECTIVE
grande *masc & fem*
a big garden
un jardín grande
a big house
una casa grande
Have you got it in a bigger size?
¿Tiene una talla más grande?

Language tip
Shorten **grande** *to* **gran** *before a singular noun.*

a big problem
un gran problema
my big brother
mi hermano mayor
her big sister
su hermana mayor

bike NOUN
1 la **bici** *fem* (bicycle)
by bike
en bici
2 la **moto** *fem* (motorbike)

Language tip
Even though it ends in **-o**, **la moto** *is a feminine noun.*

bikini NOUN
el **bikini** *masc*

bill NOUN
la **cuenta** *fem* (in restaurant, hotel)
Can we have the bill, please?
¿Nos puede traer la cuenta, por favor?

billion NOUN
mil millones *masc pl*
a billion dollars
mil millones de dólares

Language tip
Be careful! The translation of **billion** *is not* **billón**.

bin NOUN
1 la **papelera** *fem* (wastepaper basket)

Put your chewing gum in the bin.
Tira el chicle a la papelera.
2 el **cubo de la basura** masc (rubbish bin)
The bin is in the kitchen.
El cubo de la basura está en la cocina.

bingo NOUN
el **bingo** masc
We're going to play bingo.
Vamos a jugar al bingo.

Language tip
In Spanish, you need to add **al** or **a la** before the name of the sport or game.

biology NOUN
la **biología** fem

bird NOUN
el **pájaro** masc

Biro® NOUN
el **boli** masc

birthday NOUN
el **cumpleaños**
masc (PL los **cumpleaños**)
My birthday is the third of May.
Mi cumpleaños es el tres de mayo.
When's your birthday?
¿Cuándo es tu cumpleaños?

Happy Birthday!
¡Feliz cumpleaños!

Language tip
Have you noticed the upside-down exclamation mark at the start of Spanish exclamations?

birthday cake NOUN
la **tarta de cumpleaños** fem

birthday card NOUN
la **tarjeta de cumpleaños** fem
I got ten birthday cards.
He recibido diez tarjetas de cumpleaños.

birthday party NOUN
la **fiesta de cumpleaños** fem
Would you like to come to my birthday party?
¿Quieres venir a mi fiesta de cumpleaños?

biscuit NOUN
la **galleta** fem
Would you like a biscuit?
¿Quieres una galleta?

bit NOUN
a bit
un poco
I'm a bit tired.
Estoy un poco cansado.

to **bite** VERB
1 morder (with teeth)
My dog doesn't bite.
Mi perro no muerde.
Stop biting your nails!
¡Deja de morderte las uñas!
2 picar (insect)
I've been bitten by something.
Me ha picado algo.

black

black can be an adjective or a noun.

A ADJECTIVE
negro masc
negra fem
She's black.
Es negra.
a black jacket
una chaqueta negra

Language tip
Colour adjectives come after the noun in Spanish.

B NOUN
el **negro** masc
He's dressed in black.
Va vestido de negro.

blackberry NOUN
la **mora** *fem*
    We picked blackberries.
    Cogimos moras.

blackboard NOUN
la **pizarra** *fem*
    Look at the blackboard!
    ¡Mira la pizarra!

black coffee NOUN
1 el **café solo** *masc (small)*
2 el **café americano** *masc*
    (large)

Did you know…?
un café solo *is a very small strong black coffee while* **un café americano** *is a mug of weaker black coffee.*

blackcurrant NOUN
la **grosella negra** *fem*
    blackcurrant jam
    mermelada de grosella negra

blank

blank *can be an adjective or a noun.*

A ADJECTIVE
en blanco
    a blank sheet of paper
    un folio en blanco
B NOUN
el **espacio en blanco** *masc*
    Fill in the blanks.
    Rellena los espacios en blanco.

blanket NOUN
la **manta** *fem*

blazer NOUN
el **blazer** *masc*
    a navy blazer
    un blazer azul marino

to **bless** VERB
    Bless you!
    ¡Salud!

Did you know…?
In Spain, people say **¡salud!** *when someone sneezes.*

blew VERB ▷ see **blow**

blind

blind *can be an adjective or a noun.*

A ADJECTIVE
ciego *masc*
ciega *fem*
    My grandfather is blind.
    Mi abuelo es ciego.
    a blind man
    un ciego
B NOUN
la **persiana** *fem*
    Open the blinds!
    ¡Sube las persianas!

to **blindfold** VERB
    I'm going to blindfold you.
    Te voy a vendar los ojos.

block NOUN
    a block of flats
    un bloque de pisos

blog NOUN
el **blog** *masc*

blonde ADJECTIVE
rubio *masc*
rubia *fem*
    She's got blonde hair.
    Tiene el pelo rubio.

blood NOUN
la **sangre** *fem*

blouse NOUN
la **blusa** *fem*
    a white blouse
    una blusa blanca

to **blow** VERB
soplar
    The wind is blowing.
    Está soplando el viento.

Stop when I blow the whistle!
¡Para cuando toque el silbato!
Blow your nose!
¡Suénate la nariz!

> **Language tip**
> In Spanish you usually use an article like **el**, **la** or **los**, **las** with parts of the body.

Blow out the candles!
¡Apaga las velas!

blue

> **blue** can be an adjective or a noun.

A ADJECTIVE
azul masc & fem
The sky is blue.
El cielo es azul.
a blue dress
un vestido azul

> **Language tip**
> Colour adjectives come after the noun in Spanish.

B NOUN
el **azul** masc
Blue is my favourite colour.
El azul es mi color preferido.

board NOUN
la **pizarra** fem (blackboard, whiteboard)
on the board
en la pizarra

board game NOUN
el **juego de mesa** masc

boarding school NOUN
el **internado** masc
I go to boarding school.
Voy a un internado.

boat NOUN
1 el **barco** masc (ferry, liner)
by boat
en barco
2 el **bote** masc (rowing boat, dinghy)

body NOUN
el **cuerpo** masc

boiled ADJECTIVE
cocido masc
cocida fem
boiled potatoes
patatas cocidas
a boiled egg
un huevo pasado por agua

bomb NOUN
la **bomba** fem

bonfire NOUN
la **hoguera** fem

> **Did you know…?**
> In Spain, people do not celebrate **Bonfire Night** but it is traditional in many places to celebrate **la noche de San Juan** (Saint John's Eve) with a public bonfire on the 23rd of June.

book

> **book** can be a noun or a verb.

A NOUN
1 el **libro** masc (printed)
Open your books at page ten.
Abrid los libros por la página diez.
2 el **cuaderno** masc (exercise book)
Write the words in your books.
Escribid las palabras en los cuadernos.
B VERB
to book
reservar
I want to book a seat.
Quiero reservar un asiento.

bookcase NOUN
la **librería** fem

> **Language tip**
> In Spanish, **la librería** is also the word for **bookshop**.

booklet NOUN
el **folleto** masc

bookshelf NOUN
la **estantería** fem
on the bookshelves
en las estanterías

bookshop NOUN
la **librería** fem

boot NOUN
1 la **bota** fem
I like your boots!
¡Me gustan tus botas!
football boots
botas de fútbol
2 el **maletero** masc (of car)
It's in the boot.
Está en el maletero.

border NOUN
la **frontera** fem (of country)

bored ADJECTIVE
aburrido masc
aburrida fem
I'm bored.
Estoy aburrido.

boring ADJECTIVE
aburrido masc

aburrida fem
a boring programme
un programa aburrido
This game is pretty boring, isn't it?
Este juego es bastante aburrido, ¿verdad?

born ADJECTIVE
I was born in 2000.
Nací en el 2000.

to **borrow** VERB
Can I borrow your pen?
¿Me dejas tu boli?

> ### Language tip
> Notice how the action is reversed in Spanish. You would normally use **¿me dejas...?** or **¿me prestas...?** when you want to borrow something.

boss NOUN
el **jefe** masc
la **jefa** fem

bossy ADJECTIVE
mandón masc (PL **mandones**)
mandona fem

both PRONOUN, ADJECTIVE
los **dos** masc pl
las **dos** fem pl
Adam and Daniel, you're both late!
Adam y Daniel, ¡habéis llegado tarde los dos!
Peter and Laura have both got a rabbit.
Tanto Peter como Laura tienen un conejo.

to **bother** VERB
molestar
I'm sorry to bother you.
Siento molestarle.

Don't bother!
¡No te preocupes!

bottle NOUN
la **botella** fem
a bottle of mineral water
una botella de agua mineral

bottom NOUN
1 la **parte de abajo** *fem*
(*of page, list*)
Look at the bottom of the page.
Mira en la parte de abajo de la página.
2 el **fondo** *masc* (*of container, bag, sea*)
My pen's at the bottom of my bag.
Mi boli está en el fondo del bolso.
3 el **trasero** *masc* (*bum*)

bought VERB ▷*see* **buy**

bow

bow *can be a noun or a verb.*

A NOUN
1 el **lazo** *masc* (*in ribbon, string*)
Tie a bow!
¡Haz un lazo!
She's wearing a pink bow in her hair.
Lleva un lazo rosa en el pelo.
2 el **arco** *masc* (*for archery*)
a bow and arrow
un arco y una flecha
B VERB
to bow
hacer una reverencia

bowl NOUN
el **tazón** *masc* (PL los **tazones**)
a bowl of soup
un tazón de sopa

bowling NOUN
los **bolos** *masc pl*
Do you want to come bowling?
¿Quieres venir a jugar a los bolos?

box NOUN
1 la **caja** *fem* (*container*)
a box of matches
una caja de cerillas
a cardboard box
una caja de cartón
2 la **casilla** *fem* (*in questionnaire*)
Tick the boxes.
Marca las casillas.

boxer NOUN
el **boxeador** *masc*

boxer shorts PL NOUN
los **bóxers** *masc pl*

boxing NOUN
el **boxeo** *masc*
I don't like boxing.
No me gusta el boxeo.

Boxing Day NOUN
el **día después de Navidad** *masc*
on Boxing Day
el día después de Navidad

boy NOUN
1 el **niño** *masc* (*young*)
a boy of six
un niño de seis años
2 el **chico** *masc* (*older*)
Well done, boys!
¡Muy bien, chicos!

boyfriend NOUN
el **novio** *masc*
Have you got a boyfriend?
¿Tienes novio?

bra NOUN
el **sujetador** *masc*

brace NOUN
  el **aparato dental** *masc*
    She wears a brace.
    Lleva un aparato dental.

bracelet NOUN
  la **pulsera** *fem*

bracket NOUN
  el **paréntesis** *masc* (PL los
    paréntesis)
    in brackets
    entre paréntesis

brain NOUN
  el **cerebro** *masc*

brainy ADJECTIVE
  listo *masc*
  lista *fem*
    Marina is very brainy.
    Marina es muy lista.

branch NOUN
  la **rama** *fem* (of tree)

brand-new ADJECTIVE
  flamante *masc & fem*
    It's brand-new.
    Es flamante.

brass band NOUN
  la **banda de música** *fem*

brave ADJECTIVE
  valiente *masc & fem*
    Be brave!
    ¡Sé valiente!

bread NOUN
  el **pan** *masc*
    Would you like some bread?
    ¿Quieres pan?
    bread and butter
    pan con mantequilla

break

> **break** *can be a noun or a verb.*

A NOUN
1 el **descanso** *masc* (in activity)
2 el **recreo** *masc* (at school)
  during morning break
  durante el recreo de la mañana

B VERB
  to break
  romper
    You're going to break it.
    Lo vas a romper.
    Who broke the window?
    ¿Quién rompió el cristal?
    Richard has broken his arm.
    Richard se ha roto el brazo.

> *Language tip*
> *In Spanish you usually use an article like* **el**, **la** *or* **los**, **las** *with parts of the body.*

to **break down** VERB
  averiarse
    The bus has broken down.
    El autobús se ha averiado.
    Our car broke down.
    Se nos averió el coche.

to **break up** VERB
  **We break up next
  Wednesday.**
  Empezamos las vacaciones el
  miércoles que viene.

breakfast NOUN
  el **desayuno** *masc*
    Breakfast is at eight o'clock.
    El desayuno es a las ocho.
    I have cereal for breakfast.
    Tomo cereales para el desayuno.
    to have breakfast
    desayunar
    When do you have breakfast?
    ¿A qué hora desayunas?

break time NOUN
  el **recreo** *masc*
    at break time
    en el recreo

breaststroke NOUN
  la **braza** *fem*
    I can do the breaststroke.
    Sé nadar a braza.

breath NOUN
  Take a deep breath!
  ¡Respira hondo!

brick NOUN
el **ladrillo** *masc*
a brick wall
una pared de ladrillo

bride NOUN
la **novia** *fem*
the bride and groom
los novios

bridegroom NOUN
el **novio** *masc*

bridesmaid NOUN
la **dama de honor** *fem*

bridge NOUN
el **puente** *masc*

bright ADJECTIVE
vivo *masc*
viva *fem*
a bright colour
un color vivo
bright blue
azul vivo
a bright blue shirt
una camisa azul vivo

> **Language tip**
> When you describe something as **bright blue**, **bright red** and so on, neither the colour nor **vivo** changes its ending to agree with the noun.

brilliant ADJECTIVE
estupendo *masc*
estupenda *fem*
We're going to London. — Brilliant!
Nos vamos a Londres. — ¡Estupendo!

to **bring** VERB
traer
Could you bring me a glass of water?
¿Me podrías traer un vaso de agua?

Bring the money tomorrow.
Trae el dinero mañana.

to **bring back** VERB
devolver
You must bring them back tomorrow.
Tienes que devolverlos mañana.

Britain NOUN
Gran Bretaña *fem*
in Britain
en Gran Bretaña

British

> **British** *can be an adjective or a noun.*

A ADJECTIVE
británico *masc*
británica *fem*
She's British.
Es británica.
B NOUN
the British
los británicos

> **Language tip**
> **británico** *is not spelled with a capital letter in Spanish.*

British Isles PL NOUN
las **Islas Británicas** *fem pl*

broccoli NOUN
el **brécol** *masc*
Would you like some broccoli?
¿Quieres brécol?

brochure NOUN
el **folleto** *masc*

broke VERB ▷*see* **break**

broken
A ADJECTIVE
roto *masc*
rota *fem*
It's broken.
Está roto.
He's got a broken arm.
Tiene un brazo roto.
B VERB ▷*see* **break**

bronze NOUN
el **bronce** masc
the bronze medal
la medalla de bronce

brother NOUN
el **hermano** masc
my big brother
mi hermano mayor
I've got one brother and two sisters.
Tengo un hermano y dos hermanas.
I haven't got any brothers or sisters.
No tengo hermanos.

Have you got any brothers or sisters?
¿Tienes hermanos?

brought VERB ▷see **bring**

brown

brown can be an adjective or a noun.

A ADJECTIVE
1 **marrón** masc & fem
(PL **marrones**)
My shoes are brown.
Mis zapatos son marrones.
I've got brown eyes.
Tengo los ojos marrones.

Language tip
Colour adjectives come after the noun in Spanish.

2 **castaño** masc
castaña fem (hair)
I've got brown hair.
Tengo el pelo castaño.
She's got light brown hair.
Tiene el pelo castaño claro.
3 **moreno** masc
morena fem (tanned)
Liz is very brown.
Liz está muy morena.
B NOUN
el **marrón** masc
Do you have these shoes in brown?

¿Tiene estos zapatos en marrón?

brown bread NOUN
el **pan integral** masc

Brownie NOUN
la **exploradora** fem
I'm a Brownie.
Soy exploradora.

bruise NOUN
el **moretón** masc (PL los **moretones**)
You've got a bruise.
Tienes un moretón.

brush

brush can be a noun or a verb.

A NOUN
el **cepillo** masc
a brush and comb
un cepillo y un peine
B VERB
to brush
cepillar
I brush my pony.
Cepillo a mi pony.
I brush my hair.
Me cepillo el pelo.
I brush my teeth every night.
Me cepillo los dientes todas las noches.

Language tip
In Spanish you usually use an article like **el**, **la** or **los**, **las** with parts of the body.

bubble gum NOUN
el **chicle** masc

bucket NOUN
el **cubo** masc
my bucket and spade
mi cubo y mi pala

bug NOUN
el **virus** masc (PL los **virus**)
Amy's got a bug.
Amy tiene un virus.

buggy NOUN
la **sillita de paseo** *fem*

to **build** VERB
construir
> **My dad is building a garage.**
> Mi padre está construyendo un garaje.

building NOUN
el **edificio** *masc*
> **a tall building**
> un edificio alto

built VERB ▷see **build**

bull NOUN
el **toro** *masc*
> **There's a bull in the field.**
> Hay un toro en el prado.

bully NOUN
el **abusón** *masc* (PL los **abusones**)
la **abusona** *fem*

bum NOUN
el **trasero** *masc*

bun NOUN
el **bollo** *masc*
> **I'd like a bun.**
> Quiero un bollo.

bunch NOUN
el **ramo** *masc*
> **a bunch of flowers**
> un ramo de flores

bunches PL NOUN
las **coletas** *fem pl*
> **She has bunches.**
> Lleva coletas.

bunk beds PL NOUN
las **literas** *fem pl*

burger NOUN
la **hamburguesa** *fem*
> **a burger and chips**
> una hamburguesa y patatas fritas

burglar NOUN
el **ladrón** *masc* (PL los **ladrones**)
la **ladrona** *fem*

bus NOUN
el **autobús** *masc* (PL los **autobuses**)
> **I go to school by bus.**
> Voy al colegio en autobús.
> **the school bus**
> el autobús escolar

> **by bus**
> en autobús

bus driver NOUN
el **conductor de autobús** *masc*
la **conductora de autobús** *fem*
> **My uncle's a bus driver.**
> Mi tío es conductor de autobús.

> **Language tip**
> *When you are talking about people's jobs in Spanish, you do not use an article.*

bus station NOUN
la **estación de autobuses** *fem* (PL las **estaciones de autobuses**)

bus stop NOUN
la **parada de autobús** *fem*

business NOUN
1 los **negocios** *masc pl (activity)*
   He's away on business.
   Está en viaje de negocios.
   a business trip
   un viaje de negocios
2 la **empresa** *fem (company)*
   My mum has her own business.
   Mi madre tiene su propia empresa.

busy ADJECTIVE
ocupado *masc*
ocupada *fem*
   My mother is always busy.
   Mi madre siempre está ocupada.

but CONJUNCTION
pero
   Thanks, but I'm not hungry.
   Gracias, pero no tengo hambre.

butcher's NOUN
la **carnicería** *fem*

butter NOUN
la **mantequilla** *fem*

butterfly NOUN
la **mariposa** *fem*

button NOUN
el **botón** *masc* (PL los **botones**)

to **buy** VERB

comprar
   What are you going to buy?
   ¿Qué vas a comprar?
   I'm going to buy a present for Tim.
   Voy a comprar un regalo para Tim.

by PREPOSITION
1 **por** *(person)*
   a meal prepared by Helen
   una comida preparada por Helen
2 **de** *(artist)*
   a painting by Picasso
   un cuadro de Picasso
   a book by J.K. Rowling
   un libro de J.K. Rowling
3 **al lado de** *(place)*
   Where's the library? — It's by the post office.
   ¿Dónde está la biblioteca? — Está al lado de Correos.
4 **en** *(transport)*
   We're going by car.
   Vamos en coche.

by car
en coche
by train
en tren
by bus
en autobús

bye EXCLAMATION
¡adiós!

English

Spanish

a
b
c
d
e
f
g
h
i
j
k
l
m
n
o
p
q
r
s
t
u
v
w
x
y
z

C c

cab NOUN
el **taxi** *masc*

cabbage NOUN
la **col** *fem*

café NOUN
la **cafetería** *fem*

cafeteria NOUN
el **restaurante autoservicio** *masc* (PL los **restaurantes autoservicio**)

cage NOUN
la **jaula** *fem*

cagoule NOUN
el **chubasquero** *masc*

cake NOUN
1 el **pastel** *masc (individual)*
2 la **tarta** *fem (bigger)*
I'm going to bake a cake.
Voy a hacer una tarta.
a piece of cake
un trozo de tarta

calculator NOUN
la **calculadora** *fem*

calendar NOUN
el **calendario** *masc*

calf NOUN
el **ternero** *masc*

call

call *can be a verb or a noun.*

A VERB
to call
llamar

Everyone calls her Fi.
Todos la llaman Fi.
Call this number.
Llama a este número.
Call the police!
¡Llama a la policía!
My cat is called Fluffy.
Mi gato se llama Fluffy.
What's your cat called?
¿Cómo se llama tu gato?
What are your brothers called?
¿Cómo se llaman tus hermanos?

What are you called?
¿Cómo te llamas?
I'm called Helen.
Me llamo Helen.
I am going to call the register.
Voy a pasar lista.

B NOUN
la **llamada** *fem*
Thanks for your call.
Gracias por tu llamada.
Give me a call.
Llámame.

to **call back** VERB
volver a llamar
I'll call you back later.
Te volveré a llamar más tarde.

call centre NOUN
el **servicio de atención telefónica** *masc*
My sister works in a call centre in London.
Mi hermana trabaja en un servicio de atención telefónica de Londres.

calm ADJECTIVE
tranquilo *masc*
tranquila *fem*

to **calm down** VERB
Calm down, Paul!
¡Tranquilo, Paul!
Calm down, Janet!
¡Tranquila, Janet!
Calm down, children!
¡Tranquilos, niños!

calves PL NOUN
los **terneros** *masc pl (young cattle)*

camcorder NOUN
la **videocámara** *fem*

came VERB ▷ *see* **come**

camera NOUN
la **cámara** *fem*
**I've got a
new camera.**
Tengo una
cámara
nueva.

camera phone NOUN
el **móvil con cámara** *masc*

camp NOUN
el **campamento** *masc*

camping NOUN
to go camping
ir de camping
We're going camping.
Vamos a ir de camping.

Language tip
In Spanish, the word **camping** on
its own means **campsite**. To talk
about the activity, you need to say
ir de camping.

campsite NOUN
el **camping** *masc* (PL los
campings)
**The campsite is next to the
river.**
El camping está al lado del río.

can

can *can be a noun or a verb.*

A NOUN
la **lata** *fem*
a can of Coke
una lata de Coca-Cola
B VERB
1 **poder** *(be able to)*
I can't go.
No puedo ir.
Can I come in?
¿Puedo entrar?
Can you open the door?
¿Puedes abrir la puerta?

Language tip
You don't always translate **can**.

I can't see it.
No lo veo.
**Can you speak English? —
No, I can't.**
¿Hablas inglés? — No.

I can.
Puedo.
I can't.
No puedo.
Can you?
¿Puedes?

2 **saber** *(know how to)*
I can swim.
Sé nadar.
I can't ride a bike.
No sé montar en bicicleta.

Canada NOUN
Canadá *masc*

Canadian

Canadian *can be an adjective or
a noun.*

A ADJECTIVE
canadiense *masc & fem*

She's Canadian
Es canadiense.

B NOUN
el/la **canadiense** *masc/fem*

> **Language tip**
> **canadiense** *is not spelled with a capital letter in Spanish.*

canal NOUN
el **canal** *masc*

to **cancel** VERB
cancelar
> **We've got to cancel our trip to London.**
> Tenemos que cancelar nuestro viaje a Londres.

cancer NOUN
el **cáncer** *masc*
> **He's got cancer.**
> Tiene cáncer.

candle NOUN
la **vela** *fem*

canoe NOUN
la **canoa** *fem*

canoeing NOUN
> **to go canoeing**
> **hacer piragüismo**
> **We're going canoeing.**
> Vamos a hacer piragüismo.

can-opener NOUN
el **abrelatas** *masc* (PL los **abrelatas**)

can't VERB ▷*see* **can**

canteen NOUN
la **cafetería** *fem*
> **I eat in the canteen.**
> Yo como en la cafetería.

cap NOUN
la **gorra** *fem*

capital
NOUN
1 la **capital**
fem (city)
> **Madrid is the capital of Spain.**
> Madrid es la capital de España.

2 la **mayúscula** *fem (letter)*
> **Write your address in capitals.**
> Escribe tu dirección en mayúsculas.

capital letter NOUN
la **mayúscula** *fem*

captain NOUN
el **capitán** *masc* (PL los **capitanes**)
la **capitana** *fem*
> **She's captain of the hockey team.**
> Es capitana del equipo de hockey.

caption NOUN
la **leyenda** *fem*

car NOUN
el **coche** *masc*
> **We've got a new car.**
> Tenemos un coche nuevo.
> **by car**
> en coche
> **We're going there by car.**
> Vamos allí en coche.

caravan NOUN
la **caravana** *fem*

caravan site NOUN
el **camping de caravanas** *masc*

card NOUN
1 la **carta** *fem (playing card)*
> **They are playing cards.**
> Están jugando a las cartas.

> **Language tip**
> *In Spanish, you need to give* **a las** *before* **cartas**.

2 la **tarjeta** *fem (for birthday, Christmas)*
> **I got lots of cards.**
> He recibido muchas tarjetas.

> **Did you know...?**
> *In Spain, people don't generally send as many cards as we do in Britain.*

cardboard NOUN
el **cartón** *masc*

card game NOUN
el **juego de cartas** *masc*

cardigan NOUN
la **rebeca** *fem*
a green cardigan
una rebeca verde

care

> **care** *can be a noun or a verb.*

A NOUN
el **cuidado** *masc*
with care
con cuidado
B VERB
to care: **I don't care!**
¡No me importa!

careful ADJECTIVE
to be careful
tener cuidado
Be careful, Gordon!
¡Ten cuidado, Gordon!

carefully ADVERB
con cuidado
Fold the paper carefully.
Dobla el papel con cuidado.
Think carefully, Hazel!
¡Piénsatelo bien, Hazel!
Listen carefully, children!
¡Escuchad con atención, niños!

careless ADJECTIVE
a careless mistake
un error por descuido

caretaker NOUN
el **bedel** *masc*

> ### Language tip
> *When talking about people's jobs in Spanish, you do not use an article.*

carol NOUN

a Christmas carol
un villancico

car park NOUN
el **parking** *masc* (PL los **parkings**)

carpet NOUN
la **moqueta** *fem (fitted)*
My bedroom carpet is blue.
La moqueta de mi habitación es azul.

carriage NOUN
el **vagón** *masc* (PL los **vagones**)

carrier bag NOUN
la **bolsa de asas** *fem*

carrot NOUN
la **zanahoria** *fem*

to **carry** VERB
llevar
I'll carry your bag.
Yo te llevo la bolsa.

to **carry on** VERB
seguir
Carry on, Diane!
¡Sigue, Diane!

carton NOUN
el **cartón** *masc* (PL los **cartones**)
a carton of milk
un cartón de leche

cartoon NOUN
1 los **dibujos animados** *masc pl (on television)*
I watch cartoons on Saturdays.
Veo los dibujos animados los sábados.
2 la **viñeta** *fem (strip cartoon)*

case NOUN
la **maleta** *fem (suitcase)*
That's my case!
¡Ésa es mi maleta!

English Spanish

a b **c** d e f g h i j k l m n o p q r s t u v w x y z

casserole NOUN
el **guiso** *masc*

cassette NOUN
la **cinta** *fem*

castle NOUN
el **castillo** *masc*
Dover Castle
el castillo de Dover

casual ADJECTIVE
informal *masc & fem*
I prefer casual clothes.
Prefiero la ropa informal.

cat NOUN
el **gato** *masc*
la **gata** *fem*
Have you got a cat?
¿Tienes gato?

to **catch** VERB
coger
Catch!
¡Cógelo!
Which bus do you catch?
¿Qué autobús coges tú?
My cat catches birds.
Mi gato atrapa pájaros.

cathedral NOUN
la **catedral** *fem*

Catholic

> **Catholic** can be an adjective or a noun.

A ADJECTIVE
católico *masc*
católica *fem*
B NOUN
el **católico** *masc*
la **católica** *fem*
I'm a Catholic.
Soy católico.

> **Language tip**
> **católico** is not spelled with a capital letter in Spanish.

cauliflower NOUN
la **coliflor** *fem*

cave NOUN
la **cueva** *fem*

CD NOUN
el **CD** *masc* (PL los **CDs**)

CD player NOUN
el **reproductor de CDs** *masc*

CD-Rom NOUN
el **CD-Rom** *masc*

ceiling NOUN
el **techo** *masc*

> **Did you know...?**
> Did you know that **el techo** can also be the word for **roof**?

to **celebrate** VERB
celebrar
Let's celebrate!
¡Vamos a celebrarlo!

celery NOUN
el **apio** *masc*

cellar NOUN
el **sótano** *masc*
The cellar is damp.
El sótano está húmedo.
a wine cellar
una bodega

cello NOUN
el **violonchelo** *masc*
I play the cello.
Toco el violonchelo.

cemetery NOUN
el **cementerio** *masc*

cent NOUN
el **céntimo** *masc* (division of euro)
two euros and twenty cents
dos euros y veinte céntimos

centigrade ADJECTIVE
centígrado *masc*
centígrada *fem*
twenty degrees centigrade
veinte grados centígrados

centimetre NOUN
el **centímetro** *masc*

central heating NOUN
la **calefacción central** *fem*

centre NOUN
el **centro** *masc*
in the centre
en el centro
The office is in the centre of town.
La oficina está en el centro de la ciudad.
a sports centre
un polideportivo

century NOUN
el **siglo** *masc*
the twenty-first century
el siglo veintiuno

cereal NOUN
los **cereales** *masc pl*
I have cereal for breakfast.
Desayuno cereales.

certain ADJECTIVE
1 **cierto** *masc*
cierta *fem*
a certain person
una cierta persona
2 **seguro** *masc*
segura *fem* (sure)
I'm not certain.
No estoy seguro.

certainly ADVERB
Certainly!
¡Por supuesto!
Certainly not!
¡Por supuesto que no!

certificate NOUN
el **certificado** *masc*

chain NOUN
la **cadena** *fem*

a silver chain
una cadena de plata

chair NOUN
1 la **silla** *fem*
There's a table and four chairs in the kitchen.
Hay una mesa y cuatro sillas en la cocina.
2 el **sillón** *masc* (PL los **sillones**)
(*armchair*)
There are two chairs and a sofa in the lounge.
Hay dos sillones y un sofá en el salón.

chalk NOUN
la **tiza** *fem*
a piece of chalk
una tiza

champagne NOUN
el **champán** *masc*
a glass of champagne
una copa de champán

champion NOUN
el **campeón** *masc* (PL los **campeones**)
la **campeona** *fem*
Mike is the champion!

¡Mike es el campeón!

championship NOUN
el **campeonato** *masc*

chance NOUN
la **oportunidad** *fem*
I'll give you another chance.
Te daré otra oportunidad.
No chance!
¡Ni en broma!

You're taking a chance!
¡Te estás arriesgando!

change

> **change** *can be a verb or a noun.*

A VERB
to change
1 **cambiar**
I'd like to change fifty pounds.
Quiero cambiar cincuenta libras.
How you've changed!
¡Cuánto has cambiado!
2 **cambiar de** *(swap)*
Change places!
¡Cambiad de sitio!
I want to change my cards.
Quiero cambiar de cartas.
I've changed my mind.
He cambiado de idea.
3 **cambiarse** *(get changed)*
I must go and change.
Tengo que ir a cambiarme.
B NOUN
el **cambio** *masc*
I haven't got any change.
No tengo cambio.

changeable ADJECTIVE
variable *masc & fem*
The weather is changeable.
El tiempo está variable.

changing room NOUN
1 el **vestuario** *masc (in school)*
2 el **probador** *masc (in shop)*

Channel NOUN
the English Channel
el Canal de la Mancha

channel NOUN
la **cadena** *fem (on TV)*
There's football on the other channel.
Hay fútbol en la otra cadena.

Channel Islands PL NOUN
the Channel Islands
las Islas del Canal de la Mancha

Channel Tunnel NOUN
the Channel Tunnel
el túnel del Canal de la Mancha *masc*

chapter NOUN
el **capítulo** *masc*

character NOUN
el **personaje** *masc*
Harriet is the main character.
Harriet es el personaje principal.

> ### Language tip
> Even though **el personaje** *is a masculine noun, you can use it to refer to a woman or girl.*

charge NOUN
an extra charge
un suplemento
There's no charge.
No hay que pagar nada.
to be in charge
ser el responsable
Who is in charge?
¿Quién es el responsable?

charity NOUN
la **organización benéfica** *fem*
We give the money to charity.
Donamos el dinero a una organización benéfica.

chart NOUN
el **gráfico** *masc*
We're making a chart.
Estamos haciendo un gráfico.

charter flight NOUN
el **vuelo chárter** *masc*

to chase VERB
perseguir
My dog chases cats.
Mi perro persigue a los gatos.

to chat VERB
charlar
Paul chats a lot.
Paul charla mucho.
Stop chatting.
Dejad de charlar.

cheap ADJECTIVE
barato *masc*
barata *fem*
> **It's cheaper by bus.**
> Es más barato en autobús.

cheat

> *cheat can be a verb or a noun.*

A VERB
to cheat
hacer trampa
> **You're cheating!**
> ¡Estás haciendo trampa!

B NOUN
el **tramposo** *masc*
la **tramposa** *fem*
> **Patrick, you're a cheat!**
> ¡Patrick, eres un tramposo!

to **check** VERB
comprobar
> **Check your spelling.**
> Comprobad la ortografía.

to **check in** VERB
facturar *(at airport)*
> **What time do I have to check in?**
> ¿A qué hora tengo que facturar?

checked ADJECTIVE
de cuadros
> **a checked shirt**
> una camisa de cuadros

checkout NOUN
la **caja** *fem*
> **at the checkout**
> en la caja

cheek NOUN
la **mejilla** *fem*
> **He kissed her on the cheek.**
> Le dio un beso en la mejilla.

cheeky ADJECTIVE
descarado *masc*
descarada *fem*
> **Don't be cheeky, Nigel!**
> ¡No seas descarado, Nigel!

cheer

> *cheer can be a noun or a verb.*

A NOUN
> **There was a loud cheer.**
> Hubo una fuerte ovación.
> **Three cheers for the captain!**
> ¡Viva el capitán!
> **Cheers!**
> ¡Salud!/¡Gracias!

Language tip
Translate **cheers!** *as* **¡salud!** *when making a toast. Use* **¡gracias!** *instead when thanking someone.*

> **Cheers, everyone!**
> ¡Salud, por todos!
> **Cheers, Tony! That's very kind of you.**
> ¡Gracias, Tony! Eres muy amable.

B VERB
to cheer
gritar entusiasmado
> **The crowd was cheering.**
> La multitud estaba gritando entusiasmada.

Cheer up!
¡Anímate!

cheerful ADJECTIVE
alegre *masc & fem*

cheerio EXCLAMATION
¡hasta luego!

cheese NOUN
el **queso** *masc*
> **a cheese sandwich**
> un sándwich de queso

chef NOUN
el **chef** *masc*

chemist NOUN
1 la **farmacia** *fem (shop)*

English

Spanish

a b **c** d e f g h i j k l m n o p q r s t u v w x y z

You get it from the chemist.
Lo compras en la farmacia.
the chemist's
la farmacia

Did you know…?

Spanish chemists are identifiable by a red or green cross outside the shop. If you want to buy cosmetics or toiletries, go to a **perfumería** *instead.*

2 el **farmacéutico** *masc*
la **farmacéutica** *fem*
(pharmacist)

chemistry NOUN
la **química** *fem*
the chemistry teacher
el profesor de química

cherry NOUN
la **cereza** *fem*
I love cherries.
Me encantan
las cerezas.

chess NOUN
el **ajedrez**
masc
I can play chess.
Sé jugar al ajedrez.

Language tip

In Spanish, you need to add **al** *or* **a la** *before the name of the game.*

chest NOUN
el **pecho** *masc*

chest of drawers NOUN
la **cómoda** *fem*

chewing gum NOUN
el **chicle** *masc*
Put your chewing gum in the bin!
¡Tira el chicle a la papelera!

chick NOUN
el **pollito** *masc*

chicken NOUN
el **pollo** *masc*

Chicken and chips, please.
Pollo con patatas fritas, por favor.

chickenpox NOUN
la **varicela** *fem*
Paul has got chickenpox.
Paul tiene varicela.

child NOUN
1 el **niño** *masc (boy)*
la **niña** *fem (girl)*
Goodbye children!
¡Adiós, niños!
2 el **hijo** *masc (son)*
la **hija** *fem (daughter)*
They've got three children.
Tienen tres hijos.

child minder NOUN
el **cuidador de niños** *masc*
la **cuidadora de niños** *fem*

children PL NOUN
1 los **niños** *masc pl (boys and girls)*
Where are the children?
¿Dónde están los niños?
2 los **hijos** *masc pl (sons and daughters)*
They've got three children.
Tienen tres hijos.

chilly ADJECTIVE
It's chilly today.
Hace frío hoy.

chip NOUN
la **patata frita** *fem*
I'd like some chips.
Quiero patatas fritas.

chocolate NOUN
1 el **chocolate** *masc*
I love chocolate.
Me encanta el
chocolate.
**a chocolate
cake**
una tarta de chocolate
a chocolate ice cream
un helado de chocolate

2 el **bombón** *masc* (PL los **bombones**) *(sweet)*
a box of chocolates
una caja de bombones

choice NOUN
la **elección** *fem*
I had no choice.
No tenía elección.
You have to make a choice.
Tienes que elegir.

choir NOUN
el **coro** *masc*
I sing in the school choir.
Canto en el coro de la escuela.

to **choose** VERB
elegir
It's difficult to choose.
Es difícil elegir.

chop NOUN
la **chuleta** *fem*
a pork chop
una chuleta de cerdo

chose VERB ▷ *see* **choose**

chosen VERB ▷ *see* **choose**

christening NOUN
el **bautizo** *masc*

Christian name NOUN
el **nombre de pila** *masc*

Christmas NOUN
la **Navidad** *fem*
at Christmas
en Navidad

> **Happy Christmas!**
> ¡Feliz Navidad!

> *Language tip*
> Have you noticed the upside-down

exclamation mark at the start of Spanish exclamations?

Christmas cake NOUN
el **pastel de Navidad** *masc*

> *Did you know…?*
> In Spain it's traditional to eat **el roscón de Reyes** on 6th January. Hidden in this fruit-studded ring-shaped cake is a little figure or other surprise that is meant to bring good luck to the person that finds it.

Christmas card NOUN
la **tarjeta de Navidad** *fem*

Christmas Day NOUN
el **día de Navidad** *masc*

Christmas dinner NOUN
la **comida de Navidad** *fem*

> *Did you know…?*
> In Spain, people usually have their special Christmas meal on Christmas Eve.

Christmas Eve NOUN
la **Nochebuena** *fem*

> *Did you know…?*
> In Spain, it's often **los Reyes Magos** (the Three Kings) rather than **Papá Noel** (Father Christmas) who bring children their presents. They come on 5th January rather than on 24th December.

Christmas present NOUN
el **regalo de Navidad** *masc*

Christmas tree NOUN
el **árbol de Navidad** *masc*

church NOUN
la **iglesia** *fem*

cider NOUN
la **sidra** *fem*

cigarette NOUN
el **cigarrillo** *masc*

cinema NOUN
el **cine** *masc*

English Spanish

a b c d e f g h i j k l m n o p q r s t u v w x y z

I'm going to the cinema this evening.
Voy a ir al cine esta noche.

circle NOUN
el **círculo** *masc*
Stand in a cicle.
Poneos de pie formando un círculo.

circus NOUN
el **circo** *masc*

citizenship NOUN
la **ciudadanía** *fem*

city NOUN
la **ciudad** *fem*
I live in a city.
Vivo en una ciudad.
the city centre
el centro de la ciudad
It's in the city centre.
Está en el centro de la ciudad.

clap

clap can be a verb or a noun.

A VERB
to clap
aplaudir
The audience was clapping.
El público estaba aplaudiendo.
Clap your hands!
¡Haced palmas!
B NOUN
Give Cordy a clap.
Dadle un aplauso a Cordy.

clarinet NOUN
el **clarinete** *masc*
I play the clarinet.
Toco el clarinete.

class NOUN
la **clase** *fem*
Martin is in my class.
Martin está en mi clase.
I go to dancing classes.
Voy a clases de baile.

classroom NOUN
el **aula** *fem*

Language tip
Even though it's a feminine noun, remember that you use **el** *and* **un** *with* **aula**.

classroom assistant NOUN
el **profesor de apoyo** *masc*
la **profesora de apoyo** *fem*

clean

clean can be an adjective or a verb.

A ADJECTIVE
limpio *masc*
limpia *fem*
a clean shirt
una camisa limpia
The bath isn't very clean.
La bañera no está muy limpia.
B VERB
to clean
limpiar
I'm cleaning the cooker.
Estoy limpiando la cocina.
Clean the board please!
¡Borrad la pizarra, por favor!
I clean my teeth twice a day.
Me lavo los dientes dos veces al día.

Language tip
In Spanish you usually use an article like **el**, **la** *or* **los**, **las** *with parts of the body.*

cleaner NOUN
el **señor de la limpieza** *masc*
la **señora de la limpieza** *fem*

clear ADJECTIVE
claro *masc*
clara *fem*
a clear explanation
una explicación clara

clementine NOUN
la **mandarina** *fem*

clever ADJECTIVE
listo *masc*
lista *fem*

Diane is very clever.
Diane es muy lista.

to **click** VERB
  clicar
    Click on the icon.
    Clica en el icono.

climate NOUN
  el **clima** *masc*

> **Language tip**
> *Even though it ends in* **-a**, **el clima** *is a masculine noun.*

  We have a terrible climate.
  Tenemos un clima espantoso.

to **climb** VERB
  1 **escalar** *(mountain)*
    I want to climb that mountain.
    Quiero escalar esa montaña.
  2 **subirse a** *(tree, wall)*
    Can you climb that tree?
    ¿Puedes subirte a ese árbol?

cloakroom NOUN
  1 el **guardarropa** *masc (for coats)*

> **Language tip**
> *Even though it ends in* **-a**, **el guardarropa** *is a masculine noun.*

  2 el **servicio** *masc (toilet)*

clock NOUN
  el **reloj** *masc*
    Look at the clock.
    Mira al reloj.

> **Language tip**
> *Did you know that* **reloj** *is also the word for a* **watch**?

close

> **close** *can be a verb or an adverb.*

  A VERB
    to close
    cerrar

  Please close the door.
  Por favor, cierra la puerta.
  Close your books, children.
  Cerrad los libros, niños.
  What time does the pool close?
  ¿A qué hora cierra la piscina?
  B ADVERB
    cerca
    The shops are very close.
    Las tiendas están muy cerca.
    My house is close to the school.
    Mi casa está cerca del colegio.
    Come closer, Daniel.
    Acércate más, Daniel.

closed ADJECTIVE
  cerrado *masc*
  cerrada *fem*
    The door's closed.
    La puerta está cerrada.

clothes PL NOUN
  la **ropa** *fem*
    I'd like to buy some new clothes.
    Quiero comprarme ropa nueva.

> **Language tip**
> *Even though* **clothes** *is a plural word in English, you use* **ropa** *in the singular in Spanish.*

cloud NOUN
  la **nube** *fem*
    There are some black clouds.
    Hay nubes negras.

cloudy ADJECTIVE
  nublado *masc*
  nublada *fem*
    It's cloudy today.
    Está nublado hoy.

clown NOUN
  el **payaso** *masc*
  la **payasa** *fem*

club NOUN
1 el **club** *masc (organization)*
a football club
un club de fútbol
2 *(in cards)*
clubs
los tréboles *masc pl*
the ace of clubs
el as de tréboles

coach NOUN
1 el **autocar** *masc (vehicle)*
by coach
en autocar
We're going by coach.
Vamos en autocar.
2 el **entrenador** *masc*
la **entrenadora** *fem (person)*

coach station NOUN
la **estación de autobuses** *fem*

coal NOUN
el **carbón** *masc*

coast NOUN
la **costa** *fem*
It's on the west coast of Scotland.
Está en la costa oeste de Escocia.

coat NOUN
el **abrigo** *masc*
I'm wearing a blue coat.
Llevo un abrigo azul.

cocoa NOUN
el **cacao** *masc*

coconut NOUN
el **coco** *masc*

coffee NOUN
el **café** *masc*
I like coffee.
Me gusta el café.
I'd like a white coffee.
Quiero un café con leche.

coin NOUN
la **moneda** *fem*
a two-euro coin
una moneda de dos euros

Coke® NOUN
la **Coca-Cola**® *fem*
a can of Coke
una lata de Coca-Cola

cold

> **cold** *can be an adjective or a noun.*

A ADJECTIVE
frío *masc*
fría *fem*
The water's cold.
El agua está fría.

> **It's cold today.**
> Hace frío hoy.
> **I'm cold.**
> Tengo frío.
> **I'm not cold.**
> No tengo frío.
> **Are you cold?**
> ¿Tienes frío?

B NOUN *(illness)*
I've got a cold.
Estoy resfriado.
Julie's got a cold.
Julie está resfriada.

coleslaw NOUN
la **ensalada de col, zanahoria, cebolla y mayonesa**

collar NOUN
1 el **cuello**
masc (on clothing)
2 el **collar**
masc
(for dog, cat)

to **collect**
VERB
1 **recoger** *(pick up)*
Collect the books please, Ryan.

Recoge los libros, por favor, Ryan.

2 coleccionar *(as hobby)*
I collect stamps.
Colecciono sellos.

collection NOUN
la **colección** *fem* (PL las **colecciones**)

college NOUN
la **universidad** *fem (university)*
Do you want to go to college?
¿Quieres ir a la universidad?
a technical college
una escuela técnica

colour

| colour *can be a noun or a verb.* |

A NOUN
el **color** *masc*
What colour are the curtains?
¿De qué color son las cortinas?
What colour eyes has he got?
¿De qué color tiene los ojos?

What colour is it?
¿De qué color es?

B VERB
to colour
pintar
I'm going to colour the house yellow.
Voy a pintar la casa de amarillo.

comb

| comb *can be a noun or a verb.* |

A NOUN
el **peine** *masc*
B VERB
to comb
peinar
to comb one's hair
peinarse
I comb my hair every day.
Me peino todos los días.
I'm combing my hair.
Me estoy peinando.

to **come** VERB
1 venir
Come with me, June.
Ven conmigo, June.

Language tip
Use **ir** (go) *rather than* **venir** *when you tell someone you're coming to join them.*

Can I come too?
¿Puedo ir yo también?
I'll come with you.
Iré contigo.
2 llegar *(arrive)*
The bus is coming.
Ya llega el autobús.
The letter came this morning.
La carta llegó esta mañana.

I'm coming!
¡Ya voy!
Come on!
¡Vamos!

to **come back** VERB
volver
Come back, Basil!
¡Vuelve, Basil!

to **come from** VERB
ser de
Where do you come from?
¿De dónde eres?

to **come in** VERB
entrar
Can I come in?
¿Puedo entrar?

Come in!
¡Pasa!

comfortable ADJECTIVE
cómodo *masc*
cómoda *fem (person, shoes, chair)*
Make yourself comfortable.
Ponte cómodo.

comic NOUN
el **cómic** *masc* (PL los **cómics**)
(magazine)

comma NOUN
la **coma** *fem*

common ADJECTIVE
común *masc & fem* (PL
comunes)
**'Davies' is a very common
surname.**
'Davies' es un apellido muy
común.

compared ADJECTIVE
compared with
en comparación con
**Oxford is small compared
with London.**
Oxford es pequeño en
comparación con Londres.

competition NOUN
el **concurso** *masc*

competitor NOUN
el/la **concursante** *masc/fem*

complete

> **complete** *can be an adjective or
> a verb.*

A ADJECTIVE
completo *masc*
completa *fem*
B VERB
to complete
completar
**Complete the following
phrases.**
Completa las frases siguientes.

completely ADVERB
completamente

complicated ADJECTIVE
complicado *masc*
complicada *fem*

comprehension NOUN
el **ejercicio de comprensión**
masc

comprehensive school
NOUN
el **instituto de secundaria**
masc

computer NOUN
el **ordenador**
masc

computer game NOUN
el **juego de ordenador** *masc*
I like computer games.
Me gustan los juegos de
ordenador.

computer room NOUN
la **sala de informática** *fem*

concert NOUN
el **concierto** *masc*

cone NOUN
el **cucurucho** *masc*
an ice-cream cone
un cucurucho de helado

congratulations
PL NOUN
la **enhorabuena** *fem*
Congratulations!
¡Enhorabuena!

conservatory NOUN
el **patio cubierto** *masc*

constant ADJECTIVE
constante *masc & fem*

contact lens NOUN
la **lentilla** *fem*
I wear contact lenses.
Llevo lentillas.

container NOUN
el **recipiente** *masc*
a plastic container
un recipiente de plástico

contest NOUN
el **concurso** *masc*

contestant NOUN
el/la **concursante** *masc/fem*

continent NOUN
el **continente** *masc*
How many continents are there?
¿Cuántos continentes hay?
the Continent
Europa
on the Continent
en Europa

continental breakfast NOUN
el **desayuno europeo** *masc*

to **continue** VERB
seguir
Continue with your work, children!
¡Seguid con vuestro trabajo, niños!

conversation NOUN
la **conversación** *fem* (PL las **conversaciones**)

cook

cook *can be a verb or a noun.*

A VERB
to cook
1 cocinar
I can cook.
Sé cocinar.
I can't cook.
No sé cocinar.
2 cocer (*potatoes, rice etc*)
Cook the pasta for ten minutes.
Cocer la pasta durante diez minutos.

B NOUN
el **cocinero** *masc*
la **cocinera** *fem*
Matthew's an excellent cook.
Matthew es un excelente cocinero.

cookbook NOUN
el **libro de cocina** *masc*

cooked ADJECTIVE
cocido *masc*
cocida *fem*

cooker NOUN
la **cocina** *fem*
a gas cooker
una cocina de gas

cooking NOUN
la **cocina** *fem*
I like cooking.
Me gusta la cocina.

cool ADJECTIVE
1 fresquito *masc*
fresquita *fem* (*quite cold*)
It's cooler in the shade.
Hace más fresquito en la sombra.
2 guay (*super*)
Cool!
¡Guay!
What a cool T-shirt!
¡Qué camiseta más guay!

copy

copy *can be a noun or a verb.*

A NOUN
la **copia** *fem*
I'll make a copy.
Haré una copia.
B VERB
to copy
copiar
Copy the words off the board.
Copiad las palabras de la pizarra.

cork NOUN
el **corcho** *masc*

corkscrew NOUN
el **sacacorchos** *masc* (PL los **sacacorchos**)

English Spanish

a
b
c
d
e
f
g
h
i
j
k
l
m
n
o
p
q
r
s
t
u
v
w
x
y
z

corner NOUN
1 el **rincón** *masc* (PL los
rincones) *(in room)*
in a corner of the room
en un rincón de la habitación
2 la **esquina**
fem (of street)
on a street corner
en una esquina de la calle

cornflakes PL NOUN
los **copos de maíz** *masc pl*

correct

> **correct** *can be an adjective or a*
> *verb.*

A ADJECTIVE
correcto *masc*
correcta *fem*
That's correct.
Eso es correcto.
the correct answer
la respuesta correcta
B VERB
to correct
corregir
I have to correct the spelling.
Tengo que corregir la ortografía.

correction NOUN
la **corrección** *fem* (PL las
correcciones)

correctly ADVERB
correctamente

corridor NOUN
el **pasillo** *masc*
in the corridor
en el pasillo

to **cost** VERB
costar
It costs two euros.
Cuesta dos euros.

> **How much does it cost?**
> ¿Cuánto cuesta?

costume NOUN
el **disfraz** *masc* (PL los **disfraces**)
(fancy-dress)

Mum's making me a clown costume.
Mi madre me está haciendo un disfraz de payaso.

cottage NOUN
la **casa de campo** *fem*

cotton NOUN
el **algodón** *masc*
a cotton shirt
una camisa de algodón

couch NOUN
el **sofá** *masc*

cough

> **cough** *can be a noun or a verb.*

A NOUN
la **tos** *fem*
I've got a cough.
Tengo tos.
B VERB
to cough
toser
I can't stop coughing.
No dejo de toser.

could VERB
Could I make a phone call?
¿Puedo hacer una llamada?
Could you open the door?
¿Puedes abrir la puerta?
Could I have a kilo of potatoes?
¿Me da un kilo de patatas?
Could I have an orange juice?
¿Me pone un zumo de naranja?

Could I...?
¿Puedo...?
Could you...?
¿Puedes...?

to **count** VERB
contar
    Count from one to twenty.
    Cuenta del uno al veinte.

counter NOUN
1 el **mostrador** *masc (in shop)*
2 la **ficha** *fem (in game)*
    Take ten yellow counters.
    Coge diez fichas amarillas.

country NOUN
1 el **país** *masc (Spain, Britain etc)*
    Spain is a big country.
    España es un país grande.
    the border between the two countries
    la frontera entre los dos países
2 el **campo** *masc (countryside)*
    I live in the country.
    Vivo en el campo.

countryside NOUN
el **campo** *masc*

in the countryside
en el campo

couple NOUN
    a couple of
    un par de
    a couple of days
    un par de días
    a young couple
    una pareja joven

courgette NOUN
el **calabacín** *masc* (PL los **calabacines**)

course NOUN
1 el **plato** *masc (of meal)*
    the main course
    el plato principal
    the first course
    el primer plato
2 el **curso** *masc (lessons)*
    an English course
    un curso de inglés
    Do you love me? —
    Of course I do!
    ¿Me quieres? — ¡Claro que sí!
    Of course not!
    ¡Claro que no!

of course
claro

court NOUN
la **pista** *fem*
    There are two tennis courts.
    Hay dos pistas de tenis.

cousin NOUN
el **primo** *masc*
la **prima** *fem*

cover

cover *can be a noun or a verb.*

A NOUN
1 la **funda** *fem (of duvet)*
2 la **tapa** *fem (of book)*
B VERB
    to cover
    cubrir
    The roof is covered with snow.
    El techo está cubierto de nieve.

cow NOUN
la **vaca** *fem*

crab NOUN
el **cangrejo** *masc*

cracker NOUN
la **galleta salada** *fem (biscuit)*

Did you know...?
In Spain, people don't pull crackers at Christmas.

crash NOUN
el **accidente** *masc*
a car crash
un accidente de coche

crawl NOUN
el **crol** *masc*
I can do the crawl.
Sé nadar a crol.

crazy ADJECTIVE
loco *masc*
loca *fem*
Are you crazy?
¿Estás loco?

cream

> **cream** *can be a noun or an adjective.*

A NOUN
la **nata** *fem*
strawberries and cream
fresas con nata
B ADJECTIVE
de color crema (*cream-coloured*)
a cream shirt
una camisa de color crema

cream cake NOUN
el **pastel de nata** *masc*
two cream cakes
dos pasteles de nata

credit card NOUN
la **tarjeta de crédito** *fem*

cress NOUN
los **berros** *masc pl*
I'm growing cress.
Estoy cultivando berros.

crew cut NOUN
el **pelo rapado** *masc*
He's got a crew cut.
Lleva el pelo rapado.

cricket NOUN
el **críquet** *masc*
I play cricket.
Juego al críquet.

> *Language tip*
> In Spanish, you need to add **al** or **a la** *before the name of the game or sport.*

cricket bat NOUN
el **bate de críquet** *masc*

crisps PL NOUN
las **patatas fritas** *fem pl*
a bag of crisps
una bolsa de patatas fritas

cross

> **cross** *can be a verb, noun or adjective.*

A VERB
to cross
cruzar
Cross the road at the lights.
Cruza la calle por el semáforo.
B NOUN
la **cruz** *fem* (PL las **cruces**)
Put a tick or a cross.
Poned una señal o una cruz.
C ADJECTIVE
enfadado *masc*
enfadada *fem*
She is cross.
Está enfadada.

crossing NOUN
la **travesía** *fem*
the crossing from Plymouth to Santander
la travesía de Plymouth a Santander

crossroads NOUN
el **cruce** *masc*
at the crossroads
en el cruce

crossword NOUN
el **crucigrama** *masc*
I like doing crosswords.
Me gusta hacer crucigramas.

Language tip
Even though it ends in **-a,** **el crucigrama** *is a masculine noun.*

crowd NOUN
la **multitud** *fem*

crowded ADJECTIVE
lleno de gente *masc*
llena de gente *fem*
The pool is crowded on Saturdays.
La piscina está llena de gente los sábados.

crown NOUN
la **corona** *fem*

crutch NOUN
la **muleta** *fem*

to **cry** VERB
llorar *(weep)*

Why are you crying?
¿Por qué lloras?

cub NOUN
1 el **cachorro** *masc (young animal)*
a lion cub
un cachorro de león
2 el **lobato** *masc (scout)*

cube NOUN
el **cubo** *masc*

cucumber NOUN
el **pepino** *masc*

cup NOUN
la **taza** *fem*
a cup of tea
una taza de té
a paper cup
un vaso de papel

cupboard NOUN
el **armario** *masc*
What's in the cupboard?
¿Qué hay en el armario?

curious ADJECTIVE
curioso *masc*
curiosa *fem*

curly ADJECTIVE
rizado *masc*
rizada *fem*
She's got curly hair.
Tiene el pelo rizado.

currant NOUN
la **pasa** *fem*
I don't like currants.
No me gustan las pasas.

curriculum NOUN
el **plan de estudios** *masc*

curry NOUN
el **curry** *masc*
chicken curry
el pollo al curry

curtain NOUN
la **cortina** *fem*
Draw the curtains, please.
Corre las cortinas, por favor.

cushion NOUN
el **cojín** *masc* (PL los **cojines**)

custard NOUN
las **natillas** *fem pl*

custom NOUN
la **costumbre** *fem*
It's an old custom.
Es una vieja costumbre.

customer NOUN
el **cliente** *masc*
la **clienta** *fem*

to **cut** VERB
  cortar
    I'll cut the cake.
    Yo cortaré la tarta.
    Mind you don't cut yourself!
    ¡Ten cuidado de no cortarte!

cutlery NOUN
  los **cubiertos** *masc pl*

to **cycle** VERB
  montar en bici
    I like cycling.
    Me gusta montar en bici.

I cycle to school.
Voy en bici al colegio.

cycle lane NOUN
  el **carril-bici** *masc* (PL los carriles-bici)

cycling NOUN
  el **ciclismo** *masc*

cyclist NOUN
  el/la **ciclista** *masc/fem*

D d

dad NOUN
1 el **padre** *masc*
   my dad
   mi padre
   **my mum
   and dad**
   mis padres

2 el **papá**
   masc (used as a name)
   Let's ask Dad.
   ¡Vamos a preguntarle a papá!

daddy NOUN
   el **papá** *masc*
   Hello Daddy!
   ¡Hola, papá!

daffodil NOUN
   el **narciso** *masc*

daily ADVERB
   diariamente
   **The pool is open daily from
   nine a.m. to six p.m.**
   La piscina está abierta
   diariamente de nueve de la
   mañana a seis de la tarde.

damn EXCLAMATION
   ¡maldita sea!

damp ADJECTIVE
   húmedo *masc*
   húmeda *fem*

dance

dance *can be a noun or a verb.*

A NOUN
   el **baile** *masc*

It's a new dance.
Es un nuevo baile.
**Are you going to the dance
tonight, Tony?**
¿Vas a ir al baile esta noche,
Tony?
B VERB
   to dance
   bailar
   Can you dance?
   ¿Sabes bailar?
   I like dancing.
   Me gusta bailar.

dancer NOUN
   el **bailarín** *masc* (PL los
   bailarines)
   la **bailarina** *fem*

danger NOUN
   el **peligro** *masc*
   in danger
   en peligro
   His life is in danger.
   Su vida está en peligro.

dangerous ADJECTIVE
   peligroso *masc*
   peligrosa *fem*

dark

dark *can be an adjective or a noun.*

A ADJECTIVE
   oscuro *masc*
   oscura *fem*
   She's got dark hair.
   Tiene el pelo oscuro.
   We wear dark green skirts.
   Llevamos unas faldas verde
   oscuro.

Language tip

When you describe something as **dark
green**, **dark blue** *and so on, neither
the colour nor* **oscuro** *changes its
ending to agree with the noun.*

some dark blue curtains
unas cortinas azul oscuro
It's dark in here.
Está oscuro aquí dentro.
It's dark at six o'clock.
Es de noche a las seis.
It's getting dark.
Se está haciendo de noche.

B NOUN
la **oscuridad** fem
I'm afraid of the dark.
Me da miedo la oscuridad.

darling NOUN
cariño masc
Thank you, darling!
¡Gracias, cariño!

Language tip
cariño still ends in **-o** even when it refers to a woman or girl.

dart NOUN
el **dardo** masc
Do you want to play darts?
¿Quieres jugar a los dardos?

Language tip
In Spanish, you need to add **a los** before **dardos**.

date NOUN
la **fecha** fem (day)
What's the date on the letter?
¿Qué fecha pone en la carta?
my date of birth
mi fecha de nacimiento

What's the date today?
¿A cuántos estamos hoy?

daughter NOUN
la **hija** fem

day NOUN
el **día** masc
I'm going to London for three days.
Voy a ir tres días a Londres.
during the day
durante el día
It's Richard's birthday the day after tomorrow.
Pasado mañana es el cumpleaños de Richard.
It's my day off.
Es mi día libre.

the days of the week
los días de la semana
every day
todos los días
all day
todo el día
What day is it today?
¿Qué día es hoy?
the day after tomorrow
pasado mañana
the day before yesterday
antes de ayer

Language tip
Even though it ends in **-a**, **el día** is a masculine noun.

dead ADJECTIVE
muerto masc
muerta fem
He's dead.
Está muerto.

deaf ADJECTIVE
sordo masc
sorda fem
She's deaf.
Es sorda.

deal

deal can be a noun or a verb.

A NOUN
el **trato** masc
It's a deal!

¡Trato hecho!
a great deal
mucho
**a great deal
of money**
mucho
dinero
B VERB
to deal
repartir *(cards)*
It's your turn to deal.
Te toca repartir a ti.

dear ADJECTIVE
1 **querido** *masc*
querida *fem (in letters to
friends)*
Dear Julia, ...
Querida Julia: ...
Dear Mum and Dad, ...
Queridos papás: ...
2 **estimado** *masc*
estimada *fem (in formal letters)*
Dear Mrs Blanco, ...
Estimada Sra. Blanco: ...

Language tip
*Did you notice that there's a colon
(:) at the end of the opening line of
a letter in Spanish, not a comma?*

death NOUN
la **muerte** *fem*

December NOUN
diciembre *masc*
My birthday's in December.
Mi cumpleaños es en
diciembre.
**It's the sixth of December
today.**
Hoy es seis de diciembre.

in December
en diciembre
on the fifth of December
el cinco de diciembre

Language tip
*Months are not spelled with a
capital letter in Spanish.*

to **decide** VERB
decidir
**I have decided to go to the
party.**
He decidido ir a la fiesta.
I can't decide.
No puedo decidirme.

decision NOUN
la **decisión** *fem* (PL las
decisiones)
We need to take a decision.
Tenemos que tomar una
decisión.

deck NOUN
la **cubierta** *fem*
on deck
en cubierta

deckchair NOUN
la **tumbona** *fem*

to **decorate** VERB
1 **decorar** *(with decorations)*
**We decorate the classroom
for Christmas.**
Decoramos la clase para la
Navidad.
2 **pintar** *(paint)*
**Mum's going to decorate my
bedroom.**
Mi madre va a pintar mi
habitación.
3 **empapelar** *(paper)*
**Mum's going to decorate my
bedroom.**
Mi madre va a empapelar mi
habitación.

Language tip
*There's no single verb meaning both
'to paint' and 'to paper' in Spanish.
Use one or the other or **pintar y
empapelar** together if you mean
both.*

decorations PL NOUN
los **adornos** *masc pl*
Christmas decorations
adornos de Navidad

deep ADJECTIVE
1 **profundo** *masc*
  profunda *fem (water, hole, cut)*
  Is it deep?
  ¿Es profundo?
  Take a deep breath, girls!
  ¡Respirad hondo, chicas!
2 **espeso** *masc*
  espesa *fem (snow, mud)*
  a deep layer of snow
  una espesa capa de nieve

deer NOUN
  el **ciervo** *masc*

defence NOUN
  la **defensa** *fem*
  I play in defence.
  Juego en la
  defensa.

defender NOUN
  el/la **defensa**
  masc/fem (in sport)

definite ADJECTIVE
1 **definitivo** *masc*
  definitiva *fem (fixed)*
  I haven't got any definite plans.
  No tengo ningún plan definitivo.
2 **seguro** *masc*
  segura *fem (certain)*
  Maybe, it's not definite.
  Quizás, no es seguro.

definitely ADVERB
  sin duda
  He's definitely the best player.
  Es sin duda el mejor jugador.
  Definitely!
  ¡Claro que sí!

degree NOUN
1 el **grado** *masc (measurement)*
  a temperature of thirty degrees
  una temperatura de treinta grados
2 la **licenciatura** *fem*
  (qualification)

a degree in maths
una licenciatura en
matemáticas

delayed ADJECTIVE
  retrasado *masc*
  retrasada *fem*
  All flights are delayed.
  Todos los vuelos están
  retrasados.

delicatessen NOUN
  la **charcutería fina** *fem*

delicious ADJECTIVE
  buenísimo *masc*
  buenísima *fem*
  The chocolate mousse is delicious!
  ¡La mousse de chocolate está
  buenísima!

to **deliver** VERB
1 **repartir** *(mail, newspapers)*
  I deliver newspapers.
  Yo reparto periódicos.
2 **entregar** *(order, goods)*
  They'll deliver my new bed on Friday.
  Me van a entregar la cama
  nueva el viernes.

denim NOUN
  a denim jacket
  una cazadora vaquera

dentist NOUN
  el/la **dentista** *masc/fem*
  I'm going to the dentist.
  Voy a ir al dentista.
  Brian is a dentist.
  Brian es dentista.

> **Language tip**
> *Did you notice that* **dentista** *still
> ends in* -a *even when referring to a
> man? Remember that in Spanish,
> you do not use an article with
> people's jobs.*

department NOUN
1 la **sección** *fem (PL las
  secciones) (in shop)*

the shoe department
la sección de calzado

2 el **departamento** *masc*
(of school, university)
He works in the English department.
Trabaja en el departamento de inglés.

department store NOUN
los **grandes almacenes** *masc pl*
This is my favourite department store.
Éstos son mis grandes almacenes favoritos.

departure NOUN
la **salida** *fem*

departure lounge NOUN
la **sala de embarque** *fem*

to **depend** VERB
It depends.
Depende.
depending on the weather
dependiendo del tiempo

Language tip
Even though we say **to depend on** *in English, remember that in Spanish they say* **depender de***.*

deposit NOUN
1 la **señal** *fem (part payment)*
You have to pay a deposit when you book.
Hay que dejar una señal para hacer la reserva.
2 el **depósito** *masc (when hiring something)*
You get the deposit back when you return the bike.
Recuperas el depósito cuando devuelves la bici.

depressed ADJECTIVE
deprimido *masc*
deprimida *fem*
I feel depressed.
Me encuentro deprimido.

deputy head NOUN
el **subdirector** *masc*
la **subdirectora** *fem*

to **describe** VERB
describir
Can you describe the man you saw?
¿Puedes describir al hombre que viste?

Language tip
Don't forget the personal **a** *in examples such as this last one.*

Describe yourself.
Descríbete.

description NOUN
la **descripción** *fem* (PL las **descripciones**)

Language tip
Have you noticed that words ending in **-tion** *in English often have Spanish counterparts ending in* **-ción***?*

desert NOUN
el **desierto** *masc*

desert island NOUN
la **isla desierta** *fem*

to **deserve** VERB
merecerse
You deserve a prize, Beth.
Te mereces un premio, Beth.

design

design can be a noun or a verb.

A NOUN
el **modelo** *masc*
a simple design
un modelo simple

B VERB
to design
diseñar

designer NOUN
el **diseñador** *masc*
la **diseñadora** *fem*

designer clothes PL NOUN
la **ropa de diseño** *fem*

> **Language tip**
> *Even though we always talk about clothes in the plural in English, in Spanish they use **la ropa** in the singular.*

desk NOUN
1 la **mesa** *fem (in school, office)*
my desk
mi mesa

2 el **mostrador** *masc (in hotel, at airport)*

dessert NOUN
el **postre** *masc*
for dessert
de postre

destination NOUN
el **destino** *masc*

detached house NOUN
la **casa independiente** *fem*

detail NOUN
el **detalle** *masc*
in detail
con detalle

detective NOUN
el/la **detective** *masc/fem*

detective story NOUN
la **novela policíaca** *fem*

detention NOUN
You'll get a detention!
¡Te vas a quedar castigado después de clase!

to develop VERB
revelar
I want to have this film developed.
Quiero revelar este carrete.

diabetic NOUN
el **diabético** *masc*
la **diabética** *fem*
I'm a diabetic.
Soy diabética.

diagonal ADJECTIVE
diagonal *masc & fem*

diagram NOUN
el **diagrama** *masc*

> **Language tip**
> *Even though it ends in **-a**, el **diagrama** is a masculine noun.*

to dial VERB
marcar
Dial the number.
Marca el número.

dialogue NOUN
el **diálogo** *masc*

diamond NOUN
el **diamante** *masc*
a diamond ring
un anillo de diamantes
the ace of diamonds
el as de diamantes

diary NOUN
1 la **agenda** *fem (for appointments)*
I've got her phone number in my diary.
Tengo su número de teléfono en mi agenda.
2 el **diario** *masc (personal record)*
I keep a diary.
Estoy escribiendo un diario.

dice NOUN
el **dado** *masc*

a b c **d** e f g h i j k l m n o p q r s t u v w x y z

Throw the dice, Sonia.
Tira los dados, Sonia.

dictionary NOUN
el **diccionario** *masc*
Look in the dictionary.
Mira en el diccionario.

did VERB ▷*see* **do**

didn't (= did not) ▷*see* **do**

to **die** VERB
morir
He died last year.
Murió el año pasado.
She's dying.
Se está muriendo.

diesel NOUN
el **gasoil** *masc*

diet

> **diet** *can be a noun or a verb.*

A NOUN
1 la **dieta** *fem*
a healthy diet
una dieta sana
2 el **régimen** *masc* (PL los
regímenes) *(for slimming)*
My dad's on a diet.
Mi padre está a régimen.
Are you on a diet?
¿Estás a régimen?
B VERB
to diet
hacer régimen
My mum's dieting.
Mi madre está haciendo
régimen.

difference NOUN
la **diferencia** *fem*

What's the difference?
¿Cuál es la diferencia?
**the difference between
Barcelona and Madrid**
la diferencia entre Barcelona
y Madrid

different ADJECTIVE
diferente *masc & fem*
We are very different.
Somos muy diferentes.
**Dublin is different from
London.**
Dublín es diferente de Londres.

> **Language tip**
> *Don't forget that there's only one* **f**
> *in the Spanish word* **diferente**.

difficult ADJECTIVE
difícil *masc & fem*
It's difficult.
Es difícil.
a difficult question
una pregunta difícil

> **Language tip**
> *Don't forget that there's only one* **f**
> *in the Spanish word* **difícil**.

difficulty NOUN
la **dificultad** *fem*
without difficulty
sin dificultad

to **dig** VERB
cavar
My dog digs lots of holes.
Mi perro cava muchos hoyos.
**The children are digging in
the sand.**
Los niños están haciendo hoyos
en la arena.

English Spanish

a b c **d** e f g h i j k l m n o p q r s t u v w x y z

digital ADJECTIVE
digital *masc & fem*
  a digital camera
  una cámara digital
  digital radio
  la radio digital
  digital television
  la televisión digital

dinghy NOUN
  a rubber dinghy
  una lancha neumática

dining room NOUN
  el **comedor** *masc*

dinner NOUN
1 la **comida** *fem (midday meal)*
  Dinner's ready!
  ¡La comida está lista!
  We always go home for dinner.
  Siempre vamos a comer a casa.
  We usually have dinner at one o'clock.
  Normalmente comemos a la una.

> **Language tip**
> *Only use* **la comida** *and the verb* **comer** *when talking about a midday meal.*

2 la **cena** *fem (evening meal)*
  There's a good film on after dinner.
  Echan una película buena después de la cena.
  What are we having for dinner tonight?
  ¿Qué hay para cenar esta noche?
  We usually have dinner at seven o'clock.
  Normalmente cenamos a las siete.

> **Language tip**
> *Only use* **la cena** *and the verb* **cenar** *when talking about an evening meal.*

dinner lady NOUN
  la **señora que ayuda en el comedor** *fem*

dinner time NOUN
1 la **hora de comer** *fem (for midday meal)*
2 la **hora de cenar** *fem (for evening meal)*

> **Did you know…?**
> *The Spanish tend to have their meals much later than in Britain, with the lunchtime meal around 2pm and the evening meal around 9pm or 10pm.*

dinosaur NOUN
  el **dinosaurio** *masc*

direct ADJECTIVE
  directo *masc*
  directa *fem*
    the most direct route
    la ruta más directa

direction NOUN
  la **dirección** *fem* (PL las **direcciones**)
    We're going in the wrong direction.
    Vamos en la dirección equivocada.
    Let's ask somebody for directions.
    Vamos a pedirle a alguien que nos indique el camino.

> **Language tip**
> *Have you noticed that words ending in* -**tion** *in English often have Spanish counterparts ending in* -**ción**?

dirty ADJECTIVE
  sucio *masc*
  sucia *fem*
    The house is very dirty.
    La casa está muy sucia.

disabled ADJECTIVE
  discapacitado *masc*
  discapacitada *fem*
    disabled people
    los discapacitados

to **disagree** VERB
I disagree!
¡No estoy de acuerdo!
He disagrees with me.
No está de acuerdo conmigo.

disappointed ADJECTIVE
decepcionado *masc*
decepcionada *fem*
We are very disappointed.
Estamos muy decepcionados.

disappointment NOUN
la **decepción** *fem* (PL las **decepciones**)

disaster NOUN
el **desastre** *masc*
It's a disaster!
¡Es un desastre!

discipline NOUN
la **disciplina** *fem*

disc jockey NOUN
el/la **disc-jockey** *masc/fem*
(PL los/las **disc-jockeys**)

disco NOUN
el **baile** *masc*
There's a disco at school tonight.
Hay un baile en el colegio esta noche.
disco music
la música disco

discussion NOUN
la **discusión** *fem*
(PL las **discusiones**)

to **disguise** VERB
disfrazar
He was disguised as a policeman.
Iba disfrazado de policía.

disgusting
ADJECTIVE
asqueroso *masc*
asquerosa *fem*

It looks disgusting.
Tiene un aspecto asqueroso.

dish NOUN
el **plato** *masc (meal, plate)*
a vegetarian dish
un plato vegetariano
to wash the dishes
fregar los platos
I always wash the dishes.
Yo siempre friego los platos.

dishwasher NOUN
el **lavavajillas** *masc* (PL los **lavavajillas**)

disk NOUN
el **disco** *masc*

dislike NOUN
my likes and dislikes
lo que me gusta y lo que no

distance NOUN
la **distancia** *fem*
a distance of ten kilometres
una distancia de diez kilómetros
in the distance
a lo lejos

to **distract** VERB
distraer
Don't distract him, Poppy.
No lo distraigas, Poppy.

district NOUN
1 el **barrio** *masc (of town)*
2 la **región** *fem* (PL las **regiones**) *(of country)*

to **disturb** VERB
molestar
I'm sorry to disturb you.
Siento molestarte.
'Do not disturb'
'No molestar'

to **dive** VERB
tirarse de cabeza
I like diving.
Me gusta tirarme de cabeza.
He dived into the water.
Se tiró al agua de cabeza.

to **divide** VERB
dividir
   Divide the pastry in half.
   Divide la masa en dos.
   Twelve divided by three is four.
   Doce dividido entre tres son cuatro.
   Divide into two groups!
   ¡Dividíos en dos grupos!

diving board NOUN
   el **trampolín** *masc* (PL los **trampolines**)

divorced ADJECTIVE
   divorciado *masc*
   divorciada *fem*
   My parents are divorced.
   Mis padres están divorciados.

DIY NOUN
   el **bricolaje** *masc*
   He likes doing DIY.
   Le gusta hacer bricolaje.

dizzy ADJECTIVE
   mareado *masc*
   mareada *fem*
   I feel dizzy.
   Estoy mareada.

DJ NOUN
   el/la **DJ** *masc/fem* (PL los/las **DJs**)

to **do** VERB
   hacer
   What are you going to do this evening?
   ¿Qué vas a hacer esta noche?
   My brother does judo.
   Mi hermano hace yudo.
   I haven't done my homework.
   No he hecho mis deberes.
   Who did that?
   ¿Quién hizo eso?
   That'll do, thanks.
   Así está bien, gracias.

> **Language tip**
> *You often use* **do** *to form questions in English. Don't use* **hacer** *like this in Spanish. Just use the normal form of the verb and make your voice go up at the end. Don't forget the opening and closing question marks in written Spanish.*

   Do you speak English? — Yes, I do.
   ¿Hablas inglés? — Sí.
   Do you like horses? — No, I don't.
   ¿Te gustan los caballos? — No.
   Where does he live?
   ¿Dónde vive?
   What do you do in your free time?
   ¿Qué haces en tu tiempo libre?

> **Language tip**
> *Just use* **no** *to make sentences negative.*

   I don't understand.
   No entiendo.
   She doesn't like dogs.
   No le gustan los perros.

> **Language tip**
> *Use* **¿no?** *to check information where in English we'd say* **don't you?**, **doesn't he?** *and so on.*

   You go swimming on Fridays, don't you?
   Tú vas a nadar los viernes, ¿no?

> **Language tip**
> *You can also use* **¿verdad?** *to check information.*

   It doesn't matter, does it?
   No importa, ¿verdad?

What are you doing?
¿Qué estás haciendo?
I'm not doing anything.
No estoy haciendo nada.
... don't you?
... ¿no?
... do you?
... ¿verdad?

to **do up** VERB
1 **atarse** *(tie)*
Do up your shoes!
¡Átate los cordones!
2 **abrocharse** *(fasten)*
Do up your coat!
¡Abróchate el abrigo!
Do up your zip!
¡Súbete la cremallera!

> *Language tip*
>
> *In Spanish you usually use an article like **el**, **la** or **los**, **las** with clothes you are wearing.*

doctor NOUN
el **médico** *masc*
la **médica** *fem*
I'd like to be a doctor.
Me gustaría ser médico.

> *Language tip*
>
> *When talking about people's jobs in Spanish, you do not use an article.*

She's a doctor.
Es médica.
I need to see a doctor.
Tengo que ver a un médico.

> *Language tip*
>
> *Don't forget the personal **a** in examples like this one.*

dodgems PL NOUN
los **coches de choque** *masc pl*

does VERB ▷ *see* **do**

doesn't (= **does not**) ▷ *see* **do**

dog NOUN
el **perro** *masc*
Have you got a dog?
¿Tienes perro?

doll NOUN
la **muñeca** *fem*

dollar NOUN
el **dólar** *masc*

dolphin
NOUN
el **delfín** *masc*
(PL los **delfines**)

dominoes PL NOUN
Let's have a game of dominoes.
Vamos a echar una partida al dominó.

done VERB ▷ *see* **do**

donkey NOUN
el **burro** *masc*
la **burra** *fem*

don't (= **do not**) . ▷ *see* **do**

door NOUN
la **puerta** *fem*
the first door on the right
la primera puerta a la derecha

dormitory NOUN
el **dormitorio** *masc*

dot NOUN
el **punto** *masc*
My email address is loveday at collins dot co dot U-K (loveday@collins.co.uk).
Mi e-mail es loveday arroba collins punto co punto U-K (loveday@collins.co.uk).

double ADJECTIVE
doble *masc & fem*
a double helping
una ración doble

double bed NOUN
la **cama de matrimonio** *fem*

English Spanish

a
b
c
d
e
f
g
h i j k l m n o p q r s t u v w x y z

English **Spanish**

a b c d e f g h i j k l m n o p q r s t u v w x y z

double room NOUN
la **habitación doble** *fem* (PL las **habitaciones dobles**)

double-decker bus NOUN
el **autobús de dos pisos** *masc* (PL los **autobuses de dos pisos**)

to **doubt** VERB
dudar
I doubt it.
Lo dudo.

doughnut NOUN
el **donut** (PL los **donuts**)

down

> **down** *can be an adverb, preposition or adjective.*

A ADVERB
abajo
It's down in the cellar.
Está abajo en el sótano.
It's down there.
Está ahí abajo.
Don't look down!
¡No mires hacia abajo!

B PREPOSITION
He ran down the road.
Corrió calle abajo.
I live just down the road.
Vivo aquí cerca en esta calle.

C ADJECTIVE
I'm feeling a bit down.
Me siento un poco deprimido.
The computer's down.
El ordenador no funciona.

to **download** VERB
descargar
You can download the file.
Puedes descargar el archivo.

downstairs ADVERB
abajo
The bathroom's downstairs.
El baño está abajo.
I'm downstairs!
¡Estoy abajo!

dozen NOUN
la **docena** *fem*

two dozen
dos docenas
a dozen eggs
una docena de huevos

dragon NOUN
el **dragón** *masc*
(PL los **dragones**)

drama NOUN
el **teatro** *masc*
Drama is my favourite subject.
Teatro es mi asignatura favorita.

drank VERB ▷see **drink**

draughts NOUN
las **damas** *fem pl*
Do you want to play draughts?
¿Quieres jugar a las damas?

> **Language tip**
> In Spanish, you need to add **a las** before **damas**.

draw

> **draw** *can be a verb or a noun.*

A VERB
to draw
1 **dibujar** *(with pencil, pen)*
I can't draw.
No sé dibujar.
Draw a house, everyone.
Dibujad todos una casa.
I'm drawing a picture.
Estoy haciendo un dibujo.
2 **empatar** *(in game)*
We drew two all.
Empatamos a dos.

B NOUN
el **empate** *masc (in game)*
It's a draw between the boys and the girls.
Es un empate entre los niños y las niñas.

drawer NOUN
el **cajón** *masc* (PL los **cajones**)

drawing NOUN
1 el **dibujo** *masc* (picture)
2 (activity)
I like drawing.
Me gusta dibujar.

drawing pin NOUN
la **chincheta** *fem*

dream NOUN
el **sueño** *masc*
Sweet dreams, darling!
¡Felices sueños, cariño!
a bad dream
un mal sueño

dress

dress *can be a noun or a verb.*

A NOUN
el **vestido** *masc*
Laura is wearing a white dress.
Laura lleva un vestido blanco.
B VERB
to get dressed
vestirse
I'm getting dressed.
Me estoy vistiendo.
Go and get dressed.
Ve a vestirte.

to **dress up** VERB
disfrazarse
I'm going to dress up as a princess.
Voy a disfrazarme de princesa.

dressed ADJECTIVE
vestido *masc*
vestida *fem*
I'm not dressed yet.
Todavía no estoy vestido.
How was he dressed?
¿Cómo iba vestido?

She was dressed in a green sweater and jeans.
Iba vestida con un jersey verde y unos vaqueros.

drew VERB ▷ see **draw**

drink

drink *can be a verb or a noun.*

A VERB
to drink
beber
What would you like to drink?
¿Qué quieres beber?
B NOUN
la **bebida** *fem*
a cold drink
una bebida fría
a hot drink
una bebida caliente
Would you like a drink?
¿Quieres beber algo?

drive

drive *can be a noun or a verb.*

A NOUN
1 (in car)
Let's go for a drive.
Vamos a dar una vuelta en el coche.
It's a twenty-minute drive to school.
El colegio está a veinte minutos en coche.
2 (of house)
You can park your car in the drive.
Puedes aparcar en la entrada de la casa.
B VERB
to drive
1 **conducir** (as skill)
She's learning to drive.
Está aprendiendo a conducir.
Can you drive?
¿Sabes conducir?
2 **ir en coche** (go by car)
Are you going by train? — No, we're driving.

¿Vais en tren? — No, vamos en coche.

3 llevar en coche *(take by car)*
My mother drives me to school.
Mi madre me lleva en coche al colegio.

driver NOUN
el **conductor** *masc*
la **conductora** *fem*
She's an excellent driver.
Es una conductora excelente.

driving licence NOUN
el **carnet de conducir** *masc*
(PL los **carnets de conducir**)

drop

> **drop** *can be a noun or a verb.*

A NOUN
la **gota** *fem*
a drop of water
una gota de agua
B VERB
to drop
dejar caer
Don't drop that glass, will you!
No dejes caer ese vaso, ¿vale?

drove VERB ▷ *see* drive

drug NOUN
1 la **medicina** *fem (medicine)*
They need food and drugs.
Necesitan alimentos y medicinas.
2 la **droga** *fem (illegal)*
hard drugs
drogas duras
It's crazy to take drugs.
Es una locura drogarse.

drum NOUN
el **tambor** *masc*
an African drum
un tambor africano
I play drums.
Toco la batería.

drum kit NOUN
la **batería** *fem*

drummer NOUN
el/la **batería** *masc/fem*

drunk ADJECTIVE
borracho *masc*
borracha *fem*

dry

> **dry** *can be an adjective or a verb.*

A ADJECTIVE
1 seco *masc*
seca *fem (not wet)*
The paint isn't dry yet.
La pintura no está seca todavía.
2 sin lluvias *(without rain)*
a long dry period
una larga temporada sin lluvias
B VERB
to dry
1 secar

> *Language tip*
> Use **secar** *to talk about drying objects, animals and babies.*

Can you dry the dishes?
¿Puedes secar los platos?
2 secarse

> *Language tip*
> Use **secarse** *when something dries.*

Let the glue dry.
Deja que se seque el pegamento.

> *Language tip*
> Use **secarse** *when someone dries themselves or their own hair, hands, feet, etc.*

Dry yourself on this towel.
Sécate con esta toalla.
I need to dry my hair.
Tengo que secarme el pelo.
Have you dried your hands?
¿Te has secado las manos?

duck NOUN
el **pato** *masc*

due ADJECTIVE
The plane is due in half an hour.
El avión llegará dentro de media hora.
When's the baby due?
¿Para cuándo nacerá el niño?
due to
debido a
We can't go out due to the bad weather.
No podemos salir debido al mal tiempo.

dug VERB ▷ see **dig**

dull ADJECTIVE
It's dull today.
Hace un día gris hoy.

dummy NOUN
el **chupete** masc (for baby)

dungeon NOUN
la **mazmorra** fem

during PREPOSITION
durante
during the day
durante el día

dustbin NOUN
el **cubo de la basura** masc

duty-free shop NOUN
la **tienda libre de impuestos** fem

duvet NOUN
el **edredón nórdico** masc (PL los **edredones nórdicos**)

DVD NOUN
el **DVD** masc (PL los **DVDs**)
I've got that film on DVD.
Tengo esa película en DVD.

DVD player NOUN
el **reproductor de DVD** masc

dwarf NOUN
el **enano** masc

E e

each

each *can be an adjective or a pronoun.*

A ADJECTIVE
cada *masc & fem*
each day
cada día

Language tip
Even though **cada** *ends in* -a, *you can use it with a masculine noun.*

B PRONOUN
cada uno *masc*
cada una *fem*
They have ten points each.
Tienen diez puntos cada uno.
The towels cost five pounds each.
Las toallas cuestan cinco libras cada una.
Take one card each.
Coged una carta cada uno.
We write to each other.
Nos escribimos.

ear NOUN
1 la **oreja** *fem (outer part)*
I want to have my ears pierced.
Quiero hacerme agujeros en las orejas.
2 el **oído** *masc (inner part)*
My ears are aching.
Me duelen los oídos.

earache NOUN
I've got earache.
Me duele el oído.

early ADVERB
1 **temprano** *(early in the day)*
I get up early.
Me levanto temprano.
I go to bed early.
Me acuesto temprano.

2 **pronto** *(ahead of time)*
Come early to get a good seat.
Llega pronto para conseguir un buen sitio.

to earn VERB
ganar
She earns ten pounds an hour.
Gana diez libras a la hora.

earring NOUN
el **pendiente** *masc*
diamond earrings
pendientes de diamantes
a pair of earrings
unos pendientes

earth NOUN
la **tierra** *fem*

east

east *can be an adjective or a noun.*

A ADJECTIVE
este

Language tip
When it means 'east', **este** *never changes its ending no matter what it describes. Adjectives that behave like this are called 'invariable adjectives'.*

the east coast
la costa este
B NOUN
el **este** *masc*
in the east
en el este

Easter NOUN
la **Semana Santa** *fem*
at Easter
en Semana Santa
the Easter holidays
las vacaciones de Semana Santa
Easter Saturday
el Sábado Santo
Easter Sunday
el Domingo de Resurrección

Happy Easter!
¡Felices Pascuas!

Did you know...?
Many places in Spain have festivals during **Semana Santa** *(Easter week). These usually involve religious floats and processions of people wearing robes and hoods which cover their faces.*

Easter egg NOUN
el **huevo de Pascua** *masc*
a big Easter egg
un gran huevo de Pascua

easy ADJECTIVE
fácil *masc & fem*
It's easy!
¡Es fácil!

to **eat** VERB
comer
I eat a lot of sweets.
Como muchos caramelos.
Would you like something to eat?
¿Quieres comer algo?

edge NOUN
el **borde** *masc*
on the edge of the table
en el borde de la mesa

Edinburgh NOUN
Edimburgo *masc*
Andrew lives in Edinburgh.
Andrew vive en Edimburgo.

education NOUN
la **educación** *fem*

effect NOUN
el **efecto** *masc*

effort NOUN
el **esfuerzo** *masc*
You have to make an effort.
Tienes que hacer un esfuerzo.

e.g. ABBREVIATION
p.ej. (= *por ejemplo*)

egg NOUN
el **huevo** *masc*
a boiled egg
un huevo pasado por agua
a hard-boiled egg
un huevo cocido
scrambled eggs
huevos revueltos
a fried egg
un huevo frito

eight NUMBER
ocho
eight euros
ocho euros

She's eight.
Tiene ocho años.

Language tip
In English you can say **she's eight** *or* **she's eight years old**. *In Spanish you can only say* **tiene ocho años**. *Have you noticed that in Spanish you need to use the verb* **tener** *to talk about somebody's age?*

eighteen NUMBER
dieciocho
eighteen euros
dieciocho euros

He's eighteen.
Tiene dieciocho años.

Language tip
In English you can say **he's eighteen** *or* **he's eighteen years**

old. *In Spanish you can only say* **tiene dieciocho años**. *Have you noticed that in Spanish you need to use the verb* **tener** *to talk about somebody's age?*

eighteenth NUMBER
dieciocho

on the eighteenth floor
en el piso dieciocho
It's my brother's eighteenth birthday on Saturday.
Mi hermano cumple dieciocho años el sábado.
My birthday's the eighteenth of August.
Mi cumpleaños es el dieciocho de agosto.
Today's the eighteenth of May.
Hoy es dieciocho de mayo.

on the eighteenth of June
el dieciocho de junio

Language tip
*Use the same set of numbers that you use for counting (**uno**, **dos**, **tres** and so on) when giving Spanish dates.*

eighth NUMBER
octavo *masc*
octava *fem*

on the eighth floor
en el octavo piso
My birthday's the eighth of May.
Mi cumpleaños es el ocho de mayo.
It's the eighth of June today.
Hoy es ocho de junio.

on the eighth of April
el ocho de abril

Language tip
*Use the same set of numbers that you use for counting (**uno**, **dos**, **tres** and so on) when giving Spanish dates.*

eighty NUMBER
ochenta

My grandmother is eighty.
Mi abuela tiene ochenta años.

Language tip
*In English you can say **she's eighty** or **she's eighty years old**. In Spanish you can only say **tiene ochenta años**. Have you noticed that in Spanish you need to use the verb **tener** to talk about somebody's age?*

Eire NOUN
la **República de Irlanda** *fem*

either ADVERB, CONJUNCTION, PRONOUN
tampoco

I don't like milk, and I don't like eggs either.
No me gusta la leche ni tampoco me gustan los huevos.
I haven't got any money. — I haven't either.
No tengo dinero. — Ni yo tampoco.
I don't like either of them.
No me gusta ninguno de los dos.
either ... or ...
o ... o ...
You can have either ice cream or yoghurt.
Puedes tomar o helado o yogur.

elastic band NOUN
la **goma elástica** *fem*

elbow NOUN
el **codo** *masc*

I've hurt my elbow.
Me he hecho daño en el codo.

Language tip
*In Spanish you usually use an article like **el**, **la** or **los**, **las** with parts of the body.*

elder ADJECTIVE
mayor *masc & fem*
my elder sister
mi hermana mayor

elderly ADJECTIVE
mayor *masc & fem*
an elderly gentleman
un señor mayor
the elderly
los ancianos

eldest ADJECTIVE
mayor *masc & fem*
my eldest brother
mi hermano mayor
He's the eldest.
Él es el mayor.

election NOUN
la **elección** *fem* (PL las **elecciones**)
the election of the new mayor
la elección del nuevo alcalde
The elections will be in May.
Las elecciones serán en mayo.

electric ADJECTIVE
eléctrico *masc*
eléctrica *fem*

an electric guitar
una guitarra eléctrica

electrician NOUN
el/la **electricista** *masc/fem*
He's an electrician.
Es electricista.

Language tip
When talking about people's jobs in Spanish, you do not use an article.

electricity NOUN
la **electricidad** *fem*

electronic ADJECTIVE
electrónico *masc*
electrónica *fem*

elegant ADJECTIVE
elegante *masc & fem*

elephant NOUN
el **elefante** *masc*

eleven NUMBER
once
eleven euros
once euros

I'm eleven.
Tengo once años.

Language tip
*In English you can say **I'm eleven** or **I'm eleven years old**. In Spanish you can only say **tengo once años**. Have you noticed that in Spanish you need to use the verb **tener** to talk about somebody's age?*

eleventh NUMBER
undécimo *masc*
undécima *fem*
on the eleventh floor
en el undécimo piso
My birthday's the eleventh of June.
Mi cumpleaños es el once de junio.
It's the eleventh of December today.
Hoy es once de diciembre.

English Spanish

a b c **d e** f g h i j k l m n o p q r s t u v w x y z

a
b
c
d
e
f
g
h
i
j
k
l
m
n
o
p
q
r
s
t
u
v
w
x
y
z

on the eleventh of January
el once de enero

Language tip
*Use the same set of numbers that you use for counting (**uno**, **dos**, **tres** and so on) when giving Spanish dates.*

else ADVERB
más
nobody else
nadie más
nothing else
nada más
Would you like anything else?
¿Quieres algo más?
I don't want anything else.
No quiero nada más.
somebody else
otra persona

email

email *can be a noun or a verb.*

A NOUN
el **e-mail** *masc* (PL los **e-mails**)
by email
por e-mail
Send your friend an email.
Envíale un e-mail a tu amigo.
B VERB
to email
mandar un e-mail a
I'll email you.
Te mandaré un e-mail.

email address NOUN
el **e-mail** *masc* (PL los **e-mails**)
My email address is loveday at collins dot co dot U-K (loveday@collins.co.uk).
Mi e-mail es loveday arroba collins punto co punto U-K (loveday@collins.co.uk).

embarrassed ADJECTIVE
I was really embarrassed.
Me dio mucha vergüenza.

embarrassing ADJECTIVE
incómodo *masc*
incómoda *fem*
an embarrassing situation
una situación incómoda

emergency NOUN
la **emergencia** *fem*
This is an emergency!
¡Es una emergencia!
in an emergency
en caso de emergencia

emergency exit NOUN
la **salida de emergencia** *fem*

empty

empty *can be an adjective or a verb.*

A ADJECTIVE
vacío *masc*
vacía *fem*
The cage is empty.
La jaula está vacía.
B VERB
to empty
vaciar
Can you empty the wastepaper basket?
¿Puedes vaciar la papelera?

to **encourage** VERB
animar
Encourage your team!
¡Anima a tu equipo!

encyclopedia NOUN
la **enciclopedia** *fem*

end

end *can be a noun or a verb.*

A NOUN
el **final** *masc*
the end of the lesson
el final de la clase
at the end of the street
al final de la calle

in the end
al final

B VERB
to end
terminar
What time does the lesson end?
¿A qué hora termina la clase?

ending NOUN
el **final** *masc*
It's a great film, especially the ending.
Es una película estupenda, sobre todo el final.

enemy NOUN
el **enemigo** *masc*
la **enemiga** *fem*

energetic ADJECTIVE
lleno de energía *masc*
llena de energía *fem*

energy NOUN
la **energía** *fem*

engaged ADJECTIVE
1 **ocupado** *masc*
ocupada *fem* (busy)
The toilet is engaged.
El baño está ocupado.
Her phone is always engaged.
Su teléfono está siempre comunicando.
2 **prometido** *masc*
prometida *fem* (to be married)
My brother is engaged.
Mi hermano está prometido.
She's engaged to Rob.
Está prometida con Rob.

engagement NOUN
el **compromiso** *masc* (to be married)

engagement ring NOUN
el **anillo de compromiso** *masc*

engine NOUN
1 el **motor** *masc* (of car, machine)

2 la **locomotora** *fem* (train)

engineer NOUN
el **ingeniero** *masc*
la **ingeniera** *fem*
He's an engineer.
Es ingeniero.

Language tip
When talking about people's jobs in Spanish, you do not use an article.

England NOUN
Inglaterra *fem*
I live in England.
Vivo en Inglaterra.
Are you coming to England?
¿Vienes a Inglaterra?

English

English *can be an adjective or a noun.*

A ADJECTIVE
inglés *masc* (PL **ingleses**)
inglesa *fem*
I'm English.
Soy inglés.
English food is different.
La comida inglesa es diferente.
English people
los ingleses

He's English.
Es inglés.
She's English.
Es inglesa.

B NOUN
el **inglés** *masc*
Do you speak English?
¿Hablas inglés?
the English
los ingleses

Language tip
inglés *is not spelled with a capital letter in Spanish.*

Englishman NOUN
el **inglés** *masc* (PL los **ingleses**)
an Englishman
un inglés

Language tip
inglés *is not spelled with a capital letter in Spanish.*

Englishwoman NOUN
la **inglesa** *fem* (PL las **inglesas**)
an Englishwoman
una inglesa

Language tip
inglesa *is not spelled with a capital letter in Spanish.*

to **enjoy** VERB
I enjoy learning English.
Me gusta aprender inglés.
Did you enjoy the film?
¿Te gustó la película?
to enjoy oneself
divertirse
Did you enjoy yourself?
¿Te divertiste?

enjoyable ADJECTIVE
agradable *masc & fem*

enormous ADJECTIVE
enorme *masc & fem*

enough

enough *can be an adjective, pronoun or adverb.*

A ADJECTIVE
suficiente *masc & fem*
enough time
tiempo suficiente
I haven't got enough money.
No tengo dinero suficiente.

Language tip
You can also use **bastante**, *which goes before the noun.*

I haven't got enough money.
No tengo bastante dinero.
B PRONOUN
bastante *masc & fem*

Have you got enough?
¿Tienes bastante?
I've had enough!
¡Ya está bien!

That's enough.
Ya basta.

C ADVERB
This hat isn't big enough.
Este sombrero no es lo suficientemente grande.
Is your coffee hot enough?
¿Tu café está lo suficientemente caliente?

to **enter** VERB
I'm going to enter the competition.
Voy a participar en el concurso.

enthusiasm NOUN
el **entusiasmo** *masc*

enthusiastic ADJECTIVE
entusiasta *masc & fem*

entrance NOUN
la **entrada** *fem*
I'll wait for you by the entrance.
Te esperaré en la entrada.

entrance exam NOUN
la **prueba de acceso** *fem*

entry NOUN
la **entrada** *fem*
'no entry'
'prohibida la entrada'

entry phone NOUN
el **portero automático** *masc*

envelope NOUN
el **sobre** *masc*

envious ADJECTIVE
envidioso *masc*
envidiosa *fem*

environment NOUN
el **medio ambiente** *masc*

episode NOUN
el **capítulo** *masc*

equal

> **equal** *can be an adjective or a verb.*

A ADJECTIVE
igual *masc & fem*
Cut the pizza into six equal pieces.
Corta la pizza en seis trozos iguales.

B VERB
to equal
ser igual a
Two times three equals six.
Dos por tres es igual a seis.

to **equalize** VERB
empatar
Henry has equalized.
Henry ha empatado.

equipment NOUN
el **equipo** *masc*
lots of equipment
mucho equipo

error NOUN
el **error** *masc*
a small error
un pequeño error

escalator NOUN
la **escalera mecánica** *fem*
Is there an escalator?
¿Hay escalera mecánica?

to **escape** VERB
escaparse
A lion has escaped.
Se ha escapado
un león.

especially ADVERB
sobre todo
It's very hot, especially in summer.
Hace mucho calor, sobre todo en verano.

essay NOUN
el **trabajo** *masc*
a history essay
un trabajo de historia

essential ADJECTIVE
esencial *masc & fem*
It's essential to bring warm clothes.
Es esencial traer ropa de abrigo.

euro NOUN
el **euro** *masc*

Europe NOUN
Europa *fem*

European ADJECTIVE
europeo *masc*
europea *fem*

> *Language tip*
> **europeo** *is not spelled with a capital letter in Spanish.*

even

> **even** *can be an adverb or an adjective.*

A ADVERB
incluso
I like all animals, even snakes.
Me gustan todos los animales, incluso las serpientes.

B ADJECTIVE
an even number
un número par

evening NOUN
1 la **tarde** *fem (early evening)*

> *Language tip*
> *Use* **la tarde** *in the early evening while it's still light.*

at six o'clock in the evening
a las seis de la tarde

this evening at about six thirty
esta tarde, a eso de las seis y media
2 la **noche** *fem (after dark)*

Language tip
Use **la noche** *for later in the evening, particularly after dark.*

at nine o'clock in the evening
a las nueve de la noche
tomorrow evening
mañana por la noche
yesterday evening
ayer por la noche
Good evening!
¡Buenas noches!

Language tip
Change **noche** *and* **noches** *to* **tarde** *and* **tardes** *if it's very early in the evening.*

evening class NOUN
la **clase nocturna** *fem*
My mother goes to an evening class.
Mi madre va a una clase nocturna.

event NOUN
el **acontecimiento** *masc*
an important event
un acontecimiento importante

ever ADVERB
alguna vez *(in questions)*
Have you ever been to France?
¿Has estado alguna vez en Francia?
for the first time ever
por primera vez
Nothing ever happens.
Nunca pasa nada.

every ADJECTIVE
every pupil
todos los alumnos
I talk to her every day.
Hablo con ella todos los días.
I do judo every week.
Hago yudo todas las semanas.

every time
cada vez

every day
todos los días
every night
todas las noches
every week
todas las semanas

everybody PRONOUN
todos *masc pl*
todas *fem pl*
Good morning everybody!
¡Buenos días a todos!
Is everybody here?
¿Están todos?
Everybody likes sweets.
A todo el mundo le gustan los caramelos.

everyone PRONOUN
todos *masc pl*
todas *fem pl*
Good morning everyone!
¡Buenos días a todos!
Is everyone here?
¿Están todos?
Everyone likes sweets.
A todo el mundo le gustan los caramelos.

everything PRONOUN
todo *masc*
Everything's fine!
¡Todo está bien!
Is that everything?
¿Eso es todo?

everywhere ADVERB
por todas partes
I looked everywhere, but I couldn't find it.
Miré por todas partes, pero no lo encontré.
There are cats everywhere!
¡Hay gatos por todas partes!

exact ADJECTIVE
exacto *masc*
exacta *fem*

exactly ADVERB
exactamente
Our trainers are exactly the same.
Nuestras zapatillas de deporte son exactamente iguales.
not exactly
no exactamente
It's exactly ten o'clock.
Son las diez en punto.

> *Language tip*
> *Have you noticed that the Spanish equivalent of the English -ly ending is -**mente**? It's added to the feminine form of the adjective.*

exam NOUN
el **examen** *masc* (PL los **exámenes**)
an English exam
un examen de inglés

example NOUN
el **ejemplo** *masc*
for example
por ejemplo

excellent ADJECTIVE
excelente *masc & fem*
Excellent!
¡Excelente!

except PREPOSITION
excepto
everyone except me
todos menos yo

to **exchange** VERB
cambiar
I want to exchange the book for a video.
Quiero cambiar el libro por un vídeo.

exchange rate NOUN
el **tipo de cambio** *masc*

excited ADJECTIVE
entusiasmado *masc*
entusiasmada *fem*

exciting ADJECTIVE
emocionante *masc & fem*

an exciting film
una película emocionante

exclamation mark NOUN
el **signo de admiración** *masc*

to **excuse** VERB

> **Excuse me!**
> ¡Perdón!

exercise NOUN
el **ejercicio** *masc*

exercise book NOUN
el **cuaderno** *masc*

exhausted ADJECTIVE
agotado *masc*
agotada *fem*

Clare is exhausted.
Clare está agotada.

exhibition NOUN
la **exposición** *fem* (PL las **exposiciones**)

exit NOUN
la **salida** *fem*
Where is the exit?
¿Dónde está la salida?

English Spanish

a b c d e f g h i j k l m n o p q r s t u v w x y z

to expect VERB
1 esperar *(wait for)*
I'm expecting a phone call.
Estoy esperando una llamada.
She's expecting a baby.
Está esperando un hijo.
2 imaginarse *(imagine)*
I expect he'll be late.
Me imagino que llegará tarde.

expedition NOUN
la **expedición** *fem* (PL las **expediciones**)

expensive ADJECTIVE
caro *masc*
cara *fem*
It's too expensive.
Es demasiado caro.

experience NOUN
la **experiencia** *fem*
an interesting experience
una experiencia interesante

experiment NOUN
el **experimento** *masc*

expert NOUN
el **experto** *masc*
la **experta** *fem*
She's a computer expert.
Es una experta en informática.

Matthew is an expert cook.
Matthew es un experto cocinero.

to explain VERB
explicar
I'll explain it in English.
Te lo explicaré en inglés.

explanation NOUN
la **explicación** *fem* (PL las **explicaciones**)
a clear explanation
una explicación clara

to explode VERB
explotar
It's going to explode!
¡Va a explotar!

explosion NOUN
la **explosión** *fem* (PL las **explosiones**)

extension NOUN
1 la **extensión** *fem* (PL las **extensiones**) *(phone)*
Extension 3137, please.
Con la extensión 3137, por favor.
2 *(of building)*
We're having an extension built.
Nos están construyendo una ampliación de la casa.

extra

extra *can be an adjective or an adverb.*

A ADJECTIVE
1 *(additional)*
an extra blanket
una manta más
2 *(not included)*
Breakfast is extra.
El desayuno no está incluido.
B ADVERB
to pay extra
pagar más
You have to pay extra for a room with a sea view.
Si quieres una habitación con vistas al mar tienes que pagar más.
It costs extra.
Lleva un suplemento aparte.

extremely ADVERB
  sumamente

eye NOUN
  el **ojo** masc
    I've got blue eyes.
    Tengo los ojos azules.
    What colour eyes has he got?
    ¿De qué color tiene los ojos?
    She opened her eyes.
    Abrió los ojos.

Language tip
In Spanish you usually use an article
like **el**, **la**, or **los**, **las** with parts of
the body.

eyebrow NOUN
  la **ceja** fem

eyelash NOUN
  la **pestaña** fem
    She's got very long eyelashes.
    Tiene las pestañas muy largas.

eyelid NOUN
  el **párpado** masc

eyesight NOUN
  la **vista** fem

English

Spanish

a
b
c
d
e
f
g
h
i
j
k
l
m
n
o
p
q
r
s
t
u
v
w
x
y
z

F f

fabulous ADJECTIVE
fantástico masc
fantástica fem

face NOUN
la **cara** fem
His face is red.
Tiene la cara roja.

> **Language tip**
> In Spanish you usually use an article like **el**, **la** or **los**, **las** with parts of the body.

face cloth NOUN
la **toallita** fem

facilities PL NOUN
las **instalaciones** fem pl

fact NOUN
el **hecho** masc
an interesting fact
un hecho interesante
in fact
en realidad

factory NOUN
la **fábrica** fem
My mum works in a factory.
Mi madre trabaja en una fábrica.

to **fail** VERB
suspender
She's going to fail her exams.
Va a suspender los exámenes.

fair

> **fair** can be an adjective or a noun.

A ADJECTIVE
1 **justo** masc
justa fem (right)
That's not fair.
Eso no es justo.
2 **rubio** masc
rubia fem (blonde)
He's got fair hair.

Tiene el pelo rubio.
B NOUN
la **feria** fem
Are you going to the fair?
¿Vas a ir a la feria?

fair-haired ADJECTIVE
Nina is fair-haired.
Nina tiene el pelo rubio.

fairly ADVERB
bastante
That's fairly good.
Eso está bastante bien.

fairy NOUN
la **hada** fem

fairy tale NOUN
el **cuento de hadas** masc

to **fall** VERB
caerse
Mind you don't fall!
¡Ten cuidado de no caerte!
to fall asleep
quedarse dormido
I'm falling asleep.
Me estoy quedando dormido.

to **fall off** VERB
caerse de
He's going to fall off the wall.
Se va a caer del muro.

false ADJECTIVE
falso masc
falsa fem

True or false?
¿Verdadero o falso?

family NOUN
la **familia** *fem*
my family
mi familia
the whole family
toda la
familia

the Crooks family
la familia Crooks

famous ADJECTIVE
famoso *masc*
famosa *fem*

fan NOUN
1 el **ventilador** *masc (electric)*
2 el **abanico** *masc (hand-held)*
3 el/la **hincha** *masc/fem*
(enthusiast)
football fans
los hinchas de fútbol

to **fancy** VERB
Do you fancy an ice cream?
¿Te apetece un helado?
I fancy watching a film.
Me apetece ver una película.
I fancy that girl.
Me gusta esa chica.

fantastic ADJECTIVE
fantástico *masc*
fantástica *fem*

far ADVERB

1 **lejos** (distant)
It isn't very far.
No está muy lejos.
far from
lejos de
It isn't far from here.
No está lejos de aquí.

Is it far?
¿Está lejos?
No, it isn't far.
No, no está lejos.
It's too far.
Está demasiado lejos.

2 **mucho** (much)
That's far better!
¡Eso está mucho mejor!

farm NOUN
la **granja** *fem*

farmer NOUN
el **agricultor** *masc*
la **agricultora** *fem*
He's a farmer.
Es agricultor.

Language tip
*When talking about people's jobs
in Spanish, you do not use an article.*

farmhouse NOUN
la **granja** *fem*

fashion NOUN
la **moda** *fem*
These shoes are in fashion.
Estos zapatos están de moda.

fashionable ADJECTIVE
de moda
This style is very fashionable.
Este estilo está muy de moda.
**Jane wears fashionable
clothes.**
Jane se viste a la moda.

fashion show NOUN
el **desfile de moda** *masc*

fast

fast can be an adverb or an adjective.

A ADVERB
rápido
**You
walk fast.**
Andas rápido.
B ADJECTIVE
rápido
masc

English

Spanish

a
b
c
d
e
f
g
h
i
j
k
l
m
n
o
p
q
r
s
t
u
v
w
x
y
z

rápida *fem*
a fast car
un coche rápido
fast food
la comida rápida

to **fasten** VERB
abrocharse
Fasten your seat belts, please.
Abróchense los cinturones de seguridad, por favor.

fat ADJECTIVE
gordo *masc*
gorda *fem*
They're both fat.
Los dos están gordos.

father NOUN
el **padre** *masc*
my father
mi padre
my mother and father
mis padres

Father Christmas NOUN
Papá Noel *masc*

Did you know…?
In Spain it's often **los Reyes Magos** *(the Three Kings) who bring children their presents. And instead of Christmas Eve they come on the night of the fifth of January, so children open their presents on the sixth.*

Father's Day NOUN
el **día del Padre** *masc*

fault NOUN
la **culpa** *fem*
It's your fault!
¡Es culpa tuya!
It wasn't my fault.
No fue culpa mía.

favour NOUN
el **favor** *masc*
Could you do me a favour?
¿Me podrías hacer un favor?

favourite ADJECTIVE
favorito *masc*

favorita *fem*
Blue's my favourite colour.
El azul es mi color favorito.

feather NOUN
la **pluma** *fem*

February NOUN
febrero *masc*
My birthday's the fourteenth of February.
Mi cumpleaños es el catorce de febrero.
It's the eighth of February today.
Hoy es ocho de febrero.

in February
en febrero
on the fifth of February
el cinco de febrero

Language tip
Months are not spelled with a capital letter in Spanish.

to **feed** VERB
dar de comer a
I'm going to feed the cat.
Voy a darle de comer al gato.

to **feel** VERB
encontrarse
I don't feel well.
No me encuentro bien.
I feel like …
Me apetece …
I feel like going for a walk.
Me apetece dar un paseo.
Do you feel like an ice cream?
¿Te apetece un helado?

feet PL NOUN
los **pies** *masc pl*
My feet are cold.
Tengo los pies fríos.

Language tip
In Spanish you usually use an article like **el**, **la** *or* **los**, **las** *with parts of the body.*

fell VERB ▷see **fall**

felt-tip pen NOUN
el **rotulador** *masc*
> **Can I borrow your felt-tip pens?**
> ¿Me dejas tus rotuladores?

female NOUN
la **hembra** *fem*
> **Is it a male or a female?**
> ¿Es macho o hembra?

feminine ADJECTIVE
femenino *masc*
femenina *fem*

fence NOUN
la **valla** *fem*

ferret NOUN
el **hurón** *masc* (PL los **hurones**)

ferry NOUN
el **ferry** *masc* (PL los **ferrys**)

to **fetch** VERB
ir a buscar
> **Can you fetch my bag?**
> ¿Puedes ir a buscar mi bolso?
> **Mum always fetches us from school.**
> Mamá siempre nos va a buscar al colegio.

few ADJECTIVE, PRONOUN
a few
unos pocos

> *Language tip*
>
> *Remember to change* **unos pocos** *to* **unas pocas** *when describing or referring to a feminine noun.*

> **a few hours**
> unas pocas horas

> **How many potatoes do you want? — Just a few.**
> ¿Cuántas patatas quieres? — Solo unas pocas.
> **quite a few people**
> bastante gente
> **I've got fewer sweets than Jim.**
> Tengo menos caramelos que Jim.
> **Who's got the fewest cards?**
> ¿Quién tiene menos cartas?

fiancé NOUN
el **prometido** *masc*
> **He's her fiancé.**
> Es su prometido.

fiancée NOUN
la **prometida** *fem*
> **She's his fiancée.**
> Es su prometida.

field NOUN
el **campo** *masc*
> **a football field**
> un campo de fútbol
> **a field of wheat**
> un campo de trigo

fifteen NUMBER
quince
> **fifteen euros**
> quince euros

> **I'm fifteen.**
> Tengo quince años.

> *Language tip*
>
> *In English you can say* **I'm fifteen** *or* **I'm fifteen years old**. *In Spanish you can only say* **tengo quince años**. *Have you noticed that in Spanish you need to use the verb* **tener** *to talk about somebody's age?*

fifteenth NUMBER
quince
> **on the fifteenth floor**
> en el piso quince
> **Today's the fifteenth of July.**
> Hoy es quince de julio.

My birthday's the fifteenth of August.
Mi cumpleaños es el quince de agosto.

on the fifteenth of November
el quince de noviembre

Language tip
*Use the same set of numbers that you use for counting (**uno**, **dos**, **tres** and so on) when giving Spanish dates.*

fifth NUMBER
quinto *masc*
quinta *fem*
on the fifth floor
en el quinto piso
Today's the fifth of April.
Hoy es cinco de abril.
My birthday's the fifth of March.
Mi cumpleaños es el cinco de marzo.

on the fifth of August
el cinco de agosto

Language tip
*Use the same set of numbers that you use for counting (**uno**, **dos**, **tres** and so on) when giving Spanish dates.*

fifty NUMBER
cincuenta
My aunt is fifty.
Mi tía tiene cincuenta años.

Language tip
*In English you can say **she's fifty** or **she's fifty years old**. In Spanish you can only say **tiene cincuenta años**. Have you noticed that in Spanish you need to use the verb **tener** to talk about somebody's age?*

fight

fight *can be a noun or a verb.*

A NOUN
la **pelea** *fem*
B VERB
to fight
pelearse
Two boys are fighting.
Dos niños se están peleando.

figure NOUN
la **cifra** *fem*
Shall I write it in figures or in words?
¿Lo escribo en cifras o en palabras?

file NOUN
1 la **carpeta** *fem (folder)*
Keep the leaflets in your file.
Guarda los folletos en tu carpeta.
2 el **archivo** *masc (on computer)*

to **fill** VERB
llenar

Can you fill the glass?
¿Puedes llenar la copa?

to **fill in** VERB
rellenar
You have to fill in the gaps in the sentences.
Hay que rellenar los huecos de las frases.

filling NOUN
el **empaste** *masc (in tooth)*

film NOUN
1 la **película** *fem (movie)*
Is it a good film?
¿Es una buena película?
2 el **carrete** *masc (for camera)*
I'd like to have this film developed.
Quiero revelar este carrete.

film star NOUN
la **estrella de cine** *fem*
   Eddie Murphy is a film star.
   Eddie Murphy es una estrella de cine.

final

A ADJECTIVE
último *masc*
última *fem*
   the final minutes
   los últimos minutos
B NOUN
la **final** *fem*
   The final is tomorrow.
   La final es mañana.

finally ADVERB
finalmente

to **find** VERB
encontrar
   My brother wants to find a job.
   Mi hermano quiere encontrar trabajo.

fine ADJECTIVE
bien

   That's fine, thanks.
   Eso está bien, gracias.
   How are you? — I'm fine.
   ¿Qué tal estás? — Estoy bien.

finger NOUN
el **dedo** *masc*
   my little finger
   mi dedo meñique
   My finger is hurting.
   Me duele el dedo.

fingernail NOUN
la **uña** *fem*

to **finish** VERB
terminar
   I've got to finish my homework.
   Tengo que terminar los deberes.
   I've finished!
   ¡He terminado!
   Is it finished?
   ¿Está terminado?

fire NOUN
1 el **fuego** *masc*
   You mustn't play with fire.
   No hay que jugar con el fuego.
2 el **incendio** *masc* (accidental)
   There's a fire in the wood.
   Hay un incendio en el bosque.

fire engine NOUN
el **coche de bomberos** *masc*

fire extinguisher NOUN
el **extintor** *masc*

fire fighter NOUN
el **bombero** *masc*
la **bombera** *fem*
   He's a fire fighter.
   Es bombero.

fireplace NOUN
la **chimenea** *fem*

fire station NOUN
el **parque de bomberos** *masc*

fireworks PL NOUN
los **fuegos artificiales** *masc pl*
There are fireworks this evening.
Hay fuegos artificiales esta noche.

first

> **first** *can be an adjective, noun or adverb.*

A ADJECTIVE
primero *masc*
primera *fem*
the first time
la primera vez

> ### Language tip
> Shorten **primero** to **primer** *before a masculine singular noun.*

the first day
el primer día
to come first
quedar primero
Rachel came first in the race.
Rachel quedó primera en la carrera.
Who's first?
¿Quién va primero?
Me first!
¡Yo primero!

B NOUN
at first
al principio
It's easy at first.
Es fácil al principio.
My birthday's the first of October.
Mi cumpleaños es el uno de octubre.
Today's the first of June.
Hoy es uno de junio.

> **on the first of September**
> el uno de septiembre

> ### Language tip
> Use the same set of numbers that you use for counting (**uno**, **dos**, **tres** and so on) when giving Spanish dates.

C ADVERB
primero
First write your names.
Primero escribid vuestros nombres.
first of all
en primer lugar

first aid NOUN
los **primeros auxilios** *masc pl*

first name NOUN
el **nombre de pila** *masc*

fish

> **fish** *can be a noun or a verb.*

A NOUN
1 el **pescado** *masc (as food)*
I don't like fish.
No me gusta el pescado.
2 el **pez** *masc* (PL los **peces**) *(animal)*
I caught three fish.
Pesqué tres peces.
B VERB
to go fishing
ir a pescar
Let's go fishing.
Vamos a pescar.

fish fingers PL NOUN
las **varitas de merluza** *fem pl*

fishing NOUN
la **pesca** *fem*
I like fishing.
Me gusta la pesca.

fishing boat NOUN
la **barca de pesca** *fem*

fishing rod NOUN
la **caña de pescar** *fem*

fish tank NOUN
el **acuario** *masc*

fit

> **fit** *can be a verb or an adjective.*

A VERB

to fit
caber
It doesn't fit in the kitchen.
No cabe en la cocina.
These trousers don't fit me.
Estos pantalones no me están
bien.
B ADJECTIVE
en forma (healthy)

He's fit.
Está en forma.

five NUMBER
cinco
   five euros
   cinco euros

She's five.
Tiene cinco años.

Language tip
In English you can say **she's five** or
she's five years old. In Spanish
you can only say **tiene cinco años**.
Have you noticed that in Spanish
you need to use the verb **tener** to
talk about somebody's age?

to **fix** VERB
arreglar
   Can you fix my bike?
   ¿Me puedes arreglar la bici?

fizzy ADJECTIVE
con gas
   I don't like fizzy drinks.
   No me gustan las bebidas con
   gas.

flag NOUN
la **bandera** fem

flame NOUN
la **llama** fem

flan NOUN
1 la **tarta** fem (sweet)
   a raspberry flan
   una tarta de frambuesa

Language tip
Be careful! The translation of **flan** is
not the same as **flan**.

2 el **pastel** masc (savoury)
   a cheese and onion flan
   un pastel de queso y cebolla

flannel NOUN
la **toallita** fem

flash NOUN
   a flash of lightning
   un relámpago

flask NOUN
el **termo** masc

flat

flat can be an adjective or a noun.

A ADJECTIVE
1 **plano** masc
   plana fem (level)
   a flat roof
   un tejado plano
   flat shoes
   zapatos planos
2 **pinchado** masc
   pinchada fem (tyre)
   I've got a flat tyre.
   Tengo una rueda pinchada.
B NOUN
   el **piso** masc
   She lives in a flat.
   Vive en un piso.

flavour NOUN
el **sabor** masc
   **Which flavour of ice cream
   would you like?**
   ¿De qué sabor quieres el
   helado?

a
b
c
d
e
f
g
h
i
j
k
l
m
n
o
p
q
r
s
t
u
v
w
x
y
z

fleece NOUN
el **forro polar** masc

flew VERB ▷ see **fly**

flight NOUN
el **vuelo** masc
What time is the flight to London?
¿A qué hora es el vuelo a Londres?

floor NOUN
1 el **suelo** masc (of room)
on the floor
en el suelo
Sit on the floor, Jenny.
Siéntate en el suelo, Jenny.
2 la **planta** fem (storey)
the ground floor
la planta baja
the first floor
la primera planta
on the third floor
en la tercera planta

florist NOUN
el/la **florista** masc/fem
He's a florist.
Es florista.
a florist's
una floristería

flour NOUN
la **harina** fem

flower NOUN
la **flor** fem

flu NOUN
la **gripe** fem
Nathan has got flu.
Nathan tiene gripe.

fluent ADJECTIVE
My sister speaks fluent Spanish.
Mi hermana habla español con fluidez.

flute NOUN
la **flauta** fem
I play the flute.
Toco la flauta.

to **flush** VERB
to flush the toilet
tirar de la cadena

fly

fly can be a verb or a noun.

A VERB
to fly
1 **ir en avión** (go by plane)
I'm going to fly to Florida.
Voy a ir a Florida en avión.
2 **volar** (with wings)
A bee was flying around the room.
Había una abeja volando por la habitación.
B NOUN
la **mosca** fem

fog NOUN
la **niebla** fem

foggy ADJECTIVE
a foggy day
un día de niebla

It's foggy.
Hay niebla.

to **fold** VERB
doblar
Fold the paper in half.
Dobla el papel por la mitad.

folder NOUN
la **carpeta** fem

to **follow** VERB
seguir
Follow me, Kevin.
Sígueme, Kevin.

following ADJECTIVE
siguiente masc & fem
the following day
el día siguiente

food NOUN
la **comida** fem
I like Spanish food.
Me gusta la comida española.
We need to buy some food.
Necesitamos comprar comida.

food processor NOUN
el **robot de cocina** *masc*

foot NOUN
el **pie** *masc*
> **My feet are hurting.**
> Me duelen los pies.

Language tip

*In Spanish you usually use an article like **el**, **la** or **los**, **las** with parts of the body.*

> **on foot**
> a pie
> **Richard is six foot tall.**
> Richard mide seis pies de altura.

football NOUN
1 el **fútbol** *masc* (game)
> **I like playing football.**
> Me gusta jugar al fútbol.
> **Do you want to play football, boys?**
> ¿Queréis jugar al fútbol, niños?

Language tip

*In Spanish, you need to add **al** or **a la** before the name of the sport.*

2 el **balón** *masc* (PL los **balones**) (ball)
> **Jason's got a new football.**
> Jason tiene un balón nuevo.

football boots PL NOUN
las **botas de fútbol** *fem pl*

footballer NOUN
el/la **futbolista** *masc/fem*
> **He's a footballer.**
> Es futbolista.

Language tip

When talking about people's jobs in Spanish, you do not use an article.

football player NOUN
el **jugador de fútbol** *masc*
la **jugadora de fútbol** *fem*
> **David Beckham is a famous football player.**
> David Beckham es un jugador de fútbol famoso.

football shirt NOUN
la **camiseta de fútbol** *fem*

footpath NOUN
el **sendero** *masc*

footstep NOUN
el **paso** *masc*

for PREPOSITION
1 **para** (intended for, destined for)
> **a present for me**
> un regalo para mí
> **the train for London**
> el tren para Londres
> **I'll do it for you.**
> Yo te lo haré.
> **What's the Spanish for 'lion'?**
> ¿Cómo se dice 'lion' en español?
> **It's time for lunch.**
> Es la hora de comer.

> **What's it for?**
> ¿Para qué es?
> **B for Barcelona**
> B de Barcelona

2 **por** (in exchange for)
> **I'll give it to you for five pounds.**
> Te lo doy por cinco libras.
> **He bought it for ten euros.**
> Lo compró por diez euros.
3 (for a period of)
> **We're going there for three weeks.**
> Vamos a pasar ahí tres semanas.

Language tip

*You can often use the verb **llevar** to talk about how long you've been doing something.*

> **I have been learning Spanish for six months.**
> Llevo seis meses aprendiendo español.

Language tip

But there are other ways of saying how long you've been doing something.

I haven't seen her for two years.
No la veo desde hace dos años.

forbidden ADJECTIVE
prohibido *masc*
prohibida *fem*
> **Smoking is forbidden.**
> Está prohibido fumar.

forecast NOUN
> **the weather forecast**
> el pronóstico del tiempo
> **What's the forecast for today?**
> ¿Cuál es el pronóstico para hoy?

forehead NOUN
la frente *fem*

foreign ADJECTIVE
extranjero *masc*
extranjera *fem*

foreigner NOUN
el **extranjero** *masc*
la **extranjera** *fem*
> **He's a foreigner.**
> Es extranjero.

forest NOUN
1 el **bosque** *masc (wood)*
2 la **selva** *fem (tropical)*

to **forget** VERB
olvidarse

> ### Language tip
> *To say* **I've forgotten …** *use* **se me ha olvidado** *when you've forgotten one thing and* **se me han olvidado** *when you've forgotten two or more things.*

> **I've forgotten his name.**
> Se me ha olvidado su nombre.
> **I've forgotten my keys.**
> Se me han olvidado las llaves.
> **Don't forget!**
> ¡Que no se te olvide!
> **to forget to do something**
> olvidarse de hacer algo
> **I forgot to post the letter.**
> Me olvidé de echar la carta.

fork NOUN
el **tenedor** *masc*

form NOUN
el **impreso** *masc*
> **You have to fill in the form.**
> Tienes que rellenar el impreso.

fortnight NOUN
> **a fortnight**
> dos semanas
> **I'm going on holiday for a fortnight.**
> Me voy dos semanas de vacaciones.

fortunately ADVERB
afortunadamente

forty NUMBER
cuarenta
> **My father is forty.**
> Mi padre tiene cuarenta años.

> ### Language tip
> *In English you can say* **he's forty** *or* **he's forty years old**. *In Spanish you can only say* **tiene cuarenta años**. *Have you noticed that in Spanish you need to use the verb* **tener** *to talk about somebody's age?*

forward ADVERB
hacia adelante
> **a step forward**
> un paso hacia adelante
> **to move forward**
> avanzar
> **Move forward two spaces.**
> Avanza dos casillas.

fought VERB ▷ *see* **fight**

found VERB ▷ *see* **find**

fountain NOUN
la **fuente** *fem*

fountain pen NOUN
la **pluma estilográfica** *fem*

four NUMBER
cuatro
> **four euros**
> cuatro euros

He's four.
Tiene cuatro años.

Language tip
*In English you can say **he's four** or **he's four years old**. In Spanish you can only say **tiene cuatro años**. Have you noticed that in Spanish you need to use the verb **tener** to talk about somebody's age?*

fourteen NUMBER
catorce
> **fourteen euros**
> catorce euros

I'm fourteen.
Tengo catorce años.

Language tip
*In English you can say **I'm fourteen** or **I'm fourteen years old**. In Spanish you can only say **tengo catorce años**. Have you noticed that in Spanish you need to use the verb **tener** to talk about somebody's age?*

fourteenth NUMBER
catorce
> **on the fourteenth floor**
> en el piso catorce
> **My birthday's the fourteenth of January.**
> Mi cumpleaños es el catorce de enero.
> **Today's the fourteenth of July.**
> Hoy es catorce de julio.

on the fourteenth of August
el catorce de agosto

Language tip
*Use the same set of numbers that you use for counting (**uno**, **dos**, **tres** and so on) when giving Spanish dates.*

fourth NUMBER
cuarto *masc*
cuarta *fem*
> **on the fourth floor**
> en el cuarto piso
> **My birthday's the fourth of December.**
> Mi cumpleaños es el cuatro de diciembre.
> **Today's the fourth of October.**
> Hoy es cuatro de octubre.

on the fourth of June
el cuatro de junio

Language tip
*Use the same set of numbers that you use for counting (**uno**, **dos**, **tres**, **cuatro** and so on) when giving Spanish dates.*

fox NOUN
el **zorro** *masc*

frame NOUN
el **marco** *masc*
> **a photo frame**
> un marco de fotos

freckles PL NOUN
las **pecas** *fem pl*

free ADJECTIVE
1 **gratis** *(free of charge)*

Language tip
***gratis** never changes its ending no matter what it describes.*

> **a free brochure**
> un folleto gratis
2 **libre** *masc & fem (not taken)*
> **Excuse me, is this seat free?**
> Perdón, ¿está libre este asiento?

freezer NOUN
el **congelador** *masc*

freezing ADJECTIVE
helado *masc*
helada *fem*
> **I'm freezing!**
> ¡Estoy helado!

English
Spanish

a
b
c
d
e
f
g
h i j k
l
m
n
o
p
q
r
s
t
u
v
w
x
y
z

406

It's absolutely freezing!
¡Hace un frío que pela!

French beans PL NOUN
las **judías verdes** *fem pl*

French fries PL NOUN
las **patatas fritas** *fem pl*

fresh ADJECTIVE
fresco *masc*
fresca *fem*
I need some fresh air.
Necesito un poco de aire fresco.

Friday NOUN
el **viernes** *masc*
It's Friday today.
Hoy es viernes.

on Friday
el viernes
on Fridays
los viernes
every Friday
todos los viernes
last Friday
el viernes pasado
next Friday
el viernes que viene

Language tip
Days are not spelled with a capital letter in Spanish.

fridge NOUN
el **frigorífico** *masc*

fried ADJECTIVE
frito *masc*
frita *fem*
a fried egg
un huevo frito

friend NOUN
el **amigo** *masc*
la **amiga** *fem*
my friend George
mi amigo George
my friend Natasha
mi amiga Natasha

friendly ADJECTIVE
simpático *masc*

simpática *fem*
She's very friendly.
Es muy simpática.

frightened ADJECTIVE
to be frightened
tener miedo
I'm not frightened.
No tengo miedo.
Alison is frightened of spiders.
A Alison le dan miedo las arañas.

I'm frightened!
¡Tengo miedo!

fringe NOUN
el **flequillo** *masc*
She's got a fringe.
Lleva flequillo.

Frisbee®
NOUN
el **disco volador** *masc*

from PREPOSITION
de
She comes from Bristol.
Es de Bristol.
a letter from my friend
una carta de mi amiga

Language tip
de *combines with* **el** *to form* **del**.

We aren't very far from the centre.
No estamos muy lejos del centro.
from ... to ...
desde ... hasta ...
from London to New York
desde Londres hasta Nueva York
the numbers from one to ten
los números del uno al diez

Where are you from?
¿De dónde eres?
I'm from Birmingham.
Soy de Birmingham.

front

front *can be a noun or an adjective.*

A NOUN
la **parte delantera** *fem*
the front of the house
la parte delantera de la casa
in front of
delante de
in front of the house
delante de la casa
B ADJECTIVE
de delante
the front row
la fila de delante

front door NOUN
la **puerta principal** *fem*

frontier NOUN
la **frontera** *fem*

frost NOUN
la **helada** *fem*

frosty ADJECTIVE
a frosty morning
una mañana de helada

It's frosty today.
Ha helado hoy.

frozen ADJECTIVE
1 **congelado** *masc*
congelada *fem (food)*
frozen peas
guisantes congelados
2 **helado** *masc*
helada *fem (lake, fingers)*
I'm frozen.
Estoy helado.

fruit NOUN
la **fruta** *fem*
I like fruit.
Me gusta la fruta.
a piece of fruit
una fruta

fruit juice NOUN
el **zumo de frutas** *masc*

fruit salad NOUN
la **macedonia** *fem*

to **fry** NOUN
freír

frying pan NOUN
la **sartén** *fem* (PL las **sartenes**)

full ADJECTIVE
lleno *masc*
llena *fem*
The bottle's full.
La botella está llena.
I'm full.
Estoy lleno.

full stop NOUN
el **punto** *masc*

fun NOUN
to have fun
pasárselo bien
Are you having fun?
¿Te lo estás pasando bien?

It's fun!
¡Es divertido!
Have fun!
¡Que te diviertas!

funfair NOUN
la **feria** *fem*

funny ADJECTIVE
divertido *masc*
divertida *fem*
It was very funny.
Fue muy divertido.

fur NOUN
1 la **piel** *fem (used in clothing)*
a fur coat
un abrigo de piel
2 el **pelo** *masc (of animal)*
the dog's fur
el pelo del perro

furious ADJECTIVE
furioso *masc*
furiosa *fem*

Dad is furious with me.
Papá está furioso conmigo.

furniture NOUN
los **muebles** *masc pl*
We've got new furniture.
Tenemos muebles nuevos.
a piece of furniture
un mueble

> **Language tip**
> *Use* **un mueble** *to refer to one piece of furniture and* **muebles** *in the plural to talk about* **furniture** *in general.*

future NOUN
el **futuro** *masc*
What are your plans for the future?
¿Qué planes tienes para el futuro?
Be more careful in future.
De ahora en adelante ten más cuidado.

a b c d e **f** g h i j k l m n o p q r s t u v w x y z

G g

game NOUN
   1 el **juego** *masc*
   Let's play a game.
   Vamos a jugar a algún juego.
   a game of chess
   una partida de ajedrez
   2 el **partido** *masc (match)*
   The game is tomorrow.
   El partido es mañana.
   a game of football
   un partido de fútbol

games PL NOUN
   la **educación física** *fem (at school)*
   I like games.
   Me gusta la educación física.

gang NOUN
   1 la **banda** *fem (of thieves, troublemakers, bullies)*
   2 la **pandilla** *fem (of friends)*

gap NOUN
   el **hueco** *masc*
   You have to fill in the gaps in the sentences.
   Hay que rellenar los huecos de las frases.

garage NOUN
   el **garaje** *masc*

garden NOUN
   el **jardín** *masc* (PL los **jardines**)
   We haven't got a garden.
   No tenemos jardín.

gardener NOUN
   el **jardinero** *masc*
   la **jardinera** *fem*

gardening NOUN
   la **jardinería** *fem*

garlic NOUN
   el **ajo** *masc*
   I don't like garlic.
   No me gusta el ajo.
   a clove of garlic
   un diente de ajo

gas NOUN
   el **gas** *masc*

gas cooker NOUN
   la **cocina de gas** *fem*

gate NOUN
   1 el **portón** *masc* (PL los **portones**) *(wooden)*
   Please close the gate.
   Por favor, cierre el portón.
   2 la **verja** *fem (metal)*
   There's a cow by the gate.
   Hay una vaca al lado de la verja.
   3 la **puerta** *fem (at airport)*
   Please go to gate seven.
   Diríjanse a la puerta siete.

gave VERB ▷ *see* **give**

GCSE NOUN
   el **Título de Graduado en Educación Secundaria** *masc*

> **Did you know...?**
> *Exams in Spain are different from those in the UK. In Spain, the qualification you can get at sixteen is the* **Título de Graduado en Educación Secundaria**.

general knowledge NOUN
   la **cultura general** *fem*
   a general knowledge quiz
   un concurso de cultura general

generous ADJECTIVE
   generoso *masc*

English Spanish

a b c d e f g h i j k l m n o p q r s t u v w x y z

generosa *fem*
> **That's very generous of you.**
> Eso es muy generoso de tu parte.

genius NOUN
> el **genio** *masc*
> **She's a genius!**
> ¡Es un genio!

> *Language tip*
> *Did you notice that you still use the masculine **un genio** even when referring to a woman or girl?*

gentleman NOUN
> el **caballero** *masc*

gents NOUN
> el **baño de caballeros** *masc*
> **Where is the 'gents', please?**
> ¿Dónde está el baño de caballeros, por favor?

geography NOUN
> la **geografía** *fem*
> **I like geography.**
> Me gusta la geografía.

gerbil NOUN
> el **gerbo** *masc*

German measles NOUN
> la **rubeola** *fem*
> **He's got German measles.**
> Tiene rubeola.

to **get** VERB
> **1** **recibir** *(receive)*
> **He always gets lots of presents.**
> Siempre recibe muchos regalos.
> **What did you get for your birthday?**
> ¿Qué te regalaron para tu cumpleaños?

> **How much pocket money do you get?**
> ¿Cuánto te dan de paga?
> **I get five pounds a week.**
> Me dan cinco libras a la semana.
> **2** **comprar** *(buy)*
> **Can you get me a smoothie?**
> ¿Me puedes comprar un batido?
> **Mum's getting me a PlayStation.**
> Mamá me va a comprar una play.
> **3** **conseguir** *(obtain)*
> **We couldn't get any tickets for the match.**
> No logramos conseguir entradas para el partido.
> **4** **ir a buscar** *(fetch)*
> **I'll get my coat.**
> Voy a buscar el abrigo.
> **5** **llegar** *(arrive)*
> **How do you get to the castle, please?**
> ¿Cómo se llega al castillo, por favor?
> **What time do we get there?**
> ¿A qué hora llegamos allí?
> **6** **to have got** ▷ *see* **got**

to **get away** VERB
> **escaparse**
> **Quick! He's getting away!**
> ¡Rápido! ¡Que se escapa!

to **get back** VERB
> **volver**
> **What time will you get back?**
> ¿A qué hora volverás?

to **get in** VERB
> **entrar**
> **Get in, boys!**
> ¡Entrad, chicos!
> **Get in the car, Ruth.**
> Entra en el coche, Ruth.

to **get off** VERB
> **bajarse de**
> **Where do we get off the train?**
> ¿Dónde nos bajamos del tren?

to **get on** VERB
1 **subirse a** (bus, train)
I get on the bus at the station.
Me subo al autobús en la estación.
2 **montarse en** (bike)
I got on my bike.
Me monté en mi bici.

How are you getting on?
¿Cómo te va?

to **get out** VERB
1 **salir** (of room, building, car)
Get out!
¡Salid!
2 **sacar** (book, object)
Get your book out, Darren.
Saca tu libro, Darren.

to **get up** VERB
levantarse
What time do you get up?
¿A qué hora te levantas?
I get up early.
Me levanto temprano.

ghost NOUN
el **fantasma** masc

Language tip
Even though it ends in -a, el fantasma is a masculine noun.

giant NOUN
el **gigante** masc
la **giganta** fem

gift NOUN
el **regalo** masc
Christmas gifts
regalos de Navidad

gift shop NOUN
la **tienda de regalos** fem

gigantic ADJECTIVE
gigantesco masc
gigantesca fem

ginger ADJECTIVE
I've got ginger hair.
Soy pelirrojo.

Language tip
*If you're a girl, say **soy pelirroja** instead.*

giraffe NOUN
la **jirafa** fem

girl NOUN
1 la **niña** fem (young)
a five-year-old girl
una niña de cinco años
2 la **chica** fem (older)
a sixteen-year-old girl
una chica de dieciséis años

girlfriend NOUN
la **novia** fem
She's his girlfriend.
Es su novia.

to **give** VERB
1 **dar**
Give me the book, please.
Dame el libro, por favor.
Give the books to Lisa.
Dale los libros a Lisa.
2 **regalar** (as gift)
What are you giving Charlie?
¿Qué le vas a regalar a Charlie?
My parents gave me a bike.
Mis padres me regalaron una bici.

to **give out** VERB
repartir
Will you give out the books, please, Mike?
¿Quieres repartir los libros, por favor, Mike?

given VERB ▷see **give**

English
Spanish

a
b
c
d
e
f
g
h
i
j
k
l
m
n
o
p
q
r
s
t
u
v
w
x
y
z

English Spanish

a b c d e f **g** h i j k l m n o p q r s t u v w x y z

glad ADJECTIVE
contento *masc*
contenta *fem*
> **She's glad she's won.**
> Está contenta de haber ganado.

glass NOUN
1 el **vaso** *masc (beaker)*
> **I'd like a glass of milk.**
> Quiero un vaso de leche.
2 la **copa** *fem (with stem)*
> **a glass of wine**
> una copa de vino
3 el **vidrio** *masc (material)*

glasses PL NOUN
las **gafas** *fem pl*

> **I wear glasses.**
> Llevo gafas.

globe NOUN
el **globo terráqueo** *masc*
> **We've got a globe in the classroom.**
> Tenemos un globo terráqueo en la clase.

glove NOUN
el **guante** *masc*
> **a pair of gloves**
> unos guantes

glue NOUN
el **pegamento** *masc*

go

> **go** *can be a noun or a verb.*

A NOUN
> **It's my go.**
> Me toca a mí.
> **Whose go is it?**
> ¿A quién le toca?
B VERB
> **to go**
> **ir**

> **I don't want to go to school.**
> No quiero ir al colegio.
> **I don't go to school on Saturdays.**
> No voy al colegio los sábados.
> **Where are you going?**
> ¿Adónde vas?
> **I went to London.**
> Fui a Londres.
> **Where did you go yesterday?**
> ¿Dónde fuiste ayer?
> **He's gone.**
> Se ha ido.

> ***Language tip***
>
> *In the same way that we say* **I'm going to** *and* **we're going to** *and so on to talk about the future in English, in Spanish they use* **voy a** *and* **vamos a** *and so on.*

> **I'm going to win.**
> Voy a ganar.
> **We're going to visit our cousins on Friday.**
> Vamos a visitar a nuestros primos el viernes.
> **I'm not going to play.**
> No voy a jugar.

to **go away** VERB
irse
> **Go away!**
> ¡Vete!

to **go back** VERB
1 **retroceder** *(in game)*
> **Go back three spaces.**
> Retrocede tres casillas.
2 **volver** *(return)*
> **Go back to your seats, boys!**
> ¡Volved a vuestro sitio, chicos!
> **Let's go back to the beginning.**
> Volvamos al principio.

to **go down** VERB
bajar
> **Let's go down to the cellar.**
> Vamos a bajar al sótano.

to **go forward** VERB
avanzar

Go forward three spaces, James.
Avanza tres casillas, James.

to **go in** VERB
entrar
Let's go in.
Vamos a entrar.

to **go on** VERB
1 **seguir** (continue)
Shall I go on?
¿Sigo?
Go on, don't stop.
Sigue, no pares.
2 **pasar** (happen)
What's going on?
¿Qué está pasando?

to **go out** VERB
salir
Are you going out tonight?
¿Vas a salir esta noche?
Peter's going out with Kim.
Peter está saliendo con Kim.

to **go past** VERB
pasar por
We're going past the cathedral.
Estamos pasando por la catedral.
Go past the station and turn right.
Pasa la estación y gira a la derecha.

to **go up** VERB
subir
I'm going up to my room.
Voy a subir a mi habitación.

goal NOUN
el **gol** masc
It's a goal!
¡Es un gol!
He's scored a goal!
¡Ha marcado un gol!

goalkeeper NOUN
el **portero** masc
la **portera** fem
He's the goalkeeper.
Es el portero.

goat NOUN
la **cabra** fem

God NOUN
Dios masc

godfather NOUN
el **padrino** masc
my godfather
mi padrino

godmother NOUN
la **madrina** fem
my godmother
mi madrina

goggles PL NOUN
las **gafas de natación** fem pl (for swimming)
I've got new goggles.
Tengo unas gafas de natación nuevas.

gold

gold can be a noun or an adjective.

A NOUN
el **oro** masc
B ADJECTIVE
de oro
a gold necklace
un collar de oro

goldfish NOUN
el **pez de colores** masc (PL los peces de colores)
I've got five goldfish.
Tengo cinco peces de colores.

golf NOUN
el **golf** masc
My dad plays golf.
Mi padre juega al golf.

golf club NOUN
1 el **palo de golf** masc (stick)
2 el **club de golf** masc (place)

golf course NOUN
el **campo de golf** masc

gone VERB ▷see go

English Spanish

a
b
c
d
e
f
g
h
i
j
k
l
m
n
o
p
q
r
s
t
u
v
w
x
y
z

good ADJECTIVE
  bueno *masc*
  buena *fem*
    That's a good idea.
    Ésa es una buena idea.
    It's a very good film.
    Es una película muy buena.

> **Language tip**
>
> *Shorten* **bueno** *to* **buen** *before a masculine singular noun.*

    We've got a good teacher.
    Tenemos un buen profesor.
    Pablo's very good at English.
    Pablo es muy bueno en inglés.
    Be good, Andrew!
    ¡Pórtate bien, Andrew!

It's good.
Es bueno.
Good morning!
¡Buenos días!
Good morning everyone!
¡Buenos días a todos!
Good afternoon!
¡Buenas tardes!
Good evening!
¡Buenas tardes!/¡Buenas noches!
Good night!
¡Buenas noches!
Good luck!
¡Buena suerte!

> **Language tip**
>
> *If you want to wish someone a* **good evening** *in the early evening, use* **¡buenas tardes!** *instead of* **¡buenas noches!**

goodbye EXCLAMATION
  ¡adiós!

Good Friday NOUN
  el **Viernes Santo** *masc*

good-looking ADJECTIVE
  guapo *masc*
  guapa *fem*
    Wayne is very good-looking.
    Wayne es muy guapo.

gorgeous ADJECTIVE
1 **guapísimo** *masc*
  guapísima *fem (person)*
  Isn't she gorgeous!
  ¿Verdad que es guapísima?
2 **excelente** *masc & fem*
  (weather)
  The weather's gorgeous.
  El tiempo es excelente.

got VERB
1 **to have got**
  tener
  I've got a dog
  and two cats.
  Tengo un perro y dos gatos.

  I haven't got a mobile phone.
  No tengo móvil.
  Elaine has got fair hair.
  Elaine tiene el pelo rubio.
  How many have you got?
  ¿Cuántos tienes?

I've got a cat.
Tengo un gato.
I haven't got a dog.
No tengo perro.
Have you got a sister?
¿Tienes una hermana?
She's got long hair.
Tiene el pelo largo.

2 **to have got to**
  tener que
  I've got to go to the dentist.
  Tengo que ir al dentista.
  You've got to take a card,
  Christine.
  Tienes que coger una carta,
  Christine.
  You've got to be careful,
  children.

Tenéis que tener cuidado, niños.
3 ▷see **get**

government NOUN
el **gobierno** *masc*

grade NOUN
la **nota** *fem*
very good grades
muy buenas notas

gradually ADVERB
poco a poco

graffiti NOUN
las **pintadas** *fem pl*
There's a lot of graffiti.
Hay muchas pintadas.

gram NOUN
el **gramo** *masc*

two hundred grams of cheese
doscientos gramos de queso

grammar NOUN
la **gramática** *fem*

grandchild NOUN
el **nieto** *masc*
la **nieta** *fem*
her grandchildren
sus nietos

granddad NOUN
el **abuelo** *masc*
my granddad
mi abuelo

granddaughter NOUN
la **nieta** *fem*
He has two granddaughters.
Tiene dos nietas.

grandfather NOUN
el **abuelo** *masc*
my grandfather
mi abuelo

grandma NOUN
la **abuela** *fem*
her grandma
su abuela

grandmother NOUN
la **abuela** *fem*
his grandmother
su abuela

grandpa NOUN
el **abuelo** *masc*
my grandpa
mi abuelo

grandparents PL NOUN
los **abuelos** *masc pl*
my grandparents
mis abuelos

grandson NOUN
el **nieto** *masc*
her grandsons
sus nietos

granny NOUN
la **abuela** *fem*
my granny
mi abuela

grapefruit NOUN
el **pomelo** *masc*
I don't like grapefruit.
No me gusta el pomelo.

grapefruit juice NOUN
el **zumo de pomelo** *masc*

grapes PL NOUN
las **uvas** *fem pl*
a kilo of grapes
un kilo de uvas

grass NOUN
1 la **hierba** *fem* (plant)
2 el **césped** *masc* (lawn)
The children are playing on the grass.
Los niños están jugando en el césped.

grated ADJECTIVE
rallado *masc*
rallada *fem*

grated cheese
queso rallado

grateful ADJECTIVE
agradecido *masc*
agradecida *fem*
> **We're very grateful.**
> Le estamos muy agradecidos.

gravy NOUN
> **I'd like some gravy.**
> Quiero un poco de jugo de carne.

great ADJECTIVE
estupendo *masc*
estupenda *fem*
> **We're going to New York. — Great!**
> Vamos a ir a Nueva York. — ¡Estupendo!

> **That's great!**
> ¡Eso es estupendo!

Great Britain NOUN
Gran Bretaña *fem*
> **We live in Great Britain.**
> Vivimos en Gran Bretaña.

greedy ADJECTIVE
glotón *masc* (PL **glotones**)
glotona *fem*
> **Don't be so greedy, Tina.**
> No seas tan glotona, Tina.

green

> **green** *can be an adjective or a noun.*

A ADJECTIVE
verde *masc & fem*
> **It's green.**
> Es verde.
> **I've got green eyes.**
> Tengo los ojos verdes.

> *Language tip*
> *Colour adjectives come after the noun in Spanish.*

B NOUN
el **verde** *masc*
> **Green is my favourite colour.**
> El verde es mi color favorito.

green beans PL NOUN
las **judías verdes** *fem pl*

greengrocer's NOUN
la **verdulería** *fem*

> **at the greengrocer's**
> en la verdulería

greenhouse NOUN
el **invernadero** *masc*

grew VERB ▷ *see* **grow**

grey

> **grey** *can be an adjective or a noun.*

A ADJECTIVE
gris *masc & fem*
> **It's grey.**
> Es gris.
> **a grey skirt**
> una falda gris
> **She's got grey hair.**
> Tiene el pelo gris.

> *Language tip*
> *Colour adjectives come after the noun in Spanish.*

B NOUN
el **gris** *masc*
> **He's dressed in grey.**
> Va vestido de gris.

to **grin** VERB
sonreír
> **Why are you grinning like that?**
> ¿Por qué estás sonriendo de esa manera?

grocer's NOUN
la **tienda de comestibles** *fem*
> **I'm going to the grocer's.**
> Voy a la tienda de comestibles.

English
Spanish

groom NOUN
el **novio** *masc*

ground NOUN
1 el **suelo** *masc*
We sat on the ground.
Nos sentamos en el suelo.
2 la **tierra** *fem (earth)*
The ground is wet.
La tierra está mojada.
3 el **campo** *masc (sports ground)*
Where's the football ground?
¿Dónde está el campo de fútbol?

on the ground
en el suelo

ground floor NOUN
la **planta baja** *fem*
This is the ground floor.
Ésta es la planta baja.
The toilets are on the ground floor.
Los baños están en la planta baja.

on the ground floor
en la planta baja

group NOUN
el **grupo** *masc*
Get into groups of four.
Formad grupos de cuatro.

to **grow** VERB
1 **crecer** *(get bigger)*
Grass grows fast.
La hierba crece rápido.
2 **cultivar** *(gardiner)*
I'm growing a sunflower.
Estoy cultivando un girasol.

to **grow up** VERB
What do you want to be when you grow up, Sandra?
¿Qué quieres ser cuando seas mayor, Sandra?

to **growl** VERB
gruñir
My dog growls a lot.
Mi perro gruñe mucho.

grown VERB ▷*see* **grow**

grown-up NOUN
el **adulto** *masc*
la **adulta** *fem*
the grown-ups
los adultos

guard dog NOUN
el **perro guardián** *masc* (PL los perros guardianes)

guarantee NOUN
la **garantía** *fem*

to **guess** VERB
adivinar
Guess what this is!
¡Adivina lo que es esto!

guest NOUN
el **invitado** *masc*
la **invitada** *fem*
our Spanish guests
nuestros invitados españoles

guide NOUN
1 el/la **guía** *masc/fem (tourist guide)*
He works as a guide at the castle.
Trabaja de guía en el castillo.
2 la **exploradora** *fem (girl guide)*

guidebook NOUN
la **guía** *fem*

guide dog NOUN
el **perro guía** *masc*

guinea pig NOUN
el **conejillo de Indias** *masc*
I've got a guinea pig.
Tengo un conejillo de Indias.

guitar NOUN
la **guitarra** *fem*
I play the guitar.
Toco la guitarra.

gun NOUN
la **pistola** *fem*

417

a
b
c
d
e
f
g
h
i
j
k
l
m
n
o
p
q
r
s
t
u
v
w
x
y
z

guy NOUN
you guys
vosotros
What do you guys think?
¿Vosotros qué pensáis?
Hurry up you guys!
¡Vamos chicos, daos prisa!

gym NOUN
1 la **gimnasia** *fem (school subject)*
We've got gym today.
Hoy tenemos gimnasia.

2 el **gimnasio** *masc (place)*
My mum goes to the gym.
Mi madre va al gimnasio.

gymnastics NOUN
la **gimnasia** *fem*
I like gymnastics.
Me gusta la gimnasia.
I do gymnastics.
Hago gimnasia.

H h

had VERB ▷ see **have**

hadn't (= had not) ▷ see **have**

hail

> **hail** *can be a noun or a verb.*

A NOUN
el **granizo** *masc*
B VERB
to hail
granizar
It's hailing.
Está granizando.

hair NOUN
el **pelo** *masc*
He's got black hair.
Tiene el pelo negro.
My cat has long hair.
Mi gato tiene el pelo largo.
You've had your hair cut!
¡Te has cortado el pelo!
I want to wash my hair.
Quiero lavarme la cabeza.

> **Language tip**
> *In Spanish you usually use an article like el, la or los, las with parts of the body.*

hairbrush NOUN
el **cepillo** *masc*

haircut NOUN
el **corte de pelo** *masc*
That's a nice haircut!
¡Qué corte de pelo tan bonito!
to have a haircut
cortarse el pelo
I need to have a haircut.
Tengo que cortarme el pelo.

hairdresser NOUN
el **peluquero** *masc*
la **peluquera** *fem*

He's a hairdresser.
Es peluquero.

> **Language tip**
> *When talking about people's jobs in Spanish, you do not use an article.*

the hairdresser's
la peluquería
at the hairdresser's
en la peluquería

hairstyle NOUN
el **peinado** *masc*
You've got a new hairstyle.
Llevas un nuevo peinado.

half

> **half** *can be a noun, adjective or adverb.*

A NOUN
1 la **mitad** *fem (fraction)*
half of the class
la mitad de la clase
to cut something in half
cortar algo por la mitad

two and a half
dos y medio
half an hour
media hora
half past ten
las diez y media
half a kilo
medio kilo

2 el **billete para niños** *masc (ticket)*
A half to the town centre, please.
Un billete para niños para el centro, por favor.
B ADJECTIVE
medio *masc*
media *fem*

a b c d e f g **h** i j k l m n o p q r s t u v w x y z

a half portion
media ración

c ADVERB
medio
I'm half Scottish.
Soy medio escocés.

> *Language tip*
> *When you use **medio** before an adjective its ending never changes.*

half-brother NOUN
el **hermanastro** *masc*
my half-brother
mi hermanastro

half-sister NOUN
la **hermanastra** *fem*
my half-sister
mi hermanastra

half-term NOUN
las **vacaciones de mitad de trimestre** *fem*

> *Did you know…?*
> *In Spain, students don't have half-term as such. However, in winter some schools have **la semana blanca**, or 'white week' the perfect opportunity for many to take off for the ski slopes.*

half-time NOUN
el **descanso** *masc*

hall NOUN
1 el **salón de actos** *masc* (assembly hall)
2 la **entrada** *fem* (entrance hall)

Hallowe'en NOUN
la **víspera de Todos los Santos** *fem*

> *Did you know…?*
> ***Hallowe'en** is not celebrated in Spain, but All Saints' Day (1st November) is a public holiday and the day when people often visit family graves. In Latin America 1st/2nd November often means colourful and fun fiestas with skulls, skeletons, and symbols of death everywhere in honour*

of **el Día de los Muertos (The Day of the Dead** *or* **All Souls' Day).**

ham NOUN
el **jamón** *masc* (PL los **jamones**)
a ham sandwich
un sándwich de jamón de York

> *Did you know…?*
> *In Spain you'll come across two main types of ham: **jamón serrano**, which is the more expensive cured ham, and the softer **jamón de York**, also known as **jamón dulce**, which is boiled and similar to British ham.*

hamburger NOUN
la **hamburguesa** *fem*
I'd like a hamburger.
Quiero una hamburguesa.

hammer NOUN
el **martillo** *masc*

hamster NOUN
el **hámster** *masc* (PL los **hámsters**)

hand NOUN
1 la **mano** *fem* (of person)

> *Language tip*
> *Even though it ends in -**o**, **la mano** is a feminine noun.*

Put up your hand if you know the answer.
Levantad la mano si sabéis la respuesta.

> *Language tip*
> *In Spanish you usually use an article like **el**, **la** or **los**, **las** with parts of the body.*

Can you give me a hand?
¿Me puedes echar una mano?
2 la **aguja** *fem* (of clock)

to **hand in** VERB
entregar
Hand in your books.
Entregad vuestros libros.

to **hand out** VERB
repartir
> **Hand out the books, Ahmed.**
> Reparte los libros, Ahmed.

handbag NOUN
el **bolso** masc

handball NOUN
el **balonmano** masc
> **Can we play handball?**
> ¿Podemos jugar al balonmano?

> *Language tip*
> *In Spanish, you need to add **al** or*
> ***a la** before the name of the sport.*

handkerchief NOUN
el **pañuelo** masc
> **Have you got a handkerchief?**
> ¿Tienes un pañuelo?

handle NOUN
1 el **asa** fem (of cup, briefcase)

> *Language tip*
> *Even though it's a feminine noun,*
> *remember that you use **el** and **un***
> *with **asa**.*

> **the handles**
> las asas
2 el **picaporte** masc (of door)

handsome ADJECTIVE
guapo masc
guapa fem
> **Paul is very handsome.**
> Paul es muy guapo.

handwriting NOUN
la **letra** fem
> **He has nice handwriting.**
> Tiene una letra bonita.

to **hang** VERB
colgar

to **hang on** VERB
esperar
> **Hang on a minute please.**
> Espera un minuto, por favor.

hangman NOUN
el **ahorcado** masc (game)

> **to play hangman**
> jugar al ahorcado

> *Language tip*
> *In Spanish, you need to add **al** or*
> ***a la** before the name of the game.*

to **happen** VERB
pasar
> **What's happening?**
> ¿Qué está pasando?

happy ADJECTIVE
contento masc
contenta fem
> **Beatrice**
> **is happy.**
> Beatrice
> está contenta.

> **The children are happy.**
> Los niños están contentos.

Happy birthday!
¡Feliz cumpleaños!
Happy Mother's Day!
¡Feliz día de la madre!
Happy Christmas!
¡Feliz Navidad!
Happy New Year!
¡Feliz Año Nuevo!

> *Language tip*
> *Have you noticed the upside-down*
> *exclamation mark at the start of*
> *Spanish exclamations?*

harbour NOUN
el **puerto** masc

hard

> *hard can be an adjective or an*
> *adverb.*

A ADJECTIVE
1 **difícil** masc & fem (difficult)
> **This question's too hard for**
> **me.**
> Esta pregunta es demasiado
> difícil para mí.

English
Spanish

a
b
c
d
e
f
g
h
i
j
k
l
m
n
o
p
q
r
s
t
u
v
w
x
y
z

421

English Spanish

a b c d e f g **h** i j k l m n o p q r s t u v w x y z

422

2 duro *masc*
dura *fem (not soft)*
This chair is very hard.
Esta silla es muy dura.

B ADVERB
mucho
Diane works hard.
Diane trabaja mucho.

hard disk NOUN
el **disco duro** *masc*

hardly ADVERB
casi
hardly ever
casi nunca
hardly anything
casi nada

has VERB ▷ *see* **have**

hasn't (= **has not**) ▷ *see* **have**

hat NOUN
1 el **sombrero** *masc*
2 el **gorro** *masc (knitted)*
a woolly hat
un gorro de lana

to **hate** VERB
odiar
I hate maths.
Odio las matemáticas.

to **have** VERB
1 tener
I have a bike.
Tengo una bici.
He has blue eyes.
Tiene los ojos azules.

I've got a bike.
Tengo una bici.
He has got blue eyes.
Tiene los ojos azules.
I haven't got any pets.
No tengo mascota.
Have you got a sister? —
Yes, I have.
¿Tienes una hermana? — Sí.

Have you got any sweets? —
No, I haven't.
¿Tienes caramelos? — No.

I've got ...
Tengo ...
I haven't got
No tengo ...
Have you got...?
¿Tienes...?
Yes, I have.
Sí.
No, I haven't.
No.

2 haber *(used to form tenses)*
I have done the shopping.
He hecho las compras.
He hasn't seen it.
No lo ha visto.
They've arrived.
Han llegado.
**Have you done your
homework?** — **Yes, I have.**
¿Has hecho los deberes? — Sí.

3 tomar *(eat, drink)*
What are you going to have?
¿Qué vas a tomar?
I'll have a white coffee.
Voy a tomar un café con leche.
**What time do you have
breakfast?**
¿A qué hora desayunas?

4 to have a shower
ducharse
I have a shower every day.
Me ducho todos los días.

5 to have a bath
bañarse
I'll have a bath.
Me voy a bañar.

6 to have to
tener que
You have to be careful.
Tienes que tener cuidado.
She has to do her homework.
Tiene que hacer los deberes.
Do I have to?
¿Tengo que hacerlo?
You have to …
Tienes que …
You have got to …
Tienes que …

haven't (= **have not**) ▷see **have**

hay fever NOUN
la **alergia al polen** *fem*

hazelnut NOUN
la **avellana** *fem*

he PRONOUN
él
He's got a radio but I haven't.
Él tiene una radio pero yo no.

Language tip
he *isn't usually translated unless it's emphatic.*

He works in a bank.
Trabaja en un banco.

head NOUN
1 la **cabeza** *fem (of person)*
Mind your head!
¡Cuidado con la cabeza!

Language tip
In Spanish you usually use an article like **el**, **la** *or* **los**, **las** *with parts of the body.*

Heads or tails? — Heads.
¿Cara o cruz? — Cara.
2 el **director** *masc*
la **directora** *fem (headteacher)*

headache NOUN
I've got a headache.
Me duele la cabeza.

headmaster NOUN
el **director** *masc*

headmistress NOUN
la **directora** *fem*

head teacher NOUN
el **director** *masc*
la **directora** *fem*

health NOUN
la **salud** *fem*

healthy ADJECTIVE
sano *masc*
sana *fem*
a healthy diet
una dieta sana

to **hear** VERB
oír
I can't hear.
No oigo.
I can't hear you.
No te oigo.
Can you hear the difference?
¿Notas la diferencia al oírlo?

heart NOUN
el **corazón** *masc* (PL los **corazones**)
the ace of hearts
el as de corazones

heat NOUN
el **calor** *masc*

heater NOUN
la **estufa** *fem*
an electric heater
una estufa eléctrica

heavy ADJECTIVE
pesado *masc*
pesada *fem*
This bag's very heavy.
Esta bolsa es muy pesada.

he'd
1 (= **he had**) ▷see **have**
2 (= **he would**) ▷see **would**

hedgehog NOUN
el **erizo** *masc*

English Spanish

a
b
c
d
e
f
g
h
i
j
k
l
m
n
o
p
q
r
s
t
u
v
w
x
y
z

heel NOUN
1 el **tacón** masc (PL los **tacones**) (of shoe)
high heels
tacones altos
2 el **talón** masc (PL los **talones**) (of foot, sock)

height NOUN
1 la **estatura** fem (of person)
2 la **altura** fem (of object, person)

held VERB ▷ see hold

helicopter NOUN
el **helicóptero** masc

he'll (= he will) ▷ see will

hello EXCLAMATION
¡hola!

Did you know…?
If you ring a Spanish person up, they'll probably answer the phone with **¿Dígame?** or **¿Diga?** They won't say **¡hola!**

helmet NOUN
el **casco** masc

help

help can be a verb or a noun.

A VERB
to help
ayudar
Can you help me?
¿Me puedes ayudar?
Help yourself!
¡Sírvete!

Help!
¡Socorro!

B NOUN
la **ayuda** fem
Do you need any help?
¿Necesitas ayuda?

hen NOUN
la **gallina** fem

her

her can be an adjective or a pronoun.

A ADJECTIVE
su masc & fem (PL **sus**)

Language tip
Remember to use **su** before a singular noun and **sus** before a plural one.

her name
su nombre
her house
su casa
her cats
sus gatos
her aunts
sus tías

Language tip
You usually translate **her** using **el**, **la**, etc before parts of the body or clothes, particularly when using a reflexive verb.

She took off her coat.
Se quitó el abrigo.

B PRONOUN
1 **la** (direct object)
I love her.
La quiero.
Do you know her?
¿La conoces?
Look at her!
¡Mírala!
2 **le** (indirect object)

Language tip
Use **le** when **her** means **to her**.

I gave her a book.
Le di un libro.
What did you say to her?
¿Qué le dijiste?

Language tip
Change **le** to **se** when combining it with a direct object pronoun like **lo**.

I'll tell her.
Se lo diré.

We've already handed it over to her.
Ya se lo hemos entregado.

Language tip
Because *se* can mean **to him**, **to them** *and* **to you** *as well as* **to her**, *you can add* **a ella** *(to her) after the verb for clarity.*

I'm going to give it to her.
Voy a dárselo a ella.

3 ella *(after prepositions)*
It's for her.
Es para ella.
He's next to her.
Está al lado de ella.

Language tip
Use **ella** *in comparisons.*

I'm older than her.
Soy mayor que ella.

Language tip
Use **ella** *after the verb* **ser**.

It must be her.
Debe de ser ella.
It's her.
Es ella.

here ADVERB
aquí
I live here.
Yo vivo aquí.
Here he is!
¡Aquí está!
Here's Helen.
Aquí está Helen.
Here are the books.
Aquí tienes los libros.

hers PRONOUN
el **suyo** *masc*
la **suya** *fem*

Language tip
Because **suyo** *can also mean* **his**, **theirs**, *and* **yours**, *you can avoid confusion by using* **de ella** *instead.*

That's not Mandy's coat. Hers is here.
Aquél no es el abrigo de Mandy. El suyo está aquí.
Those aren't Marian's boots. Hers are here.
Aquéllas no son las botas de Marian. Las suyas están aquí.

Language tip
After **ser** *you can usually just use* **suyo**, **suya**, **suyos** *or* **suyas** *to agree with the noun referred to.*

Is this hers?
¿Es suyo esto?
These boots are hers.
Estas botas son suyas.
Whose is this? — It's hers.
¿De quién es esto? — Es suyo.

Language tip
Because **suyo** *can also mean* **his**, **theirs** *and* **yours**, *you can avoid confusion by using* **de ella** *instead.*

Whose is this? — It's hers.
¿De quién es esto? — Es de ella.

a friend of hers
un amigo suyo

herself PRONOUN
1 se *(reflexive use)*
She's hurt herself.
Se ha hecho daño.
My cat washes herself a lot.
Mi gata se lava mucho.
2 sí misma *(after preposition)*
She talked about herself.
Habló de sí misma.
3 ella misma *(for emphasis)*
She did it herself.
Lo hizo ella misma.
She lives by herself.
Ella vive sola.

by herself
sola

he's
1 (= **he is**) ▷*see* **be**
2 (= **he has**) ▷*see* **have**

hi EXCLAMATION
¡hola!

hiccups NOUN
el **hipo** masc
I've got hiccups.
Tengo hipo.

to **hide** VERB
1 **esconder**
Mum hides the biscuits.
Mamá esconde las galletas.
2 **esconderse** (hide oneself)
Hide!
¡Escóndete!
Daniel is hiding under the bed.
Daniel está escondido debajo de la cama.

hide-and-seek NOUN
el **escondite** masc
Let's play hide-and-seek!
¡Vamos a jugar al escondite!

> **Language tip**
> In Spanish, you need to add **al** or **a la** before the name of the game.

high ADJECTIVE
alto masc
alta fem
It's too high.
Es demasiado alto.
How high is Mount Everest?
¿Cuál es la altura del Everest?
The wall is two metres high.
El muro tiene dos metros de altura.

high jump NOUN
el **salto de altura** masc

high-rise NOUN
la **torre de pisos** fem
I live in a high-rise.
Vivo en una torre de pisos.

high school NOUN
el **instituto** masc

high street NOUN
la **calle principal** fem

hiking NOUN
We're going to go hiking.
Vamos a ir de excursión al campo.

hill NOUN
la **colina** fem

him PRONOUN
1 **lo** (direct object)
I love him.
Lo quiero.
Do you know him?
¿Lo conoces?
Look at him!
Míralo.

> **Language tip**
> In some parts of Spain you'll hear people using **le** instead of **lo**.

2 **le** (indirect object)

> **Language tip**
> Use **le** when **him** means **to him**.

I gave him a book.
Le di un libro.
What did you say to him?
¿Qué le dijiste?

> **Language tip**
> Change **le** to **se** when combining it with a direct object pronoun like **lo**.

I'll tell him.
Se lo diré.
We've already handed it over to him.
Ya se lo hemos entregado.

> **Language tip**
> Because **se** can mean **to her**, **to them** and **to you** as well as **to him**, you can add **a él** (to him) after the verb for clarity.

I'm going to give it to him.
Voy a dárselo a él.
3 **él**

> **Language tip**
> Use **él** after a preposition.

It's for him.
Es para él.

She's next to him.
Ella está al lado de él.

Language tip
*Use **él** in comparisons.*

I'm older than him.
Soy mayor que él.

Language tip
*Use **él** after the verb **ser**.*

It must be him.
Debe de ser él.
It's him.
Es él.

himself PRONOUN

1 **se** *(reflexive use)*
He's hurt himself.
Se ha hecho daño.
The cat is washing himself.
El gato está lavándose.

2 **sí mismo** *(after preposition)*
He talked about himself.
Habló de sí mismo.

3 **él mismo** *(for emphasis)*
He did it himself.
Lo hizo él mismo.
He lives by himself.
Vive solo.

by himself
solo

hip NOUN
la **cadera** *fem*

hippo
NOUN

el **hipopótamo** *masc*

to hire VERB
alquilar
You can hire bikes.
Se pueden alquilar bicis.

his

his *can be an adjective or a pronoun.*

A ADJECTIVE
su *masc & fem* (PL **sus**)

Language tip
*Remember to use **su** with singular nouns and **sus** with plural ones.*

his name
su nombre
his house
su casa
his cats
sus gatos
his aunts
sus tías

Language tip
*You usually translate **his** using **el**, **la**, etc before parts of the body or clothes, particularly when using a reflexive verb.*

He took off his coat.
Se quitó el abrigo.

B PRONOUN
el **suyo** *masc*
la **suya** *fem*

Language tip
*Remember that the choice of **el suyo**, **la suya**, **los suyos** or **las suyas** depends entirely on the thing or things referred to.*

That's not Mike's coat. His is here.
Aquél no es el abrigo de Mike. El suyo está aquí.
Those aren't Martin's boots. His are here.
Aquéllas no son las botas de Martin. Las suyas están aquí.

Language tip
*After **ser** you can usually just use **suyo**, **suya**, **suyos** or **suyas** to agree with the noun referred to.*

Is this his?
¿Esto es suyo?
These boots are his.
Estas botas son suyas.
Whose is this? — It's his.
¿De quién es esto? — Es suyo.

Language tip

Because **suyo** *can also mean* **hers,** **theirs** *and* **yours,** *you can avoid confusion by using* **de él** *instead.*

Whose is this? — It's his.
¿De quién es esto? — Es de él.

a friend of his
un amigo suyo

history NOUN
la **historia** *fem*
History is my favourite subject.
La historia es mi asignatura favorita.

hit

hit *can be a verb or a noun.*

A VERB
to hit
pegar
Don't hit me!
¡No me pegues!
He's hitting his brother.
Le está pegando a su hermano.

Language tip

Don't forget the personal **a** *in examples like this one.*

B NOUN
1 el **éxito** *masc (success)*
Take That's latest hit
el último éxito de Take That
2 el **acierto** *masc (on internet)*
I got a lot of hits.
Tuve muchos aciertos.

hobby NOUN
la **afición** *fem* (PL las **aficiones**)
What are your hobbies?
¿Cuáles son tus aficiones?

hockey NOUN
el **hockey** *masc*
I play hockey.
Juego al hockey.

Language tip

In Spanish, you need to add **al** *or* **a la** *before the name of the sport.*

to **hold** VERB
1 **sostener** *(hold on to)*
Can you hold the baby?
¿Puedes sostener al niño?
2 **sujetar** *(keep in position)*
Can you hold the ladder?
¿Puedes sujetar la escalera?
3 **llevar en la mano** *(carry)*
He's holding a gun.
Lleva una pistola en la mano.
Hold hands!
¡Cogeos de la mano!

to **hold on** VERB
esperar
Hold on a minute!
¡Espera un momento!

to **hold up** VERB
Hold up your hands.
Levantad las manos.

Language tip

In Spanish you usually use an article like **el,** **la** *or* **los,** **las** *with parts of the body.*

hole NOUN
el **agujero** *masc*

holiday NOUN
1 las **vacaciones** *fem pl*
our holiday in France
nuestras vacaciones en Francia
When are you going on holiday?
¿Cuándo te vas de vacaciones?
We are on holiday.
Estamos de vacaciones.
in the school holidays
durante las vacaciones escolares

on holiday
de vacaciones
the school holidays
las vacaciones escolares

2 la **fiesta** *fem (public holiday)*
Monday is a holiday.
El lunes es fiesta.

holly NOUN
  el **acebo** *masc*
home NOUN
  la **casa** *fem*
    Is Chris at home?
    ¿Está Chris en casa?
    What time do you get home?
    ¿A qué hora llegas a casa?
    I get home at five o'clock.
    Llego a casa a las cinco.
    to go home
    irse a casa
    I've got to go home.
    Tengo que irme a casa.

  at home
  en casa
  Let's go home.
  Vámonos a casa.

homesick ADJECTIVE
    I'm homesick.
    Echo de menos mi casa.

homework NOUN
  los **deberes** *masc pl*
    We have too much homework.
    Tenemos demasiados deberes.
    my geography homework
    mis deberes de geografía

honey NOUN
  la **miel** *fem*

honeymoon NOUN
  la **luna de miel** *fem*

hood NOUN
  la **capucha** *fem*

hook NOUN
  el **gancho** *masc*

hooray EXCLAMATION
  ¡hurra!

to **hop** VERB
  saltar a la pata coja
    Hop!
    ¡Salta a la pata coja!
    children hopping on one leg
    niños saltando a la pata coja

to **hope** VERB
  esperar
    I'm hoping to go to Spain.
    Espero ir a España.
    I hope that's okay.
    Espero que eso esté bien.

  I hope so.
  Espero que sí.
  I hope not.
  Espero que no.

hopeless ADJECTIVE
    I'm hopeless at maths.
    Soy un negado para las matemáticas.
    She's hopeless at biology.
    Es una negada para la biología.
    You're hopeless, Louise!
    ¡No tienes remedio, Louise!

horrible ADJECTIVE
  horrible *masc & fem*

horror film NOUN
  la **película de terror** *fem*

horse NOUN
  el **caballo** *masc*

    I can ride a horse.
    Sé montar a caballo.

hospital NOUN
  el **hospital** *masc*
    My grandmother is in hospital.
    Mi abuela está en el hospital.

hot ADJECTIVE
  1 **caliente** *masc & fem*
    a hot bath
    un baño caliente
    I'm too hot.
    Tengo mucho calor.

a
b
c
d
e
f
g
h
i
j
k
l
m
n
o
p
q
r
s
t
u
v
w
x
y
z

It's very hot today.
Hace mucho calor hoy.
The weather is hotter in Spain.
En España hace más calor.

I'm hot.
Tengo calor.
It's hot.
Hace calor.

2 picante (spicy)
a very hot curry
un curry muy picante

hot chocolate NOUN
el **chocolate caliente** masc

hot dog NOUN
el **perrito caliente** masc

hotel NOUN
el **hotel** masc
We're staying at a hotel near the beach.
Nos alojamos en un hotel cerca de la playa.

hour NOUN
la **hora** fem
an hour and ten minutes
una hora y diez minutos
an hour and a half
una hora y media

a quarter of an hour
un cuarto de hora
half an hour
media hora
two and a half hours
dos horas y media

house NOUN
la **casa** fem (building)
You've got a nice house.
Tienes una casa bonita.
Do you want to play at my house?
¿Quieres jugar en mi casa?

at my house
en mi casa

housewife NOUN
el **ama de casa** fem (PL las **amas de casa**)

Language tip

Even though it's a feminine noun, remember that you use **el** and **un** with **ama de casa**.

how ADVERB
cómo
How do you say 'apple' in Spanish?
¿Cómo se dice 'apple' en español?
How do you spell your name?
¿Cómo se escribe tu nombre?
How many...?
¿Cuántos...?
How many pupils are there in the class?
¿Cuántos alumnos hay en la clase?
How many apples are there?
¿Cuántas manzanas hay?
How much...?
¿Cuánto...?
How much sugar would you like?
¿Cuánto azúcar quieres?
How much is it?
¿Cuánto es?
How old is your brother?
¿Cuántos años tiene tu hermano?

How are you?
¿Cómo estás?
How old are you?
¿Cuántos años tienes?
How many?
¿Cuántos?
How much?
¿Cuánto?

Language tip

Don't forget the accent on question words like **cómo** and **cuántos** nor the upside-down question mark at the start of questions.

hug

hug can be a noun or a verb.

A NOUN
el **abrazo** *masc*
a big hug
un fuerte abrazo
Give me a hug.
Dame un abrazo.

Did you know...?
*Spanish speakers sometimes end letters, postcards, and emails to friends with **un abrazo** (a hug) or **un fuerte abrazo** (a big hug).*

B VERB
to hug
abrazar

huge ADJECTIVE
enorme *masc & fem*

human ADJECTIVE
humano *masc*
humana *fem*
a human being
un ser humano

hundred NOUN
a hundred
cien

Language tip
*When translating **a hundred** or **one hundred** use **cien** before words for things and people.*

a hundred euros
cien euros
a hundred students
cien estudiantes

Language tip
*Use **cien** before **mil** (thousand).*

one hundred thousand
cien mil

Language tip
*When translating **a hundred and** use **ciento**.*

one hundred and one
ciento uno
one hundred and twenty-five
ciento veinticinco

Language tip
There are special words for two hundred, three hundred and so on.

two hundred
doscientos
three hundred and fifty people
trescientas cincuenta personas
five hundred and one
quinientos uno
hundreds of people
cientos de personas

hung VERB ▷*see* **hang**

hungry ADJECTIVE
to be hungry
tener hambre
Are you hungry?
¿Tienes hambre?

I'm hungry.
Tengo hambre.
I'm not hungry.
No tengo hambre.

hunting NOUN
la **caza** *fem*
I'm against hunting.
Estoy en contra de la caza.

hurry NOUN
to be in a hurry
tener prisa
I'm in a hurry!
¡Tengo prisa!

to **hurry up** VERB
Hurry up, Paul!
¡Date prisa, Paul!
Hurry up, children!
¡Daos prisa, niños!

to **hurt** VERB
You're hurting me!
¡Me estás haciendo daño!
Have you hurt yourself?
¿Te has hecho daño?

My leg hurts.
Me duele la pierna.

Language tip
In Spanish you usually use an article like **el**, **la** *or* **los**, **las** *with parts of the body.*

That hurts.
Eso duele.

husband NOUN
el **marido** *masc*

hut NOUN
la **cabaña** *fem*

hymn NOUN
el **himno** *masc*

hyphen NOUN
el **guión** *masc* (PL los **guiones**)

I i

I PRONOUN
> **yo**
>> **He's got a bike but I haven't.**
>> Él tiene una bici pero yo no.
>> **Ann and I**
>> Ann y yo

> *Language tip*
>
> **I** *isn't usually translated before a verb unless it's emphatic.*

>> **I speak English.**
>> Hablo inglés.
>> **I play the flute.**
>> Toco la flauta.

ice NOUN
> el **hielo** *masc*

ice cream NOUN
> el **helado** *masc*
>> **Would you like an ice cream?**
>> ¿Quieres un helado?
>> **vanilla ice cream**
>> helado de vainilla

ice cube NOUN
> el **cubito de hielo** *masc*

ice lolly NOUN
> el **polo** *masc*

ice rink NOUN
> la **pista de patinaje** *fem*

ice-skating NOUN
> el **patinaje sobre hielo** *masc*
>> **an ice-skating championship**
>> un campeonato de patinaje sobre hielo
>> **I like ice-skating.**
>> Me gusta patinar sobre hielo.

ICT NOUN
> la **informática** *fem*

icy ADJECTIVE
>> **The roads are icy.**
>> Las carreteras están cubiertas de hielo.

I'd
> 1 (= **I had**) ▷ *see* **have**
> 2 (= **I would**) ▷ *see* **would**

idea NOUN
> la **idea** *fem*
>> **Good idea!**
>> ¡Buena idea!
>> **I have no idea.**
>> No tengo ni idea.

identical ADJECTIVE
> **idéntico** *masc*
> **idéntica** *fem*
>> **They're identical.**
>> Son idénticos.

idiot NOUN
> el/la **idiota** *masc/fem*

if CONJUNCTION
> **si**
>> **You can have it if you like.**
>> Te lo puedes quedar si quieres.
>> **Do you know if he's there?**
>> ¿Sabes si él está allí?
>> **if I were you**
>> yo que tú

I'll (= **I will**) ▷ *see* **will**

ill ADJECTIVE
> **enfermo** *masc*
> **enferma** *fem*
>> **Melissa is ill.**
>> Melissa está enferma.

I'm (= **I am**) ▷ *see* **be**

imagination NOUN
> la **imaginación** *fem*

to **imagine** VERB
> **imaginar**

Imagine you have lots of money.
Imagina que tienes mucho dinero.

to **imitate** VERB
imitar
   Imitate the sound.
   Imita el sonido.

immediately ADVERB
inmediatamente
   I'll do it immediately.
   Lo haré inmediatamente.

immigrant NOUN
   el/la **inmigrante** *masc/fem*

impatient ADJECTIVE
   impaciente *masc & fem*
     Don't be so impatient, Sasha.
     No seas tan impaciente, Sasha.

important ADJECTIVE
   importante *masc & fem*
     Today's an important day.
     Hoy es un día importante.

impossible ADJECTIVE
   imposible *masc & fem*
     Sorry, it's impossible.
     Lo siento, es imposible.

> **Language tip**
> *Don't forget that there's only one **s** in the Spanish word **imposible**.*

to **improve** VERB
mejorar
   You need to improve your work.
   Tienes que mejorar tu trabajo.

in

> **in** *can be a preposition or an adverb.*

A PREPOSITION
1 en
   in the house
   en la casa
   What can you see in the picture?
   ¿Qué ves en la foto?

in England
en Inglaterra
in hospital
en el hospital
in 2007
en el 2007

in London
en Londres
in Spain
en España
in English
en inglés
in Spanish
en español

2 de
   the tallest person in the family
   la persona más alta de la familia
   She's the oldest in the class.
   Ella es la mayor de la clase.
   at six o'clock in the evening
   a las seis de la tarde

   the boy in the blue shirt
   el chico de la camisa azul

B ADVERB
   He isn't in.
   No está.

inch NOUN
   la **pulgada** *fem*
     six inches
     seis pulgadas

> **Did you know…?**
> **Inches**, **feet** and **yards** *aren't used in Spain. Use* **centímetros** *(centimetres) and* **metros** *(metres) instead.*

English
Spanish

included ADJECTIVE
incluido *masc*
incluida *fem*
> **Service is not included.**
> La propina no está incluida.

including PREPOSITION

> *Language tip*
>
> **including** *is often translated by* **incluido***, which, as it's an adjective, changes to* **incluida***,* **incluidos** *or* **incluidas** *to agree with the noun that goes with it.*

> **Everybody came, including Jack.**
> Vinieron todos, incluido Jack.
> **Everybody came, including Sophie.**
> Vinieron todos, incluida Sophie.
> **There are fifteen people, not including me.**
> Hay quince personas, sin incluirme a mí.

incredible ADJECTIVE
increíble *masc & fem*
> **That's incredible!**
> ¡Eso es increíble!

indeed ADVERB
> **Thank you very much indeed!**
> ¡Muchísimas gracias!

indoor ADJECTIVE
> **an indoor swimming pool**
> una piscina cubierta

indoors ADVERB
dentro
> **She's indoors.**
> Está dentro.

inexpensive ADJECTIVE
barato *masc*
barata *fem*

> **an inexpensive hotel**
> un hotel barato

infant school NOUN
la primaria *fem*
> **He's going to start infant school.**
> Va a empezar primaria.

infection NOUN
la infección *fem* (PL las infecciones)
> **an ear infection**
> una infección de oído

information NOUN
la información *fem*
> **I need some information.**
> Necesito información.
> **information about Ireland**
> información sobre Irlanda

ingredient NOUN
el ingrediente *masc*
> **a list of ingredients**
> una lista de ingredientes

inhabitant NOUN
el/la habitante *masc/fem*

inhaler NOUN
el inhalador *masc*

initials PL NOUN
las iniciales *fem pl*
> **My initials are G-A-C.**
> Mis iniciales son G-A-C.

injection NOUN
la inyección *fem* (PL las inyecciones)

to **injure** VERB
herir
> **Was anyone injured?**
> ¿Resultó alguien herido?

injury NOUN
la herida *fem*
> **a serious injury**
> una herida grave

ink NOUN
la tinta *fem*

a b c d e f g h **i** j k l m n o p q r s t u v w x y z

435

English Spanish

a b c d e f g h i j k l m n o p q r s t u v w x y z

to **inquire** VERB
to inquire about something
informarse acerca de algo
I'm going to inquire about train times.
Voy a informarme acerca del horario de los trenes.

inquisitive ADJECTIVE
curioso masc
curiosa fem

insect NOUN
el **insecto** masc

inside

> **inside** can be an adverb or a preposition.

A ADVERB
dentro
They're inside.
Están dentro.
B PREPOSITION
dentro de
inside the house
dentro de la casa

inspector NOUN
el **inspector** masc
la **inspectora** fem

instance NOUN
for instance
por ejemplo

instantly ADVERB
al instante

instead ADVERB
instead of
en vez de
Eat fruit instead of sweets.
Come fruta en vez de caramelos.
instead of me
en mi lugar

Language tip
When talking about people's jobs in Spanish, you do not use an article.

The pool was closed so we played tennis instead.
La piscina estaba cerrada así que jugamos al tenis.
There's no apple juice. Do you want orange juice instead?
No hay zumo de manzana. ¿Quieres de naranja?

instructions PL NOUN
las **instrucciones** fem pl
Follow the instructions.
Sigue las instrucciones.

instructor NOUN
el **monitor** masc
la **monitora** fem (swimming, skiing)
She's a skiing instructor.
Es monitora de esquí.
He's a driving instructor.
Es profesor de autoescuela.

Language tip
When talking about people's jobs in Spanish, you do not use an article.

instrument NOUN
el **instrumento** masc

Do you play an instrument?
¿Tocas algún instrumento?

intelligent ADJECTIVE
inteligente masc & fem
You're very intelligent.
Eres muy inteligente.

Language tip
Don't forget that there's only one **l** in the Spanish word **inteligente**.

interest NOUN
1 el **interés** masc (PL los **intereses**)

to lose interest in something
perder el interés por algo
She shows interest in languages.
Se interesa por los idiomas.
2 la **afición** *fem* (PL las **aficiones**)
My main interest is music.
Mi mayor afición es la música.

interested ADJECTIVE
I'm not interested.
No me interesa.
I'm not interested in football.
No me interesa el fútbol.
Are you interested?
¿Te interesa?

interesting ADJECTIVE
interesante *masc & fem*
It's a very interesting story.
Es una historia muy interesante.

international ADJECTIVE
internacional *masc & fem*
an international school
un colegio internacional

internet NOUN
the internet
Internet

on the internet
en Internet

internet café NOUN
el **cibercafé** *masc*

to **interrupt** VERB
interrumpir
Don't interrupt, Anthony!
¡No interrumpas, Anthony!

interval NOUN
el **descanso** *masc*

during the interval
durante el descanso

interview NOUN
la **entrevista** *fem*

interviewer NOUN
el **entrevistador** *masc*
la **entrevistadora** *fem*

into PREPOSITION
1 **a** *(to)*
I'm going into town.
Voy a la ciudad.
Translate it into English.
Tradúcelo al inglés.
2 **en** *(in)*
He got into the car.
Se metió en el coche.
Divide into two groups.
Dividíos en dos grupos.

to **introduce** VERB
presentarse
I'd like to introduce you to Julia.
Quiero presentarte a Julia.
Can you introduce yourselves?
¿Podéis presentaros vosotros mismos?

inventor NOUN
el **inventor** *masc*
la **inventora** *fem*

invisible ADJECTIVE
invisible *masc & fem*

invitation NOUN
la **invitación** *fem* (PL las **invitaciones**)
Thank you for the invitation.
Gracias por la invitación.

to **invite** VERB
invitar
Thank you for inviting me.
Gracias por invitarme.
I'm going to invite Graham to my party.
Voy a invitar a Graham a mi fiesta.

Language tip
Don't forget the personal a in examples like this one.

iPod® NOUN
el **iPod**® *masc*

Ireland NOUN
Irlanda *fem*
I live in Ireland.
Vivo en Irlanda.
I'm from Ireland.
Soy de Irlanda.

in Ireland
en Irlanda
I'm going to Ireland.
Voy a Irlanda.

Irish

Irish can be an adjective or a noun.

A ADJECTIVE
irlandés *masc* (PL **irlandeses**)
irlandesa *fem*
I'm Irish.
Soy irlandés.
I like Irish music.
Me gusta la música irlandesa.
Irish people
los irlandeses

He's Irish.
Es irlandés.
She's Irish.
Es irlandesa.

B NOUN
el **irlandés** *masc* (language)
Do you speak Irish?
¿Hablas irlandés?

the Irish
los irlandeses

Language tip
irlandés *is not spelled with a capital letter in Spanish.*

Irishman NOUN
el **irlandés** *masc* (PL los irlandeses)

Language tip
irlandés *is not spelled with a capital letter in Spanish.*

Irishwoman NOUN
la **irlandesa** *fem*

Language tip
irlandesa *is not spelled with a capital letter in Spanish.*

iron

iron can be a noun or a verb.

A NOUN
1 el **hierro** *masc* (metal)
an iron gate
un portón de hierro
2 la **plancha** *fem* (for clothes)
B VERB
to iron
planchar
I can iron a shirt.
Sé planchar una camisa.

ironing NOUN
to do the ironing
planchar

irritating ADJECTIVE
irritante *masc & fem*

is VERB ▷see **be**

Islam NOUN
el **Islam** *masc*

island NOUN
la **isla** *fem*

isle NOUN
the Isle of Man
la Isla de Man

the Isle of Wight
la Isla de Wight

isn't (= **is not**) ▷ see **be**

it PRONOUN
1 *(subject)*

Language tip
*When **it** is the subject of a verb, it isn't translated into Spanish.*

Where's my book? — It's on the table.
¿Dónde está mi libro? —
Está en la mesa.
Where's my notebook? — It's in your bag.
¿Dónde está mi libreta? —
Está en tu bolsa.
It's easy.
Es fácil.
It's incredible!
¡Es increíble!

It's expensive.
Es caro.
It's one o'clock.
Es la una.
It's two o'clock.
Son las dos.
It's me.
Soy yo.
It's hot.
Hace calor.

2 **lo** *masc*
la *fem (direct object)*

Language tip
*Remember to use **lo** to refer to a masculine noun and **la** to refer to a feminine one.*

There's one cake left. Do you want it?
Queda un pastel. ¿Lo quieres?
It's a good film. Have you seen it?
Es una buena película. ¿La has visto?
This is my new jumper. Do you like it?

Éste es mi jersey nuevo.
¿Te gusta?

itch VERB
picar

My arm itches.
Me pica el brazo.

Language tip
*In Spanish you usually use an article like **el**, **la** or **los**, **las** with parts of the body.*

it'd
1 (= **it had**) ▷ see **have**
2 (= **it would**) ▷ see **would**

item NOUN
el **artículo** *masc*

it'll (= **it will**) ▷ see **will**

it's
1 (= **it is**) ▷ see **be**
2 (= **it has**) ▷ see **have**

its ADJECTIVE
su *masc & fem* (PL **sus**)

Language tip
*Remember to use **su** with singular nouns and **sus** with plural ones.*

Everything is in its place.
Cada cosa está en su sitio.
This model has its disadvantages.
Este modelo tiene sus desventajas.
What's its name?
¿Cómo se llama?

itself PRONOUN
by itself
solo
She left the cat by itself.
Dejó al gato solo.

Language tip
*Don't forget the personal **a** in examples like this one.*

I've (= **I have**) ▷ see **have**

English Spanish

a
b
c
d
e
f
g
h
i
j
k
l
m
n
o
p
q
r
s
t
u
v
w
x
y
z

J j

jab NOUN
la **inyección** fem (PL las **inyecciones**)

jack NOUN
la **jota** fem
the jack of hearts
la jota de corazones

jacket NOUN
la **chaqueta** fem
a white jacket
una chaqueta blanca

jacket potato NOUN
la **patata asada con piel** fem

jail NOUN
la **cárcel** fem
in jail
en la cárcel

jam NOUN
la **mermelada** fem
strawberry jam
mermelada de fresa

jam jar NOUN
el **tarro de mermelada** masc

janitor NOUN
el/la **conserje** masc/fem
He's a janitor.
Es conserje.

> **Language tip**
> When talking about people's jobs in Spanish, you do not use an article.

January NOUN
enero masc
My birthday's in January.
Mi cumpleaños es en enero.
It's the sixth of January today.
Hoy es seis de enero.

in January
en enero
on the fifth of January
el cinco de enero

> **Language tip**
> Months are not spelled with a capital letter in Spanish.

jealous ADJECTIVE
celoso masc
celosa fem
Anne is jealous.
Anne está celosa.
She's jealous of Kate.
Le tiene envidia a Kate.

jeans PL NOUN
los **vaqueros** masc pl
I've got some new jeans.
Tengo unos vaqueros nuevos.
a pair of jeans
unos vaqueros

jelly NOUN
la **gelatina** fem

jersey NOUN
el **jersey** masc (PL los **jerseys**)

Jew NOUN
el **judío** masc
la **judía** fem

jewel NOUN
la **joya** fem

jewellery NOUN
las **joyas** fem pl

Jewish ADJECTIVE
judío masc
judía fem

He's Jewish.
Es judío.
She's Jewish.
Es judía.

English
Spanish

jigsaw NOUN
el **rompecabezas** *masc* (PL los **rompecabezas**)
I like doing jigsaws.
Me gusta hacer rompecabezas.

job NOUN
el **trabajo** *masc*
He's got an interesting job.
Tiene un trabajo interesante.
She's looking for a job.
Está buscando trabajo.

jogging NOUN
el **footing** *masc*
She goes jogging.
Hace footing.

joke NOUN
1 el **chiste** *masc* (funny story)
He told me a joke.
Me contó un chiste.
2 la **broma** *fem* (trick)
It was only a joke.
Era solo una broma.

jotter NOUN
el **bloc** *masc* (MASC PL los **blocs**)

journalist NOUN
el/la **periodista** *masc/fem*
He's a journalist.
Es periodista.

journey NOUN
el **viaje** *masc*
I don't like long journeys.
No me gustan los viajes largos.

judge

judge can be a noun or a verb.

A NOUN
el **juez** *masc*
la **jueza** *fem*
B VERB
to judge
hacer de juez en
Who's going to judge the competition?
¿Quién va a hacer de juez en el concurso?

judo NOUN
el **yudo** *masc*
I do judo.
Hago yudo.

juggler NOUN
el/la **malabarista** *masc/fem*

juice NOUN
el **zumo** *masc*
I'd like some orange juice.
Quiero zumo de naranja.

July NOUN
julio *masc*
My birthday is in July.
Mi cumpleaños es en julio.
It's the fourth of July today.
Hoy es cuatro de julio.

in July
en julio
on the fourteenth of July
el catorce de julio

441

to **jump** VERB
saltar
>**Jump!**
>¡Salta!

jumper NOUN
>el **jersey** *masc* (PL los **jerseys**)
>**a dark green jumper**
>un jersey verde oscuro

June NOUN
>**junio** *masc*
>**My birthday is in June.**
>Mi cumpleaños es en junio.
>**It's the eighteenth of June today.**
>Hoy es dieciocho de junio.

>**in June**
>en junio
>**on the fourth of June**
>el cuatro de junio

junior NOUN
>**the juniors**
>los alumnos de los primeros cursos

junior school NOUN
>el **colegio de primaria** *masc*

junk food NOUN
>la **comida basura** *fem*

just ADVERB
1 **justo**
>**just after Christmas**
>justo después de Navidad
>**just now**
>en este momento
>**I'm busy just now.**
>Estoy ocupada en este momento.
>**I'm just coming!**
>¡Ya voy!
2 **sólo** (*only*)
>**It's just a suggestion.**
>Es sólo una sugerencia.

>**Just a moment, please.**
>Un momento, por favor.
3 **to have just done something**
>**acabar de hacer algo**
>**I've just done it.**
>Acabo de hacerlo.
>**He's just arrived.**
>Acaba de llegar.

K k

kangaroo NOUN
el **canguro** *masc*

karaoke NOUN
el **karaoke** *masc*

karate NOUN
el **karate** *masc*
I do karate.
Hago karate.

keen ADJECTIVE
entusiasmado *masc*
entusiasmada *fem*
He's not very keen.
No está muy entusiasmado.
I'm very keen on football.
Me gusta mucho el fútbol.
I'm not very keen on spinach.
No me gustan mucho las
espinacas.

> ### Language tip
> Remember that you use **me gusta…**
> to say that you're keen on one thing
> and **me gustan…** to say that you're
> keen on two or more things.

to **keep** VERB
1 quedarse con *(have)*
You can keep it.
Puedes quedarte con él.
Keep the receipt.
Quédate con el recibo.
2 quedarse *(stay)*
Keep still!
¡Quédate quieto!
Keep quiet!
¡Estaros callados!

to **keep on** VERB
seguir

Keep on singing.
Seguid cantando.

keep-fit NOUN
la **gimnasia** *fem*
**The keep-fit class is on
Tuesday.**
La clase de gimnasia es el
martes.

kept VERB ▷ *see* **keep**

kettle NOUN
el **hervidor** *masc*

key NOUN
la **llave** *fem*
Where are my keys?
¿Dónde están mis llaves?

keyboard NOUN
el **teclado** *masc*

kick

> **kick** *can be a noun or a verb.*

A NOUN
la **patada** *fem*
B VERB
to kick
dar una patada a
He kicked me!
¡Me dio una patada!
Kick the ball.
Dale una patada al balón.

kid NOUN
el **niño** *masc*
la **niña** *fem (child)*
the kids
los niños

to **kill** VERB
matar
My cat kills birds.
Mi gato mata pájaros.

English **Spanish**

a
b
c
d
e
f
g
h
i
j
k
l
m
n
o
p
q
r
s
t
u
v
w
x
y
z

kilo NOUN
el **kilo** *masc*
two euros a kilo
dos euros el kilo

kilometre NOUN
el **kilómetro** *masc*

kilt NOUN
la **falda escocesa** *fem*

kind

kind *can be an adjective or a noun.*

A ADJECTIVE
amable *masc & fem*
She's a kind lady.
Es una señora amable.
That's very kind of you.
Es muy amable de tu parte.
B NOUN
el **tipo** *masc*
It's a kind of sausage.
Es un tipo de salchicha.

kindergarten NOUN
el **jardín de infancia** *masc* (PL
los **jardines de infancia**)

king NOUN
el **rey** *masc*
the king of hearts
el rey de corazones
the king and queen
los reyes

kiss

kiss *can be a noun or a verb.*

A NOUN
el **beso** *masc*
Give me a kiss.
Dame un beso.

Did you know…?
Did you know that Spanish speakers sometimes end emails, postcards, and letters to friends with **un beso** *(a kiss) or* **besos** *(kisses)?*

B VERB
to kiss
besar

Kiss me.
Bésame.

kit NOUN
el **equipo** *masc*
Don't forget your gym kit.
Que no se te olvide el equipo de gimnasia.

kitchen NOUN
la **cocina** *fem*
She's in the kitchen.
Está en
la cocina.

kite NOUN
la **cometa** *fem*

kitten NOUN
el **gatito** *masc*
la **gatita** *fem*

knee NOUN
la **rodilla** *fem*

to **kneel** VERB
arrodillarse

knew VERB ▷*see* **know**

knickers PL NOUN
las **bragas** *fem pl*
Your knickers are showing!
¡Se te ven las bragas!
a pair of knickers
unas bragas

knife NOUN
el **cuchillo** *masc*

to **knit** VERB
hacer punto
I can knit.
Sé hacer punto.
She's knitting a scarf.
Se está haciendo una bufanda de punto.

knives PL NOUN
los **cuchillos** *masc pl*
knives, forks and spoons
cuchillos, tenedores y cucharas

knob NOUN
1 el **pomo** *masc* (on door)

2 el **botón** *masc* (PL los **botones**)
(*on radio, TV*)

to **knock** VERB
llamar
> **Someone's knocking at the door.**
> Alguien está llamando a la puerta.

to **know** VERB

1 **saber** (*fact*)
> **It's a long way. — Yes, I know.**
> Está lejos. — Sí, ya lo sé.
> **Who knows the answer?**
> ¿Quién sabe la respuesta?

I don't know.
No lo sé.

2 **conocer** (*person, place*)
> **I know her.**
> La conozco.
> **I don't know him.**
> No lo conozco.

> **Do you know Tom?**
> ¿Conoces a Tom?
> **I know Madrid well.**
> Conozco bien Madrid.

knowledge NOUN
el **conocimiento** *masc*

Koran NOUN
el **Corán** *masc*

Ll

label NOUN
la **etiqueta** *fem*

lace NOUN
el **cordón** *masc* (PL los **cordones**)
(of shoe)
Tie your laces.
Átate los cordones.

> **Language tip**
> In Spanish you usually use an article
> like **el**, **la** or **los**, **las** with clothes
> you are wearing.

ladder NOUN
la **escalera de mano** *fem*

lady NOUN
la **señora** *fem*
an old lady
una señora
mayor
a young lady
una joven
**Ladies and
gentlemen ...**
Señoras y caballeros ...
Where is the 'ladies'?
¿Dónde está el baño de señoras?

laid VERB
▷ see **lay**

lain VERB
▷ see **lie**

lake NOUN
el **lago** *masc*

lamb NOUN
el **cordero** *masc*
a lamb chop
una chuleta de cordero

lamp NOUN
la **lámpara** *fem*

land

> **land** *can be a noun or a verb.*

A NOUN
la **tierra** *fem*
on land
en tierra
B VERB
to land
aterrizar
**The plane lands at nine
o'clock.**
El avión aterriza a las nueve.

lane NOUN
el **camino** *masc*
a country lane
un camino de campo
the fast lane
el carril de adelantamiento

language NOUN
el **idioma** *masc*
**Spanish isn't a difficult
language.**
El español no es un idioma
difícil.

> **Language tip**
> Even though it ends in **-a**, **el
> idioma** is a masculine noun.

language laboratory
NOUN
el **laboratorio de idiomas**
masc

lap NOUN
on my lap
en mi regazo

laptop NOUN
el **ordenador portátil** *masc*

large ADJECTIVE
grande *masc & fem*
a large house
una casa grande
a large dog
un perro grande

> **Language tip**
> **grande** *normally follows the noun when it means 'large'. However, when it does go before a singular noun, it is shortened to* **gran**.
>
> **a large number of people**
> un gran número de personas

> **Language tip**
> *Be careful! The translation of* **large** *is not* **largo**.

last

> **last** *can be an adjective or an adverb.*

A ADJECTIVE
  último *masc*
  última *fem*
    the last time
    la última vez
    He arrived last night.
    Llegó anoche.
    We've got here at last!
    ¡Por fin hemos llegado!

> **last Friday**
> el viernes pasado
> **last week**
> la semana pasada
> **last year**
> el año pasado
> **last night**
> anoche
> **at last**
> por fin

B ADVERB
  en último lugar *(in last place)*
  He always comes last.
  Siempre llega en último lugar.
  I've lost my bag. — When did you last see it?
  He perdido el bolso. — ¿Cuándo lo viste por última vez?

late ADVERB, ADJECTIVE
  tarde
    I go to bed late.
    Me acuesto tarde.
    to be late

llegar tarde
You're going to be late!
¡Vas a llegar tarde!
Sorry I'm late!
¡Siento llegar tarde!
I'm late for school.
Voy tarde para el colegio.

later ADVERB
  más tarde
    I'll do it later.
    Lo haré más tarde.

> **See you later!**
> ¡Hasta luego!

latest ADJECTIVE
  último *masc*
  última *fem*
    their latest album
    su último álbum

Latin NOUN
  el **latín** *masc*
    I do Latin.
    Hago latín.

to laugh VERB
  reírse
    Why are you laughing?
    ¿Por qué os reís?

lawn NOUN
  el **césped** *masc*

lawnmower NOUN
  la **cortadora de césped** *fem*

lawyer NOUN
  el **abogado** *masc*
  la **abogada** *fem*
    My mother's a lawyer.
    Mi madre es abogada.

> **Language tip**
> *When talking about people's jobs in Spanish, you do not use an article.*

to lay VERB
  1 poner
    Lay your cards on the table.
    Pon tus cartas sobre la mesa.
    to lay the table
    poner la mesa

It's Sylvia's turn to lay the table.
Le toca a Sylvia poner la mesa.
2 ▷ see **lie**

lazy ADJECTIVE
vago *masc*
vaga *fem*
My sister is very lazy.
Mi hermana es muy vaga.

lead

> **lead** *can be a noun or a verb.*

A NOUN
1 to be in the lead
ir en cabeza
Our team is in the lead.
Nuestro equipo va en cabeza.
2 el **cable** *masc (cable)*
3 la **correa** *fem (of dog)*
B VERB
to lead
llevar
This street leads to the station.
Esta calle lleva a la estación.

leaf NOUN
la **hoja** *fem*

to **lean out** VERB
asomarse
Don't lean out of the window.
No te asomes a la ventana.

to **lean over** VERB
inclinarse
Don't lean over too far.
No te inclines demasiado.

leap year NOUN
el **año bisiesto** *masc*

to **learn** VERB
aprender
I'm learning Spanish.
Estoy aprendiendo español.
I'm learning to ski.
Estoy aprendiendo a esquiar.

least ADVERB, ADJECTIVE, PRONOUN
menos

> **Language tip**
> **menos** *never changes its ending.*

the least expensive hotel
el hotel menos caro
the least expensive camera
la cámara menos cara
the least expensive hotels
los hoteles menos caros
Who's got the least money?
¿Quién tiene menos dinero?
It will cost at least two hundred pounds.
Costará al menos doscientas libras.

at least
al menos

leather NOUN
el **cuero** *masc*
It's made of leather.
Es de cuero.
a black leather jacket
una chaqueta de cuero negra

to **leave** VERB
1 **dejar** *(object)*
Don't leave your bag in the car.
No dejes el bolso en el coche.
I've left my book at home.
Me he dejado el libro en casa.
2 **salir** *(depart)*
The bus leaves at eight.
El autobús sale a las ocho.
3 **irse** *(go away)*
He's already left.
Ya se ha ido.

leaves PL NOUN
las **hojas** *fem pl*

led VERB ▷ see **lead**

leek NOUN
el **puerro** *masc*

left

> **left** *can be an adjective, adverb, noun or verb.*

A ADJECTIVE

1 **izquierdo** *masc*
izquierda *fem (not right)*
Stretch out your left arm.
Estira el brazo izquierdo.
on the left side of the road
en el lado izquierdo de la calle

2 *(remaining)*
I've got fifteen euros left.
Me quedan quince euros.
How many cards have you got left?
¿Cuántas cartas te quedan?
I haven't got any money left.
No me queda dinero.

B ADVERB
a la izquierda
Turn left.
Gira a la izquierda.
Take the next left.
Toma la siguiente a la izquierda.

C NOUN
la **izquierda** *fem*
It's on the left.
Está a la izquierda.
the house on the left
la casa de la izquierda

D VERB ▷ *see* **leave**

left-hand ADJECTIVE
the left-hand side
la izquierda
It's on the left-hand side.
Está a la izquierda.

left-handed ADJECTIVE
zurdo *masc*
zurda *fem*
Tina is left-handed.
Tina es zurda.

left-luggage office NOUN
la **consigna** *fem*

leftovers PL NOUN
las **sobras** *fem pl*

leg NOUN
1 la **pierna** *fem (of person)*
She has a broken leg.
Tiene una pierna rota.

I've hurt my leg.
Me he hecho daño en la pierna.

> *Language tip*
> In Spanish you usually use an article like **el**, **la** or **los**, **las** with parts of the body.

2 la **pata** *fem (of animal, table)*
It's got a wobbly leg.
Tiene una pata que cojea.
a chicken leg
un muslo de pollo

leggings PL NOUN
las **mallas** *fem pl*

leisure centre NOUN
el **polideportivo** *masc*

lemon NOUN
el **limón** *masc*
(PL los **limones**)

lemonade NOUN
la **gaseosa** *fem*

to **lend** VERB
dejar
Can you lend me a pencil?
¿Me puedes dejar un lápiz?

less ADJECTIVE, ADVERB, PRONOUN
menos

> *Language tip*
> **menos** never changes its ending.

Less noise, please!
¡Menos ruido, por favor!
A bit less, please.
Un poco menos, por favor.

> *Language tip*
> You normally translate **less than** *as* **menos que**.

I've got less than him!
¡Tengo menos que él!
I'm less nervous than I was.
Ahora estoy menos nervioso que antes.

Language tip
Use **menos de** instead before numbers.

It costs **less than** ten euros.
Cuesta menos de diez euros.

lesson NOUN
1 la **clase** fem
una clase de inglés
an English lesson
Each lesson lasts forty minutes.
Cada clase dura cuarenta minutos.
2 la **lección** fem (PL las **lecciones**) (in book)

to **let** VERB
1 **dejar** (allow)
Let me see.
Déjame ver.
Let me go!
¡Suéltame!
I'll let you know.
Ya te lo diré.
2 (in suggestions)

Language tip
let's ... is often translated by **vamos a ...** when making a suggestion.

Let's send him an email!
¡Vamos a enviarle un e-mail!

Language tip
vamos is also used to mean **let's go**.

Let's go to the park!
¡Vamos al parque!

Language tip
Alternatively you can make suggestions using **¿por qué no...?**, which literally means 'why not...?'.

Let's send him an email!
¿Por qué no le enviamos un e-mail?
Let's go to the park!
¿Por qué no vamos al parque?

Let's go!
¡Vamos!

Let's start now!
¡Vamos a empezar ahora!

letter NOUN
1 la **carta** fem (note)
I'm writing a letter to my friend.
Le estoy escribiendo una carta a mi amigo.
2 la **letra** fem (of alphabet)
It's a five-letter word.
Es una palabra de cinco letras.

letterbox NOUN
el **buzón** masc (PL los **buzones**)

Did you know...?
In Spain **letterboxes** tend to be metal boxes in which the postman leaves mail rather than the hole in the door that is common in the UK.

lettuce NOUN
la **lechuga** fem

level NOUN
el **nivel** masc

liar NOUN
el **mentiroso** masc
la **mentirosa** fem

library NOUN
la **biblioteca** fem

Language tip
Be careful! The translation of **library** is not **librería**.

licence NOUN
el **permiso** masc
a fishing licence
un permiso de pesca
a driving licence
un carnet de conducir

to **lick** VERB
lamer
The dog is licking me.
El perro me está lamiendo.

lid NOUN
la **tapa** *fem*

to **lie**

lie can be a verb or a noun.

A VERB
1 **mentir** *(tell lies)*
She's lying.
Está mintiendo.
2 **estar tumbado** *(lie down)*
He is lying on the sofa.
Está tumbado en el sofá.
B NOUN
la **mentira** *fem*
That's a lie!
¡Eso es mentira!

life NOUN
la **vida** *fem*

life jacket NOUN
el **chaleco salvavidas** *masc*
(PL los **chalecos salvavidas**)

lift

lift can be a verb or a noun.

A VERB
to lift
levantar
It's too heavy, I can't lift it.
Pesa demasiado, no puedo
levantarlo.
B NOUN
1 el **ascensor** *masc (to another
floor)*
The lift isn't working.
El ascensor no funciona.
2 *(in car)*
**Can you give me a lift to the
station?**
¿Me puedes llevar a la estación?

light

*light can be an adjective, noun or
verb.*

A ADJECTIVE
1 **ligero** *masc*
ligera *fem (in weight)*
as light as a feather
tan ligero como una pluma
2 **claro** *masc*
clara *fem (in colour)*
light blue socks
calcetines azul claro

Language tip

*When you describe something as
light blue, **light green** and so on,
neither the colour nor **claro** changes
its ending to agree with the noun.*

some light green curtains
unas cortinas verde claro
B NOUN
la **luz** *fem* (PL las **luces**)
Switch on the light.
Enciende la luz.
Switch off the light.
Apaga la luz.
Turn right at the lights.
Gira a la derecha al llegar al
semáforo.
C VERB
to light
encender
Let's light the fire.
Vamos a encender
el fuego.

light bulb
NOUN
la **bombilla**
fem

lighter NOUN
el **mechero** *masc*

lighthouse NOUN
el **faro** *masc*

lightning NOUN
los **relámpagos** *masc pl*
**There was thunder and
lightning.**
Había truenos y relámpagos.
a flash of lightning
un relámpago

like

> **like** *can be a verb or a preposition.*

A VERB
  to like
1 I like ...
  Me gusta .../Me gustan ...

> *Language tip*
>
> *Remember that you use* **me gusta**
> *... to say you like one thing and* **me**
> **gustan** *... to say you like two or*
> *more things.*

  I like milk.
  Me gusta la leche.
  I don't like riding.
  No me gusta montar a caballo.
  I like cherries.
  Me gustan las cerezas.
  I don't like grapes.
  No me gustan las uvas.
  Do you like coffee?
  ¿Te gusta el café?
  Do you like sweets?
  ¿Te gustan los caramelos?
  I like Paul.
  Paul me cae bien.
2 **querer** *(want)*
  Yes, if you like.
  Sí, si quieres.
  I'd like an orange juice,
  please.
  Quiero un zumo de naranja,
  por favor.
  I'd like some chips.
  Quiero patatas fritas.
  What would you like for
  breakfast?
  ¿Qué quieres desayunar?
  Would you like to go for a
  walk?
  ¿Quieres ir a dar un paseo?
  What would you like, Madam?
  ¿Qué desea, señora?

> **I'd like ...**
> Quiero ...

B PREPOSITION
  como

  a city like London
  una ciudad como Londres
  I look like my brother.
  Me parezco a mi hermano.
  What's Madrid like?
  ¿Cómo es Madrid?
  What's the weather like?
  ¿Cómo está el tiempo?
  like this
  así

likely ADJECTIVE
  probable *masc & fem*
    That's not very likely.
    Eso no es muy probable.

line NOUN
  la **línea** *fem*
    a straight line
    una línea recta

lion NOUN
  el **león** *masc*
  (PL los
  leones)

lip NOUN
  el **labio** *masc*

lipstick NOUN
  la **barra de**
  labios *fem*

liquid NOUN
  el **líquido** *masc*

list

> **list** *can be a noun or a verb.*

A NOUN
  la **lista** *fem*
    a shopping list
    una lista de la compra
B VERB
  to list
  hacer una lista de
  List your hobbies.
  Haz una lista de tus aficiones.

to **listen** VERB
escuchar
  Are you listening, Sonia?
  ¿Estás escuchando, Sonia?

to listen to something
escuchar algo
Listen to this, everybody!
¡Escuchad todos esto!

Listen to me, children!
¡Escuchadme, niños!

Language tip
Have you noticed that in Spanish you don't need a preposition after the verb **escuchar**?

litre NOUN
el **litro** *masc*

litter NOUN
la **basura** *fem*
Don't leave litter.
No dejéis basura.

litter bin
NOUN
la **papelera** *fem*

little

little *can be an adjective or a pronoun.*

A ADJECTIVE
1 **pequeño** *masc*
pequeña *fem (small)*
a little girl
una niña pequeña
2 **poco** *masc*
poca *fem (in quantity)*
We've got very little time.
Tenemos muy poco tiempo.
B PRONOUN
a little
un poco
How much would you like? —
Just a little.
¿Cuánto quieres? —
Solo un poco.
There's very little left.
Queda muy poco.

to **live** VERB
vivir
Where do you live?
¿Dónde vives?

I live here.
Vivo aquí.
I live in Edinburgh.
Vivo en Edimburgo.
I live with my grandmother.
Vivo con mi abuela.
My parents don't live together any more.
Mis padres ya no viven juntos.

living room NOUN
la **sala de estar** *fem*

lizard NOUN
la **lagartija** *fem*

load

load *can be a noun or a verb.*

A NOUN
loads of
un montón de
loads of people
un montón de gente
loads of money
un montón de dinero
B VERB
to load
cargar

loaf NOUN
a loaf of bread
un pan
two loaves of bread
dos panes
a French loaf
una barra de pan

lock

lock *can be a noun or a verb.*

A NOUN
la **cerradura** *fem*
The lock is broken.
La cerradura está rota.
B VERB
to lock
cerrar con llave
I must lock the door.
Tengo que cerrar la puerta con llave.

locker NOUN
la **taquilla** *fem*
> **Leave your books in your locker.**
> Deja los libros en la taquilla.

log NOUN
el **tronco** *masc*

to **log in** VERB
conectarse
> **I can't log in.**
> No puedo conectarme.

to **log off** VERB
desconectarse
> **I've forgotten how to log off.**
> He olvidado cómo desconectarme.

to **log on** VERB
conectarse
> **Have you logged on yet?**
> ¿Te has conectado ya?

to **log out** VERB
desconectarse
> **Please log out now.**
> Por favor, desconéctate ahora.

lollipop NOUN
el **pirulí** *masc* (PL los **pirulís**)

> ### Did you know…?
> Schools in Spain don't have **lollipop men** or **lollipop ladies** to help children cross the roads.

London NOUN
Londres *masc*
> **in London**
> en Londres
> **to London**
> a Londres
> **I'm from London.**
> Soy de Londres.

lonely ADJECTIVE
solo *masc*
sola *fem*
> **to feel lonely**
> sentirse solo
> **He feels lonely.**
> Se siente sola.

long ADJECTIVE
largo *masc*
larga *fem*
> **She's got long hair.**
> Tiene el pelo largo.
> **There's a long queue.**
> Hay una larga cola.
> **How long is the flight?**
> ¿Cuánto dura el vuelo?

> **How long does it take?**
> ¿Cuánto tiempo se tarda?
> **It takes a long time.**
> Se tarda mucho tiempo.
> **How long is it?**
> ¿Cuánto mide de largo?
> **It's two hundred metres long.**
> Mide doscientos metros de largo.

loo NOUN
el **baño** *masc*
> **Where's the loo?**
> ¿Dónde está el baño?
> **Can I go to the loo?**
> ¿Puedo ir al baño?

look

> **look** *can be a noun or a verb.*

A NOUN
> **to have a look**
> **echar un vistazo**
> **Have a look at this!**
> ¡Echa un vistazo a esto!

B VERB
to look

1 **mirar**
> **Look, children!**
> ¡Mirad, niños!
> **to look at something**
> mirar algo
> **Look at the picture.**
> Mira la foto.
> **Look at me, Simon.**
> Mírame, Simon.

2 *(seem)*
> **That cake looks nice.**
> Esa tarta tiene buena pinta.

Look!
¡Mira!
Look at the board.
Mirad a la pizarra.
Look out!
¡Cuidado!

to **look after** VERB
cuidar
   I look after my little sister.
   Cuido a mi hermana pequeña.

Language tip
*Don't forget the personal **a** in examples like this one.*

to **look for** VERB
buscar
   What are you looking for?
   ¿Qué estás buscando?
   I'm looking for my rubber.
   Estoy buscando mi goma de borrar.
   We're looking for Daniel.
   Estamos buscando a Daniel.

Language tip
*Don't forget the personal **a** in examples like this one.*

to **look up** VERB
consultar
   You'll need to look up the words in the dictionary.
   Tendrás que consultar las palabras en el diccionario.

lorry NOUN
   el **camión** *masc* (PL los camiones)

lorry driver NOUN
   el **camionero** *masc*
   la **camionera** *fem*
   He's a lorry driver.
   Es camionero.

Language tip
When talking about people's jobs in Spanish, you do not use an article.

to **lose** VERB
perder

I've lost my purse.
He perdido mi monedero.
Our team always loses.
Nuestro equipo siempre pierde.
to get lost
perderse
We got lost in the wood.
Nos perdimos en el bosque.

loser NOUN
   el **perdedor** *masc*
   la **perdedora** *fem*

lost VERB ▷see **lose**

lot NOUN
   a lot
   mucho
   She talks a lot.
   Habla mucho.
   Do you like football? — Not a lot.
   ¿Te gusta el fútbol? — No mucho.
   How many friends have you got? — A lot.
   ¿Cuántos amigos tienes? — Muchos.
   a lot of
   mucho
   We haven't got a lot of time.
   No tenemos mucho tiempo.

Language tip
*Remember to change the ending of **mucho** to agree with what it describes.*

   She's got a lot of books.
   Tiene muchos libros.
   He's got lots of experience.
   Tiene mucha experiencia.

Thanks a lot.
Muchas gracias.

lottery NOUN
   la **lotería** *fem*
   I hope I win the lottery.
   Espero que me toque la lotería.
   a lottery ticket
   un billete de lotería

loud ADJECTIVE
alto *masc*
alta *fem*
> **The television is too loud.**
> La televisión está demasiado alta.
> **Speak louder!**
> ¡Habla más alto!

lounge NOUN
el **salón** *masc* (PL los **salones**)

love

> **love** *can be a noun or a verb.*

A NOUN
> el **amor** *masc*
> **her love for animals**
> su amor por los animales
> **She's in love.**
> Está enamorada.
> **She's in love with Mike.**
> Está enamorada de Mike.
> **Give Emma my love.**
> Dale recuerdos a Emma de mi parte.
> **Love, Peter.**
> Un abrazo, Peter.

B VERB
> **to love**
1 **querer** *(person)*
> **Do you love me?**
> ¿Me quieres?
> **Everybody loves her.**
> Todos la quieren.
> **I love Roger.**
> Quiero a Roger.

> **Language tip**
> *Don't forget the personal **a** in examples like this one.*

2 *(thing)*
> **I love chocolate.**
> Me encanta el chocolate.
> **I love skiing.**
> Me encanta esquiar.
> **I love roses.**
> Me encantan las rosas.

> **Language tip**
> *Remember that you use **me encanta** ... to say you love one thing and **me encantan** ... to say you love two or more things.*

> **I love you.**
> Te quiero.
> **Love from ...**
> Un abrazo de ...

lovely ADJECTIVE
bonito *masc*
bonita *fem*
> **They've got a lovely house.**
> Tienen una casa bonita.
> **It's a lovely day.**
> Hace un día bonito.
> **Have a lovely time!**
> ¡Que lo paséis bien!

low ADJECTIVE
bajo *masc*
baja *fem*
> **a low price**
> un precio bajo

luck NOUN
la **suerte** *fem*
> **She doesn't have much luck.**
> No tiene mucha suerte.

> **Good luck!**
> ¡Buena suerte!
> **Bad luck!**
> ¡Qué mala suerte!

> **Language tip**
> *Have you noticed the upside-down exclamation mark at the start of Spanish exclamations?*

luckily ADVERB
afortunadamente

lucky ADJECTIVE
> **to be lucky**
> **tener suerte**
> **You're lucky!**
> ¡Tienes suerte!
> **Sarah is lucky, she's going to Ireland.**

Sarah tiene suerte, se va a
Irlanda.
Black cats are lucky.
Los gatos negros traen suerte.
a lucky horseshoe
una herradura de la suerte

luggage NOUN
el **equipaje** masc
Have you got any luggage?
¿Tienes equipaje?

lump NOUN
1 el **trozo** masc (piece)
a lump of cheese
un trozo de queso
2 el **chichón** masc (PL los
chichones) (bump)
**He's got a lump on his
forehead.**
Tiene un chichón en la frente.

> ### Language tip
> *In Spanish you usually use an article
> like el, la or los, las with parts of
> the body.*

lunch NOUN
la **comida** fem
Lunch is nearly ready.
La comida está casi lista.
I go home for lunch.
Voy a casa a
comer.

It's time for lunch.
Es hora de comer.
to have lunch
comer
**We have lunch at twelve
thirty.**
Comemos a las doce y media.

lying VERB ▷see **lie**

M m

machine NOUN
la **máquina** *fem*

mad ADJECTIVE
1 **loco** *masc*
  loca *fem (insane)*
  You're mad!
  ¡Estás loco!
  He's mad about football.
  Está loco por el fútbol.
  She's mad about horses.
  Le encantan los caballos.
2 **furioso** *masc*
  furiosa *fem (angry)*
  He's mad at me for losing his watch.
  Está furioso conmigo por haber perdido su reloj.

Madam NOUN
la **señora** *fem*
  Excuse me, Madam.
  Perdone, señora.

made VERB ▷*see* **make**

Madrid NOUN
Madrid *masc*
  in Madrid
  en Madrid
  to Madrid
  a Madrid
  Luis is from Madrid.
  Luis es de Madrid.

magazine NOUN
la **revista** *fem*

magic

> *magic can be an adjective or a noun.*

A ADJECTIVE
1 **mágico** *masc*
  mágica *fem*
  a magic wand
  una varita mágica

a magic trick
un truco de magia
2 **fantástico** *masc*
  fantástica *fem (brilliant)*
  It was magic!
  ¡Fue fantástico!
B NOUN
la **magia** *fem*
  by magic
  por magia

magician
NOUN

el **mago** *masc*
la **maga** *fem*

magnifying glass NOUN
la **lupa** *fem*

mail

> *mail can be a noun or a verb.*

A NOUN
el **correo** *masc*
  You've got some mail.
  Tienes correo.
  by mail
  por correo
B VERB
  to mail
  enviar un e-mail a *(email)*
  I'll mail my friend.
  Voy a enviar un e-mail a mi amigo.

main ADJECTIVE
principal *masc & fem*
  the main problem
  el problema principal
  The hotel is on the main road.
  El hotel está en la carretera principal.

major ADJECTIVE
   muy importante
   a major change
   un cambio muy importante
   a major problem
   un problema serio

Majorca NOUN
   Mallorca *fem*

make

> **make** *can be a noun or a verb.*

A NOUN
   la **marca** *fem*
   What make is that car?
   ¿De qué marca es ese coche?
B VERB
   to make
1 **hacer**
   I'm going to make a cake.
   Voy a hacer un pastel.

They are making a lot of noise.
Están haciendo mucho ruido.
He made it himself.
Lo hizo él solo.
I make my bed every morning.
Me hago la cama todas las mañanas.
Two and two make four.
Dos y dos son cuatro.
Four take away two, what does that make?
Si a cuatro le quitamos dos, ¿cuánto queda?

> **made in Spain**
> fabricado en España
> **It's made of iron.**
> Es de hierro.

2 **ganar** *(earn)*
   He makes a lot of money.
   Gana mucho dinero.

to **make up** VERB
   inventar
   You're making it up!
   ¡Te lo estás inventando!

make-up NOUN
   el **maquillaje** *masc*

male ADJECTIVE
1 **macho** *(animal)*

> *Language tip*
> **macho** *never changes its ending when it's used to describe a noun.*

   a male tortoise
   una tortuga macho
2 **varón** *masc (on forms)*
   Sex: male.
   Sexo: varón.

man NOUN
   el **hombre** *masc*
   an old man
   un hombre mayor

to **manage** VERB
   arreglárselas
   It's okay, I can manage.
   Está bien, yo me las arreglo.
   I can't manage all that.
   No puedo acabar con todo eso.
   to manage to do something
   conseguir hacer algo
   I managed to fix my bike.
   Conseguí arreglar mi bicicleta.

manager NOUN
1 el **director** *masc*
   la **directora** *fem (of company)*
2 el **encargado** *masc*
   la **encargada** *fem (of shop, restaurant)*
   I'd like to speak to the manager.
   Quiero hablar con el encargado.
3 el/la **gerente** *masc/fem (of hotel)*
4 el **entrenador** *masc*
   la **entrenadora** *fem (of team)*

English Spanish

a
b
c
d
e
f
g
h i j
k
l
m
n
o
p
q
r
s
t
u
v
w
x
y
z

manageress NOUN
  1 la **encargada** *fem (of shop, restaurant)*
  2 la **gerente** *fem (of hotel)*

manners PL NOUN
  los **modales** *masc pl*
    good manners
    buenos modales
    Her manners are appalling.
    Tiene muy malos modales.
    It's bad manners to speak with your mouth full.
    Es de mala educación hablar con la boca llena.

many ADJECTIVE, PRONOUN
  muchos *masc pl*
  muchas *fem pl*

    He hasn't got many friends.
    No tiene muchos amigos.
    I haven't bought many magazines.
    No he comprado muchas revistas.
    How many...?
    ¿Cuántos...?

> ### Language tip
> *Don't forget the accent on question words like* **cuántos** *nor the upside-down question mark at the start of questions.*

    How many sisters have you got?
    ¿Cuántas hermanas tienes?
    That's too many.
    Ésos son demasiados.
    You ask too many questions!
    ¡Haces demasiadas preguntas!

> **How many?**
> ¿Cuántos?

Not many
No muchos.
too many
demasiados

map NOUN
  1 el **mapa** *masc (of country, area)*
    a map of Spain
    un mapa de España

> ### Language tip
> *Even though it ends in* -a, **el mapa** *is a masculine noun.*

  2 el **plano** *masc (of town)*
    a map of London
    un plano de Londres

marathon NOUN
  el **maratón** *masc* (PL los **maratones**)
    the London marathon
    el maratón de Londres

marbles PL NOUN
  las **canicas** *fem pl*
    Do you want to play marbles?
    ¿Quieres jugar a las canicas?

> ### Language tip
> *In Spanish, you need to add* **a las** *before* **canicas**.

March NOUN
  marzo *masc*
    My birthday's in March.
    Mi cumpleaños es en marzo.
    It's the twenty-ninth of March today.
    Hoy es veintinueve de marzo.

> **in March**
> en marzo
> **on the fifth of March**
> el cinco de marzo

> ### Language tip
> *Months are not spelled with a capital letter in Spanish.*

margarine NOUN
  la **margarina** *fem*

margin NOUN
el **margen** *masc* (PL los **márgenes**)
Write notes in the margin.
Escribid anotaciones en el margen.

mark

mark *can be a noun or a verb.*

A NOUN
1 la **nota** *fem (at school)*
I get good marks in English.
Saco buenas notas en inglés.
2 la **mancha** *fem (stain)*
You've got a mark on your shirt.
Tienes una mancha en la camisa.

On your marks, get set, go!
¡En sus marcas, preparados, listos, ya!

B VERB
to mark
corregir
She's got books to mark.
Tiene cuadernos para corregir.

market NOUN
el **mercado** *masc*

marmalade NOUN
la **mermelada de naranja** *fem*

Language tip
Don't forget to say **de naranja** *if you mean 'orange marmalade'.* **La mermelada** *on its own just means 'jam'.*

marriage NOUN
el **matrimonio** *masc*

married ADJECTIVE
casado *masc*
casada *fem*
They are not married.
No están casados.
She's married to my cousin.
Está casada con mi primo.
to get married
casarse

They want to get married.
Quieren casarse.
My sister's getting married in June.
Mi hermana se va a casar en junio.
a married couple
un matrimonio

to **marry** VERB
casarse con
He wants to marry her.
Quiere casarse con ella.

marvellous ADJECTIVE
estupendo *masc*
estupenda *fem*
She's a marvellous cook.
Es una cocinera estupenda.
The weather was marvellous.
Hizo un tiempo estupendo.

masculine ADJECTIVE
masculino *masc*
masculina *fem*

mashed potatoes PL NOUN
el **puré de patatas** *masc*
sausages and mashed potatoes
salchichas con puré de patatas

mask NOUN
la **máscara** *fem*

mass NOUN
1 el **montón** *masc* (PL los **montones**)
a mass of books and papers
un montón de libros y papeles
We've got masses of homework today.
Hoy tenemos montones de deberes.
2 la **misa** *fem (in church)*
We go to mass on Sundays.
Vamos a misa los domingos.

a b c d e f g h i j k l **m** n o p q r s t u v w x y z

461

a b c d e f g h i j k l **m** n o p q r s t u v w x y z

massive ADJECTIVE
enorme *masc & fem*

masterpiece NOUN
la **obra maestra** *fem*

mat NOUN
el **felpudo** *masc (doormat)*
Wipe your feet on the mat.
Límpiate los pies en el felpudo.

> *Language tip*
> *In Spanish you usually use an article like* **el**, **la** *or* **los**, **las** *with parts of the body.*

match

> **match** *can be a noun or a verb.*

A NOUN
1 la **cerilla** *fem (for striking)*
a box of matches
una caja de cerillas
2 el **partido** *masc (game)*
a football match
un partido de fútbol
B VERB
to match
1 **hacer juego con** *(go with)*
The jacket matches the trousers.
La chaqueta hace juego con los pantalones.
2 **hacer corresponder con** *(put with)*
Match the words to the pictures.
Une las palabras con su imagen correspondiente.

matching ADJECTIVE
a juego
My bedroom has matching wallpaper and curtains.
Mi habitación tiene el papel y las cortinas a juego.

mate NOUN
el **amigo** *masc*
la **amiga** *fem (friend)*
He's my mate.
Es mi amigo.

material NOUN
la **tela** *fem (cloth)*
It's made of red material.
Está hecho de tela roja.

maths NOUN
las **matemáticas** *fem*

matter

> **matter** *can be a noun or a verb.*

A NOUN
What's the matter? Why are you crying?
¿Qué pasa? ¿Por qué estás llorando?
What's the matter with him?
¿Qué le pasa?
B VERB
to matter: **It doesn't matter.**
No importa.

mattress NOUN
el **colchón** *masc* (PL los **colchones**)

maximum ADJECTIVE
máximo *masc*
máxima *fem*

May NOUN
mayo *masc*
My birthday's in May.
Mi cumpleaños es en mayo.
It's the eleventh of May today.
Hoy es once de mayo.

> **in May**
> en mayo
> **on the fifth of May**
> el cinco de mayo

Language tip
Months are not spelled with a capital letter in Spanish.

may VERB
May I come in?
¿Puedo entrar?
She may not come.
Puede que no venga.

maybe ADVERB
a lo mejor
maybe not
a lo mejor no
Maybe she's at home.
A lo mejor está en casa.

mayonnaise NOUN
la **mayonesa** *fem*

mayor NOUN
el **alcalde** *masc*
la **alcaldesa** *fem*

maze NOUN
el **laberinto** *masc*

me PRONOUN
1 me
Do you love me?
¿Me quieres?
Can you help me?
¿Me puedes ayudar?
Wait for me!
¡Espérame!
Are you looking for me?
¿Me estás buscando?
Can you give it to me?
¿Me lo puedes dar?
He wants to talk to me.
Quiere hablar conmigo.
2 mí

Language tip
*Use **mí** after a preposition.*

Is it for me?
¿Es para mí?
You're after me.
Tú vas detrás de mí.

Language tip
*Remember that **with me** translates as **conmigo**.*

He was with me.
Estaba conmigo.
3 yo

Language tip
*Use **yo** after the verb **ser**.*

It's me.
Soy yo.

Language tip
*Use **yo** in comparisons.*

He's taller than me.
Es más alto que yo.

It's me.
Soy yo.
Me too.
Yo también.
Excuse me!
¡Perdóname!

meal NOUN
la **comida** *fem*

mean

mean *can be a verb or an adjective.*

A VERB
to mean
significar
What does 'complete' mean?
¿Qué significa 'complete'?
I don't know what it means.
No sé lo que significa.
What do you mean?
¿Qué quieres decir?
That's not what I mean.
Eso no es lo que quiero decir.

What does it mean?
¿Qué significa?

B ADJECTIVE
1 tacaño *masc*
tacaña *fem* (with money)
He's too mean to buy presents.

Es demasiado tacaño para comprar regalos.
2 mezquino masc
mezquina fem (unkind)
You're being mean to me.
Estás siendo mezquina conmigo.

meaning NOUN
el **significado** masc

measles NOUN
el **sarampión** masc

to **measure** VERB
medir
Measure the length.
Medid la longitud.

meat NOUN
la **carne** fem
I don't eat meat.
No como carne.

Mecca NOUN
La Meca fem

mechanic NOUN
el **mecánico** masc
la **mecánica** fem
He's a mechanic.
Es mecánico.

> **Language tip**
> When talking about people's jobs in Spanish, you do not use an article.

medal NOUN
la **medalla** fem
the gold medal
la medalla de oro

medical

> **medical** can be an adjective or a noun.

A ADJECTIVE
She's a medical student.
Es estudiante de medicina.
B NOUN
You have to have a medical.
Necesitas hacerte una revisión médica.

medicine NOUN
la **medicina** masc
What's this medicine for?
¿Para qué es esta medicina?
I want to study medicine.
Quiero estudiar medicina.

Mediterranean NOUN
the Mediterranean
el Mediterráneo masc

medium ADJECTIVE
mediano masc
mediana fem
a man of medium height
un hombre de estatura mediana
Small, medium or large?
¿Pequeño, mediano o grande?

medium-sized ADJECTIVE
de tamaño medio
a medium-sized town
una ciudad de tamaño medio

to **meet** VERB
1 encontrarse con (by chance)
I met Paul in town.
Me encontré con Paul en el centro.
2 (by arrangement)
I'm meeting my friends at the swimming pool.
He quedado con mis amigos en la piscina.
Let's meet in front of the tourist office.
¿Por qué no quedamos delante de la oficina de turismo?
3 conocer (get to know)
He met Tim at a party.
Conoció a Tim en una fiesta.

> **Language tip**
> Don't forget the personal **a** after **conocer** when you name the person.

Have you met Amy?
¿Conoces a Amy?
Where did you two meet?

¿Dónde os conocisteis vosotros dos?

4 recoger *(pick up)*
I'll meet you at the station.
Te recogeré en la estación.

meeting NOUN
la **reunión** *fem* (PL las **reuniones**)
their first meeting
su primera reunión

melon NOUN
el **melón** *masc* (PL los **melones**)

to **melt** VERB
derretirse
The snow is melting.
La nieve se está derritiendo.

member
NOUN
el **socio** *masc*
la **socia** *fem*
a member of our club
un socio de nuestro club

memory NOUN
1 la **memoria** *fem* (*for facts, words*)
I haven't got a good memory.
No tengo buena memoria.
2 el **recuerdo** *masc* (*of past*)
some happy memories
algunos recuerdos felices

men PL NOUN
los **hombres** *masc pl*

to **mend** VERB
arreglar
Can you mend it?
¿Puedes arreglarlo?

to **mention** VERB
Thank you! — Don't mention it!
¡Gracias! — ¡De nada!

menu NOUN
1 la **carta** *fem* (*in restaurant*)
Could I have the menu please?
¿Me trae la carta por favor?

2 el **menú** *masc* (*on computer*)

merry ADJECTIVE

Merry Christmas!
¡Feliz Navidad!

Language tip
Have you noticed the upside-down exclamation mark at the start of Spanish exclamations?

merry-go-round NOUN
el **tiovivo** *masc*

mess NOUN
el **desorden** *masc*
What a mess!
¡Qué desorden!
My bedroom's in a mess.
Mi habitación está desordenada.

message NOUN
el **mensaje** *masc*

met VERB ▷see **meet**

metal NOUN
el **metal** *masc*

method NOUN
el **método** *masc*

metre NOUN
el **metro** *masc*
I can swim two hundred metres.
Puedo nadar doscientos metros.
I'm one metre thirty tall.
Mido un metro treinta.

metric ADJECTIVE
métrico *masc*
métrica *fem*

mice PL NOUN
los **ratones** *masc pl*

microphone NOUN
el **micrófono** *masc*

microscope NOUN
el **microscopio** *masc*

microwave NOUN
el **microondas** *masc* (PL los **microondas**)

midday NOUN
el **mediodía** *masc*
It's midday.
Es mediodía.

> **at midday**
> al mediodía

> ### Language tip
> *Even though it ends in* **-a**, **el mediodía**, *like* **día**, *is a masculine noun.*

middle NOUN
el **centro** *masc*
Come into the middle, Andrew.
Ven al centro, Andrew.
in the middle of the road
en medio de la carretera
in the middle of the night
en mitad de la noche

middle-aged ADJECTIVE
de **mediana edad**
a middle-aged man
un hombre de mediana edad

middle name NOUN
el **segundo nombre** *masc*
It's my middle name.
Es mi segundo nombre.

midge NOUN
el **mosquito** *masc*

midnight NOUN
la **medianoche** *fem*
It's midnight.
Es medianoche.

> **at midnight**
> a medianoche

might VERB
I might, I might not.
Puede que sí, puede que no.

> ### Language tip
> **puede que sí, puede que no**
> *literally means 'maybe, maybe not'.*

It might rain.
Puede que llueva.

migraine NOUN
la **jaqueca** *fem*
I've got a migraine.
Tengo jaqueca.

mild ADJECTIVE
suave *masc & fem*
The winters are quite mild.
Los inviernos son bastante suaves.
It's mild today.
No hace mucho frío hoy.

mile NOUN
la **milla** *fem*
It's five miles from here.
Está a cinco millas de aquí.
We walked miles!
¡Caminamos durante kilómetros!

> ### Did you know…?
> *In Spain distances are measured in kilometres. A mile is about 1.6 kilometres.*

milk NOUN
la **leche** *fem*
tea with milk
té con leche

milkman NOUN
el **lechero** *masc*

> ### Language tip
> *When talking about people's jobs in Spanish, you do not use an article.*

milk shake NOUN
  el **batido** *masc*

millimetre NOUN
  el **milímetro** *masc*

million NOUN
  el **millón** *masc* (PL los **millones**)
    a million times
    un millón de veces
    two million
    dos millones

millionaire NOUN
  el **millonario** *masc*
  la **millonaria** *fem*

mince NOUN
  la **carne picada** *fem*

Did you know...?
Mince pies are not eaten in Spain.

mind

mind *can be a verb or a noun.*

A VERB
  to mind: **Do you mind if I**
  open the window?
  ¿Le importa si abro la ventana?

  Mind the step!
  ¡Cuidado con el escalón!

I don't mind.
No me importa.
Never mind!
¡No importa!

B NOUN
  I've changed my mind.
  He cambiado de idea.
  Make your mind up!
  ¡Decídete ya!

mine

mine *can be a pronoun or a noun.*

A PRONOUN
  el **mío** *masc*
  la **mía** *fem*

Language tip
Remember that the choice of **el**
mío, **la mía**, **los míos**, *or* **las**
mías *depends entirely on the thing*
or things referred to and not on the
person who owns it or them.

  That's not my coat. Mine is
  here.
  Ése no es mi abrigo. El mío está
  aquí.
  Those aren't my boots. Mine
  are here.
  Ésas no son mis botas. Las mías
  están aquí.

Language tip
After **ser**, *you can often just use*
mío, **mía**, **míos** *or* **mías** *to agree*
with the noun referred to.

  This scarf is mine.
  Esta bufanda es mía.
  These books are mine.
  Estos libros son míos.

a friend of mine
una amigo mío
It's mine.
Es mío.

B NOUN
  la **mina** *fem*
  a coal mine
  una mina de carbón

mineral water NOUN
  el **agua mineral** *fem*
    A mineral water for me,
    please.
    Para mí agua mineral, por favor.

Language tip
Even though it's a feminine noun,
remember that you use **el** *and* **un**
with **agua**.

minibus NOUN
el **microbús** *masc* (PL los **microbuses**)

minimum ADJECTIVE
mínimo *masc*
mínima *fem*

miniskirt NOUN
la **minifalda** *fem*

minister NOUN
1 el **ministro** *masc*
la **ministra** *fem (in government)*
2 el **pastor** *masc*
la **pastora** *fem (in church)*

minor ADJECTIVE
de poca importancia
a minor problem
un problema de poca importancia
a minor injury
una herida leve

mint NOUN
1 el **caramelo de menta** *masc (sweet)*
2 la **hierbabuena** *fem (plant)*
mint sauce
salsa con hierbabuena

minus PREPOSITION
menos
Seventeen minus three is fourteen.
Diecisiete menos tres son catorce.
It's minus two degrees outside.
Fuera hace dos grados bajo cero.

minute NOUN
el **minuto** *masc*
Wait a minute!
¡Espera un minuto!

mirror NOUN
el **espejo** *masc*

to **misbehave** VERB
portarse mal
She's misbehaving.
Se está portando mal.
Don't misbehave, Patrick!
¡No te portes mal, Patrick!

mischief NOUN
las **travesuras** *fem pl*
My little sister's always up to mischief.
Mi hermana pequeña siempre está haciendo travesuras.

miserable ADJECTIVE
1 **muy triste** *masc & fem (person)*
You're looking miserable.
Pareces muy triste.
2 **deprimente** *masc & fem (weather)*
The weather was miserable.
El tiempo fue deprimente.

Miss NOUN
1 la **señorita** *fem*
Yes, Miss.
Sí, señorita.
2 **Srta.** *(in addresses)*
Miss Jones
Srta. Jones

> **Language tip**
> *Don't forget the dot at the end of Spanish abbreviations.*

to **miss** VERB
1 **perder**
Hurry or you'll miss the bus.
Date prisa o perderás el autobús.
Miss a turn.
Pierde un turno.
2 **echar de menos** *(long for)*
I miss you.
Te echo de menos.
He misses his family.
Echa de menos a su familia.

> **Language tip**
> *Don't forget the personal **a** in examples like this one.*

missing ADJECTIVE
  perdido *masc*
  perdida *fem*
    the missing piece
    la pieza perdida *fem*
    to be missing
    faltar
    My rucksack is missing.
    Falta mi mochila.
    Two children are missing.
    Faltan dos niños.

mist NOUN
  la **neblina** *fem*

mistake NOUN
  el **error** *masc*
    She only made two mistakes.
    Solo cometió dos errores.
    a spelling mistake
    una falta de ortografía
    by mistake
    por error
    I took his bag by mistake.
    Cogí su bolso por error.

mistletoe NOUN
  el **muérdago** *masc*

misty ADJECTIVE
  de neblina
    a misty morning
    una mañana de neblina

    It's misty.
    Hay neblina.

to **mix** VERB
  mezclar
    Mix the flour with the sugar.
    Mezclar la harina con el
    azúcar.

to **mix up** VERB
  confundir
    He always mixes me up with
    my sister.
    Siempre me confunde con mi
    hermana.

mixed ADJECTIVE
  mixto *masc*
  mixta *fem*

    a mixed school
    un colegio mixto

mixture NOUN
  la **mezcla** *fem*

mix-up NOUN
  el **lío** *masc*

mobile NOUN
  el **móvil** *masc*
    I haven't got a mobile.
    No tengo móvil.

mobile phone NOUN
  el **teléfono móvil** *masc*

Have you got a mobile phone?
¿Tienes teléfono móvil?

model

model *can be a noun or an adjective.*

A NOUN
1 la **maqueta** *fem (small version)*
  I'm making a model of the castle.
  Estoy haciendo una maqueta del castillo.
2 el/la **modelo** *masc/fem (person)*
  She's a famous model.
  Es una modelo famosa.
B ADJECTIVE
  a model plane
  una maqueta de avión

a model railway
una vía férrea en miniatura

modern ADJECTIVE
moderno *masc*
moderna *fem*

moment NOUN
el **momento** *masc*
Wait a moment, Mike.
Espera un momento, Mike.
Could you wait a moment?
¿Puedes esperar un momento?
in a moment
dentro de un momento
I'm a bit busy at the moment.
Estoy algo ocupado en este momento.

Just a moment!
¡Un momento!
at the moment
en este momento

Monday NOUN
el **lunes** *masc*
It's Monday today.
Hoy es lunes.

on Monday
el lunes
on Mondays
los lunes
every Monday
cada lunes
last Monday
el lunes pasado
next Monday
el lunes que viene

Language tip
Days are not spelled with a capital letter in Spanish.

money NOUN
el **dinero** *masc*

I haven't got enough money.
No tengo suficiente dinero.
I need to change some money.
Necesito cambiar dinero.

monk NOUN
el **monje** *masc*

monkey NOUN
el **mono** *masc*

monster NOUN
el **monstruo** *masc*

month NOUN
el **mes** *masc*
two months
dos meses
at the end of the month
a final de mes

this month
este mes
next month
el mes que viene
last month
el mes pasado
every month
cada mes
What month is it?
¿Qué mes es?

monument NOUN
el **monumento** *masc*

mood NOUN
el **humor** *masc*
She's in a bad mood.
Está de mal humor.
He's in a good mood.
Está de buen humor.

moon NOUN
la **luna** *fem*
the moon and the stars
la luna y las estrellas

moped NOUN
el **ciclomotor** *masc*

more ADVERB, ADJECTIVE, PRONOUN
más
more difficult
más difícil
Could you speak more slowly?
¿Puedes hablar más despacio?
There are more girls in the class.
Hay más chicas en la clase.
Do you want some more tea?
¿Quieres más té?
Would you like some more, Luke?
¿Quieres más, Luke?
There isn't any more.
Ya no queda más.
Two more minutes!
¡Dos minutos más!

Language tip
You normally translate **more than** *using* **más que**.

more than me
más que yo
He's more intelligent than me.
Es más inteligente que yo.
more than that
más que eso

Language tip
Use **más de** *instead before numbers.*

I've got more than fifty euros.
Tengo más de cincuenta euros.

a bit more
un poco más
more ... than
más ... que

morning NOUN
la **mañana** *fem*
on Saturday morning
el sábado por la mañana

all morning
toda la mañana
Are they staying all morning?
¿Se quedan toda la mañana?

this morning
esta mañana
tomorrow morning
mañana por la mañana
yesterday morning
ayer por la mañana
every morning
todas las mañanas
at seven o'clock in the morning
a las siete de la mañana

mosque NOUN
la **mezquita** *fem*

mosquito NOUN
el **mosquito** *masc*
a mosquito bite
una picadura de mosquito

most ADVERB, ADJECTIVE, PRONOUN

Language tip
When **most** *goes with an adjective or verb, it usually translates as* **más**.

the most expensive restaurant
el restaurante más caro
the most expensive restaurants
los restaurantes más caros
Stephen talks the most.
Stephen es el que más habla.
He got the most votes.
Fue él que sacó más votos.

Language tip
You can usually use **la mayoría de** *to translate* **most of** *with a plural noun.*

most of my friends
la mayoría de mis amigos
most of them
la mayoría
most Spanish people
la mayoría de los españoles

Language tip
Use **la mayor parte de** *to translate* **most of** *with a singular noun.*

most of the time
la mayor parte del tiempo
most of the class
la mayor parte de la clase
at the most
como máximo
two hours at the most
dos horas como máximo

motel NOUN
el **motel** *masc*

moth NOUN
la **mariposa nocturna** *fem*

mother NOUN
la **madre** *fem*
my mother
mi madre
your mother
tu madre
my mother and father
mis padres

Mother's Day NOUN
el **día de la Madre**
It's Mother's Day on Sunday.
El domingo es el día de la Madre.

Happy Mother's Day!
¡Feliz día de la Madre!

Language tip
Have you noticed the upside-down exclamation mark at the start of Spanish exclamations?

motor NOUN
el **motor** *masc*

motorbike NOUN
la **moto** *fem*

Language tip
Even though it ends in **-o**, **la moto** *is a feminine noun.*

motorboat NOUN
la **lancha motora** *fem*

motorcycle NOUN
la **motocicleta** *fem*

motorcyclist NOUN
el/la **motociclista** *masc/fem*

motorist NOUN
el/la **automovilista** *masc/fem*

motorway NOUN
la **autopista** *fem*
on the motorway
en la autopista

mountain NOUN
la **montaña** *fem*

mountain bike NOUN
la **bicicleta de montaña** *fem*

mouse NOUN
el **ratón** *masc* (PL los **ratones**)

mouse mat NOUN
la **alfombrilla del ratón** *fem*

mousse NOUN
la **mousse** *fem*
chocolate mousse
la mousse de chocolate

moustache NOUN
el **bigote** *masc*
He's got a moustache.
Tiene bigote.

mouth NOUN
la **boca** *fem*
Open your mouth.
Abre la boca.

Language tip

In Spanish you usually use an article
like **el**, **la** or **los**, **las** with parts of
the body.

move

move *can be a noun or a verb.*

A NOUN
el **turno** *masc*
It's your move.
Es tu turno.
Get a move on, Sebastian!
¡Muévete, Sebastian!
B VERB
to move
1 **mover** *(object)*
**Could you move your stuff
please?**
¿Puedes mover tus cosas, por
favor?
2 **moverse** *(change position)*
Don't move!
¡No te muevas!
You moved!
¡Te has movido!
Move forward two spaces!
¡Adelanta dos casillas!

to **move over** VERB
correrse
Could you move over a bit?
¿Puedes correrte un poco?

movement NOUN
el **movimiento** *masc*

MP NOUN
el **diputado** *masc*
la **diputada** *fem*
She's an MP.
Es diputada.

Language tip

When talking about people's jobs in
Spanish, you do not use an article.

MP3 NOUN
el **MP3**

an MP3 player
un reproductor de MP3

Mr NOUN
1 el **señor** *masc*
Good morning, Mr Jones.
¡Buenos días, señor Jones!
Mr Jones wants to see you.
El señor Jones quiere verte.
Mr and Mrs Carrasco are here.
Los señores Carrasco están aquí.
2 **Sr.** *(in addresses)*
Mr Silvestre
Sr. Silvestre
Mr and Mrs Ruiz
Srs. Ruiz

Language tip

Don't forget the dot at the end of
Spanish abbreviations.

Mrs NOUN
1 la **señora** *fem*
Good morning, Mrs Jones.
¡Buenos días, señora Jones!
Mrs Jones wants to see you.
La señora Jones quiere verte.
2 **Sra.** *(in addresses)*
Mrs Silvestre
Sra. Silvestre

Language tip

Don't forget the dot at the end of
Spanish abbreviations.

Ms NOUN
1 la **señora** *fem*
Ms Smith is here.
La señora Smith está aquí.
2 **Sra.** *(in addresses)*

Did you know…?

There isn't a specific word for **Ms** in
Spanish. Just use **Sra.**

English

Spanish

a
b
c
d
e
f
g
h
i
j
k
l
m
n
o
p
q
r
s
t
u
v
w
x
y
z

English

Spanish

a
b
c
d
e
f
g
h
i
j
k
l
m
n
o
p
q
r
s
t
u
v
w
x
y
z

much ADJECTIVE, ADVERB, PRONOUN
mucho *masc*
mucha *fem*
> **not much**
> no mucho
> **I haven't got much money.**
> No tengo mucho dinero.
> **I don't want very much milk.**
> No quiero mucha leche.
> **I don't like sport much.**
> No me gusta mucho el deporte.
> **I don't want much.**
> No quiero mucho.
> **I like England very much.**
> Me gusta muchísimo Inglaterra.
> **How much?**
> ¿Cuánto?
> **How much money have you got?**
> ¿Cuánto dinero tienes?
> **How much jam is left?**
> ¿Cuánta mermelada queda?

Language tip

Don't forget the accent on question words like **cuánto** *nor the upside-down question mark at the start of questions.*

> **How much does it cost?**
> ¿Cuánto cuesta?
> **How much do you want?**
> ¿Cuánto quieres?
> **How much is it all together?**
> ¿Cuánto es todo junto?
> **It costs too much.**
> Cuesta demasiado.
> **That's too much!**
> ¡Eso es demasiado!
> **too much butter**
> demasiada mantequilla

How much?
¿Cuánto?
not much
no mucho
too much
demasiado
Thank you very much.
Muchas gracias.

mud NOUN
el **barro** *masc*

muddy ADJECTIVE
cubierto de barro *masc*
cubierta de barro *fem*

mug NOUN
el **tazón** *masc* (PL los **tazones**)
> **Do you want a cup or a mug?**
> ¿Quieres una taza o un tazón?

to **multiply** VERB
multiplicar
> **Multiply six by three.**
> Multiplica seis por tres.
> **Two multiplied by three is six.**
> Dos multiplicado por tres son seis.

mum NOUN
1 la **madre** *fem*
> **my mum**
> mi madre
> **my mum and dad**
> mis padres
2 la **mamá** *fem* (used as name)
> **Hi, Mum.**
> Hola, mamá.
> **I'll ask Mum.**
> Se lo preguntaré a mamá.

mummy NOUN
la **mamá** *fem*
> **Hello, Mummy!**
> ¡Hola, mamá!

mumps NOUN
las **paperas** *fem pl*
> **Teresa has got mumps.**
> Teresa tiene paperas.

murder NOUN
el **asesinato** *masc*

muscle NOUN
el **músculo** *masc*

museum NOUN
el **museo** *masc*

mushroom NOUN
1 el **champiñón** *masc* (PL los **champiñones**) *(button mushroom)*
2 la **seta** *fem* *(open-cup mushroom)*

music NOUN
la **música** *fem*
I like listening to music.
Me gusta escuchar música.

musical instrument NOUN
el **instrumento musical** *masc*
Can you play a musical instrument?
¿Sabes tocar algún instrumento musical?

musician NOUN
el **músico** *masc*
la **música** *fem*

Muslim NOUN
el **musulmán** *masc* (PL los **musulmanes**)
la **musulmana** *fem*
He's a Muslim.
Es musulmán.

> **Language tip**
> *Remember that **musulmán** is not spelled with a capital letter in Spanish.*

mussel NOUN
el **mejillón** *masc* (PL los **mejillones**)

must VERB
1 **tener que** *(have to)*
You must be careful, Edward.
Tienes que tener cuidado, Edward.
You must listen, children.
Tenéis que escuchar, niños.
2 **deber de** *(in guesses)*
You must be tired.
Debes de estar cansado.

mustard NOUN
la **mostaza** *fem*

mustn't (= **must not**) ▷ *see* **must**

my ADJECTIVE
mi *masc & fem* (PL **mis**)

> **Language tip**
> *Remember to use **mi** before a singular noun and **mis** before a plural one.*

my father
mi padre
my friend Alicia
mi amiga Alicia
my parents
mis padres

> **Language tip**
> *In Spanish you usually use an article like **el**, **la** or **los**, **las** with parts of the body and clothes.*

I wash my face in the morning.
Me lavo la cara por las mañanas.
I'm going to wear my shorts today.
Voy a llevar los pantalones cortos hoy.

myself PRONOUN
1 **me** *(reflexive use)*
I've hurt myself.
Me he hecho daño.
I like to look at myself in the mirror.
Me gusta mirarme en el espejo.

I'm enjoying myself.
Me estoy divirtiendo.

2 mí *(after preposition)*
I'll tell you about myself.
Te contaré sobre mí.

3 yo mismo *(for emphasis)*
I made it myself.
Lo hice yo mismo.
by myself
solo

I don't like travelling by myself.
No me gusta viajar solo.

mysterious ADJECTIVE
misterioso *masc*
misteriosa *fem*

mystery NOUN
el **misterio** *masc*

N n

nail NOUN
1 la **uña** *fem (fingernail)*
   Don't bite your nails!
   ¡No te muerdas las uñas!

> **Language tip**
> In Spanish you usually use an article like **el**, **la** or **los**, **las** with parts of the body.

2 el **clavo** *masc (for hammering)*

nailfile NOUN
la **lima de uñas** *fem*

nail varnish NOUN
el **esmalte de uñas** *masc*

naked ADJECTIVE
desnudo *masc*
desnuda *fem*

name NOUN
el **nombre** *masc*
   a pretty name
   un nombre bonito
   What's your cat's name?
   ¿Cómo se llama tu perro?

   His name's Max.
   Se llama Max.

> **What's your name?**
> ¿Cómo te llamas?
> **My name is Ruth.**
> Me llamo Ruth.

nanny NOUN
la **niñera** *fem*
   She's a nanny.
   Es niñera.

> **Language tip**
> When talking about people's jobs in Spanish, you do not use an article.

napkin NOUN
la **servilleta** *fem*

narrow ADJECTIVE
estrecho *masc*
estrecha *fem*
   a narrow street
   una calle estrecha

nasty ADJECTIVE
malo *masc*
mala *fem*
   Don't be nasty!
   ¡No seas malo!

> **Language tip**
> Shorten **malo** to **mal** before a masculine singular noun.

   a nasty smell
   un mal olor
   a nasty cold
   un resfriado terrible
   He's a nasty man.
   Es un hombre con mala idea.

nationality NOUN
la **nacionalidad** *fem*

natural ADJECTIVE
natural *masc & fem*

nature NOUN
la **naturaleza** *fem*

naughty ADJECTIVE
travieso *masc*
traviesa *fem*
   Naughty girl!
   ¡Qué chica más traviesa!

a
b
c
d
e
f
g
h
i
j
k
l
m
n
o
p
q
r
s
t
u
v
w
x
y
z

Don't be naughty!
¡No seas malo!

navy NOUN
la **armada** *fem*
He's in the navy.
Está en la armada.

navy-blue

navy-blue *can be an adjective or a noun.*

A ADJECTIVE
azul marino

Language tip
azul marino *never changes its endings to agree with the noun it describes.*

a navy-blue skirt
una falda azul marino
B NOUN
el **azul marino** *masc*

near

near *can be an adverb, adjective or preposition.*

A ADVERB, ADJECTIVE
1 **cerca**

Language tip
Use **cerca** *when saying that something or someone is near. As it's an adverb, it never changes its ending.*

It's fairly near.
Está bastante cerca.
2 **cercano** *masc*
cercana *fem*

Language tip
Use the adjective **cercano, cercana,** *etc in noun phrases.*

the nearest village
el pueblo más cercano
Where's the nearest service station?
¿Dónde está la gasolinera más cercana?

The nearest shops are three kilometres away.
Las tiendas más cercanas están a tres kilómetros.
B PREPOSITION
cerca de *(close to)*
I live near Liverpool.
Vivo cerca de Liverpool.
near my house
cerca de mi casa
near here
cerca de aquí
Is there a bank near here?
¿Hay un banco cerca de aquí?

Language tip
Another way of saying **near here** *is* **por aquí cerca**.

Is there a supermarket near here?
¿Hay un supermercado por aquí cerca?

nearby ADVERB
cerca
There's a supermarket nearby.
Hay un supermercado cerca.

nearly ADVERB
casi
Dinner's nearly ready.
La cena está casi lista.
I'm nearly ten.
Tengo casi diez años.

neat ADJECTIVE
1 **ordenado** *masc*
ordenada *fem (room, desk)*
a neat room
una habitación ordenada
2 **claro** *masc*
clara *fem (writing)*
She has very neat writing.
Tiene una letra muy clara.

necessary ADJECTIVE
necesario *masc*
necesaria *fem*

neck NOUN
el **cuello** *masc*

I've hurt my neck.
Me he hecho daño en el cuello.

necklace NOUN
   el **collar** *masc*
      a diamond necklace
      un collar de diamantes

to **need** VERB
   necesitar
      I need a rubber.
      Necesito una goma de borrar.

      to need to
      tener que
      I need to wash the dishes.
      Tengo que fregar los platos.

needle NOUN
   la **aguja** *fem*

neighbour NOUN
   el **vecino** *masc*
   la **vecina** *fem*
      the neighbours' garden
      el jardín de los vecinos

neighbourhood NOUN
   el **barrio** *masc*

neither PRONOUN, CONJUNCTION, ADVERB
   ni una cosa ni otra
      **Carrots or peas? —
      Neither, thanks.**
      ¿Zanahorias o guisantes? —
      Ni una cosa ni otra, gracias.

neither ... nor ...
ni ... ni ...
   **Neither Sarah nor Julia is
   coming to the party.**
   Ni Sarah ni Julia vienen a la
   fiesta.

Neither do I.
Yo tampoco.
Neither have I.
Yo tampoco.

nephew NOUN
   el **sobrino** *masc*
      her nephew
      su sobrino

nerve NOUN
   el **nervio** *masc*
      She gets on my nerves.
      Me pone de los nervios.

nervous ADJECTIVE
   nervioso *masc*
   nerviosa *fem*
      **I bite my nails when I'm
      nervous.**
      Cuando estoy nervioso me
      muerdo las uñas.

Net NOUN
      the Net
      Internet
      I like to surf the Net.
      Me gusta navegar por Internet.

netball NOUN

never ADVERB
   nunca
      **When are you going to phone
      him? — Never!**
      ¿Cuándo vas a telefonearle? —
      ¡Nunca!
      I never go to the cinema.
      Nunca voy al cine.
      We never see them.
      No los vemos nunca.

Language tip
*Don't forget to put **no** before the verb when putting **nunca** after it.*

new ADJECTIVE
nuevo *masc*
nueva *fem*

Language tip
*When **new** means **brand-new**, you usually put **nuevo** after the noun.*

a new skirt
una falda nueva

Language tip
*When **new** means **replacement** rather than **brand-new**, you usually put **nuevo** before the noun.*

her new boyfriend
su nuevo novio

news NOUN
1 la **noticia** *fem*

Language tip
*Use **noticia** in the singular when you're referring to a single piece of news.*

That's wonderful news!
¡Eso es una noticia estupenda!
2 las **noticias** *fem pl*

Language tip
*Use **noticias** in the plural when you're referring to more than one piece of news or to a news bulletin.*

It was on the news.
Salió en las noticias.

newsagent's NOUN
la **tienda de periódicos**

Did you know…?
*In Spain you'll come across **kioscos**, newsstands on the street which sell newspapers, magazines, and other items.*

newspaper NOUN
el **periódico** *masc*

New Year NOUN
New Year's Day
el Día de Año Nuevo
New Year's Eve
la Nochevieja

Happy New Year!
¡Feliz Año Nuevo!

Did you know…?
*In Spain, it's traditional to see the New Year in by eating **doce uvas** (twelve grapes) for good luck as the clock strikes midnight.*

next

next can be an adjective or adverb.

A ADJECTIVE
1 **próximo** *masc*
próxima *fem (in sequence)*
the next time
la próxima vez
Who's next?
¿A quién le toca?
I'm next.
Me toca a mí.
2 **que viene** *(coming)*
next Saturday
el sábado que viene

next year
el año que viene
next week
la semana que viene
next summer
el verano que viene

3 **They live next door.**
Viven al lado.
the flat next door
el piso de al lado

B ADVERB

1 después (afterwards)
What shall I do next?
¿Qué hago después?

2 next to
al lado de
It's next to the bank.
Está al lado del banco.
I sit next to my friend.
Me siento al lado de mi amigo.

next-door ADJECTIVE
de al lado
the next-door flat
el piso de al lado

nice ADJECTIVE

1 simpático masc
simpática fem (friendly)
Your parents are very nice.
Tus padres son muy simpáticos.

2 amable masc & fem (kind)
She was always very nice to me.
Siempre fue muy amable conmigo.

3 bonito (pretty)
Granada is a nice town.
Granada es una ciudad bonita.
What a nice dress!
¡Qué vestido más bonito!

4 bueno (good)
The soup is very nice.
La sopa está muy buena.

> ### Language tip
> Shorten **bueno** to **buen** before a masculine singular noun.
>
> **nice weather**
> buen tiempo

> **Have a nice time!**
> ¡Que te diviertas!
> **It's a nice day.**
> Hace buen día.

niece NOUN
la **sobrina** fem
his niece
su sobrina

night NOUN
la **noche** fem
I want a room for two nights.
Quiero una habitación para dos noches.
We arrived last night.
Llegamos anoche.

> **last night**
> anoche
> **tomorrow night**
> mañana por la noche

nightie NOUN
el **camisón** masc (PL los camisones)

nightmare NOUN
la **pesadilla** fem
I have nightmares.
Tengo pesadillas.

nil NOUN
el **cero** masc
We won two-nil.
Ganamos dos a cero.

nine NUMBER
nueve
nine euros
nueve euros

> **She's nine.**
> Tiene nueve años.

> ### Language tip
> In English you can say **she's nine** or **she's nine years old**. In Spanish you can only say **tiene nueve años**. Have you noticed that in Spanish you need to use the verb **tener** to talk about somebody's age?

English
Spanish

a
b
c
d
e
f
g
h
i
j
k
l
m
n
o
p
q
r
s
t
u
v
w
x
y
z

481

English Spanish

a b c d e f g h i j k l m **n** o p q r s t u v w x y z

nineteen NUMBER
diecinueve
nineteen euros
diecinueve euros

She's nineteen.
Tiene diecinueve años.

Language tip
In English you can say **she's nineteen** or **she's nineteen years old**. In Spanish you can only say **tiene diecinueve años**. Have you noticed that in Spanish you need to use the verb **tener** to talk about somebody's age?

nineteenth NUMBER
diecinueve
on the nineteenth floor
en la planta diecinueve
We break up on the nineteenth of December.
Empezamos las vacaciones el diecinueve de diciembre.
It's the nineteenth of February today.
Hoy es diecinueve de febrebro.

on the nineteenth of August
el diecinueve de agosto

Language tip
Use the same set of numbers that you use for counting (**uno**, **dos**, **tres** and so on) when giving Spanish dates.

ninety NUMBER
noventa
My gran is ninety.
Mi abuela tiene noventa años.

Language tip
In English you can say **he's ninety** or **he's ninety years old**. In Spanish you can only say **tiene noventa años**. Have you noticed that in Spanish you need to use the verb **tener** to talk about somebody's age?

ninth NUMBER
noveno masc
novena fem
on the ninth floor
en la planta novena
My birthday's the ninth of April.
Mi cumpleaños es el nueve de abril.
It's the ninth of July today.
Hoy es nueve de julio.

on the ninth of February
el nueve de febrero

Language tip
Use the same set of numbers that you use for counting (**uno**, **dos**, **tres** and so on) when giving Spanish dates.

no

no can be an adverb or an adjective.

A ADVERB
no
Are you coming? — No, I'm not.
¿Vienes? — No.
Can you swim? — No, I can't.
¿Sabes nadar? — No.
B ADJECTIVE
There are no trains on Sundays.
No hay trenes los domingos.
'no smoking'
'prohibido fumar'

nobody PRONOUN
nadie
Who's going with you? — Nobody.
¿Quién va contigo? — Nadie.
Nobody saw me.
Nadie me vio.
Nobody came.
Nadie vino.

Language tip
nadie often goes before the verb. If you're putting it after the verb,

remember to use the construction **no ... nadie**.

There's nobody in the classroom.
No hay nadie en la clase.

to **nod** VERB
decir que sí con la cabeza

noise NOUN
el **ruido** *masc*
Please make less noise.
Por favor, haced menos ruido.

noisy ADJECTIVE
ruidoso *masc*
ruidosa *fem*
the noisiest city in the world
la ciudad más ruidosa del mundo

none PRONOUN
1 ninguno *masc*
ninguna *fem*

Language tip
When **none** *refers to things you can count, such as* **girls** *or* **friends**, *Spanish uses the singular* **ninguno**.

How many girls? — None.
¿Cuántas chicas? — Ninguna.
None of these pens work.
No funciona ninguno de estos bolígrafos.
There are none left.
No queda ninguno.

Language tip
Don't forget to put **no** *before the verb when putting* **ninguno** *after it.*

2 nada

Language tip
When **none** *refers to something you cannot count, such as* **cheese** *or* **milk**, *Spanish uses* **nada**, *which is also singular. Don't forget to put* **no** *before the verb when putting* **nada** *after it.*

There's none left.
No queda nada.

nonsense NOUN
las **tonterías** *fem pl*
She talks a lot of nonsense.
Dice muchas tonterías.

noodles PL NOUN
los **fideos** *masc pl*

noon NOUN
las **doce del mediodía** *fem pl*
It's noon.
Son las doce del mediodía.

at noon
a las doce del mediodía

no one PRONOUN
nadie
Who's going with you? — No one.
¿Quién va contigo? — Nadie.
No one saw me.
Nadie me vio.
No one came.
Nadie vino.

Language tip
nadie *often goes before the verb. If you're putting it after the verb, remember to use the construction* **no ... nadie**.

There's no one in the classroom.
No hay nadie en la clase.

nor CONJUNCTION
neither ... nor
ni ... ni
neither Jack nor Jimmy
ni Jack ni Jimmy

Nor do I.
Yo tampoco.
Nor have I.
Yo tampoco.

normal ADJECTIVE
normal *masc & fem*
at the normal time
a la hora normal

north

> **north** *can be an adjective or a noun.*

A ADJECTIVE
norte

> *Language tip*
>
> **norte** *never changes its ending no matter what it describes. Did you know that adjectives that behave like this are called 'invariable adjectives'?*

the north coast
la costa norte
B NOUN
el **norte** *masc*
in the north
en el norte

Northern Ireland NOUN
Irlanda del Norte *fem*
in Northern Ireland
en Irlanda del Norte
to Northern Ireland
a Irlanda del Norte
I'm from Northern Ireland.
Soy de Irlanda del Norte.

North Pole NOUN
el **Polo Norte** *masc*

North Sea NOUN
el **mar del Norte** *masc*

nose NOUN
la **nariz** *fem* (PL las **narices**)
My nose is blocked.
Tengo la nariz tapada.

> *Language tip*
>
> *In Spanish you usually use an article like* **el**, **la** *or* **los**, **las** *with parts of the body.*

nosy ADJECTIVE
curioso *masc*
curiosa *fem*

not ADVERB
no
Are you coming or not?
¿Vienes o no?
It's not raining.
No está lloviendo.
I don't like cheese.
No me gusta el queso.
He can't drive.
No sabe conducir.
Sit down everybody! Not you, June.
¡Sentaos todos! Tú no, June.
Have you finished? — Not yet.
¿Has terminado? — Todavía no.

> **not yet**
> todavía no
> **not you**
> tú no
> **Thank you! — Not at all!**
> ¡Gracias! — ¡De nada!

note NOUN
1 la **nota** *fem* (message)
I'll write her a note.
Le escribiré una nota.
2 el **billete** *masc* (banknote)

notebook NOUN
el **cuaderno** *masc*

notepad NOUN
el **bloc** *masc* (PL los **blocs**)

notepaper NOUN
el **papel de cartas** *masc*

nothing PRONOUN
nada
What's wrong? — Nothing.
¿Qué pasa? — Nada.

> *Language tip*
>
> *Don't forget to put* **no** *before the verb when putting* **nada** *after it.*

Nothing's the matter.
No pasa nada.
He does nothing.
No hace nada.

notice

notice *can be a noun or a verb.*

A NOUN
el **anuncio** *masc*

Language tip
Be careful! The translation of **notice** *is not* **noticia**.

B VERB
to notice
darse cuenta de
Don't worry, he won't notice anything.
No te preocupes. No se dará cuenta de nada.

notice board NOUN
el **tablón de anuncios** *masc*
(PL los **tablones de anuncios**)

noun NOUN
el **sustantivo** *masc*

novel NOUN
la **novela** *fem*

November NOUN
noviembre *masc*
My birthday's in November.
Mi cumpleaños es en noviembre.
It's the eleventh of November today.
Hoy es once de noviembre.

in November
en noviembre
on the fifth of November
el cinco de noviembre

Language tip
Months are not spelled with a capital letter in Spanish.

now ADVERB
ahora
What are you doing now?
¿Qué estás haciendo ahora?

I'm rather busy just now.
Estoy bastante ocupado en este momento.

not now
ahora no
just now
en este momento
now and then
de vez en cuando
from now on
de ahora en adelante

nowhere ADVERB
a ningún sitio
Where did you go? — Nowhere.
¿Dónde fuiste? — A ningún sitio.
There's nowhere to go in the evenings.
No hay ningún sitio adonde ir por la noche.

number NOUN
1 el **número** *masc* (of house, telephone)
They live at number five.
Viven en el número cinco.
What's your phone number?
¿Cuál es tu número de teléfono?
2 la **cantidad** *fem* (of people, things)
a large number of people
una gran cantidad de personas
3 la **cifra** *fem* (figure)
the second number
la segunda cifra

nun NOUN
la **monja** *fem*

nurse NOUN
el **enfermero** *masc*
la **enfermera** *fem*
I want to be a nurse.
Quiero ser enfermera.

Language tip
When talking about people's jobs in Spanish, you do not use an article.

nursery NOUN
la **guardería** *fem*
My sister goes to nursery.
Mi hermana va a la guardería.

nursery school NOUN
la **escuela infantil** *fem*
My little sister goes to nursery school.

Mi hermana pequeña va a la escuela infantil.

nut NOUN
el **fruto seco** *masc*
I like nuts.
Me gustan los frutos secos.
a bowl of nuts
un cuenco de frutos secos

O o

oats PL NOUN
la **avena** *fem*

Language tip
avena *is a singular word.*

obedient ADJECTIVE
obediente *masc & fem*

to **obey** VERB
cumplir
    **You must obey the
    rules of the game.**
    Tienes que cumplir
    las reglas del juego.

object NOUN
el **objeto** *masc*

obstacle NOUN
el **obstáculo** *masc*

obvious ADJECTIVE
evidente *masc & fem*
    That's obvious!
    ¡Eso es evidente!

occasion NOUN
la **ocasión** *fem* (PL las
ocasiones)
    a special occasion
    una ocasión especial
    on several occasions
    en varias ocasiones

occasionally ADVERB
de vez en cuando

occupation NOUN
la **ocupación** *fem* (PL las
ocupaciones)

ocean NOUN
el **océano** *masc*
    the Atlantic Ocean
    el océano Atlántico
    the Pacific Ocean
    el océano Pacífico

Language tip
océano *is not spelled with a capital
letter in names of oceans.*

o'clock ADVERB
    at four o'clock
    a las cuatro
    It's one o'clock.
    Es la una.
    It's five o'clock.
    Son las cinco.

October NOUN
octubre *masc*
    My birthday's in October.
    Mi cumpleaños es en octubre.
    **It's the eleventh of October
    today.**
    Hoy es once de octubre.

in October
en octubre
on the fifth of October
el cinco de octubre

Language tip
*Months are not spelled with a
capital letter in Spanish.*

odd ADJECTIVE
  1 **raro** *masc*
    rara *fem* (strange)
    That's odd!
    ¡Eso es raro!
  2 **impar** *masc & fem* (not even)
    an odd number
    un número impar

of PREPOSITION
de
    a bottle of water
    una botella de agua
    a kilo of oranges
    un kilo de naranjas
    a boy of ten
    un niño de diez años

a b c d e f g h i j k l m n o p q r s t u v w x y z

the end of the film
el final de la película

> **Language tip**
> **de** combines with **el** to form **del**.

a photo of the school
una foto del colegio
Do you want some of them?
¿Quieres algunos de ellos?
a friend of mine
un amigo mío
That's very kind of you.
Eso es muy amable de tu parte.
There are three of us.
Somos tres.
There are seven of them.
Son siete.

off

> **off** can be an adjective, preposition or adverb.

A ADJECTIVE
1 **apagado** masc
apagada fem (switched off)
The light is off.
La luz está apagada.
2 **cerrado** masc
cerrada fem (turned off)
Is the tap off?
¿Está cerrado el grifo?
3 (cancelled)
The match is off.
El partido se ha cancelado.
4 (absent)
He's off today.
Hoy no ha venido.
Dad's got the day off tomorrow.
Papá no trabaja mañana.
5 (not available)
The soup's off.
No hay sopa.
6 (milk)
The milk's off.
La leche está cortada.
B PREPOSITION
He's off school.
No ha ido al colegio./
No ha venido al colegio.

> **Language tip**
> **he's off school** has two translations depending on whether someone hasn't gone to school or they haven't come to school. Look at the examples.

David's upstairs, he's off school today.
David está arriba, hoy no ha ido al colegio.
Ryan isn't here, he's off school today.
Ryan no está aquí, hoy no ha venido al colegio.
C ADVERB
Off you go, Jack!
¡Hala Jack, vete!

offer

> **offer** can be a verb or a noun.

A VERB
to offer
ofrecer
Can you offer Teresa something to drink?
¿Puedes ofrecerle a Teresa algo de beber?
B NOUN
la **oferta** fem
There's a special offer on dictionaries.
Hay una oferta especial de diccionarios.

office NOUN
la **oficina** fem
She works in an office.
Trabaja en una oficina.

often ADVERB
a menudo

We often go to London.
Vamos a menudo a Londres.
It often rains.
Llueve a menudo.

English

Spanish

How often do you clean your teeth?

¿Con qué frecuencia te lavas los dientes?

oil NOUN
  el **aceite** *masc*

OK EXCLAMATION, ADJECTIVE
  = **okay**

okay

> **okay** *can be an exclamation or an adjective.*

  A EXCLAMATION
  ¡de acuerdo!
    I'll go tomorrow. — Okay!
    Iré mañana. — ¡De acuerdo!
  B ADJECTIVE
  bien

> *Language tip*
> **bien** *never changes its ending.*

    I'm okay thanks.
    Estoy bien, gracias.
    Is everything okay?
    ¿Está todo bien?
    Do you like school? — It's okay.
    ¿Te gusta el colegio? — No está mal.
    Is that okay with you?
    ¿Estás de acuerdo con eso?

> **Okay!**
> ¡De acuerdo!
> **Are you okay?**
> ¿Estás bien?

old ADJECTIVE
  viejo *masc*
  vieja *fem*
    an old dog
    un perro viejo
    an old house
    una casa vieja
    old shoes
    zapatos viejos

> *Language tip*
> *It sounds more polite if you describe someone as* **mayor** *rather than* **viejo**.

    an old man
    un hombre mayor
    an old lady
    una señora mayor
    old people
    los mayores

> *Language tip*
> **mayor** *can also mean* **older** *or* **oldest** *while* **mayor que** *means* **older than**.

    my older sister
    mi hermana mayor
    my oldest brother
    mi hermano mayor
    Damian's the oldest in the class.
    Damian es el mayor de la clase.
    I'm older than you.
    Soy mayor que tú.
    She's two years older than me.
    Ella tiene dos años más que yo.

> **How old are you?**
> ¿Cuántos años tienes?
> **He's ten years old.**
> Tiene diez años.

old age pensioner NOUN
  el **jubilado** *masc*
  la **jubilada** *fem*
    She's an old age pensioner.
    Ella está jubilada.

Olympic ADJECTIVE
  olímpico *masc*
  olímpica *fem*
    the Olympic Games
    los Juegos Olímpicos

omelette NOUN
  la **tortilla** *fem*

on

> **on** *can be an adjective or a preposition.*

  A ADJECTIVE
  1 **encendido** *masc*
    encendida *fem* (switched on)
    The light is on.
    La luz está encendida.

a
b
c
d
e
f
g
h
i
j
k
l
m
n
o
p
q
r
s
t
u
v
w
x
y
z

2 **abierto**
abierta (tap)
The tap is on.
El grifo está abierto.

B PREPOSITION

1 **en**
Your books are on the table.
Tus libros están en la mesa.
on the wall
en la pared
I go to school on my bike.
Voy al colegio en bici.
Is there anything on television?
¿Hay algo en la televisión?
I'm on the phone.
Estoy hablando por teléfono.

2 **sobre** (about)
a book on Ghandi
un libro sobre Ghandi

3 (with days and dates)

Language tip
Just give **el** with a particular day or date.

on Monday
el lunes
on the fifteenth of June
el quince de junio

Language tip
To say **on Sundays**, **on Tuesdays**, and so on, use **los**.

on Sundays
los domingos
on Tuesdays
los martes

4 (in expressions)
It's on the right.
Está a la derecha.
They're on holiday.
Están de vacaciones.

on Friday
el viernes
on Fridays
los viernes
on June 20th
el 20 de junio
on Christmas Day
el día de Navidad
on holiday
de vacaciones
on the left
a la izquierda

once ADVERB
una **vez**
once a week
una vez por semana
only once
solo una vez
Come here at once!
¡Ven aquí enseguida!
Everybody answered at once.
Todo el mundo contestó a la vez.
once more
otra vez

one NUMBER, PRONOUN
1 **un** masc (before noun)
una fem

Language tip
Use **un** before a masculine noun and **una** before a feminine noun.

one day
un día
one hour
una hora
I've got one brother and one sister.
Tengo un hermano y una hermana.

She's one.
Tiene un año.

Language tip
In English you can say **she's one** or **she's one year old**. In Spanish you can only say **tiene un año**. Have you noticed that in Spanish you need to use the verb **tener** to talk about somebody's age?

2 uno *masc (not before noun)*
una *fem*
This sweater is too big, I need a smaller one.
Este jersey es demasiado grande. Necesito uno más pequeño.
This T-shirt is too small, I need a bigger one.
Esta camiseta es demasiado pequeña. Necesito una más grande.
Which packet do you want? — The big one.
¿Qué paquete quieres? — El grande.
Which card do you want? — The red one.
¿Qué carta quieres? — La roja.
one, two, three, four, five ...
uno, dos, tres, cuatro, cinco ...
It's one o'clock.
Es la una.

onion NOUN
la **cebolla** *fem*

only

only *can be an adjective or an adverb.*

A ADJECTIVE
único
masc
única
fem

my only dress
mi único vestido
my only clean T-shirt
mi única camiseta limpia
I'm an only child.
Soy hijo único.
Tracy is an only child.
Tracy es hija única.

B ADVERB
sólo
only ten euros
sólo diez euros
I've only got two cards.

Sólo tengo dos cartas.
He's only three.
Sólo tiene tres años.

Language tip
*Traditionally, the adverb **sólo** was written with an accent to distinguish it from the unaccented adjective **solo**, meaning 'alone'. Nowadays, you don't have to give the accent unless the sentence would be confusing otherwise.*

open

open *can be an adjective or a verb.*

A ADJECTIVE
abierto *masc*
abierta *fem*
The supermarket is open on Sunday mornings.
El supermercado está abierto los domingos por la mañana.

B VERB
to open
abrir
Can I open the window?
¿Puedo abrir la ventana?
Open your books.
Abrid vuestros libros.
What time does the bank open?
¿A qué hora abre el banco?

opening hours PL NOUN
el **horario de apertura** *masc*

operation NOUN
la **operación** *fem* (PL las **operaciones**)
He is recovering from an operation.
Se está recuperando de una operación.
My mum's going to have an operation.
Van a operar a mi madre.

opinion NOUN
la **opinión** *fem* (PL las **opiniones**)
in my opinion
en mi opinión

What's your opinion?
¿Tú qué opinas?

opponent NOUN
el **adversario** masc
la **adversaria** fem

opportunity NOUN
la **oportunidad** fem
It's a good opportunity.
Es una buena oportunidad.

opposite

opposite *can be an adjective, noun, adverb or preposition.*

A ADJECTIVE
contrario masc
contraria fem
It's in the opposite direction.
Está en la dirección contraria.

B NOUN
the opposite
lo contrario
the opposite of good
lo contrario de bueno

C ADVERB
enfrente
They live opposite.
Viven enfrente.

D PREPOSITION
enfrente de
the girl sitting opposite me
la niña que está sentada enfrente de mí

or CONJUNCTION
1 o
Would you like tea or coffee?
¿Quieres té o café?
Hurry up or you'll miss the bus.
Date prisa o perderás el autobús.

Language tip
Change **o** *to* **u** *before words starting with* **o-** *or* **ho-**.

seven or eight
siete u ocho
men or women
mujeres u hombres

2 ni *(in negatives)*
I don't eat meat or fish.
No como carne ni pescado.

oral NOUN
el **examen oral** masc (PL los **exámenes orales**)
I've got my Spanish oral soon.
Tengo mi examen oral de español pronto.

orange

orange *can be a noun or an adjective.*

A NOUN
1 la **naranja** fem *(fruit)*
a big orange
una naranja grande
2 el **naranja**
masc *(colour)*
Orange is my favourite colour.
El naranja es mi color favorito.

Language tip
When it means the colour **orange**, **el naranja**, *like all colours in Spanish, is masculine.*

B ADJECTIVE
naranja

Language tip
The colour **naranja** *never changes its ending no matter what it describes. Don't forget that colour adjectives come after the noun in Spanish.*

orange curtains
cortinas naranja

orange juice NOUN
el **zumo de naranja** masc

orchestra NOUN
la **orquesta** fem
I play in the school orchestra.
Toco en la orquesta del colegio.

order

order *can be a noun or a verb.*

A NOUN

1 el **orden** *masc (sequence)*
Put the words in alphabetical order, children.
Poned las palabras en orden alfabético, niños.
The words are not in the right order.
Las palabras no están en el orden correcto.

2 *(in restaurant)*
The waiter took our order.
El camarero tomó nota de lo que queríamos.

3 la **orden** *fem* (PL las **órdenes**) *(command)*

'out of order'
'no funciona'

B VERB
to order
pedir
Are you ready to order?
¿Ya saben lo que van a pedir?

ordinary ADJECTIVE
normal *masc & fem*
an ordinary day
un día normal

to **organize** VERB
organizar
We are organizing a trip to London.
Estamos organizando un viaje a Londres.

original ADJECTIVE
original *masc & fem*
It's a very original idea.
Es una idea muy original.

orphan NOUN
el **huérfano** *masc*
la **huérfana** *fem*

other

other *can be an adjective or a pronoun.*

A ADJECTIVE
otro *masc*
otra *fem*

on the other side of the street
al otro lado de la calle
the other day
el otro día

Language tip
The translation of **the other one** *depends on whether you're referring to something masculine or feminine. Use* **el otro** *for something masculine and* **la otra** *for something feminine.*

This knife? — No, the other one.
¿Este cuchillo? — No, el otro.
This spoon? — No, the other one.
¿Esta cuchara? — No, la otra.

B PRONOUN
el **otro** *masc*
la **otra** *fem*
Get into twos, one behind the other.
Poneos de dos en dos, uno detrás del otro.
Where are the others?
¿Dónde están los otros?

ought VERB

Language tip
To translate **ought to***, you need to use the conditional tense of the verb* **deber***.*

I ought to phone my parents.
Debería llamar a mis padres.

our ADJECTIVE
  nuestro *masc*
  nuestra *fem*
    our dog
    nuestro perro
    our house
    nuestra casa
    our friends
    nuestros amigos
    our plants
    nuestras plantas

Language tip
*You usually translate **our** using **el**, **la**, etc before parts of the body or clothes, particularly when using a reflexive verb.*

    We took off our coats.
    Nos quitamos los abrigos.

ours PRONOUN
  el **nuestro** *masc*
  la **nuestra** *fem*

Language tip
*Remember that the choice of **el nuestro**, **la nuestra**, **los nuestros** or **las nuestras** depends entirely on the thing or things referred to.*

    That's not our car. Ours is here.
    Aquél no es nuestro coche. El nuestro está aquí.
    Those aren't our backpacks. Ours are here.
    Aquéllas no son nuestras mochilas. Las nuestras están aquí.

Language tip
*After **ser** you can usually just use **nuestro**, **nuestra**, **nuestros** or **nuestras** to agree with the noun referred to.*

    Is this ours?
    ¿Es nuestro esto?
    These cases are ours.
    Estas maletas son nuestras.
    Whose is this? — It's ours.

    ¿De quién es esto? — Es nuestro.

ourselves PRONOUN
  1 **nos** *(reflexive)*
    We enjoyed ourselves.
    Nos divertimos.
  2 **nosotros mismos** *masc pl*
    nosotras mismas *fem pl*
    (for emphasis)
    We did it ourselves!
    ¡Lo hicimos nosotros mismos!
    by ourselves
    solos
    We want to do it by ourselves.
    Queremos hacerlo solos.

out

out can be an adverb or an adjective.

A ADVERB
  1 **fuera** *(not at home)*
    Derek's out.
    Derek está fuera.
    I'm going out.
    Voy a salir.
    He was coming out of the cinema.
    Estaba saliendo del cine.
    Can you get the paints out of the cupboard?
    ¿Puedes sacar las pinturas del armario?
  2 **eliminado** *masc*
    eliminada *fem (in game)*

Language tip
***eliminado** is an adjective, so remember that it needs to agree with the person it refers to.*

    You're out, Lucy!
    ¡Estás eliminada, Lucy!

'way out'
'salida'

B ADJECTIVE
  apagado *masc*
  apagada *fem (turned off)*

All the lights are out.
Todas las luces están apagadas.

outdoor ADJECTIVE
  al aire libre
    outdoor activities
    actividades al aire libre
    an outdoor swimming pool
    una piscina exterior

outdoors ADVERB
  al aire libre

outer space NOUN
  el **espacio** masc
    a monster from outer space
    un monstruo del espacio

outside

  outside can be an adverb or a
  preposition.

  A ADVERB
    fuera
    It's very cold outside.
    Hace mucho
    frío fuera.
  B PREPOSITION
    fuera de
    outside
    the school
    fuera del
    colegio

oven NOUN
  el **horno** masc

over

  over can be a preposition or an
  adjective.

  A PREPOSITION
  1 **más de** (more than)
    **There were over five hundred
    people at the concert.**
    Había más de quinientas
    personas en el concierto.
    Are you over ten?
    ¿Tienes más de diez años?
    The temperature is over

thirty degrees.
La temperatura supera los
treinta grados.
  2 **durante** (during)
    over Christmas
    durante la Navidad
  3 **al otro lado de** (across)
    The baker's is over the road.
    La panadería está al otro lado de
    la calle.
  4 **encima de** (above)
    **There's a mirror over the
    washbasin.**
    Encima del lavabo hay un espejo.

Language tip

Use **por encima de** instead when
there is movement **over** something.

    The ball went over the wall.
    La pelota pasó por encima del
    muro.
    a bridge over the river
    un puente sobre el río

  over here
  aquí
  over there
  allí
  all over Scotland
  por toda Escocia

  B ADJECTIVE (finished)
    The match is over.
    Se ha terminado el partido.

overcast ADJECTIVE
  cubierto masc
  cubierta fem
    The sky was overcast.
    El cielo estaba cubierto.

overhead projector NOUN
  el **retroproyector** masc

to **owe** VERB
  deber
    He owes me five pounds.
    Me debe cinco libras.

owl NOUN
  el **búho** masc

own ADJECTIVE
propio *masc*
propia *fem*
> **I've got my own bathroom.**
> Tengo mi propio cuarto de baño.
> **I'd like a room of my own.**
> Quiero una habitación para mí
> solo.
> **He lives on his own.**
> Vive solo.

on his own
solo
on her own
sola

owner NOUN
el **propietario** *masc*
la **propietaria** *fem*

P p

pack

> **pack** *can be a verb or a noun.*

A VERB
to pack
hacer las maletas
I have to pack.
Tengo que hacer las maletas.

B NOUN
1 el **pack** *masc (of goods)*
a pack of six
un pack de seis
2 el **paquete** *masc (packet)*
3 la **baraja** *fem (of cards)*
a pack of cards
una baraja de cartas

packed lunch NOUN
I take a packed lunch to school.
Me llevo la comida al colegio.

packet NOUN
el **paquete** *masc*
a packet of crisps
una bolsa de patatas fritas

page NOUN
la **página** *fem*
on page ten
en la página diez
Look at page six, everyone.
Mirad todos en la página seis.

paid VERB ▷*see* pay

pain NOUN
1 el **dolor** *masc*
a terrible pain
un dolor horrible
2 **to be a pain**
ser un pesado
He's a pain.
Es un pesado.

> **Language tip**
> *Change* **un pesado** *to* **una pesada** *if you're referring to a girl.*

My little sister is a pain.
Mi hermana pequeña es una pesada.

paint

> **paint** *can be a noun or a verb.*

A NOUN
la **pintura** *fem*
red paint
pintura roja
'wet paint'
'recién pintado'
B VERB
to paint
pintar
I'm going to paint it green.
Lo voy a pintar de verde.

paintbrush NOUN
1 el **pincel** *masc (for artwork)*
2 la **brocha** *fem (for walls, ceiling)*

painting NOUN
1 el **cuadro** *masc (picture)*
a painting by Picasso
un cuadro de Picasso
2 la **pintura** *fem (activity)*
I like painting.
Me gusta la pintura.

pair NOUN
el **par** *masc*
a pair of shoes
un par de zapatos
a pair of trousers
unos pantalones
two pairs of trousers
dos pantalones
a pair of jeans
unos vaqueros
in pairs
por parejas
We work in pairs.
Trabajamos por parejas.

English **Spanish**

a b c d e f g h i j k l m n o p q r s t u v w x y z

Can you get into pairs?
¿Podéis colocaros por parejas?

pal NOUN
el **amigo** *masc*
la **amiga** *fem*

palace
NOUN
el **palacio** *masc*

pale ADJECTIVE
1 **pálido** *masc*
pálida *fem*
She looks very pale.
Está muy pálida.
2 **claro** *masc*
clara *fem (in colour)*
pale blue
azul claro
a pale blue shirt
una camisa azul claro

some pale green curtains
unas cortinas verde claro

pan NOUN
1 la **cacerola** *fem (saucepan)*
2 la **sartén** *fem* (PL las **sartenes**)
(frying pan)

pancake NOUN
la **tortita** *fem*

Pancake Day NOUN
el **Martes de Carnaval** *masc*

to **panic** VERB
Don't panic!
¡Tranquilo!

pantomime NOUN
la **pantomima navideña** *fem*

pants PL NOUN
1 los **calzoncillos** *masc pl*
(for men, boys)
a pair of pants
unos calzoncillos
2 las **braguitas** *fem pl*
(for women, girls)
a pair of pants
unas braguitas

paper NOUN
1 el **papel** *masc*
Have you got a pencil and
some paper?
¿Tienes lápiz y papel?
a paper towel
una servilleta de papel
a piece of paper
un papel

2 el **periódico**
masc (newspaper)

paper boy
NOUN
el **repartidor
de periódicos** *masc*

paper girl NOUN
la **repartidora de
periódicos** *fem*

parade NOUN
el **desfile** *masc*

paragraph NOUN
el **párrafo** *masc*

parcel NOUN
el **paquete** *masc*

pardon
NOUN
Pardon?
¿Cómo?

parents
PL NOUN
los **padres**
masc pl
my parents
mis padres

Language tip
Be careful! The translation of **parents** is not **parientes**.

park

park *can be a noun or a verb.*

A NOUN
el **parque** *masc*
There's a nice park.
Hay un parque bonito.
B VERB
to park
aparcar
It's difficult to park.
Es difícil aparcar.

parking NOUN
'**no parking**'
'prohibido aparcar'

parrot NOUN
el **loro** *masc*

part NOUN
1 la **parte** *fem*
The first part is easy.
La primera parte es fácil.
2 **to take part in something**
participar en algo
I'm taking part in the competition.
Participo en el concurso.

partly ADVERB
en parte

partner NOUN
1 el **compañero** *masc*
la **compañera** *fem (in game, role play)*
2 la **pareja** *fem (in dance, relationship)*

Language tip
Even though **la pareja** *is a feminine word, you can use it to refer to a man.*

part-time ADJECTIVE, ADVERB
a tiempo parcial
a part-time job
un trabajo a tiempo parcial
She works part-time.
Trabaja a tiempo parcial.

party NOUN
la **fiesta** *fem*
I'm going to a party on Saturday.
Voy a una fiesta el sábado.
a birthday party
una fiesta de cumpleaños
a Christmas party
una fiesta de Navidad

to **pass** VERB
1 **pasar** *(give)*
Pass the ball, Nina!
¡Pasa la pelota, Nina!
Could you pass me the salt?
¿Me puedes pasar la sal?
2 **pasar por delante de**
(go past)
You pass the post office.
Pasas por delante de Correos.

passenger NOUN
el **pasajero** *masc*
la **pasajera** *fem*

Passover NOUN
la **Pascua Judía** *fem*
at Passover
en la Pascua Judía

passport NOUN
el **pasaporte** *masc*
Have you got your passport?
¿Llevas tu pasaporte?

English

Spanish

a
b
c
d
e
f
g
h
i
j
k
l
m
n
o
p
q
r
s
t
u
v
w
x
y
z

password NOUN
la **contraseña** *fem*

past

past can be a preposition or a noun.

A PREPOSITION
1 después de *(after)*
It's on the right, just past the station.
Está a la derecha, justo después de la estación.
2 *(with times)*
It's quarter past one.
Es la una y cuarto.
It's half past ten.
Son las diez y media.
It's quarter past nine.
Son las nueve y cuarto.
It's ten past eight.
Son las ocho y diez.
at ten past five
a las cinco y diez

> **half past eight**
> las ocho y media
> **quarter past ten**
> las diez y cuarto

B NOUN
el **pasado** *masc*
in the past
en el pasado

pasta NOUN
la **pasta** *fem*
Pasta is easy to cook.
La pasta es fácil de cocinar.

path NOUN
1 el **camino** *masc (in garden, town)*
Follow the path.
Sigue el camino.
2 el **sendero** *masc (in woods)*

patience NOUN
la **paciencia** *fem*

He hasn't got much patience.
No tiene mucha paciencia.

patient

patient can be a noun or an adjective.

A NOUN
el/la **paciente** *masc/fem*
B ADJECTIVE
paciente *masc & fem*
The teacher is very patient.
El maestro es muy paciente.
Be patient, Joshua.
Ten paciencia, Joshua.

patio NOUN
el **patio** *masc*

pattern NOUN
el **diseño** *masc*
a simple pattern
un diseño sencillo

pause NOUN
la **pausa** *fem*

pavement NOUN
la **acera** *fem*
on the pavement
en la acera

paw NOUN
la **pata** *fem*

pay

pay can be a noun or a verb.

A NOUN
la **paga** *fem*
What is the pay?
¿Cuánto es la paga?
B VERB
to pay
pagar
Who's going to pay?
¿Quién va a pagar?
Where do I pay?
¿Dónde pago?
to pay for something
pagar algo
I've paid for my ticket.
He pagado mi entrada.

I paid ten euros for the book.
Pagué diez euros por el libro.
to pay attention
prestar atención

Pay attention, Hayley!
¡Presta atención, Hayley!
Pay attention, everybody!
¡Prestad todos atención!

PC NOUN
el **PC** masc
I have a PC at home.
Tengo un PC en casa.

PE NOUN
la **educación física** fem
We have PE twice a week.
Tenemos educación física dos
veces por semana.

pea NOUN
el **guisante** masc
a tin of peas
una lata de guisantes

peace NOUN
la **paz** fem

peach NOUN
el **melocotón** masc (PL los
melocotones)
a kilo of peaches
un kilo de melocotones

peanut NOUN
el **cacahuete** masc
a packet of peanuts
un paquete de cacahuetes

peanut butter NOUN
la **mantequilla de
cacahuete** fem
a peanut butter sandwich
un bocadillo de mantequilla de
cacahuete

pear NOUN
la **pera** fem
**Which would you like, a pear
or an apple?**
¿Qué es lo que quieres: una pera
o una manzana?

pebble NOUN
el **guijarro** masc

pedal NOUN
el **pedal** masc

peg NOUN
1 el **gancho** masc (for coats)
2 la **pinza de la ropa** fem
(clothes peg)

pen NOUN
el **bolígrafo** masc
Can I borrow your pen?
¿Me dejas tu bolígrafo?

pence PL NOUN
los **peniques** masc pl

pencil NOUN
el **lápiz** masc (PL los **lápices**)
in pencil
a lápiz
coloured pencils
lápices de colores

pencil case NOUN
el **estuche** masc

pencil sharpener NOUN
el **sacapuntas** masc (PL los
sacapuntas)

penfriend NOUN
el **amigo por
correspondencia** masc
la **amiga por
correspondencia** fem
**I'm Emma, your English
penfriend.**
Soy Emma, tu amiga por
correspondencia inglesa.

penknife NOUN
la **navaja** fem

penny NOUN
el **penique** masc

pensioner NOUN
el/la **pensionista** masc/fem

people PL NOUN
1 la **gente** fem
The people are nice.

English Spanish

a b c d e f g h i j k l m n o **p** q r s t u v w x y z

La gente es simpática.
a lot of people
mucha gente
There are too many people here.
Aquí hay demasiada gente.

> *Language tip*
> *Remember that **gente** is a singular word in Spanish.*

2 las **personas** *fem pl* (*individuals*)
Four people can play.
Pueden jugar cuatro personas.
How many people are there in your family?
¿Cuántas personas forman tu familia?

> *Language tip*
> *In English you can say **tall people**, **rich people** etc. In Spanish you say the equivalent of **the tall**, **the rich** etc.*

tall people
los altos
rich people
los ricos
Spanish people
los españoles

pepper NOUN
1 la **pimienta** *fem* (*spice*)
Pass the pepper, please.
Pásame la pimienta, por favor.
2 el **pimiento** *masc* (*vegetable*)
a red pepper
un pimiento rojo

per PREPOSITION
por
per day
por día

per cent ADVERB
por ciento
fifty per cent
cincuenta por ciento

perfect ADJECTIVE
perfecto *masc*

perfecta *fem*
Raquel speaks perfect English.
Raquel habla un inglés perfecto.

performance NOUN
la **representación** *fem* (PL las **representaciones**)
The performance starts at two o'clock.
La representación empieza a las dos.

perfume NOUN
el **perfume** *masc*
a bottle of perfume
un frasco de perfume

perhaps
ADVERB
a lo mejor
Perhaps he's ill.
A lo mejor está enfermo.

period NOUN
el **periodo** *masc*
the holiday period
el periodo de vacaciones

permission NOUN
el **permiso** *masc*
Have you got permission?
¿Tienes permiso?

person NOUN
la **persona** *fem*
She's a very nice person.
Es una persona muy simpática.

personality NOUN
la **personalidad** *fem*

pet NOUN
la **mascota** *fem*
Have you got a pet?
¿Tienes alguna mascota?

petrol NOUN
la **gasolina** *fem*
unleaded petrol
gasolina sin plomo

pet shop NOUN
la **tienda de animales** *fem*

phone

> **phone** *can be a noun or a verb.*

A NOUN
el **teléfono** *masc*
Where's the phone?
¿Dónde está el teléfono?
She's on the phone at the moment.
Ahora mismo está al teléfono.
Can I use the phone, please?
¿Puedo llamar por teléfono, por favor?

B VERB
to phone
llamar
I'll phone you tomorrow.
Mañana te llamo.
I have to phone my mum.
Tengo que llamar a mi madre.
Who are you phoning?
¿A quién llamas?

> **Language tip**
> *Don't forget the personal **a** in examples like the last two.*

phone box NOUN
la **cabina telefónica** *fem*

phone call NOUN
la **llamada** *fem*
She gets lots of phone calls.
Recibe muchas llamadas.
Can I make a phone call?
¿Puedo hacer una llamada?

phonecard NOUN
la **tarjeta telefónica** *fem*

phone number NOUN
el **número de teléfono** *masc*
What's your phone number?
¿Cuál es tu número de teléfono?

photo NOUN
la **foto** *fem*
This is a photo of my family.
Ésta es una foto de mi familia.
I want to take some photos.
Quiero hacer unas fotos.
I want to take a photo of you.
Quiero hacerte una foto.

> **Language tip**
> *Even though it ends in **-o**, **la foto** is a feminine noun.*

photocopier NOUN
la **fotocopiadora** *fem*

photocopy

> **photocopy** *can be a noun or a verb.*

A NOUN
la **fotocopia** *fem*
It's only a photocopy.
Es solo una fotocopia.

B VERB
to photocopy
fotocopiar
You can photocopy it.
Puedes fotocopiarlo.

photograph NOUN
la **fotografía** *fem*

physics NOUN
la **física** *fem*
She teaches physics.
Ella da clases de física.

pianist NOUN
el/la **pianista** *masc/fem*

piano NOUN
el **piano** *masc*

I play the piano.
Toco el piano.
I have piano lessons.
Tomo clases de piano.

pick

> **pick** *can be a noun or a verb.*

A NOUN
Take your pick!
¡Escoge el que quieras!
B VERB
to pick
1 **escoger** *(choose)*
Pick a card, Murray!
¡Escoge una carta, Murray!
Pick three girls and three boys.
Escoge a tres niños y tres niñas.

> **Language tip**
> *Don't forget the personal* **a** *in examples like this one.*

2 **coger** *(fruit, flowers)*
I like picking strawberries.
Me gusta coger fresas.

to **pick up** VERB
1 **recoger** *(collect)*
We can come to the airport to pick you up.
Podemos ir al aeropuerto a recogerte.
2 **coger** *(take)*
Pick up another card, William!
¡Coge otra carta, William!

> **Language tip**
> *Use* **tomar** *instead of* **coger** *if talking to someone from Latin America.*

3 **aprender** *(learn)*
I hope I'll pick up some Spanish.
Espero aprender un poco de español.

picnic NOUN
el **picnic** *masc*
I like picnics.
Me gustan los picnics.
to have a picnic

hacer un picnic
We had a picnic on the beach.
Hicimos un picnic en la playa.

picture NOUN
1 la **foto** *fem (photo)*
This is a picture of my family.
Ésta es una foto de mi familia.

> **Language tip**
> *Even though it ends in* **-o**, **la foto** *is a feminine noun.*

2 el **cuadro** *masc (painting)*
a famous picture
un cuadro famoso
3 el **dibujo** *masc (drawing)*
I'll draw a picture.
Haré un dibujo.
Draw a picture of your pet, Lisa.
Haz un dibujo de tu mascota, Lisa.
4 la **ilustración** *fem* (PL las **ilustraciones**) *(illustration)*
Look at the picture.
Mira la ilustración.

pie NOUN
la **tarta** *fem*
an apple pie
una tarta de manzana

piece NOUN
el **trozo** *masc*
A small piece, please.
Un trozo pequeño, por favor.

pierced ADJECTIVE
I've got pierced ears.
Tengo los agujeros hechos en las orejas.
I want to get my ears pierced.
Quiero hacerme los agujeros en las orejas.

> **Language tip**
> *In Spanish you usually use an article like* **el**, **la** *or* **los**, **las** *with parts of the body.*

pig NOUN
el **cerdo** *masc*

pigeon NOUN
la **paloma** fem

piggy bank NOUN
la **hucha** fem

pigtail NOUN
la **trenza** fem
She's got pigtails.
Lleva trenzas.

pile NOUN
el **montón** masc (PL los
montones)
a pile of books
un montón de libros

pill NOUN
la **píldora** fem

pillow NOUN
la **almohada** fem

pilot NOUN
el/la **piloto** masc/fem
She's a pilot.
Es piloto.

> **Language tip**
> Even though **piloto** ends in **-o**, you
> can use it to refer to a woman.
> Remember that in Spanish, you do
> not use an article with people's jobs.

pineapple NOUN
la **piña** fem

pink

> **pink** can be an adjective or a noun.

A ADJECTIVE
rosa

> **Language tip**
> The colour **rosa** never changes its
> ending no matter what it describes.
> Don't forget that colour adjectives
> come after the noun in Spanish.

a pink dress
un vestido rosa
B NOUN
el **rosa** masc
Pink is my favourite colour.
El rosa es mi color favorito.

> **Language tip**
> When it means the colour **pink**, **el
> rosa**, like all colours in Spanish, is
> masculine.

pint NOUN
la **pinta** fem
a pint of milk
una pinta de leche

> **Did you know...?**
> In Spain liquids are measured in
> litres and centilitres. A pint is about
> 0.6 litres.

pipe NOUN
la **tubería** fem (for water)

pirate NOUN
el/la **pirata** masc/fem
**a pirate
DVD**
un DVD
pirata

pitch NOUN
el **campo** masc
a football pitch
un campo de fútbol

pity NOUN
What a pity she can't come!
¡Qué pena que no pueda venir!

> **What a pity!**
> ¡Qué pena!

pizza NOUN
la **pizza** fem

place NOUN
el **sitio** masc
It's a quiet place.
Es un sitio tranquilo.
**There are a lot of interesting
places to visit.**
Hay un montón de sitios
interesantes que visitar.
Can I change places?

a
b
c
d
e
f
g
h
i
j
k
l
m
n
o
p
q
r
s
t
u
v
w
x
y
z

¿Puedo cambiarme de sitio?
Carol, change places with Harry!
¡Carol, cámbiate de sitio con Harry!

plain ADJECTIVE
liso *masc*
lisa *fem (not patterned)*
a plain grey fabric
una tela gris lisa

plain chocolate NOUN
el **chocolate amargo** *masc*

plait NOUN
la **trenza** *fem*
She wears her hair in a plait.
Lleva el pelo recogido en una trenza.

> **Language tip**
> In Spanish you usually use an article like **el**, **la** or **los**, **las** with parts of the body.

plan

> **plan** can be a noun or a verb.

A NOUN
1 el **plan** *masc*
Have you got any plans for the holidays?
¿Tienes planes para las vacaciones?
2 el **plano** *masc (map)*
a plan of the school
un plano del colegio
B VERB
to plan
planear
We're planning a trip to the States.
Estamos planeando hacer un viaje a Estados Unidos.

plane NOUN
el **avión** *masc* (PL los **aviones**)
by plane
en avión

plant NOUN
la **planta** *fem*

plaster NOUN
la **tirita** *fem*

plastic

> **plastic** can be a noun or an adjective.

A NOUN
el **plástico** *masc*
It's made of plastic.
Es de plástico.
B ADJECTIVE
de plástico
a plastic bag
una bolsa de plástico

plate NOUN
el **plato**
masc

platform NOUN
el **andén** *masc* (PL los **andenes**)
I'll wait for you on the platform, ok?
Te espero en el andén, ¿vale?

> **Did you know…?**
> At railway stations in Spain, it is the track rather than the platform that's numbered.

on platform seven
en la vía siete

play

> **play** can be a verb or a noun.

A VERB
to play
1 **jugar**
He's playing with his friends.
Está jugando con sus amigos.
2 **jugar a** *(sport, game)*
I play football.
Juego al fútbol.
Can you play chess?
¿Sabes jugar al ajedrez?

3 **tocar** *(instrument)*
I play the guitar.
Toco la guitarra.
What sort of music do they play?
¿Qué tipo de música tocan?

4 **poner** *(CD)*
Why don't you play that CD that you like?
¿Por qué no pones ese CD que te gusta?

B NOUN
la **obra** *fem*
a play by Shakespeare
una obra de Shakespeare

player NOUN
el **jugador** *masc*
la **jugadora** *fem*
a football player
un jugador de fútbol

playground NOUN
1 el **patio de recreo** *masc*
(at school)
2 los **columpios** *masc pl*
(in park)

playgroup NOUN
la **guardería** *fem*

playing card NOUN
la **carta** *fem*

playing field
NOUN
el **campo de deportes** *masc*

playtime NOUN
el **recreo** *masc*
at playtime
en el recreo

please EXCLAMATION
por favor
Two coffees, please.
Dos cafés, por favor.

Did you know…?
In Spanish you don't use **por favor** *as often as you'd say* **please** *in English. Speakers often show politeness by phrasing requests as a question.*

I'd like a lemonade, please.
¿Me pone una gaseosa?
Can we have the bill, please?
¿Nos puede traer la cuenta?
Can you open the door for me, please?
¿Me puede abrir la puerta?

Yes, please!
¡Sí, por favor!

pleased ADJECTIVE
contento *masc*
contenta *fem*
My mother isn't pleased.
Mi madre no está contenta.

pleasure NOUN
el **gusto** *masc*
with pleasure
con mucho gusto

plenty NOUN
I've got plenty.
Tengo de sobra.
You've got plenty of time.
Tienes tiempo de sobra.

That's plenty, thanks.
Así está bien, gracias.

to **plug in** VERB
enchufar
Is it plugged in?
¿Está enchufado?
It isn't plugged in.
No está enchufado.

plum NOUN
la **ciruela** *fem*
plum jam
mermelada de ciruela

plump ADJECTIVE
regordete *masc & fem*

plural NOUN
el **plural** *masc*

a
b
c
d
e
f
g
h
i
j
k
l
m
n
o
p
q
r
s
t
u
v
w
x
y
z

English **Spanish**

a b c d e f g h i j k l m n o **P** q r s t u v w x y z

in the plural
en plural

plus PREPOSITION
más
> **Four plus three equals seven.**
> Cuatro más tres son siete.

p.m. ABBREVIATION
1 **de la tarde** (in the afternoon or evening)
> **at two p.m.**
> a las dos de la tarde
2 **de la noche** (at night)
> **at ten p.m.**
> a las diez de la noche

> *Language tip*
> Use **de la tarde** at times when it's still light and **de la noche** at times when it's dark.

poached egg NOUN
el **huevo escalfado** *masc*

pocket NOUN
el **bolsillo** *masc*
> **It's in my pocket.**
> Lo tengo en el bolsillo.

pocket money NOUN
la **paga** *fem*
> **I get two pounds a week pocket money.**
> Me dan dos libras a la semana de paga.

poem NOUN
el **poema** *masc*

> *Language tip*
> Even though it ends in **-a**, **el poema** is a masculine noun.

point

> point can be a noun or a verb.

A NOUN
1 el **punto** *masc*
> **You've got five points.**
> Tienes cinco puntos.
> **What's the point?**
> ¿Para qué?

> **What's the point of leaving so early?**
> ¿Para qué vamos a salir tan pronto?
2 la **coma** *fem* (in decimals)
> **two point five (2.5)**
> dos coma cinco (2,5)

> *Did you know…?*
> In Spanish you use a comma instead of a point in decimal numbers.

B VERB
> **to point**: **Which cake? Can you point to it?**
> ¿Qué pastel? ¿Puedes señalarlo?
> **The guide pointed out the Columbus monument to us.**
> El guía nos señaló dónde estaba el monumento a Colón.

poison NOUN
el **veneno** *masc*

poisonous ADJECTIVE
venenoso *masc*
venenosa *fem*
> **a poisonous snake**
> una serpiente venenosa

police PL NOUN
la **policía** *fem*
> **The police are usually very helpful.**
> La policía suele ser de mucha ayuda.

> *Language tip*
> **policía** is a singular word in Spanish.

police car NOUN
el **coche de policía** *masc*

policeman NOUN
el **policía** *masc*
> **He's a policeman.**
> Es policía.

Language tip
When talking about people's jobs in Spanish, you do not use an article.

police station NOUN
la **comisaría** *fem*

policewoman NOUN
la **policía** *fem*
She's a policewoman.
Es policía.

Language tip
When talking about people's jobs in Spanish, you do not use an article.

polite ADJECTIVE
educado *masc*
educada *fem*
He's a very polite boy.
Es un chico muy educado.

polluted ADJECTIVE
contaminado *masc*
contaminada *fem*

pollution NOUN
la **contaminación** *fem*

polo shirt NOUN
el **polo** *masc*

pond NOUN
el **estanque** *masc*
There's a pond in our garden.
Hay un estanque en nuestro jardín.

pony
NOUN
el **pony** *masc*
(PL los **ponys**)

ponytail NOUN
la **coleta** *fem*
I've got a ponytail.
Llevo una coleta.

pony trekking NOUN
I go pony trekking.
Voy de excursión en pony.

pool NOUN
1 la **piscina** *fem* (swimming pool)
There's a pool.
Hay una piscina.
2 el **billar** *masc* (game)
Can you play pool?
¿Sabes jugar al billar?

poor ADJECTIVE
pobre *masc & fem*
They're very poor.
Son muy pobres.

Language tip
*In noun phrases you put **pobre** before the noun when you mean **unlucky**.*

Poor David, he's very unlucky!
¡Pobre David, tiene muy mala suerte!

Language tip
*You put **pobre** after the noun when you mean **not wealthy**.*

a poor family
una familia pobre

popcorn NOUN
las **palomitas de maíz** *fem*

Pope NOUN
el **Papa** *masc*

pop group NOUN
el **grupo de pop** *masc*
What's your favourite pop group?
¿Cuál es tu grupo de pop favorito?

pop music NOUN
la **música pop** *fem*

poppy NOUN
la **amapola** *fem*

pop song NOUN
la **canción pop** *fem* (PL las **canciones pop**)

popular ADJECTIVE
She's a very popular girl.

Es una chica que gusta a todo el mundo.

porch NOUN
el **porche** *masc*

pork NOUN
la **carne de cerdo** *fem*
I don't eat pork.
No como carne de cerdo.
a pork chop
una chuleta de cerdo

port NOUN
el **puerto** *masc*

portable ADJECTIVE
portátil *masc & fem*
a portable TV
un televisor portátil

portion NOUN
la **ración** *fem* (PL las **raciones**)
a large portion of chips
una ración grande de patatas fritas

posh ADJECTIVE
de lujo
a posh hotel
un hotel de lujo

positive ADJECTIVE
seguro *masc*
segura *fem*
Are you positive, Geoffrey?
¿Estás seguro, Geoffrey?

possibility NOUN
It's a possibility.
Es posible.

possible ADJECTIVE
posible *masc & fem*
as soon as possible
lo antes posible

> **Language tip**
> *Don't forget that there's only one* **s** *in the Spanish word* **posible**.

post

> **post** *can be a noun or a verb.*

A NOUN
el **correo** *masc*

Is there any post for me?
¿Hay correo para mí?
B VERB
to post
enviar por correo
I've got some cards to post.
Tengo que enviar por correo algunas postales.
Can you post this letter for me?
¿Me echas esta carta al correo?

postbox NOUN
el **buzón** *masc* (PL los **buzones**)

postcard NOUN
la **postal** *fem*
Thank you for the postcard, Jill.
Gracias por la postal, Jill.

postcode NOUN
el **código postal** *masc*
What is your postcode?
¿Cuál es tu código postal?

poster NOUN
el **póster** *masc* (PL los **pósters**)
I've got posters on my bedroom walls.
Tengo pósters en las paredes de mi habitación.

postman NOUN
el **cartero**
masc

He's a postman.
Es cartero.

> **Language tip**
> *When talking about people's jobs in Spanish, you do not use an article.*

post office NOUN
la **oficina de Correos** *fem*
Where's the post office, please?
¿Dónde está la oficina de Correos, por favor?

potato NOUN
la **patata** *fem*
mashed potatoes
el puré de patatas
boiled potatoes
patatas cocidas
a baked potato
una patata asada

potato salad NOUN
la **ensaladilla de patatas** *fem*

pottery NOUN
la **cerámica** *fem*

pound NOUN
la **libra** *fem*
How many euros do you get for a pound?
¿Cuántos euros equivalen a una libra?
a pound of tomatoes
una libra de tomates

Did you know…?
In Spain measurements are in grams and kilograms. One pound is about 450 grams.

to **pour** VERB
1 **echar** *(pour out)*
She poured some water into the pan.
Echó un poco de agua en la olla.
2 **diluviar** *(with rain)*
It's pouring.
Está diluviando.

powerful ADJECTIVE
poderoso *masc*
poderosa *fem*

practically ADVERB
prácticamente
It's practically impossible.
Es prácticamente imposible.

practice NOUN
el **entrenamiento** *masc*
football practice
entrenamiento de fútbol
I've got to do my piano practice.
Tengo que hacer mis ejercicios de piano.

to **practise** VERB
1 **practicar** *(instrument, language)*
I ought to practise more.
Debería practicar más.
I practise my flute every evening.
Practico con la flauta todas las noches.
I like practising my Spanish.
Me gusta poner en práctica el español.
2 **entrenar** *(do training)*
The team practises on Thursdays.
El equipo entrena los jueves.

prawn NOUN
la **gamba** *fem*

to **pray** VERB
rezar
Let's pray for them.
Rezemos por ellos.
Let us pray.
Oremos.

prayer NOUN
la **oración** *fem* (PL las **oraciones**)

precisely ADVERB
at ten a.m. precisely
a las diez en punto de la mañana

to **prefer** VERB
preferir
Which would you prefer?
¿Cuál prefieres?
Which do you prefer, tennis or football?
¿Qué prefieres, el tenis o el fútbol?
I prefer English to geography.
Prefiero el inglés a la geografía.

pregnant ADJECTIVE
embarazada *fem*
   She's six months pregnant.
   Está embarazada de seis
   meses.

prep NOUN
los **deberes** *masc pl*
   history prep
   los deberes de historia

to **prepare** VERB
preparar
   She's preparing dinner.
   Está preparando la cena.

prep school NOUN
el **colegio privado** *masc*

preposition NOUN
la **preposición** *fem* (PL las
preposiciones)

present

> **present** *can be an adjective or a noun.*

A ADJECTIVE
  presente *masc & fem*
   Ten present, two absent.
   Diez presentes, dos faltas.
   **He was present at the
   meeting.**
   Asistió a la reunión.
   the present tense
   el presente *masc*
B NOUN
1 el **regalo** *masc (gift)*
   **I'm going to give Julia a
   present.**
   Le voy a hacer un regalo a Julia.
   I got lots of presents.
   Me hicieron muchos regalos.

2 el **presente** *masc (time)*
   the present and the future
   el presente y el futuro

president NOUN
el **presidente** *masc*
la **presidenta** *fem*

to **pretend** VERB
   Pretend you are in a café.
   Haz como si estuvieras en una
   cafetería.

> ***Language tip***
> *Be careful! The translation of*
> **pretend** *is not* **pretender**.

pretty

> **pretty** *can be an adjective or an
> adverb.*

A ADJECTIVE
1 **guapo** *masc*
   guapa *fem (good-looking)*
   She's very pretty.
   Es muy guapa.
   Sarah is prettier than Irene.
   Sarah es más guapa que Irene.
   **She's the prettiest girl in the
   class.**
   Es la chica más guapa de la
   clase.
2 **bonito** *masc*
   bonita *fem (lovely)*
   a pretty blouse
   una blusa bonita
B ADVERB
bastante
   It's pretty old.
   Es bastante viejo.
   **The weather was pretty
   awful.**
   Hizo un tiempo bastante
   horrible.

previous ADJECTIVE
anterior *masc & fem*
   the previous day
   el día anterior

price NOUN
el **precio** *masc*

priest NOUN
el **sacerdote** *masc*

primary school NOUN
la **escuela primaria** *fem*
I am at primary school.
Estoy en la escuela primaria.

prince NOUN
el **príncipe** *masc*
the Prince of Wales
el Príncipe de Gales

princess NOUN
la **princesa** *fem*
Princess Anne
la princesa Ana

> **Did you know...?**
> In Spain a princess who is not the heir to the throne is called an **infanta** *rather than a* **princesa** *while a prince who is not the heir to the throne is an* **infante**.

to **print** VERB
1 **escribir en letra de imprenta** *(write)*
Print your name.
Escribe tu nombre en letra de imprenta.
2 **imprimir** *(on machine)*

printer NOUN
la **impresora** *fem*

prison NOUN
la **cárcel** *fem*
in prison
en la cárcel

private ADJECTIVE
privado *masc*
privada *fem*
a private letter
una carta privada
I have private lessons.
Tomo clases particulares.

private school NOUN
el **colegio privado** *masc*

prize NOUN
el **premio** *masc*
The prize is one hundred euros.
El premio son cien euros.
You can win a prize.
Puedes ganar un premio.

prize-giving NOUN
la **entrega de premios** *fem*

prizewinner NOUN
el **ganador** *masc*
la **ganadora** *fem*

probably ADVERB
probablemente
probably not
probablemente no

problem NOUN
el **problema** *masc*
Is there a problem?
¿Hay algún problema?

> **Language tip**
> Even though it ends in **-a**, **el problema** *is a masculine noun.*

What's the problem?
¿Qué pasa?

> **No problem!**
> ¡No importa!

procession NOUN
la **procesión** *fem* (PL las **procesiones**)

profession NOUN
la **profesión** *fem* (PL las **profesiones**)

professor NOUN
el **catedrático** *masc*
la **catedrática** *fem*

> **Language tip**
> Be careful! The translation of **professor** is not **profesor**.

profit NOUN
el **beneficio** *masc*

program NOUN
el **programa** *masc*

a computer program
un programa informático

Language tip
Even though it ends in -a, el programa is a masculine noun.

programme NOUN
el **programa** *masc*
my favourite TV programme
mi programa favorito de la tele
Would you like a programme?
¿Quieres un programa?

Language tip
Even though it ends in -a, el programa is a masculine noun.

progress NOUN
You're making progress, Edward!
¡Estás progresando, Edward!

projector NOUN
el **proyector** *masc*

promise

promise *can be a noun or a verb.*

A NOUN
la **promesa** *fem*
I'll make you a promise.
Te haré una promesa.
That's a promise!
¡Es una promesa!

B VERB
to promise
prometer
I promise!
¡Lo prometo!
I'll write, I promise!
¡Escribiré, lo prometo!

prompt

prompt *can be an adjective or an adverb.*

A ADJECTIVE
rápido *masc*
rápida *fem*
a prompt reply
una rápida respuesta

B ADVERB
at eight o'clock prompt
a las ocho en punto

pronoun NOUN
el **pronombre** *masc*

to **pronounce** VERB
pronunciar
How do you pronounce that word?
¿Cómo se pronuncia esa palabra?

pronunciation NOUN
la **pronunciación** *fem*
Your pronunciation is good!
¡Tienes una buena pronunciación!

proper ADJECTIVE
adecuado *masc*
adecuada *fem (suitable)*
the proper equipment
el equipo adecuado
You should eat a proper breakfast.
Deberías desayunar como Dios manda.

properly ADVERB
correctamente
I can't pronounce it properly.
No puedo pronunciarlo correctamente.

Protestant

Protestant *can be an adjective or a noun.*

A ADJECTIVE
protestante *masc & fem*
B NOUN
el/la **protestante** *masc/fem*
I'm a Protestant.
Soy protestante.

Language tip
In Spanish protestante is not spelled with a capital letter. Remember that you do not use an article with people's religions in Spanish.

proud ADJECTIVE
orgulloso *masc*
orgullosa *fem*
   Her parents are proud of her.
   Sus padres están orgullosos de
   ella.

prune NOUN
   la **ciruela pasa** *fem*

PTO ABBREVIATION
(= **please turn over**)
   sigue

pub NOUN
   el **pub** *masc*

public

> **public** *can be a noun or an
> adjective.*

A NOUN
   el **público** *masc*
   **The castle is open to the
   public.**
   El castillo está abierto al público.
B ADJECTIVE
   público *masc*
   pública *fem*
   a public swimming pool
   una piscina pública

publicity NOUN
   la **publicidad** *fem*

public school NOUN
   el **colegio privado** *masc*

public transport NOUN
   el **transporte público** *masc*
   by public transport
   en transporte público

pudding NOUN
   el **postre** *masc*
   Would you like a pudding?
   ¿Quieres postre?
   What's for pudding?
   ¿Qué hay de postre?

to **pull** VERB
   tirar
   Pull!
   ¡Tira!

pullover NOUN
   el **jersey** *masc* (PL los **jerseys**)
   What colour is your pullover?
   ¿De qué color es tu jersey?

pump NOUN
   1 la **bomba** *fem (for pumping)*
   a bicycle pump
   una bomba de bicicleta
   2 la **zapatilla de deporte** *fem*
   (shoe)
   Have you got your pumps?
   ¿Tienes tus zapatillas de
   deporte?

to **pump up** VERB
   inflar
   Pump up your tyres!
   ¡Infla tus ruedas!

pumpkin NOUN
   la **calabaza** *fem*

to **punch** VERB
   dar un puñetazo a
   He punched me!
   ¡Me dio un puñetazo!

punctual ADJECTIVE
   puntual *masc & fem*
   Be punctual!
   ¡Sé puntual!

punctuation NOUN
   la **puntuación** *fem*

punishment NOUN
   el **castigo** *masc*

pupil NOUN
   el **alumno** *masc*
   la **alumna** *fem*

There are twenty-two pupils in my class.
Hay veintidós alumnos en mi clase.

puppet NOUN
la **marioneta** *fem*

puppy NOUN
el **cachorro** *masc*

pure ADJECTIVE
puro *masc*
pura *fem*
It's pure water.
Es agua pura.

purple

purple *can be an adjective or a noun.*

A ADJECTIVE
morado *masc*
morada *fem*
a purple skirt
una falda morada

Language tip

Colour adjectives come after the noun in Spanish.

B NOUN
el **morado** *masc*
Purple is my favourite colour.
El morado es mi color favorito.

purpose NOUN
on purpose
a propósito
You're doing it on purpose.
Lo estás haciendo a propósito.

to **purr** VERB
ronronear
The cat is purring.
El gato está ronroneando.

purse NOUN
el **monedero** *masc*
I've lost my purse.
He perdido mi monedero.

to **push** VERB
empujar
Push!
¡Empuja!

pushchair NOUN
la **sillita de paseo** *fem*

to **put** VERB
poner
Where shall I put my things?
¿Dónde pongo mis cosas?
Don't forget to put your name on the paper.
No te olvides de poner tu nombre en la hoja.
She's putting the baby to bed.
Está acostando al niño.
Put your chewing gum in the bin.
Tira el chicle a la papelera.

to **put away** VERB
guardar
Put your things away, children.
Guardad vuestras cosas, niños.

to **put back** VERB
poner en su sitio
Don't forget to put it back.
No te olvides de ponerlo en su sitio.

to **put down** VERB
soltar *(stop holding)*
Put the bags down for a moment.
Suelta las bolsas un momento.
Put down a card.
Suelta una carta.
Put your hands down.
Bajad las manos.

Language tip

*In Spanish you usually use an article like **el**, **la** or **los**, **las** with parts of the body.*

to **put off** VERB
1 **apagar** *(switch off)*
Shall I put the light off?
¿Apago la luz?
2 **distraer** *(distract)*
Stop putting me off!
¡Deja de distraerme!

to **put on** VERB
1 **ponerse** *(clothes)*
I'll put my coat on.
Me pondré el abrigo.

> **Language tip**
>
> *In Spanish you usually use an article like* **el**, **la** *or* **los**, **las** *with clothes you are wearing.*

2 **encender** *(switch on)*
Shall I put the light on?
¿Enciendo la luz?

to **put up** VERB
1 **colgar** *(hang)*
I'll put the poster up on my wall.
Colgaré el póster en la pared.
2 **subir** *(raise)*
They've put up the price.
Han subido el precio.
Put up your hand if you know the answer.
Que levante la mano el que sepa la respuesta.

puzzle NOUN
el **rompecabezas** *masc* (PL los **rompecabezas**)

puzzled ADJECTIVE
perplejo *masc*
perpleja *fem*
You look puzzled.
Parece que te has quedado perplejo.

pyjamas PL NOUN
el **pijama** *masc*
my pyjamas
mi pijama
I've got some new pyjamas.
Tengo un pijama nuevo.
a pair of pyjamas
un pijama

> **Language tip**
>
> *In Spanish* **el pijama** *is a singular word.*

Q q

quad bike NOUN
el **quad** *masc*

quality NOUN
1 la **calidad** *fem (of work, product)*
good quality towels
toallas de buena calidad
2 la **cualidad** *fem (of person)*
She's got lots of good qualities.
Tiene un montón de buenas cualidades.

quantity NOUN
la **cantidad** *fem*

to **quarrel** VERB
pelearse
They're always quarrelling.
Siempre se están peleando.

quarter NOUN
la **cuarta parte** *fem*
a quarter of the class
una cuarta parte de la clase
It's a quarter to one.
Es la una menos cuarto.
It's a quarter past six.
Son las seis y cuarto.
at a quarter to eight
a las ocho menos cuarto

three quarters
tres cuartos
a quarter of an hour
un cuarto de hora
three quarters of an hour
tres cuartos de hora
a quarter past ten
las diez y cuarto
a quarter to eleven
las once menos cuarto

queen NOUN
la **reina** *fem*
Queen Elizabeth
la reina Isabel

Did you know…?
Did you know that Spanish speakers translate the names of the British royal family into Spanish?

the queen of hearts
la reina de corazones

question NOUN
1 la **pregunta** *fem (query)*
Are there any questions?
¿Hay alguna pregunta?
Can I ask a question?
¿Puedo hacer una pregunta?
2 la **cuestión** *fem* (PL las **cuestiones**) *(matter)*
That's a difficult question.
Ésa es una cuestión complicada.

question mark NOUN
el **signo de interrogación** *masc*

questionnaire NOUN
el **cuestionario** *masc*

queue

queue *can be a noun or a verb.*

A NOUN
la **cola** *fem*
There's a very long queue.
Hay una cola muy larga.
B VERB
to queue
hacer cola
You have to queue.
Tienes que hacer cola.

quick ADJECTIVE
rápido *masc*
rápida *fem*
a quick lunch
una comida rápida
It's quicker by train.
Es más rápido en tren.

Be quick, Laura!
¡Date prisa, Laura!
Be quick, girls!
¡Daos prisa, niñas!

quickly ADVERB
rápido
    Am I speaking too quickly?
    ¿Estoy hablando demasiado
    rápido?

quiet ADJECTIVE
1 **callado** *masc*
   callada *fem (not chatty)*
   You're very quiet, Julia.
   Estás muy callada, Julia.

> ### Language tip
> When **be quiet** means 'fall silent',
> you translate it using the verb
> **callarse**.

   Be quiet all of you, I'm
   thinking!
   ¡Callaos todos, que estoy
   pensando!

Be quiet, Jeremy!
¡Cállate, Jeremy!
Quiet!
¡Silencio!

2 **tranquilo** *masc*
   tranquila *fem (peaceful)*
   a quiet place
   un lugar tranquilo
   a quiet weekend
   un fin de semana tranquilo

quietly ADVERB
1 **en voz baja** *(in a low voice)*
   Talk quietly.
   Hablad en voz baja.
2 **sin hacer ruido** *(noiselessly)*
   Shut the door quietly, Sophie.
   Cierra la puerta sin hacer ruido,
   Sophie.

quilt NOUN
el **edredón** *masc*
   (PL los **edredones**)

quite ADVERB
1 **bastante** *(rather)*
   It's quite expensive.
   Es bastante caro.
   It's quite warm today.
   Hace bastante calor hoy.
   It's quite a long way.
   Está bastante lejos.
   quite a lot of money
   bastante dinero
2 **totalmente** *(completely)*
   I'm quite sure he's coming.
   Estoy totalmente seguro de que
   viene.
   Are you ready, Lorna? — Not
   quite.
   ¿Estás lista, Lorna? — No del
   todo.

quite good
bastante bueno

quiz NOUN
el **concurso** *masc*

a
b
c
d
e
f
g
h
i
j
k
l
m
n
o
p
q
r
s
t
u
v
w
x
y
z

R r

rabbi NOUN
el **rabino** *masc*
la **rabina** *fem*

rabbit NOUN
el **conejo** *masc*

race NOUN
la **carrera** *fem*
a cycle race
una carrera ciclista
Let's have a race!
¡Vamos a echar una carrera!

racing car NOUN
el **coche de carreras** *masc*

racket NOUN
la **raqueta** *fem*
my tennis racket
mi raqueta de tenis

radiator NOUN
el **radiador** *masc*

radio NOUN
la **radio** *fem*
I heard it on the radio.
Lo escuché en la radio.

> ### *Language tip*
> Even though it ends in **-o**, **la radio** is a feminine noun.

raffle NOUN
la **rifa** *fem*

raffle ticket NOUN
la **papeleta para la rifa** *fem*
Do you want to buy a raffle ticket?
¿Quieres comprar una papeleta para la rifa?

rage NOUN
to be in a rage
estar furioso

> ### *Language tip*
> Change **furioso** to **furiosa** *if it's a woman or girl who's in a rage.*

She's in a rage.
Está furiosa.

rail NOUN
by rail
en tren

railway NOUN
el **ferrocarril** *masc*

railway line NOUN
la **línea de ferrocarril** *fem*

railway station NOUN
la **estación de trenes** *fem* (PL
las **estaciones de trenes**)

rain

> **rain** *can be a noun or a verb.*

A NOUN
la **lluvia** *fem*
in the rain
bajo la lluvia
B VERB
to rain
llover
It's going to rain.
Va a llover.
It rains a lot here.
Llueve mucho aquí.

> **It's raining.**
> Está lloviendo.

rainbow NOUN
el **arco iris** *masc*

raincoat NOUN
el **impermeable** *masc*

rainy ADJECTIVE
lluvioso *masc*
lluviosa *fem*
a rainy day
un día lluvioso

to **raise** VERB
levantar
Raise your left arm, everyone.
Levantad todos el brazo izquierdo.
to raise money
recaudar fondos
We're raising money for a new gym.
Estamos recaudando fondos para un gimnasio nuevo.

raisin NOUN
la **pasa** *fem*

Ramadan NOUN
el **Ramadán** *masc*

ramp NOUN
la **rampa** *fem*

ran VERB ▷ *see* **run**

random ADJECTIVE
at random
al azar
Pick a card at random.
Escoge una carta al azar.

rang VERB ▷ *see* **ring**

range NOUN
la **gama** *fem*
There's a wide range of colours.
Hay una amplia gama de colores.

rap NOUN
el **rap** *masc* (poetry)

rare ADJECTIVE
1 **raro** *masc*
rara *fem* (unusual)
2 **poco hecho** *masc*
poco hecha *fem* (steak)

rarely ADVERB
raras veces

raspberry NOUN
la **frambuesa** *fem*
raspberry jam
mermelada de frambuesa

rat NOUN
la **rata** *fem*

rather ADVERB
1 **bastante** (quite)
Twenty pounds! That's rather expensive!
¡Veinte libras! ¡Eso es bastante caro!
2 **I'd rather ...**
Preferiría ...
I'd rather stay in tonight.
Preferiría no salir esta noche.
Would you like a sweet? — I'd rather have an apple.
¿Quieres un caramelo? — Preferiría una manzana.
Which would you rather have?
¿Cuál prefieres?
Would you rather have water or orange juice?
¿Prefieres agua o zumo de naranja?

ravenous ADJECTIVE
I'm ravenous!
¡Estoy muerto de hambre!

> **Language tip**
> Change **muerto** to **muerta** if you're a girl.

raw ADJECTIVE
crudo *masc*
cruda *fem*

razor NOUN
la **maquinilla de afeitar** *fem*

English Spanish

a b c d e f g h i j k l m n o p q **r** s t u v w x y z

RE NOUN
la **religión** fem

reach

> **reach** can be a noun or a verb.

A NOUN
Mum keeps the biscuits out of reach.
Mi madre guarda las galletas fuera de nuestro alcance.
The hotel is within easy reach of the town centre.
El hotel está a poca distancia del centro de la ciudad.

B VERB
to reach
llegar a
We hope to reach London by five o'clock.
Esperamos llegar a Londres para las cinco.
I can't reach the top shelf.
No llego a la estantería de arriba.

to **read** VERB
leer
I don't read much.
No leo mucho.
Have you read 'The Prisoner of Azkaban'?
¿Has leído 'El prisionero de Azkaban'?

to **read out** VERB
leer en voz alta
I'll read out the names.
Leeré en voz alta los nombres.

reading NOUN
la **lectura** fem
Reading is one of my hobbies.
La lectura es una de mis aficiones.

ready
ADJECTIVE
listo masc
lista fem

Breakfast is ready.
El desayuno está listo.
She's nearly ready.
Ella está casi lista.
Are you ready, children?
¿Estáis listos, niños?

Ready, steady, go!
¡Preparados, listos, ya!

real ADJECTIVE
1 **verdadero** masc
verdadera fem (true)
Her real name is Cordelia.
Su verdadero nombre es Cordelia.
2 **auténtico** masc
auténtica fem (genuine)
It's real leather.
Es piel auténtica.

to **realize** VERB
darse cuenta de
Do you realize what time it is?
¿Te das cuenta de la hora que es?

really ADVERB
1 **muy** (very)
She's really nice.
Es muy simpática.
It's really hot today.
Hoy hace mucho calor.
2 **de verdad** (genuinely)
I'm learning German. — Really?
Estoy aprendiendo alemán. — ¿De verdad?
Do you want to go? — Not really.
¿Quieres ir? — La verdad es que no.

reason NOUN
la **razón** fem (PL las **razones**)

reasonable ADJECTIVE
razonable masc & fem
Be reasonable, Joyce!
¡Sé razonable, Joyce!

receipt NOUN
el **recibo** masc
Keep your receipt.
Guarda tu recibo.

Language tip
Be careful! The translation of
receipt *is not* **receta.**

to **receive** VERB
recibir
 I received your letter
 yesterday.
 Recibí tu carta ayer.

recent ADJECTIVE
reciente *masc & fem*

recently ADVERB
recientemente
 He's been ill recently.
 Ha estado enfermo recientemente.

reception NOUN
1 la **recepción** *fem (desk)*
 Please leave your key at
 reception.
 Por favor, deje su llave en
 recepción.
2 la **celebración** *fem* (PL las
 celebraciones) *(party)*
 The reception will be at a
 big hotel.
 La celebración será en un gran
 hotel.

receptionist NOUN
el/la **recepcionista** *masc/fem*
 She's a receptionist.
 Es recepcionista.

Language tip
*When talking about people's jobs in
Spanish, you do not use an article.*

recipe NOUN
la **receta** *fem*
 a recipe
 book
 un libro
 de recetas

to **reckon** VERB
creer
 What do you reckon?
 ¿Tú qué crees?

to **recognize** VERB
reconocer
 Do you recognize this boy?
 ¿Reconoces a este chico?

Language tip
Don't forget the personal **a** *in
examples like this one.*

to **recommend** VERB
recomendar
 What do you recommend?
 ¿Qué me recomienda?
 I recommend the soup.
 Le recomiendo la sopa.

Language tip
*In Spanish you usually say who
you're recommending something to.
Can you find words for 'to me' and
'to you' above?*

record

record *can be a noun or a verb.*

A NOUN
 el **récord** *masc (in sport)*
 the world record
 el récord mundial
B VERB
 to record
 grabar
 We're going to record the
 song.
 Vamos a grabar la canción.

Language tip
Be careful! The translation of **to
record** *is not* **recordar.**

recorder NOUN
la **flauta dulce** *fem*
 I play the recorder.
 Toco la flauta dulce.

rectangle
NOUN
el **rectángulo**
 masc

to **recycle**
VERB
reciclar

red

> **red** *can be an adjective or a noun.*

A ADJECTIVE
rojo *masc*
roja *fem*
a red rose
una rosa roja

Language tip

Colour adjectives come after the noun in Spanish.

The traffic lights are red.
El semáforo está en rojo.
Gerald's got red hair.
Gerald es pelirrojo.

B NOUN
el **rojo** *masc*
Red is my favourite colour.
El rojo es mi color favorito.

to **redecorate** VERB

1 **empapelar de nuevo**
(with wallpaper)
I'd like to redecorate my room.
Quiero empapelar de nuevo mi habitación.

2 **pintar de nuevo** *(with paint)*
I'd like to redecorate my room.
Quiero pintar de nuevo mi habitación.

Language tip

There's no single verb meaning both 'to paint' and 'to paper' in Spanish.

red-haired ADJECTIVE
pelirrojo *masc*
pelirroja *fem*

redhead NOUN
el **pelirrojo** *masc*
la **pelirroja** *fem*

to **redo** VERB
rehacer
I need to redo my homework.
Tengo que rehacer mis deberes.

reduced ADJECTIVE
at a reduced price
a un precio rebajado

reduction NOUN
la **rebaja** *fem*
a five-percent reduction
una rebaja del cinco por ciento

referee NOUN
el **árbitro** *masc*
la **árbitra** *fem*

reflexive ADJECTIVE
a reflexive verb
un verbo reflexivo

refrigerator
NOUN
el **frigorífico**
masc

refugee NOUN
el **refugiado**
masc
la **refugiada** *fem*

to **refuse** VERB
negarse
She's refusing to say anything.
Se niega a decir nada.

regards PL NOUN
los **recuerdos** *masc pl*
Give my regards to Lucy.
Dale recuerdos a Lucy.
Tim sends his regards.
Tim manda recuerdos.

region NOUN
la **región** *fem* (PL las **regiones**)
in this region
en esta región

register NOUN
I'm going to call the register.
Voy a pasar lista.

registration NOUN
after registration
después de pasar lista

regular ADJECTIVE
1 **regular** *masc & fem*
at regular intervals
a intervalos regulares
a regular verb
un verbo regular
You should take regular exercise.
Deberías hacer ejercicio con regularidad.
2 **normal** *masc & fem (medium)*
a regular portion of fries
una porción normal de patatas fritas

rehearsal NOUN
el **ensayo** *masc*

reindeer NOUN
el **reno** *masc*

relation NOUN
el/la **pariente** *masc/fem*
my relations
mis parientes
I've got relations in London.
Tengo parientes en Londres.

relative NOUN
el/la **pariente** *masc/fem*
all her relatives
todos sus parientes
I've got relatives in Manchester.
Tengo parientes en Manchester.

to **relax** VERB
relajarse
Mum's relaxing in front of the TV.
Mi madre se está relajando delante de la tele.
Relax! Everything's fine.
¡Tranquilo! No pasa nada.

Language tip
Change **tranquilo** *to* **tranquila** *if talking to a woman or girl.*

relaxed ADJECTIVE
relajado *masc*
relajada *fem*

relaxing ADJECTIVE
relajante *masc & fem*
Cooking is very relaxing.
Cocinar es muy relajante.

relay race NOUN
la **carrera de relevos** *fem*
We won the relay race.
Ganamos la carrera de relevos.

reliable ADJECTIVE
fiable *masc & fem*
a reliable car
un coche fiable
He's not very reliable.
No es muy fiable.

relief NOUN
el **alivio** *masc*
What a relief!
¡Qué alivio!

religion NOUN
la **religión** *fem* (PL las **religiones**)
What religion are you?
¿De qué religión eres?

religious ADJECTIVE
religioso *masc*
religiosa *fem*

to **rely on** VERB
confiar en
I'm relying on you.
Confío en ti.

remark NOUN
el **comentario** *masc*

to **remember** VERB
acordarse de
I can't remember his name.
No me acuerdo de su nombre.
Sorry, I can't remember.
Lo siento, no me acuerdo.
Did you remember to lock the door?
¿Te acordaste de cerrar la puerta con llave?

> **Language tip**
> In Spanish you often say **no te olvides** (don't forget) instead of **remember**.

Remember to write your names on the form.
No os olvidéis de escribir vuestro nombre en el impreso.

to **remind** VERB
recordar
Remind me to speak to Daniel.
Recuérdame que hable con Daniel.
She reminds me of you.
Me recuerda a ti.

remote control NOUN
el **mando a distancia** masc

to **remove** VERB
quitar
Please remove your bag from my seat.
Por favor, quita tu bolsa de mi asiento.

rent

rent can be a noun or a verb.

A NOUN
el **alquiler** masc
She has to pay the rent.
Tiene que pagar el alquiler.
B VERB
to **rent**
alquilar
We are going to rent a villa.
Vamos a alquilar un chalet.

to **repair** VERB
arreglar
Can you repair them?
¿Puedes arreglarlos?

to **repeat** VERB
repetir
Can you repeat that, please?
¿Puedes repetir eso, por favor?

Repeat after me, everyone.
Repetid todos después de mí.

reply

reply can be a noun or a verb.

A NOUN
la **respuesta** fem
I got no reply to my letter.
No recibí respuesta a mi carta.
B VERB
to reply
contestar
I hope you will reply soon.
Espero que contestes pronto.
She always replies to my letters.
Siempre contesta a mis cartas.

report NOUN
1 el **boletín de evaluación** masc (PL los **boletines de evaluación**) (school report)

> **Language tip**
> Although **el boletín de evaluación** is the Spanish for **school report**, Spanish children usually just talk about their **notas**, literally 'marks'.

I usually get a good report.
Normalmente saco buenas notas.
2 el **reportaje** masc (news report)

request NOUN
la **solicitud** fem

reservation NOUN
la **reserva** fem
I've got a reservation.
Tengo una reserva.
I'd like to make a reservation.
Quisiera hacer una reserva.

reserve

reserve can be a noun or a verb.

A NOUN
el/la **suplente** masc/fem

I was a reserve in the game last Saturday.
Estaba de suplente en el partido del sábado.

B VERB
to reserve
reservar
I'd like to reserve a table for tomorrow evening.
Quisiera reservar una mesa para mañana por la noche.

reserved ADJECTIVE
reservado *masc*
reservada *fem*
This seat is reserved.
Este asiento está reservado.

resolution NOUN
Have you made any New Year's resolutions?
¿Tienes buenos propósitos para el Año Nuevo?

resort NOUN
el **centro turístico** *masc*
It's a resort on the Costa del Sol.
Es un centro turístico de la Costa del Sol.
a ski resort
una estación de esquí

responsibility NOUN
la **responsabilidad** *fem*
It's your responsibility.
Es tu responsabilidad.

> *Language tip*
> *Have you noticed that* **responsabilidad** *has an 'a' in it in Spanish?*

responsible ADJECTIVE
responsable *masc & fem*

> *Language tip*
> *Remember that the Spanish word ends in 'able' rather than 'ible'.*

He's responsible for booking the tickets.
Es responsable de reservar las entradas.
It's a responsible job.
Es un puesto de responsabilidad.

rest

> **rest** *can be a noun or a verb.*

A NOUN
1 el **descanso** *masc* (break)
five minutes' rest
cinco minutos de descanso
Can we have a rest?
¿Podemos descansar?
I need a rest.
Necesito descansar.
2 *(remainder)*
the rest
el resto
I'll do the rest.
Yo haré el resto.
the rest of the money
el resto del dinero
B VERB
to rest
descansar

restaurant NOUN
el **restaurante** *masc*

We don't often go to restaurants.
No solemos ir a restaurantes.

result NOUN
el **resultado** *masc*
my exam results
los resultados de los exámenes

> *Language tip*
> *Change* **los exámenes** *to* **el examen** *if you're talking about only one exam.*

What was the result? — One-nil.
¿Cuál fue el resultado? — Uno a cero.

to **retire** VERB
jubilarse
> He's going to retire.
> Va a jubilarse.

retired ADJECTIVE
jubilado *masc*
jubilada *fem*
> She's retired.
> Está jubilada.

retirement NOUN
la **jubilación** *fem*

return

> **return** *can be a noun or a verb.*

A NOUN
1 la **vuelta** *fem*
> **after our return**
> después de nuestra vuelta
> **the return journey**
> el viaje de vuelta
2 la **ida y vuelta** *fem (ticket)*
> **A return to Glasgow, please.**
> Una ida y vuelta a Glasgow, por favor.

> **Many happy returns!**
> ¡Que cumplas muchos más!

> *Language tip*
> Have you noticed the upside-down exclamation mark at the start of Spanish exclamations?

B VERB
to return
1 **volver** *(come back)*
> **I've just returned from holiday.**
> Acabo de volver de vacaciones.
2 **devolver** *(give back)*
> **I've got to return this book to the library.**
> Tengo que devolver este libro a la biblioteca.

reverse ADJECTIVE
inverso *masc*
inversa *fem*

> **in reverse order**
> en orden inverso

to **revise** VERB
estudiar para un examen
> **I haven't started revising for my exams yet.**
> Todavía no he empezado a estudiar para los exámenes.

revision NOUN
> **Have you done a lot of maths revision?**
> ¿Has estudiado mucho para el examen de matemáticas?

reward NOUN
la **recompensa** *fem*
> **There's a thousand-euro reward.**
> Hay una recompensa de mil euros.

rhubarb NOUN
el **ruibarbo** *masc*

rhythm NOUN
el **ritmo** *masc*

rib NOUN
la **costilla** *fem*

ribbon NOUN
la **cinta** *fem*

rice NOUN
el **arroz** *masc*
> **Would you like some rice?**
> ¿Quieres arroz?

rich ADJECTIVE
rico *masc*
rica *fem*
> **He's very rich.**
> Es muy rico.

to **rid** VERB
to get rid of
deshacerse de

I need to get rid of my chewing gum.
Necesito deshacerme del chicle.

ride

ride can be a noun or a verb.

A NOUN *(on horse)*
to go for a ride
ir a montar a caballo
Would you like to go for a ride?
¿Te gustaría ir a montar a caballo?
I'm going for a ride on my bike.
Voy a ir a dar una vuelta en bici.

B VERB
to ride
1 montar a caballo
(on horse)
I'm learning to ride.
Estoy aprendiendo a montar a caballo.
2 to ride a bike
montar en bici
Can you ride a bike?
¿Sabes montar en bici?

rider NOUN

1 el jinete *masc (man, boy)*
He's a good rider.
Es un buen jinete.
2 la amazona *fem (woman, girl)*
She's a good rider.
Es una buena amazona.

ridiculous ADJECTIVE

ridículo *masc*
ridícula *fem*
Don't be ridiculous, Fiona!
¡No seas ridícula, Fiona!

riding NOUN

I like riding.
Me gusta montar a caballo.

riding school NOUN

la **escuela de equitación** *fem*

right

right can be an adjective, adverb or noun.

A ADJECTIVE
1 correcto *masc*
correcta *fem (correct)*
That's the right answer!
¡Ésa es la respuesta correcta!
It isn't the right size.
No es la talla correcta.
We're on the right train.
Estamos en el tren correcto.
2 *(true)*
That's right!
¡Es verdad!
You're right, Luke.
Tienes razón, Luke.
3 derecho *masc*
derecha *fem (not left)*
Hold out your right hand.
Extiende la mano derecha.

B ADVERB
1 correctamente *(correctly)*
Am I pronouncing it right?
¿Lo pronuncio correctamente?
2 a la derecha *(to the right)*
Turn right at the traffic lights.
Gira a la derecha en el semáforo.

C NOUN
on the right
a la derecha
a step to the right
un paso a la derecha

You're right.
Tienes razón.
Right! Let's get started.
¡Bueno! ¡Empecemos!
Turn right.
Gira a la derecha.

right-hand ADJECTIVE

the right-hand side
la derecha
It's on the right-hand side.
Está a la derecha.

English

Spanish

a
b
c
d
e
f
g
h
i
j
k
l
m
n
o
p
q
r
s
t
u
v
w
x
y
z

right-handed ADJECTIVE
diestro *masc*
diestra *fem*
Tim is right-handed.
Tim es diestro.

ring

> **ring** *can be a noun or a verb.*

A NOUN
1 el **anillo** *masc*
(for finger)
a gold ring
un anillo
de oro
**a diamond
ring**
un anillo de
diamantes
a wedding ring
una alianza de boda
2 el **círculo** *masc (circle)*
Stand in a ring.
Poneos formando un círculo.
B VERB
to ring
1 **llamar** *(phone)*
You can ring me at home.
Me puedes llamar a casa.
2 **sonar** *(make sound)*
The phone's ringing.
El teléfono está sonando.

ringtone NOUN
el **tono de llamada** *masc*

rink NOUN
1 la **pista de hielo** *fem (for
ice-skating)*
2 la **pista de patinaje** *fem
(for roller-skating)*

ripe ADJECTIVE
maduro *masc*
madura *fem*
a ripe peach
un melocotón maduro

to **rise** VERB
subir

risk NOUN
el **riesgo** *masc*
It's a big risk.
Es un gran riesgo.

rival

> **rival** *can be a noun or an adjective.*

A NOUN
el/la **rival** *masc/fem*
our rivals
nuestros rivales
B ADJECTIVE
rival *masc & fem*
a rival gang
una banda rival

river NOUN
el **río** *masc*
across the river
al otro lado del río
the River Amazon
el río Amazonas

> ### *Language tip*
> In Spanish **río** is not spelled with a
> capital letter in names of rivers.

road NOUN
1 la **carretera** *fem*
**There's a lot of traffic on the
roads.**
Hay mucho tráfico en las
carreteras.
2 la **calle** *fem (street)*
They live across the road.
Viven al otro lado de la calle.

road sign NOUN
la **señal de tráfico** *fem*

roadworks PL NOUN
las **obras** *fem pl*

roast ADJECTIVE
asado *masc*
asada *fem*
roast chicken
pollo asado
roast potatoes
patatas asadas

Did you know…?

In Spanish the translation of **roast potatoes** *and* **baked potatoes** *is the same. If you want to specify, you can say* **patatas asadas con la piel** *for* **baked potatoes**.

rob VERB
robar *(person)*
I've been robbed!
¡Me han robado!
to rob a bank
asaltar un banco
They're robbing the bank!
¡Están asaltando el banco!

robber NOUN
el **ladrón** *masc* (PL los **ladrones**)
la **ladrona** *fem*
a bank robber
un ladrón de bancos

robbery NOUN
el **robo** *masc*
There have been a lot of robberies in my neighbourhood.
Ha habido muchos robos en mi barrio.
a bank robbery
un asalto a un banco

rock NOUN
1 la **roca** *fem (boulder)*
2 el **rock** *masc (music)*
a rock concert
un concierto de rock
He's a rock star.
Es una estrella del rock.
3 *(sweet)*
a stick of rock
un palo de caramelo

rocket NOUN
el **cohete** *masc*

rod NOUN
la **caña** *fem*

rode VERB ▷ *see* **ride**

role play NOUN
el **juego de rol** *masc*

We're going to do a role play.
Vamos a hacer un juego de rol.

roll

roll *can be a noun or a verb.*

A NOUN
el **bollito** *masc (of bread)*
a ham roll
un bollito con jamón
B VERB
to roll: **Roll the dice.**
Lanza los dados.

Rollerblades® PL NOUN
los **patines en línea** *masc pl*
a pair of Rollerblades
unos patines en línea

rollercoaster NOUN
la **montaña rusa** *fem*

roller skates PL NOUN
los **patines de ruedas** *masc pl*

roller-skating NOUN
to go roller-skating
ir a patinar
Do you want to go roller-skating?
¿Quieres ir a patinar?

Roman Catholic NOUN
el **católico** *masc*
la **católica** *fem*
He's a Roman Catholic.
Es católico.

Language tip

católico *is not spelled with a capital letter. Remember that you do not use an article with people's religions in Spanish.*

romantic ADJECTIVE
romántico *masc*
romántica *fem*

roof NOUN
el **tejado** *masc*

room NOUN
1 la **habitación** *fem* (PL las **habitaciones**) *(in house)*

My room is the smallest.
Mi habitación es la más pequeña.
a single room
una habitación individual
a double room
una habitación doble
the biggest room in the house
la habitación más grande de la casa

Language tip
*You can also use **el cuarto** to refer to a room.*

My room is the smallest.
Mi cuarto es el más pequeño.
2 el **aula** *fem (in school)*

Language tip
*Even though it's a feminine noun, remember that you use **el** and **un** with **aula**.*

the music room
el aula de música
3 el **sitio** *masc (space)*
Is there room for me?
¿Hay sitio para mí?

rope NOUN
la **cuerda** *fem*

rose NOUN
la **rosa** *fem*
a bouquet of roses
un ramo de rosas

rough ADJECTIVE
áspero *masc*
áspera *fem*

roughly ADVERB
aproximadamente
It weighs roughly twenty kilos.
Pesa unos veinte kilos aproximadamente.

round

round *can be an adjective, preposition or noun.*

A ADJECTIVE
redondo *masc*
redonda *fem*
a round table
una mesa redonda
B PREPOSITION
alrededor de
Sit round the table.
Sentaos alrededor de la mesa.
It's just round the corner.
Está aquí a la vuelta de la esquina.
round here
por aquí cerca
Is there a chemist's round here?
¿Hay una farmacia por aquí cerca?
C NOUN
la **vuelta** *fem (of tournament)*
the next round
la siguiente vuelta
a round of golf
un partido de golf

roundabout NOUN
1 el **tiovivo** *masc (merry-go-round)*
2 la **rotonda** *fem (at road junction)*

rounders NOUN

Did you know…?

Rounders *isn't played in Spain. The nearest game for which there is a Spanish translation is **el béisbol** or **baseball**.*

row

row can be a noun or a verb.

A NOUN
1 la **hilera** *fem*
   a row of houses
   una hilera de casas
2 la **fila** *fem (of seats)*
   Our seats are in the front row.
   Nuestros asientos están en la primera fila.
3 el **jaleo** *masc (noise)*
   What a row!
   ¡Menudo jaleo!
B VERB
   to row
   remar
   I can row.
   Sé remar.

rowing boat NOUN
la **barca de remos** *fem*

royal ADJECTIVE
real *masc & fem*

rubber NOUN
la **goma de borrar** *fem*
   Can I borrow your rubber?
   ¿Me dejas tu goma de borrar?

rubber band NOUN
la **goma elástica** *fem*

rubbish

rubbish can be a noun or an adjective.

A NOUN
1 la **basura** *fem (garbage)*
   Where shall I put the rubbish?
   ¿Dónde pongo la basura?
2 las **estupideces** *fem pl (nonsense)*
   Don't talk rubbish!
   ¡No digas estupideces!
B ADJECTIVE *(useless)*
   They're a rubbish team!
   ¡Son un equipo que no vale nada!

The film was rubbish.
La película no valía nada.

rubbish bin NOUN
el **cubo de la basura** *masc*

rucksack NOUN
la **mochila** *fem*

rude ADJECTIVE
grosero *masc*
grosera *fem*
   Don't be rude!
   ¡No seas grosero!
   a rude word
   una palabrota

rug NOUN
1 la **alfombra** *fem (carpet)*
2 la **manta de viaje** *fem (travelling rug)*

rugby NOUN
el **rugby** *masc*
   I play rugby.
   Juego al rugby.

> **Language tip**
> *In Spanish, you need to add **al** or **a la** before the name of the sport.*

ruin

ruin can be a noun or a verb.

A NOUN
   la **ruina** *fem*
   the ruins of the castle
   las ruinas del castillo
B VERB
   to ruin
   estropear
   You'll ruin your shoes.
   Te vas a estropear los zapatos.

> **Language tip**
> *In Spanish you usually use an article like **el**, **la** or **los**, **las** with clothes you are wearing.*

rule NOUN
1 la **regla** *fem (of game)*
   the rules of the game
   las reglas del juego

English

Spanish

a
b
c
d
e
f
g
h
i
j
k
l
m
n
o
p
q
r
s
t
u
v
w
x
y
z

English **Spanish**

a
b
c
d
e
f
g
h
i
j
k
l
m
n
o
p
q
r
s
t
u
v
w
x
y
z

2 *(regulations)*
the rules
las normas
It's against the rules.
Va contra las normas.

ruler NOUN
la **regla** *fem*
Can I borrow your ruler?
¿Me dejas tu regla?

run

> **run** *can be a noun or a verb.*

A NOUN
to go for a run
ir a correr
Do you want to go for a run?
¿Quieres ir a correr?
I did a ten-kilometre run.
Corrí diez kilómetros.
B VERB
to run
1 correr *(move fast)*
Run!
¡Corre!
I ran two kilometres.
Corrí dos kilómetros.
She's running.
Está corriendo.

2 organizar *(organize)*
They run English courses.
Organizan cursos de inglés.

rung VERB ▷ *see* **ring**

runner NOUN
el **corredor** *masc*
la **corredora** *fem*

runner-up NOUN
el **segundo** *masc*
la **segunda** *fem*

running NOUN
Running is my favourite sport.
Correr es mi deporte favorito.

rush

> **rush** *can be a noun or a verb.*

A NOUN
la **prisa** *fem*
I'm in a rush.
Tengo prisa.
B VERB
to rush
apurarse
There's no need to rush.
No hay por qué apurarse.

rush hour NOUN
la **hora punta** *fem*
in the rush hour
en la hora punta

S s

Sabbath NOUN
el **sábado** *masc (Jewish)*

sack NOUN
el **saco** *masc*

sad ADJECTIVE
triste *masc & fem*
Don't be sad.
No estés triste.

sadly ADVERB
1 **lamentablemente**
(unfortunately)
Sadly, we haven't got time.
Lamentablemente, no tenemos
tiempo.
2 **con tristeza** *(sorrowfully)*
'She's gone,' he said sadly.
–Se ha ido, dijo con tristeza.

safe ADJECTIVE
seguro *masc*
segura *fem*
This car isn't safe.
Este coche no es seguro.
We're safe here.
Aquí estamos seguros.
Put it in a safe place.
Ponlo en un lugar seguro.
**Don't worry, it's perfectly
safe.**
No te preocupes, no tiene el
menor peligro.
You're safe now.
Ya estás a salvo.

safety NOUN
la **seguridad** *fem*

safety pin NOUN
el **imperdible** *masc*

said VERB ▷ *see* **say**

sailing NOUN
la **vela** *fem*
His hobby is sailing.

Es aficionado a la vela.
to go sailing
hacer vela
I'd like to go sailing.
Me gustaría hacer vela.

sailing boat NOUN
el **barco de vela** *masc*

sailor NOUN
el **marinero** *masc*

saint NOUN
el **santo** *masc*
la **santa** *fem*

Language tip
The masculine form **Santo** is
shortened to **San** before names
other than **Domingo** and **Tomás**.

Saint John
San Juan
Saint Thomas
Santo Tomás

salad NOUN
la **ensalada** *fem*
Would you like some salad?
¿Quieres ensalada?

salad cream NOUN
la **mayonesa** *fem*

salad dressing NOUN
la **vinagreta** *fem*

salary NOUN
el **sueldo** *masc*

sale NOUN
1 la **venta** *fem (transaction)*
'for sale'
'a la venta'
2 las **rebajas** *fem pl (with bargains)*
There's a sale on this week.
Hay rebajas esta semana.

salmon NOUN
el **salmón** *masc* (PL los **salmones**)

salt NOUN
la **sal** *fem*

same

> **same** *can be an adjective or pronoun.*

A ADJECTIVE
mismo *masc*
misma *fem*
the same class
la misma clase
We've got the same colour T-shirts.
Tenemos las camisetas del mismo color.
B PRONOUN
They're exactly the same.
Son exactamente iguales.
Our trainers are the same.
Nuestras zapatillas son iguales.
It's not the same.
No es lo mismo.

sand NOUN
la **arena** *fem*

sandal NOUN
la **sandalia** *fem*
a pair of sandals
unas sandalias

sand castle NOUN
el **castillo de arena** *masc*

sandwich NOUN
el **sándwich** *masc*
a cheese sandwich
un sándwich de queso

sang VERB ▷ *see* **sing**

Santa Claus NOUN
Papá Noel *masc*

satchel NOUN
la **cartera** *fem*

satisfied ADJECTIVE
satisfecho *masc*
satisfecha *fem*

Saturday NOUN
el **sábado** *masc*
It's Saturday today.
Hoy es sábado.
I've got a Saturday job.
Tengo un trabajo los sábados.

on Saturday
el sábado
on Saturdays
los sábados
every Saturday
todos los sábados
last Saturday
el sábado pasado
next Saturday
el sábado que viene

Language tip
Days are not spelled with a capital letter in Spanish.

sauce NOUN
la **salsa** *fem*

saucepan NOUN
el **cazo** *masc*

saucer NOUN
el **platito** *masc*

sausage NOUN
la **salchicha** *fem*
sausages and chips
salchichas con patatas fritas

to **save** VERB
1 **ahorrar** *(money, time)*

English Spanish

a b c d e f g h i j k l m n o p q r s t u v w x y z

I'm saving for a new bike.
Estoy ahorrando para una bici nueva.
It'll save time.
Ahorrará tiempo.
2 **salvar** *(rescue)*
He saved my life.
Me salvó la vida.
3 **guardar** *(on computer)*
Don't forget to save the file.
No te olvides de guardar el archivo.

to **save up** VERB
ahorrar
I'm saving up for a new bike.
Estoy ahorrando para una bici nueva.

savoury
ADJECTIVE
salado
masc
salada *fem*
Is it sweet or savoury?
¿Es dulce o salado?

saw VERB ▷ *see* **see**

to **say** VERB
decir
Say hello, Matthew.
Di hola, Matthew.
What did you say?
¿Qué dijiste?
I said no.
Dije que no.
Could you say that again, please?
¿Puedes repetir eso, por favor?
I don't know how to say it in Spanish.
No sé cómo se dice en español.

How do you say 'hello' in Spanish?
¿Cómo se dice 'hello' en español?

scar NOUN
la **cicatriz** *fem* (PL las **cicatrices**)
He's got a scar on his face.
Tiene una cicatriz en la cara.

Language tip
In Spanish you usually use an article like **el**, **la** *or* **los**, **las** *with parts of the body.*

scared ADJECTIVE
to be scared
tener miedo
Don't be scared.
No tengas miedo.
I'm scared of dogs.
Me dan miedo los perros.

I'm scared!
¡Tengo miedo!

scarf NOUN
la **bufanda** *fem*

scary ADJECTIVE
It was really scary.
Daba mucho miedo.
a scary film
una película de miedo

scenery NOUN
el **paisaje** *masc*

school NOUN
el **colegio** *masc*
I love school.
Me encanta el colegio.
The children are at school.
Los niños están en el colegio.
I go to school by bike.
Voy al colegio en bici.
the school library
la biblioteca del colegio
There's no school next week.
La semana que viene no hay clase.

at school
en el colegio

schoolbag NOUN
la **cartera** fem

schoolboy NOUN
el **colegial** masc

schoolchildren PL NOUN
los **colegiales** masc pl

schoolgirl NOUN
la **colegiala** fem

school holidays PL NOUN
las **vacaciones escolares** fem pl

school uniform NOUN
el **uniforme del colegio** masc

science NOUN
la **ciencia** fem

scientist NOUN
el **científico** masc
la **científica** fem

scissors PL NOUN
las **tijeras** fem pl
a pair of scissors
unas tijeras

scooter NOUN
1 el **patinete** masc (child's toy)
2 la **Vespa**® fem (motorcycle)

score

score can be a noun or a verb.

A NOUN
What's the score?
¿Cómo va el partido?

The score was three nil.
El partido acabó tres a cero.
B VERB
to score
1 **marcar** (goal)
I scored a goal.
Marqué un gol.
2 **obtener** (point)
City School scored fifty points.
El colegio City obtuvo cincuenta puntos.
3 **llevar el tanteo** (keep score)
Who's going to score?
¿Quién va a llevar el tanteo?

Scot NOUN
el **escocés** masc (PL los escoceses)
la **escocesa** fem

Scotland NOUN
Escocia fem
Glasgow is in Scotland.
Glasgow está en Escocia.
I'm from Scotland.
Soy de Escocia.

Scotsman NOUN
el **escocés** masc (PL los escoceses)

> *Language tip*
> **escocés** is not spelled with a capital letter in Spanish.

Scotswoman NOUN
la **escocesa** fem

> *Language tip*
> **escocesa** is not spelled with a capital letter in Spanish.

Scottish ADJECTIVE
escocés masc (PL **escoceses**)
escocesa fem
He's Scottish.
Es escocés.

> *Language tip*
> **escocés** is not spelled with a capital letter in Spanish.

Scout NOUN
  el **boy scout** *masc*
  la **girl scout** *fem*
    I'm in the Scouts.
    Estoy en los scouts.

scrambled eggs PL NOUN
  los **huevos revueltos** *masc pl*

scrapbook NOUN
  el **álbum de recortes** *masc*

to **scream** VERB
  chillar

screen NOUN
  la **pantalla** *fem*

screw NOUN
  el **tornillo** *masc*

screwdriver NOUN
  el **destornillador** *masc*

sea NOUN
  el **mar** *masc*
    I live by the sea.
    Vivo al lado del mar.

> **Language tip**
> **mar** *is usually masculine but you may come across some expressions where it's feminine.*

seafood NOUN
  el **marisco** *masc*

seagull NOUN
  la **gaviota** *fem*

seashore NOUN
  la **orilla del mar** *fem*

    on the seashore
    a la orilla del mar

seasick ADJECTIVE
  to get seasick
  marearse en barco
  I get seasick.
  Me mareo en barco.

seaside NOUN
  la **playa** *fem*
    at the seaside
    en la playa

season NOUN
  la **estación del año** *fem* (PL las **estaciones del año**)
    What's your favourite season?
    ¿Cuál es tu estación del año preferida?

season ticket NOUN
  el **abono de temporada** *masc*

seat NOUN
  el **asiento** *masc*
    I'd like a seat by the window.
    Quiero un asiento al lado de la ventana.
    Go back to your seat, Mike!
    ¡Vuelve a tu sitio, Mike!

second

> **second** *can be an adjective or a noun.*

A ADJECTIVE
  segundo *masc*
  segunda *fem*
  on the second page
  en la segunda página
  Tim came second.
  Tim llegó el segundo.

B NOUN
  el **segundo** *masc*
  It'll only take a second.
  Solo tardará un segundo.
  My birthday's the second of July.
  Mi cumpleaños es el dos de julio.
  Today's the second of June.
  Hoy es dos de junio.

on the second of March
el dos de marzo

Language tip
*Use the same set of numbers that you use for counting (**uno**, **dos**, **tres** and so on) when giving Spanish dates.*

secondary school
NOUN
el **instituto** *masc*

secret

secret can be a noun or an adjective.

A NOUN
el **secreto** *masc*
It's a secret.
Es un secreto.
Can you keep a secret?
¿Me guardas un secreto?

in secret
en secreto

B ADJECTIVE
secreto *masc*
secreta *fem*
a secret passage
un pasadizo secreto

secretary NOUN
el **secretario** *masc*
la **secretaria** *fem*
She's a secretary.
Es secretaria.

Language tip
When talking about people's jobs in Spanish, you do not use an article.

secretly ADVERB
en secreto

to **see** VERB
ver
We're going to see Granny and Grandpa.
Vamos a ir a ver a los abuelos.

I can see her car.
No veo su coche.
I can't see anything.
No veo nada.
Can you see the difference?
¿Ves la diferencia?

Language tip
*Don't forget the personal **a** in examples like the following.*

I saw Catriona yesterday.
Vi a Catriona ayer.
Have you seen Paul?
¿Has visto a Paul?

See you!
¡Hasta luego!
See you tomorrow!
¡Hasta mañana!
See you soon!
¡Hasta pronto!

seed NOUN
la **semilla** *fem*
poppy seeds
semillas de amapola
sunflower seeds
pipas de girasol

Did you know...?
*Did you know that sunflower seeds, often referred to just as **pipas**, are a popular Spanish snack?*

to **seem** VERB
parecer
She seems tired.
Parece cansada.
There seems to be a problem.
Parece que hay un problema.

seen VERB ▷ see **see**

seesaw NOUN
el **balancín** masc (PL los **balancines**)

selfish ADJECTIVE
egoísta masc & fem
Don't be so selfish, Charles.
No seas tan egoísta, Charles.

> **Language tip**
> Even though **egoísta** ends in **-a**, you can use it to describe a man or boy.

self-service ADJECTIVE
autoservicio

> **Language tip**
> **autoservicio** never changes its ending no matter what it describes.

The café is self-service.
La cafetería es autoservicio.
a self-service restaurant
un autoservicio

to **sell** VERB
vender
He's selling his car.
Vende su coche.
The tickets are sold out.
Las entradas están agotadas.

Sellotape® NOUN
la **cinta adhesiva** fem

semicircle NOUN
el **semicírculo** masc
Get into a semicircle.
Formad un semicírculo.

semicolon NOUN
el **punto y coma** masc (PL los **punto y coma**)

semi-final NOUN
la **semifinal** fem

to **send** VERB
enviar
I'm going to send Sally a postcard.
Voy a enviarle una postal a Sally.

Send me an email.
Envíame un e-mail.
My friend has sent me some photos.
Mi amigo me ha enviado algunas fotos.

senior school NOUN
el **instituto de enseñanza secundaria** masc

sense of humour NOUN
el **sentido del humor** masc
Our teacher has a sense of humour.
Nuestro profesor tiene sentido del humor.
He has no sense of humour.
No tiene sentido del humor.

sensible ADJECTIVE
sensato masc
sensata fem
Be sensible, Amy!
¡Sé sensata, Amy!

> **Language tip**
> Be careful! The translation of **sensible** is not **sensible**.

sent VERB ▷ see **send**

sentence NOUN
la **oración** fem (PL las **oraciones**)
What does this sentence mean?
¿Qué significa esta oración?

separate ADJECTIVE
aparte masc & fem
Put the green cards in a separate pile.
Pon las tarjetas verdes en una pila aparte.

English Spanish

a b c d e f g h i j k l m n o p q r s t u v w x y z

September NOUN
septiembre *masc*
   My birthday's in September.
   Mi cumpleaños es en septiembre.
   It's the twelfth of September today.
   Hoy es doce de septiembre.

> **in September**
> en septiembre
> **on the fifth of September**
> el cinco de septiembre

> *Language tip*
> *Months are not spelled with a capital letter in Spanish.*

sequence NOUN
   el **orden** *masc* (PL los **órdenes**)
   Put the pictures in sequence, Peter.
   Pon las fotos en orden, Peter.

series NOUN
   la **serie** *fem*
   a TV series
   una serie de TV

serious ADJECTIVE
   serio *masc*
   seria *fem*
   You look very serious.
   Estás muy serio.
   Are you serious?
   ¿En serio?

to **serve** VERB
   servir
   They're serving lunch now.
   Están sirviendo la comida ahora.
   It serves you right.
   Te está bien empleado.

service NOUN
1 el **servicio** *masc (in restaurant)*
   Service is included.
   El servicio está incluido.
2 el **oficio religioso** *masc (in church)*

service charge NOUN
   el **servicio** *masc*

There's no service charge.
El servicio va incluido.

service station NOUN
   la **estación de servicio** *fem*
   (PL las **estaciones de servicio**)

serviette NOUN
   la **servilleta** *fem*

to **set** VERB
1 **poner**
   I normally set the alarm for seven.
   Normalmente pongo el despertador para las siete.
   Could you set the table?
   ¿Puedes poner la mesa?
2 **ponerse** *(sun)*
   The sun is setting.
   El sol se está poniendo.

to **set off** VERB
   salir
   What time are you setting off?
   ¿A qué hora sales?

settee NOUN
   el **sofá** *masc*

to **settle down** VERB
   calmarse
   Settle down, children!
   ¡Calmaos, niños!

seven NUMBER
   siete
   seven euros
   siete euros
   I get up at seven o'clock.
   Me levanto a las siete.

> **She's seven.**
> Tiene siete años.

> *Language tip*
> *In English you can say **she's seven** or **she's seven years old**. In Spanish you can only say **tiene siete años**.*

Have you noticed that in Spanish you need to use the verb **tener** *to talk about somebody's age?*

seventeen NUMBER
diecisiete
seventeen euros
diecisiete euros

He's seventeen.
Tiene diecisiete años.

Language tip
In English you can say **he's seventeen** *or* **he's seventeen years old**. *In Spanish you can only say* **tiene diecisiete años**. *Have you noticed that in Spanish you need to use the verb* **tener** *to talk about somebody's age?*

seventeenth NUMBER
diecisiete
on the seventeenth floor
en la planta diecisiete
We break up on the seventeenth of December.
Empezamos las vacaciones el diecisiete de diciembre.
Today's the seventeenth of March.
Hoy es diecisiete de marzo.

on the seventeenth of January
el diecisiete de enero

Language tip
Use the same set of numbers that you use for counting (**uno**, **dos**, **tres** *and so on) when giving Spanish dates.*

seventh NUMBER
1 **séptimo** *masc*
séptima *fem*
on the seventh floor
en la séptima planta
My birthday's the seventh of February.
Mi cumpleaños es el siete de febrero.
It's the seventh of April today.
Hoy es siete de abril.

on the seventh of August
el siete de agosto

Language tip
Use the same set of numbers that you use for counting (**uno**, **dos**, **tres** *and so on) when giving Spanish dates.*

seventy NUMBER
setenta
My grandma is seventy.
Mi abuela tiene setenta años.

Language tip
In English you can say **she's seventy** *or* **she's seventy years old**. *In Spanish you can only say* **tiene setenta años**. *Have you noticed that in Spanish you need to use the verb* **tener** *to talk about somebody's age?*

several ADJECTIVE
varios *masc pl*
varias *fem pl*
Several children are absent.
Varios niños no han venido.

sewing NOUN
la **costura** *fem*
I like sewing.
Me gusta la costura.

shade NOUN
la **sombra** *fem*
It was thirty-five degrees in the shade.
Hacía treinta y cinco grados a la sombra.

shadow
NOUN
la **sombra**
fem
my shadow
mi sombra

to **shake** VERB
1 **temblar** *(tremble)*
My hands are shaking.
Me tiemblan las manos.

English | Spanish

a b c d e f g h i j k l m n o p q r s t u v w x y z

2 sacudir *(on purpose)*
She shook the rug.
Sacudió la alfombra.
to shake hands with somebody
darle la mano a alguien
Shake hands with your best friend!
¡Dale la mano a tu mejor amigo!
Spanish people shake hands a lot.
Los españoles se dan mucho la mano.

shall VERB

Shall I shut the window?
¿Cierro la ventana?
Shall I go first?
¿Empiezo yo?
Shall I put the light on?
¿Enciendo la luz?

shame NOUN

What a shame!
¡Qué pena!

shampoo NOUN
el **champú** *masc*
a bottle of shampoo
un bote de champú

shape NOUN
la **forma** *fem*

to **share** VERB
compartir
I share a room with my brother.
Comparto la habitación con mi hermano.

sharp ADJECTIVE

afilado *masc*
afilada *fem*
Be careful, it's sharp.
Ten cuidado que está afilado.

she PRONOUN
ella
She's got a radio but I haven't.
Ella tiene una radio pero yo no.

She's very nice.
Es muy simpática.

she'd
1 (= **she had**) ▷ *see* **have**
2 (= **she would**) ▷ *see* **would**

sheep NOUN
la **oveja** *fem*

sheet NOUN
la **sábana** *fem*
clean sheets
sábanas limpias
a sheet of paper
una hoja de papel

shelf NOUN
el **estante** *masc*
the top shelf
el estante de arriba

she'll (= **she will**) ▷ *see* **will**

shell NOUN
la **concha** *fem*

English Spanish

shelves PL NOUN
los **estantes** *masc pl*

she's
1 (= **she is**) ▷ see **be**
2 (= **she has**) ▷ see **have**

Shetland Islands
PL NOUN
las **Islas Shetland** *fem pl*

to **shine** VERB
brillar
The sun is shining.
El sol brilla.

ship NOUN
el **barco** *masc*

shirt NOUN
la **camisa** *fem*
a white shirt
una camisa
blanca

shocking ADJECTIVE
escandaloso *masc*
escandalosa *fem*
It's shocking!
¡Es escandaloso!

shoe NOUN
el **zapato** *masc*
I've got new shoes.
Tengo unos zapatos nuevos.
Put on your shoes.
Ponte los zapatos.

Language tip
In Spanish you usually use an article
like el, la or los, las with clothes
you are wearing.

shoelace NOUN
el **cordón** *masc* (PL los **cordones**)

shoe shop NOUN
la **zapatería** *fem*

shop NOUN
la **tienda** *fem*
The shop is shut.
La tienda está cerrada.
a sports shop
una tienda de deportes

shop assistant NOUN
el **dependiente** *masc*
la **dependienta** *fem*
She's a shop assistant.
Es dependienta.

Language tip
When talking about people's jobs in
Spanish, you do not use an article.

shopkeeper NOUN
el **tendero** *masc*
la **tendera** *fem*

shopping NOUN
la **compra** *fem*
I do the shopping for my
granny.
Le hago la compra a mi abuela.
I go shopping with my
friends.
Me voy de compras con mis
amigas.
Can you get the shopping
from the car?
¿Puedes traer las bolsas de la
compra del coche?

shopping bag NOUN
la **bolsa de la compra** *fem*

shopping centre NOUN
el **centro comercial** *masc*

short ADJECTIVE
1 corto *masc*
corta *fem (not long)*
a short skirt
una falda corta
short hair
el pelo corto
a short walk
un paseo corto

English Spanish

a b c d e f g h i j k l m n o p q r s t u v w x y z

2 bajo *masc*
baja *fem* (not tall)
She's quite short.
Es bastante baja.

shorts PL NOUN
los **pantalones cortos** *masc pl*
My shorts are green.
Mis pantalones cortos son
verdes.
a pair of shorts
unos pantalones cortos

short-sighted ADJECTIVE
miope *masc & fem*

shoulder NOUN
el **hombro** *masc*

should VERB
You should try it.
Deberías intentarlo.
You shouldn't do that.
No deberías hacer eso.

to **shout** VERB
gritar

**Don't
shout,
children!**
¡Niños,
no gritéis!

to **show** VERB
enseñar
Show me!
¡Enséñame!
Shall I show you the photos?
¿Te enseño las fotos?

shower NOUN
1 la **ducha** *fem* (for washing)
She's in the shower.
Está en la ducha.
to have a shower
ducharse
I'm going to have a shower.
Voy a ducharme.
2 el **chaparrón** *masc* (PL los
chaparrones) (rain)
It's just a shower.
Es solo un chaparrón.

Shrove Tuesday NOUN
el **Martes de Carnaval** *masc*

Did you know...?
*During the week before Lent, all over
Spain and Latin America there are
fiestas and fancy-dress parades,
with the main celebrations taking
place on* **Martes de Carnaval**
(literally 'Carnival Tuesday').

to **shrug** VERB
to shrug one's shoulders
encogerse de hombros
She shrugged her shoulders.
Se encogió de hombros.

to **shuffle** VERB
You have to shuffle the cards.
Tienes que barajar las cartas.

shut

shut can be a verb or an adjective.

A VERB
to shut
cerrar
What time do the shops shut?
¿A qué hora cierran las tiendas?
**Open your mouth and shut
your eyes.**
Abre la boca y cierra los ojos.

Language tip
*In Spanish you usually use an article
like* **el**, **la** *or* **los**, **las** *with parts of the
body.*

B ADJECTIVE
cerrado *masc*
cerrada *fem*
The door is shut.
La puerta está cerrada.

shy ADJECTIVE
tímido *masc*
tímida *fem*
He's very shy.
Es muy tímido.

sick ADJECTIVE
enfermo *masc*
enferma *fem* (unwell)

He is sick.
Está enfermo.
I'm going to be sick.
Voy a devolver.
I feel sick.
Tengo ganas de devolver.

side NOUN
1 el **lado** *masc (of object, building, street)*
on this side
en este lado
It's on this side of the street.
Está en este lado de la calle.
2 el **equipo** *masc (team)*
He's on my side.
Está en mi equipo.

sightseeing NOUN

We're going to go sightseeing.
Vamos a ir a visitar monumentos.

sign

sign *can be a noun or a verb.*

A NOUN
la **señal** *fem*
a road sign
una señal de tráfico
B VERB
to sign
firmar
Sign here, please.
Firma aquí, por favor.

signal NOUN
la **señal** *fem*

signature NOUN
la **firma** *fem*

sign language NOUN
el **lenguaje de signos** *masc*

silence NOUN
el **silencio** *masc*

silk

silk *can be a noun or an adjective.*

A NOUN
la **seda** *fem*
B ADJECTIVE
de seda
a silk scarf
un pañuelo de seda

silly ADJECTIVE
tonto *masc*
tonta *fem*
Don't be silly, Ian!
¡No seas tonto, Ian!

silver

silver *can be a noun or an adjective.*

A NOUN
la **plata** *fem*
gold and silver
oro y plata
B ADJECTIVE
de plata
a silver chain
una cadena de plata
a silver medal
una medalla de plata

similar ADJECTIVE
parecido *masc*
parecida *fem*
His sweater's similar to mine.
Su jersey es parecido al mío.

simple ADJECTIVE
sencillo *masc*
sencilla *fem*
It's very simple.
Es muy sencillo.

since PREPOSITION
desde
since Christmas
desde Navidad
since then
desde entonces

sincerely ADVERB
Yours sincerely ...
Le saluda atentamente ...

English Spanish

a b c d e f g h i j k l m n o p q r s t u v w x y z

Language tip
Use **Le saluda atentamente** *when writing to one person.* Use **Les saluda atentamente** *when writing to more than one person.*

to sing VERB
cantar
> **I sing in the choir.**
> Canto en el coro.

singer NOUN
el/la **cantante** *masc/fem*

single

single can be an adjective or a noun.

A ADJECTIVE
1 individual *masc & fem*
> **a single room**
> una habitación individual
> **a single bed**
> una cama individual

B NOUN
el **billete de ida** *masc*
> **A single to Barcelona, please.**
> Uno de ida a Barcelona, por favor.

singular NOUN
> **in the singular**
> en singular

sink NOUN
el **fregadero** *masc (kitchen sink)*

sir NOUN
el **señor** *masc*
> **Yes, sir.**
> Sí, señor.

sister NOUN
la **hermana** *fem*
> **my little sister**
> mi hermana pequeña
> **my big sister**
> mi hermana mayor
> **I've got one sister.**
> Tengo una hermana.
> **I haven't got any sisters.**
> No tengo hermanas.

Have you got any brothers or sisters?
¿Tienes hermanos?

to sit VERB
sentarse
> **I want to sit next to my friend.**
> Quiero sentarme al lado de mi amigo.
> **Can I sit here?**
> ¿Puedo sentarme aquí?
> **Brian is sitting next to Megan.**
> Brian está sentado al lado de Megan.

Language tip
Change **está sentado** *to* **está sentada** *if it's a girl or woman who is sitting somewhere.*

to sit down VERB
sentarse
> **Sit down, Anthony.**
> Siéntate, Anthony.

Sit down, children.
Niños, sentaos.

site NOUN
1 el **sitio web** *masc (website)*
2 el **camping** *masc (campsite)*

sitting room NOUN
el **salón** *masc* (PL los **salones**)

situation NOUN
la **situación** *fem* (PL las **situaciones**)

six NUMBER
seis
> **six euros**
> seis euros

She's six.
Tiene seis años.

Language tip
In English you can say **she's six** *or* **she's six years old**. *In Spanish you can only say* **tiene seis años**. *Have*

*you noticed that in Spanish you need to use the verb **tener** to talk about somebody's age?*

sixteen NUMBER
dieciséis
    sixteen euros
    dieciséis euros

He's sixteen.
Tiene dieciséis años.

Language tip
*In English you can say **he's sixteen** or **he's sixteen years old**. In Spanish you can only say **tiene dieciséis años**. Have you noticed that in Spanish you need to use the verb **tener** to talk about somebody's age?*

sixteenth NUMBER
dieciséis
    on the sixteenth floor
    en la planta dieciséis
    We break up on the sixteenth of December.
    Empezamos las vacaciones el dieciséis de diciembre.
    Today's the sixteenth of January.
    Hoy es dieciséis de enero.

on the sixteenth of August
el dieciséis de agosto

Language tip
*Use the same set of numbers that you use for counting (**uno**, **dos**, **tres** and so on) when giving Spanish dates.*

sixth NUMBER
sexto *masc*
sexta *fem*
    on the sixth floor
    en la sexta planta
    My birthday's the sixth of October.
    Mi cumpleaños es el seis de octubre.

It's the sixth of November today.
Hoy es seis de noviembre.

on the sixth of August
el seis de agosto

Language tip
*Use the same set of numbers that you use for counting (**uno**, **dos**, **tres** and so on) when giving Spanish dates.*

sixty NUMBER
sesenta

My aunt is sixty.
Mi tía tiene sesenta años.

Language tip
*In English you can say **she's sixty** or **she's sixty years old**. In Spanish you can only say **tiene sesenta años**. Have you noticed that in Spanish you need to use the verb **tener** to talk about somebody's age?*

size NOUN
    la **talla** *fem*
        It's the right size.
        Es la talla correcta.

to **skate** VERB
1 **patinar** *(roller-skate)*
    I can't skate.
    No sé patinar.
2 **patinar sobre hielo** *(ice-skate)*
    I like skating.
    Me gusta patinar sobre hielo.

skateboard NOUN
    el **monopatín** *masc* (PL los **monopatines**)

English | **Spanish**

a b c d e f g h i j k l m n o p q r s t u v w x y z

skateboarding NOUN
el **skateboard** _masc_
I like skateboarding.
Me gusta el skateboard.
I'm going skateboarding with Gavin.
Voy a hacer skateboard con Gavin.

skating NOUN
I go skating every Saturday.
Voy a patinar todos los sábados.

skeleton NOUN
el **esqueleto** _masc_

ski

ski _can be a verb or a noun._

A VERB
to ski
esquiar
Can you ski?
¿Sabes esquiar?
B NOUN
el **esquí** _masc_ (PL los **esquís**)

ski boots PL NOUN
las **botas de esquí** _fem pl_

ski lift NOUN
el **telesilla** _masc_

Language tip
Even though it ends in **-a**, **el telesilla** is a masculine noun.

ski slope NOUN
la **pista de esquí** _fem_

skiing NOUN
Do you like skiing?
¿Te gusta esquiar?
I'm going on a skiing holiday.
Voy a ir de vacaciones a esquiar.

skin NOUN
la **piel** _fem_

skinny
ADJECTIVE
flaco _masc_
flaca _fem_

skipping rope NOUN
la **comba** _fem_

skirt NOUN
la **falda** _fem_
a black skirt
una falda negra

sky NOUN
el **cielo** _masc_
The sky is blue.
El cielo es azul.

to **slam** VERB
Don't slam the door.
No des portazos.

sledge NOUN
el **trineo** _masc_

sledging NOUN
Let's go sledging!
¡Vamos a montarnos en trineo!

to **sleep** VERB
dormir
My cat sleeps in a box.
Mi gato duerme en una caja.
Did you sleep well, Sonia?
¿Dormiste bien, Sonia?

sleeping bag NOUN
el **saco de dormir** _masc_

sleepover NOUN
My friend is coming for a sleepover tonight.
Mi amigo viene a dormir a mi casa esta noche.
We're going to Camilla's for a sleepover.
Vamos a quedarnos a dormir en casa de Camilla.

sleepy ADJECTIVE
I'm sleepy.
Tengo sueño.

sleeve NOUN
la **manga** _fem_
a shirt with long sleeves
una camisa de manga larga
a shirt with short sleeves
una camisa de manga corta

slept VERB ▷see **sleep**

slice NOUN
1 la **rebanada** *fem (of bread)*
2 el **trozo** *masc (of cake)*

slide NOUN
1 el **tobogán** *masc* (PL los **toboganes**) *(in playground)*
2 el **pasador del pelo** *masc (hair slide)*
3 la **diapositiva** *fem (photo)*

slight ADJECTIVE
ligero *masc*
ligera *fem*
   a slight fever
   una ligera fiebre
   a slight problem
   un pequeño problema

slightly ADVERB
ligeramente

slim

> **slim** *can be an adjective or a verb.*

A ADJECTIVE
   delgado *masc*
   delgada *fem*
   She's slimmer now.
   Ahora está más delgada.
B VERB
   to slim
   adelgazar
   I'm trying to slim.
   Estoy intentando adelgazar.

slipper NOUN
la **zapatilla** *fem*
   a pair of slippers
   unas zapatillas
   Put on your slippers.
   Ponte las zapatillas.

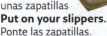

> *Language tip*
> In Spanish you usually use an article like **el**, **la** or **los**, **las** with clothes you are wearing.

slow ADJECTIVE
lento *masc*

lenta *fem*
   The music is too slow.
   La música es demasiado lenta.

slowly ADVERB
despacio
   Could you speak more slowly?
   ¿Puedes hablar más despacio?

smack NOUN

> **smack** *can be a noun or a verb.*

A NOUN
   el **cachete** *masc*
B VERB
   to smack
   dar un cachete a

small ADJECTIVE
pequeño *masc*
pequeña *fem*
   This skirt is too small for me.
   Esta falda me está demasiado pequeña.

smart ADJECTIVE
1 **elegante** *masc & fem (elegant)*
   smart clothes
   ropa elegante
2 **listo** *masc*
   lista *fem (clever)*
   She's very smart.
   Es muy lista.

smart phone NOUN
el **smartphone**

smell

> **smell** *can be a noun or a verb.*

A NOUN
   el **olor** *masc*
   a nice smell
   un buen olor
B VERB
   to smell
   oler
   Mmm, that smells nice!
   ¡Uy, qué bien huele eso!

smile

> **smile** *can be a noun or a verb.*

A NOUN
la **sonrisa** *fem*
a beautiful smile
una bonita sonrisa
B VERB
to smile
sonreír
Why are you smiling?
¿Por qué sonríes?

smiley NOUN
el **smiley** *masc*

to **smoke** NOUN
fumar
I don't smoke.
Yo no fumo.
He's smoking.
Está fumando.

smoking NOUN
Smoking is bad for you.
Fumar es malo para la salud.
'no smoking'
'prohibido fumar'

smoothie NOUN
el **batido de frutas** *masc*

snack NOUN
You can get a snack in the canteen.
Puedes picar algo en la cafetería.

snack bar NOUN
la **cafetería** *fem*

snail NOUN
el **caracol** *masc*

snake NOUN
la **serpiente** *fem*

to **sneeze** VERB
estornudar

snooker NOUN
el **billar** *masc*
I play snooker.
Juego al billar.

> *Language tip*
> In Spanish, you need to add **al** or
> **a la** *before the name of the sport.*

to **snore** VERB
roncar
He's snoring.
Está roncando.

snow

> **snow** *can be a noun or a verb.*

A NOUN
la **nieve** *fem*
B VERB
to snow
nevar
It's going to snow.
Va a nevar.
It snows a lot in the mountains.
Nieva mucho en las montañas.

It's snowing.
Está nevando.

snowball NOUN
la **bola de nieve** *fem*

snowboarding NOUN
el **snowboard** *masc*
I like snowboarding.
Me gusta hacer snowboard.

snowflake NOUN
el **copo de nieve** *masc*

snowman NOUN
el **muñeco de nieve** *masc*
I'm going to make a snowman.
Voy a hacer un muñeco de nieve.

so

> **so** *can be an adverb or a conjunction.*

A ADVERB
tan
You talk so fast.
Hablas tan rápido.

It's so difficult.
Es tan difícil.
so much
tanto
I love you so much.
Te quiero tanto.
I've got so many things to do today.
Tengo tantas cosas que hacer hoy.
B CONJUNCTION
así que
It's Raymond's birthday, so I've got him a present.
Es el cumpleaños de Raymond, así que tengo un regalo para él.
I play football. — So do I.
Yo juego al fútbol. — Yo también.
Is Lisa winning? — I think so.
¿Va ganando Lisa? — Creo que sí.

so do I
yo también
so have I
yo también
so am I
yo también
I think so.
Creo que sí.
I don't think so.
Creo que no.
I hope so.
Eso espero.

soap NOUN
el **jabón** masc
a bar of soap
una pastilla de jabón

soccer NOUN
el **fútbol** masc

sock NOUN
el **calcetín** masc (PL los **calcetines**)
I'm wearing white socks.
Llevo calcetines blancos.
a pair of socks
un par de calcetines

sofa NOUN
el **sofá** masc

soft ADJECTIVE
1 **suave** masc & fem (voice, texture)
2 **blando** masc
blanda fem (pillow, bed, ball)

soft drink NOUN
el **refresco** masc

soil NOUN
la **tierra** fem

sold VERB ▷see **sell**

soldier NOUN
el **soldado** masc
He's a soldier.
Es soldado.

Language tip
When talking about people's jobs in Spanish, you do not use an article.

some

some can be an adjective or a pronoun.

A ADJECTIVE
1 **algunos** masc pl
algunas fem pl (a few)

Language tip
*When **some** refers to something plural and means the same as 'a few', you can use **algunos** or **algunas** depending on whether the word is masculine or feminine.*

Some children are absent.
Algunos niños no están.
I need some nails.
Necesito algunos clavos.
I've got some sweets.
Tengo algunos caramelos.

Language tip
*However, when **some** is followed by a plural word, it is often not translated.*

I need some nails.
Necesito clavos.
I've got some sweets.
Tengo caramelos.

2 *(a little)*

> **Language tip**
> When **some** *refers to something you can't count, it usually isn't translated.*

Would you like some bread?
¿Quieres pan?
I need some sellotape.
Necesito celo.
3 algún *masc*
alguna *fem (one)*
some day
algún día
B PRONOUN
1 algunos *masc pl*
algunas *fem pl (a few)*
some of my friends
algunos de mis amigos
Have you got all her books? — I've got some of them.
¿Tienes todos sus libros? — Tengo algunos.
I've got some, but not many.
Tengo algunos, pero no muchos.

> **Language tip**
> When the number of things referred to is unimportant, **some** *usually isn't translated.*

Chips? — No thanks, I've still got some.
¿Patatas fritas? — No, gracias, todavía tengo.
2 *(a little)*

> **Language tip**
> When **some** *refers to something you can't count, it usually isn't translated.*

Would you like some coffee? — No thanks, I've already got some.
¿Quieres café? — No gracias, ya tengo.

> **Language tip**
> However, you can often use **un poco**, *which literally means 'a little'.*

I've got a bar of chocolate. Would you like some?
Tengo una tableta de chocolate.
¿Quieres un poco?

> **I've got some.**
> Tengo.
> **Would you like some?**
> ¿Quieres?

somebody PRONOUN
alguien
Somebody asked after you.
Alguien preguntó por ti.

someone PRONOUN
alguien
Someone asked after you.
Alguien preguntó por ti.

something PRONOUN
algo
Are you looking for something?
¿Estás buscando algo?
I can see something green.
Veo algo verde.

sometimes ADVERB
a veces
sometimes, but not very often
a veces, pero no muy a menudo

somewhere ADVERB
en alguna parte
It's somewhere in the classroom.
Está en alguna parte de la clase.
I've got to go somewhere.
Tengo que ir a alguna parte.

son NOUN
el **hijo** *masc*
her son
su hijo

song NOUN
la **canción** *fem* (PL las
canciones)
We're going to sing a song.
Vamos a cantar una canción.

soon ADVERB
pronto
It'll soon be lunchtime.
Pronto será la hora de comer.
very soon
muy pronto
**Please tell me as soon as
possible.**
Por favor, dímelo lo antes posible.

as soon as possible
lo antes posible
Write soon!
¡Escribe pronto!

sore ADJECTIVE
It's sore.
Duele.
My head is sore.
Me duele la cabeza.

Language tip

*In Spanish you usually use an article
like* **el**, **la** *or* **los**, **las** *with parts of
the body.*

sorry EXCLAMATION
¡Lo siento!
I'm really sorry.
Lo siento mucho.
I'm sorry, I can't.
Lo siento, no puedo.
I'm sorry I'm late.
Siento llegar tarde.

Sorry!
¡Lo siento!

sort NOUN
el **tipo** *masc*
What sort of bike have you got?
¿Qué tipo de bici tienes?

sound

sound *can be a noun or a verb.*

A NOUN
1 el **ruido** *masc* (noise)
the sound of footsteps
el ruido de pasos
Don't make a sound!
¡No hagas ruido!
2 el **volumen** *masc* (volume)
Can I turn the sound down?
¿Puedo bajar el volumen?
B VERB
to sound
parecer
That sounds interesting.
Eso parece interesante.
That sounds like a good idea.
Eso parece una buena idea.

soup NOUN
la **sopa** *fem*
**vegetable
soup**
sopa de
verduras

sour ADJECTIVE
agrio *masc*
agria *fem*

south

south *can be an adjective or a
noun.*

A ADJECTIVE
sur

Language tip

sur *never changes its ending no
matter what it describes. Did you
know that adjectives that behave
like this are called 'invariable
adjectives'?*

the south coast
la costa sur
B NOUN
el **sur** *masc*
in the south
en el sur

the south of Spain
el sur de España
Málaga is in the south of Spain.
Málaga está en el sur de España.

southern ADJECTIVE
southern England
el sur de Inglaterra

South Pole NOUN
the South Pole
el Polo Sur *masc*

souvenir NOUN
el **recuerdo** *masc*
a souvenir shop
una tienda de recuerdos

space NOUN
1 el **sitio** *masc (room)*
There's a lot of space.
Hay mucho sitio.
Leave a space for a drawing.
Deja un sitio para un dibujo.
2 el **espacio** *masc (outer space)*
3 la **casilla** *fem (in game)*
Go back three spaces.
Retrocede tres casillas.

spaceship NOUN
la **nave espacial** *fem*

spade NOUN
1 la **pala** *fem*
a bucket and spade
un cubo y una pala

> **Language tip**
> Be careful! The translation of **spade** is not **espada**.

2 *(in cards)*
spades
las picas *fem pl*

the ace of spades
el as de picas

spaghetti NOUN
los **espaguetis** *masc pl*

Spain NOUN
España *fem*
Seville is in Spain.
Sevilla está en España.
He lives in Spain.
Vive en España.
We're going to Spain.
Vamos a ir a España.
They are from Spain.
Son de España.

Spanish

> **Spanish** *can be an adjective or a noun.*

A ADJECTIVE
español *masc*
española *fem*
a Spanish girl
una chica española
our Spanish teacher
nuestro profesor de español
my Spanish book
mi libro de español
Spanish people
los españoles

> **He's Spanish.**
> Es español.
> **She's Spanish.**
> Es española.

B NOUN
el **español** *masc*
Do you speak Spanish?
¿Hablas español?

> **Did you know…?**
> *Did you know that Spanish is also called* **el castellano** *because it originated in* **Castilla** *in central Spain? Depending where you are in the country, you'll also hear other languages, such as* **el catalán**, **el gallego**, *and* **el vasco**, *but* **el castellano**

is understood and used throughout the country too.

the Spanish
los españoles

Language tip
español *is not spelled with a capital letter in Spanish.*

spare room NOUN
la **habitación de invitados** *fem* (PL las **habitaciones de invitados**)

spare time NOUN
el **tiempo libre** *masc*
What do you do in your spare time?
¿Qué haces en tu tiempo libre?

sparkling ADJECTIVE
con gas
sparkling water
agua con gas
sparkling wine
vino espumoso

to **speak** VERB
hablar
Could you speak more slowly, please?
¿Puedes hablar más despacio, por favor?

I speak English.
Hablo inglés.
Do you speak English?
¿Hablas inglés?

special ADJECTIVE
especial *masc & fem*

speciality NOUN
la **especialidad** *fem*

specially ADVERB
sobre todo
It rains a lot, specially in winter.
Llueve mucho, sobre todo en invierno.

spectator NOUN
el **espectador** *masc*
la **espectadora** *fem*

speech NOUN
el **discurso** *masc*
The headmaster made a speech.
El director dio un discurso.

speed NOUN
la **velocidad** *fem*

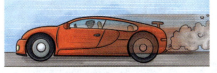

a ten-speed bike
una bici de diez velocidades

speedboat NOUN
la **lancha motora** *fem*

to **spell** VERB
1 escribir *(in writing)*
How do you spell that?
¿Cómo se escribe eso?
2 deletrear *(out loud)*
Can you spell that please?
¿Puedes deletrear eso, por favor?

spelling NOUN
la **ortografía** *fem*
a spelling mistake
una falta de ortografía

to **spend** VERB
1 gastar *(money)*
I spent twenty pounds on presents.
Gasté veinte libras en regalos.
2 pasar *(time)*
We are going to spend two weeks in Scotland.
Vamos a pasar dos semanas en Escocia.

spicy ADJECTIVE
picante *masc & fem*

spider NOUN
la **araña** *fem*

spinach NOUN
las **espinacas** *fem pl*
I don't like spinach.
No me gustan las espinacas.

spite NOUN
in spite of
a pesar de
in spite of the weather
a pesar del tiempo

to **split** VERB
1 **dividirse** *(separate)*
Split into two groups.
Dividíos en dos grupos.
2 **compartir** *(share)*
**Let's split the money
between us.**
Vamos a compartir el dinero
entre nosotros.

spoiled ADJECTIVE
mimado *masc*
mimada *fem*
a spoiled child
un niño mimado

spoilsport NOUN
el/la **aguafiestas** *masc/fem* (PL
los/las **aguafiestas**)
Don't be a spoilsport!
¡No seas aguafiestas!

spoilt ADJECTIVE
mimado *masc*
mimada *fem*
a spoilt child
un niño mimado

spoke VERB ▷ *see* **speak**

spoken VERB ▷ *see* **speak**

sponge NOUN
la **esponja** *fem*

sponge bag NOUN
la **bolsa de aseo** *fem*

sponge cake NOUN
el **bizcocho** *masc*

to **sponsor** VERB
**I'm doing a sponsored
ten-mile walk in aid of the
homeless.**
Voy a caminar diez millas para
conseguir donativos en beneficio
de los sin techo.

Did you know…?
In Spain it isn't usual to sponsor
people to go on walks, swims, and
so on for charity.

spoon NOUN
la **cuchara** *fem*
I haven't got a spoon.
No tengo cuchara.

sport NOUN
el **deporte** *masc*
What's your favourite sport?
¿Cuál es tu deporte favorito?
**Football is my favourite
sport.**
El fútbol es mi deporte favorito.
What sports do you play?
¿Qué deportes practicas?

sports bag NOUN
la **bolsa de deportes** *fem*

sports car NOUN
el **coche deportivo** *masc*

spot

spot *can be a noun or a verb.*

A NOUN
1 el **lunar** *masc (dot)*
a red dress with white spots
un vestido rojo con lunares
blancos
2 el **grano** *masc (pimple)*
He's covered in spots.
Está lleno de granos.
B VERB
to spot
encontrar *(find)*
**Can you spot the odd one
out?**
¿Puedes encontrar el que no es
como los demás?

spring NOUN
la **primavera** *fem*
It's the first day of spring.
Es el primer día de la primavera.

in spring
en primavera

springtime NOUN
la **primavera** *fem*

in springtime
en primavera

spy NOUN
el/la **espía** *masc/fem*

square NOUN
1 el **cuadrado** *masc (shape)*
a square and a triangle
un cuadrado y un triángulo
2 la **plaza** *fem (in town)*
There's a statue in the middle of the square.
Hay una estatua en mitad de la plaza.

squash NOUN
1 *(drink)*
orange squash
la naranjada
2 el **squash** *masc (game)*
I play squash.
Juego al squash.

Language tip
In Spanish, you need to add **al** or **a la** before the name of the sport.

squirrel NOUN
la **ardilla** *fem*

stable NOUN
la **cuadra** *fem*

stack NOUN
la **pila** *fem*
a stack of books
una pila de libros

stadium NOUN
el **estadio** *masc*

staff NOUN
1 el **personal** *masc (personnel)*

2 el **profesorado** *masc*
(of school)

staffroom NOUN
la **sala de profesores** *fem*

staircase NOUN
la **escalera** *fem*

stairs PL NOUN
la **escalera** *fem*
Go down the stairs.
Baja la escalera.
Go up the stairs.
Sube la escalera.

stamp NOUN
el **sello** *masc*
a Spanish stamp
un sello español
My hobby is stamp collecting.
Mi afición es coleccionar sellos.

stamp album NOUN
el **álbum de sellos** *masc*

stamp collection NOUN
la **colección de sellos** *fem* (PL
las **colecciones de sellos**)

to **stand** VERB
Stand in a line.
Poneos en fila.
Stand over there, Andrew.
Quédate ahí de pie, Andrew.
I'm standing by the door.
Estoy de pie junto a la puerta.

to **stand for** VERB
ser la abreviatura de
'EU' stands for 'European Union'.
'EU' es la abreviatura de 'European Union'.

to **stand up** VERB
ponerse de pie
Stand up, Christine!
¡Ponte de pie, Christine!

stapler NOUN
la **grapadora** *fem*

star NOUN
la **estrella** *fem*

the moon and the stars
la luna y las estrellas
He's a TV star.
Es una estrella de la TV.

Language tip
*Did you notice that you can use **una estrella** even when referring to a man?*

start

start *can be a verb or a noun.*

A VERB
to start
1 **empezar** *(begin)*
What time does it start?
¿A qué hora empieza?
It starts with a P.
Empieza por P.

Language tip
*When **start** is followed by another verb it is translated by **empezar a**.*

You can start writing now.
Podéis empezar a escribir ahora.

Let's start.
Empecemos.
Start now, children.
¡Niños, empezad ahora!

2 **crear** *(set up)*
We want to start a football team.
Queremos crear un equipo de fútbol.
B NOUN
el **principio** *masc (beginning)*
at the start of the film
al principio de la película
at the start of December
a primeros de diciembre
Shall we make a start?
¿Empezamos ya?

starter NOUN
la **entrada** *fem (dish)*

to starve VERB
I'm starving!
¡Tengo mucha hambre!

station NOUN
la **estación** *fem* (PL las **estaciones**)
Where's the station?
¿Dónde está la estación?

statue NOUN
la **estatua** *fem*

stay

stay *can be a verb or a noun.*

A VERB
to stay
quedarse
Stay here, Daniel!
¡Quédate aquí, Daniel!
We stayed in London for three days.
Nos quedamos tres días en Londres.
We're going to stay with friends.
Vamos a quedarnos a dormir con unos amigos.
Why don't you stay the night?
¿Por qué no os quedáis a dormir?
B NOUN
la **estancia** *fem*
my stay in England
mi estancia en Inglaterra

to stay in VERB
quedarse en casa
I'm staying in tonight.
Esta noche me quedo en casa.

steak NOUN
el **filete** *masc*
I'd like steak and chips.
Quiero un filete con patatas.

to steal VERB
1 **quitar** *(take)*

Who's stolen my pencil case?
¿Quién me ha quitado el estuche?
2 robar *(thief)*
Our car's been stolen.
Nos han robado el coche.

step NOUN
1 el **paso** *masc (movement)*
a step backwards
un paso atrás
Take a step forward, boys.
Dad un paso hacia adelante, chicos.
2 el **escalón** *masc* (PL los **escalones**)
Mind the step.
Cuidado con el escalón.

stepbrother NOUN
el **hermanastro** *masc*
his stepbrother
su hermanastro

stepfather NOUN
el **padrastro** *masc*
my stepfather
mi padrastro

stepmother NOUN
la **madrastra** *fem*
my stepmother
mi madrastra

stepsister NOUN
la **hermanastra** *fem*
my stepsister
mi hermanastra

stew NOUN
el **estofado** *masc*

stewardess NOUN
1 la **auxiliar de vuelo** *fem (on plane)*
2 la **camarera** *fem (on boat)*

to **stick** VERB
pegar
Stick the stamps on the envelope.
Pega los sellos en el sobre.

to **stick out** VERB
Don't stick out your tongue!
¡No saques la lengua!

sticker NOUN
la **pegatina** *fem*

still

> **still** *can be an adverb or an adjective.*

A ADVERB
todavía
You've still got two cards.
Todavía tienes dos cartas.
I'm still hungry.
Todavía tengo hambre.
B ADJECTIVE
Keep still, Ben!
¡No te muevas, Ben!
Sit still, David!
¡Siéntate ahí quieto, David!

> **Language tip**
> Change **quieto** to **quieta** *if you're talking to a girl.*

stitch NOUN
el **punto** *masc*
I've got five stitches.
Me han dado cinco puntos.

stomach NOUN
el **estómago** *masc*

stomachache NOUN
I've got stomachache.
Me duele el estómago.

stone NOUN
la **piedra** *fem*
The boys are throwing stones.
Los niños están tirando piedras.
a stone wall
un muro de piedra
I weigh five stone.
Peso unos treinta y dos kilos.

Did you know…?
In Spain, weight is given in kilos.
A **stone** *is about 6.3 kilos.*

stool NOUN
la **banqueta** *fem*

stop

stop *can be a verb or a noun.*

A VERB
to stop
parar
Stop, that's enough!
¡Para, ya basta!
Stop talking, children.
Parad de hablar, niños.
My dad wants to stop smoking.
Mi padre quiere dejar de fumar.

Stop it!
¡Ya basta!

B NOUN
la **parada** *fem*
a bus stop
una parada de autobús

storey NOUN
la **planta** *fem*
a three-storey building
un edificio de tres plantas

storm NOUN
la **tormenta** *fem*

stormy
ADJECTIVE
stormy weather
tiempo tormentoso

story NOUN
1 la **historia** *fem (spoken)*
I'm going to tell you a story.
Os voy a contar una historia.
2 el **cuento**
masc
(written)

stove NOUN
la **cocina** *fem*

straight

straight *can be an adjective or an adverb.*

A ADJECTIVE
1 **recto** *masc*
recta *fem*
a straight line
una línea recta
2 **lacio** *masc*
lacia *fem (hair)*
I've got straight hair.
Tengo el pelo lacio.
B ADVERB
straight away
en seguida
straight on
todo recto

Go straight on.
Sigue recto.

strange ADJECTIVE
extraño *masc*
extraña *fem*
That's strange!
¡Eso es extraño!
a strange dream
un sueño extraño

stranger NOUN
el **desconocido** *masc*
la **desconocida** *fem*
Don't talk to strangers.
No hables con desconocidos.
I'm a stranger here.
Soy de fuera.

Language tip
Be careful! The translation of **stranger** *is not* **extranjero**.

strap NOUN
1 el **tirante** *masc (of bra, dress)*
2 la **correa** *fem (of watch, camera, suitcase)*
I need a new strap for my watch.
Necesito una correa nueva para mi reloj.

straw NOUN
1 la **pajita** *fem (for drinking)*
2 la **paja** *fem (material)*

strawberry NOUN
la **fresa** *fem*
   strawberry jam
   mermelada de fresa
   a strawberry ice cream
   un helado de fresa

stream NOUN
el **arroyo** *masc*

street
NOUN
la **calle** *fem*
   in the street
   en la calle

to **stretch** VERB
1 **estirarse**
   The dog woke up and stretched.
   El perro se despertó y se estiró.
2 **estirar** *(arms, legs)*
   Stretch your arms!
   ¡Estirad los brazos!
   Shall we go out and stretch our legs?
   ¿Salimos a estirar las piernas?

> **Language tip**
> *In Spanish you usually use an article like **el**, **la** or **los**, **las** with parts of the body.*

strict ADJECTIVE
estricto *masc*
estricta *fem*

strike NOUN
la **huelga** *fem*
   They are on strike.
   Están en huelga.

string NOUN
la **cuerda** *fem*
   a piece of string
   una cuerda

stripe NOUN
la **raya** *fem*

stripy ADJECTIVE
de rayas
   a stripy shirt
   una camisa de rayas

strong ADJECTIVE
fuerte *masc & fem*
   She's very strong.
   Es muy fuerte.

student NOUN
el/la **estudiante** *masc/fem*
   I'm a student.
   Soy estudiante.

> **Language tip**
> *When talking about people's jobs in Spanish, you do not use an article.*

to **study** VERB
estudiar
   My sister's studying for her exams.
   Mi hermana está estudiando para sus exámenes.

stuff NOUN
las **cosas** *fem pl*
   Have you got all your stuff?
   ¿Tienes todas tus cosas?

stuffy ADJECTIVE
   It's stuffy in here.
   Hay un ambiente muy cargado aquí.

stupid ADJECTIVE
estúpido *masc*
estúpida *fem*
   a stupid joke
   un chiste estúpido

subject NOUN
la **asignatura** *fem*
   What's your favourite subject?
   ¿Cuál es tu asignatura favorita?

subtitles PL NOUN
los **subtítulos** *masc pl*
   a Spanish film with English subtitles
   una película española con subtítulos en inglés

to **subtract** VERB
restar
Subtract three from five.
Réstale tres a cinco.

suburb NOUN
el **barrio de las afueras** *masc*
a suburb of London
un barrio de las afueras de Londres
They live in the suburbs.
Viven en las afueras.

success NOUN
el **éxito** *masc*
The party was a great success.
La fiesta fue un gran éxito.

> ***Language tip***
> *Be careful! The translation of* **success** *is not* **suceso**.

such ADVERB
tan
such nice people
gente tan simpática
such a long journey
un viaje tan largo
We've got such a lot of work.
Tenemos mucho trabajo.
such as
como
towns such as Alicante and Valencia
ciudades como Alicante y Valencia

sudden ADJECTIVE
repentino *masc*
repentina *fem*
a sudden change
un cambio repentino

suddenly ADVERB
de repente

suede NOUN
el **ante** *masc*
a suede jacket
una chaqueta de ante

sugar NOUN

el **azúcar** *masc*
Do you take sugar?
¿Tomas azúcar?
More sugar?
¿Más azúcar?

suggestion NOUN
la **sugerencia** *fem*
Have you got any suggestions?
¿Tienes alguna sugerencia?

suit

suit *can be a noun or a verb.*

A NOUN
1 el **traje** *masc (man's)*
2 el **traje de chaqueta** *masc (woman's)*
B VERB
to suit
sentar bien a
Pink doesn't suit me.
El rosa no me sienta bien.

suitcase NOUN
la **maleta** *fem*

sum NOUN
la **suma** *fem*
I like doing sums.
Me gusta hacer sumas.
She's good at sums.
Se le da bien el cálculo.

summer NOUN
el **verano** *masc*
It's very hot in summer.
Hace mucho calor en verano.
We're going to Greece this summer.
Vamos a ir a Grecia este verano.

in summer
en verano
this summer
este verano
last summer
el verano pasado

summer holidays PL NOUN
las **vacaciones de verano**
fem pl
in the summer holidays
en las vacaciones de verano

summertime NOUN
el **verano** *masc*

in summertime
en verano

sun NOUN
el **sol** *masc*
in the
sun
al sol

to **sunbathe** VERB
tomar el sol
I like sunbathing.
Me gusta tomar el sol.

sunburnt ADJECTIVE
to get sunburnt
quemarse con el sol
I got sunburnt.
Me quemé con el sol.

Sunday NOUN
el **domingo** *masc*
It's Sunday today.
Hoy es domingo.

on Sunday
el domingo
on Sundays
los domingos
every Sunday
cada domingo
last Sunday
el domingo pasado

next Sunday
el domingo que viene

Language tip
Days are not spelled with a capital letter in Spanish.

Sunday school NOUN
la **catequesis** *fem*

sunflower NOUN
el **girasol** *masc*

sung VERB ▷*see* **sing**

sunglasses PL NOUN
las **gafas de sol** *fem pl*
a pair of sunglasses
unas gafas de sol

sunny ADJECTIVE
It's a sunny day.
Hace un día de sol.

It's sunny.
Hace sol.

sunshine NOUN
el **sol** *masc*
lots of sunshine
mucho sol

super ADJECTIVE
estupendo *masc*
estupenda *fem*

supermarket NOUN
el **supermercado** *masc*
We do our shopping at the supermarket.
Hacemos la compra en el supermercado.

supper NOUN
la **cena** *fem*

supply teacher NOUN
el **profesor sustituto** *masc*
la **profesora sustituta** *fem*
She's a supply teacher.
Es profesora sustituta.

Language tip
When talking about people's jobs in Spanish, you do not use an article.

English Spanish

a b c d e f g h i j k l m n o p q r s t u v w x y z

to **support** VERB
  ser de
    I support Real Madrid.
    Soy del Real Madrid.
    What team do you support?
    ¿De qué equipo eres?

supporter NOUN
  el **aficionado** masc
  la **aficionada** fem
    a Liverpool supporter
    un aficionado del Liverpool

to **suppose** VERB
  suponer
    I suppose he's right.
    Supongo que tiene razón.
    You're not supposed to do that, Teresa.
    No deberías hacer eso, Teresa.

sure ADJECTIVE
  seguro masc
  segura fem
    Are you sure, Helen?
    ¿Estás segura, Helen?

I'm not sure.
No estoy seguro.

surf

surf can be a noun or a verb.

A NOUN
  las **olas** fem pl (in sea)
B VERB
  to surf
1 **hacer surf**
    I like to go surfing at the weekends.
    Los fines de semana me gusta hacer surf.
2 **to surf the Net**
   navegar por Internet

surface NOUN
  la **superficie** fem

surfboard NOUN
  la **tabla de surf** fem

surfing NOUN
  el **surf** masc

  I go surfing.
  Hago surf.

surname NOUN
  el **apellido** masc
    What's your surname?
    ¿Cuál es tu apellido?

surprise NOUN
  la **sorpresa** fem
    What a surprise!
    ¡Vaya sorpresa!

survey NOUN
  la **encuesta** fem
    We're doing a survey on pets.
    Estamos haciendo una encuesta sobre las mascotas.

to **suspend** VERB
  expulsar temporalmente
    He's been suspended.
    Lo han expulsado temporalmente.

to **swallow** VERB
  tragar

swam VERB ▷ see **swim**

swan NOUN
  el **cisne** masc

to **swap** VERB
  cambiar
    Do you want to swap?
    ¿Quieres que cambiemos?
    I'll swap you my stamps for your stickers.
    Te cambiaré mis sellos por tus pegatinas.
    Let's swap places.
    Vamos a cambiarnos de sitio.

sweat

sweat can be a verb or a noun.

A VERB
  to sweat
  sudar
B NOUN
  el **sudor** masc

sweater NOUN
el **jersey** *masc* (PL los **jerseys**)
a white sweater
un jersey blanco

sweatshirt NOUN
la **sudadera** *fem*
a green sweatshirt
una sudadera verde

sweet

> **sweet** *can be a noun or an adjective.*

A NOUN
1 el **caramelo** *masc (toffee, mint etc)*
a bag of sweets
una bolsa de caramelos
2 el **postre** *masc (pudding)*
Sweets: ice cream or chocolate mousse
Postres: helado o mousse de chocolate

B ADJECTIVE
1 **dulce** *masc & fem (sugary)*
It's too sweet.
Está demasiado dulce.
2 **encantador** *masc*
encantadora *fem (delightful)*
Isn't she sweet?
¿Verdad que es encantadora?

sweetcorn NOUN
el **maíz dulce** *masc*

swim

> **swim** *can be a verb or a noun.*

A VERB
to swim
nadar
Can you swim?
¿Sabes nadar?
I can swim.
Sé nadar.
I can't swim.
No sé nadar.

B NOUN
I want to go for a swim.
Quiero ir a nadar.

swimmer NOUN
el **nadador** *masc*
la **nadadora** *fem*
She's a good swimmer.
Es una buena nadadora.

swimming NOUN
la **natación** *fem*
Do you like swimming?
¿Te gusta la natación?
I go swimming on Wednesdays.
Voy a nadar los miércoles.

swimming costume
NOUN
el **traje de baño** *masc*

swimming pool NOUN
la **piscina** *fem*

swimming trunks PL NOUN
el **bañador** *masc*
I've got new swimming trunks.
Tengo un bañador nuevo.

swimsuit NOUN
el **traje de baño** *masc*

swing NOUN
el **columpio** *masc*

switch

> **switch** *can be a noun or a verb.*

A NOUN
el **interruptor** *masc*
Where's the switch?
¿Dónde está el interruptor?
B VERB
to switch
cambiar de

Switch partners!
¡Cambiad de pareja!

to **switch off** VERB
apagar
Switch off the computer, Jane.
Apaga el ordenador, Jane.

to **switch on** VERB
encender
Switch on the light, Neil.
Enciende la luz, Neil.

to **swop** VERB
cambiar
Do you want to swop?
¿Quieres que cambiemos?
Let's swop places.
Vamos a cambiar de sitio.

sword NOUN
la **espada** fem

swum VERB ▷see **swim**

symbol NOUN
el **símbolo** masc

sympathetic ADJECTIVE
comprensivo masc
comprensiva fem

Language tip
Be careful! The translation of **sympathetic** is not **simpático**.

system NOUN
el **sistema** masc

Language tip
Even though it ends in -**a**, **el sistema** is a masculine noun.

T t

table NOUN
1 la **mesa** *fem (piece of furniture)*
It's on the table.
Está en
la mesa.
2 la **tabla**
fem (chart)
**the three
times table**
la tabla del tres

tablecloth NOUN
el **mantel** *masc*

tablespoon NOUN
la **cuchara grande** *fem*

table tennis NOUN
el **tenis de mesa** *masc*
I can play table tennis.
Sé jugar al tenis de mesa.

Language tip
*In Spanish, you need to add **al** or
a la before the name of the sport or
game.*

tail NOUN
1 el **rabo** *masc (of dog)*
The dog wagged its tail.
El perro movía el rabo.

Language tip
*In Spanish you usually use an article
like **el**, **la** or **los**, **las** with parts of
the body.*

2 la **cola** *fem (of horse, bird, fish)*

Heads or tails?
¿Cara o cruz?

to **take** VERB
1 **coger**
Take a card, Susan.
Coge una carta, Susan.
Who has taken my ruler?
¿Quién ha cogido mi regla?

**Take the first turning on
the right.**
Coge el primer desvío a la
derecha.
Let's take the bus.
Vamos a coger el autobús.

Language tip
*Don't use **coger** in Latin America as
it's considered rude in some places.
Use verbs like **tomar** and **agarrar**
instead.*

2 **tomar** *(food, medicine)*
I don't take sugar.
No tomo azúcar.
3 **llevar** *(take along)*
**Mum's going to take me to
the fair.**
Mi madre me va a llevar a la
feria.
**Don't forget to take your
camera.**
No te olvides de llevarte la
cámara.
4 **durar** *(last)*
**How long does the journey
take?**
¿Cuánto dura el viaje?
It takes about an hour.
Se tarda más o menos una hora.

to **take away** VERB
**Thirty take away nine is
twenty-one.**
Treinta menos nueve son
veintiuno.

to **take back** VERB
devolver
**I'm going to take this book
back to the library.**
Voy a devolver este libro a la
biblioteca.

to **take down** VERB
quitar

a
b
c
d
e
f
g
h
i
j
k
l
m
n
o
p
q
r
s
t
u
v
w
x
y
z

English
Spanish

569

Take the posters down.
Quita los pósters.

to **take off** VERB
quitarse *(clothes)*
Take your coat off.
Quítate el abrigo.

> **Language tip**
> *In Spanish you usually use an article*
> *like* **el**, **la** *or* **los**, **las** *with clothes*
> *you are wearing.*

to **take out** VERB
sacar
Can you take the key out of the lock?
¿Puedes sacar la llave de la cerradura?
I take the dog out at about six o'clock.
Saco al perro a pasear sobre las seis.

taken ▷ *see* take

takeoff NOUN
el **despegue** *masc*

tale NOUN
el **cuento** *masc*

talk

> **talk** *can be a verb or a noun.*

A VERB
to talk
hablar
You talk too much.
Hablas demasiado.

Today we're going to talk about Spain.
Hoy vamos a hablar de España.
B NOUN
Let's have a talk about it.
Vamos a hablar de eso.

talkative ADJECTIVE
hablador *masc*
habladora *fem*

tall ADJECTIVE
alto *masc*
alta *fem*
Ian is tall.
Ian es alto.
My sister is taller than me.
Mi hermana es más alta que yo.
Mark is the tallest in the class.
Mark es el más alto de la clase.
a very tall building
un edificio muy alto

> **How tall are you?**
> ¿Cuánto mides?
> **I'm one metre thirty tall.**
> Mido un metro treinta.

tan NOUN
el **bronceado** *masc*
She's got an amazing tan.
Tiene un bronceado increíble.

tangerine NOUN
la **mandarina** *fem*

tap NOUN
el **grifo** *masc*
Turn on the tap.
Abre el grifo.
the hot tap
el grifo del agua caliente

tap-dancing NOUN
el **claqué** *masc*

target NOUN
la **diana** *fem*

tart NOUN
la **tarta** *fem*
a jam tart
una tarta de mermelada

tartan
ADJECTIVE
de cuadros escoceses
a tartan scarf
una bufanda de cuadros escoceses

taste

> *taste can be a noun or a verb.*

A NOUN
   el **sabor** *masc*
   It's got a strange taste.
   Tiene un sabor extraño.
   Would you like a taste?
   ¿Quieres probarlo?
B VERB
   to taste
1 **probar** *(try)*
   Would you like to taste it?
   ¿Quieres probarlo?
2 **It tastes nice.**
   Tiene buen sabor.
   It tastes of fish.
   Sabe a pescado.

tasty ADJECTIVE
   sabroso *masc*
   sabrosa *fem*

tattoo NOUN
   el **tatuaje** *masc*

taught VERB ▷ *see* **teach**

taxi NOUN
   el **taxi** *masc*
   by taxi
   en taxi

taxi driver NOUN
   el/la **taxista** *masc/fem*

> **Language tip**
> *When talking about people's jobs in Spanish, you do not use an article.*

tea
1 NOUN
   el **té** *masc*
   a cup of tea
   una taza de té
   tea with milk
   té con leche
   Would you like some tea?
   ¿Quieres un té?
2 la **cena** *fem (evening meal)*
   What's for tea?
   ¿Qué hay de cena?

   to have tea
   cenar
   We're having tea.
   Estamos cenando.

tea bag NOUN
   la **bolsita de té** *fem*

to teach VERB
   enseñar
   Mrs Morris teaches us English.
   Mrs Morris nos enseña inglés.
   My cousin is teaching me to play the guitar.
   Mi primo me está enseñando a tocar la guitarra.

teacher NOUN
1 el **maestro** *masc*
   la **maestra** *fem (in primary school)*
   Mr Price is our teacher.
   Mr Price es nuestro maestro.
2 el **profesor** *masc*
   la **profesora** *fem (in secondary school)*
   a maths teacher
   un profesor de matemáticas
   She's a teacher.
   Es profesora.

> **Language tip**
> *When talking about people's jobs in Spanish, you do not use an article.*

team NOUN
   el **equipo** *masc*
   a football team
   un equipo de fútbol
   She's in my team.
   Está en mi equipo.
   We're going to divide the class into two teams.
   Vamos a dividir la clase en dos equipos.

teaspoon NOUN
   la **cucharilla** *fem*

tear

> *tear can be a noun or a verb.*

A NOUN
   la **lágrima** *fem*

B VERB
to tear
romper
Be careful or you'll tear the page.
Ten cuidado que vas a romper la página.

teatime NOUN
la **hora de cenar** fem (supper time)
at teatime
a la hora de cenar

tea towel NOUN
el **paño de cocina** masc

technology NOUN
la **tecnología** fem

teddy bear
NOUN
el **osito de peluche**
masc

teenager NOUN
el/la **adolescente** masc/fem

teens PL NOUN
He's in his teens.
Es un adolescente.
She's in her teens.
Es una adolescente.

tee-shirt NOUN
la **camiseta** fem

teeth PL NOUN
los **dientes** masc pl
I clean my teeth three times a day.
Me lavo los dientes tres veces al día.

telephone NOUN
el **teléfono** masc

telephone call NOUN
la **llamada telefónica** fem

telephone number NOUN
el **número de teléfono** masc
What's your telephone number?
¿Cuál es tu número de teléfono?

television NOUN
la **televisión** fem
on television
en la televisión
What's on television?
¿Qué hay en la televisión?
I haven't got a television in my room.
No tengo televisión en mi habitación.

television programme
NOUN
el **programa de televisión** *masc*

to **tell** VERB
1 **decir** (say)
Tell me why, Janice.
Dime por qué, Janice.
I'm going to tell my mum.
Se lo voy a decir a mi madre.
2 **contar** (recount)
I'm going to tell you a story.
Te voy a contar una historia.
I'll tell you about myself.
Te contaré cosas sobre mí.

to **tell off** VERB
regañar
She tells me off if I'm late.
Me regaña si llego tarde.

telly NOUN
   la **tele** fem
      I watch telly a lot.
      Veo mucho la tele.
      on telly
      en la tele

temperature NOUN
   1 la **temperatura** fem (in centigrade etc)
   2 la **fiebre** fem (fever)
      I've got a temperature.
      Tengo fiebre.

ten NUMBER
   diez
      ten euros
      diez euros
      It's ten to three.
      Son las tres menos diez.
      It's ten past two.
      Son las dos y diez.

I'm ten.
Tengo diez años.

Language tip
*In English you can say **I'm ten** or **I'm ten years old**. In Spanish you can only say **tengo diez años**. Have you noticed that in Spanish you need to use the verb **tener** to talk about somebody's age?*

tennis NOUN
   el **tenis** masc
      I play tennis.
      Juego al tenis.

Language tip
*In Spanish, you need to add **al** or **a la** before the name of the sport.*

tennis ball NOUN
   la **pelota de tenis** fem

tennis court NOUN
   la **pista de tenis** fem

tennis racket NOUN
   la **raqueta de tenis** fem

tennis player NOUN
   el **jugador de tenis** masc

   la **jugadora de tenis** fem

tenpin bowling NOUN
   los **bolos** masc pl
      Do you want to go tenpin bowling?
      ¿Quieres jugar a los bolos?

Language tip
*In Spanish, you need to add **a los** before **bolos**.*

tent NOUN
   la **tienda de campaña** fem

tenth NUMBER
   décimo masc
   décima fem
      on the tenth floor
      en el décimo piso
      My birthday's the tenth of April.
      Mi cumpleaños es el diez de abril.
      It's the tenth of July today.
      Hoy es diez de julio.

on the tenth of August
el diez de agosto

Language tip
*Use the same set of numbers that you use for counting (**uno**, **dos**, **tres** and so on) when giving Spanish dates.*

term NOUN
   el **trimestre** masc
      It will soon be the end of term.
      Pronto será el final del trimestre.

terraced house NOUN
   la **casa adosada** fem

terrible ADJECTIVE
   terrible masc & fem
      My English is terrible.
      Mi inglés es terrible.

terrified ADJECTIVE
   aterrorizado masc
   aterrorizada fem

I was terrified!
¡Estaba aterrorizado!

test NOUN
la **prueba** *fem*
I've got a test tomorrow.
Tengo una prueba mañana.

text

text can be a noun or a verb.

A NOUN
1 el **texto** *masc (in book)*
2 el **mensaje de texto** *masc*
(from mobile)
B VERB
to text
enviar un mensaje a
I'll text you when I get there.
Te envío un mensaje cuando llegue.

textbook NOUN
el **libro de texto** *masc*
an English textbook
un libro de texto de inglés

text message
NOUN
el **mensaje de texto**
masc

than
CONJUNCTION
que
She's taller than me.
Es más alta que yo.
Are you older than him?
¿Eres mayor que él?

thanks EXCLAMATION
gracias
No thanks.
No, gracias.
Thanks for helping me.
Gracias por ayudarme.

thank you EXCLAMATION
gracias

Thank you very much.
Muchas gracias.

that

that can be a pronoun, adjective or conjunction.

A PRONOUN
1 **ése** *masc*
ésa *fem*
eso *neuter*
That's my brother.
Ése es mi hermano.
That's my friend Sonia.
Ésa es mi amiga Sonia.

> *Language tip*
>
> Use the neuter form **eso** when **that** refers to something vague, something not very specific or to an object you don't recognize.

That's right! Well done.
¡Eso es! Bien hecho.

> *Language tip*
>
> Instead of **ése**, **ésa** and **eso**, use **aquél**, **aquélla** and **aquello** to talk about something or someone that's quite far away.

That's my French teacher over there.
Aquél es mi profesor de francés.

What's that?
¿Qué es eso?
Who's that? — It's Stephen.
¿Quién es ése? — Es Stephen.
Who's that? — It's Sarah.
¿Quién es ésa? — Es Sarah.
I know that.
Lo sé.

> *Language tip*
>
> Traditionally, the pronouns **ése**, **ésa**, **aquél** and **aquélla** were written with an accent to distinguish them from the unaccented adjective forms. Nowadays, you don't have to give the accents unless the sentence would be confusing otherwise.

a b c d e f g h i j k l m n o p q r s **t** u v w x y z

2 **que** *(relative)*
the man that lives here
el hombre que vive aquí
the girl that I saw
la chica que vi

Language tip
*We sometimes leave out **that** in English sentences like these, but you can't ever leave out the **que** in Spanish.*

B ADJECTIVE
ese *masc*
esa *fem*
that dog
ese perro
that woman
esa mujer
This man? — No, that one.
¿Este hombre? — No, ése.
This chair? — No, that one.
¿Esta silla? — No, ésa.

Language tip
*Instead of **ese** and **esa**, use **aquel** and **aquella** to talk about something or someone that's quite far away.*

Look at that car over there!
¡Mira aquel coche!

C CONJUNCTION
que
I think that it's raining.
Creo que está lloviendo.

Language tip
*We sometimes leave out **that** in English sentences like this one. Don't ever leave out the **que** in Spanish.*

I think that Henry is ill.
Creo que Henry está enfermo.

the ARTICLE
el *masc*
la *fem*
los *masc pl*
las *fem pl*

Language tip
*Use **el** with a masculine singular noun and **la** with a feminine*

singular noun. Use **los** with a masculine plural noun and **las** with a feminine plural noun.

the boy
el chico
the girl
la chica

the children
los niños
the oranges
las naranjas

Language tip
*a combines with **el** to form **al** while de combines with **el** to form **del**.*

We're going to the theatre.
Vamos al teatro.
a photo of the dog
una foto del perro

theatre NOUN
el **teatro** *masc*

their ADJECTIVE
su *masc & fem* (PL **sus**)

Language tip
*Remember to use **su** before a singular noun and **sus** before a plural one.*

their house
su casa
their parents
sus padres

Language tip
*In Spanish you usually use an article like **el**, **la** or **los**, **las** with clothes or parts of the body.*

They took off their coats.
Se quitaron los abrigos.

a
b
c
d
e
f
g
h
i
j
k
l
m
n
o
p
q
r
s
t
u
v
w
x
y
z

They are washing their hands.
Se están lavando las manos.

theirs PRONOUN
el **suyo** *masc*
la **suya** *fem*

> ### *Language tip*
> *Remember that the choice of* **el suyo**, **la suya**, **los suyos** *or* **las suyas** *depends entirely on the thing or things referred to.*

That isn't the Smiths' car. Theirs is red.
Aquél no es el coche de los Smith. El suyo es rojo.
Those aren't the twins' books. Theirs are here.
Aquéllos no son los libros de los gemelos. Los suyos están aquí.

> ### *Language tip*
> *After* **ser** *you can usually just use* **suyo**, **suya**, **suyos** *or* **suyas** *to agree with the noun referred to.*

Is this theirs?
¿Es suyo esto?
This house is theirs.
Esta casa es suya.
These cases are theirs.
Estas maletas son suyas.
Whose is this? — It's theirs.
¿De quién es esto? — Es suyo.

> ### *Language tip*
> *Because* **suyo** *can also mean* **his**, **hers** *and* **yours**, *you can avoid confusion by using* **de ellos/de ellas** *instead.*

Whose is this? — It's theirs.
¿De quién es esto? — Es de ellos.

> **a friend of theirs**
> un amigo suyo

them PRONOUN
1 los *masc*
las *fem pl (direct object)*
Where are the horses? I can't see them.

¿Dónde están los caballos?
No los veo.
There are some more biscuits in the cupboard. Do you want them?
Hay más galletas en el armario. ¿Las quieres?
I like these socks. I think I'll buy them.
Me gustan estos calcetines. Creo que me los voy a comprar.
2 les *(indirect object)*

> ### *Language tip*
> *Use* **les** *when* **them** *means* **to them** *or* **for them**.

Can you give them a message?
¿Les puedes dar un mensaje?
I'm going to buy them a present.
Les voy a comprar un regalo.

> ### *Language tip*
> *Change* **les** *to* **se** *when combining it with a direct object pronoun like* **lo**.

I'll tell them.
Se lo diré.

> ### *Language tip*
> *Because* **se** *can mean* **to him**, **to her** *and* **to you** *as well as* **to them**, *you can add* **a ellos/a ellas** *(to them) after the verb for clarity.*

I'm going to give it to them.
Voy a dárselo a ellos.
3 ellos *masc pl*
ellas *fem pl (after preposition)*
It's not for you, it's for them.
No es para ti, es para ellos.
Teresa and Victoria are here, and Graham's with them.
Teresa y Victoria están aquí, y Graham está con ellas.

> ### *Language tip*
> *Use* **ellos** *and* **ellas** *in comparisons.*

I'm older than them.
Soy mayor que ellos.

a
b
c
d
e
f
g
h
i
j
k
l
m
n
o
p
q
r
s
t
u
v
w
x
y
z

> **Language tip**
> Use **ellos** and **ellas** *after the verb* **ser**.

It must be them.
Deben de ser ellos.
It's them.
Son ellos.

theme park NOUN
el **parque temático** *masc*

themselves PRONOUN
1 **se** *(reflexive use)*
They're enjoying themselves.
Se están divirtiendo.
They have hurt themselves.
Se han hecho daño.
2 **sí mismos** *masc pl*
sí mismas *fem pl (after preposition)*
They talked about themselves.
Hablaron de sí mismos.
3 **ellos mismos** *masc pl*
ellas mismas *fem pl (for emphasis)*
They did it themselves.
Lo hicieron ellos mismos.
The girls did it all by themselves.
Las chicas lo hicieron todo ellas mismas.

then CONJUNCTION
luego
I get dressed. Then I have breakfast.
Me visto. Luego desayuno.

there ADVERB
1 **ahí** *(not far away)*
Put it there, on the table.
Ponlo ahí, en la mesa.
up there
ahí arriba
down there
ahí abajo
2 **allí** *(further away)*
I'm going there on Friday.
El viernes voy allí.
3 **there is ...**
hay ...

There's a new boy in the class.
Hay un chico nuevo en la clase.
there are ...
hay ...
There are ten chairs in the room.
Hay diez sillas en la habitación.
How many biscuits are there?
¿Cuántas galletas hay?
There are lots.
Hay muchas.
There aren't many.
No hay muchas.

> **over there**
> por ahí
> **There he is!**
> ¡Ahí está!
> **There they are!**
> ¡Ahí están!
> **There is ...**
> Hay ...
> **There are ...**
> Hay ...

these
A ADJECTIVE
estos *masc pl*
estas *fem pl*
these shoes
estos zapatos

these tables
estas mesas
Which books do you need? — These ones.
¿Qué libros necesitas? — Éstos.
B PRONOUN
éstos *masc pl*
éstas *fem pl*
If you need felt-tips, I've got these.
Si necesitas rotuladores, tengo éstos.

Of course we've got apples.
Look at these!
Claro que tenemos manzanas.
¡Mira éstas!

they PRONOUN
ellos *masc pl*
ellas *fem pl*
We went to the cinema,
but they didn't.
Nosotros fuimos al cine, pero
ellos no.
I spoke to my sisters and they
agree with me.
Hablé con mis hermanas y ellas
están de acuerdo conmigo.

Where are your friends? —
They're over there.
¿Dónde están tus amigos? —
Están allí.

they'd
  1 (= they had) ▷ see **have**
  2 (= they would) ▷ see **would**

they'll (= they will) ▷ see **will**

they're (= they are) ▷ see **be**

they've (= they have) ▷ see **have**

thick ADJECTIVE
  grueso *masc*
  gruesa *fem*
  a thick
  slice
  una
  rebanada
  gruesa

thief NOUN
  el **ladrón** *masc* (PL los **ladrones**)
  la **ladrona** *fem*

thin ADJECTIVE
  1 **delgado** *masc*
    delgada *fem (person)*
    I'm quite thin.
    Soy bastante delgado.
  2 **fino** *masc*
    fina *fem (slice, book)*
    a thin slice
    una rebanada fina

thing NOUN
  la **cosa** *fem*
  I've got lots of things to do.
  Tengo muchas cosas que hacer.
  my things
  mis cosas

to **think** VERB
  1 **pensar**
    What do you think?
    ¿Qué piensas?
    Think carefully, Harry.
    Piénsalo bien, Harry.
    I'll think about it.
    Lo pensaré.
  2 **creer** *(believe)*
    I think he's here.
    Creo que está aquí.

I think so.
Creo que sí.
I don't think so.
Creo que no.

third NUMBER
  tercero *masc*
  tercera *fem*
  It's the third time.
  Es la tercera vez.
  I came third.
  Llegué el tercero.

Language tip

*Shorten **tercero** to **tercer** before a masculine singular noun.*

> **the third prize**
> el tercer premio
> **My birthday's the third of September.**
> Mi cumpleaños es el tres de septiembre.
> **It's the third of December today.**
> Hoy es tres de diciembre.

on the third of March
el tres de marzo

Language tip

*Use the same set of numbers that you use for counting (**uno**, **dos**, **tres** and so on) when giving Spanish dates.*

thirsty ADJECTIVE
> **to be thirsty**
> **tener sed**
> **Are you thirsty?**
> ¿Tienes sed?
> **I'm not thirsty.**
> No tengo sed.

I'm thirsty.
Tengo sed.

thirteen NUMBER
> **trece**
> **thirteen euros**
> trece euros

I'm thirteen.
Tengo trece años.

Language tip

*In English you can say **I'm thirteen** or **I'm thirteen years old**. In*

*Spanish you can only say **tengo trece años**. Have you noticed that in Spanish you need to use the verb **tener** to talk about somebody's age?*

thirteenth NUMBER
> **trece**
> **on the thirteenth floor**
> en la planta trece
> **We break up on the thirteenth of December.**
> Empezamos las vacaciones el trece de diciembre.
> **Today's the thirteenth of May.**
> Hoy es trece de mayo.

on the thirteenth of August
el trece de agosto

Language tip

*Use the same set of numbers that you use for counting (**uno**, **dos**, **tres** and so on) when giving Spanish dates.*

thirtieth NUMBER
> **treinta**
> **My birthday's the thirtieth of March.**
> Mi cumpleaños es el treinta de marzo.
> **Today's the thirtieth of July.**
> Hoy es treinta de julio.

on the thirtieth of August
el treinta de agosto

Language tip

*Use the same set of numbers that you use for counting (**uno**, **dos**, **tres** and so on) when giving Spanish dates.*

thirty NUMBER
> **treinta**
> **thirty euros**
> treinta euros
> **My aunt is thirty.**
> Mi tía tiene treinta años.

English Spanish

a
b
c
d
e
f
g
h
i
j
k
l
m
n
o
p
q
r
s
t
u
v
w
x
y
z

Language tip
In English you can say **she's thirty** *or* **she's thirty years old**. *In Spanish you can only say* **tiene treinta años**. *Have you noticed that in Spanish you need to use the verb* **tener** *to talk about somebody's age?*

this

this *can be an adjective or a pronoun.*

A ADJECTIVE
este *masc*
esta *fem*
this book
este libro
this man
este hombre
this time
esta vez
Which book do you want? — This one.
¿Qué libro quieres? — Éste.
That card? — No, this one.
¿Esa tarjeta? — No, ésta.

B PRONOUN
éste *masc*
ésta *fem*
esto *neuter*
This is my room.
Éste es mi cuarto.
This is my class.
Ésta es mi clase.

Language tip
Use the neuter form **esto** *when* **this** *refers to something vague, something not very specific or to an object you don't recognize.*

Look at this.
Mira esto.

this morning
esta mañana
this year
este año
this afternoon
esta tarde

What's this?
¿Qué es esto?

Language tip
Traditionally, the pronouns **éste** *and* **ésta** *were written with an accent to distinguish them from the unaccented adjective forms shown in the previous category. Nowadays, you don't have to give the accents unless the sentence would be confusing otherwise.*

those

A ADJECTIVE
esos *masc pl*
esas *fem pl*
those shoes
esos zapatos
those chairs
esas sillas

Language tip
Instead of **esos** *and* **esas**, *use* **aquellos** *and* **aquellas** *if you're talking about people or things that are quite far away.*

Look at those boys over there!
¡Mira a aquellos chicos!
Which books do you need? — Those ones.
¿Qué libros necesitas? — Ésos.

B PRONOUN
ésos *masc pl*
ésas *fem pl*
Those aren't my boots.
Ésas no son mis botas.

Language tip
Instead of **ésos** *and* **ésas**, *use* **aquéllos** *and* **aquéllas** *to talk about people or things that are quite far away.*

Those are my classmates over there.
Aquéllos son mis compañeros de clase.

> **Language tip**
> *Traditionally, the pronouns **ésos**, **ésas**, **aquéllos** and **aquéllas** were written with an accent to distinguish them from the unaccented adjective forms shown in the previous category. Nowadays, you don't have to give the accents unless the sentence would otherwise be confusing.*

thought VERB ▷*see* **think**

thousand NOUN
a thousand
mil
a thousand euros
mil euros
two thousand pounds
dos mil libras
thousands of people
miles de personas

three NUMBER
tres
three euros
tres euros

> **She's three.**
> Tiene tres años.

> **Language tip**
> *In English you can say **she's three** or **she's three years old**. In Spanish you can only say **tiene tres años**. Have you noticed that in Spanish you need to use the verb **tener** to talk about somebody's age?*

throat NOUN
la **garganta** *fem*
I've got a sore throat.
Me duele la garganta.

through PREPOSITION
por
Our cat always comes in through the window.
Nuestro gato siempre entra por la ventana.
I know her through my sister.
La conozco por mi hermana.

to **throw** VERB
tirar
Throw me the ball.
Tírame la pelota.

to **throw away** VERB
tirar
Don't throw it away!
¡No lo tires!

thumb NOUN
el **pulgar** *masc*
She sucks her thumb.
Se chupa el pulgar.

> **Language tip**
> *In Spanish you usually use an article like **el**, **la** or **los**, **las** with parts of the body.*

thunder NOUN
los **truenos** *masc pl*
There was thunder and lightning.
Hubo rayos y truenos.

thunderstorm NOUN
la **tormenta** *fem*

Thursday NOUN
el **jueves** *masc*
It's Thursday today.
Hoy es jueves.

> **on Thursday**
> el jueves
> **on Thursdays**
> los jueves
> **every Thursday**
> cada jueves
> **last Thursday**
> el jueves pasado
> **next Thursday**
> el jueves que viene

> **Language tip**
> *Days are not spelled with a capital letter in Spanish.*

tick

> **tick** *can be a noun or a verb.*

A NOUN
la **señal** *fem*
Put a tick or a cross.
Pon una señal o una cruz.

B VERB
to tick
señalar
Tick the right box.
Señala la casilla correcta.

ticket NOUN
1 la **entrada** *fem (for concert, cinema, museum)*
a cinema ticket
una entrada para el cine
2 el **billete** *masc (for bus, train, plane)*
a bus ticket
un billete de autobús

ticket office NOUN
la **taquilla** *fem*

tidy

> **tidy** *can be an adjective or a verb.*

A ADJECTIVE
ordenado *masc*
ordenada *fem*
My room is tidy.
Mi cuarto está ordenado.
It's tidier now.
Ahora está más ordenado.

B VERB
to tidy
ordenar
You must tidy your room.
Tienes que ordenar tu cuarto.

to **tidy up** VERB
Don't forget to tidy up afterwards, children.
No olvidéis ordenarlo todo después, niños.

tie

> **tie** *can be a noun or a verb.*

A NOUN
1 la **corbata** *fem (for neck)*
2 el **empate** *masc (in match)*
It's a tie.
Es un empate.
B VERB
to tie
atar
Let's tie the balloons to the door!
¡Vamos a atar los globos a la puerta!
Tie your laces.
Átate los cordones.

tiger NOUN
el **tigre** *masc*

tight ADJECTIVE
1 **estrecho** *masc*
estrecha *fem (too small)*
This dress is a bit tight.
Este vestido es un poco estrecho.
2 **ceñido** *masc*
ceñida *fem (close-fitting)*
a tight skirt
una falda ceñida

tights PL NOUN
las **medias** *fem pl*
I'm wearing black tights.
Llevo medias negras.
a pair of tights
unas medias

till

> **till** *can be a noun or a preposition.*

A NOUN
la **caja** *fem*

at the till
en la caja
B PREPOSITION
hasta
He's staying till Monday.
Se queda hasta el lunes.
from nine till five
de nueve a cinco

time NOUN
1 la **hora** *fem (on clock)*
What time is it?
¿Qué hora es?
It's time to go.
Es hora de irse.
What time...?
¿A qué hora...?
What time do you get up?
¿A qué hora te levantas?
What time does the train arrive?
¿A qué hora llega el tren?
2 el **tiempo** *masc (amount of time)*
I'm sorry, I haven't got time.
Lo siento, no tengo tiempo.
3 la **vez** *fem* (FEM PL las **veces**)
(occasion)
three times
tres veces
this time
esta vez
next time
la próxima vez
the first time
la primera vez
two at a time
dos a la vez
Two times two is four.
Dos por dos son cuatro.

What time is it?
¿Qué hora es?
It's lunch time.
Es la hora de comer.
How many times?
¿Cuántas veces?
Have a good time, Amanda!
¡Que lo pases bien, Amanda!

timetable NOUN
el **horario** *masc*

tin NOUN
la **lata** *fem*
a tin of soup
una lata de sopa

tin opener NOUN
el **abrelatas** *masc* (MASC PL los **abrelatas**)

tinsel NOUN
el **espumillón** *masc*

tiny ADJECTIVE
minúsculo *masc*
minúscula *fem*

tip NOUN
1 la **propina** *fem (for waiter, taxi driver)*
It's a tip for the waiter.
Es una propina para el camarero.
2 el **consejo** *masc (piece of advice)*

tiptoe NOUN
on tiptoe
de puntillas
He's standing on tiptoe.
Está de puntillas.

tired ADJECTIVE
cansado *masc*
cansada *fem*
I'm tired.
Estoy cansado.

tiring ADJECTIVE
cansado *masc*
cansada *fem*
Doing so much running is tiring.
Es cansado correr tanto.

tissue NOUN
el **Kleenex**® *masc*

English Spanish

a b c d e f g h i j k l m n o p q r s t u v w x y z

Have you got a tissue?
¿Tienes un Kleenex?

title NOUN
el **título** *masc*

to PREPOSITION
1 a
We're going to London.
Vamos a Londres.

Language tip
a *combines with* **el** *to form* **al**.

Can I go to the toilet?
¿Puedo ir al servicio?
I go to school with my friend.
Voy al colegio con mi amigo.
I'm going round to Mary's.
Voy a casa de Mary.
Give it to Jane!
¡Dáselo a Jane!

to my house
a mi casa
to the supermarket
al supermercado

2 de *(for)*
the train to London
el tren de Londres
the plane to Madrid
el avión de Madrid
3 hasta *(up to)*
Count to ten, everyone.
Contad todos hasta diez.
from nine o'clock to half past three
desde las nueve hasta las tres y media
4 para *(in order to)*
I'm doing it to help you.
Lo hago para ayudarte.

Language tip
Don't forget that **to** *is often just part of the infinitive form of the verb.*

to eat
comer
to work
trabajar

I want to buy a new camera.
Quiero comprar una cámara nueva.

toast NOUN
las **tostadas** *fem pl*
Would you like some toast?
¿Quieres tostadas?
a piece of toast
una tostada

toaster NOUN
la **tostadora** *fem*

toastie NOUN
el **sándwich caliente** *masc*

today ADVERB
hoy
What's the date today?
¿Hoy qué día es?
It's Monday today.
Hoy es lunes.

toe NOUN
el **dedo del pie** *masc*

Language tip
On its own **dedo** *means 'finger'. So the Spanish* **dedo del pie** *literally means 'foot finger'!*

toffee NOUN
el **caramelo** *masc*

together ADVERB
juntos *masc pl*
juntas *fem pl*

Language tip
The Spanish word **juntos** *is an adjective so must agree with the noun.*

Mary and Barbara are going to go there together.
Mary y Barbara van a ir allí juntas.

toilet NOUN
1 el **servicio** *masc (in school, café etc)*
Can I go to the toilet?
¿Puedo ir al servicio?
2 el **baño** *masc (in private house)*

toilet paper NOUN
el **papel higiénico** *masc*

told VERB ▷*see* **tell**

tomato NOUN
el **tomate** *masc*
a kilo of tomatoes
un kilo de tomates
tomato soup
sopa de tomate

tomorrow ADVERB
mañana
Let's go swimming tomorrow.
Vamos a nadar mañana.

tomorrow morning
mañana por la mañana
tomorrow afternoon
mañana por la tarde
tomorrow night
mañana por la noche
the day after tomorrow
pasado mañana
See you tomorrow.
Hasta mañana.

tongue NOUN
la **lengua** *fem*

tonight ADVERB
esta noche
Are you going out tonight?
¿Vas a salir esta noche?

tonsillitis NOUN
la **amigdalitis** *fem*

too ADVERB
1 **también** (*as well*)
My sister is coming too.
Mi hermana también viene.

Me too.
Yo también.

2 **demasiado** (*very*)
The water's too hot.
El agua está demasiado caliente.
You're too late.
Llegas demasiado tarde.

Daniel, you talk too much.
Daniel, hablas demasiado.
It costs too much.
Cuesta demasiado.

Language tip
*When **too much** and **too many** are used to describe nouns, remember to make them agree.*

too much noise
demasiado ruido
too much water
demasiada agua
too many mistakes
demasiadas faltas

tooth NOUN
el **diente** *masc*

toothache NOUN
I've got toothache.
Me duelen las muelas.

toothbrush NOUN
el **cepillo de dientes** *masc*

toothpaste NOUN
la **pasta de dientes** *fem*

top

top *can be a noun or an adjective.*

A NOUN
1 el **top** *masc* (*T-shirt, sweater, etc*)
a black skirt and a white top
una falda negra y un top blanco
2 la **parte de arriba** *fem*
(*highest part*)
at the top of the page
en la parte de arriba de la página
on top of
encima de
It's on top of the fridge.
Está encima de la nevera.
3 la **cima** *fem* (*of mountain*)
the top of Snowdon
la cima de Snowdon
4 el **tapón** *masc* (PL los **tapones**)
(*of bottle*)
B ADJECTIVE
He always gets top marks in English.

a
b
c
d
e
f
g
h i j
k
l
m
n
o
p
q
r
s
t
u
v
w
x
y
z

Siempre saca las mejores notas en inglés.
the top floor
el piso de arriba

torch NOUN
la **linterna** *fem*

tortoise NOUN
la **tortuga**
fem

total NOUN
el **total** *masc*

to **touch** VERB
tocar
Don't touch that!
¡No toques eso!

tour NOUN
la **visita** *fem*
a tour of the museum
una visita al museo

tourism NOUN
el **turismo** *masc*

tourist NOUN
el/la **turista** *masc/fem*
There are lots of tourists.
Hay muchos turistas.

> **Language tip**
> Even though it ends in **-a**, you can use **turista** to refer to a man or boy.

tourist information office NOUN
la **oficina de turismo** *fem*

towards PREPOSITION
hacia
Come towards me.
Ven hacia mí.

towel NOUN
la **toalla** *fem*

tower NOUN
la **torre** *fem*
a tower block
una torre de pisos

town NOUN
la **ciudad** *fem*
It's a beautiful town.
Es una ciudad muy bonita.
the town centre
el centro de la ciudad
I'm going into town.
Voy al centro.

toy NOUN
el **juguete** *masc*

toy shop NOUN
la **juguetería** *fem*

tracksuit NOUN
el **chándal** *masc* (PL los chándals)

tractor NOUN
el **tractor** *masc*

tradition NOUN
la **tradición** *fem* (PL las tradiciones)

traffic NOUN
el **tráfico** *masc*
There's a lot of traffic.
Hay mucho tráfico.

traffic lights PL NOUN
el **semáforo** *masc*
Turn right at the traffic lights.
Gira a la derecha en el semáforo.

train NOUN
el **tren** *masc*
by train
en tren
We're going by train.
Vamos en tren.

trainers PL NOUN
las **zapatillas de deporte** *fem pl*
a pair of trainers
unas zapatillas de deporte

training NOUN
el **entrenamiento** *masc*

tram NOUN
el **tranvía** *masc*

> **Language tip**
> *Even though it ends in* **-a**, **el tranvía** *is a masculine noun.*

trampoline NOUN
la **cama elástica** *fem*

to **translate** VERB
traducir
I can translate the menu into English.
Puedo traducir la carta al inglés.

translation NOUN
la **traducción** *fem* (PL las **traducciones**)

trap NOUN
la **trampa** *fem*

travel agent's NOUN
la **agencia de viajes** *fem*

travelling NOUN
I love travelling.
Me encanta viajar.

tray NOUN
la **bandeja** *fem*

treasure NOUN
el **tesoro** *masc*

tree NOUN
el **árbol** *masc*

triangle NOUN
el **triángulo** *masc*

trick NOUN
el **truco** *masc*
I can do magic tricks.
Sé hacer trucos de magia.

trip NOUN
el **viaje** *masc*
We're going on a trip to London.
Vamos a hacer un viaje a Londres.

> **Have a good trip!**
> ¡Buen viaje!

trolley NOUN
el **carrito** *masc*

trouble NOUN
el **problema** *masc*
The trouble is, it's too expensive.
El problema es que es demasiado caro.
Peter is always getting into trouble.
Peter siempre se está metiendo en problemas.

> **Language tip**
> *Even though it ends in* **-a**, **el problema** *is a masculine noun.*

trousers PL NOUN
los **pantalones** *masc pl*
I'm wearing black trousers.
Llevo unos pantalones negros.
He's changing his trousers.
Se está cambiando de pantalones.

truck NOUN
el **camión** *masc* (PL los **camiones**)

true ADJECTIVE
That's true.
Eso es verdad.
That's not true.
Eso no es verdad.

> **True or false?**
> ¿Verdadero o falso?

trumpet NOUN
la **trompeta** *fem*
She plays the trumpet.
Toca la trompeta.

trunks PL NOUN
el **bañador** *masc*
I've got new trunks.
Tengo un bañador nuevo.

truth NOUN
la **verdad** *fem*
Tell me the truth.
Dime la verdad.

try

> **try** *can be a verb or a noun.*

A VERB
to try
1 **intentar** *(attempt)*
Try to remember.
Intenta acordarte.
I'm going to try.
Voy a intentarlo.
You're not trying, Richard.
No estás haciendo el esfuerzo
suficiente, Richard.
2 **probar** *(taste)*
Would you like to try some?
¿Quieres probar un poco?
B NOUN
el **intento** *masc*
his third try
su tercer intento

> **Good try!**
> ¡No ha estado mal!
> **Can I have a try?**
> ¿Puedo intentarlo yo?

to **try on** VERB
probarse
Can I try it on?
¿Puedo probármelo?

T-shirt NOUN
la **camiseta** *fem*
Put on your T-shirt.
Ponte la camiseta.

> **Language tip**
> *In Spanish you usually use an article
> like el, la or los, las with clothes
> you are wearing.*

Tube NOUN
the Tube
el metro

Tuesday NOUN
el **martes** *masc*
It's Tuesday today.
Hoy es martes.

> **on Tuesday**
> el martes
> **on Tuesdays**
> los martes
> **every Tuesday**
> cada martes
> **last Tuesday**
> el martes pasado
> **next Tuesday**
> el martes que viene

> **Language tip**
> *Days are not spelled with a capital
> letter in Spanish.*

tummy NOUN
la **barriga** *fem*

tummy ache NOUN
I've got tummy ache.
Me duele la barriga.

tuna NOUN
el **atún** *masc*
a tuna salad
una ensalada con atún

tune NOUN
la **melodía** *fem*
I know the tune.
Conozco la melodía.

tunnel NOUN
el **túnel** *masc*

turkey NOUN
el **pavo** *masc*

turn

> **turn** *can be a noun or a verb.*

A NOUN
el **turno** *masc*
You miss a turn.
Pierdes un turno.

Whose turn is it?
¿A quién le toca?
It's my turn!
¡Me toca!

B VERB
to turn
girar
Turn right at the lights.
Gira a la derecha en el semáforo.

to **turn off** VERB
1 apagar *(switch off)*
Could you turn off the light?
¿Puedes apagar la luz?
2 cerrar *(tap)*
Turn off the tap, please.
Cierra el grifo, por favor.

to **turn on** VERB
1 encender *(switch on)*
Could you turn on the light?
¿Puedes encender la luz?
2 abrir *(tap)*
Turn on the tap, please.
Abre el grifo, por favor.

to **turn over** VERB
dar la vuelta a
Turn over the cards, everyone.
Dadle todos la vuelta a las cartas.

to **turn round** VERB
darse la vuelta
Turn round, children!
¡Daos la vuelta, niños!

TV NOUN
la **tele** *fem*
on TV
en la tele

twelfth NUMBER
doce
on the twelfth floor
en la planta doce
We break up on the twelfth of April.
Empezamos las vacaciones el doce de abril.
Today's the twelfth of June.
Hoy es doce de junio.

on the twelfth of August
el doce de agosto

Language tip
*Use the same set of numbers that you use for counting (**uno**, **dos**, **tres** and so on) when giving Spanish dates.*

twelve NUMBER
doce
twelve euros
doce euros
I have lunch at twelve o'clock.
Como a las doce.
It is twelve thirty.
Son las doce y media.

twelve o'clock
las doce
I'm twelve.
Tengo doce años.

English

Spanish

a
b
c
d
e
f
g
h
i
j
k
l
m
n
o
p
q
r
s
t
u
v
w
x
y
z

589

> **Language tip**
> In English you can say **I'm twelve** or **I'm twelve years old**. In Spanish you can only say **tengo doce años**. Have you noticed that in Spanish you need to use the verb **tener** to talk about somebody's age?

twentieth NUMBER
veinte
> **the twentieth floor**
> el piso veinte
> **My birthday's the twentieth of October.**
> Mi cumpleaños es el veinte de octubre.
> **Today's the twentieth of April.**
> Hoy es veinte de abril.

> **on the twentieth of May**
> el veinte de mayo

> **Language tip**
> Use the same set of numbers that you use for counting (**uno**, **dos**, **tres** and so on) when giving Spanish dates.

twenty NUMBER
veinte
> **twenty euros**
> veinte euros
> **It's twenty to two.**
> Son las dos menos veinte.

> **It's twenty past eleven.**
> Son las once y veinte.

> **He's twenty.**
> Tiene veinte años.

> **Language tip**
> In English you can say **he's twenty** or **he's twenty years old**. In Spanish you can only say **tiene veinte años**. Have you noticed that in Spanish you need to use the verb **tener** to talk about somebody's age?

twice ADVERB
dos veces

twin NOUN

> **Language tip**
> In Spanish you usually use different words for identical and non-identical twins

1 el **mellizo** masc
la **melliza** fem (not identical)
> **They're twins.**
> Son mellizos.
> **her twin sister**
> su hermana melliza
2 el **gemelo** masc
la **gemela** fem (identical twin)
> **They're identical twins.**
> Son gemelos.
> **my twin sister**
> mi hermana gemela

twin room NOUN
la **habitación con dos camas** fem (PL las **habitaciones con dos camas**)

twinned ADJECTIVE
hermanado masc
hermanada fem
> **Veracruz is twinned with Valencia.**
> Veracruz está hermanada con Valencia.

two NUMBER
dos
> **two euros**
> dos euros
> **It's two o'clock.**
> Son las dos.
> **Get into twos.**
> Poneos en grupos de dos.

She's two.
Tiene dos años.

Language tip
In English you can say **she's two** *or* **she's two years old**. *In Spanish you can only say* **tiene dos años**. *Have you noticed that in Spanish you need to use the verb* **tener** *to talk about somebody's age?*

type NOUN
el **tipo** *masc*
What type of camera have you got?
¿Qué tipo de cámara tienes?

tyre NOUN
el **neumático** *masc*

a
b
c
d
e
f
g
h
i
j
k
l
m
n
o
p
q
r
s
t
u
v
w
x
y
z

U u

UFO NOUN
el **OVNI** *masc*

ugly ADJECTIVE
feo *masc*
fea *fem*

UK NOUN (= **United Kingdom**)
el **Reino Unido** *masc*
in the UK
en el Reino Unido
to the UK
al Reino Unido
I live in the UK.
Vivo en el Reino Unido.

Ulster NOUN
el **Ulster** *masc*

umbrella NOUN
1 el **paraguas** *masc* (PL los
   paraguas) *(for rain)*
2 la **sombrilla** *fem (sun
   umbrella)*

umpire NOUN
el **árbitro** *masc*
la **árbitra** *fem*

unbelievable ADJECTIVE
increíble *masc & fem*
That's unbelievable!
¡Eso es increíble!]

uncle NOUN
el **tío** *masc*
my uncle
mi tío
my uncles and aunts
mis tíos

uncomfortable ADJECTIVE
incómodo *masc*
incómoda *fem*
**The seats are very
uncomfortable.**
Los asientos son muy
incómodos.

under PREPOSITION
1 **debajo de**

> **Language tip**
> When something is positioned under
> something, use **debajo de**.

The cat's under the table.
El gato está debajo de la mesa.

under there
ahí debajo
2 **por debajo de**

> **Language tip**
> After verbs which express movement
> (like 'go' and 'run') use **por debajo
> de**.

**The tunnel goes under the
river.**
El túnel pasa por debajo del río.
3 **menos de** *(less than)*
**It costs under twenty
pounds.**
Cuesta menos de veinte libras.
children under ten
niños de menos de diez años

underground

> **underground** *can be a noun,
> adjective or adverb.*

A NOUN
el **metro** *masc*
by underground
en metro

the London underground
el metro de Londres

B ADJECTIVE
subterráneo *masc*
subterránea *fem*
an underground car park
un parking subterráneo

C ADVERB
bajo tierra
Moles live underground.
Los topos viven bajo tierra.

underneath

underneath *can be a preposition or an adverb.*

A PREPOSITION
1 debajo de

Language tip
When something is positioned underneath something, use **debajo de**.

The key's underneath the mat.
La llave está debajo del felpudo.

2 por debajo de

Language tip
After verbs which express movement (like 'go' and 'run') use **por debajo de**.

The footpath goes underneath the bridge.
El sendero pasa por debajo del puente.

B ADVERB
debajo
Look underneath, Rachel!
¡Mira debajo, Rachel!

to **understand** VERB
entender
I don't understand this word.
No entiendo esta palabra.
Do you understand, Tim?
¿Lo entiendes, Tim?

I don't understand.
No lo entiendo.
Do you understand?
¿Lo entiendes?

understood VERB ▷*see* **understand**

underwear NOUN
la **ropa interior** *fem*

undone ADJECTIVE
desatado *masc*
desatada *fem*
Your laces are undone.
Llevas los cordones desatados.

Language tip
In Spanish you usually use an article like **el**, **la** *or* **los**, **las** *with clothes you are wearing.*

undressed ADJECTIVE
to get undressed
desnudarse
I'm getting undressed.
Me estoy desnudando.

unemployed ADJECTIVE
parado *masc*
parada *fem*
He's unemployed.
Está parado.

unfair ADJECTIVE
injusto *masc*
injusta *fem*
That's unfair!
¡Eso es injusto!

unfashionable ADJECTIVE
pasado de moda *masc*
pasada de moda *fem*

to **unfold** VERB
desplegar
Unfold the map.
Despliega el mapa.

unforgettable ADJECTIVE
inolvidable *masc & fem*

unfortunately ADVERB
lamentablemente
Unfortunately it's too late.
Lamentablemente es demasiado tarde.
Unfortunately not.
Lamentablemente no.

English

Spanish

a
b
c
d
e
f
g
h
i
j
k
l
m
n
o
p
q
r
s
u
v
w
x
y
z

unhappy ADJECTIVE
to be unhappy
no estar contento
She's unhappy at school.
No está contenta en el colegio.
You look unhappy.
Pareces triste.

uniform NOUN
el **uniforme** *masc*
We wear school uniform.
Llevamos uniforme al colegio.

Did you know…?
Uniforms aren't worn in most Spanish state schools but they are in most Spanish private schools.

Union Jack NOUN
la **bandera del Reino Unido** *fem*

United Kingdom NOUN
el **Reino Unido** *masc*
to the United Kingdom
al Reino Unido
in the United Kingdom
en el Reino Unido

United States NOUN
los **Estados Unidos** *masc pl*
in the United States
en Estados Unidos
to the United States
a Estados Unidos

universe NOUN
el **universo** *masc*

university NOUN
la **universidad** *fem*
She's at university.
Está en la universidad.
Do you want to go to university?
¿Quieres ir a la universidad?
Lancaster University
la universidad de Lancaster

unless CONJUNCTION
a menos que

Don't do it unless your mum tells you to.
No lo hagas a menos que tu madre te lo diga.

Language tip
*a menos que is followed by a form of the verb called the subjunctive. Alternatively, you can often use **si no** (if not) and an ordinary form of the verb instead.*

I'll have that biscuit, unless you want it.
Yo cogeré esa galleta, si no la quieres tú.

unlikely ADJECTIVE
poco probable *masc & fem*
It's possible, but unlikely.
Es posible, pero poco probable.

unlucky ADJECTIVE
to be unlucky
tener mala suerte/traer mala suerte

Language tip
to be unlucky has two translations depending on whether it means 'to have bad luck' or 'to bring bad luck'. Look at the examples.

I'm always unlucky.
Siempre tengo mala suerte.
It's unlucky to walk under a ladder.
Trae mala suerte pasar por debajo de una escalera.
Thirteen is an unlucky number.
El trece trae mala suerte.

to **unpack** VERB
deshacer las maletas
Have you unpacked?
¿Has deshecho las maletas?
I'm going to unpack my suitcase.
Voy a deshacer la maleta.

unpleasant ADJECTIVE
desagradable *masc & fem*

unpopular ADJECTIVE

poco popular *masc & fem*

unpredictable ADJECTIVE
impredecible *masc & fem*
> **The weather is unpredictable.**
> El tiempo es impredecible.

unreliable ADJECTIVE
poco fiable *masc & fem*
> **Our car is unreliable.**
> Nuestro coche es poco fiable.

unsuitable ADJECTIVE
inadecuado *masc*
inadecuada *fem*

untidy ADJECTIVE
desordenado *masc*
desordenada *fem*
> **My bedroom's always untidy.**
> Mi habitación siempre está desordenada.
> **My writing is untidy.**
> Tengo mala letra.

until PREPOSITION
hasta
> **He's here until tomorrow.**
> Está aquí hasta mañana.
> **The supermarket is open until ten.**
> El supermercado está abierto hasta las diez.
> **not until tomorrow**
> hasta mañana no
> **When will it be ready? — Not until next week.**
> ¿Cuándo estará listo? — Hasta la semana que viene no.
> **from ... until**
> de ... a
> **from nine until five**
> de nueve a cinco
> **from the tenth until the fourteenth of May**
> del diez al catorce de mayo

unusual ADJECTIVE
poco común *masc & fem* (PL **poco comunes**)
> **It's an unusual name.**
> Es un nombre poco común.

up

> **up** *can be an adverb, adjective or preposition.*

A ADVERB
1 hacia arriba *(upwards)*
> **She looked up.**
> Miró hacia arriba.
2 arriba *(at a higher level)*
> **He's up on the roof.**
> Está arriba en el tejado.
> **It's up there.**
> Está allí arriba.
> **I'll come up later.**
> Subo más tarde.
> **up to**
> hasta
> **Let's count up to fifty.**
> Vamos a contar hasta cincuenta.
> **up to now**
> hasta ahora
> **It's up to you.**
> Lo que tú quieras.
> **What's up with her?**
> ¿Qué le pasa?

> **up there**
> allí arriba
> **up here**
> aquí arriba

B ADJECTIVE
> **I'm always up before eight.**
> Siempre me levanto antes de las ocho.
> **He's not up yet.**
> Todavía no se ha levantado.
C PREPOSITION *(along)*
> **We could walk up the road to the bus stop.**
> Podríamos subir por la carretera hasta la parada del autobús.
> **The post office is up the road.**
> Correos está más arriba.
> **The cat is on the roof.**
> El gato está subido al tejado.

a
b
c
d
e
f
g
h
i
j
k
l
m
n
o
p
q
r
s
t
u
v
w
x
y
z

upper ADJECTIVE
superior *masc & fem*
on the upper floor
en el piso superior

upset

> **upset** *can be an adjective or a verb.*

A ADJECTIVE
disgustado *masc*
disgustada *fem*
She's still a bit upset.
Todavía está un poco disgustada.
I've got an upset stomach.
Tengo mal el estómago.

B VERB
to upset
dar un mal rato a
I don't want to upset my granny.
No quiero dar un mal rato a mi abuela.

upside down ADVERB
al revés
That painting is upside down.
Ese cuadro está al revés.

upstairs ADVERB
arriba
Where's your coat? — It's upstairs.
¿Dónde está tu abrigo? — Está arriba.

up-to-date ADJECTIVE
moderno *masc*
moderna *fem*

upwards ADVERB
hacia arriba

urgent ADJECTIVE
urgente *masc & fem*
Is it urgent?
¿Es urgente?

US NOUN (= **United States**)
los **EE.UU.** *masc pl*
in the US
en EE.UU.
to the US
a EE.UU.
from the US
desde EE.UU.

> **Language tip**
>
> As **EE.UU.** *stands for* **Estados Unidos**, *why are there two Es and two Us? It's to show that the abbreviation refers to something plural. Compare* **JJ.OO.** *for* **Juegos Olímpicos** *(Olympic Games).*

us PRONOUN
1 nos *(direct and indirect object)*
He hates us.
Nos odia.
Tell us the story.
Cuéntanos la historia.
to us
nos
She's going to write to us.
Va a escribirnos.
2 nosotros *masc pl*
nosotras *fem pl*

> **Language tip**
>
> Use **nosotros** and **nosotras** *after prepositions.*

Come with us.
Ven con nosotros.

> **Language tip**
>
> Use **nosotros** and **nosotras** *in comparisons.*

He's older than us.
Es mayor que nosotros.

> **Language tip**
>
> Use **nosotros** and **nosotras** *after the verb* **ser**.

It's us.
Somos nosotros.

USA NOUN
(= **United States of America**)
los **EE.UU.** *masc pl*
in the USA
en EE.UU.
to the USA
a EE.UU.
from the USA
desde EE.UU.

Language tip

As **EE.UU.** *stands for* **Estados Unidos**, *why are there two Es and two Us? It's to show that the abbreviation refers to something plural. Compare* **JJ.OO.** *for* **Juegos Olímpicos** *(Olympic Games).*

---

use

---
use *can be a verb or a noun.*

A VERB
to use
usar
Can we use a dictionary in the exam?
¿Podemos usar un diccionario en el examen?
Somebody is using the computer.
Alguien está usando el ordenador.
Can I use your phone?
¿Puedo llamar por teléfono?
Can I use the toilet?
¿Puedo ir al baño?
B NOUN
It's no use.
Es inútil.

to **use up** VERB
gastar
We've used up all the paint.
Hemos gastado toda la pintura.

used ADJECTIVE
I'm used to getting up early.
Estoy acostumbrado a levantarme temprano.

I'm used to it.
Estoy acostumbrado.
I'm not used to it.
No estoy acostumbrado.

---

useful ADJECTIVE
útil *masc & fem*

useless ADJECTIVE
to be useless
no servir para nada
This map is useless.
Este mapa no sirve para nada.

usual ADJECTIVE
habitual *masc & fem*
my usual seat
mi asiento habitual
She's late, as usual.
Llega tarde, como siempre.

---
as usual
como siempre

---

usually ADVERB
normalmente
I usually wear trousers.
Normalmente llevo pantalones.

utility room NOUN
el **lavadero** *masc*

V v

vacancy NOUN *(in hotel)*
'Vacancies'
'Quedan plazas'
'No vacancies'
'Completo'

vacuum cleaner NOUN
la **aspiradora** *fem*

Valentine card NOUN
la **tarjeta del día de los enamorados** *fem*

Valentine's Day NOUN
el **día de los enamorados** *masc*

valley NOUN
el **valle** *masc*

valuable ADJECTIVE
de **valor**
a valuable picture
un cuadro de valor

van NOUN
la **camioneta** *fem*

vandal NOUN
el **vándalo** *masc*

vandalism NOUN
el **vandalismo** *masc*

vanilla NOUN
la **vainilla** *fem*

a vanilla ice cream
un helado de vainilla

varied ADJECTIVE
variado *masc*
variada *fem*

variety NOUN
la **variedad** *fem*

various ADJECTIVE
varios *masc pl*
varias *fem pl*
There are various possibilities.
Existen varias posibilidades.

vase NOUN
el **jarrón** *masc* (PL los **jarrones**)

vegan NOUN
el **vegetariano estricto** *masc*
la **vegetariana estricta** *fem*
I'm a vegan.
Soy vegetariano estricto.

vegetable NOUN
la **verdura** *fem*
vegetable soup
sopa de verduras
Would you like some vegetables?
¿Queréis verduras?

vegetarian

vegetarian *can be an adjective or a noun.*

A ADJECTIVE
vegetariano *masc*
vegetariana *fem*
vegetarian lasagne
lasaña vegetariana
B NOUN
el **vegetariano** *masc*
la **vegetariana** *fem*
I'm a vegetarian.
Soy vegetariano.

verb NOUN
el **verbo** *masc*

very ADVERB
muy
very tall
muy alto
not very interesting
no muy interesante
It's very hot.
Hace mucho calor.
I love you very much.
Te quiero mucho.

very soon
muy pronto
very much
mucho
I'm very sorry.
Lo siento mucho.

vest NOUN
la **camiseta** *fem*

vet NOUN
el **veterinario** *masc*
la **veterinaria** *fem*
She's a vet.
Es veterinaria.

Language tip
When talking about people's jobs in Spanish, you do not use an article.

vicar NOUN
el **pastor** *masc*
la **pastora** *fem*

video

video *can be a noun or a verb.*

A NOUN
el **vídeo** *masc* (*film, cassette, machine*)

We're going to watch a video.
Vamos a ver un vídeo.
B VERB
to video
grabar en vídeo
We're going to video the concert.
Vamos a grabar el concierto en vídeo.

video game NOUN
el **videojuego** *masc*
I like playing video games.
Me gusta jugar con videojuegos.

video recorder NOUN
el **vídeo** *masc*

video shop NOUN
el **videoclub** *masc*

view NOUN
la **vista** *fem*
There's an amazing view.
Hay una vista increíble.

village NOUN
el **pueblo** *masc*
in the village
en el pueblo

vinegar NOUN
el **vinagre** *masc*

vineyard NOUN
el **viñedo** *masc*

violent ADJECTIVE
violento *masc*
violenta *fem*

violin NOUN
el **violín** *masc*
I play the violin.
Toco el violín.

English Spanish

a
b
c
d
e
f
g
h
i
j
k
l
m
n
o
p
q
r
s
t
u
v
w
x
y
z

virus NOUN
el **virus** masc (PL los **virus**)

visit

visit can be a noun or a verb.

A NOUN
la **visita** fem
a visit to Edinburgh castle
una visita al castillo de
Edimburgo
B VERB
to visit
visitar
**We're going to visit the
castle.**
Vamos a visitar el castillo.
**I'm going to visit some
friends.**
Voy a visitar a unos amigos.

Language tip

*Don't forget the personal **a** in
examples like this one.*

visitor NOUN
el **invitado** masc

la **invitada** fem
**Today we've got a Spanish
visitor.**
Hoy tenemos un invitado
español.

vocabulary NOUN
el **vocabulario** masc

voice NOUN
la **voz** fem (PL las **voces**)

volleyball NOUN
el **voleibol** masc
**We play volleyball
sometimes.**
A veces jugamos al voleibol.

Language tip

*In Spanish, you need to add **al** or
a la before the name of the sport.*

volunteer NOUN
el **voluntario** masc
la **voluntaria** fem

vowel NOUN
la **vocal** fem

W w

waist NOUN
la **cintura** *fem*

waistcoat NOUN
el **chaleco** *masc*

to **wait** VERB
esperar
Wait Alison, it's not your turn.
Espera, Alison, que no es tu turno.

Wait for me!
¡Espérame!
Wait a minute!
¡Espera un momento!

waiter NOUN
el **camarero** *masc*

waiting room NOUN
la **sala de espera** *fem*

waitress NOUN
la **camarera** *fem*

to **wake up** VERB
despertarse
Wake up, Peter!
¡Despiértate, Peter!

Wales NOUN
Gales *masc*
Swansea is in Wales.
Swansea está en Gales.
Bronwen is from Wales.
Bronwen es de Gales.
the Prince of Wales
el Príncipe de Gales

walk

walk *can be a verb or a noun.*

A VERB
to walk
caminar
He walks fast.
Camina rápido.

I walked ten kilometres.
Caminé diez kilómetros.
Are you walking or going by bus?
¿Vas a ir a pie o en autobús?
B NOUN
el **paseo** *masc*
Would you like to go for a walk?
¿Quieres ir a dar un paseo?
It's a five-minute walk to the town centre.
Se tarda cinco minutos andando hasta el centro.

walking NOUN
My parents like walking.
A mis padres les gusta caminar.

wall NOUN
1 la **pared** *fem (inside building)*
There are posters on the wall.
Hay pósters en la pared.

2 el **muro** *masc (outer wall, garden wall)*
Tony is sitting on the wall.
Tony está sentado en el muro.

wallet NOUN
la **cartera** *fem*

walnut NOUN
la **nuez** *fem* (FEM PL las **nueces**)

to **want** VERB
querer
Do you want a piece of cake?
¿Quieres un trozo de tarta?

I don't want to play.
No quiero jugar.
What do you want to do tomorrow?
¿Qué quieres hacer mañana?

What do you want, Judith?
¿Qué quieres, Judith?
What do you want, boys?
¿Que queréis, niños?

war NOUN
  la **guerra** fem

wardrobe NOUN
  el **armario** masc

warm ADJECTIVE
1 **cálido** masc
  cálida fem (weather)
  warm weather
  tiempo cálido
  It's warm today.
  Hoy hace calor.
  warm clothes
  ropa de abrigo

2 **caliente**
  masc & fem (bath, water, hands)

It's warm.
Hace calor.
I'm warm.
Tengo calor.

was VERB ▷see **be**

to **wash** VERB
1 **lavar** (thing)
  He washes his car every Sunday.
  Lava el coche todos los domingos.
2 **lavarse** (get washed)
  At eight I get up, wash and get dressed.
  A las ocho me levanto, me lavo y me visto.
  I'm going to wash my hands.
  Me voy a lavar las manos.
  I want to wash my hair.
  Quiero lavarme la cabeza.

Wash your hands!
¡Lávate las manos!

Language tip
In Spanish you usually use an article like **el**, **la** *or* **los**, **las** *with parts of the body.*

washbasin NOUN
  el **lavabo** masc

washing machine NOUN
  la **lavadora** fem

washing-up NOUN
  to do the washing-up
  fregar los platos
  Who's going to do the washing-up?
  ¿Quién va a fregar los platos?
  I often do the washing-up.
  Muchas veces friego yo los platos.

wasn't (= **was not**) ▷see **be**

wasp NOUN
  la **avispa** fem

waste NOUN
  It's a waste of time.
  Es una pérdida de tiempo.

wastepaper basket NOUN
  la **papelera** fem
  Put your chewing gum in the wastepaper basket.
  Tira tu chicle a la papelera.

watch

watch *can be a noun or a verb.*

A NOUN
  el **reloj** masc
  I haven't got a watch.
  No tengo reloj.

Language tip
Did you know that **un reloj** *is also* **a clock**?

B VERB
  to watch
1 **mirar** (look at)

Watch what I do.
Mira lo que hago.

Watch me, Mum!
¡Mírame, mamá!

2 ver (television, programme, match)
He watches television every day.
Ve la televisión todos los días.

to **watch out** VERB
tener cuidado
You need to watch out.
Tienes que tener cuidado.

Watch out!
¡Cuidado!

water NOUN
el **agua** fem

Language tip
Even though it's a feminine noun, remember that you use **el** *and* **un** *with* **agua**.

The water was very cold.
El agua estaba muy fría.
a glass of water
un vaso de agua

Language tip
Be careful! The translation of **water** *is not* **wáter**.

wave

wave *can be a noun or a verb.*

A NOUN
la **ola** fem
There are big waves sometimes.
A veces hay olas grandes.
B VERB
to wave
1 saludar con la mano (in greeting)
They're waving at us.
Nos están saludando con la mano.

2 to wave goodbye
decir adiós con la mano
Let's wave goodbye.
Vamos a decir adiós con la mano.

wavy ADJECTIVE
wavy hair
pelo ondulado

way NOUN
1 el **camino** masc. (to place)
I don't know the way.
No sé el camino.
Ask the way.
Pregunta el camino.
Can you tell me the way to the station?
¿Me puedes decir cómo se llega a la estación?

It's a long way.
Está lejos.
Which way is it?
¿Por dónde está?
It's this way.
Es por aquí.

2 la **forma** fem (manner)
What's the best way to learn Spanish?
¿Cuál es la mejor forma de aprender español?

Language tip
As **la manera** *and* **el modo** *mean the same as* **la forma**, *you could alternatively say* **la mejor manera** *or* **el mejor modo** *to mean* **the best way**.

He looked at me in a strange way.
Me miró de forma extraña.
Do it this way, Katy.
Hazlo así, Katy.
by the way
a propósito
No way!
¡Ni hablar!

way in NOUN
la **entrada** fem

way out NOUN
la **salida** *fem*
> **Where's the way out?**
> ¿Dónde está la salida?

we PRONOUN
nosotros *masc pl*
nosotras *fem pl*
> **Shall we do it?**
> ¿Lo hacemos nosotros?

Language tip
we *isn't usually translated unless it's emphatic.*

> **We do sport in the afternoon.**
> Hacemos deporte por la tarde.

to **wear** VERB
llevar
> **He's wearing a hat.**
> Lleva un sombrero.
> **I wear glasses.**
> Llevo gafas.
> **What's she wearing?**
> ¿Qué lleva puesto?

weather NOUN
el **tiempo** *masc*
> **What's the weather like today?**
> ¿Qué tiempo hace hoy?
> **The weather isn't very nice.**
> No hace muy buen tiempo.

What's the weather like?
¿Qué tiempo hace?
The weather's nice.
Hace buen tiempo.

weather forecast NOUN
el **pronóstico del tiempo** *masc*

Web NOUN
the Web
Internet *masc/fem*
Look on the Web.
Mira en Internet.

la **webcam** NOUN
la **webcam**

website NOUN
el **sitio web** *masc*

we'd
1 (= we would) ▷ *see* **would**
2 (= we had) ▷ *see* **have**

wedding NOUN
la **boda** *fem*
> **It's my cousin's wedding today.**
> Hoy es la boda de mi prima.

wedding anniversary NOUN
el **aniversario de boda** *masc*

Wednesday NOUN
el **miércoles** *masc*
> **It's Wednesday today.**
> Hoy es miércoles.

on Wednesday
el miércoles
on Wednesdays
los miércoles
every Wednesday
cada miércoles
last Wednesday
el miércoles pasado
next Wednesday
el miércoles que viene

Language tip
Days are not spelled with a capital letter in Spanish.

week NOUN
la **semana** *fem*
> **two weeks**
> dos semanas

this week
esta semana
last week
la semana pasada
every week
cada semana
next week
la semana que viene
in a week's time
dentro de una semana

weekday NOUN
on weekdays
los días entre semana

weekend NOUN
el **fin de semana** *masc*
What are you doing at the weekend?
¿Qué vas a hacer el fin de semana?
The shops are closed at weekends.
Las tiendas cierran los fines de semana.

at weekends
los fines de semana
last weekend
el fin de semana pasado
next weekend
el fin de semana que viene

welcome ADJECTIVE
Welcome!
¡Bienvenido!

Language tip
Remember to change **¡bienvenido!** to **¡bienvenida!** if you're welcoming a girl or woman. Similarly, change it to **¡bienvenidos!** if you're welcoming a mixed group or a group of men.

Welcome to Scotland!
¡Bienvenido a Escocia!

Thank you! — You're welcome!
¡Gracias! — ¡De nada!

we'll (= we will) ▷ see **will**

well

well can be an adverb or an adjective.

A ADVERB
bien
The team is playing well.
El equipo está jugando bien.
as well
también
We're going to London as well as Manchester.
Vamos a Londres y también a Manchester.
B ADJECTIVE
to be well
estar bien

Language tip
bien *never changes its ending no matter who or what it describes.*

He isn't well.
No está bien.
I'm not very well at the moment.
No estoy muy bien en este momento.
How are you? — I'm very well, thank you.
¿Cómo estás? — Estoy muy bien, gracias.

Well done!
¡Bien hecho!
Get well soon!
¡Que te mejores pronto!

Language tip
Have you noticed the upside-down exclamation mark at the start of Spanish exclamations?

well-behaved ADJECTIVE
well-behaved children
niños que se portan bien
He's very well-behaved.
Se porta muy bien.

wellies PL NOUN
las **botas de agua** *fem pl*

wellingtons PL NOUN
las **botas de agua** *fem pl*

English
Spanish

a
b
c
d
e
f
g
h
i
j
k
l
m
n
o
p
q
r
s
t
u
v
w
x
y
z

well-known ADJECTIVE
conocido *masc*
conocida *fem*
    a well-known film star
    un conocido artista de cine

Welsh

Welsh *can be an adjective or a noun.*

A ADJECTIVE
galés *masc* (PL **galeses**)
galesa *fem*
a Welsh town
una ciudad galesa
Welsh people
los galeses

He's Welsh.
Es galés.
She's Welsh.
Es galesa.

B NOUN
el **galés** *masc (language)*
the Welsh
los galeses

Language tip
*galés is not spelled with a capital
letter in Spanish.*

Welshman NOUN
el **galés** *masc* (PL los **galeses**)

Language tip
*galés is not spelled with a capital
letter in Spanish.*

Welshwoman NOUN
la **galesa** *fem*

Language tip
*galesa is not spelled with a capital
letter in Spanish.*

went VERB ▷ *see* **go**

were VERB ▷ *see* **be**

we're (= **we are**) ▷ *see* **be**

weren't (= **were not**) ▷ *see* **be**

west

west *can be an adjective or a noun.*

A ADJECTIVE
oeste

Language tip
oeste *never changes its ending no
matter what it describes. Did you
know that adjectives that behave
like this are called 'invariable
adjectives'?*

the west coast
la costa oeste
B NOUN
el **oeste** *masc*
in the west
en el oeste

western NOUN
la **película del oeste** *fem*
I like westerns.
Me gustan las películas del
oeste.

wet ADJECTIVE
mojado *masc*
mojada *fem*
wet clothes
ropa mojada
I'm wet.
Estoy mojado.
It's wet today.
Hoy está lloviendo.

what

what *can be a pronoun or an
adjective.*

A PRONOUN
1 qué
What are you doing, boys?
¿Qué estáis haciendo, chicos?
What's the matter?
¿Qué pasa?
What's this?
¿Qué es esto?

Language tip
Use ¿qué es...? *in 'what is...?'
questions when asking for an
explanation or definition.*

Ask her what they are.
Pregúntale qué son.

2 cuál (PL **cuáles**)
What's the capital of Spain?
¿Cuál es la capital de España?

Language tip
You usually use ***¿cuál es...?*** *in 'what is...?' questions when asking for specific information rather than an explanation or definition.*

3 lo que

Language tip
Use ***lo que*** *when* **what** *is not a question word. Because* **que** *is not a question word here, it does not have an accent.*

I saw what happened.
Vi lo que pasó.

What?
¿Qué?
What is it?
¿Qué es?
What do you want?
¿Qué quieres?
What's the weather like?
¿Qué tiempo hace?
What's your name?
¿Cómo te llamas?
What's your phone number?
¿Cuál es tu número de teléfono?

B ADJECTIVE
qué

Language tip
qué *never changes its ending.*

What letter does it start with?
¿Por qué letra empieza?
What colour is it?
¿De qué color es?
What a pretty house!
¡Qué casa más bonita!
What delicious cherries!
¡Qué cerezas tan ricas!
What time is it?
¿Qué hora es?

What day is it today?
¿Qué día es hoy?

Language tip
Don't forget the written accent on question words like **qué** *and* **cuál** *or the upside-down question mark at the start of questions.*

wheel NOUN
la **rueda** *fem*

wheelchair NOUN
la **silla de ruedas** *fem*

when ADVERB
1 cuándo (*in questions*)
When's your birthday?
¿Cuándo es tu cumpleaños?

Language tip
Don't forget the written accent on question words like **¿cuándo...?** *or the upside-down question mark at the start of questions.*

2 cuando (*in other sentences*)
When it rains, we stay in the classroom.
Cuando llueve nos quedamos en la clase.

where ADVERB, CONJUNCTION
1 dónde (*in questions*)
Where's Emma today?
¿Dónde está hoy Emma?
Where are you going?
¿A dónde vas?

Where do you live?
¿Dónde vives?

> **Language tip**
> *Don't forget the written accent on question words like ¿dónde...? or the upside-down question mark at the start of questions.*

2 donde *(in other sentences)*
the house where I live
la casa donde vivo

whether CONJUNCTION
si
I don't know whether to go or not.
No sé si ir o no.

which

> **which** *can be an adjective or a pronoun.*

A ADJECTIVE
qué

> **Language tip**
> **qué** *never changes its ending.*

Which flavour do you want?
¿Qué sabor quieres?
Which number is it?
¿Qué número es?
Which one would you like?
¿Cuál quieres?
Which ones would you like?
¿Cuáles quieres?

> **Language tip**
> *Don't forget the written accent on question words like ¿qué...? and ¿cuál...? nor the upside-down question mark at the start of questions.*

B PRONOUN
1 cuál (PL **cuáles**) *(in questions)*
Which would you like?
¿Cuál quieres?
Which is your car?
¿Cuál es tu coche?
Which are your suitcases?
¿Cuáles son tus maletas?
Which do you prefer, cricket or football?
¿Qué te gusta más, el críquet o el fútbol?

2 que *(relative)*
the car which we sold
el coche que vendimos

> **Language tip**
> *After a preposition* **que** *becomes* **el que**, **la que**, **los que** *or* **las que** *to agree with the noun referred to.*

the film which I was telling you about
la película de la que te hablaba

while

> **while** *can be a conjunction or a noun.*

A CONJUNCTION
mientras
While you're here, we can do some sightseeing.
Mientras estás aquí podemos hacer un poco de turismo.
You hold the torch while I look inside.
Aguanta la linterna mientras yo miro dentro.
B NOUN
a while
un rato
a while ago
hace un rato
after a while
después de un rato

whipped cream NOUN
la **nata montada** *fem*

whiskers PL NOUN
los **bigotes** *masc pl*

white

> **white** *can be an adjective or a noun.*

A ADJECTIVE
blanco *masc*
blanca *fem*
He's wearing white trousers.
Lleva pantalones blancos.
My shirt is white.
Mi camisa es blanca.
He's got white hair.
Tiene el pelo blanco.

> **Language tip**
>
> *Colour adjectives come after the noun in Spanish.*

B NOUN
  el **blanco** *masc*
  The bride is wearing white.
  La novia va vestida de blanco.

whiteboard NOUN
  la **pizarra blanca** *fem*
  an interactive whiteboard
  una pizarra interactiva

white coffee NOUN
  el **café con leche** *masc*

> **Did you know…?**
>
> **el café con leche** *is made with hot milk. If you'd like a short, strong white coffee, ask for* **un cortado** *instead.*

Whitsun NOUN
  Pentecostés *masc*

who PRONOUN
  1 quién (PL **quiénes**) *(in questions)*
  Who wants to start?
  ¿Quién quiere empezar?
  Who's that?
  ¿Quién es ése?
  Who are they?
  ¿Quiénes son?

> **Language tip**
>
> *Don't forget the written accent on question words like* **¿quién…?** *nor the upside-down question mark at the start of questions.*

  2 que *(relative)*
  the girl who lives there
  la chica que vive allí

whole ADJECTIVE
  todo *masc*
  toda *fem*

  the whole class
  toda la clase
  the whole afternoon
  toda la tarde
  the whole world
  el mundo entero

whose PRONOUN, ADJECTIVE
  de quién *(in questions)*
  Whose pencil case is this?
  ¿De quién es este estuche?
  Whose turn is it?
  ¿De quién es el turno?

> **Whose is this?**
> ¿De quién es esto?

why ADVERB
  por qué
  Why are you crying?
  ¿Por qué lloras?
  Why not?
  ¿Por qué no?
  **Why don't you eat meat? —
  Because I don't like it.**
  ¿Por qué no comes carne? —
  Porque no me gusta.

> **Language tip**
>
> *The Spanish translations for* **why** *and* **because** *are very similar. When it is used to ask a question,* **¿por qué?** *is two separate words and has an accent on the* **qué**.

  That's why I can't go.
  Por eso no puedo ir.

wide ADJECTIVE
  ancho *masc*
  ancha *fem*
  a wide road
  una calle ancha

widow NOUN
  la **viuda** *fem*

widower NOUN
  el **viudo** *masc*

wife NOUN
  la **mujer** *fem*
  She's his wife.
  Es su mujer.

Language tip

Did you know that **la mujer** *is also the Spanish for* **woman**?

wifi NOUN
el **wifi** *masc*

wild ADJECTIVE
salvaje *masc & fem*
a wild animal
un animal salvaje

will VERB
1 *(forming future)*
It will soon be my birthday.
Pronto será mi cumpleaños.
We'll get there quite late.
Llegaremos bastante tarde.
It won't rain.
No lloverá.
2 *(in requests and offers)*
Will you help me?
¿Me ayudas?
I'll make the coffee.
Yo hago el café.

to **win** VERB
ganar
Who is winning?
¿Quién va ganando?
I've won!
¡He ganado!

wind NOUN
el **viento** *masc*
There is a lot of wind.
Hace mucho viento.

window NOUN
1 la **ventana** *fem*
Look out of the window, boys.
Mirad por la ventana, chicos.
a shop window
un escaparate
2 el **cristal** *masc (pane)*
He's broken the window.
Ha roto el cristal.

windy ADJECTIVE
a windy day
un día de viento

It's windy.
Hace viento.

wine NOUN
el **vino** *masc*
a bottle of wine
una botella de vino
a glass of wine
una copa de vino
white wine
vino blanco
red wine
vino tinto

winner NOUN
el **ganador** *masc*
la **ganadora** *fem*

winning ADJECTIVE
the winning team
el equipo ganador

winter NOUN
el **invierno** *masc*
last winter
el invierno
pasado

in winter
en invierno

winter sports PL NOUN
los **deportes de invierno**
masc pl

wintertime NOUN
el **invierno** *masc*

in wintertime
en el invierno

wish

wish *can be a noun or a verb.*

A NOUN
el **deseo** *masc*
Make a wish!
¡Pide un deseo!
With best wishes, Lily
Un abrazo, Lily

Best wishes
Un abrazo

B VERB
to wish
desear
He wished her a happy birthday.
Le deseó feliz cumpleaños.
I wish I could go with you!
¡Ojalá pudiera ir contigo!

Language tip
Ojalá *is followed by a form of the verb called the subjunctive.*

witch NOUN
la **bruja** *fem*

with PREPOSITION
1 con
Tea with milk?
¿Té con leche?
We're going to stay with friends.
Nos vamos a quedar con unos amigos.
I live with my dad.
Vivo con mi padre.

Language tip
Remember that **with me** *translates as* **conmigo**.

Come with me.
Ven conmigo.
It begins with 'b'.
Empieza por 'b'.
2 de *(in descriptions)*
a woman with blue eyes
una mujer de ojos azules

without PREPOSITION
sin
I drink coffee without sugar.
Bebo el café sin azúcar.
without speaking
sin hablar

Language tip
Just use **sin** *on its own to translate* **without a**.

without a coat
sin abrigo

witness NOUN
el/la **testigo** *masc/fem*

Language tip
Did you notice that the feminine form **la testigo** *still ends in* **-o**?

wives
PL NOUN
las **mujeres**
fem pl

wolf NOUN
el **lobo** *masc*

woman NOUN
la **mujer** *fem*
three women and two men
tres mujeres y dos hombres

won VERB ▷ *see* **win**

to **wonder** VERB
preguntarse
I wonder where Caroline is.
Me pregunto dónde está Caroline.

wonderful ADJECTIVE
maravilloso *masc*
maravillosa *fem*

won't (= **will not**) ▷ *see* **will**

wood NOUN
1 la **madera** *fem (substance)*
It's made of wood.
Es de madera.
2 el **bosque** *masc (place)*
We went for a walk in the wood.
Fuimos a pasear por el bosque.

wool NOUN
la **lana** *fem*
It's made of wool.
Es de lana.

English Spanish

a b c d e f g h i j k l m n o p q r s t u v **w** x y z

word NOUN
la **palabra** *fem*
I've forgotten the word.
Se me ha olvidado la palabra.
What's the word for 'shop' in Spanish?
¿Cómo se dice 'shop' en español?
We're going to learn the words of a song.
Vamos a aprendernos la letra de una canción.

work

work *can be a verb or a noun.*

A VERB
to work

1 **trabajar** *(person)*
She works in a shop.
Trabaja en una tienda.
2 **funcionar** *(machine, plan)*
The heating isn't working.
La calefacción no funciona.
B NOUN
el **trabajo** *masc*
He's at work at the moment.
Está en el trabajo en estos momentos.
I've got a lot of work to do.
Tengo mucho trabajo que hacer.
to go to work
ir a trabajar
He goes to work at eight o'clock.
Va a trabajar a las ocho.

at work
en el trabajo

worker NOUN
el **trabajador** *masc*

la **trabajadora** *fem*
She's a good worker.
Es una buena trabajadora.

worksheet NOUN
la **hoja de ejercicios** *fem*

world NOUN
el **mundo** *masc*
the whole world
el mundo entero
He's the world champion.
Es el campeón del mundo.

worried ADJECTIVE
preocupado *masc*
preocupada *fem*
She's very worried.
Está muy preocupada.

to **worry** VERB
preocuparse
He worries too much.
Se preocupa demasiado.

worse ADJECTIVE, ADVERB
peor *masc & fem*
The weather is worse in Scotland.
El tiempo está peor en Escocia.
I'm feeling worse.
Me siento peor.

worst ADJECTIVE, ADVERB, NOUN
peor *masc & fem*
I always get the worst mark.
Siempre saco la peor nota.
Darren behaves worst.
Darren es el que peor se porta.
She's the worst in the class.
Es la peor de la clase.
Chemistry is my worst subject.
La química es lo que peor se me da.

worth ADJECTIVE
It's worth a lot of money.
Vale mucho dinero.

Language tip

In Spanish, **valer mucho** *has two meanings. It can mean* **to be worth a lot** *or* **to cost a lot**.

It's worth it.
Vale la pena.

would VERB
1 (in offers, requests)

> **Language tip**
> Use the verb **querer** to ask what someone would like or to say what you would like.

What would you like, dear?
¿Qué quieres, cielo?
My friend would like a sandwich.
Mi amigo quiere un bocadillo.
Would you like to play with me?
¿Quieres jugar conmigo?
I'd like a hot chocolate, please.
Quiero una taza de chocolate, por favor.
2 (in polite orders)

> **Language tip**
> Use the verb **poder** to ask someone to do something.

Would you close the door, please?
¿Puedes cerrar la puerta, por favor?

wrapping paper NOUN
el **papel de envolver** masc

to write VERB
escribir
She's writing a story.
Está escribiendo un cuento.
I'm going to write to my friend.
Le voy a escribir a mi amigo.
Write your names.
Escribid vuestro nombre.
Write to me soon, Sandra.
Escríbeme pronto, Sandra.

Write soon!
¡Escribe pronto!

> **Language tip**
> Have you noticed the upside-down exclamation mark at the start of Spanish exclamations?

to write down VERB
apuntar
I'll write down the address.
Apuntaré la dirección.
Can you write it down for me, please?
¿Me lo puedes apuntar, por favor?

writer NOUN
el **escritor** masc
la **escritora** fem
He's a writer.
Es escritor.

> **Language tip**
> When talking about people's jobs in Spanish, you do not use an article.

writing NOUN
la **letra** fem
I can't read your writing.
No entiendo tu letra.

written VERB ▷see write

wrong

> **wrong** can be an adjective or an adverb.

A ADJECTIVE
1 **incorrecto** masc
incorrecta fem (answer, information)

This answer is **wrong.**
Esta respuesta es incorrecta.
That's the **wrong** answer.
Ésa no es la respuesta correcta.
I got three questions **wrong.**
Me equivoqué en tres preguntas.

2 **equivocado** *masc*
equivocada *fem (person)*
You're **wrong!**
¡Estás equivocado!
You're looking at the **wrong page.**
Estás mirando en la página equivocada.

B ADVERB
mal
You're saying it **wrong.**
Lo estás diciendo mal.
Have I spelled it **wrong?**
¿Lo he escrito mal?

What's **wrong?**
¿Qué pasa?
What's **wrong** with you?
¿Qué te pasa?

wrote VERB ▷*see* **write**

X x

Xmas NOUN
la **Navidad** *fem*

X-ray

> **X-ray** *can be a verb or a noun.*

A VERB
to X-ray
hacer una radiografía de
They're going to X-ray my leg.
Me van a hacer una radiografía de la pierna.

They X-rayed my arm.
Me hicieron una radiografía del brazo.

> *Language tip*
> *In Spanish you usually use an article like **el**, **la** or **los**, **las** with parts of the body.*

B NOUN
la **radiografía** *fem*
I'm going to have an X-ray.
Me voy a hacer una radiografía.

xylophone NOUN
el **xilófono** *masc*

Y y

yacht NOUN
1 el **barco de vela**
   masc (sailing boat)
2 el **yate** masc (luxury motorboat)

yard NOUN
   el **patio** masc
   in the yard
   en el patio

to **yawn** VERB
   bostezar

year NOUN
1 el **año** masc
   a hundred years
   cien años
   an eight-year-old child
   un niño de ocho años

> **this year**
> este año
> **last year**
> el año pasado
> **next year**
> el año que viene
> **I'm ten years old.**
> Tengo diez años.

2 el **curso** masc (school year)
   What year are you in?
   ¿En qué curso estás?
   I'm in Year Six.
   Estoy en sexto.
   She's in Year Five.
   Está en quinto.

> **Did you know…?**
> In Spain, children start primary
> school at six and go on to secondary
> school at twelve. Compulsory
> education ends at sixteen but they
> can stay on at school till they're
> eighteen to do their **Bachillerato**.

yellow

> **yellow** can be an adjective or a noun.

A ADJECTIVE
   amarillo masc
   amarilla fem
   I'm wearing
   yellow shorts.
   Llevo unos pantalones
   cortos amarillos.

> **Language tip**
> Colour adjectives come after the
> noun in Spanish.

B NOUN
   el **amarillo** masc
   Yellow is my favourite colour.
   El amarillo es mi color favorito.

yes ADVERB
   sí
   Do you like it? — Yes.
   ¿Te gusta? — Sí.
   Orange juice? — Yes, please.
   ¿Zumo de naranja? — Sí, por favor.
   Answer yes or no.
   Responde sí o no.

yesterday ADVERB
   ayer
   When? — Yesterday.
   ¿Cuándo? — Ayer.
   I was absent yesterday.
   Ayer no vine.

> **yesterday morning**
> ayer por la mañana
> **yesterday afternoon**
> ayer por la tarde
> **yesterday evening**
> ayer por la noche

> **Language tip**
> Translate **yesterday evening** by
> **ayer por la tarde** instead if you're
> talking about a time when it was
> still light.

yet ADVERB
1 **todavía** *(in negatives)*
I haven't finished yet.
Todavía no he terminado.
2 **ya** *(in questions)*
Have you finished yet, children?
¿Habéis terminado ya, niños?

Not yet.
Todavía no.

yoga NOUN
el **yoga** *masc*

yoghurt NOUN
el **yogur** *masc*

you PRONOUN

Language tip
There are different Spanish words for **you** *depending on whether it refers to one person or more than one person and how formal you are with them. The translation also depends on whether* **you** *is a subject (see senses 1–4) or an object (see mainly senses 5–8). The notes that follow each translation will help you find the word you need.*

1 **tú** *masc & fem*

Language tip
Use **tú** *to refer to just one friend, family member or person your own age when* **you** *is the subject of the verb.*

You've got a cat but I haven't.
Tú tienes un gato pero yo no.

Language tip
But remember that **you** *isn't usually translated unless it's emphatic.*

You've got a new computer, haven't you?
Tienes un ordenador nuevo, ¿verdad?

Language tip
Also use **tú** *in comparisons.*

She's younger than you.
Es más joven que tú.

Language tip
Use **ti** *instead after a preposition like* **para** *or* **de***.*

It's for you, James.
Es para ti, James.
I'll go with you.
Iré contigo.

for you
para ti
with you
contigo

2 **vosotros** *masc pl*
vosotras *fem pl*

Language tip
Use **vosotros** *and* **vosotras** *to refer to two or more friends, family members or people your own age when* **you** *is the subject of the verb.*

You've got time but I haven't.
Vosotros tenéis tiempo pero yo no.

Language tip
But remember that **you** *isn't usually translated unless it's emphatic.*

You've got a new car, haven't you?
Tenéis un coche nuevo, ¿verdad?

Language tip
Use **vosotros/vosotras** *in comparisons.*

They are younger than you two.
Son más jóvenes que vosotros dos.

Language tip
Also use **vosotros/vosotras** *after a preposition like* **para** *or* **de***.*

It's for you, girls.
Es para vosotras, niñas.
3 **usted** *masc & fem*

a b c d e f g h i j k l m n o p q r s t u v w x y z

617

Language tip
*Use **usted** to refer to just one person that you treat with respect, for example your teacher or an older person, when **you** is the subject of the verb.*

You have a lot of books but I haven't.
Usted tiene muchos libros pero yo no.

Language tip
*But remember that, like the other subject pronouns, **usted** is often omitted.*

Have you got any more paints, Miss?
¿Tiene más pinturas, señorita?

Language tip
*Use **usted** in comparisons.*

She isn't as nice as you.
No es tan simpática como usted.

Language tip
*Also use **usted** after a preposition like **para** or **de**.*

It's for you, Mr Smith.
Es para usted, señor Smith.

4 ustedes *masc & fem pl*

Language tip
*Use **ustedes** to refer to two or more people that you treat with respect, for example your teachers or older people, when **you** is the subject of the verb.*

You have a lot of books but we haven't.
Ustedes tienen muchos libros pero nosotros no.

Language tip
*But remember that, like the other subject pronouns, **ustedes** is often omitted.*

You've got a huge garden, haven't you?
Tienen un jardín enorme, ¿verdad?

Language tip
*Use **ustedes** in comparisons.*

They aren't as nice as you.
No son tan simpáticos como ustedes.

Language tip
*Use **ustedes** after a preposition like **para** or **de**.*

They are for you, Mr and Mrs Smith.
Son para ustedes, señor y señora Smith.

5 te *masc & fem*

Language tip
*Use **te** instead of **tú** to refer to just one friend, family member or person your own age when **you** is the object of the verb.*

I love you.
Te quiero.
I'll give it to you.
Te lo daré.

6 os *masc & fem pl*

Language tip
*Use **os** instead of **vosotros/vosotras** to refer to two or more friends, family members or people your own age when **you** is the object of the verb.*

I know you, Tracy and Sheila.
Os conozco, Tracy y Sheila.
I'll give it to you, boys.
Os lo daré, chicos.

7 lo *masc*
la *fem*

Language tip
*Use **lo** and **la** to refer to just one person that you treat with respect, for example, your teacher or an older person, when **you** is the object of the verb. **lo** and **la** are the direct object pronouns that correspond to **usted**.*

I can see you, sir.
Lo veo, señor.

I can see you, Miss.
La veo, señorita.

Language tip

Use **le** *instead (for both masculine and feminine) when* **you** *means 'to you' or 'for you' and is the indirect object of the verb.*

I'll give you my exercise book.
Le daré mi cuaderno.
I'll write to you.
Le escribiré.

Language tip

Change **le** *to* **se** *when combining it with a direct object pronoun like* **lo**, **la**, **los** *or* **las**.

I'll give it to you.
Se lo daré.

8 **los** *masc pl*
las *fem pl*

Language tip

Use **los** *and* **los** *to refer to two or more people that you treat with respect, for example your teachers or older people, when* **you** *is the object of the verb.* **los** *and* **las** *are the direct object pronouns that correspond to* **ustedes**.

May I help you?
¿Los puedo ayudar?

Language tip

Use **les** *instead (for both masculine plural and feminine plural) when* **you** *means 'to you' or 'for you' and is the indirect object of the verb.*

I'll give you the keys.
Les daré las llaves.
I'll write to you.
Les escribiré.

Language tip

Change **les** *to* **se** *when combining it with a direct object pronoun like* **lo**, **la**, **los** *or* **las**.

I'll give them to you.
Se las daré.

you'd
1 (= **you would**) ▷ *see* **would**
2 (= **you had**) ▷ *see* **have**

you'll (= **you will**) ▷ *see* **will**

young ADJECTIVE
joven *masc & fem* (PL **jóvenes**)
You're too young.
Eres demasiado joven.
They're younger than me.
Son más jóvenes que yo.
She's the youngest in the class.
Es la más joven de la clase.
my youngest brother
mi hermano menor
Stephen's the youngest.
Stephen es el menor.

your ADJECTIVE
1 **tu** *masc & fem* (PL **tus**) *(to someone you call 'tú')*

Language tip

Remember to use **tu** *before a singular noun and* **tus** *before a plural one.*

Is that your brother?
¿Es ése tu hermano?
your friend Helen
tu amiga Helen
your parents
tus padres
Wash your hands, Tim.
Lávate las manos, Tim.

Language tip

Remember that **tú** *with an accent means 'you' while* **tu** *without an accent means 'your'.*

2 **vuestro** *masc*
vuestra *fem (to people you call 'vosotros')*

English Spanish

a b c d e f g h i j k l m n o p q r s t u v w x y z

Is that your car?
¿Es ése vuestro coche?
Is this your house?
¿Es ésta vuestra casa?
Write your names.
Escribid vuestros nombres.
Put on your coats, children.
Poneos los abrigos, niños.

3 **su** *masc & fem* (PL **sus**) *(to people you call 'usted' and 'ustedes')*

your house
su casa
When's your birthday, Miss?
¿Cuándo es su cumpleaños, señorita?
Here are your books, Miss.
Aquí tiene sus libros, señorita.

you're (= you are) ▷ see **be**

yours PRONOUN
1 el **tuyo** *masc*
la **tuya** *fem (to someone you call 'tú')*

That isn't your coat. Yours is here.
Aquél no es tu abrigo. El tuyo está aquí.
Those aren't your boots. Yours are here.
Aquéllas no son tus botas. Las tuyas están aquí.

Is this yours, Frank?
¿Esto es tuyo, Frank?
Whose is this? — It's yours.
¿De quién es esto? — Es tuyo.
a friend of yours
un amigo tuyo

2 el **vuestro** *masc*
la **vuestra** *fem (to people you call 'vosotros')*

That isn't your car. Yours is here.
Aquél no es vuestro coche. El vuestro está aquí.
Those aren't your exercise books. Yours are here.
Aquéllos no son vuestros cuadernos. Los vuestros están aquí.

These sweets are yours.
Estos caramelos son vuestros.
a friend of yours
un amigo vuestro

3 el **suyo** *masc*
la **suya** *fem (to people you call 'usted' and 'ustedes')*

English

Spanish

That isn't your coat. Yours is here.
Aquél no es su abrigo. El suyo está aquí.
Those aren't your boots. Yours are here.
Aquéllas no son sus botas. Las suyas están aquí.

Is this yours, sir?
¿Esto es suyo, señor?
These tickets are yours.
Estas entradas son suyas.
Whose is this? — It's yours.
¿De quién es esto? — Es suyo.
a friend of yours
un amigo suyo
Yours sincerely
Le saluda atentamente

yourself PRONOUN
1 **te** *(to someone you call 'tú')*
You'll make yourself sick!
¡Te vas a marear!
Are you enjoying yourself?
¿Te estás divirtiendo?

Tell me about yourself!
¡Háblame de ti!

Do it yourself!
¡Hazlo tú mismo!
2 **se** *(to someone you call 'usted')*
Are you enjoying yourself?
¿Se está divirtiendo?

Tell me about yourself!
¡Hábleme de usted!

Help yourself, Mrs Day!
¡Sírvase usted misma, señora Day!

yourselves PRONOUN
1 **os** *(to people you call 'vosotros')*
Did you enjoy yourselves?
¿Os divertisteis?

Tell me about yourselves!
¡Habladme de vosotros!

Do it yourselves!
¡Hacedlo vosotros mismos!
2 **se** *(to people you call 'ustedes')*
Are you enjoying yourselves?
¿Se están divirtiendo?

Tell me about yourselves!
¡Háblenme de ustedes!

Help yourselves!
¡Sírvanse ustedes mismos!

youth club NOUN
el **club juvenil** *masc*

a b c d e f g h i j k l m n o p q r s t u v w x **y** z

youth hostel NOUN
  el **albergue juvenil** *masc*
    We're going to stay at a youth hostel.
    Nos vamos a alojar en un albergue juvenil.

you've (= you have) ▷*see* **have**

yummy ADJECTIVE
  buenísimo *masc*
  buenísima *fem*

Z z

zebra NOUN
la **cebra** *fem*

zebra crossing NOUN
el **paso de peatones** *masc*

zero NOUN
el **cero** *masc*

zip NOUN
la **cremallera** *fem*

zoo NOUN
el **zoo** *masc*
We went to the zoo on Saturday.
Fuimos al zoo el sábado.